Adolescence
Development, Diversity, and Context

Series Editor
Richard M. Lerner
Tufts University

A GARLAND SERIES

Series Contents

The Editors of this series are grateful to the several colleagues who facilitated our work on this series. Foremost, we are grateful to the authors of the selections reprinted in this volume. Their scholarship has shaped the study of adolescent development and we appreciate greatly their allowing us to include their work in this book.

We are especially grateful to Sofia T. Romero, Editor at the Boston College Center for Child, Family, and Community Partnerships, and to Imma De Stefanis, Graduate Research Assistant at the Center, for all their many contributions. Ms. Romero provided us with sage and professional editorial advice. Her wisdom, judgment, and skills enhanced the quality of our work and made it much more productive. Sr. De Stefanis collaborated extensively with us in the selection and organization of the scholarship included in the series. Her knowledge of and enthusiasm for the study of adolescence was an invaluable asset in our work.

We appreciate as well the excellent work of Carole Puccino, Editor at Garland Publishing. Her productivity and organizational skill enabled the volume to be produced with efficiency and quality. Finally, we thank Leo Balk, Vice President of Garland, for his enthusiasm for this project and for his support, encouragment, and guidance.

Adolescents and Their Families
Structure, Function, and Parent-Youth Relationships

Edited, with an introduction by

Richard M. Lerner
Tufts University

Domini R. Castellino
University of North Carolina – Chapel Hill

GARLAND PUBLISHING, INC.
A MEMBER OF THE TAYLOR & FRANCIS GROUP
New York & London
1999

Library of Congress Cataloging-in-Publication Data

Adolescents and their families : structure, function, and parent-youth
relationships / edited, with an introduction by Richard M. Lerner,
Domini R. Castellino.
       p.   cm. — (Adolescence : development, diversity, and context
; 4)
       Includes bibliographical references.
       ISBN 0-8153-3293-9 (alk. paper)
       1. Teenagers—United States—Family relationships. 2. Teenagers
—United States—Social conditions. 3. Parent and teenager—United
States. 4. Minority teenagers—United States. 5. Adolescence—
United States. I. Lerner, Richard M. II. Castellino, Domini R.
(Domini Rose) III. Series: Adolescence (New York, N.Y.) ; 4.
HQ796.A33533 1999
305.235'0973—dc21   99-33729
                                                        CIP

Printed on acid-free, 250-year-life paper
Manufactured in the United States of America

Contents

viii   CONTENTS

Introduction

Adolescents and Their Families:
A View of the Issues

*Richard M. Lerner, **Domini R. Castellino*

The adolescent period is marked by changes in the biological, psychological, cognitive, and social dimensions of the individual, as well as by changes in the adolescents' multilevel context (i.e., the peers, family, school, and other institutions in his or her ecology). Adolescence is a dynamic period, one which exemplifies the importance of understanding the relations between the developing individual and his or her changing context. The relations which characterize the adolescent period legitimate the study of adolescence from a developmental systems framework (Lerner and Castellino, 1998). The articles included in this volume represent the current range of scholarship pertaining to adolescents and their families, and exemplify the use of such an approach.

The articles underscore the continual importance of the family across adolescence. Consistent with a developmental systems perspective, the articles emphasize that the relations between the developing person and this key feature of his or her context are critical for understanding variation in development and positive and negative outcomes of this period of life (e.g., Bronfenbrenner, 1986; Lerner, 1998). Thus, rather than focusing theoretical and empirical emphasis solely on the individual (e.g., his or her genes, personality, intelligence, or motivation) as a basis for variation in important life outcomes, or only on various levels of the context, such as family structure or function, scholars have focused on the role of individual-family relations in accounting for outcomes of development in adolescence.

In emphasizing the developmental systems perspective, the articles in this volume underscore the importance of the themes that are reflected throughout this series: the significance of studying adolescent-context relations, the notion of developmental diversity, and the links among theory, research, and application.

The Family as a Context and Family Processes

This volume is divided into four sections. The first section addresses the family as an important context for development in general, and focuses on the influence of family processes such as parenting and parent-child interaction. The first article (Bronfenbrenner, 1986) sets a frame for the articles that follow. Bronfenbrenner underscores the importance of evaluating individual-context relations in order to better understand the development of children during this phase of life. He outlines critical features of the context — such as parental employment, the school and peer settings, and the larger community — that impact the functioning of families with respect to fostering optimal developmental outcomes. Bronfenbrenner points out how more macro-ecological features of the context can influence the family and, in turn, how this broader context can affect and be affected by intrafamilial processes such as divorce. These ideas are illustrated in the research presented in the articles that follow Bronfenbrenner's presentation.

Phinney and Chavira (1995) point to the importance of examining the cultural context within which socialization of the child occurs. Consistent with a developmental systems perspective, they acknowledge the importance of the interactions between the individual and his or her context for developmental outcomes. As such, Phinney and Chavira suggest that the cultural context of the individual — specifically the particular ethnicity that determines one's cultural heritage, history, and status within society — is likely to influence developmental outcomes. This article, as well as the ones by Harrison et al. (1990) and by McAdoo (1995) underscore, then, the significance of diversity in development, a central theme reflected in all the volumes in the series; as well, the articles point to the crucial need to appreciate the diversity of family contexts that can further healthy adolescent development.

Other articles in the first section highlight the pervasive themes of the series as well. For example, articles by Eccles et al. (1993) and Larson et al. (1996) also address the importance of diverse adolescent-context relations in understanding outcomes for youth. For instance, Eccles and her colleagues discuss the relationship of adolescent-context fit in accounting for negative developmental outcomes during this period. They point out that a "mismatch" between the needs of the adolescent and the opportunities presented to him or her in both the family and school context may account for variations in the difficulty experienced by many adolescents during this period of life. This work exemplifies the need to appraise, in an integrated manner, both the developing person and his or her environment in order to better understand development during adolescence.

Articles in this first section (Baumrind, 1991; Steinberg et al., 1991) also address the influence of parenting styles on adolescent adjustment. The normative developmental transition that occurs during adolescence, involving change from a more 'child-like' to a more 'adult-like' behavioral, cognitive, and emotional repertoire, includes role changes within the family and, particularly, in the entitlements given to, and in the obligations placed upon, youth within the family context (Baumrind, 1991). For instance, in addition to other transitions during this period, such as the biological changes that accompany puberty (Petersen, 1987), and the challenges regarding school transitions and achievement (Simmons and Blyth, 1987), adolescents are faced with increasing independence from parents and, subsequently, changing parent-adolescent relations (Grotevant and Cooper, 1986). The articles in this section provide details of these changing relations between parents and their adolescents, and highlight the importance of parenting and parenting style for developmental outcomes during this period of life. For example, Baumrind (1991) reports that authoritative parents generate competence in their adolescents and are able to successfully protect their youth from drug use.

Variations in Family Structure and Function

Section Two focuses on variations in family structure and function and their impact on adolescent development. As indicated in Volume 1 of this series, both interindividual differences and intraindividual changes in development characterize this phase of life. Thus, multiple pathways exist for negotiating the adolescent period (Offer, 1969). The articles in this section highlight how family structure and function influence these features of adolescent development. For example, several articles (Hetherington, 1991; Buchanan et al., 1991; Smetana, 1993) discuss the influence of divorce on adolescents' outcomes such as depression, anxiety, and deviant behavior. In turn, Lerner and Galambos (1985) detail the importance of the mother's satisfaction with her role as either a working or non-working mother for the interactions she has with her child. These articles address the issue of diversity in family structure and how such diversity relates to development during the adolescent period.

Family and Economic Stress

Articles in the third section by McLoyd (1989), Taylor and Roberts (1995), and Ge et al. (1992) address the influence of economic hardship on adolescent adjustment and well-being. These articles point to both the risks associated with economic stress, and the ways in which individual and contextual factors can enable adolescents to overcome economic hardships. The adolescent-context relations identified as being involved in this variation in developmental outcomes have important implications for intervention research and for policies and programs aimed at aiding youth in overcoming the challenges of poverty. This knowledge is critical during the adolescent period in particular, since "poverty and economic distress may impede the completion of important developmental tasks during adolescence" (Taylor and Roberts, 1995, pp. 1585).

For example, research has found that poor children are at risk for depression, low self-confidence, peer conflict, and conduct problems (McLoyd and Wilson, 1991; Klerman, 1991). Further, poverty has been linked with such negative outcomes as school failure, underemployability, welfare dependency, and violent crime (McLoyd and Wilson, 1991; Schorr, 1991).

Teenage Parenting

In the last section of this volume, the issue of teenage parenting — of families started by adolescents — is discussed. Teenage parenting continues to be a pressing social concern in the United States, and the articles focus on the intergenerational bases of such parenting and on the meaning of parenting among adolescent fathers. Given the negative life outcomes that have been associated with adolescent parenthood, such as school dropout, economic dependency, and high fertility (Furstenberg et al., 1990), it is critical to evaluate the individual and contextual factors that influence both the occurrence of teenage parenting and the impact that becoming a parent during the adolescent period has on later development. The issues involved in teenage parenting highlight, then, the importance of understanding the diversity of developmental pathways in addressing how knowledge about adolescent development can be applied to policies and programs aimed at enhancing the lives of youth and their families.

Conclusions

The need to focus on the changing relations between the individual and his/her changing context is critical for the understanding of human development across life. The bi-directional relationship between an active individual and a changing context must be the focus of developmental analyses in order to generate data that adequately reflect the broad range of individual differences that exist across human life (Lerner, 1998). These ideas are exemplified in the research presented in this volume.

Taken together, the articles illustrate the continued salience of the family across the adolescent period. Moreover, in embedding adolescent-family relations within other levels or contexts, and by discussing the family in relation to the life span of parents, youth, and the children youth may themselves have, this volume highlights the importance of focusing on the relations between adolescents, their families, and the broader ecological context in order to study development across this period of life. This integrative perspective is critical both to understand youth and families and to improve development outcomes of the relations adolescents have with their parents and their own children.

Richard M. Lerner holds the Bergstrom Chair in Applied Developmental Science at Tufts University. A developmental psychologist, Lerner received a Ph.D. in 1971 from the City University of New York. He has been a fellow at the Center for Advanced Study in the Behavioral Sciences and is a fellow of the American Association for the Advancement of Science, the American Psychological Association, the American Psychological Society, and the American Association of Applied and Preventive Psychology. Prior to joining Tufts University, he was on the faculty and held administrative posts at Michigan State University, Pennsylvania State University, and Boston College, where he was the Anita L. Brennan Professor of Education and the director of the Center for Child, Family, and Community Partnerships. During the 1994–95 academic year Lerner held the Tyner Eminent Scholar Chair in the Human Sciences at Florida State University. Lerner is the author or editor of 40 books and more than 275 scholarly articles and chapters, including his 1995 book, *America's Youth in Crisis: Challenges and Options for Programs and Policies*. He edited Volume 1, on "Theoretical models of human development," for the fifth edition of the *Handbook of Child Psychology*. He is known for his theory of, and research about, relations between life-span human development and contextual or ecological change. He is the founding editor of the *Journal of Research on Adolescence* and of the new journal, *Applied Developmental Science*.
** Domini R. Castellino is an NICHD Postdoctoral Fellow of the Carolina Consortium on Human Development at the Center for Developmental Science at the University of North Carolina-Chapel Hill. Dr. Castellino received her bachelors degree in Human Development and Family Studies from the Pennsylvania State University and earned her masters and Ph.D. degrees in Developmental Psychology at Michigan State University. Her research interests include

developmental theory, parent-child relations, maternal employment issues, and adolescent career development.

References[1]

Klerman, L.V. (1991). The health of poor children: Problems and programs. In A.C. Huston (Ed.), *Children in poverty: Child development and public policy* (pp. 1–22). Cambridge, UK: Cambridge University Press.

Lerner, R.M. (1998). Theories of human development: Contemporary perspectives. In R.M. Lerner (Ed.), *Theoretical models of human development.* Volume 1 of the *Handbook of child psychology* (5th ed., pp. 1–24). Editor in chief: W. Damon. New York: Wiley.

McLoyd, V.C., and Wilson, L. (1991). The strain of living poor: Parenting, social support, and child mental health. In A.C. Huston (Ed.), *Children in poverty: Child development and public policy* (pp.105–135). Cambridge, UK: Cambridge University Press.

Offer, D. (1969). *The psychological world of the teen-ager.* New York: Basic Books.

Petersen, A.C. (1987). The nature of biological psychosocial interactions: The sample case of early adolescence. In R.M. Lerner and T.T. Foch (Eds.), *Biological-psychosocial interactions in early adolescence* (pp. 35–61). Hillsdale, NJ: Lawrence Erlbaum Associates.

Schorr, L. B. (1991). Effective programs for children growing up in concentrated poverty. In A.C. Huston (Ed.), *Children in poverty: Child development and public policy* (pp. 26–281). Cambridge, UK: Cambridge University Press.

Simmons, R.G., and Blyth, D.A. (1987). *Moving into adolescence.* New York: Aldine DeGruyter.

Footnote

[1]This list provides reference only to citations not included in this volume.

Developmental Psychology
1986, Vol. 22, No. 6, 723–742

Ecology of the Family as a Context for Human Development: Research Perspectives

Urie Bronfenbrenner
Cornell University

This review collates and examines critically a theoretically convergent but widely dispersed body of research on the influence of external environments on the functioning of families as contexts of human development. Investigations falling within this expanding domain include studies of the interaction of genetics and environment in family processes; transitions and linkages between the family and other major settings influencing development, such as hospitals, day care, peer groups, school, social networks, the world of work (both for parents and children), and neighborhoods and communities; and public policies affecting families and children. A second major focus is on the patterning of environmental events and transitions over the life course as these affect and are affected by intrafamilial processes. Special emphasis is given to critical research gaps in knowledge and priorities for future investigation.

The purpose of this article is to document and delineate promising lines of research on external influences that affect the capacity of families to foster the healthy development of their children. The focus differs from that of most studies of the family as a context of human development, because the majority have concentrated on intrafamilial processes of parent–child interaction, a fact that is reflected in Maccoby and Martin's (1983) recent authoritative review of research on family influences on development. By contrast, the focus of the present analysis can be described as "once removed." The research question becomes: How are intrafamilial processes affected by extrafamilial conditions?

Paradigm Parameters

In tracing the evolution of research models in developmental science, Bronfenbrenner and Crouter (1983) distinguished a series of progressively more sophisticated scientific paradigms for investigating the impact of environment on development. These paradigms provide a useful framework for ordering and analyzing studies bearing on the topic of this review. At the most general level, the research models vary simultaneously along two dimensions. As applied to the subject at hand, the first pertains

to the structure of the external systems that affect the family and the manner in which they exert their influence. The second dimension relates to the degree of explicitness and differentiation accorded to intrafamilial processes that are influenced by the external environment.

External Systems Affecting the Family

Research paradigms can be distinguished in terms of three different environmental systems that can serve as sources of external influence on the family.

Mesosystem models. Although the family is the principal context in which human development takes place, it is but one of several settings in which developmental process can and do occur. Moreover, the processes operating in different settings are not independent of each other. To cite a common example, events at home can affect the child's progress in school, and vice versa. Despite the obviousness of this fact, it was not until relatively recently that students of development began to employ research designs that could identify the influences operating, in both directions, between the principal settings in which human development occurs. The term *mesosystem* has been use to characterize analytic models of this kind (Bronfenbrenner, 1979). The results of studies employing this type of paradigm in relation to the family are summarized below, in the section "Mesosystem Models."

Exosystem models. The psychological development of children in the family is affected not only by what happens in the other environments in which children spend their time but also by what occurs in the other settings in which their parents live their lives, especially in a place that children seldom enter—the parents' world of work. Another domain to which children tend to have limited access is the parents' circle of friends and acquaintances—their social network. Such environments "external" to the developing person are referred to as "exosystems." The findings of investigations employing exosystem designs are reviewed below, in the section "Exosystem Models."

This review is based on a longer background paper prepared at the request of the Human Learning and Behavior Branch of the National Institute of Child Health and Human Development in connection with the development of their Five Year Plan for Research.

I am indebted to the following colleagues for their constructive criticism of the original document: Josephine Arastah, Mavis Hetherington, Richard Lerner, Jeylan T. Mortimer, Joseph H. Pleck, Lea Pulkinnen, Michael Rutter, Klaus Schneewind, and Diana Slaughter. Appreciation is also expressed to Gerri Jones for typing innumerable revisions of this manuscript.

Correspondence concerning this article should be sent to Urie Bronfenbrenner, Department of Human Development and Family Studies, Cornell University, Ithaca, New York 14853.

Chronosystem models. Traditionally in developmental science, the passage of time has been treated as synonymous with chronological age; that is, as a frame of reference for studying psychological changes within individuals as they grow older. Especially during the past decade, however, research on human development has projected the factor of time along a new axis. Beginning in the mid 1970s, an increasing number of investigators have employed research designs that take into account changes over time not only within the person but also in the environment and—what is even more critical—that permit analyzing the dynamic relation between these two processes. To distinguish such investigations from more traditional longitudinal studies focusing exclusively on the individual, I have proposed the term *chronosystem* for designating a research model that makes possible examining the influence on the person's development of changes (and continuities) over time in the environments in which the person is living (Bronfenbrenner, 1986a).

The simplest form of chronosystem focuses around a life transition. Two types of transition are usefully distinguished: normative (school entry, puberty, entering the labor force, marriage, retirement) and nonnormative (a death or severe illness in the family, divorce, moving, winning the sweepstakes). Such transitions occur throughout the life span and often serve as a direct impetus for developmental change. Their relevance for the present review, however, lies in the fact that they can also influence development indirectly by affecting family processes.

A more advanced form of chronosystem examines the cumulative effects of an entire sequence of developmental transition over an extended period of the person's life—what Elder (1974, 1985) has referred to as the life course. During the past decade, studies of the impact of personal and historical life events on family processes and on their developmental outcomes have received increasing attention. Several of these investigations have yielded findings of considerable substantive and theoretical significance. These are described, along with other relevant researches employing a chronosystem design, below ("Chronosystem Models").

Family Processes in Context

With respect to explicitness and complexity, research paradigms can again be differentiated at three successive levels.

Social address model. At the first level, the family processes are not made explicit at all, because the paradigm is limited to the comparison of developmental outcomes for children or adults living in contrasting environments as defined by geography (e.g., rural vs. urban, Japan vs. the United States), or by social background (socioeconomic status, ethnicity, religion, etc.). Hence the name "social address" (Bronfenbrenner, 1979). Given their restricted scope, social address models have a number of important limitations summarized in the following passage:

> No explicit consideration is given . . . to intervening structures or processes through which the environment might affect the course of development. One looks only at the social address—that is, the environmental label—with no attention to what the environment is like, what people are living there, what they are doing, or how the activities taking place could affect the child. (Bronfenbrenner & Crouter, 1983, pp. 361–362)

Despite these shortcomings, social address models remain one of the most widely used paradigms in the study of environmental influences on development. Two reasons may account for their scientific popularity. The first is their comparative simplicity, both at a conceptual and an operational level. Indeed, they can be, and sometimes have been, employed without doing very much thinking in advance, a procedure, alas, that is reflected in the product. But social address models, when appropriately applied, can also serve as a helpful scientific tool. Precisely because of their simplicity, they can be implemented easily and quickly. Hence, they may often be the strategies of choice for exploring uncharted domains. Like the surveyor's grid, they provide a useful frame for describing at least the surface of the new terrain. A case in point is their application in identifying developmental outcomes associated with what Bronfenbrenner and Crouter (1983) have called the "new demography"—single parents, day care, mothers in the labor force, remarriage, or (perhaps soon) fathers in the role of principal caregiver.

Process-context model. Paradigms at this second level explicitly provide for assessing the impact of the external environment on particular family processes. As documented in Bronfenbrenner and Crouter's analysis (1983), such paradigms represent a fairly recent scientific development, appearing in a reasonably full form only in the late 1960s and early 1970s. Because the corresponding research designs tend to be more complex than those employed in social address models, a concrete illustration may be helpful. For this purpose, I have selected one of the earliest examples of its kind, but one that still deserves to be emulated as a model for future research. In a series of researches growing out of his doctoral dissertation, Tulkin and his colleagues (Tulkin, 1973a, 1973b, 1977; Tulkin & Cohler, 1973, Tulkin & Covitz, 1975; Tulkin & Kagan, 1972) sought to go beyond the label of social class in order to discover its manifestations in family functioning. The first study focused on families with an infant under one year of age. To control for the child's sex and ordinal position, the sample was limited to firstborn girls, first studied when they were 10 months old. The initial publication (Tulkin & Kagan, 1972), based on home observations, reported that middle-class mothers engaged in more reciprocal interactions with their infants, especially in verbal behavior, and provided them with a greater variety of stimulation. The second study (Tulkin & Cohler, 1973) documented parallel differences in maternal attitudes; middle-class mothers were more likely to subscribe to statements stressing the importance of perceiving and meeting the infant's needs, the value of mother–child interaction, and the moderate control of aggressive impulses. Furthermore, the correlations between maternal behavior and attitudes were substantially greater in middle-class than in lower-class families. Next, in two experiments, Tulkin (1973a, 1973b) found that middle-class infants cried more when separated from their mothers, but were better able to discriminate the mother's voice from that of an unfamiliar female from the same social class. Finally, several years later, Tulkin and Covitz (1975) reassessed the same youngsters after they had entered school. The children's performance on tests of mental ability and language skill showed significant relationships to prior measures of reciprocal mother–infant interaction, strength of maternal attachment, and voice recognition when the children had been 10 months old. Once again, the observed

2

correlations were higher for middle-class families. Even more important from a developmental perspective, the relationships of maternal behavior at 10 months to the child's behavior at age 6 were considerably greater than the contemporaneous relationships between both types of variables in the first year of life. The investigators, however, were quick to reject the hypothesis of a delayed "sleeper effect." Rather, they argued that mothers who engage in adaptive reciprocal activity with their infants at early ages are likely to continue to do so as the child gets older, thus producing a cumulative trend.

Although a number of other investigators of socialization and social class have observed mother–child interaction, Tulkin's work remains unique in combining three critical features: (a) an emphasis on social class differences in *process* rather than merely in outcome; (b) demonstration of the key role played by child rearing values and the higher correspondence between parental values and behavior among middle-class than working-class families; and (c) evidence of developmental effects over time.

Person-process-context model. As its name indicates, the next and last process paradigm adds a new, third element to the system. Although the process-context model represented a significant advance over its predecessors, it was based on an unstated assumption—namely, that the impact of a particular external environment on the family was the same irrespective of the personal characteristics of individual family members, including the developing child. The results of the comparatively few studies that have employed a triadic rather than solely dyadic research paradigm call this tacit assumption into question. Research by Crockenberg (1981) illustrates both the model and its message. Working with a middle-class sample, she found that the amount of social support received by mothers from their social network when their infants were 3 months old was positively related to the strength of the child's attachment to its mother at one year of age. The beneficial impact of social support varied systematically, however, as a function of the infant's temperament. It was strongest for mothers with the most irritable infants and minimal for those whose babies were emotionally calm. In addition, the author emphasizes that "the least irritable infants appear somewhat impervious to the low support environments which disrupt the development of their more irritable peers . . . the easy babies in this study were unlikely to develop insecure attachments even when potentially unfavorable social milieus existed" (p. 862).

As documented subsequently in this review, the personal characteristics of parents, especially of fathers, are of no less—and perhaps even greater—importance than those of the child in determining the positive or negative impact of the external environment on family processes and their developmental outcomes.

Although research paradigms in the study of development-in-context have become progressively more complex over time both with respect to the analysis of family processes and of environmental systems, this does not mean that the correlation applies at the level of individual studies. Indeed, the opposite is often the case. Thus one encounters chronosystem designs that still rely primarily on social address models for analyzing data, and, conversely, person-process-context designs that give no consideration to the length of time that a family has been exposed to a particular environmental context (for example, unemployment). Moreover, seldom in either instance is there recognition of the ambiguity of interpretation produced by the failure to use a more sophisticated design. Fortunately, a number of studies, reported below, do employ paradigms that are comparatively advanced on both dimensions and, thereby, produce a correspondingly rich scientific yield.

Mesosystem Models

Ecology of Family Genetics

Studies of twins have typically reported correlations between IQ scores of identical twins reared apart that are quite substantial and appreciably greater than those for fraternal twins reared in the same home. Thus Bouchard and McGue (1981), in their comprehensive review of studies of family resemblance in cognitive ability, report an average weighted correlation of .72 for the former group versus .60 for the latter. Such findings are typically interpreted as testifying to the primacy of genetic influences in the determination of intelligence (e.g., Burt, 1966; Jensen, 1969, 1980; Loehlin, Lindzey, & Spuhler, 1975). Underlying this interpretation is the assumption that twins reared apart are experiencing widely different environments, so that the substantial similarity between them must be attributable primarily to their common genetic endowment. A mesosystem model calls this assumption into question on the ground that, even though they are not living in the same home, the twins may share common environments in other settings. To test this assumption, Bronfenbrenner (1975) recalculated correlations based on subgroups of twins sharing common environments as follows:

1. Among 35 pairs of separated twins for whom information was available about the community in which they lived, the correlation in Binet IQ for those raised in the same town was .83, for those brought up in different towns, .67.

2. In another sample of 38 separated twins, the correlation for those attending the same school in the same town was .87, for those attending schools in different towns, .66.

3. When the communities in the preceding samples were classified as similar versus dissimilar on the basis of size and economic base (e.g., mining vs. agricultural), the correlation for separated twins living in similar communities was .86; for those residing in dissimilar localities, .26.

Subsequently, Taylor (1980) independently replicated the same pattern of findings in an analysis based on a reclassification of cases from the same studies as well as additional data from others.

Genetics-environment interaction in family processes

The pioneering investigation in this domain is one that has been much criticized on technical grounds by proponents of the hereditarian view (e.g., Jensen, 1973), but as a research paradigm it broke new ground. In the late 1930s, Skeels and his colleagues (Skeels & Dye, 1939; Skeels et al., 1938; Skodak & Skeels, 1949) published the first stage of what was to become a classical longitudinal study (Skeels, 1966). The investigators compared mental development of children brought up from an early age in adoptive families and in a control group of young-sters raised by their biological parents. Building on earlier work in this area (Burks, 1928; Leahy, 1935), the investigation is important in three respects. First, following Burks, the researchers demonstrated, and took into account, the influence of selective placement (the tendency of children of more intelligent biological parents to be placed in more advantaged adoptive homes). Second, Skeels and his associates showed that, while parent-child correlations in intellectual performance were appreciably higher in biological families than in adoptive families, the mean IQ of the adopted children was 20 points higher than that of their natural parents. This phenomenon has since been replicated both in the United States (Scarr & Weinberg, 1976) and in Europe (Schiff et al., 1981, 1982). Third, and the most relevant for present purposes, Skeels and his colleagues gathered and analyzed critical data of a type never before examined in adoptive families—the nature of the home environments and parental behaviors that accounted for the more advanced development of children placed for adoption in middle-class families (Skodak & Skeels, 1949).

An even clearer example of the multiplicative effect of environmental and genetic forces are the Danish and American adoptive studies of the origins of criminal behavior. Taking advantage of the unusually complete multigenerational demographic and health statistics available in Denmark, Hutchings, and Mednick (1977) compared the incidence of criminal offenses for males adopted early in life and for their biological and adoptive fathers. Among adopted men for whom neither father had a criminal record, 12% had a criminal record of their own. If either the biological or the adoptive father had a criminal record, the rate rose appreciably (21% and 19%, respectively). If both fathers had recorded offenses, the proportion jumped to 36%.

An American study (Crowe, 1974) reported a more precise multiplicative effect; among adult adoptees whose mothers had a criminal record, the only ones who had criminal records themselves were those who had spent considerable time in institutions or foster homes prior to adoption. This effect was independent of age of adoption, because children transferred at the same ages directly from the biological to the adoptive family did not have criminal records later in life. Crowe's research provides a telling example of how a rather complex mesosystem effect can be demonstrated by applying a fairly simple social address model.

The use of more advanced and differentiated research design for the study of genetics–environment interaction in development is still comparatively rare. A striking finding demonstrates by contradiction the paucity of our knowledge in this sphere. The modest but significant association between family background factors in childhood and subsequent educational and occupational achievement in adulthood has been documented many times. Yet, it is only two years ago that Scarr and McAvay (1984) reported an important qualification with respect to this often cited relationship. Exploiting the methodological leverage provided by a longitudinal study of brothers and sisters brought up in adoptive and biologically related families, the investigators demonstrated that, within biological families, such family background characteristics are much more predictive for sons than for daughters.

The Family and the Hospital

Given the critical importance that hospital care can play in the life and development of young children, it is surprising that so little attention has been paid to the relationship between the hospital and the home as a moderating influence on the child's recuperation. The importance of this relation is illustrated by the results of two studies. Scarr-Salapatek and Williams (1973) assessed the effects of an experimental program carried out with a sample of black mothers and their premature infants from extremely deprived socioeconomic backgrounds. In addition to providing special sensory stimulation procedures by hospital staff, the program involved home visits to the mothers in which they were given instruction, demonstration, and practice in observing, caring for, and carrying out a variety of activities with their infants. At one year of age, the latter showed an IQ score 10 points higher than that of randomly selected control groups, and achieved an average level of 95, thus bringing them to "nearly normal levels of development" (p. 99).

An earlier experiment with an older aged group yielded equally impressive results. Prugh and his colleagues (1953) took advantage of a planned change in hospital practice to conduct a comparative study of the reaction of children and their parents to contrasting modes of ward operation. The control group consisted of children admitted and discharged over a 4-month period prior to the introduction of the contemplated change. They experienced "traditional practices of ward management" (p. 75) in which parents were restricted to weekly visiting periods of two hours each. The experimental group, admitted during the succeeding period, could receive visits from parents at any time. Parents were also encouraged to participate in ward care. Greater emotional distress was observed among the children in the control group, both before and as late as a year after discharge from the hospital.

The Family and Day Care

As pointed out by Belsky and his colleagues in a series of comprehensive reviews (Belsky 1985; Belsky & Steinberg, 1978; Belsky, Steinberg, & Walker, 1982), researchers on day care have limited themselves almost exclusively to the direct effects on the child while neglecting possibly even more powerful influences on family processes. In his most recent review of the few studies that depart from this pattern, Belsky (1985) qualifies previous more optimistic assessments regarding effects of infant day care on the formation of mother–infant attachment. After analyzing several recent investigations, Belsky (1984) concludes as follows:

> These new data lead me to modify conclusions that have been arrived at in past reviews in order to underscore the potentially problematical nature of early entry into community-based, as opposed to university-based day care . . . There seems to be cause for concern about early entry to the kind of day care that is available in most communities. (p. 11)

An additional study by Thompson, Lamb, and Estes (1982) lends support to Belsky's caveat. These investigators report data from a middle-class sample showing that stability of secure attachment between 12 and 19 months was lower among infants placed in day care or whose mother had returned to work during the first year. The effect for day care was greater than that for maternal employment.

The Family and the Peer Group

In the middle 1960s and early 1970s, a series of studies, conducted both in the United States and other countries (Bronfenbrenner, 1967; Bronfenbrenner, Devereux, Suci, & Rodgers, 1965; Devereux, 1965, 1966; Devereux, Bronfenbrenner, & Rodgers, 1969; Rodgers, 1971), demonstrated powerful and often opposite effects of parental and peer influences on the development of children and youth. Especially instructive is the comparative investigation by Kandel and Lesser (1972), who found that Danish adolescents and youth, in contrast to American teenagers, paradoxically exhibited both greater independence from and closer and warmer relationships with their parents and other adults as opposed to peers, with a corresponding reduction in antisocial behavior. More recently, the developmental importance of the interface between family and peer group has been corroborated in studies focusing on the antecedents of antisocial behavior in adolescence and the entrapment of youth in juvenile delinquency, alcoholism, and substance use (Boehnke et al., 1983; Gold & Petronio, 1980; Jessor, 1986; Kandel, 1986; Pulkkinen, 1983a, 1983b).

Particularly revealing are three recent investigations that have used more sophisticated designs to reveal the interplay between family structure and functioning on the one hand, and indexes of peer group deviance on the other. Thus Dornbusch and his colleagues (1985) first show that, with effects of socioeconomic status held constant, adolescents from mother-only households are more likely than their age-mates from two-parent families to engage in adult disapproved activities (such as smoking, school misbehavior, and delinquency). They then demonstrate that a key process involved in this relationship is the contrasting pattern of decision-making prevailing in the two types of family structure, with more unilateral decisions (parent alone, child alone) predominating in the single-parent setting. Substantial difference in antisocial behavior still remained after control for patterns of decision-making. These differences were considerably reduced, however, by the presence of a second adult in the single-parent home, *except* in those cases in which the second adult was a stepparent, when the effect was reversed. In other words, having a stepparent increased the likelihood of socially deviant behavior. The effect of the child's own characteristics on the family process is reflected in the fact that all of the above relationships, especially the disruptive influence of a stepparent, were more pronounced for boys than for girls.

A subsequent study by Steinberg (1985) not only replicates the above pattern of findings but further illuminates the nature of the processes involved by using a measure not of the frequency of antisocial behavior per se such but of susceptibility to peer-group pressure for such activity. Finally, in his most recent report, Steinberg (1986) introduces a caveat to conclusions drawn from prior studies of the growing phenomenon of the "latchkey child." Using a conventional "social address" model, these investigations had failed to detect any behavioral difference between such children and those who came home from school to a house in which the parent was present. By employing a person-process-context mesosystem model, Steinberg identified as a crucial variable the extent of parental monitoring and "remote control" of the child's activities in the parent's absence. For example, children whose parents knew their whereabouts were less susceptible to antisocial peer influence. Where such parental monitoring was weak, latchkey children were indeed at greater risk of becoming involved in socially deviant behavior. And once again, the importance of the characteristics of the child was reflected in the fact that males were more susceptible to antisocial influences than females and were less responsive to the moderating effect of increased parental control or monitoring.

Family and School

Research in this sphere has been heavily one-sided. Although there have been numerous investigations of the influence of the family on the child's performance and behavior in school, as yet no researchers have examined how school experiences affect the behavior of children and parents in the home. Several studies, however, have explored how the relation between these two settings might affect children's behavior and development in school environments (Becker & Epstein, 1982; Bronfenbrenner, 1974; Burns, 1982; Collins, Moles, & Cross, 1982; Epstein, 1983a, 1984; Hayes & Grether, 1969; Henderson, 1981; Heyns, 1978; Lightfoot, 1978; Medrich et al., 1982; Smith, 1968; Tangri & Leitsch, 1982). Smith's study (1968) is especially noteworthy. She carried out a planned experiment involving a series of ingenious strategies for increasing home–school linkages that brought about significant gains in academic achievement in a sample of approximately 1,000 elementary pupils from low-income, predominantly black families.

Almost all of these investigations, however, including Smith's, have focused on techniques of parent involvement rather than on the associated processes taking place within family and classroom and their joint effects on children's learning and development. A notable exception is Epstein's research on "Longitudinal Effects of Family-School-Person Interactions on Student Outcomes" (1983a, 1983b). Working with a sample of almost 1,000 eighth graders, she examined the joint impact of family and classroom processes on change in pupil's attitudes and their academic achievement during the transition between the last year of middle school and the first year of high school. Children from homes or classrooms affording greater opportunities for communication and decision-making not only exhibited greater initiative and independence after entering high school, but also received higher grades. Family processes were considerably more powerful in producing change than classroom procedures. School influences were nevertheless effective, especially for pupils from families who had not emphasized intergenerational communication in the home or the child's participation in decision-making. The effects of family and school processes were greater than those attributable to socioeconomic status or race.

Exosystem Models

In modern, industrialized societies, there are three exosystems that are especially likely to affect the development of the child, primarily thorough their influence on family processes.

The first of these is the parents' workplace, the second parents' social networks, and the third community influences on family functioning.

Family and Work

In their review of research on the effects of parental work on children, Bronfenbrenner and Crouter (1982) pointed out that, until very recently, researchers have treated the job situation of mothers and fathers as separate worlds having no relation to each other and, presumably, leading to rather different results. For mothers, it was the fact of being employed that was thought to be damaging to the child, whereas for fathers it was being unemployed that was seen as the destructive force. Because of this "division of labor," the principal research findings in each domain are most conveniently summarized under separate headings.

Parental Employment and Family Life

The first studies in this sphere appeared in the late 1930s and dealt with the impact on the family of the father's loss of a job during the Great Depression (Angell, 1936; Cavan & Ranck, 1938; Komarovsky, 1940; Morgan, 1939). The husband's unemployment resulted in a loss of status within the family, a marked increase in family tensions and disagreements, and a decrease in social life outside the home. At the same time, the father became increasingly unstable, moody, and depressed. In these early studies, no reference was made to any effects of these disruptive processes on the children; the latter were treated simply as participants playing secondary roles in the family drama. It was not until the 1970s that Elder (1974) began his exploitation of archival data to trace the life course of "Children of the Great Depression" (1974). Because he also employed a more powerful chronosystem paradigm for this purpose, Elder's findings will be presented in a later section, in which such models and their results are reviewed.

In 1958, Miller and Swanson called attention to another aspect of the father's work situation that appeared to affect parental childrearing attitudes and practices. The investigators distinguished between two main types of work organization: bureaucratic and entrepreneurial. The first, represented by large-scale businesses, was characterized by relatively more secure conditions of work, manifested by such features as regular hours, stabilized wages, unemployment insurance, and retirement funds. The second, exemplified by small-scale family-owned businesses, involved greater initiatives, competitiveness, risk taking, and insecurity regarding the future. Miller and Swanson reported that wives of men from bureaucratic backgrounds described styles of upbringing that were more permissive and laid greater stress on the development of interpersonal skills; by contrast, wives of husbands working in entrepreneurial settings were found to be more concerned with individual achievement and striving. A decade later, similar findings based on Miller and Swanson's occupational dichotomy were obtained by Caudill and Weinstein in Japan (1969).

The hypothesis that the structure and content of activities in the father's job can influence the family's childrearing values has been investigated by Kohn and his colleagues. In his first study, Kohn (1969) demonstrated that working-class men whose jobs typically required compliance with authority tended to hold values that stressed obedience in their children; by contrast, middle-class fathers expected self-direction and independence, the qualities called for by the demands of their occupation. Occupational values were also reflected in both parents' childrearing practices. Subsequently, Kohn and Schooler (1973, 1978, 1982, 1983) examined the nature of work in a more fine-grained analysis, focusing on the dimension of "occupational self-direction"—the extent to which a job requires complex skills, autonomy, and lack of routinization—and its relation to worker's "intellectual flexibility" as measured in a series of standardized tests. Using causal modeling techniques with longitudinal data, the investigators demonstrated that the occupational self-direction of a job could affect one's intellectual flexibility 10 years later. This finding was subsequently replicated in a comparative study including samples both from the United States and Poland (Slomezynski, Miller, & Kohn, 1981).

The key question left unresolved in the work of Kohn and his colleagues concerns the last step in the developmental sequence that he posits: Does the opportunity for self-direction in the parent's job, and the intellectual flexibility that it generates, influence the actual child rearing behavior of the parents and, thereby, affect the development of the child? The one study I have been able to find that bears on this issue did not yield very powerful results. Using data from a sample of several hundred 12th-graders, Morgan, Alwin, and Griffin (1979) found the expected association between father's occupation and mother's childrearing values. But when these value measures were related to various aspects of the adolescent's academic career, the findings presented a somewhat mixed picture. Neither the adolescents' school grades, academic self-esteem, expected educational and occupational attainment, nor their generalized sense of personal control were affected. The mother's childrearing values, however, did predict the child's curriculum placement (measured on a continuum from vocational-commercial courses to college preparation), as well as the young person's involvement in school activities. The latter finding, however, held only for white students, not for blacks. Note that even in this study, no data are available on the parents' behavior, which constitutes a critical link in the postulated causal chain.

A closer approximation of the processes involved appears in a longitudinal research conducted by Mortimer and her colleagues (Mortimer, 1974, 1975, 1976; Mortimer & Kumka, 1982; Mortimer & Lorence, 1979; Mortimer, Lorence, & Kumka, 1982). Applying Kohn's theoretical schema in a reanalysis of panel study data, the investigators were able to demonstrate a strong tendency for sons to choose an occupation similar to their fathers', as defined along dimensions of work autonomy and the function of work activities. The most effective transmission of occupational value and choice occurred under a combination of a prestigious parental role model and a close father–son relationship. Mortimer's most recent study (1986) establishes the mediating role of the family in adult development by documenting that, compared to men who remained single, men who married during the decade following graduation had greater career stability, income, and work autonomy and exhibited greater job satisfaction. There was substantial evidence that these findings were not attributable to selection processes. The special strength of Mortimer's work lies in the inclusion of family relationships as intervening links in her model.

A third line of investigation, emerging in the middle 1960s, reflects a significant elaboration in the latent structure of research designs in this sphere. The earliest studies in this domain focused on the effects of conflicting time schedules. For example, Mott, Mann, McLoughlin, and Warwick (1965) found that workers on the late afternoon shift rarely saw their school-age children during the work week. The job of discipline fell to the mother, and the shortage of time shared by both parents produced family conflicts over what to do with that time. A subsequent study (Landy, Rosenberg, and Sutton-Smith, 1969) examined the impact on daughters of the fathers' working on a night shift. The daughters of men so employed showed significantly lower scores in tests of academic achievement.[1]

Kanter (1977) introduced the concept of "work absorption" to describe the extent to which work made demands on one's physical and mental energy. In the same year, Heath (1977) studied the effects of this phenomenon and reported that it had a "narrowing effect" on men who had little time for nonwork activities, including spending time with their children. Work absorption tended to generate guilt and increased irritability and impatience in dealing with the child. Two studies have gone a step further to demonstrate the interaction between work and family as a two-way system, with "spillover," in both directions, of tensions, satisfactions, and modes of interaction (Crouter, 1984; Piotrkowski, 1979).

Finally, Bohen and Viveros-Long (1981) exploited an experiment of nature to investigate the impact of flexible work hours (flexitime) on family life. They compared two federal agencies engaged in similar work and staffed by similar personnel, but differing in arrangement of working hours. In one agency the employees worked a conventional schedule from 9:00 a.m. to 5:00 p.m.; in the other, they could choose to arrive within a 2-hr range in the morning and adjust their leaving time accordingly. The results of the experiment were somewhat ironic. Measures of family strain and participation in home activities showed a significant difference favoring flexitime for only one group of families—those without children. One proposed explanation is that flexitime arrangements did not go far enough to meet the complex scheduling problems experienced by today's parents. A second interpretation suggests that the flexible time may have been used for activities outside the home unrelated to childrearing, such as recreation, socializing, or moonlighting. Unfortunately, no data were available to verify either hypothesis.

Maternal Employment and the Family

As documented in three recent reviews (Bronfenbrenner & Crouter, 1982; Hoffman, 1980, 1983), an analysis of research in this sphere reveals a consistent contrast, summarized in the following passage:

> By 1980 there had accumulated an appreciable body of evidence indicating that the mother's work outside the home tends to have a salutary effect on girls, but may exert a negative influence on boys . . . The results indicate that daughters from families in which the mother worked tended to admire their mothers more, had a more

positive conception of the female role, and were more likely to be independent . . . None of these trends was apparent for boys. Instead, the pattern of findings, especially in recent investigations, suggests that the mother's working outside the home is associated with a lower academic achievement for sons in middle-class but not in low-income families . . . A similar tendency for maternal employment to have a negative influence on the development of boys was apparent in investigations conducted as far back as the 1930s. (Bronfenbrenner & Crouter, 1982, pp. 51-52)

The processes underlying this complex but consistent set of findings are illuminated in a study by Bronfenbrenner, Alvarez, and Henderson (1984). The basic data consisted of parents' free descriptions of their 3-year-old children. A systematic content analysis revealed that the most flattering portrait of a daughter was painted by mothers who were working full-time, but this was also the group that portrayed the son in the least favorable terms. A further breakdown by mother's educational status indicated that the enthusiastic view of a daughter in the full-time group occurred only among those mothers who had some education beyond high school. In the light of both quantitative and qualitative findings, the authors make the following interpretative comment: "The pattern brings to mind the picture of an aspiring professional woman who already sees her three-year-old daughter as an interesting and competent person potentially capable of following in her mother's footsteps" (p. 1,366). The most salient feature of the findings for sons was the exceptionally positive description given by mothers working part-time, in contrast to the much lower evaluation offered by those fully employed. The advantages of part-time employment, so far as maternal perceptions are concerned, were appreciably greater for a son that for a daughter. The results of interviews with fathers (conducted separately) revealed the same highly differentiated profile, but in somewhat lower relief.[2]

Revealing as the foregoing studies are of the dynamics of the family-work exosystem, they fail to take account of what turns out to be a critical third dimension–that of continuity versus change in employment status over time. Research bearing on this issue is discussed below.

Parental Support Networks

Investigations in this domain first began to appear in the 1970s. In a study of child neglect among low-income families

---

[1] A growing phenomenon in this regard that has received surprisingly little research attention is paternal employment requiring frequent and extended absence from the home. Results from one of the few studies of the developmental effects of this pattern, Tiller's (1958) investigation of Norwegian sailor and whaler families, suggests that the outcomes may be rather different from those observed for children of divorced, separated, or widowed parents.

[2] Regarding the basis for the observed sex differences in the effects of maternal employment, the authors speculate as follows: "One possible explanation draws on the recurrent and generally accepted finding in research on early sex differences (Maccoby & Jacklin, 1974) that male infants tend to be more physically active from birth and hence require more control and supervision. Full-time work may limit opportunities for such necessary monitoring. Viewed from this perspective, the findings suggest that the reported sex difference in effects of maternal employment derive from the cumulative interaction of familial, organismic, and employment factors evolving in a larger socioeconomic context" (p. 1371).

Giovanni and Billingsley (1970) found that neglect was less frequent among families characterized by strong kinship networks and regular church attendance. The authors conclude the "among low-income people, neglect would seem to be a social problem that is as much a manifestation of social and community conditions as it is of any individual parent's pathology" (p. 204). Corroborative data come from a large-scale correlational analysis of child abuse reports and socioeconomic and demographic information for the 58 counties in New York State (Garbarino, 1976). In the investigator's words, "a substantial proportion of the variance in rates of child abuse/maltreatment among New York State counties . . . was found to be associated with the degree to which mothers do not possess adequate support systems for parenting and are subjected to economic stress." (p. 185)

Subsequent research in this sphere has continued to focus almost exclusively on mothers of young children, particularly mothers in specially vulnerable groups such as teen-age mothers, single-parent mothers, or families living in poverty. In general, these studies revealed that support was more likely to come from kin than nonkin, with the father being the principal source of help, even in single-parent households; the mother's mother was next in line, followed by other relatives, and then friends, neighbors, and professionals (Belle, 1981; Brown, Bhrolchin, & Harris, 1975; Crockenberg, in press-a, in press-b; Tietjen & Bradley, 1982). In the area of attitudes, Tietjen and Bradley (1982) found that mothers who had access to stronger social networks during their pregnancy reported lower levels of stress, anxiety, and depression, a better marital adjustment, and a more positive attitude toward their pregnancy. Support from the husband was more effective than that from friends, neighbors, or relatives outside the home. Studies conducted of families with young infants revealed that low family support evoked maternal attitudes of hostility, indifference, and rejection of the infant (Colletta, 1981), whereas mothers experiencing help and comfort, primarily from the immediate family and relatives, felt less stress and had more positive attitudes toward themselves and their babies (Aug & Bright, 1970; Colletta, 1981, 1983; Colletta & Gregg, 1981; Colletta and Lee, 1983; Mercer, Hackley, & Bostrom, in press). In the realm of maternal behavior, mothers receiving higher levels of social support responded more quickly when their infants cried (Crockenberg, 1984a, 1984b) and provided more adequate caretaking behavior (Epstein, 1980; Wandersman & Unger, 1983).

With respect to the behavior of the children themselves, Furstenberg & Crawford (1978) has documented effects of family support on the child's social and emotional development. Working with a predominantly black sample of teen-age mothers, he found that children of mothers who continued to live with their families of origin experienced fewer behavior problems, showed less antisocial behavior, and scored higher on cognitive tests than did children of teenage mothers who lived alone without adult relatives.

A more differentiated picture of sources of external support, stress, and their interaction emerges from a study by Crnic and his colleagues (1983). These investigators devised separate indexes of stress and of support experienced by the mother from the beginning of her pregnancy until the infant had been home for 1 month. Moreover, the measure of support distinguished

between help coming from three different sources: the mother's husband (or partner), friends, and other persons in the neighborhood or community. The analysis revealed that both environmental stress and environmental support had independent effects on the family. Maternal attitudes were influenced most; social support was associated with more positive orientations, stress with more negative ones. Effects on both the mother's and the infant's behavior, when observed after a 3-month interval, were less powerful, but still significant. Mothers who had received higher levels of support when the infants had been 1 month old were more responsive and positive in interacting with the child 3 months later. Correspondingly, the babies acted more responsively and positively toward their mothers and gave clearer cues regarding their emotional state, needs, and desires. The infant's behavior was affected somewhat more than the mother's. The findings with respect to source of support were equally instructive. Whereas support from either spouse, friends, or community was about equally influential in increasing maternal levels of satisfaction, support from the father had an appreciably stronger and more general effect on the actual behavior of both mother and child than did help from friends or community. Finally, environmental stresses and supports interacted with each other, with support serving to buffer the disruptive effects of stress.

An analogous interaction effect appears in a study of the impact of environmental stress and social support in single- and two-parent families (Weinraub & Wolf, 1983); stress proved to be more debilitating and social support more effective when the mother was not married. Once again, it would appear that social support is most potent under conditions of stress.

This conclusion must be qualified, however, in the light of a subsequent study by Crockenberg (in press-b) with an extremely deprived sample—a group of teenage mothers who were also unmarried, uneducated, poor, and predominantly Black and Mexican-American. Her findings indicate that, for mothers living under highly stressful conditions, social networks not only cease to exert a positive influence but can even become a source of stress.

A similar result is reported in a recent article by Riley and Eckenrode (in press). In a study of stresses and supports in mothers' lives, the investigators found that the influence of social networks on psychological well-being shifted in direction from positive to negative as a function of three kinds of factors: (a) reduced socioeconomic status, (b) the occurrence of misfortune in the lives of significant others (e.g., a close relative suffers an accident), or (c) low levels of belief either in one's capacity to influence one's own life (i.e., locus of control) or in the probable success vs failure of one's own help-seeking efforts.

Processes and outcomes of social support are set within a still broader social context in Crockenberg's most recent study (1985), in which she compared English teenage mothers with a matched sample of their American counterparts. She found that "English mothers engaged in more smiling and eye contact, less frequent routine contact, and responded more quickly to their babies' crying than did American mothers" (p. 422). Control of possibly confounding variables through regression analysis pointed to the amount and type of social support as the factor accounting for the difference. Crockenberg elaborates as follows:

8

In the United States most mothers rely on private doctors to serve their own and their children's health needs. . . . Public health nurses or social workers may be assigned to families in need of special assistance, but there is no comprehensive system designed to provide health-related and child care advice to parents. . . . In contrast, through the National Health Service, England incorporates community-based social support for parents in a comprehensive program of health care. This care begins before the child's birth and continues through his school years. . . . Midwives provide postnatal care for mothers and babies after they leave the hospital following delivery, and home health visitors see new mothers on a regular basis. . . . In England, mothers had only to be home and open their doors. (pp. 414–425)

Although this provocative cultural contrast clearly requires replication, in terms of research design it provides an excellent example of the power of a process-context model for analyzing external influences on family processes and their developmental effects.

The Family and the Community

The outstanding studies in this domain have been those conducted by Rutter and his colleagues, beginning with their classical comparison of rates of mental disorder in inner-London and the Isle of Wight (Rutter et al., 1975; Rutter & Quinton, 1977). In order to control for possible effects of migration, the investigators confined their samples to children of parents born and bred only in the given area. Their findings reveal that rates of psychiatric disorder were much more frequent in the metropolis. Nor could the observed effects be explained by any community differences with respect to ethnicity, social class, or demographic factors (Quinton, 1980; Rutter & Madge, 1976). Indeed, the same social class position appeared to have a different significance in urban versus rural environments, with low socioeconomic status being a much stronger predictor of mental illness in the city than in the country. In the light of this series of findings, Rutter concluded: "It seemed that there must be something about living in the city which predisposed to mental disorder" (1981, p. 612).

What is this "something?" Rutter's own efforts to answer this question have yielded results of particular relevance for child development. For example, taking advantage of the longitudinal design of the London–Isle of Wight study, Rutter (1981) analyzed community differences as a joint function of age of onset and type of disorder.

The results were striking in showing that the biggest difference between London and the Isle of Wight applied to *chronic* disorders of *early* onset. . . . The least difference was found with psychiatric conditions beginning in adolescence for the first time. Moreover, the difference also mainly applied to disorders associated with serious family difficulties. In short, the problems most characteristic of city children were those beginning early, lasting a long time, and accompanied by many other problems in the family. (Rutter, 1981, p. 613, italics in original)

These findings raise the possibility that the observed community differences may simply reflect the aggregation of vulnerable families. To clarify this issue, Rutter and Quinton (1977) compared rates of psychiatric disorder in different neighborhoods controlling for such factors as the proportion of low status, low-income families, and single-parent households. They found that families were affected irrespective of their background characteristics, so that, in general, persons living in a vulnerable area shared a higher risk of psychiatric disorder. In short, to use Rutter's words, the effect was to some extent ecological as well as individual.

Such an effect can operate in two ways. It can impinge on children directly, or indirectly through the child's family. To investigate these possibilities, Rutter and his colleagues (1975, 1977) developed an index of "family adversity" including such factors as marital discord and dissolution, mental disorder or criminality in the parents, large family size, and other conditions known to be associated with higher levels of psychiatric disturbance and social deviance. Again, the results were striking, but now in the opposite direction. With the degree of family adversity controlled, the difference between London and the Isle of Wight in rates of child psychiatric illness all but disappeared. The authors interpret this result as indicating that the main adverse effects of city life on children are indirect, resulting from the disruption of the families in which they live.

Similar evidence of indirect effects on the child via the family have also been found for juvenile delinquency. The relevant research has been summarized by Rutter and Giller (1983). For example, using a longitudinal design that permitted control for prior characteristics both of the child and of the family, West (1982) was able to demonstrate that delinquency rates for boys declined after the family moved out of London. As Rutter notes in a personal communication (1984) what is lacking in studies of this kind (including his own) is an identification of the particular features of an area that produce the given effect, and the process through which the effect takes place. "It is all very well to note the 'stresses' of inner-city life, but what is needed is to determine just what it is that makes inner-city life stressful for some families in some circumstances. Personally, I would see this as the most important needed direction for future research."

Finally, whereas the indirect effects of urban residence appear to be negative for social and emotional development, particularly in young children, there is evidence that the direct influence of the city environment may be beneficial for intellectual development among *older* children. The principal support for this conclusion comes from a two-stage investigation carried out in rural and urban areas of Switzerland. The first study (Meili & Steiner, 1965) was conducted with 11-year-old school children. The researchers found that performance in both intelligence and achievement tests increased as a direct function of the amount of industry and traffic present in the area. The relationship was still significant after controlling for social class, but the influence of the latter variable was more powerful than that of locality. Four years later, in a follow-up study, Vatter (1981) undertook to investigate the nature of the more immediate influences accounting for this result. Drawing on earlier work by Klineberg (1935, 1938) and Wheeler (1942), Vatter hypothesized that the superior cognitive functioning observed in city children was a product of exposure to richer and more differentiated cultural environment typifying the urban scene. To investigate his "stimulus hypothesis," Vatter obtained information from his subjects about their daily activities within the community, and about the nature of existing community facilities (for example, availability and use of libraries, learning opportunities outside the home, etc.). In support of the author's hypothe-

9

sis, there was a significant positive relation between indexes of the community environment and mental test scores. Moreover, community factors appeared to exert a stronger influence than intrafamilial variables (median r of .41 vs. .26). Vatter acknowledges, however, that his design did not permit adequate control for migration effects, because his follow-up study did not include all of the original cases, and it was impossible to identify and reanalyze Time 1 data for the Time 2 sample.[3]

Chronosystem Models

The impact of a single life transition on family processes and the development of the child is well illustrated in the work of Hetherington and her colleagues (Hetherington, 1981; Hetherington, Cox, & Cox, 1978), which traced the progressive impact of divorce on the mother–child relationship and the child's behavior in school. The disruptive effects of separation reached their peak 1 year afterward and declined through the second year, although the divorced mothers never gained as much influence with the child as their married counterparts wielded. Two of Hetherington's findings illustrate the power of exosystem forces in influencing family processes. First, the mother's effectiveness in dealing with the child was directly related to the amount of support received from third parties such as friends, relatives, and especially her exhusband. Second, the disruptive effects of divorce were exacerbated in those instances in which the separation was accompanied by the mother's entry into the work force.

The potentially destabilizing impact of extrafamilial transitions on intrafamilial processes is elegantly demonstrated in a doctoral dissertation by Moorehouse (1986). This researcher employed a two-stage model in order to investigate how stability versus change over time in the mother's work status during the child's preschool years affected patterns of mother–child communication, and how these patterns in turn influenced the child's achievement and social behavior in the first year of school. The complex nature of the feedback systems operating in the family–workplace–school interface is illustrated by the following seemingly paradoxical sequence of findings;

1. As reflected by grades and teacher ratings, the children experiencing the greatest difficulty in adapting to school were those whose mother was working full time. This relationship remained significant after control for mother's education.

2. As hypothesized, the generally positive relationship between mother's communicative activities at home and the child's performance at school varied systematically as a function of the mother's work status, and was strongest among the children of mothers working full time. In the author's words,

> Rather than weakening the effectiveness of the mother–child system, a full-time job appears to increase the positive impact of this system on the child's school competence . . . When high levels of communicative activities are maintained, these children are as competent, or more competent, than their peers with mothers who work fewer hours or not at all. Thus, mother–child activities seem to compensate or prevent detrimental consequences of maternal employment for children who are first entering school. (p. 129)

3. Moorehouse carried out a comparative analysis of mothers who had maintained the same employment status over the period of the study versus those who had changed in either di-

rection: that is, working more hours, fewer hours, or none at all. The results revealed that significant effects of work status were pronounced only in the latter group. Moreover, "instability, on the whole, is associated with less favorable school outcomes than stability" (p. 89).

Moorehouse cautions that her findings should be viewed as tentative, because her sample was comparatively small (N = 112), resulting in only minimally acceptable frequencies in some of the subgroups. Nevertheless her conclusion regarding the importance of stability in the family's environment finds independent confirmation in the results of a longitudinal study in Finland conducted by Pulkkinen (Pitkanen-Pulkkinen, 1980; Pulkkinen, 1982, 1983b, 1984). The investigator examined the influence of environmental stability and change on the development of children from 8 to 14 years of age. Specifically, the "steadiness" versus "unsteadiness" of family living conditions was measured by the occurrence of events such as the following: the number of family moves, changes in day care or school arrangements, parental absences, changes in family structure, and altered conditions of maternal employment. Greater instability in the family environment was associated with greater submissiveness, aggressiveness, and anxiety among children in later childhood and adolescence, and higher rates of criminality in adulthood. Moreover, the factor of stability of family living conditions appeared to be a stronger determinant of the child's development than the family's socioeconomic status. (The relation of socioeconomic status to family stability, however, was not examined.)

A similar finding was reported in a longitudinal study carried out in Hawaii (Werner & Smith, 1982). The investigators focused special attention on a subgroup of their sample whom they designated as "Vulnerable but Invincible." These were adolescents and youth who, over the course of their lives, had been "exposed to poverty, biological risks, and family instability, and reared by parents with little education or serious mental health problems—who remained *invincible* and developed into competent and autonomous young adults who worked well, played well, loved well, and expected well" (p. 3). A major environmental factor that distinguished this group from their socioeconomically matched "nonresilient" controls was a low number of chronic, stressful life events experienced in childhood and adolescence, and the presence of an informal multigenerational network of kin.

The Hawaiian research also validated in a longitudinal design a pattern of reversing sex differences previously detectable only in fragmented fashion from cross-sectional designs (Hetherington, 1972, 1981; Hetherington & Deur, 1971). Through the first decade of life, boys appeared to be substantially more vulnerable than girls both to biological and environmental insult; during the second decade of life, however, the pattern was reversed.

> Boys seemed now more prepared for the demands of school and work . . . girls were now confronted with social pressures and sexual expectations that produced a higher rate of mental health prob-

---

[3] Similar findings were reported in an earlier study by Clausen and Kohn (1959). The correlations between neighborhood characteristics and the development of psychiatric disorders were greater in large cities than in smaller ones.

lems in later adolescence . . . often control of aggression appeared to be one of the major problems for the boys in childhood, dependency became a major problem for the girls in adolescence . . . In spite of the biological and social pressures which in this culture appeared to make each sex more vulnerable at different times, more high-risk girls than high-risk boys grow into resilient young adults. (pp. 153–154)

The reader will have observed that the investigations just described are no longer confined to the developmental impact of a single event in a person's life. Rather they examine cumulative effects of a sequence of developmental transitions over time—what Elder has referred to as the *life course.* The scientific power of this paradigm is best illustrated by Elder's now classic study of "Children of the Great Depression" (1974). To investigate the long-range effects of this experience on children's development, Elder reanalyzed archival data from two longitudinal studies that had been conducted in California with samples of children born in the early versus late 1920s (Elder, 1974, 1981, 1984). The basic design in these investigations involved the comparison of two otherwise comparable groups differentiated on the basis of whether the loss of income as a result of the Depression extended or fell short of 35%. The availability of longitudinal data made it possible to assess developmental outcomes through childhood, adolescence, and adulthood. Finally, the fact that children in one sample were born 8 years earlier than those in the other permitted a comparison of the effects of the Depression on youngsters who were adolescents when their families became economically deprived versus those who were still young children at that time.

The results for the two groups presented a dramatic contrast. Paradoxically, for youngsters who were teenagers during the Depression years, the families' economic deprivation appeared to have a salutary effect on their subsequent development, especially in the middle class. As compared with the nondeprived who were matched on pre-Depression socioeconomic status, deprived boys displayed greater desire to achieve and a firmer sense of career goals. Boys and girls from deprived homes attained greater satisfaction in life, both by their own and by societal standards. Though more pronounced for adolescents from middle-class backgrounds, these favorable outcomes were evident among their lower-class counterparts as well. Analysis of interview and observation protocols enabled Elder to identify what he regarded as a critical factor in investigating this favorable developmental trajectory: The loss of economic security forced the family to mobilize its own human resources, including its teenagers, who had to take on new roles and responsibilities both within and outside the home and to work together toward the common goal of getting and keeping the family on its feet. This experience provided effective training in initiative, responsibility, and cooperation. In the words of the banished Duke, "Sweet are the uses of adversity."

Alas, adversity was not so sweet for male children who were still preschoolers when their families suffered economic loss. The results were almost the opposite of those for boys in the earlier investigation. Compared with controls from nondeprived families, these youngsters subsequently did less well in school, showed less stable and successful work histories, and exhibited more emotional and social difficulties, some still apparent in middle adulthood. These negative outcomes were much more marked in boys than in girls and were accentuated in families from lower class backgrounds.

Subsequently, Elder and his coworkers have emphasized the importance of mediating processes and conditions within the family as the vehicles through which economic hardship reaches into the child's life and shapes the course of subsequent development (Elder, Caspi, & Downey, in press; Elder, Caspi, & van Nguyen, 1986; Elder, Van Nguyen, & Caspi, 1985). Perhaps the most important factors in this regard were the personality characteristics of fathers and children. The presence in the family of an irritable father or an irritating child significantly increased the likelihood that unemployment would have long-range negative consequences for life course development. Also critical was the marital discord that often arose, or became exacerbated, following the father's loss of a job.

In an especially revealing analysis, Elder, Caspi, and Downey (in press) have traced the impact of life course experience across four generations, and shown the effects of unstable parents and family life during the Depression on problem behavior of the children, who in turn are followed into their adult roles: work, marriage, and the raising of sons and daughters. Within a generation, it is the unstable personality of the parent, particularly the father, that gives rise to tension both in the marital relationship and the parent–child dyad. Across generations, it is disturbance in either of these family relationships that leads to the development of an unstable personality in the child as an adult.

In recent years, a number of developmental studies employing a life course perspective have yielded important research results. Some, like the researches of Scarr, Mortimer, and Pulkkinen, have already been mentioned. An additional example appears in the work of Furstenberg and Gunn (Furstenberg, 1976; Furstenberg & Brooks-Gunn, in press). These investigators have shown that, contrary to conclusions drawn from previous research, teenage pregnancy does not necessarily lead to academic and personal failure in the rest of a woman's life. A special strength of the second volume is its emphasis on the feasibility of alternative pathways that could be provided through the development of appropriate policies and programs.

Although the advantages of a chronosystem model are best achieved within the framework of a longitudinal design, important benefits can also be gleaned from cross-sectional studies that gather key retrospective data and use appropriate analytic procedures, such as causal modeling. An example is the work of Schneewind and his colleagues (1983). Their sample consisted of 570 children (ages 9–14) from schools in six German states. Data were obtained independently from both children and their parents. The productivity of such a multigenerational path analytic model is best conveyed by some illustrative findings. For example, one of the analyses focused on the environmental antecedents of two contrasting clusters of children's maladaptive behavior: aggressiveness and antisocial behavior on the one hand and anxiety and helplessness on the other. Both patterns were influenced by factors outside the child's immediate family, but in each instance the causal path was indirect rather than direct, with the parental use of corporal punishment serving as a key intervening variable. Parents most likely to employ physical discipline were those who occupied a lower socioeconomic status or who themselves had experienced an unhappy childhood. But even here the influence on parental practices was not direct but operated principally through effects on parental personality structure, marital conflict, and child rearing attitudes. Moreover, these findings, obtained from a cross-sectional sample in Germany, were strikingly similar to Elder's results from a longitudinal study in the United States.

Turning from the problematic to the constructive aspects of the child's behavior, Schneewind and his colleagues also examined the environmental and personality antecedents of children's creativity and social extravertedness as measured in psychometric tests. In both instances, a key intervening environmental variable was the family's social network. Moreover, in contrast to most American studies in which social networks are viewed as support systems influencing the family (e.g., Cochran & Brassard, 1979; Crnic et al., 1983; Crockenberg, 1981), Schneewind et al. (1983) interpreted social networks as a product of an expressive and stimulating climate within the family. This stimulating atmosphere also emerged as a major determinant both of the child's creativity (especially in girls) and social involvement (especially in boys), including establishment of the children's own social networks and their engagement in group and extracurricular activities.

Research Gaps and Opportunities

From the scientist's perspective, perhaps the most important function of a review of existing knowledge in a particular area is to identify promising directions for future investigation. As in other spheres of exploration, there is uncharted terrain at all four points of the compass.

Ecological Variations in the Expression of Genotypes

Identification of discordant phenotypes. Studies of the role of family inheritance in human development have focused almost exclusively on concordant cases; that is, the fact that persons related by blood tend to exhibit similar psychological characteristics; almost no attention has been paid to discordant instances. For example, when one twin has been diagnosed as schizophrenic, or has a criminal record, or has failed to graduate from school, but the other twin has not, what patterns of behavior or life career does this other twin exhibit? In the absence of such comparative data, investigators are prone to draw conclusions about the existence of familial genetic dispositions that are highly specific; for example, one assumes a hereditarian proclivity for criminal behavior, or particular forms of mental disorder. The possibility exists, however, that the biological predisposition may be of a more general order. The issue could be resolved by examining the nature of variation and behavior patterns exhibited by persons of identical genetic constitution in different contexts. In reviewing the research literature, I have been able to find only one investigation that examines the career lines of discordant cases. In a study of psychiatric disorders among foster home-reared children of schizophrenic mothers, Heston (1966) reports that nonschizophrenic offspring tended to be persons of unusual creativity and competence. Unfortunately, there are a number of flaws in the study design. More rigorous investigations of this kind, encompassing positive as well as negative outcomes, would not only help define the scope of genetic predispositions but also elucidate the operation of

both intra- and extrafamilial environments in shaping alternative courses of psychological development for persons of similar genetic endowment.

Child rearing processes in adoptive families. In a series of publications, Scarr and her associates (Scarr, 1981; Scarr & McCartney, 1983; Scarr & Weinberg, 1983) have argued that results of numerous studies purporting to demonstrate the environmental effect of parental behavior on children's development are in fact ambiguous because they are confounded by the genetic similarity between biological parents and their children. This similarity, Scarr contends, obtains both in the realm of perception and behavior, so that each party of the dyad is likely on genetic grounds to be especially responsive to the action (or passivity) of the other. In Scarr's view, such multiplicative effects account for most of the developmental variance within what she calls "the normal range"; that is, persons not severely damaged by organic or environmental insult. Implied in this provocative formulation is the assumption that patterns of parent–child interaction in adoptive families are quite different from those occurring among biological-related family members. Should such a difference in fact exist, it would have profound implications for the development of children raised by biological parents who possess psychological characteristics known to have a significant genetic basis. Microanalytic techniques for the analysis of parent–child interaction, such as those developed by Patterson (1982) would be particularly well-suited for the comparative study of adoptive and biological families as contrasting contexts of family functioning.

Relations Between the Family and Other Child Settings

Existing theory and research point to the importance for the child's development of the nature and strength of connections existing between the family and the various other settings that a young person enters during the first two decades of life. Of particular significance in this regard are the successive transitions into (and within) day care, peer group, school, and work. In relation to each of these extrafamilial settings, three stages of transition deserve attention:

Preexisting intersetting relationships. How is the process of transition, and its developmental effects, influenced by the presence or absence of prior connections between the two settings? Such linkages may take the form of previous social interactions between participants in the two settings (e.g., parent and teacher are friends, the child has an older sibling at school) or of information, attitudes, and expectations existing in each setting about the other.

Transition feedback. Once the child has entered the new setting, this event can markedly alter attitudes, expectations, and patterns of interaction *within* the family, especially in relation to the child. Such reorganization of the family system following the child's transition into a new role in a new setting can have even more significance for the child's development than his or her experience within the new setting.

Posttransition changes in relations between settings. The child's development may be further affected by shifts over time in the nature and extent of linkages between the family and the other principal settings in which the child spends his or her time (for example, the parents encourage or discourage the child's contact with peers; there is a decline or increase of parental interest in the child's school experience).

A particularly effective research strategy for investigating the development of relations between the family and other settings is a controlled experiment designed to create or strengthen linkages between settings (for example, the experiment by Smith, 1968, cited previously).

The foregoing consideration is applicable to setting transitions and linkages in general. In addition, the relations between the family and specific settings in the child's life deserve further comment.

Family and day care. A major gap in research in this area is the absence of studies of how children's development is affected not directly but indirectly through the role of day care as a support system for parents, especially for mothers. Although a number of research reviews have emphasized the importance of such indirect influence (e.g., Belsky, 1985), no investigation has yet been specifically focused on this issue. A second and related omission is the failure to investigate the interrelation between day care and parental employment. It seems likely that the observed developmental effects in the latter sphere may be moderated by day care as a family support system.

Family and the peer group. As documented above, previous research in this sphere has focused primarily on the family's capacity to counteract pressures toward socially deviant behavior emanating from the peer group. Yet, a number of developmental theorists, most notably Piaget (1932), have emphasized the constructive role of experience with peers for both the child's moral and cognitive development. Subsequent investigations demonstrating the powerful interplay between parent and peer influences in the genesis of antisocial behavior by no means rule out the possibility of constructive processes emanating from the same parallelogram of forces. Of particular promise is the application of chronosystem designs in tracing alternative pathways from family to peer group and then, from both of these contexts, into adult roles in the areas of school, work, family formation, parenthood, and participation in the social and political life of the community.

Family and the school. The available research evidence suggests that a powerful factor affecting the capacity of a child to learn in the classroom is the relationship existing between the family and the school. Although, as previously noted, a number of investigations have addressed this interface, the majority are descriptive rather than analytic and are limited almost entirely to the role of parents as educators, with scholastic achievement serving as the principal psychological outcome. Lacking are process-oriented field studies or experiments that trace the emergence of a broader range of characteristics and employ research designs addressed to each of the three stages of intersetting relationships set forth in the opening paragraph of this section. Of particular importance are investigations of feedback effects from school experience to family functioning.

Family and children's work experience. The developmental effects of this important life transition are only beginning to receive the attention they deserve. The gap in knowledge is all the more striking given the fact that, according to recent figures, about half of all American high school students engage in some form of paid employment. Moreover, a pioneering series of studies (Greenberger & Steinberg, in press; Greenberger,

Steinberg, & Vaux, 1981; Steinberg et al., 1982) has shown that, contrary to the expectations and recommendations of several blue ribbon panels (e.g., National Commission on Youth, 1980; President's Scientific Advisory Commission, 1979), such job involvement, rather than furthering the development of responsibility, diminishes the adolescent's involvement in the family and school, increases use of cigarettes and marijuana, generates cynical attitudes toward work, and encourages acceptance of unethical work practices. From this perspective, the role of the parents in influencing the timing, selection, and interpretation of the child's work experience, and the resulting feedback effect of such experience on the family's treatment of the child, may have considerable significance for the child's subsequent development in the adult roles of worker, spouse, parent, and citizen.

Relations Between Family Processes and Parental Participation in Other Settings of Adult Life

The directions for future research in this sphere are well indicated by the gaps in existing knowledge. These fall under two now-familiar headings.

Family and the conditions of parental work. Especially lacking in this sphere are studies examining the developmental impact of the *joint* employment patterns of father and mother. Of particular significance is conflict between the work schedules of the two parents, and the hecticness it may generate in their lives as these conditions affect the intensity and quality of parent-child interaction. A second omission is the failure to include within the same research design provision for investigating both links in the presumed causal chain: (a) the influence of parental employment on parental functioning and (b) the effect of the induced change in family processes on the behavior and development of the child. Finally, there is evidence to suggest that, as in other domains, both the sex and the age of the child may be critical in mediating the impact of parents' work. Specifically, conditions of employment may be more consequential, both positively and negatively, for younger children, although the full effect may not be observable until the children are older, and the outcome may be rather different for daughters and sons.

Family and parental social networks. Research in this sphere is plagued by the lack of clarity in the operationalization of concepts and causal processes. First, both agents and types of support need to be differentiated and related to the degree of environmental stress to which the family is subjected. Second, research designs must take into account the possibility that causal processes may actually be operating in the reverse direction, with supportive social networks being a creation rather than a condition of constructive family functioning. Finally, as in research on parents' working conditions, social network studies should be expanded to encompass the full, two-step causal sequence: first, from the network properties to family functioning (or vice-versa) and second, from family functioning to the behavior and development of the child (or vice versa).

Families in Broader Social Contexts

Five topics are especially relevant here.

Unravelling social class. An essential task is to penetrate behind the label of socioeconomic status to identify the specific elements of social structure and substance that shape the course and content of human development. This unravelling process requires the decomposition of the typically composite measures of social class into their most common components (occupational status, parental education, and family income).

Family's occupational status. In their most recent work, Kohn and his followers (Kohn & Schooler, 1978, 1982, 1983; Miller, Schooler, Kohn, & Miller, 1979, Miller & Kohn, 1983) have used causal modeling techniques in order to demonstrate that the degree of occupational self-direction in the job promotes the development of the worker's intellectual flexibility. But, no evidence is available as yet on how the opportunity for self-direction at work, and the intellectual flexibility that it engenders, relate to parental patterns of child rearing or how these, in turn, affect the behavior and development of the child. A related issue is whether and how parental experiences at work operate through the family to influence the selection, timing, and psychological content of the child's successive transitions into, and experience in, other settings such as school, peer group, and, especially, the world of work.

Parents' education. This variable takes on special significance in an ecological systems model on several counts. First, it offers a unique advantage for the analysis of causal pathways, because, unlike either occupational status or income, it usually precedes both family formation and the birth of the child, and hence provides an index of social background, separately, for each parent, that is unlikely to be influenced by subsequent family processes, and therefore can be interpreted primarily as unidirectional in its effects. Second, as revealed in the work of Tulkin and others, education appears to be an important source for parents' conceptions of the nature and capacities both of the child and of the parent at successive stages of the child's life. A more complete understanding of the connection between parental schooling and family perceptions is clearly in the interest of both developmental science and of educational policy and practice.

Family income. As this author has pointed out elsewhere (Bronfenbrenner, 1982, 1984, 1986), income plays an especially telling role in American family life because, to a greater extent than in other modern industrialized societies, the resources and services required for sustaining the health and well-being of family members and furthering the development of the child are dependent on the family's financial resources. This issue becomes critical to families that are chronically poor or in which the principal breadwinner becomes unemployed. Because of the magnitude of the resultant effect on children, this issue is given separate consideration in the final section of this review.

Families in the community. It is a striking fact, and a provocative question for the sociology of knowledge, that the overwhelming majority of systematic studies of community influences on families and children have been conducted in Europe. In addition to the British and Swiss studies reviewed above, a seminal line of investigation in France takes its impetus from the classic two volume work by Chombart de Lauwe (1959–60), "Famille et habitation," and focuses primarily on neighborhood and housing as physical environments. In German-speaking Europe, a research tradition stimulated by the Muchows' (1935) classic study of the life-span of city children has led to

investigations that are more diversified. For example, a recent compilation by Walter (1981, 1982) fills two volumes with well-designed studies by more than a score of investigators representing a variety of theoretical orientations.

The European work is distinguished not only for its quantity, but also for the comparative sophistication of the research paradigms that have been employed. Whereas American studies have been confined almost exclusively to social address models documenting associated differences in the behavior of children (Barker & Schoggen, 1973; Garbarino, 1976; Hollingshead, 1949), European investigations have focused on variations in socialization processes arising in different types of communities or neighborhoods defined by their particular physical and social characteristics. For example, in the first volume of Walter's *Region and Sozialisation*, Bargel and his associates (1981) developed the concept of "Soziotope" for classifying types of residential areas. They then applied their taxonomy both to rural and urban districts in the West German state of Nordhessen in order to demonstrate that particular styles of child rearing are associated with contrasting forms of Soziotope. The more differentiated taxonomies for describing communities developed by European researchers provide a point of departure for addressing what Rutter has designated as "the most important needed direction for future research" in the study of community influences on the family: identifying the particular features of community life that impair or enhance family functioning.

Family and geographic mobility. One key aspect of family ecology has been equally neglected by researchers in Europe and the United States—the impact on family functioning, and on children, of moving from place to place. The only research that has given at least partial attention to this problem is the previously mentioned longitudinal study by Pulkkinen (Pitkanen-Pulkinnen, 1980; Pulkinnen, 1982). Geographic mobility was one of the components in Pulkkinen's index of the instability of the family environment. This index, in turn, proved to be a major predictor of the child's subsequent development in adolescence and early adulthood. Although, to this writer's knowledge, no reliable figures exist for the United States on the frequency of moves among families with children, it seems likely that the incidence is quite high in certain occupations, for example, the military (McCubbin, Dahl, & Hunter, 1976). The much-needed studies in this area should take into account both the direct and indirect effects on the child of simultaneous disruption of established patterns of relations within the peer group, the school, and the family, as well as the subsequent processes of rebuilding linkages in the new location. Of special significance in this regard is the experience of newly immigrant families, particularly those who come from, and enter into, markedly contrasting environments with respect to values, customs, and socioeconomic conditions.

Television and the family. In terms of research, this area is truly a terra incognita. As this reviewer has written elsewhere (Bronfenbrenner, 1974a), the primary importance of television for child development may lie "not so much in the behavior it produces as the behavior it prevents," and the behavior that can be prevented is family interaction—"the talks, the games, the family festivities, and arguments through which much of the child's learning takes place and his character is formed" (p. 170). The trouble with this seemingly authoritative conclusion is that it is based almost entirely on subjective opinion. To be sure, the opinion has subsequently been echoed in two necessarily brief reviews of research on television's role in family life (Garbarino, 1975; Dorr, 1981). But, insofar as I have been able to determine, the only empirical study that has examined the effect of television on patterns of family interaction is the pioneering research of Maccoby, published more than three decades ago (1951). Her principal conclusion: "The nature of the family social life during a program could be described as 'parallel' rather than interactive, and the set does seem quite clearly to dominate family life when it is on" (p. 428). Given the massive expansion of the medium in the interim, it is clearly time to follow up on Maccoby's lead, employing research models that will be revealing not only of family processes but of the developmental outcomes that they may generate.

Family, poverty, and unemployment. Elder's follow-up studies of "Children of the Great Depression" carry special significance for the contemporary scene. As revealed in recent census data, the most rapid, and perhaps the most consequential, change taking place in American family life in the 1980s has been the widening gap between poor families and the rest of society. To quote an official census report (U.S. Bureau of the Census, 1981), recent data document "the largest decline in family income in the post-World War II period." As of March of last year (U.S. Bureau of the Census, 1985), almost a fourth (24%) of the nation's children under 3 years of age, and between 3 and 6 as well, were living in families below the "poverty line," compared to 15% for the population as a whole, and 16% for those over 65 (Bronfenbrenner, 1986b, c). The effects of the current economic trend are already being reflected in research findings (Farran & Margolis, 1983; Steinberg, Catalano, & Dooley, 1981). For example, Steinberg and his colleagues studied the impact of unemployment on 8,000 families in California in a longitudinal design. Analyses of data over a 30-month period revealed that increases in child abuse were preceded by periods of high job loss, thus confirming the authors' hypothesis that "undesirable economic change *leads* to increased child maltreatment" (p. 975). More recently, Farran and Margolis (1983) have reported yet another more subtle but no less insidious impact of parental job loss. In families in which the father had been unemployed for several months, children exhibited a significant increase in susceptibility to contagious diseases. The authors offered two explanations for these effects: (a) reduced use of preventative health services because of income loss and (b) the greater vulnerability of children to contagious diseases in response to increased family stress.

As this author has written elsewhere:

> It is the irony and limitation of our science that the greater the harm done to children, the more we stand to learn about the environmental conditions that are essential for making—and keeping—human beings human. As we enter the 1980s, there are indications that these essential conditions are being seriously undermined in broad segments of American society. It therefore becomes our professional obligation to employ the most advanced research designs at our disposal in order to forestall the tragic opportunity of significantly expanding our knowledge about the limits of the human condition for developing human beings. (Bronfenbrenner & Crouter, 1983, p. 412)

Research on the effects of child and family policy. Implied

in the above statement is the responsibility of developmental science to go beyond the analysis of the status quo in order to design and evaluate strategies that can sustain, enhance, and, where necessary, create environments that are conducive to healthy human growth. And indeed, in accord with this responsibility, during the 1960s and the 1970s a substantial number of investigators developed, carried out, and researched a variety of intervention programs that had both rehabilitation and prevention as their aims. Although some of the impressive initial gains appeared to attenuate over time (Bronfenbrenner, 1974b), more recent analyses have revealed encouraging longer-term effects. For example, children who were enrolled as preschoolers more than two decades ago subsequently showed significantly higher rates of meeting school requirements than did controls as measured by lower frequency of placement in special education classes and of retention in grade (Berrueta-Clement, Schweinhart, Barnett, Epstein, & Weikart, 1984; Consortium for Longitudinal Studies, 1983; Darlington et al., 1980). Today, preliminary reports of the most recent findings indicate that the same children, as they grew older, were better achievers in school and were more likely to graduate from high school. These experiences, in turn, predicted indexes of subsequent success as measured by such criteria as continuing one's education, being gainfully employed, or having income other than public assistance (Lazar, 1984).

Along the same line, follow-up studies of several guaranteed-income experiments conducted in the 1970s have revealed higher levels of school achievement by children of families in the randomly assigned experimental groups compared to their controls (Salkind, 1983). Also, a post hoc analysis of pregnant mothers participating in the WIC Program (Kotelchuck, 1983) showed that the treatment group had achieved the desired objective of increasing birth weight and reducing infant mortality as compared to findings for a carefully matched control group. That beneficial effects of community-based maternal care programs can extend into the realm of mother–child relations is indicated by the results of nurse home-visiting programs conducted with pregnant mothers at risk (Olds, 1983). Along with increased birth weight of babies born to teenage mothers, the experimental group, compared with carefully matched controls, showed a reduction in verified cases of child abuse, more positive maternal perceptions of the infant, and less restrictive and punitive behavior in the home.

In recent years, however, such studies of the consequences to children and parents of various forms of family policies and programs have become less frequent. Instead, the newly established field of family policy studies has shifted the focus of research attention to organizational issues. In the following passage, Bronfenbrenner and Weiss (1982) offer their assessment of the current trend as reflected in a recent collection of papers on child and family policy (Zigler, Kagan, & Klugman, 1983):

> Policy research is now a thriving enterprise encompassing such diverse and essential topics as legislation at national, state, and local levels; the evolution and nature of programs serving families and children; educational policies and practices; legal and judicial procedures; policies governing mass media; the role of advocacy in the policy process; the development of strategies for dealing with drugs, child abuse, and other social problems; the construction of childhood social indicators; and analyses of the policy process itself. Least salient in this newly evolving field is a concern that emerges

as central in an ecological perspective on human development—namely, how do policies affect the experience of those whom they are intended to serve? To put the issue more succinctly: What is the nature of the interface between policies and people. (pp. 393–394).

At a time of financial retrenchment, when many children are being placed at greater risk as a result of parental unemployment, other income losses, and reduction of health and family services, it is essential to determine which policies and programs can do most to enable families to perform the magic feat of which they alone are capable: making and keeping human beings human.

The foregoing statement has yet another significance that is at once both broader and more concrete. Taken as a whole the body of research reviewed in these pages is curiously one-sided, for its predominant focus is on the ecologies of family disorganization and developmental disarray. Yet, for every study that documents the power of disruptive environments, there is a control group that testifies to the existence and unrealized potential of ecologies that sustain and strengthen constructive processes in society, the family, and the self. Nor is there reason to believe that the progressively more powerful paradigms that have illuminated our understanding of the roots of alienation cannot be turned about to shed light on the ecologies of social and psychological integration. Herein lie the challenge, and the opportunity, for the developmental science of the future.

References

Angell, R. C. (1936). *The family encounters the Depression.* New York: Scribner.

Bargel, T., et al. (1981). Soziale und raumliche Bedingungen der Sozialisation von Kindern in verschiendenen Ergebnisse einer Befragung von Eltern in Landgemeinden und Stadtvierteln Nordhessens. In A. H. Walter (Ed.), *Region und Sozialisation: Volume 1,* (pp. 186–261). Stuttgart: Frommann-Holzboog.

Barker, R. G., & Schoggen, P. (1973). *Qualities of community life: Methods of measuring environment and behavior applied to an American and an English town.* San Francisco: Jossey-Bass.

Becker, H. J., & Epstein, J. L. (1982). *Influences on teachers' use of parent involvement at home* (Report #324). Baltimore, MD: Johns Hopkins Center for Social Organization of Schools.

Belle, D. E. (1981. April). *The social network as a source of both stress and support to low-income mothers.* Paper presented at the Biennial Meeting of the Society for Research in Child Development, Boston, MA.

Belsky, J. (1984). Two waves of day care research: Developmental effects and conditions of quality. In R. Ainslie (Ed.). *The child and the day care setting* (pp. 1–34). New York: Praeger.

Belsky, J., & Steinberg, L. D. (1978). The effects of day care: A critical review. *Child Development, 49,* 929–949.

Belsky, J., Steinberg, L. D., & Walker, A. (1982). The ecology of day care. In M. E. Lamb (Ed.), *Child rearing in nontraditional families* (pp. 71–115). Hillsdale, NJ: Erlbaum.

Berrueta-Clement, J. R., Schweinhart, L. J., Barnett, W. S., Epstein, A. S., & Weikart, D. P. (1984). *Changed lives: The effects of the Perry Preschool Program on youths through age 19.* Ypsilanti, MI: High/Scope Educational Research Foundation.

Boehnke, K., Eyferth, K., Kastner, P., Noack, P., Reitzle, M., Silbereisen, R. K., Walter, S., & Zank, S. (1983, July). *Youth development and substance use.* Paper presented at the Seventh Biennial Meeting of the International Society for the Study of Behavioral Development, Munich, Germany.

Bohen, H., & Viveros-Long, A. (1981). *Balancing jobs and family life: Do flexible working schedules help?* Philadelphia, PA: Temple University Press.

Bouchard, T. J., & McGue, M. (1981). Familial studies of intelligence: A review. *Science, 29,* 1055–1059.

Bronfenbrenner, U. (1967). Response to pressure from peers versus adults among Soviet and American school children. *International Journal of Psychology, 2,* 199–208.

Bronfenbrenner, U. (1974a). Developmental research and public policy. In J. Romanshyn (Ed.), *Social science and social welfare* (pp. 159–182). New York: Council on Social Work Education.

Bronfenbrenner, U. (1974b). Is early intervention effective? *Teachers College Record, 76,* 279–303.

Bronfenbrenner, U. (1975). Nature with Nurture: A reinterpretation of the evidence. In A. Montague (Ed.), *Race and IQ* (pp. 114–144). New York: Oxford University Press.

Bronfenbrenner, U. (1979). *The ecology of human development: Experiments by nature and design.* Cambridge, MA: Harvard University Press.

Bronfenbrenner, U. (1982). New images of children, families, and America. *Television & Children,* Winter, 1–15.

Bronfenbrenner, U. (1984). The changing family in a changing world: America first? In *The legacy of Nicholas Hobbs: Research on education and human development in the public interest, Part II. Peabody Journal of Education, 61,* 52–70.

Bronfenbrenner, U. (1986a). Recent advances in research on the ecology of human development. In R. K. Silbereisen, K. Eyferth, & G. Rudinger (Eds.), *Development as action in context: Problem behavior and normal youth development* (pp. 287–309). Heidelberg and New York: Springer-Verlag.

Bronfenbrenner, U. (1986b). Alienation and the four worlds of childhood. *Phi Delta Kappan. 67,* 430–436.

Bronfenbrenner, U. (1986c). The War on Poverty: Won or lost? America's children in poverty: 1959–1985. *Newsletter Division of Child, Youth, and Family Services, 9,* 2–3. Washington, DC: American Psychological Association.

Bronfenbrenner, U., Alvarez, W. F., & Henderson, C. R. (1984). Working and watching: Maternal employment status and parents' perceptions of their three-year-old children. *Child Development, 55,* 1362–1378.

Bronfenbrenner, U., & Crouter, A. C. (1982). Work and family through time and space. In S. B. Kamerman & C. D. Hayes (Eds.), *Families that work: Children in a changing world.* Washington, DC: National Academy Press.

Bronfenbrenner, U., & Crouter, A. C. (1983). The evolution of environmental models in developmental research. In W. Kessen (Ed.), *History, theory, and methods,* Volume 1 of P. H. Mussen (Ed.), *Handbook of child psychology* (4th ed., pp. 357–414). New York: Wiley. 357–414.

Bronfenbrenner, U., & Weiss, H. B. (1983). Beyond policies without people. In E. Zigler, S. L. Kagan, & E. Klugman (Eds.), *Children, families, and government: Perspectives on American social policy.* New York: Cambridge University Press.

Bronfenbrenner, U., Devereux, E. C., Jr., Suci, G. J., & Rodgers, R. R. (1965, April). *Adults and peers as sources of conformity and autonomy.* Paper presented at the Conference on Socialization and Competence, sponsored by the Social Science Research Council, Puerto Rico.

Brown, D. W., Bhrolchin, M., & Harris, T. (1975). Social class and psychiatric disturbance among women in urban populations. *Sociology, 9,* 225–254.

Burks, B. S. (1928). The relative influence of nature and nurture upon mental development: A comparative study of foster parent–foster child resemblance and true parent–true child resemblance. *Yearbook of the National Society for the Study of Education, 27*, 219–316.

Burns, J. (1982). *The study of parental involvement in four federal education programs: Executive summary.* Washington, DC: Department of Education, Office of Planning Budget and Evaluation.

Burt, C. (1966). The genetic determination of differences in intelligence: A study of monozygotic twins reared apart and together. *British Journal of Psychology, 57*, 137–153.

Caudill, W., & Weinstein, H. (1969). Maternal care and infant behavior in Japan and America. *Psychiatry, 32*, 12–43.

Cavan, R. S., & Ranck, K. H. (1938). *The family and the Depression: A study of 100 Chicago families.* Chicago: University of Chicago Press.

Chombart de Lauwe, P. H. (1959–60). *Famille et Habitation* (2 volumes). Paris: Centre National de la Recherche Scientifique.

Clausen, J. A., & Kohn, M. (1959). The relation of schizophrenia to the social structure of a small city. In B. Pasamanick (Ed.), *Epidemiology of mental disorder* (pp. 69–74). Washington, D.C. American Association for the Advancement of Science.

Cochran, M. M., & Brassard, J. (1979). Child development and personal social networks. *Child Development, 50*, 601–616.

Colletta, N. (1981). Social support and the risk of maternal rejection by adolescent mothers. *The Journal of Psychology, 109*, 191–197.

Colletta, N. (1983). At risk for depression: A study of young mothers. *Journal of Genetic Psychology, 142*, 301–310.

Colletta, N. D., & Gregg, C. H. (1981). Adolescent mothers' vulnerability to stress. *Journal of Nervous and Mental Diseases, 169*, 50–54.

Colletta, N. D., & Lee, D. (1983). The impact of support for Black adolescent mothers. *Journal of Family Issues, 4*, 127–143.

Collins, C., Moles, O., & Cross, M. (1982). *The home–school connection: Selected partnership programs in large cities.* Boston, MA: Institute for Responsive Education.

Crnic, K. A., Greenberg, M. C., Ragozin, A. S., Robinson, N. M., & Basham, R. (1983). Effects of stress and social supports on mothers in premature and full term infants. *Child Development, 54*, 209–217.

Crockenberg, S. B. (1981). Infant irritability, other responsiveness, and social support influences on the security of infant–mother attachment. *Child Development, 52*, 857–865.

Crockenberg, S. B. (1985). Professional support and care of infants by adolescent mothers in England and the United States. *Journal of Pediatric Psychology, 10*, 413–428.

Crockenberg, S. B. (in press-a). English teenage mothers: Attitudes, behavior, and social support. In E. J. Anthony (Ed.), *International yearbook series of the International Association for Child Psychiatry and Allied Professions.*

Crockenberg, S. B. (in press-b). Support for adolescent mothers during the postnatal period: Theory and research. In Z. Boukydis (Ed.), *Research on support for parents and infants in the postnatal period.* Norwood, NJ: Ablex.

Crouter, A. C. (1984). Participative work as an influence on human development. *Journal of Applied Developmental Psycology, 5*, 71–90.

Crowe, R. R. (1974). An adoption study of antisocial personality. *Archives of General Psychiatry, 31*, 785–791.

Darlington, R., Royce, J. M., Snipper, A. S., Murray, H. W., & Lazar, I. (1980). Preschool programs and later school comparisons of children from low-income families. *Science, 208*, 202–204.

Devereux, E. C., Jr. (1965). *Socialization in cross-cultural perspective: A comparative study of England, Germany, and the United States.* Paper read at the Ninth International Seminar on Family Research, Puerto Rico.

Devereux, E. C., Jr. (1966, May). *Authority, guilt, and conformity to adult standards among German school children: A pilot experimental study.* Paper presented to the Upstate New York Sociological Association. Rochester, New York.

Devereux, E. C., Bronfenbrenner, U., & Rodgers, R. R. (1969). Child

rearing in England and the United States: A cross-national comparison. *Journal of Marriage and the Family, 31*, 257–270.

Dorr, A. (1981, August). *Television's role in family life.* Paper presented at the meetings of the American Psychological Association, Los Angeles.

Dornbusch, S. M., Carlsmith, J. M., Bushwall, P. L., Ritter, P. L., Leiderman, H., Hastorf, A. H., & Gross, R. T. (1985). Single parents, extended households, and the control of adolescents. *Child Development, 56*, 326–341.

Elder, G. H., Jr. (1974). *Children of the Great Depression.* Chicago: University of Chicago Press.

Elder, G. H., Jr. (1981). Scarcity and prosperity in postwar childbearing: Explorations from a life course perspective. *Journal of Family History, 5*, 410–431.

Elder, G. H., Jr. (1984). Families, kin, and the life course: A sociological perspective. In R. D. Parke (Ed.), *The family.* Chicago: University of Chicago Press.

Elder, G. H., Jr. (Ed.) (1985). *Life course dynamics: Trajectories and transitions, 1968–1980.* Ithaca, NY: Cornell University Press.

Elder, G. H., Jr., Caspi, A., & Downey, G. (in press). Problem behavior and family relationships: A multigenerational analysis. In A. Sorensen, F. Weinert, & L. Sherrod (Eds.), *Human development: Interdisciplinary perspectives* Hillsdale, NJ: Erlbaum.

Elder, G. H., Jr., Caspi, A., & van Nguyen, T., (1986). Resourceful and vulnerable children: Family influences in stressful times. In R. K. Silbereisen, K. Eyferth, & G. Rudinger, (Eds.), *Development as action in context: Problem behavior and normal youth development* (pp. 169–186). Heidelberg & New York: Springer-Verlag.

Elder, G. H., Jr., Van Nguyen, T., & Caspi, A. (1985). Linking family hardship to children's lives. *Child Development, 56*, 361–375.

Epstein, A. (1980). *Assessing the child development information needed by adolescent parents with very young children.* Final report of Grant OCD-90-C-1341. Washington, DC: Office of Child Development, Department of Health, Education and Welfare (ERIC Document Reproduction Service No. ED 183286).

Epstein, J. L. (1983a). *Effects on parents of teacher practices of parent involvement.* Baltimore, MD: Center for Social Organization of Schools, Johns Hopkins University (Report #346).

Epstein, J. L. (1983b). Longitudinal effects of family-school-person interactions on student outcomes. *Research in Sociology of Education and Socialization, 4*, 101–127.

Epstein, J. L. (1984). Single-parents and the schools: The effects of marital status on parent and teacher evaluations. (Report No. 353). Baltimore, MD: Johns Hopkins University, Center for Social Organization of Schools.

Farran, D. C., & Margolis, L. H. (1983). *The impact of paternal job loss on the family.* Paper presented at the Biennial Meeting of the Society for Research in Child Development, Detroit, Michigan.

Furstenberg, F. F. (1976). *Unplanned parenthood: The social consequences of teenage child bearing.* New York: Free Press.

Furstenberg, F. F., & Brooks-Gunn (in press). *Adolescent mothers in later life.* New York: Cambridge University Press.

Furstenberg, F. F., & Crawford, A. (1978). Family support: Helping teenage mothers to cope. *Family Planning Perspectives, 10*, 322–333.

Garbarino, J. (1975). A note on the effects of televisiion viewing. In U. Bronfenbrenner & M. A. Mahoney (Eds.) *Influences on human development.* (2nd ed., pp. 397–399). Hinsdale, IL: Dryden.

Garbarino, J. (1976). A preliminary study of some ecological correlates of child abuse: The impact of socioeconomic stress on mothers. *Child Development, 47*, 178–185.

Giovannoni, J., & Billingsley, A. (1970). Child neglect among the poor: A study of parental adequacy in families of their ethnic groups. *Child Welfare, 49*, 196–204.

Gold, M., & Petronio, R. J. (1980). Delinquent behavior in adolescence.

In J. Adelson (Ed.), *Handbook of adolescent psychology.* New York: Wiley.

Greenberger, E., & Steinberg, L. D. (in press). *When teenagers work: The psychological and social costs of adolecent employment.* New York: Basic Books.

Greenberger, E., Steinberg, L. D., & Vaux, A. (1981). Adolescents who work: Health and behavioral consequences of job stress. *Developmental Psychology, 6,* 691–703.

Henderson, A. (1981). *Parent particiation—student achievement: The evidence grows.* Columbia, MO: National Committee for Citizen Education.

Hayes, D., & Grether, J. (1969). *The school year and vacation: When do children learn?* Paper presented at the Eastern Sociological Convention, New York.

Heath, D. B. (1977). Some possible effects of occupation on the maturing of professional men. *Journal of Vocational Behavior, 11,* 263–281.

Heston, L. L. (1966). Psychiatric disorders in foster home-reared children of schizophrenic mothers. *British Journal of Psychiatry, 112,* 819–825.

Hetherington, E. M. (1972). Effects of father absence on personality development in adolescent daughters. *Developmental Psychology, 7,* 313–326.

Hetherington, E. M. (1981). Children of divorce. In R. Henderson (Ed.), *Parent–child interaction.* New York: Academic Press.

Hetherington, E. M., Cox, M., & Cox, R. (1978). The aftermath of divorce. In J. H. Stevens, Jr. & M. Mathews (Eds.), *Mother–child, father–child relations.* Washington, DC: National Association for the Education of Young Children.

Hetherington, E. M., & Deur, J. (1971). The effects of father absence on child development in young children. *Young Children,* 233–248.

Heyns, B. (1978). *Summer learning and effects of schooling.* New York: Academic Press.

Hoffman, L. W. (1980). The effects of maternal employment on the academic attitudes and performance of school-age children. *School Psychology Review,* 319–335.

Hoffman, L. W. (1983). Work, family, and the socialization of the child. In R. D. Parke (Ed.), *Review of child development research. Volume 7: The family.* Chicago: University of Chicago Press.

Hollingshead, A. B. (1949). *Elmtown's youth and Elmtown revisited.* New York: Wiley.

Hutchings, B., & Mednick, S. A. (1977). Criminality in adoptees and their adoptive and biological parents: A pilot study. In S. A. Mednick & K. O. Christinesen (Eds.), *Biological bases of criminal behavior* (pp. 127–164). New York: Gardner Press.

Jensen, A. R. (1969). How much can we boost IQ and scholastic achievement? *Harvard Educational Review,* Winter, 1–123.

Jensen, A. R. (1973). Let's understand Skodak and Skeels, finally. *Educational Psychologist, 10,* 30–35.

Jensen, A. R. (1980). *Bias in mental testing.* New York: Free Press.

Jessor, R. (1986). *Adolescent problem drinking: Psychological aspects and developmental outcomes.* In R. K. Silbereisen, K. Eyferth, & G. Rudinger (Eds.), *Development as action in context: Problem behavior and normal youth development.* (pp. 241–264). Heidelberg & New York: Springer-Verlag.

Kandel, D. B. (1986). On processes of peer influence in adolescence. In R. Silbereisen, K. Eyferth, & G. Rudinger (Eds.). *Development as action in context: Problem behavior and normal youth development.* (pp. 203–228). Heidelberg & New York: Springer-Verlag.

Kandel, D. B., & Lesser, G. S. (1972). *Youth in two worlds.* San Francisco: Jossey-Bass.

Kanter, R. N. (1977). *Work and family in the United States: A critical review and agenda for research and public policy.* New York: Russell Sage.

Klineberg, O. (1935). *Negro intelligence in selective migration.* New York: Columbia University Press.

Klineberg, O. (1938). The intelligence of migrants. *American Sociological Review, 3,* 218–224.

Kohn, M. L. (1969). *Class and conformity: A study in values.* Homewood, IL: Dorsey.

Kohn, M. L., & Schooler, C. (1973). Occupational experience and psychological functioning: An assessment of reciprocal effects. *American Sociological Review, 38,* 97–118.

Kohn, M. L., & Schooler, C. (1978). The reciprocal effects of substantive complexity of work and intellectual flexibility: A longitudinal assessment. *American Journal of Sociology, 84,* 24–52.

Kohn, M. L., & Schooler, C. (1982). Job conditions and personality: A longitudinal assessment of their reciprocal effects. *American Journal of Sociology, 87,* 1257–1258.

Kohn, M. L., & Schooler, C. (1983). *Work and personality: An inquiry into the impact of social stratification.* Norwood, NJ: Ablex Press.

Komarovsky, M. (1940). *The unemployed man and his family.* New York: Dryden Press.

Kotelchuck, M. (1983). Schwarts, J. B., Anderka, N. T., & Finison, K. F. *WIC participation and pregnancy outcomes.* Unpublished manuscript, Masssachusetts Statewide Evaluation Project, Boston.

Lazar, I. (1984). Personal communication.

Leahy, A. M. (1935). Nature, nurture, and intelligence. *Genetic Psychology Monographs, 17,* 236–308.

Lightfoot, S. L. (1978). *Worlds apart: Relationships between families and school.* New York: Basic Books.

Loehlin, J. C., Lindzey, G., & Spuhler, J. N. (1975). *Race difference in intelligence.* San Francisco: Freeman.

Maccoby, E. E. (1951). Television: Its impact on school children. *Public Opinion Quarterly, 15,* 421–444.

Maccoby, E. E., & Jacklin, C. N. (1974). *The psychology of sex differences.* Stanford, CA: Stanford University Press.

McCubbin, H. I., Dahl, B. B., & Hunter, E. J. (Eds.) (1976). *Families in the military system.* New York: Sage.

Medrich, E. A., Roizen, J., Rubin, V., & Buckley, S. (1982). *The serious business of growing up: A study of children's lives outside school.* Berkeley, CA: University of California Press.

Meili, R., & Steiner, H. (1965). Eine untersuchung zum intelligenzniveau elfjahriger der deutschen schweitz. *Schweizerishe Zeitschrift fur Psychologie und ihre Anwendungen, 24,* 23–32.

Mercer, R. T., Hackley, K. C., & Bostrom, A. (in press). Social support of teenage mothers. *Birth Defects: Irugubak Article Series.*

Miller, D. R., & Swanson, G. E. (1958). *The changing American parent: A study in the Detroit areas.* New York: Wiley.

Miller, K. A., & Kohn, M. L. (1983). The reciprocal effects of job conditions and the intellectuality of leisure-time activity. In M. L. Kohn & C. Schooler, *Work and personality: An inquiry into the impact of social stratification.* Norwood, NJ: Ablex Press.

Miller, K. A., Schooler, C., Kohn, M. L., & Miller, K. A. (1979). Women and work: The psychological effects of occupational conditions. *American Journal of Sociology, 85,* 66–94.

Moorehouse, M. (1986). *The relationships among continuity in maternal employment, parent–child communicative activities, and the child's school competence.* Unpublished doctoral dissertation. Cornell University, Ithaca, N.Y.

Morgan, W. L. (1939). *The family meets the Depression.* Minneapolis: University of Minnesota Press.

Morgan, W. R., Alwin, D. F., & Griffin, L. J. (1979). Social origins, parental values, and the transmission of inequality. *American Journal of Sociology, 85,* 156–166.

Mortimer, J. T. (1974). Patterns of intergenerational occupational movements: A smallest-space analysis. *American Journal of Sociology, 79,* 1278–1299.

Mortimer, J. T. (1975). Occupational and value socialization in business and professional families. *Sociology of Work and Occupations, 2,* 29–53.

Mortimer, J. T. (1976). Social class, work, and the family: Some implications of the father's career for familial relationships and son's career decisions. *Journal of Marriage and the Family,* May, 241–256.

Mortimer, J. T., & Kumka, D. (1982). A further examination of the "occupational link hypothesis." *Sociological Quarterly, 23,* 3–16.

Mortimer, J. T., & Lorence, J. (1979). Work experience and occupational value socialization: a longitudinal study. *American Journal of Sociology, 84,* 1361–1385.

Mortimer, J. T., Lorence, J., & Kumka, D. (1982). Work and family linkages in the transition to adulthood: A panel study of highly-educated men. *Western Psychological Review, 13,* 50–68.

Mortimer, J. T., Lorence, J., & Kumka, D. (1986). *Work, family, and personality: Transition to adulthood.* Norwood, NJ: Ablex.

Mott, P. E., Mann, F. C., McLoughlin, Q., & Warwick, D. P. (1965). *Shift work: The social, psychological, and physical consequences.* Ann Arbor: University of Michigan Press.

Muchow, M., & Muchow, H. H. (1935). *Der Lebenstraum des Grosstadkindes.* Hamburg, Germany: M. Riegel.

National Commission on Youth. (1980). *The transition of youth to adulthood: A bridge too long.* Boulder, CO: Westview Press.

Olds, D. L. (1983). An intervention program for high-risk families. In R. A. Hockelman (Ed.). *Minimizing high-risk parenting* (pp. 249–268). Media, PA: Harwal.

Patterson, G. R. (1982). *Coercive family processes.* Eugene, OR: Castalia.

Piaget, J. (1932). *The moral judgment of the child.* New York: Harcourt-Brace.

Piotrkowski, C. S. (1979). *Work and the family system: A naturalistic study of working-class and lower-middle class families.* New York: Free Press.

Pitkanen-Pulkkinen, L. (1980). The child in the family. *Nirdisk Psykologi, 32,* 147–157.

President's Science Advisory Committee. (1973). *Youth: Transition to adulthood.* Chicago: University of Chicago Press.

Prugh, D. G., Staub, E. M., Sands, H. H., Kirschbaum, R. M., & Lenihan, E. A. (1953). A study of the emotional reactions of children in families to hospitalization and illness. *American Journal of Orthopsychiatry, 23,* 70–106.

Pulkkinen, L. (1982). Self-control and continuity in childhood delayed adolescence. In P. Baltes & O. Brim (Eds.), *Life span development and behavior* (Volume 4, pp. 64–102). New York: Academic Press.

Pulkkinen, L. (1983a). Finland: Search of alternatives to aggression. In A. Goldstein & M. Segall (Eds.), *Aggression in global perspective.* New York: Pergamon Press.

Pulkkinen, L. (1983b). Youthful smoking and drinking in a longitudinal perspective. *Journal of Youth and Adolescence, 12*(4), 253–283.

Pulkkinen, L. (1984). *Nuoret ja kotikasvatus* [*Youth and home ecology*] Helsinki: Otava.

Quinton, D. (1980). Family life in the inner city: Myth and reality. In M. Marland (Ed.), *Education for the inner city* (pp. 45–67). London: Heinemann.

Riley, D., & Eckenrode, J. (in press). Social ties: Costs and benefits within differing groups. *Journal of Personality and Social Psychology.*

Rodgers, R. R. (1971). Changes in parental behavior reported by children in West Germany and the United States. *Human Development, 14,* 208–224.

Rutter, M. (1981). The city and the child. *American Journal of Orthopsychiatry, 51,* 610–625.

Rutter, M., & Giller, H. J. (1983). *Juvenile delinquency: Trends and perspectives.* New York: Penguin Books.

Rutter, M., Cox, A., Tupling, C., Berger, M., & Youle, W. (1975). Attainment and adjustment in two geographical areas. I. The prevalence of psychiatric disorder. *British Journal of Psychiatry, 126,* 493–509.

Rutter, M., & Madge, N. (1976). *Cycles of disadvantage.* London: Heinemann.

Rutter, M., & Quinton, D. (1977). Psychiatric disorder—Ecological factors and concepts of causation. In H. McGurk (Ed.), *Ecological factors in human development* (pp. 173–187). Amsterdam: North-Holland.

Salkind, N. J. (1983). *Impact of a guaranteed income on children.* Paper presented at the Biennial Meeting of the Society for Research in Child Development, Detroit, Michigan.

Scarr, S. (1981). *Race, social class, and individual differences in IQ: New studies of old issues.* Hillsdale, NJ: Erlbaum.

Scarr, S., & McAvay, G. (1984). *Predicting the occupational status of young adults: A longitudinal study of brothers and sisters in adoptive and biologically-related families.* Unpublished manuscript, Department of Psychology, University of Virginia.

Scarr, S., & McCartney, K. (1983). How people make their own environments: The theory of genotype–environment effect. *Child Development, 44,* 424–436.

Scarr, S., & Weinberg, R. A. (1976). IQ test performance of black children adopted by white families. *American Psychologist, 31,* 726–739.

Scarr, S., & Weinberg, R. A. (1983). The Minnesota adoption studies: Genetic differences and malability. *Child Development, 54,* 260–267.

Scarr-Salapatek, S., Williams, M. L. (1973). The effects of early stimulation on low-birth weight infants. *Child Development, 44,* 94–101.

Schiff, M., Duyme, M., Dumaret, A., & Tomkiewicz, (1981). Enfants de travailleurs manuels adoptes par des cadres: Effet d'un changement de classe sociale sur le cursus scolaire et les notes de QI. *Travaux et Documents, 93.*

Schiff, M., Duyme, M., Dumaret, A., & Tomkiewicz, (1982). How much could we boost scholastic achievement and IQ scores? A direct answer from a French adoption study. *Cognition, 12,* 155–196.

Schneewind, K. A., Beckman, M., & Engfer, A. (1983). *Eltern und kinder.* Stuttgart: Kohlhammer.

Skeels, H. M. (1966). Adult status of children with contrasting early life experiences: A follow-up study. *Monographs of the Society for Research in Child Development, 31,* No. 105, 1–65.

Skeels, H. M., & Dye, H. B. (1939). A study of the effects of differential stimulation on mentally retarded children. *Proceedings and Addresses of the American Association on Mental Deficiency, 44,* 114–136.

Skeels, H. M., Updegraff, R., Wellman, B. L., & Williams, H. M. (1938). A study of environmental stimulation: An orphanage preschool project. *University of Iowa Studies in Child Welfare, 15*(4).

Skodak, M., & Skeels, H. M. (1949). A final follow-up study of one hundred adopted children. *The Journal of Genetic Psychology, 75,* 85–125.

Slomezynski, K. M., Miller, J., & Kohn, M. (1981). Stratification, work, and values: A Polish-United States comparison. *American Sociological Review, 46,* 720–744.

Smith, M. B. (1968). School and home: Focus on achievement. In A. H. Passow (Ed.), *Developing programs for the educationally disadvantaged.* New York: Teachers College Press.

Steinberg, L. (1985). *Single parents, stepparents, and the susceptibility of adolescents to antisocial peer pressure: When two parents are not enough.* Unpublished manuscript. University of Wisconsin, Department of Child and Family Studies.

Steinberg, L. (1986). *Latchkey children and susceptibility to peer pressure: An ecological analysis.* Unpublished manuscript. University of Wisconsin, Department of Child and Family Studies.

Steinberg, L. D., Catalano, R., & Dooley, D. (1981). Economic antecedents of child abuse and neglect. *Child Development, 52,* 975–985.

19

Steinberg, L. D., Greenberger, E., Garduque, L., Ruggiero, M., & Vaux, A. (1982). The effects of working on adolescent development. *Developmental Psychology, 18*, 385–395.

Tangri, S. S., & Leitch, M. L. (1982). *Barriers to home–school collaboration: Two case studies in junior high school.* Final Report submitted to the National Institute of Education. Washington, DC: The Urban Institute.

Taylor, H. F. (1980). *The IQ game.* New Brunswick, NJ: Rutgers University Press.

Thompson, R. A., Lamb, M. E., & Estes, D. Stability of infant–mother attachment and its relationship to changing life circumstances. *Child Development,* 1982, *53,* 144–148.

Tietjen, A. M., & Bradley, C. F. (1982). *Social networks, social support and transition to parenthood.* Unpublished paper. University of British Columbia, Vancouver, Division of Family Studies.

Tiller, P. O. (1958). Father absence and personality development of children in sailor families: A preliminary research report. In N. Anderson (Ed.), *Studies of the Family.* Göttingen: Vandenhoeck and Ruprecht.

Tulkin, S. R. (1973a). Social class differences in infants' reactions to mother's and stranger's voices. *Developmental Psychology, 8,* 137.

Tulkin, S. R. (1973b). Social class differences in attachment behaviors of ten-month-old infants. *Child Development, 44,* 171–174.

Tulkin, S. R. (1977). Social class differences in maternal and infant behavior. In P. H. Leiderman, A. Rosenfeld, & S. R. Tulkin (Eds.). *Culture and infancy* (pp. 495–557). New York: Academic Press.

Tulkin, S. R., & Cohler, B. J. (1973). Child-rearing attitudes and mother–child interaction in the first year of life. *Merrill-Palmer Quarterly, 19,* 95–106.

Tulkin, S. R., & Covitz, F. E. (1975). *Mother–infant interaction and intellectual functioning at age six.* Paper presented at the meeting of the Society for Research in Child Development, Denver.

Tulkin, S. R., & Kagan, J. (1972). Mother–child interaction in the first year of life. *Child Development, 43,* 31–41.

U.S. Bureau of the Census (1981). Current Population Reports, Series P-60, #127. *Money income and poverty status of families and persons in the United States, 1980.* Washington, DC: U.S. Government Printing Office.

U.S. Bureau of the Census (1985). Current Population Reports, Series P-60, #149. *Money income and poverty status of families and persons in the United States, 1984.* Washington, DC: U.S. Government Printing Office.

Vatter, M. (1981). Intelligenz und regionale Herkunft. Eine Langsschnittstudie im Kanton Bern. In A. H. Walter (Ed.), *Region und Sozialisation* (Volume I, pp. 56–91). Stuttgart: Frommann-Holzboog.

Walter, H. (Ed.) (1981–1982). *Region und Sozialisation* (Volumes I and II). Stuttgart: Frommann-Holzboog.

Wandersman, L. P., & Unger, D. G. (1983). *Interaction of infant difficulty and social support in adolescent mothers.* Paper presented at the Biennial Meeting of the Society for Research in Child Development, Detroit, Michigan.

Weinraub, M., & Wolf, B. M. (1983). Effects of stress and social supports on mother–child interactions in single- and two-parent families. *Child Development, 54,* 1294–1311.

Werner, E. E., & Smith, R. S. (1982). *Vulnerable but invincible.* New York: McGraw-Hill.

Wheeler, L. R. (1942). A comparative study of the intelligence of East Tennessee mountain children. *Journal of Educational Psychology, 33,* 321–334.

Zigler, E., Kagan, S. L., & Klugman, E. (1983). *Children, families, and government: Perspectives on American social policy.* New York: Cambridge University Press.

Received August 6, 1984
Revision received April 9, 1986 ■

The Influence of Parenting Style on Adolescent Competence and Substance Use

Diana Baumrind
University of California at Berkeley

An overview of the Family Socialization and Developmental Competence longitudinal program of research (FSP) is followed by a presentation of the hypotheses and findings pertaining to family patterns as determinants of adolescent competence, and of types of adolescent substance users. Data include clusters derived from comprehensive ratings of parents and their children completed independently within- and across-time periods at ages 4, 9, and 15 years. At Time 3 (T3), the sample included 139 adolescents and their parents from a predominantly affluent, well-educated, Caucasian population. Parenting types were identified that differ on the bases of commitment and balance of demandingness and responsiveness. Authoritative parents who are highly demanding and highly responsive were remarkably successful in protecting their adolescents from problem drug use, and in generating competence. Authoritative upbringing, although sufficient, is not a necessary condition to produce competent children. Casual recreational drug use was not associated with pathological attributes, either precursive or concurrent, although nonusers showed an increment in competence from Time 2 (T2) to Time 3 (T3).

In his eulogy to John P. Hill, Steinberg (1989, pp. 1-2) wrote, "G. Stanley Hall may be considered to be the 'father' of the study of adolescence, but John Hill is the person who took the field out of its infancy." This presentation

This article is based on an invited address at the Science Weekend of the American Psychological Association in New Orleans, August 12-13, 1989, in recognition of the G. Stanley Hall Award conferred by Division 7 in 1988 to the author. It does not purport to be a fully documented empirical report but instead presents an overview of the major results on the adolescent phase of the Family Socialization and Developmental Competence Project (FSP). The data drawn on for this essay are being prepared in empirical reports, two of which, on adolescent substance use, have been recently completed. I wish to acknowledge the generous support of the William T. Grant Foundation and the Institute of Human Development at Berkeley. I wish also to express my appreciation to two long-term staff members: Steven Pulos, Ph.D., for his excellent assistance with the analyses of the longitudinal data; and Margaret Tauber, Ph.D., for her help in collecting and organizing those data. Above all, thanks are due to the families who contributed their time and ideas so that their peers and progeny could profit from their experience.

Journal of Early Adolescence, Vol. 11 No. 1, February 1991 56-95

celebrates the legacy that John Hill left us in his systematic studies of family relations during early adolescence. John Hill, like G. Stanley Hall, did not promote a value-free science, but instead applied his understanding of developmental psychology to solving social problems of his day. Like Hall, John Hill held society responsible for the problems of youth, and not youth for the problems of society.

Hall's description of the unsuitability of the social environment of his day to the needs of the adolescent is oddly reminiscent of the present:

> Never has youth been exposed to such dangers of both perversion and arrest as in our own land and day. Increasing urban life with its temptations, prematurities, sedentary occupations, and passive stimuli, just when an active, objective life is most needed, early emancipation and a lessening sense for both duty and discipline, the haste to know and do all befitting man's estate before its time . . . In this environment our young people leap rather than grow into maturity. (Hall, 1905, p. xv)

Hill's integrative reviews and excellent empirical studies laid the groundwork for research on the contribution of family patterns to adolescent development and behavior. In one of his last integrative reviews, Hill (1987) noted that longitudinal data were needed to clarify the processes by which authoritative and other patterns of childrearing influence adolescents. Such data from the Family Socialization and Developmental Competence Project (FSP) will be presented on (a) the relation of family patterns to adolescent competence, and (b) familial determinants of types of adolescent substance users.

In this report, the rationale and results for each study will be presented separately. Before proceeding with these study-specific presentations, a general overview of those aspects of the FSP methodology that apply to both studies is presented to orient the reader to the sample and procedure.

REVIEW OF FSP RESEARCH STRATEGY

The children in this study came form middle-class, educationally advantaged Caucasian families residing in San Francisco East Bay communities. They were born in the mid-1960s, and their parents in the 1930s. The participants were first studied when the children were 4 years old (T1), then twice more when they were almost 10 years old (T2) and 15 years old (T3). Although at T1, by design, all families were intact, by T3 38% of the families in the sample had been divorced. Mothers worked an average of 64% of full time with one-third of the mothers working less than 25% of full time and one-third working more than 75% of full time. The third wave, that is the adolescent phase, took place between 1978 and 1980. At T3 the sample consisted of 139 adolescents and their custodial parent(s).

At each time period, one team of observers spent at least 20 hours with the child and a different team spent about 30 hours with the parents prior to completing a comprehensive set of ratings. In order to keep the data sets independent, different observers and raters were used at each time period, and for parents and children.

The adolescent data set includes assessment of physical fitness, maturational status, and nutritional status; and social, cognitive, and emotional functioning. For parents, as well as adolescents, political and social attitudes, moral judgment level and attitudes, alcohol and drug use, health practices, intellectual ability, and personal problem behavior were assessed. Each parent was interviewed for six hours, and parents were observed in interaction with their children during a home visit and a videotaped, structured family interaction. In addition, quantitative measures of the stressors that have impinged on the adolescent over the years were measured at ages 4, 9, and 15 years using a project-designed Family Stressor Index. On the basis of transcripts of the entire battery of interviews and observational procedures, two psychologists, working independently, rated each adolescent on 137 personality items (90 Q-sort items and 47 Likert-type rating items), a problem behavior checklist, and several alcohol and drug use scales. Parent interviews and observations were summarized for each parent by 153 scales (82 parent behavior rating items, and 71 personal attribute rating items).

The child or parent composites comprising the substantive domains of theoretical interest were expected to overlap somewhat, because the original hypothetical constructs within each domain were conceptually interrelated. Accordingly, the items were first grouped to yield a set of correlated clusters via the BC TRY cluster analyses procedure (Tryon & Bailey, 1970). Second order-data reduction was then conducted via principal component analysis with varimax rotations, with the number of factors retained determined by a screen test (Gorsuch, 1974). (A more detailed presentation of the methods used is provided in Baumrind, 1990a, 1990b.)

ADOLESCENT DEVELOPMENT
IN THE CONTEXT OF THE FAMILY

Hypotheses pertaining to the effects of family patterns on adolescent competence are grounded in premises concerning normal adolescent development. The normative adolescent stage transition in our society from

24

"child" to "adult" includes major role changes in the individual's position relative to others, a shift in loyalties toward peers if not away from family, and a different mix of entitlements and obligations within the family and the larger society.

Overview

According to the classic view based on psychoanalytic formulations (Blos, 1962, 1979; Douvan & Adelson, 1966; Erikson, 1959; Marcia, 1980), and Piagetian stage theory (Kohlberg, 1969; Piaget 1932/1965), identity formation during adolescence is achieved by emotional disengagement from the family and a transfer of attachment to peers. Adolescents who remain emotionally attached to parents and respectful of their authority are said to be immature or to suffer from a "foreclosed identity." According to Piaget, a young child's heteronomous view of authority as unilateral and role-bound is supplanted during adolescence by an autonomous view of authority arising from symmetrical and reciprocal relationships established among peers. Some critics of the classic view (Bellah, Madsen, Sullivan, Swidler, & Tipton, 1985; Gilligan, 1982, 1987; Lasch, 1978; Sampson, 1988), have argued that it promotes agency at the expense of communion and connectedness. It also may be argued that the classic view presumes a stable, traditional society in which paternalistic adult authority is firmly established, whereas social organization in the United States is unstable and not adequately protective of youth.

The classic view contrasts sharply with its antithesis, the transition-proneness view, put forth by contemporary researchers concerned with the prevention of "problem behavior" in a transition-prone society (e.g., Jessor & Jessor, 1978). By "transition-proneness," Jessor and his colleagues refer to a pattern of behavior that normally emerges in early adolescence — higher value on independence, increased social activism, decreased religiosity, perceived relaxation of parental standards, and increased reliance on friends relative to parents. Although adolescents value self-reliance and the ability to make their own decisions (Feather, 1980; Greenberger, 1984), these developmentally appropriate behaviors are viewed as problematic by transition-proneness theorists because they are often (but not typically) accompanied by lowered achievement, early sexual experience, and substance use. Researchers or practitioners concerned with preventing such undesirable behaviors advocate restrictive practices in order to postpone or avert problematic risk-taking behavior that is sometimes associated with movement toward independence and intensification of peer relations. Their advice, that parents keep control, conflicts with that of classic Freudian or Piagetian stage theorists, to "let go."

In his insightful essay on freedom and control in parent-child relations, Bronfenbrenner (1985) suggested that the optimal ratio of control relative to freedom within the family increases as the modal level of stability and structure in the larger society decreases. The adolescents in the present sample, although largely middle-class and therefore not exposed to risks faced by the urban poor, reached puberty during a period of societal transition in which adults as well as youth had lost confidence in societies' fiduciaries. Mothers entered the work force, marital dissolution became more acceptable, and drugs were easily available around the high school and on the city streets. In periods of social instability parents are caught on the horns of a dilemma: Adolescents, in order to become self-regulated, individuated, competent individuals, require both the freedom to explore and experiment, and protection from experiences that are clearly dangerous. The classic view emphasizes the importance of the former, the transition-proneness view the importance of the latter.

The contemporary view (Baumrind, 1987) has sought to address this dilemma. In place of the "classic" emphasis on emotional detachment from parents, or the "transition-proneness" emphasis on delaying psychosocial maturity to minimize problem behaviors, the contemporary view emphasizes (as in another transitional period, infancy) the role of security of attachment in fostering family interdependence and in facilitating adolescent self-regulation, individuation, and exploratory behavior (Hartup, 1979; Hill, 1980; Hill & Holmbeck, 1986). The contemporary view departs from the liberal, individualist view that emphasizes self-containment and autonomy, in favor of the social-context position, well articulated by Luria (1929/1978), that who persons are and will become is defined by the communities they inhabit and the activities in which they engage. From this perspective, attachment to family and community facilitates individual development at any stage. Because parents are literally a part of oneself, both genetically and as a result of socialization processes, a view of reality and self-concept that denies one's continuity with one's parents is bound to be problematic. As Ryan and Lynch (1989) have shown, secure attachment to parents fosters a healthy self-confidence during adolescence as it does at other developmental stages. Therefore, relinquishing childhood dependencies on parents does not require adolescents to distance themselves emotionally from parents nor to deny continuity with parental values.

Cooper, Grotevant, and Condon (1982, 1983) described the effective family system as one that avoids both enmeshment, in which individuality is discouraged in favor of exaggerated family harmony; and disengagement, in which family members are so separate that they have little effect on each other. They refer to the individuated adolescent or the effective parent as one who achieves a *balance* between individuality (clear, differentiated presentation of one's own point of view) and connectedness (responsiveness to, and respect for, the views of others). Similarly, Steinberg and Silverberg (1986) have claimed that for boys a subjective sense of self-reliance develops out of family relations that are neither very close nor very distant, and that resistance to peer pressure is facilitated by close but not enmeshed family ties.

Reiss, Oliveri, and Curd (1983) used a systems approach to group families into a four-category typology based on high or low scores on two problem-solving dimensions: configuration or cognitive integration of parts into a complex, patterned whole; and coordination or interpersonal integration of all family member's contributions into a harmonious whole. Their ideal (environment-sensitive) families are organized optimally to investigate both the cognitive and social dimensions of the environment because they are high on both dimensions. By contrast, the consensus-sensitive family and the achievement-sensitive family are both unbalanced: The former, high on coordination but low on configuration, is interpersonally oriented, seeking harmony at the expense of information; and the latter, low on coordination and high on configuration, is individualistically oriented at the expense of group processes. Distance-sensitive families, low on both dimensions, explore neither the inner nor the outer world.

For purposes of this study, optimal competence was defined as the integration of agency and communion. Greenberger (1984) defined psychosocial maturity during adolescence similarly. In the psychosocial literature (e.g., Bakan, 1966), *communion* refers to the need to be of service and to be included and connected, whereas *agency* refers to the drive for independence, individuality, and self-aggrandizement. The social dimensions of status (dominance, power) and love (solidarity, affiliation) that emerge as the two orthogonal axes from almost all factor analyses of human behavior (e.g. Baumrind & Black, 1967; Leary, 1957, Lonner, 1980; Wiggins, 1979) are manifestations of agency and communion.

Adolescents' personal commitment to courses of thought and action that depart from early, more stable and secure patterns is facilitated by commensurate accommodations to their changing status by parents and other significant adults. It is hypothesized that adolescents are most likely to be "optimally competent" — that is, both communal and agentic, able both to criticize and to sustain attachment to their parents — when parents are both highly demanding and highly responsive, but increase the ratio of freedom to control in order to match the developmental level of their child. *Demandingness* refers to the claims parents make on children to become integrated into the family whole, by their maturity demands, supervision, disciplinary efforts and willingness to confront the child who disobeys. *Responsiveness* refers to the extent to which parents intentionally foster individuality, self-regulation, and self-assertion by being attuned, supportive, and acquiescent to children's special needs and demands.

Parent Types Prior to Adolescence

Factor analyses of parents' behavior typically yield two dimensions, which are manifestations in parents of demandingness and responsiveness (see Maccoby & Martin, 1983, for a review). Baumrind (in press b) used these dimensions to derive a four-fold classification of parenting behavior that describes how parents reconcile the joint needs of children for nurturance and limit-setting. The operational definitions of these four prototypes — authoritative, authoritarian, permissive, and rejecting-neglecting — differ somewhat depending on social context, developmental period, and method of assessment, but share certain essential features. *Authoritative* parents are both demanding and responsive. They monitor and impart clear standards for their children's conduct. They are assertive, but not intrusive or restrictive. Their disciplinary methods are supportive rather than punitive. They want their children to be assertive as well as socially responsible, and self-regulated as well as cooperative. *Authoritarian* parents are demanding and directive, but not responsive. They are obedience- and status-oriented, and expect their orders to be obeyed without explanation. They provide an orderly environment, and a clear set of regulations, and monitor their children's activities carefully. Not all directive or traditional parents are authoritarian. *Permissive* or nondirective parents are more responsive than they are demanding. They are nontraditional and lenient, do not require mature behavior, allow considerable self-regulation, and avoid confrontation. *Rejecting-neglecting* or disengaged parents are neither demanding nor responsive. They do not structure and monitor, and are not supportive, but may be actively rejecting or else neglect their childrearing responsibilities altogether.

The consequences for children *prior* to adolescence in the *Family Socialization and Developmental Competence Project* (FSP) of these four parental styles may be summarized as follows. Children from authoritative homes have consistently been found to be more instrumentally competent — agentic, communal, and cognitively competent — than other children (for an overview see Hill, 1980, and Maccoby & Martin, 1983; for examples of empirical studies see Baumrind, 1987; Clark, 1983; Dornbusch, Ritter, Leiderman, Roberts, & Fraleigh, 1987; Steinberg, Elmen, & Mounts, 1989). The effects of authoritarian upbringing in early childhood have been found to be more harmful for (middle-class) boys than girls (Baumrind, 1971; Baumrind, 1989), for preschool White girls than Black girls (Baumrind, 1973), and for White boys than Hispanic boys (Dornbusch et al., 1987). Preschool and primary school girls from permissive homes, compared to those from authoritative homes, were markedly less self-assertive, and preschool children of both sexes were less cognitively competent. Generally speaking, children from rejecting-neglecting homes tended to be the least competent of all.

Parent Types During Adolescence: Current Study

A typology assumes that the types are more than and different from the sum of their parts. Thus, high assertive control with low supportive control is hypothesized to have a different effect on a child than would moderate levels of both variables. By considering naturally occurring patterns of interaction among variables, typological analyses often provide more meaningful information about individuals and relationships than linear analyses (Hinde & Dennis, 1986).

When their children were adolescents, parents in the FSP were classified jointly by two psychologists into six types with one of these types further subdivided (index of agreement [Kappa] was .89). The seven types represent further differentiations among the four prototypic patterns described earlier. These differentiations are particularly pertinent to family relations during adolescence. The permissive prototype which emphasizes freedom over control was subdivided into a *democratic* and a *nondirective* type, with the democratic pattern representing a more conscientious and engaged commitment to the child. The authoritarian prototype was subsumed under directive parenting which emphasizes control over freedom. In order to differentiate between parents who were directive but not autocratic in their use of power *nonauthoritarian-directive* parents, who were not high on the Intrusive (I) cluster, were grouped separately from the *authoritarian-directive* parents, who were highly intrusive. A "*good-enough*" pattern (a term first coined by Winnicot in 1965) with moderate scores on both demandingness and responsiveness, was added with the thought that this moderate level of commitment would suffice to prevent problem behavior and to assure adequate competence during the adolescent stage of development.

Three parent behavior scales were used to define the six types, with a fourth scale used to subdivide the *directive* type. These scales emerged from BC TRY cluster analyses of the T3 parent rating items and measure different forms of demandingness and responsiveness. The three scales used to define the six types are *directive/conventional control* (D/C C), containing items that assess restrictive control and conventional values; *assertive control*

(AC), containing items that assess confrontational control (that is, firm but nonrestrictive monitoring of adolescents' lifestyle and activities, and straightforward confrontation and enforcement of rules); and *supportive control* (SC), containing items that assess rational control (that is, responsive, discipline, principled use of rational explanations to influence adolescents, intellectual stimulation, and encouragement of individuation). The fourth scale, *intrusive* (I), contains items that assess officiousness, and subversion of the child's independence.

In the definitions of the parent types, families were classified as "high" or "low" if their scores were one-half standard deviation from the total mean. Medium or moderate scores are from one-half standard deviation below (medium-low) to one-half standard deviation above (medium-high) the mean. In addition to the defining variables, family types were found to differ on such factors as disorganization, percent divorced, percent time mother works, and internalizing and externalizing problem behaviors. Table 1 presents the conceptual definition of the parent types. Table 2 contrasts the parent types on the defining variables and the major additional parent variables.

Parents in the same family were classified separately on the basis of their defining scale scores, and then combined. In divorced families, the parent (and long-term partner where there was one) with whom the adolescent lived were classified. In intact families, in the few instances that parents were not classified identically, the differences on the two major defining scales were small (e.g., one parent would be authoritative [high-high] and the other democratic [high-medium]). When there was such moderate divergence, precedence was given to the mother's scores because it was known from correlational analyses (Baumrind, in press a) that mothers were more influential than fathers in affecting adolescents' (especially daughters') behavior. Five families could not be classified because the divergence was too great or the family had idiosyncratic scores. For those who could be classified, the percentage of exact agreement for mothers and fathers in the same family was 76% (index of agreement [kappa] was .58).

Results

Adolescent attributes were compared across the T3 parent types in a one-way analysis of variance. A priori contrasts were used to test differences that were predicted. Otherwise, Newman-Keuls post-hoc comparisons were used.[1]

Table 3 contrasts the parent types on the adolescent attributes. Hypotheses pertaining to the influences of each parent type on adolescent functioning are

TABLE 1: Definitions of the T3 Family Types[a]

1. *Authoritative* families (12 girls and 9 boys), by definition are both highly demanding (AC) and highly responsive (SC). In addition, they were found to be well organized, to manifest low problem behavior, stress levels, and substance use, and to disapprove of adolescent drug and alcohol use. Fourteen percent were divorced.

2. *Democratic* families (13 girls and 12 boys), by definition are highly responsive (SC), moderately demanding (AC), and not restrictive (not-high on D/C C). They are less conventional, directive, and assertive in their control than authoritative parents, but like authoritative parents are supportive, caring, personally agentic, and manifest no problem behavior or family disorganization. Twenty-eight percent were divorced.

3. *Directive* families (12 girls and 16 boys) are restrictive (medium-high to high scores on D/C C), demanding (average to medium-high scores on AC), and not responsive (medium-low to low scores on SC). They value conformity above individuality, are obedience- and status-oriented, provide an orderly environment and a clear set of regulations, and closely monitor their children's activities. *Authoritarian-directive* families (8 girls and 13 boys) are also Intrusive (I) whereas *nonauthoritarian-directive* families (4 girls and 3 boys) are not Intrusive. Fifty percent of authoritarian parents and 14% of nonauthoritarian-directive parents were divorced.

4. *Good-enough* families (7 girls and 6 boys) had medium-low to medium-high scores on D/C C, AC, and S. In addition, they did not manifest problem behavior or disorganization. Thirty-nine percent were divorced.

5. *Nondirective* families (3 girls and 4 boys) are very nonrestrictive (very low scores on D/C C) and rather responsive (medium-high scores on SC). Nondirective parents allowed considerable self-regulation, and avoided confrontation. Nondirective families were also disorganized and all but one had been divorced. Mothers were more likely to use illicit drugs and not to object to the adolescent's use of alcohol or drugs. Mothers used little assertive control, but both parents were personally agentic and manifested little personal problem behavior.

6. *Unengaged* families (12 girls and 18 boys) are neither demanding nor responsive (that is, low on both SC and AC). They do not structure or monitor. In addition, it was found that unengaged mothers were nonagentic, families were disorganized with 60% divorced, and both parents manifested problem behavior.

a. AC = assertive control, SC = supportive control, D/C C = directive/conventional control, I = intrusive.

presented followed by results. *F* tests were significant for nearly all the adolescent attributes.

The home environment that authoritative and democratic parents generate was hypothesized to be more conducive to the development of optimal competence in adolescents than that of any other type of parent. Authoritative and democratic parents, compared to other types of parents, are more rational,

Text continues on page 72

TABLE 2: Analysis of Variance of Time 3 (T3) Parent Variables by T3 Parent Types

Parent(s)	T3 Family Type[a]							F	Comparisons
	1	2	3a	3b	4	5	6		
Socialization Practices									
Directive/Conventional control[b]									Restrictive Domain
Mothers	53	46	60	61	48	37	45	16.50***	5 < 1, 2, 3a, 3b, 6; 6, 2 < 1, 3a, 3b; 1, 4 < 3a, 3b
Fathers	52	46	57	62	47	42	45	9.91***	6 < 1, 3a, 3b; 2, 4 < 3a, 3b; 1 < 3b
Assertive control[b]									Demanding Domain
Mothers	60	52	56	50	50	43	39	22.07***	5, 6 < 1, 2, 3a, 3b, 4; 2, 3b, 4 < 1; 3b < 3a
Fathers	58	49	54	55	52	50	40	9.21***	6 < 1, 2, 3a, 3b, 4; 2 < 1, 3b
									Psychologically differentiated domain
Agentic/Influential									
Mothers	58	57	48	41	50	57	43	18.64***	3a, 3b, 4, 6 < 1, 2, 5; 3b < 3a, 4; 6 < 4
Fathers	55	56	49	48	52	57	46	2.85*	3b, 6 < 1, 2
Supportive control[b]									Responsive domain
Mothers	59	59	49	41	51	53	40	40.87***	3b, 6 < 1, 2, 3a, 4, 5; 3a 4, 5 < 1, 2
Fathers	59	58	50	42	54	65	40	15.80***	3b, 6 < 1, 2, 3a, 4; 3a < 1, 2
Parent Problem Behaviors									
Internalizing									
Mothers	45	45	43	54	47	51	58	8.36***	1, 2, 3a, 4 < 3b, 6
Fathers	46	46	45	49	46	45	56	3.86*	1, 2, 3a, 3b, 4 < 6

32

								F	
Externalizing									
Mothers	45	46	45	55	45	49	57	6.62***	1, 2, 3a, 4 < 3b, 6
Fathers	46	45	45	54	46	46	56	5.48***	1, 2, 4 < 3b, 6; 3a < 6; 3a < 3b
Intrusive[b]									
Mothers	47	43	49	64	45	48	51	15.88***	2, 4 < 6; 1, 2, 3a, 4, 5, 6 < 3b
Fathers	47	45	45	60	46	45	47	6.86***	1, 2, 3a, 4, 6 < 3b
Substance Use									
									Alcohol
Alcohol User Type									
Mothers	48	52	49	50	51	47	51	0.53	
Fathers	45	50	51	46	50	51	55	3.01*	1, 3b < 6
Opposes child's alcohol use									
Mothers	54	49	56	63	47	41	48	2.57*	5 < 1, 3a, 3b
Fathers	53	48	57	55	44	41	50	2.67*	4 < 1, 3a, 3b; 2 < 3a, 3b
									Cannabis and drug
Drug user type									
Mothers	47	53	46	46	53	64	48	3.56**	1, 2, 3a, 3b, 6 < 5; 3a, 3b < 2, 4
Fathers	46	51	46	46	53	53	55	2.58*	1, 3a, 3b < 6
Opposes child's drug use									
Mothers	55	49	55	50	47	43	50	2.06*	2, 4, 5 < 1; 5 < 3a
Fathers	53	48	55	53	46	36	51	1.53	4 < 1, 3a, 3b
Family Stressors									
Family disorganization	44	47	43	50	46	56	59	9.18***	1, 2, 3a, 4 < 5, 6; 1, 3a < 3b; 3b < 6
Total stressors	46	47	49	52	48	53	58	5.37	1, 2, 3a, 3b, 4 < 6; 1, 2 < 3b, 5

(continued)

33

TABLE 2 continued

Parent(s)	T3 Family Type[a]							F	Comparisons
	1	2	3a	3b	4	5	6		
Demographics									
% time mother works	40	70	28	36	57	80	53	2.65*	*3a, 3b < 2, 5; 1 < 2, 5*
% divorced	14	28	14	33	39	86	60	3.95**	*1, 2, 3a, 3b < 6; 4 < 6*
N									
Total	21	25	7	21	13	7	30		
Mothers	21	24	7	21	12	6	28		
Fathers	18	17	7	16	9	2	13		

NOTE: Flush-left headings designate major categories of variables. Centered headings designate domains. All variables are T-scores (mean = 50, SD = 10), except the demographic variables which are expressed as percents. Post-hoc comparisons (Newman-Keuls) that are significant at $p < .05$ are printed in italics (i.e., both numbers on either side of the less-than sign must be italics) and those that are significant at $p < .10$ are in ordinary type. The higher probability level ($p < .10$) is due to the low power resulting from the small number in some of the family types. Because Type 5 has $n = 2$ for fathers, it is not included in the F tests or for comparisons including fathers only.

a. Family types: 1. authoritative, 2. democratic, 3a. nonauthoritarian-directive, 3b. authoritarian-directive, 4. good-enough, 5. nondirective, 6. unengaged.

b. The F values for the four defining variables are *not* mathematically independent of the parent types, and are presented for descriptive purposes only.

*$p < .05$; **$p < .01$; ***$p < .001$.

34

TABLE 3: Analysis of Variance of Time 3 (T3) Adolescent Psychological Attributes by T3 Parent Types

Adolescent	1	2	3a	3b	4	5	6	F	Comparisons
Competence									
Agentic									
Emancipated	50	51	42	45	50	55	53	2.63*	3a, 3b < 2, 5, 6; 3a < 1
Autonomy	52	51	42	45	49	53	53	2.65*	3a, 3b < 1, 2, 5, 6
Socially conscious	53	57	42	44	52	52	47	5.64***	3a < 2; 6 < 1, 2; 3a, 3b < 1, 2, 4, 5
General Competence									
Individuated	58	56	45	43	50	50	45	10.16***	3b, 6 < 1, 2, 4; 3a < 1, 2; 4, 5 < 1
Maturity	58	57	45	44	51	50	45	10.60***	3a, 3b, 6 < 1, 2; 4, 5 < 1
Resilient	56	56	45	45	51	49	45	6.77***	3a, 3b < 1, 2; 6 < 1, 2, 4
Optimistic	58	54	53	47	48	47	44	8.57***	3b, 4, 6, < 1, 2; 4, 5 < 1
Optimum competence	59	57	48	45	51	48	43	13.54***	3a, 3b, 4, 5 < 1, 2; 6 < 1, 2, 4; 3a < 1
General self-esteem	53	52	42	50	44	47	51	2.35*	4 < 1, 2, 6
Cognitive Competence									
Cognitively motivated	57	55	49	48	50	49	42	8.74***	3b < 1, 2; 3a, 4, 5 < 1; 6 < 1, 2, 3a, 3b, 4
Cognitively competent	56	56	51	49	49	46	42	8.66***	3b, 4, 5 < 1, 2; 6 < 1, 2, 3a, 3b, 4
Achievement oriented	56	56	52	50	49	45	42	7.85***	4, 5 < 1, 2; 6 < 1, 2, 3a, 3b, 4
Math achievement	93	93	81	75	89	86	78	2.94*	3b, 6 < 1, 2;
Girls	92	96	84	79	85	96	88	1.54	3b < 2
Boys	94	91	77	72	93	79	72	3.57*	3b, 6 < 1, 2, 4
Verbal achievement	94	93	85	75	89	86	77	3.02***	3b < 1, 2, 4; 6 < 1, 2
Girls	94	96	92	79	85	96	88	1.49	3b < 2
Boys	94	91	77	73	93	79	71	3.73*	3b, 6 < 1, 4; 3b, 6 < 2

T3 Family Type[a]

(continued)

35

TABLE 3 continued

Adolescent	1	2	3a	3b	4	5	6	F	Comparisons
						T3 Family Type[a]			
					Communal				
Self-regulated	58	56	53	47	51	45	41	12.38***	3b, 5 < 1, 2; 6 < 1, 2, 3a, 3b, 4
Prosocial	57	56	53	49	52	46	41	12.21***	3b, 5 < 1, 2; 6 < 1, 2, 3a, 3b, 4
Socially responsible	56	56	53	50	53	47	41	9.13***	6 < 1, 2, 3a, 3b, 4; 3b, 5 < 1, 2
Conformity									
Seeks adult approval	53	52	57	50	46	46	46	2.38***	4, 5 < 3a; 6 < 1, 2, 3a
Negative attitude toward drugs	52	46	57	57	47	46	47	3.82**	2, 4, 5, 6 < 3b, 3a
Girls	56	48	57	53	46	44	47	2.24	2, 4, 6 < 1
Boys	47	44	57	59	49	48	47	4.13**	1, 2, 4, 6 < 3b; 2 < 4
External locus of control	44	46	62	55	51	49	53	6.04***	1 < 3a, 3b, 4, 6; 2 < 3a, 3b, 6; 4, 5, 6 < 3a
Problem Behaviors									
Internalizing	44	45	48	53	51	50	56	6.42***	1 < 3b, 6; 2, 3 < 6; 2 < 3b
Total problem behavior	44	45	46	50	49	50	60	10.88***	1, 2 < 3b, 6; 3a, 3b, 4, 5 < 6
Alienation	45	48	50	48	55	56	52	2.40**	1 < 5, 6
Girls	46	45	47	46	61	55	50	3.54*	1, 2, 3b, 6 < 4
Boys	45	52	53	49	48	57	54	1.65	1 < 6
Externalizing	46	43	46	47	48	49	60	8.11***	1, 2, 3a, 3b, 4, 5 < 6
Illicit drug use	45	50	41	48	53	55	56	5.97***	1, 2, 3a, 3b < 6; 1, 3a < 2, 4, 5
Girls	52	62	48	56	48	58	65	4.74**	1, 2, 3b < 6; 1 < 4
Boys	48	53	45	54	61	60	64	2.26	1, 3b < 6
Alcohol use	50	57	47	55	55	59	64	5.87***	1, 3a < 2, 5, 6; 2, 3b, 4 < 6; 1 < 2
Acts out sexually	47	49	46	46	48	54	56	3.44**	1, 2, 3a, 3b, 4 < 5, 6

	1	2	3a	3b	4	5	6	F	Comparisons
Girls	46	49	46	46	49	46	59	4.29**	1, 2, 3b, 4 < 6
Boys	49	49	47	46		60	54	1.32	
Adolescent's Perception of Parent									
Restrictive	50	46	56	48	40	50		6.15***	1, 2, 4, 5, 6 < 3a, 3b; 5 < 1, 6
Loving and influential	58	56	53	47	49	45	42	14.45***	3b, 4, 5, 6 < 3a, 1, 2; 6 < 3b, 4
Exemplary	54	54	44	48	55	51	41	7.40***	3a, 3b, 6 < 1, 2, 4; 6 < 5
N									
Total	21	25	7	21	13	7	30		
Girls	12	13	(4)	8	7	(3)	12		
Boys	9	12	(3)	13	6	(4)	18		

NOTE: Flush-left headings designate major categories of variables. Centered headings designate domains. All variables are T-scores (mean = 50, $SD = 10$), except verbal and math achievement (range 0-100). Significant ($p < .05$) post-hoc comparisons (Newman-Keuls) are printed in italics (i.e., both numbers on either side of the less-than sign must be italics) and a priori comparisons (t tests) are in ordinary type. Results are presented for each gender separately whenever the results are significant for one gender and not the other. There were no significant ($p < .05$) interactions with gender. Because family Types 3a and 5 have $n < 5$ for boys and girls separately, they are not included in the F tests or for comparisons including boys and girls separately.

a. Family types: 1. authoritative, 2. democratic, 3a. nonauthoritarian-directive, 3b. authoritarian-directive, 4. good-enough, 5. nondirective, 6. unengaged.

*$p < .05$; **$p < .01$; ***$p < .001$.

consistent, and considerate, and thus are less likely to induce disruptive emotional responses (internalizing problem behavior) that interfere with complex reasoning or task performance. Because they also are more challenging and demanding of high performance, their children are expected to perform well in school (mathematics and verbal achievement) and to be motivated to excel (cognitive motivation). Because they are both agentic and communal, authoritative and democratic parents are likely to be perceived by their adolescents as loving and influential. Their children will therefore be more likely to emulate the general competence, cognitive differentiation, and prosocial behaviors these parents display, and to comply with their standards of conduct. Democratic families are lenient during adolescence because of their commitment to democratic ideology and respect for the adolescent's autonomy. Because of the difference in ideology of their parents, it was predicted that adolescents from democratic families would be more socially conscious and use substances more heavily than those from authoritative families.

Compared to their peers the adolescents from authoritative and democratic families were, as predicted, outstandingly competent (see Table 3). Both groups by comparison with their peers were individuated, mature, resilient, optimistic, and perceived their parents as loving and influential. They were cognitively motivated and achievement oriented, and had among the highest scores on verbal and mathematics achievement tests. They were also self-regulated and socially responsible and had high self-esteem and an internal locus of control. They were not alienated, and manifested minimal externalizing and internalizing problem behaviors. Adolescents from authoritative and democratic homes were not significantly more competent than their peers from other family types in all respects. For example, adolescents from authoritative and democratic families were only slightly higher in prosocial behavior than adolescents from nonauthoritarian-directive and good-enough families, and only slightly higher in academic achievement than their peers from good-enough families.

The adolescents from authoritative parents were more competent on most attributes than those from democratic parents — but seldom to a significant degree. As expected, self-reported negative attitudes toward the use of drugs were lower for girls, and actual use was higher for girls and boys from democratic families than from authoritative families. The expected difference in social consciousness for adolescents from democratic compared to authoritative families was in the predicted direction, but was not significant.

Using correlational analyses, it had already been noted that directive/ conventional control, the distinctive feature of directive parents, was associated with low externalizing problem behavior (such as drug use), and with behavioral conformity, but not with internalization of prosocial values, mature ego development, individuation, or secure attachment to parents (Baumrind, in press a). Similarly, Hauser et al. (1984) had linked constraining discourse (e.g, withholding, indifference, devaluing) characteristic of authoritarian families to lower adolescent ego development, and enabling discourse (e.g., problem solving, explaining, acceptance, and empathy) characteristic of authoritative and democratic families to higher ego development. Therefore, adolescents from directive homes, compared to their peers from authoritative and democratic families, were hypothesized to experience their parents as more restrictive and to be more concerned with eliciting adult approval, less socially conscious, more conforming, socially agentic, and individuated and to have an external locus of control. Compared to adolescents from democratic families, they were expected to be less involved with drugs and alcohol.

Adolescents from nonauthoritarian-directive and authoritarian-directive families were expected to differ in some respects. Authoritarian parents were obedience- and status-oriented and expected their orders to be obeyed without explanation. Compared to authoritative parents, authoritarian parents manifested somewhat more problem behavior and were much more officious, restrictive, and conventional, and much less supportive (see Table 2). Authoritarian parents, despite their traditional values, had more difficultly sustaining satisfying interpersonal relations with their spouses (one-half were divorced) as well as their adolescent offspring. By contrast, nonauthoritarian-directive parents manifested as little problem behavior and family disorganization as authoritative parents, and unlike authoritarian parents, were adequately caring and considerate (although not as supportive). Therefore, adolescents from authoritarian-directive homes were expected to be less optimistic and to manifest more internalizing problem behaviors than those from nonauthoritarian-directive homes.

As expected, adolescents from directive homes — both authoritarian and nonauthoritarian — were somewhat lacking in individuation, social consciousness, and autonomy, had an external locus of control, opposed drug use, and experienced their parents as restrictive (see table 3). Adolescents from nonauthoritarian-directive homes were the most concerned with seeking adult approval. They also used significantly less drugs and alcohol than any other group except those from authoritative homes. Adolescents from authoritarian homes, unlike those from nonauthoritarian-directive homes, when compared to adolescents from authoritative or democratic homes performed poorly on verbal and mathematics achievement tests and manifested more internalizing problem behavior. When directive parents are authoritarian — that is, officious and restrictive in their constraints — they retard adolescent development, and become less effective in controlling their adolescent's problem behaviors than nonauthoritarian parents, but are still somewhat effective in minimizing externalizing behavior.

Adolescents from good-enough homes were, as the name suggests, expected to be adequately but not outstandingly competent, and without serious problem manifestations. These hypotheses were confirmed (see Table 3). An unexpected and possibly unstable finding is that daughters of good-enough parents were alienated and manifested extremely low self-esteem. These girls may need something more from their good-enough parents (perhaps a sense of being special).

Nondirective parents, like democratic parents, are more responsive than they are demanding. Similar to permissive parents at early time periods, nondirective, like democratic, parents were nontraditional and lenient, and valued individuality above conformity. However, nondirective parents were even less willing than democratic parents to set limits, especially on drug use, and were more nonconforming. The differences between democratic and nondirective parents were expected to affect their adolescents in important ways. By comparison with adolescents from democratic homes, those from nondirective homes were not expected to be outstandingly competent, and instead were expected to be relatively alienated, noncommunal, nonachievement-oriented, and nonconforming, to use illicit drugs freely, and to experience their parents as nonrestrictive.

Differences were all in the expected direction (see Table 3). With power reduced by the small number of nondirective families, only differences of relatively large magnitude could be found to be significant. However, compared to adolescents from either democratic or authoritative homes, adolescents from nondirective homes were, as expected, significantly less achievement oriented despite their high intelligence (average 121), and also were somewhat less optimally competent, self-regulated, and socially responsible. They were heavier users of illicit drugs than all other adolescents except those from unengaged homes, and experienced their parents as the least restrictive.

Unengaged parents did not want to be encumbered by childrearing responsibilities. Some were actively rejecting, whereas others neglected their childrearing responsibilities altogether. By comparison with their peers, adolescents from unengaged families were expected to be antisocial, lacking self-regulation, social responsibility, and cognitive competence, to suffer from internalizing and externalizing problem behaviors, and to reject their parents as role models. These hypotheses were all confirmed (see Table 3).

Adolescents from unengaged homes differed from all other adolescents in their high incidence of externalizing problem behavior, including problem drug and alcohol use, and in their low communal behavior and cognitive competence. They had the highest levels of externalizing problem behaviors in the sample, especially of illicit drug use. Adolescents from unengaged homes were similar to adolescents from authoritarian homes in that they performed poorly on standardized achievement tests and were immature (not individuated or resilient and had an external locus of control). Girls in particular manifested internalizing problem behaviors.

In the a priori tests of the family types (Table 3), none were significant in the opposite direction, 68% were significant in the predicted direction and of a moderate to large magnitude, 20% were not significant but were in the expected direction with a moderate magnitude, and 12% were of a small magnitude and not significant (Cohen, 1977).

DETERMINANTS OF
ADOLESCENT SUBSTANCE USER TYPES

Overview

Risk-taking experimentation with illicit substances, as a class of behavior, is not necessarily pathological and indeed was normative for adolescents when these data were obtained. The term "risk-taking behavior" is used here to refer to actions undertaken intentionally and with an awareness of the risk involved. Illicit drug *experimentation* is likely to be risk-taking by this definition, whereas *habitual use* that results in dependence and withdrawal from exploratory risk-taking in most other domains is not. Although use of alcohol or drugs cannot be regarded as a health-promoting form of experimentation for adolescents, explorative risk-taking behavior during adolescence is normal and necessary (Baumrind, 1987). Therefore, sexual or drug experimentation in early adolescence was not expected to be a manifestation of early maladaptive patterns of childrearing or childhood personality. Heavy use of alcohol or illicit substances was expected to be associated with low competence and problem behavior, whereas experimental and recreational substance use was not. Heavy substance users were expected to show a decrement from T2 or T3, relative to their peers, in cognitive competence, mental health, communal behavior, and concern for adult approval, but experimental users were not. Parents of heavy users were expected to be lax, neglectful, and to manifest externalizing problem behavior including sub-

41

stance abuse, but parents of experimenters were not. (A more complete rationale for this study is provided in Baumrind, 1990b.)

Substance User Types

In order to evaluate such hypotheses, user types were compared on concurrent and antecedent child and parent variables. An adolescent drug user typology was constructed from detailed information obtained during a two hour interview (at T3) with each adolescent about dosage, frequency, and context of use of alcohol, tobacco, cannabis, and other illicit drugs. With regard to each substance the adolescent was asked who introduced her or him to the substance, what the pattern of usage by close friends and peer group was, at what age the substance was first used, and with whom, when it was last used, what effects the substance had during the first use and thereafter, the setting in which use generally took place, who the supplier was, whether use occurred on school days, and how the adolescent's school work was affected. (For further discussion of adolescent substance user typologies, see Baumrind, 1985, and Baumrind, 1990b.)

Two separate ordered, qualitative substance-user scales were constructed: one for cannabis and hard drugs, and one for alcohol. In adolescent populations, alcohol and cannabis use are highly correlated (in the present sample the two scales are correlated .70). To take these dependencies into account, the two substance-use scales were combined into a single ordered, qualitative scale composed of five main substance user types. The types are defined conceptually in Table 4 and operationally in Baumrind (1990b).

Results

Analyses included linear and nonlinear trends, a priori and post hoc comparisons, and functional decrements – that is, T3 minus T2 standard scores on the same or analogous scales. These analyses are presented fully in two articles (Baumrind, 1990a, 1990b). Here, the T3 adolescent and parent variables that relate significantly to the combined substance user types are tabled (see Tables 5 and 6). The parent and child *antecedent* attributes are summarized in text but are not tabled.

It is assumed that the substance user types refer to discrete groups of adolescents, but also that the types constitute more than a nominal scale. Unlike the parent types, substance user types clearly can be placed along a single dimension (severity of substance abuse), and thus form an ordinal scale. In addition, it is assumed that the substance user variable represents an approximation to an interval scale. Exact error-free interval scales are virtu-

42

TABLE 4: Definitions of the Combined Substance User Types

I. *Nonuser* (17 girls, 15 boys). Virtual nonuser of alcohol, cannabis, or other illicit substances. *Risk-avoidant nonusers* (Ia) avoid substance use because of irrational and unrealistic fears (e.g., "marijuana can make you crazy"), whereas *rational nonusers* (Ib) justify abstinence on specific and realistic grounds (e.g., "I don't like my mood changed chemically").

II. *Recreational user of alcohol* (14 girls, 17 boys). Light or casual recreational user of alcohol and nonuser of cannabis. Drinks no more than two ounces less than once a week. Seldom drinks alone, and does not drink to cope with stress.

III. *Experimental or casual user of cannabis* (14 girls, 12 boys). An experimental or casual user of cannabis who uses cannabis less than once a week and is not a heavy user of alcohol.

IV. *Heavy user of alcohol, drugs, or both* (13 girls, 12 boys). Habitual user of either alcohol or cannabis or both. May have preference for alcohol or illicit drugs, or may use both heavily, but not in school or so as to interfere with homework. Heavy use entails consumption of two joints of cannabis or other illicit drugs, or three ounces or more of alcohol, or somewhat less than three ounces of alcohol several times a month where the aim is to get high in order to cope.

V. *Drug-dependent users of alcohol, drugs, or both* (10 girls, 15 boys). Uses either alcohol or cannabis, or both, in such a way that use interferes with scholastic performance.

ally absent in the behavioral sciences, but fortunately approximations to an interval scale can be used with most fixed regression based models (Cohen & Cohen, 1975).

Type I nonusers (23% of the sample) were virtual nonusers of alcohol, cannabis, or other illicit substances. Parents of abstainers were expected to be conforming, directive, and conventional. Therefore, nonusers compared to users (Types III, IV, and V) were expected to be conforming, concerned with adult approval, and not gregarious. They were expected to show a relative increment from T2 to T3 in cognitive competence and prosocial behavior, but a decrement in social agency.

As expected, relative to other parents at all time periods, parents of nonusers were conforming, directive, and conventional. During adolescence, mothers opposed adolescents' use of alcohol more and worked less (girls), and parents used fewer illicit drugs than any other group. As expected, the profile of nonusers was characterized by high-average general competence, cognitive competence, and communal behavior. Compared to heavy users (Types IV and V), nonusers were lower in personal agency and problem behavior. Nonusers differed significantly from their peers in that they were

Text continues on page 85

43

TABLE 5: Analysis of Variance of Adolescent Variables by Adolescent Combined Substance User Types

Child Attributes	Combined Substance User Type					F	Comparisons	Deviation from Linearity
	I	II	III	IV	V			
Competence								
						Agentic		
Emancipated	47	46	48	53	57	6.85***	1, 2 < 4, 5; 3 < 5	1.10
Autonomy	47	47	49	53	56	4.84**	1, 2, 3 < 5; 1, 2 < 4	0.53
Gregarious	45	48	54	53	53	3.73**	1 < 3, 4, 5; 2 < 3	1.17
Seeks Peer Approval	49	48	48	51	56	3.15*	1, 2, 3 < 5	1.49
						General Competence		
Optimistic	53	53	52	48	43	5.23***	5 < 1, 2, 3, 4	1.45
Girls	55	53	54	47	38	9.34***	4 < 2, 3, 1; 5 < 1, 2, 3, 4	2.98*
Boys	50	52	50	50	47	0.51	NS	
Optimum Competence	52	52	53	49	45	2.66*	5 < 1, 3, 2	1.17
Girls	53	52	53	49	42	3.19*	5 < 1, 2, 3, 4	1.40
Boys	50	51	53	48	47	0.60	NS	
						Cognitive Competence		
Cognitively motivated	53	53	51	45	44	5.95***	4, 5 < 1, 2, 3	0.92
Girls	53	54	50	45	41	5.75***	4, 5 < 1, 2; 5 < 3	0.70
Boys	53	53	53	46	47	1.75	NS	
Cognitively competent	54	54	52	46	42	10.01***	4, 5 < 1, 2, 3	1.17
Achievement oriented	54	54	51	46	42	10.68***	4, 5 < 1, 2, 3	1.25
						Communal		
Self-regulated	53	53	52	48	43	5.64***	5 < 1, 2, 3; 4 < 1	0.94
Girls	54	54	53	49	41	4.53**	5 < 1, 2, 3, 4	1.67
Boys	53	52	50	46	44	1.79	5 < 1, 2	

	1	2	3	4	5	F	Contrast	
Prosocial	53	52	53	48	43	5.69***	5 < 1, 2, 3, 4	1.71
Girls	53	52	54	49	39	5.12**	5 < 1, 2, 3, 4	2.56
Boys	52	52	53	47	45	1.59	5 < 1	
Socially responsible	52	52	53	49	43	4.72**	5 < 1, 2, 3, 4	2.14
Girls	53	51	54	49	38	4.70**	5 < 1, 2, 3, 4	2.88*
Boys	52	53	53	48	47	1.22	NS	
Conformity								
Seeks adult approval	55	54	46	46	45	8.15***	3, 4, 5 < 1, 2	1.99
Girls	58	57	46	46	42	6.82***	3, 4, 5 < 1, 2	0.95
Boys	53	52	46	47	48	2.11	3 < 1, 2	1.09
Negative attitude toward drugs	57	54	48	46	41	17.39***	3, 4, 5 < 1, 2; 5 < 3, 4	0.68
Problem Behaviors								
Internalizing	50	49	47	50	56	2.70*	1, 2, 4, 3 < 5	2.43
Girls	49	48	46	49	58	2.72*	1, 2, 3, 4 < 5	2.36
Boys	52	49	48	51	54	0.63	NS	
Total problem behavior	48	47	47	51	61	11.45***	1, 2, 3, 4 < 5	5.66**
Alienation	47	49	49	50	56	3.05*	1, 2, 3, 4 < 5	0.91
Externalizing	46	45	48	52	63	21.93***	1, 2 < 4, 5; 3, 4, < 5	6.82***
Acts out sexually	47	46	48	53	59	10.68***	1, 2 < 4, 5; 3, 4 < 5	2.57
Adolescent's Perception of Parent								
Observer's ratings of adolescent's perception of parents as:								
Restrictive								
Fathers	55	50	47	.47	50	3.00*	3, 4 < 1	2.42

(continued)

45

TABLE 5 continued

Child Attributes	Combined Substance User Type					F	Comparisons	Deviation from Linearity
	I	II	III	IV	V			
Loving & influential								
Mothers	54	56	52	47	40	15.35***	*4, 5 < 1, 2; 5 < 3, 4*	3.21*
Fathers	55	56	50	46	40	17.28***	*3, 4, 5 < 1, 2; 5 < 3, 4*	2.05
Adolescent's ratings of parents as:								
Exemplary								
Mothers	49	54	53	49	45	2.97*	*5 < 2, 3*	2.98*
Fathers	51	52	53	50	44	3.40*	*5 < 1, 2, 3, 4*	2.24
Girls	51	56	51	53	39	5.01**	*5 < 1, 2, 3, 4*	4.07*
Boys	51	49	55	47	47	1.34	*5 < 3*	
N								
Total	32	31	26	25	25			
Girls	17	14	14	13	10			
Boys	15	17	12	12	15			

NOTE: Only variables with a significant ANOVA or a priori comparison are included. Flushed left headings designate major kinds of variables. Centered headings designate domains. Other names are variable names. All variables are T scores ($M = 50$, SD = 10). All variables are standardized across girls and boys. Significant ($p < .05$) comparisons (Newman-Keuls) are printed in italics (i.e., both numbers on either side of the less-than sign must be in italics), and significant a priori comparisons (t tests) in ordinary type. Results are presented for each gender separately only when there is a significant interaction with gender or the results are significant for one gender and not the other. F values printed in italics signify an ANOVA with a significant interaction with gender ($p < .05$).
*$p < .05$; **$p < .01$; ***$p < .001$.

TABLE 6: Analysis of Variance of Time 3 Parent Variables by Combined Substance User Types

Parent(s)	Combined Substance User Type					F	Comparisons	Deviation from Linearity
	I	II	III	IV	V			
Socialization Practices								
						Restrictive domain		
Directive/Conventional Control								
Mothers	58	50	51	46	44	8.02***	2, 3, 4, 5 < 1; 5 < 2, 3	1.79
						Demanding domain		
Assertive Control								
Mothers	55	53	53	47	40	12.99***	4, 5 < 1, 2, 3; 5 < 4	2.62+
						Psychologically differentiated domain		
Agentic/Influential								
Mothers	47	53	54	51	45	3.37*	1 < 2, 3; 5 < 2, 3	4.30**
Girls	47	54	54	50	42	3.04*	5 < 2, 3	3.56*
Boys	48	51	54	51	48	0.92	NS	
						Responsive domain		
Supportive Control								
Mothers	52	53	51	49	44	3.59**	5 < 1, 2, 3	1.12
Girls	52	56	52	49	41	4.81**	5 < 1, 2, 3, 4	2.26+
Boys	52	50	51	49	46	0.56	NS	

(continued)

TABLE 6 continued

Parent(s)	Combined Substance User Type					F	Comparisons	Deviation from Linearity
	I	II	III	IV	V			
Parent Problem Behaviors								
Internalizing								
Mothers	50	48	47	51	54	1.93	2, 3 < 5	0.73
Externalizing								
Fathers	47	49	49	52	56	2.86*	1, 2, 3 < 5	0.56
Girls	46	46	48	53	61	3.65*	1, 2, 3 < 5	1.03
Boys	49	51	49	51	53	0.46	NS	
Intrusive								
Mothers	53	47	50	54	47	2.62*	2, 5 < 1, 4	3.33*
Substance Use						Alcohol		
Alcohol User Type								
Fathers	47	49	50	54	54	3.08*	1, 2, < 4	0.54
Girls	49	51	49	57	53	0.95	NS	
Boys	45	44	51	52	54	3.71**	1, 2 < 5; 2 < 4	0.65
Opposes child's alcohol use								
Fathers	53	54	48	54	45	3.22**	5 < 1, 2	0.46
Mothers	55	51	47	49	45	4.33**	3, 4, 5 < 1; 5 < 2	0.68
Girls	55	52	48	47	41	3.63*	4 < 1; 5 < 1, 2	0.13
Boys	56	51	47	50	47	1.63	3, 5 < 1	
						Cannabis and Drugs		
Drug user type								
Mothers	44	45	54	53	53	5.11***	1 < 3, 4, 5; 2 < 3	2.01

	1	2	3	4	5	F	Contrast	
Girls	44	47	54	52	53	3.62*	1 < 3, 4, 5	1.29
Boys	44	49	55	51	53	1.81	1 < 3, 5	0.54
Fathers	44	48	54	53	53	4.20**	1, 2 < 3; 1, 2 < 5	
Opposes child's drug use								
Fathers	50	54	48	49	48	3.22**	5 < 1, 2	0.46
Mothers	52	51	49	48	48	4.33***	3, 4, 5 < 1; 5 < 2	0.68
Girls	51	53	49	46	47	3.63*	4 < 1; 5 < 1, 2	0.13
Boys	53	50	48	50	48	1.63	3, 5 < 1	
Family Stressors								
Family disorganization	47	47	48	48	56	3.91***	1, 2, 3, < 5	1.02
Girls	47	47	45	49	59	3.69**	1, 2, 3, 4 < 5	2.33
Boys	47	48	50	52	54	1.24	NS	
Total Stressors	47	47	50	52	57	5.62***	1, 2, 3 < 5; 1, 2 < 4	0.93
Demographics								
% Mother works	36	51	54	56	62	1.43	1 < 5	
Girls	19	40	49	72	74	4.24**	1 < 4, 5; 2 < 5	0.25
Boys	54	61	60	42	53	0.44	NS	
% Divorced	28	29	35	32	60	2.04+	1, 2, 3 < 5	
Girls	18	14	29	39	70	2.96*	1, 2, 3 < 5	0.91
Boys	40	41	42	25	53	0.53	NS	0.76

(continued)

49

TABLE 6 continued

Parent(s)	Combined Substance User Type					F	Comparisons	Deviation from Linearity
	I	II	III	IV	V			
N								
Mothers								
Total	27	29	23	22	23			
Girls	14	14	13	10	10			
Boys	13	15	10	12	13			
Fathers								
Total	23	30	23	15	21			
Girls	13	13	12	5	7			
Boys	10	17	11	10	14			

NOTE: Flush-left headings designate major kinds of variables. Centered headings designate domains. All variables are T scores ($M = 50$, $SD = 10$), except for the demographic variables which are expressed as percents. Significant ($p < .05$) post-hoc comparisons (Newman-Keuls) are printed in italics (i.e., both numbers on either side of the less-than sign must be in italics), and a priori comparisons (t tests) are in ordinary type. Results are presented for each gender separately whenever there is significant interaction with gender or the results are significant for one gender and not the other. The F value printed in italics signifies an ANOVA with a significant interaction with gender ($p < .05$).
+$p < .10$; *$p < .05$; **$p < .01$; ***$p < .001$.

50

less gregarious. According to self-reports (together with Type II adolescents) they sought adult approval and opposed the use of drugs. At age 9 years, nonusing boys were lower in social confidence but otherwise did not differ from their peers. Relative to peers, from T2 to T3, Type I boys became more competent, and Type I girls manifested less externalizing problem behavior.

Differentiations between *risk-avoidant nonusers* (Ia) and *rational nonusers* (Ib) were made on the basis of the reasons given for abstention when queried during the interview. Abstainers may have rational reasons not to use illicit drugs or may avoid all risk-taking exploration because they are fearful and immature. Risk-avoidant nonusers of cannabis or other illicit drugs stated that they abstained because of a fear of consequences, including punishment from parents or authorities and fears of global, unspecified, unrealistic effects (such as "Marijuana can make you crazy") whereas rational nonusers justified abstinence on specific and realistic bases (such as "I don't like my mood changed chemically"). It was hypothesized that risk-avoidant nonusers compared to rational nonusers of illicit drugs would be less explorative, resilient, individuated, and optimally competent and would have a more internal locus of control.

These hypotheses were all confirmed by a priori tests across gender. In addition, post-hoc comparisons indicated that during adolescence rational nonusers across-gender used less alcohol than risk-avoidant nonusers and were more intelligent. At T2, rational compared to risk-avoidant nonusers had been more socially confident, adjusted, optimally competent, cognitively competent, and had manifested even less problem behavior. Parents of rational nonusers compared to risk-avoidant nonusers, at all time periods, were more demanding and responsive. At age 9 years mothers of risk-avoidant nonusers had been more coercive, but provided less structure and intellectual stimulation than parents of rational nonusers. The two types of abstainers from illicit drugs were, as expected, different as children. The risk-avoidant children were more fearful and came from less engaged and stable homes (with a divorce rate of 29%), whereas rational nonusers were competent and came from stable homes (with a divorce rate of 2%).

Type II users (22% of sample) are recreational users of alcohol, but nonusers of cannabis. Parents of Type II adolescents were expected to be less conforming and more individuated than parents of (risk-avoidant) nonusers. As expected, adolescent recreational users of alcohol were not less competent than nonusers and differed from heavy users in a manner similar to that of nonusers.

At age 4 years they had less problem behavior, and at age 9 years the boys were more socially confident. Compared to parents of nonusers, their mothers, as expected, were less conventional and conforming at T2 and T3. At T2 both parents of Type II girls were more intellectually stimulating, and although neither parent was better educated, mothers were more individuated and self-confident. Types I and II, relative to peers who used illicit drugs, showed an increment from T2 to T3 in cognitive competence, prosocial behaviors, mental health, and concern for adult approval.

Type III users (19% of sample) are experimental or casual users of cannabis. They use cannabis, but less than once a week, and are not heavy users of alcohol. Parents of Type III adolescents were expected to be less conventional and to use more illicit drugs. Their children were expected to be more socially agentic and gregarious and less cognitively motivated, conforming, and adult-oriented than nonusers.

At T2, parents of Type III adolescents were less conventional than parents of Type I adolescents, but provided as much control and structure, and manifested as little substance use and problem behavior. By T3, both parents of Type III adolescents used more illicit drugs than parents of adolescents who did not use cannabis, which may have allowed their adolescents to experiment. Also at T1 both parents had manifested relatively more maladaptive behavior in this emotionally stable population. However, parents were as assertive and supportive in their childrearing practices as parents of lower level users. Type III adolescents differed from nonusers, as expected, in that they were more gregarious, and from both Type I and Type II adolescents in that they were less opposed to using illicit drugs and were less adult-oriented. However, the hypothesis that cannabis users, compared to nonusers of cannabis, would be less cognitively competent was not confirmed, although from T2 to T3, relative to nonusers, their verbal achievement scores decreased. Perhaps because their parents, although somewhat nonconforming, were engaged and committed, Type III adolescents were as generally competent, cognitively competent, and communal, and manifested as little problem behavior at all time periods as nonusers.

Type IV users (18% of sample) were heavy users of alcohol, drugs, or both. Their parents were expected to be unconventional, undemanding, and to manifest problem behavior. Relative to lower level users, Type IV heavy users were expected to be emancipated from adult authority, and to manifest a decrement from T2 to T3 in cognitive competence and prosocial behavior.

By comparison with nonusers of illicit drugs, mothers of Type IV adolescents, as expected, exerted less directive/conventional and assertive control. At T3, the expectations that parents would manifest significantly more personal problem behavior and illicit substance use were not confirmed, although fathers used more alcohol. However, at both T1 and T2, parents had offered less structure, and at T1 had been less demanding, confronting, and maturity-demanding, and were more frequently absent from the home, and total family stressors were higher. Fathers at T1 had lacked self-awareness and self-confidence, and, at T2, had abused alcohol more than any other group. Mothers at previous time periods had manifested more internalizing and externalizing problem behaviors, and with sons had been exceedingly officious. The divorce rate did not exceed the average. At T1 and T2, there were no differences between Type IV users and their peers. Thus prior personality characteristics did not foretell even this heavy level of use. By comparison with nonusers of illicit drugs, Type IV users showed an increment from T2 to T3 in externalizing problem behavior, a slight decrement in cognitive competence and prosocial behavior, and a large decrement in verbal achievement; and girls showed a large increment in social agency (i.e., emancipation and autonomy during adolescence). As hypothesized Type IV adolescents, relative to lower-level users, were emancipated from adult authority and lacking in cognitive motivation and achievement orientation, and girls were less optimistic.

Type V users (18% of sample) are dependent users of alcohol, drugs, or both. These substances are used heavily and during school days, and in such a way that use interferes directly with school performance. Parents of Type V adolescents were expected to be lax (low assertive control), disorganized, and nonsupportive. Type V adolescents, compared to their peers, were expected to be more emancipated from adult authority, markedly less competent and to manifest more problem behavior.

The 25 adolescents who fell into this category were qualitatively different from their peers. They were, as expected, emancipated from adult authority and alienated. Compared to peers, they lacked achievement orientation, and sharply manifested more externalizing problem behavior, including sexual acting-out. In general, the girls were especially adversely affected. They were pessimistic, antisocial, lacked general competence and cognitive motivation, and manifested internalizing problem behavior. Type V boys and girls at age 4 years, and girls at age 9 years, had manifested more total problem behavior than all other groups. Relative to peers, Type V adolescents showed a large decrement in general competence, cognitive competence, and communal behavior, and a strong increment in externalizing problem behavior. Girls lost interest in adult approval and were emancipated from adult authority. Mothers of Type V adolescents were unconventional, did not assert control, lacked personal agency and influence (with girls), and were nonsupportive. In particular families of girls were highly disorganized at T1 and T3, with 70% divorced by T3. At T2, total stress level in the family was high, and mothers lacked psychological differentiation. At both T1 and T2 mothers of girls in particular had suffered from internalizing problem behaviors, and both parents had abused alcohol. At T1, fathers of girls had been more officious and manifested more mental illness.

In the a priori tests of the substance user types (Tables 5 and 6), none were significant in the opposite direction, 76% were significant in the predicted direction and of a large or moderate magnitude, 6% were not significant but were in the expected direction with a moderate magnitude, and the remaining 18% were of a small magnitude and not significant.

When the T3 parent types were contrasted on levels of adolescent drug use, the results were highly significant. An analysis of variance of substance user categories by parent types ($F = 6.81, p < .001$) indicated that 27% of the variance in substance use could be explained by T3 parent types. In terms of the Cohen (1977) criterion, this is considered a large effect. Adolescents with the lowest use came from nonauthoritarian-directive homes, followed closely by adolescents from authoritative homes. Both parenting styles were more effective in deterring adolescent drug use than democratic or other less demanding styles. It is important to note the following: (a) Authoritative parents were at least as effective as authoritarian parents in deterring adolescent drug use; (b) significantly more heavy drug users (i.e., Types IV and V) came from democratic than from authoritative homes; and (c) heavy users (Types IV and V) from democratic families were much more competent than heavy users from other families, reinforcing the importance of parenting style as a protective factor.

CONCLUSIONS

The ecological niche assessed in this study does not include users of highly addictive drugs and reflects the liberal values that predominate in a West Coast university community. These sample characteristics should be kept in mind when considering the findings from the two typological analyses. As John Hill (1987) and Baumrind (in press b) emphasized, crucial information on adolescent development in ethnic families is lacking. Although some family processes and dynamics have been found to generalize across subcultures, life realities and culture-specific tasks, and thus to some extent, the appropriate socialization goals of each subculture, and the defining criterion of optimal competence appropriate to that subculture, will also vary.

This study did not address the long-range health and social consequences of casual drug or alcohol use during adolescence. It did address effectively the antecedent and concurrent factors associated with adolescent substance use. The presence of numerous nonlinear relations on the combined substance use scale provides strong evidence of discontinuity in personality and family factors associated with the different types. Variations along the drug usage scale were not "merely quantitative," as Jessor (1982) concluded. The pattern of psychosocial factors associated with the onset of drinking was not exactly the same as the pattern associated with the onset of cannabis use, and more important, the pattern associated with the onset of cannabis use was not the same as the pattern associated with drug-dependent use of alcohol or illicit drugs.

There was no evidence in this population that experimentation with alcohol or cannabis was associated with pathological precursors in the adolescent user or the family, a result found also by Shedler and Block (1990). Concurrent effects of casual recreational use were minimal. Abstainers and light alcohol users, unlike experimenters with illicit drugs, showed an increment from T2 to T3 in cognitive competence, prosocial behavior, and mental health. In this study, unlike the Shedler and Block study, a distinction was made between two kinds of abstainers. Only the risk-avoidant nonusers shared the negative characteristics attributed to abstainers by Shedler and Block.

Although Shedler and Block found signs in childhood of maladjustment associated with heavy substance use in adolescence, in this study signs of prior maladjustment associated with substance use were virtually absent, except for Type V adolescents. In fact, when the absolute means, standard deviations, and ranges were examined (Baumrind, 1990a) antecedent pathology was evident in only some of the Type V adolescents and in very few of the Type IV adolescents. As children, Type IV adolescents who were heavy users of alcohol, illicit drugs, or both, had shown few signs of maladjustment, and did not show serious signs of maladjustment concurrent with drug use. Only Type V drug-dependent users, who had lost the distinction between work and play, were qualitatively different from their peers: in their characteristic pattern of psychosocial attributes, including serious problem behavior; in their relative impairment in general competence and achievement motivation; and in their clearly dysfunctional upbringing.

Adolescents tend to internalize the values of their parents, whether these values are conforming or nonconforming. However, the success of nonauthoritarian-directive families in shielding their children from dysfunctional, risk-taking behavior appears to be less a consequence of their conventional values than of two factors that they share with authoritative families: strong mutual attachments that persist through adolescence, and coherent consistent management policies including supervision and discipline. Authoritative parents who, like nonauthoritarian-directive parents, are firm and committed but who in addition embrace some nontraditional beliefs are also able to shield their adolescents from dysfunctional risk-taking behavior, without the loss of assertiveness and optimism that appears in many of the adolescents from authoritarian-directive homes.

The seven parenting styles differ structurally on the bases of commitment and balance of freedom and control. Whereas unengaged and authoritative parent patterns are similar in that both are balanced, they differ greatly in their level of commitment. Authoritative families are committed (that is, their levels of responsiveness and demandingness are high as well as balanced); whereas unengaged families are not committed (that is their levels of responsiveness and demandingness are low). Good-enough parents are balanced and moderately committed. Democratic and nonauthoritarian-directive parents are as committed as authoritative parents, but are somewhat unbalanced by their ideological adherence — to freedom in the instance of democratic parents, and to control in the instance of nonauthoritarian-directive parents. Both authoritarian and nondirective families are moderately committed but very unbalanced, each in opposite directions: Authoritarian families are much more demanding than responsive, maintaining tight control and offering little freedom, and nondirective families are much more responsive than demanding, offering little control and much freedom.

Family types differed by status (divorced or intact), and family status affected adolescent functioning, especially for girls. For girls, but not for boys, those from intact families were significantly more prosocial and manifested less problem behavior and drug use than those from single or stepfamilies. Although children from divorced families manifested more problem behavior, the problems caused by marital separation are not inevitable. Thus, the few adolescents from single authoritative homes did not differ from those whose parents remained married. Although adolescents from single democratic families used more drugs that their peers from intact homes, they were as competent. By contrast, sons of single authoritarian parents were less competent than their counterparts from intact homes. Disproportionately more single families were nondirective or unengaged. Children from intact disengaged homes were as incompetent as their counterparts from single homes, but the girls used fewer drugs and manifested less internalizing problem behavior.

This study is unique, not only in its use of a typological approach to the understanding of substance use, but also in its intensive, multidimensional assessments of parent-child interaction and psychological functioning. Fiscal constraints typically place a limit on the number of families that can be studied intensively, and therefore on the magnitude of effects that can be detected. Effects of small magnitude cannot be detected with a sample as small as this one, especially when typological analyses are used. Because the effects had to be robust to be detected at all, they are large enough to be of practical use to health care practitioners, social policy planners, and educators concerned with the development of competence and the prevention of substance abuse in the socioecological niche sampled in this study.

This study does not support the view that casual use of either alcohol or cannabis is a result of personal pathology or deficient moral character, or that abusive use of illicit drugs is more harmful than abusive use of alcohol. Although in a less competent and socially advantaged population drug abuse may be associated more strongly with prior maladjustment, it is quite clear that adolescent drug abuse also may be manifested among normal adolescents when the social climate and family precursors are not protective.

The data presented here affirm the continuing importance of parents to the healthy development of their adolescents. For the socially advantaged population studied, authoritative upbringing is a sufficient but not a necessary condition to produce competent, well-adjusted children, even in divorced families. That is, well-adjusted children came from other than authoritative homes. Children from democratic homes where parents value freedom highly were as competent during adolescence, although more were heavy drug users; children from nonauthoritarian-directive homes where parents value control highly, although not as competent as others, avoided drugs altogether. Adolescents' developmental progress is held back by authoritarian, officious, or nondirective and disengaged practices, and facilitated by reciprocal, balanced, committed caregiving characteristic of both authoritative and democratic parents.

The success of authoritative parents in protecting their adolescents from problem drug use and in generating competence should be emphasized. In periods of social instability, young adolescents may need as much control as authoritative parents provide, although in less dangerous times it is generally thought that adolescents would benefit from the slight imbalance of freedom over control that democratic parents provide. Unlike any other pattern, authoritative upbringing (in this socioecological niche) consistently generated competence and deterred problem behavior in both boys and girls at all developmental stages (Baumrind, 1989). Secure in their attachment to their parents and with adequate protection from the instabilities present in the larger society, adolescents from authoritative homes showed that they simultaneously could validate the interests of personal emancipation and individuation, and the claims of their shared social norms.

NOTE

1. In Table 2, post-hoc contrasts are presented at the .05 level (in italics) and at the .10 level (in regular type face). The lower level of significance is included in Table 2 due to the small number of subjects in some parent types and the corresponding low level of power. A priori contrasts are not included in Table 2 because the information is descriptive. In Tables 3, 5, and 6, unlike Table 2, both post-hoc contrasts (in italics) and a priori contrasts (in regular type face) are presented. A priori tests are two-sided. Two-sided t tests were used to avoid Type III errors (treating as equivalent nonsignificant findings and significant findings occurring in the opposite directions). The use of two-sided t tests yields the same results as directional two-sided tests (Kaiser, 1960) when the alpha level is controlled for the number of tests conducted.

A priori tests were conducted for approximately one-third of the contrasts on which the Newman-Keuls were conducted. In Tables 2, 3, 5, and 6 the magnitude of the differences between the types may be compared with the Cohen standards for all variables that are not marked with a percent sign (only the demographic variables are reported in terms of percentages). Differences less than five and greater than or equal to two are small, less than eight and greater than or equal to five are medium, and greater than or equal to eight are large. The magnitude of the effect (that is, the proportion of variance accounted for by the types), may be estimated from the tables by the formula $(F - 1)/(F - 1 + N)/(k - 1))$ where k is the number of types (Lindman, 1974).

REFERENCES

Bakan, D. (1966). *The duality of existence: Isolation and communion in Western man.* Boston: Beacon.

Baumrind, D. (1971). Types of adolescent life-styles. *Developmental Psychology Monographs, 4*(1, Pt. 2).

Baumrind, D. (1973). The development of instrumental competence through socialization. In A. Pick (Ed.), *Minnesota Symposia on Child Psychology* (Vol. 7, pp. 3-46). Minneapolis: University of Minnesota Press.

Baumrind, D. (1985). Familial antecedents of adolescent drug use: A developmental perspective. In C. L. Jones & R. J. Battjes (Eds.), *Etiology of drug abuse: Implications for prevention* (NIDA Research Monograph No. 56, pp. 13-44; DHHS Publication No. (ADM) 85-1355). Rockville, MD: National Institute on Drug Abuse.

Baumrind, D. (1987). A developmental perspective on adolescent risk-taking behavior in contemporary America. In W. Damon (Ed.), *New directions for child development: Adolescent health and social behavior* (Vol. 37, pp. 93-126). San Francisco: Jossey-Bass.

Baumrind, D. (1989). Rearing competent children. In W. Damon (Ed.), *Child development today and tomorrow* (pp. 349-378). San Francisco: Jossey-Bass.

Baumrind, D. (in press a). Effective parenting during the early adolescent transition. In P. A. Cowan & E. M. Hetherington (Eds.), *Advances in family research* (Vol. 2). Hillsdale, NJ: Lawrence Erlbaum.

Baumrind, D. (in press b). Parenting styles and adolescent development. In R. M. Lerner, A. C. Peterson & J. Brooks-Gunn (Eds.), *Encyclopedia of Adolescence* (pp. 758-772). New York: Garland.

Baumrind, D. (1990a). Familial versus personological determinants of adolescent substance use. Manuscript submitted for publication.

Baumrind, D. (1990b). Types of middle-class adolescent substance users: Concurrent family and personality influences. Manuscript submitted for publication.

Baumrind, D., & Black, A. E. (1967). Socialization practices associated with dimensions of competence in preschool boys and girls. *Child Development, 38*, 291-327.

Bellah, R. N., Madsen, R., Sullivan, W. M., Swidler, A., & Tipton, S. M. (1985). *Habits of the heart: Individualism and commitment in American life*. Berkeley: University of California Press.

Blos, P. (1962). *On adolescence: A psychoanalytic interpretation*. Glencoe, IL: Free Press.

Blos, P. (1979). The second individuation process. In P. Blos (Ed.), *The adolescent passage: Developmental issues of adolescence* (pp. 141-170). New York: International University Press.

Bronfenbrenner, U. (1985). Freedom and discipline across the decades. In G. Becker, H. Becker, & L. Huber (Eds.), *Ordnung and Unordnung* [Order and Disorder] (pp. 326-339). Weinheim, West Germany: Beltz Berlag.

Clark, R. (1983). *Family life and school achievement: Why poor black children succeed or fail*. Chicago: University of Chicago Press.

Cohen, J. (1977). *Statistical power analysis for the behavioral sciences*. New York: Academic Press.

Cohen, J., & Cohen, P. (1975). *Applied multiple regression/correlation analysis for the behavioral sciences*. Hillsdale, NJ: Lawrence Erlbaum.

Cooper, C. R., Grotevant, H. D., & Condon, S. M. (1982). Methodological challenges of selectivity in family interaction: Addressing temporal patterns of individuation. *Journal of Marriage and the Family, 44*, 749-754.

Cooper, C. R., Grotevant, H. D., & Condon, S. M. (1983). Individuality and connectedness in the family as a context for adolescent identity formation and role-taking skill. In H. D. Grotevant and C. R. Cooper (Eds.), *New directions for child development: Adolescent development in the family* (Vol. 22, pp. 43-59). San Francisco: Jossey-Bass.

Dornbusch, S. M., Ritter, P. L., Leiderman, P. H., Roberts, D. F., & Fraleigh, M. J. (1987). The relation of parenting style to adolescent performance. *Child Development, 58*, 1244-1257.

Douvan, E., & Adelson, J. (1966). *The adolescent experience*. New York: Wiley.

Erikson, E. H. (1959). Identity and the life cycle: Selected papers. *Psychological Issues, 1*(1).

Feather, N. (1980). Values in adolescence. In J. Adelson (Ed.), *Handbook of adolescent psychology* (pp. 247-294). New York: Wiley.

Gilligan, C. (1982). *In a different voice: Psychological theory and women's development*. Cambridge: Harvard University Press.

Gilligan, C. (1987). Adolescent development reconsidered. In C. E. Irwin, Jr. (Ed.), *New directions for child development* (Vol. 37, pp. 63-92). San Francisco: Jossey-Bass.

Gorsuch, R. L. (1974) *Factor analysis*. Philadelphia, PA: W. B. Saunders.

Greenberger, E. (1984). Defining psychosocial maturity in adolescence. In P. Karoly & J. J. Steffen (Eds.), *Adolescent behavior disorders: Foundations and contemporary concerns* (rev. ed., pp. 3-39). Lexington, MA: D. C. Heath.

Hall, G. S. (1905). *Adolescence* (Vol. I, p. xv). New York: Appleton-Century-Crofts.

Hartup, W. W. (1979). The social worlds of childhood. *American Psychologist, 34*, 944-950.

Hauser, S. T., Powers, S. I., Noam, G. G., Jacobson, A. M., Weiss, B., & Follansbee, D. J. (1984). Familial contexts of adolescent ego development. *Child Development, 55*, 195-213.

Hill, J. P. (1980). The early adolescent and the family. In M. Johnson (Ed.), *The seventy-ninth yearbook of the National Society for the Study of Education* (pp. 32-55). Chicago: University of Chicago Press.

Hill, J. P. (1987). Research on adolescents and their families: Past and prospect. In C. E. Irwin (Ed.), *New directions for child development* (Vol. 37, pp. 13-31). San Francisco: Jossey-Bass.

Hill, J. P., & Holmbeck, G. N. (1986). Attachment and autonomy during adolescence. In G. Whitehurst (Ed.), *Annals of child development* (Vol. 3, pp. 145-189). Greenwich, CT: JAI.

Hinde, R. A., & Dennis, A. (1986). Categorizing individuals: An alternative to linear analysis. *International Journal of Behavioral Development*, 105-119.

Jessor, R. (1982). Critical issues in research on adolescent health promotion. In T. J. Coates, A. C. Peterson, & C. Perry (Eds.), *Promoting adolescent health: A dialogue on research and practice* (pp. 447-465). New York: Academic Press.

Jessor, R., & Jessor, S. L. (1978). Theory testing in longitudinal research on marijuana use. In D. B. Kandel (Ed.), *Longitudinal research on drug use: Empirical findings and methodological issues* (pp. 41-71). Washington, DC: Hemisphere.

Kaiser, H. F. (1960). Directional statistical decisions. *Psychological Review, 67*, 3.

Kohlberg, L. (1969). Stage and sequence: The cognitive-developmental approach to socialization. In D. A. Goslin (Ed.), *Handbook of socialization theory and research* (pp. 347-480). Chicago: Rand McNally.

Lasch, C. (1978). *The culture of narcissism: American life in an age of diminishing expectations*. New York: Norton.

Leary, T. (1957). *Interpersonal diagnosis of personality: A functional theory and methodology for personality evaluation*. New York: Ronald Press.

Lindman, H. R. (1974). *Analysis of variance in complex experimental designs*. San Francisco: Freeman.

Lonner, W. J. (1980). The search for psychological universals. In H. C. Triandis & W. W. Lambert (Eds.), *Handbook of cross-cultural psychology* (Vol. 1, pp. 143-204). Boston: Allyn & Bacon.

Luria, A. R. (1978). Paths of development of thought in the child. In M. Cole & S. Cole (Eds.), *The selected writings of A. R. Luria* (pp. 97-144). New York: Sharpe. (Original publication 1929)

Maccoby, E. E., & Martin, J. A. (1983). Socialization in the context of the family: Parent-child interaction. In E. M. Hetherington (Ed.) & P. H. Mussen (Series Ed.), *Handbook of child psychology: Vol 4. Socialization, personality and social development* (pp. 1-101). New York: Wiley.

Marcia, J. E. (1980). Identity in adolescence. In J. Addison (Ed.), *Handbook of adolescent psychology* (pp. 159-187). New York: Wiley.

Piaget, J. (1965). *Moral judgment of the child*. New York: Free Press. (Original publication 1932)

Reiss, D., Oliveri, M. E., & Curd, K. (1983). Family paradigm and adolescent social behavior. In H. D. Grotevant & C. R. Cooper (Eds.), *New directions for child development: Adolescent development in the family* (pp. 77-92). San Francisco: Jossey-Bass.

Ryan, R. M., & Lynch, J. H. (1989). Emotional autonomy versus detachment: Revisiting the vicissitudes of adolescence and young adulthood. *Child Development, 60*, 340-356.

Sampson, E. E. (1988). The debate on individualism: Indigenous psychologies of the individual and their role in personal and societal functioning. *American Psychologist, 43* 15-22.

Shedler, J., & Block, J. (1990). Adolescent drug use and psychological health: A longitudinal inquiry. *American Psychologist, 45*, 612-630.

Steinberg, L. (1989). In memorium — John P. Hill (1936-1988). *Society for Research on Adolescence Newsletter, 3*(1), 1-2.

60

Steinberg, L., Elmen, J. D., & Mounts, N. S. (1989). Authoritative parenting, psychosocial maturity, and academic success among adolescents. *Child Development, 60,* 1424-1436.

Steinberg, L., & Silverberg, S. B. (1986). The vicissitudes of autonomy in early adolescence. *Child Development, 57,* 841-851.

Tryon, R. C., & Bailey, D. E. (1970). *Cluster analysis.* New York: McGraw-Hill.

Wiggins, J. S. (1979). A psychological taxonomy of trait-descriptive terms: The interpersonal domain. *Journal of Personality and Social Psychology, 37,* 395-412.

Winnicot, D. W. (1965). *The maturational processes and the facilitating environment: Studies in the theory of emotional development.* New York: International Universities Press.

Reprint requests should be addressed to Diana Baumrind, Family Socialization Project, Institute of Human Development, 1203 Tolman Hall, University of California, Berkeley, CA 94720.

Developmental Psychology
1996, Vol. 32, No. 4, 696–706

Parental Religiosity, Family Processes, and Youth Competence in Rural, Two-Parent African American Families

Gene H. Brody, Zolinda Stoneman, and Douglas Flor
University of Georgia

A model that linked parental formal religiosity to children's academic competence and socioemotional adjustment during early adolescence was tested. The sample included 90 9- to 12-year-old African American youths and their married parents living in the rural South. The theoretical constructs in the model were measured through a multimethod, multi-informant design. Rural African American community members participated in the development of the self-report instruments and observational research methods. Greater parental religiosity led to more cohesive family relationships, lower levels of interparental conflict, and fewer externalizing and internalizing problems in the adolescents. Formal religiosity also indirectly influenced youth self-regulation through its positive relationship with family cohesion and negative relationship with interparental conflict.

In the United States, religion is an important part of the lives of many individuals. Various estimates exist concerning the percentage of the population who identify themselves as religious. The Princeton Religion Research Center (1980) reported that 94% of Americans over 18 professed a belief in God, 69% identified themselves as church members, and 57% indicated that their religious beliefs were very important to them. In the largest national survey conducted on religious affiliation in the United States, over 92% of the respondents identified themselves as religious (Goldman, 1991). Considering these statistics, it is surprising that so little empirical work has been undertaken to examine the links among religiosity, family processes, and the development of children and adolescents.

Previous research has shown that religiousness can moderate the effects of stressful life events (Pargament, 1990). A variety of social psychological studies have described the positive relationship of formal religiosity with measures of coping and internal control during periods of adversity (Balk, 1983; Palmer & Noble, 1986). Religious adults report more adaptive strategies for coping with life stresses and are more optimistic and focused in their coping efforts (Seligman, 1991). For example, religious commitment has been shown to influence the adjustment of bereaved parents, through social support processes and the finding of meaning in the loss (D. McIntosh & Spilka, 1990).

The present study was designed to define and clarify the links among religion, family processes, and young adolescents' academic and socioemotional competence among rural, two-parent African American families. These links are particularly rel-

Gene H. Brody, Zolinda Stoneman, and Douglas Flor, Program for the Study of Competence in Children and Families, University of Georgia.

This research was supported by grants from the Spencer Foundation and the National Reading Research Center.

Correspondence concerning this article should be addressed to Gene H. Brody, Program for the Study of Competence in Children and Families, Dawson Hall, University of Georgia, Athens, Georgia 30602.

evant to African American families, who consistently manifest higher levels of religiosity than do Whites (Taylor, 1988). The church contributes to cohesion in the African American community by acting as an agency of moral guidance, a conservator of political leadership, and the center of community life (Taylor & Chatters, 1991). The potential benefits of African American religious participation are underscored by research indicating that religious belief and church attendance form an important coping mechanism for negotiating the life stresses that rural African Americans are more likely than other groups to experience (Krause & Tran, 1989). The 1 million African American families who live in the rural South often lack the facilities, amenities, and services to which many urban African American families commonly have access (Lick, 1986). Many of these families are also at risk for unemployment, low wages, low education levels, substandard housing, and high infant mortality rates (Coward & Smith, 1983). As Taylor and Chatters (1991) noted, the traditional "otherworldly" emphasis of many Black churches, particularly in the rural South, was "Black religion's remedy for the deleterious effects of pervasive discrimination and racism, and the resulting psychological alienation and demoralization" (p. 106).

Religiosity, Family Relationships, and Competence Among Rural African American Youth

In Figure 1, we present an overview of the conceptual model that guided this research. This model was constructed on the basis of the hypothesis that parental religiosity gives rise to a belief system that produces norms that are directly and indirectly linked to youth competence. The norms of the religious group in which the family participates are hypothesized to promote conventional values, to facilitate interaction, and to establish strong social bonds that encourage academic and socioemotional competence. Religious participation also may be associated with more cohesive family relationships, which in turn are linked to youth competence. Each of these linkages between religiosity and youth competencies is examined in more detail below.

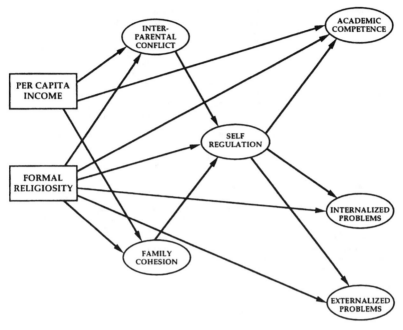

Figure 1. The hypothetical model.

Figure 1 depicts the hypothesized direct links between parental religiosity and youth academic and socioemotional competence. Hirschi (1969) hypothesized that parental formal religiosity encourages youths to establish closer ties to the conventional order, including the family and the school, and that these attachments decrease the likelihood that the youths will engage in deviant behavior while increasing the likelihood that they will engage in socially sanctioned activities. Similarly, Durkheim (1951), in his classic treatise on suicide, speculated that religiosity promotes a sense of community, helps to integrate individuals into a significant social group, and encourages commitment to group standards rather than individual choices. He hypothesized that such influences would decrease the likelihood of internalizing problems, anomie, and suicide. Numerous studies have demonstrated that, on average, youths whose parents are religious report less drug and alcohol use, and adolescent girls report beginning sexual activity at an older age, than do children of nonreligious parents (e.g., W. A. McIntosh, Fitch, Wilson, & Nyburg, 1981; Udry, 1988). Thus, the available data support the hypothesized direct links between parental religiosity and youth competence. The investigations from which they came, however, did not focus on rural African American families.

We also proposed two direct relationships between parental formal religiosity and family process variables. We predicted that family cohesion would be positively associated with religiosity, and that interparental conflict would be negatively associated with it. The belief system on which the Judeo-Christian religious tradition is based promotes a prosocial orientation toward relationships in general and family relationships in particular. The values of loving one's family and neighbors and forgiving one's enemies are prominent (Thomas & Henry, 1988; Wuthnow, 1991). In several studies, religiosity has been found to be positively associated with marital adjustment (Bahr & Chadwick, 1985; Wilson & Filsinger, 1986) and marital stability (Shrum, 1980). These findings remained robust even when "conventionality" (i.e., social desirability) is statistically controlled (Filsinger & Wilson, 1984).

We predicted that engaged, harmonious family interactions—our family cohesion construct—and interparental conflict also would serve as mediators connecting parental religiosity to youth self-regulation, academic competence, and socioemotional competence. The literature on resilience suggests that a general atmosphere of family harmony and low levels of chronic interparental conflict provide a buffer against stress, allowing the family to be more effective in their negotiations of daily hassles (Garmezy, Masten, & Tellegen, 1984; Lewis, Dlugokinski, Caputo, & Griffin, 1988). Youths whose families encourage their active engagement in supportive family relationships display impulse control (Block, 1971; Patterson, 1976), regulate their own behavior, and achieve academically (Steinberg, Lamborn, Darling, Mounts, & Dornbusch, 1994). Earlier studies have described the positive effects that supportive familial and nonfamilial relationships have on parent–child relationships and child outcomes in single-parent African American families (Stevens & Duffield, 1986; Wilson, 1984). Such effects are especially likely when another adult partner is involved in co-caregiving (Brody et al., 1994; Brown & Gary, 1988; Lewis, 1989; Wilson, 1984). Because most research on African American households has focused on those headed by single mothers, however, little is known about the links between family processes and youth competence in two-parent African American families.

The empirical literature on both African American and White families with early adolescent offspring includes few studies of the processes that mediate the effect of family relationships on youth competence. In our model, we hypothesized that family cohesion and interparental conflict will affect adolescents' outcomes through their effects on the development of self-regulation, which includes the ability to set and attain goals, to plan actions and consider their consequences, and to persist. In turn, self-regulated African American youths will be likely to display greater academic and socioemotional competence. This hypothesis is derived from the work of Greenberger (1982) and Steinberg, Elmen, and Mounts (1989), who found that differences in self-regulation differentiate academically competent adolescents beyond influences attributable to social class or academic ability.

The design used in this study allowed an examination of additional issues that will advance our understanding of the links between parental religiosity and youth outcomes in rural African American families. In the conceptual model depicted in Figure 1, we included family financial resources to determine the unique contribution of parental religiosity to family processes and youth outcomes after family financial resources are taken into account statistically. Per capita income, operationalized as the family's total annual income divided by the number of people living in the household, served as the measure of family financial resources. As the hypothesized paths in Figure 1 indicate, we postulated that per capita income would have direct effects on family processes and academic competence, as well as indirect effects, through family processes, on self-regulation and on academic and socioemotional competence.

These proposed links are consistent with findings from recent analyses of the influence of financial stress on family processes and youth outcomes in both White (Conger et al., 1992; Conger et al., 1990) and African American (Brody et al., 1994) rural families. The chronic strains associated with inadequate income induce stress, anger, frustration, and a sense of helplessness (Bruce, Takeuchi, & Leaf, 1991; Kessler, 1982; McLoyd, 1990), which in turn promote more disengaged and hostile family relationships and higher levels of externalizing and internalizing problems in youths (Conger et al., 1990; Rutter, 1990).

As the model in Figure 1 suggests, the hypothesized paths to youth outcomes from parental religiosity and per capita income differ. For reasons explained earlier, we predicted both direct and indirect links between parental religiosity and all three youth outcome variables, whereas for per capita income we predicted a direct link with academic competence only, and indirect links, through family processes, for the two socioemotional outcomes. We proposed the hypothesized direct link between per capita income and academic competence because of the influence of factors associated with per capita income, such as the quality and variety of stimulation in the home, environmentally indirect prenatal or perinatal biological factors, and nonfamily socialization factors that have been found to exert robust effects on academic performance (Wachs, 1992). The indirect links to socioemotional outcomes are based on literature that has consistently shown that economic hardship and social disadvantage clearly alter family relationships, which in turn affect the development of internalizing and externalizing problems (Conger et al., 1992; McLoyd, 1989; Patterson, Reid, & Dishion, 1992).

In the following analyses, we empirically evaluated our conceptual model with a sample of rural African American adolescents living in two-parent families. Rural African American community members participated in the development of the self-report and observational research methods; this collaborative effort resulted in the multimethod, multi-informant research design described below.

Method

Participants

Ninety African American families with married parents and a 9- to 12-year-old firstborn child (48 female and 42 male) were recruited from nonmetropolitan counties in Georgia and South Carolina. As defined by the U.S. Bureau of the Census, nonmetropolitan counties may include urbanized areas with populations of 20,000 or more; this sample, however, was drawn from rural areas with populations of less than 2,500. We sampled only counties in which 25% or more of the population was African American to ensure that a viable African American community existed within the county. Families were recruited through schools, churches, and community contacts. An African American staff member made contacts with African American community members, such as pastors and teachers, and explained the research project to them. After community members understood the purposes of the project and developed trusting relationships with the staff member, they contacted prospective participant families and informed them of the project's purpose. Each community contact gave to the research staff member the names of families who expressed interest in the project, and the staff member contacted the families. Each family was paid $60 for their participation in the study.

To enhance rapport and cultural understanding, African American students majoring in a variety of subjects served as home visitors to collect data from the families. Approximately half of the visitors were graduate students and half were undergraduates. Before data collection, the visitors received 1 month of training in administering the self-report instruments and observational procedures.

Of the 90 participating families, 17 had a per capita income of $3,300 or less ($M$ = $1,906). This, according to criteria established by the Census Bureau (U.S. Bureau of the Census, 1992), places them in the first quintile for household income, which the bureau defines as poverty status. The mean total family annual income of this group was $11,882, which was below the poverty line criterion of $12,195 set by the Census Bureau. The largest group, which included 51 families, placed in the

Table 1

Means, Standard Deviations, and Ranges for Demographic and Manifest Variables

Variable	M	SD	Range
Demographic			
Total family income ($)	29,053	11,613	2,500–55,000
Maternal age (years)	34	5.41	26–56
Paternal age (years)	37	6.24	25–62
Child's age (years)	11	1.59	9–12
Maternal education[a]	4.28	1.20	1–7
Paternal education[a]	3.80	1.26	1–7
Family size	2.22	1.01	1–6
Manifest			
Per capita income ($)	5,675	2,585	357–13,500
Formal religiosity, mothers	20.59	7.39	0–30
Formal religiosity, fathers	16.26	9.23	0–30
Conflict scale, mothers	10.58	4.29	6–24
Conflict scale, fathers	10.35	4.80	6–24
Engagement	8.58	1.71	4–14
Harmony	8.77	1.25	6–12
Self-control subscale, fathers	17.86	3.26	7–25
Self-control subscale, teachers	18.84	4.56	7–25
Self-control subscale, mothers	16.53	3.62	6–25
Actual school reading grades	4.04	0.84	1–5
WISC–R vocabulary subscale	8.71	3.37	1–25
Actual school mathematics grades	3.84	1.07	1–5
WISC–R mathematics subscale	9.35	2.48	3–15
Conduct disorder, mothers	9.79	7.58	0–31
Conduct disorder, teachers	4.81	7.39	0–16
Socialized aggression, teachers	1.24	2.59	0–16
Classroom misconduct, teachers	1.67	0.88	1–5
Antisocial subscale, mothers	9.55	3.13	4–19
Antisocial subscale, teachers	7.82	4.04	4–19
CDI, fathers	17.07	3.43	13–27
CDI, mothers	18.08	4.38	13–32
CDI, teachers	4.37	5.73	0–28

Note. WISC–R = Wechsler Intelligence Scale for Children—Revised; CDI = Childhood Depression Inventory.
[a] 1 = less than high school; 2 = high school graduate; 3 = high school equivalence diploma; 4 = technical training; 5 = junior college; 6 = college graduate; 7 = graduate school training.

Census Bureau's third income quintile with an average per capita income of $5,515. The 21 remaining families' average per capita income of $9,044 placed them in the Census Bureau's fourth income quintile. These data indicate that the sample included an economic cross-section of rural, two-parent African American families. Total family annual income ranged from $2,500 to $57,500, and per capita income ranged from $357 to $13,500. Table 1 presents the means, ranges, and standard deviations for each demographic variable.

In many families in each group, one or both spouses worked two jobs, and mothers and fathers often worked different shifts. Although this scheduling may make it more likely that at least one parent will be at home with the child, the parents consequently spend a minimal amount of time at home together. Such long working hours are apparently necessary to provide for the families' needs, given the low wages that the parents earn. In the impoverished group, four fathers and four mothers were unemployed (two fathers and one mother were unemployed because of disability). At least one parent, however, was employed in each family living in poverty.

Development of Measures With the Assistance of Community Members

We were concerned about the accurate assessment of the population we were to study, because most instruments used to evaluate family processes and individual outcomes have been developed for use with, and standardized on, White, middle-class families. Consequently, the available measures may not validly describe family dynamics among rural African Americans. We dealt with this issue through the formation of focus groups consisting of rural African American community members. Most of the group members served as peer agents for two state agencies housed on the University of Georgia campus; some of these agents recommended other African American community leaders for participation. The final focus group included 40 people from throughout Georgia who were representative of the population we planned to study. A detailed discussion of our decision to use focus groups as a means of developing culturally sensitive research methodologies, and a more extensive description of the focus group process, can be found in Brody and Stoneman (1992).

The group addressed two measurement issues, the first of which concerned the development of valid self-report instruments. Each group member rated each instrument that we planned to use on a 5-point Likert scale ranging from 1 = *not appropriate for rural African American families* through 3 = *appropriate* to 5 = *very appropriate.* Those instruments that attained a mean rating of at least 3.5 were retained. The focus groups reviewed each item on each scale and suggested wording changes, as well as the deletion of items that they perceived as unclear or irrelevant to rural African Americans.

The second issue concerned our plan to videotape family interactions. In past projects, we have found the videotaping of these interactions to be essential to the close study of family relationships. The focus group suggested that this procedure be made as nonthreatening as possible by recording no interactions involving finances or other sensitive information. From a list of activities in which families have been videotaped in past studies, the group selected game playing as the context that the families would consider most acceptable. In addition, during the first home visit, the project staff clearly explained the videotaping procedure and the reasons for its use, strongly emphasizing its confidentiality. The staff also gave particular attention to establishing rapport and putting the families at ease, a process that was emphasized throughout the project. The majority of the families cooperated freely with the taping, and only two families declined to participate in the study because of it.

Procedure

Three home visits, each lasting 2 to 3 hr, were made to each family, arranged as closely to a week apart as the families' schedules allowed. African American students visited the families in teams of two, one male and one female, to give both parents someone with whom they could identify and to whom they could comfortably relate. During home visits, therefore, the male researcher worked primarily with the father and the female researcher worked with the mother and child. During the first visit, informed consent forms were completed. The parents consented to their own and their child's participation in the study, and the child consented to his or her own participation. The parents also provided the name and location of the child's school and authorized the child's teacher to provide the researchers with information concerning the child's school performance. The following demographic information was also gathered from separate interviews with mothers and fathers: total household income, income sources, adult household members' employment status, and parents' occupations and educational levels.

On the third home visit, the mother, father, and target child were videotaped in two triadic interactions. First, they played the board game "Trouble" (Gilbert Industries, Springfield, MA) for 15 min. "Trouble" is a game in which players move pegs around a board in accordance with numbers rolled on a die; the player who gets all of his or her pegs into a "finish lane" first wins. We have used this activity extensively in our research on parent–child and sibling relations because we have found it to be both understandable and interesting to children in the age ranges with which we have worked. The focus group of community members also endorsed its use in this study because of its familiarity to the families in our sample. The observational data obtained from this activity were used to assess family interaction quality.

Second, the parents and child were videotaped while discussing an issue that had been presented to them individually by the researchers. Each family member was escorted to a different room and responded to the question, "We know that many children in this community live in homes where families are poor. Some of these children do well in life, others do not. What is the difference between children who make it in life and those who do not?" The family members then gathered in their living room, and the researchers asked them to share and discuss their answers. The focus group recommended this strategy of eliciting family interaction because the topic is of great concern to rural African American families, thus making it more likely that both parents and the child would participate actively in the discussion. The researchers then left the room and were not present during the discussions, which lasted an average of 10 min. This task, designed in accordance with key methodological considerations in current family problem-solving research, simulated a natural context in which families often engage (cf. Jacob, 1987).

At each home visit, self-report questionnaires were administered to each parent in an interview format. On the third visit, the questionnaires were administered before the observational assessments described earlier. Each interview was conducted privately between the family member and a researcher, with no other family members present or able to overhear the conversation. At no time during the presentation of the self-report instruments did the researchers assume that a family member could read. This literacy concern was one of the reasons for presenting the questionnaires in an interview format. When responses to a Likert scale were required, the family member was shown a card with a series of dots in graduated sizes that corresponded to the magnitude of the responses from which he or she was to choose and was asked to indicate his or her feelings using the dots on the card.

To collect the data needed to evaluate the child's academic and socioemotional functioning in school, we mailed to each child's classroom teacher assessment instruments with a cover letter, a copy of the signed consent form, and a stamped return envelope. Follow-up phone calls were made, and letters were sent to the teachers if they had not returned their questionnaires after 2 weeks.

Measures

Family financial resources. A single indicator—each family's per capita income—was used as a measure of financial resources. This is computed by dividing the family's annual income by the number of people in the household. The resulting figure is the amount of money available to support each person in the family. Brody et al. (1994) and Wilson (1984) used per capita income in studies of rural African American families, in which its use detected differences in socioeconomic levels that were not revealed when other measures were used. The total family income was derived by averaging the husband's and wife's reports, which were found to correlate significantly ($r = .71, p < .001$). The two reports were averaged to create a more reliable index of family financial resources.

Formal religiosity. We assessed maternal and paternal religiosity separately by using a single indicator of formal religiosity, defined as the frequency with which each parent attends church and the importance to each parent of church attendance. Each parent rated, on a 7-point Likert scale ranging from $0 = never$ to $6 = more\ than\ once\ a\ week$, the frequency with which he or she had attended church services during the previous year. Each parent also rated the importance to him or her of church attendance, using a 5-point scale ranging from $1 = not\ very\ important$ to $5 = very\ important$. For each parent, the values for the responses to these items were then multiplied, yielding the formal religiosity indicator. For both mothers and fathers, formal religiosity scores ranged from 0 to 30. The mean score for mothers was 20.59 ($SD = 7.39$) and for fathers was 16.26 ($SD = 9.23$). Most of the parents (85%) were Southern Baptists who attended church regularly. Neither mothers' nor fathers' formal religiosity was significantly correlated with per capita income (rs = .12 and .17, respectively).

Family cohesion. Family cohesion was assessed by using two observed behavioral indicators: harmony and engagement. African American student assistants received a minimum of 10 hr of training in observational coding, which included study and discussion of the coding category definitions and observation of videotaped family interactions. The coders worked in teams of two, viewing the videotapes and independently rating the interactions on the following dimensions: (a) the Conflict–Harmony scale, ranging from $1 = conflicted$ (relationships among the family members are hostile and tense, with frequent displays of negative verbal and nonverbal behavior) to $7 = harmonious$ (relationships are warmly supportive, dialogue is relaxed, members clearly work together to resolve issues, and tone is friendly); and (b) the Engagement scale, ranging from $1 = not\ at\ all\ engaged$ (family members do not speak to one another or interact with one another nonverbally) through $4 = moderately\ engaged$ (family members talk to one another or interact nonverbally with one another for approximately half of the observation period) to 7 = *highly engaged* (family members display high rates of talking and nonverbal interaction with one another). The codes were designed to focus on the interacting family as a triad, so that the family, not the individuals or dyads, would be the focus of the analyses. Because family interactions took place in two task settings, the scores for each setting were averaged across tasks to increase the reliability of the assessments (Epstein, 1979). Coders did not rate any families whose homes they had visited.

Reliability was calculated by using split-half, Spearman-Brown coefficients, computed for each possible pair of observers. Mean agreement scores were calculated across participants for each pair, and across all pairs, of observers. Estimates of reliability between raters were .86 for the Conflict–Harmony scale and .87 for the Supportiveness scale.

Interparental conflict. To assess frequency of interparental conflict in the presence of children, we asked mothers and fathers to complete the O'Leary–Porter Scale (OPS; Porter & O'Leary, 1980). The OPS is a 10-item scale with a 5-point Likert-type format that ranges from *never/very little* to *a lot.* A sample of the items includes the following: "How often has your child heard you and your spouse argue about the wife's duties, such as housework or her job?" "How often do you complain to your spouse in front of your child about the things they do?" and "How much do you argue with your spouse in front of your child?" Estimates of internal consistency were .77 for mothers and .87 for fathers.

Youth self-regulation. We assessed self-regulation by using the self-control subscale of the Children's Self-Control Scale (Humphrey, 1982). This subscale contains five items that were rated on a 5-point scale by mothers, fathers, and teachers. Adults, rather than the children, completed this assessment because the instrument's reliabilities are higher for adult reports than for child reports (Humphrey, 1982). The items were as follows: (a) thinks ahead of time about the consequences of his or her actions, (b) plans ahead before acting, (c) pays attention to what he or she is doing, (d) works toward goals, and (e) sticks to what he or she is doing, even on long, unpleasant tasks, until finished. The Cronbach alphas for mothers, fathers, and teachers were .80, .71, and .92, respectively.

Academic competence. Assessments of academic competence included reading and mathematics grades assigned by teachers (A, B, C, D, F) and the youth's scores on the vocabulary and mathematics subscales of the Wechsler Intelligence Scale for Children—Revised. The latter measures were administered individually to the target youth in his or her home, by a graduate student who had received extensive instruction in their administration. All graduate student assistants practiced administering the subscales and became proficient in their use before assessing study participants.

Externalizing problems. Mothers, fathers, and teachers completed the 10-item conduct disorder subscale from the Revised Behavior Problem Checklist (Quay & Peterson, 1987). Each item is rated on a 3-point scale, with 0 = *not a problem,* 1 = *somewhat of a problem,* and 2 = *definite problem* for the child. Sample items include "fights," "disruptive," "annoys and bothers others," "argues; quarrels," "tries to dominate others; bullies; threatens," and "deliberately cruel to others." The Cronbach alphas exceeded .90 for both parents and teachers in this sample. Parents and teachers also completed the four-item antisocial behavior subscale from the Self-Control Inventory (Humphrey, 1982), indicating on a 5-point Likert scale ranging from 1 = *little or none* to 5 = *a lot* the extent to which the target child "gets into arguments or fights with other children," "talks out of turn," "interrupts others when they are doing things," and "has trouble keeping promises to improve his/her actions." Cronbach alphas for parents exceeded .70, and for teachers, .90. The teacher-assigned classroom conduct grade (A, B, C, D, F) was included as an additional indicator.

Internalizing problems. Mothers, fathers, and teachers completed a

revised version of the Children's Depression Inventory (Kovacs, 1981). This instrument consists of 27 items. On each item, the respondents selected alternatives on a 3-point scale reflecting the degree to which they believed the child would agree with such statements as "Things bother me all the time," "I hate myself," "I am sad all the time," and "I feel like crying every day." Cronbach alphas for mothers, fathers, and teachers in this sample were .78, .70, and .90, respectively.

Results

Mean scores, standard deviations, and ranges for all study variables are displayed in Table 1. The ranges of scores were distributed evenly across each of the variables. Although the means for youth academic achievement and socioemotional functioning indicate above-average reading and math performance and few conduct and internalizing problems, the ranges of scores were distributed widely across each of the outcome dimensions. Table 2 presents, separately for mothers and fathers, the bivariate correlations between the latent constructs; coefficients below the diagonal are for fathers, and those above it are for mothers. For mothers, formal religiosity was associated positively with family cohesion and negatively with externalizing problems. Fathers' formal religiosity was positively associated with family cohesion and negatively associated with interparental conflict, externalizing problems, and internalizing problems.

The data in Table 2 also show patterns of correlations linking financial resources to family cohesion, youth self-regulation, academic competence, and both externalizing and internalizing problems. Interparental conflict and family cohesion were both linked with youth self-regulation and academic competence, and family cohesion alone was linked with externalizing and internalizing problems. Youth self-regulation had a moderate positive association with academic competence and a negative association with externalizing and internalizing problems. Academic competence was negatively associated with both externalizing and internalizing problems.

Latent variable path analysis with partial least squares (LVPLS) estimation procedures (Lohmoeller, 1989) were used to examine the hypothesized relationships depicted in the theoretical model (see Figure 1). LVPLS is part of a family of statistical procedures known as component analyses, of which principal-component analysis and canonical correlation are most well known.

Structural equation modeling with partial least squares was developed by Wold (1975) for situations in which data do not meet the highly restrictive assumptions that underlie maximum likelihood techniques such as LISREL (see Falk & Miller, 1991). The advantage of partial least squares over other analyses is that it allows the assessment of both direct and indirect effects, both of which are included in our hypotheses.

Goodness-of-fit indexes assess the extent to which the model reproduces the actual covariance matrix. The coefficient RMS COV (E, U), which stands for the root-mean-square of the covariance between the residuals of the manifest and latent variables, is an index of the overall model's fit with the raw data. This coefficient would be zero in a model that describes with complete accuracy the relationships between the variables. A coefficient above .20 indicates a poor model, and a coefficient

Table 2

Latent Variable Correlation Matrix

Variable	1	2	3	4	5	6	7	8
1. Per capita income	—	.12	−.11	.28	.25	.48	−.21	−.23
2. Formal religiosity	.17	—	−.11	.21	.04	.15	−.26	−.12
3. Interparental conflict	−.11	−.33	—	.00	−.26	−.28	.23	.17
4. Family cohesion	.28	.30	−.01	—	.27	.40	−.22	−.29
5. Child self-regulation	.25	.10	−.26	.27	—	.54	−.67	−.63
6. Academic competence	.48	.11	−.28	.40	.54	—	−.36	−.46
7. Externalizing problems	−.21	−.22	.23	−.22	−.67	−.36	—	.50
8. Internalizing problems	−.23	−.22	.18	−.28	−.63	−.46	.50	—

Note. Correlations for fathers are below the diagonal; those for mothers are above the diagonal. All correlations with a magnitude greater than .21 are significant at the .05 level ($df = 90$). All correlations with a magnitude greater than .27 are significant at the .01 level ($df = 90$).

of, for example, .02 indicates a superior one. The model presented here achieved a coefficient of .06.

As a form of data reduction, manifest variables are combined into theoretical components, resulting in multiple measurement of latent components. This capitalizes on the advantages of composited variables based on shared variance. The LVPLS program uses composite weights to create latent variables and to optimize linear relationships between predictor and predicted components. Paths between the theoretical constructs are standardized path coefficients or beta weights. Two models were evaluated: one that included maternal, and the other paternal, formal religiosity. Although our analytic procedures allow for the analysis of relatively small samples, they require an adequate number of participants for the number of composite variables in the model. Accordingly, separate models were executed for mothers and fathers. In addition, we used t tests to determine whether the composited measures differed by youth gender. Gender effects were not detected on any of the composited variables; thus, the models were not executed separately by gender of child.

The measurement model has mean commonalities (h^2) of .59 for both mothers and fathers. The factor loadings of the manifest variables and their respective latent components are presented in Table 3. These may be considered approximations of first principal-component loadings because they also take into account the hypothesized relations among the latent variables. Loadings of formal religiosity and family financial resources, measured by a single manifest variable, are necessarily 1.0. In the theoretical model presented in Figure 2, the mean R^2 values are statistically significant (all $ps < .001$). Overall, the models fit the data quite well.

The findings presented in Figure 2 indicate that greater maternal formal religiosity predicted less interparental conflict, greater family cohesion, and fewer externalizing problems. An indirect effect emerged between maternal formal religiosity and youth self-regulation, through interparental conflict and family cohesion. Indirect effects also emerged from interparental conflict and family cohesion to the youth outcome constructs, through youth self-regulation.

The paths in the model linking fathers' formal religiosity to family processes and youth outcomes were similar to those in the mothers' model. Figure 2, however, reveals one difference:

A direct path emerged between fathers' formal religiosity and youths' internalizing problems, indicating a negative association. It is also noteworthy that the path coefficient between fathers' formal religiosity and interparental conflict was three times larger than the same path for mothers.

Table 3

Component Loadings on Latent Variables

	Loading	
Variable	Fathers	Mothers
Economic resources		
Per capita income	1.00	1.00
Formal religiosity		
Maternal	1.00	1.00
Paternal	1.00	1.00
Interparental conflict		
Conflict scale, mothers (O'Leary–Porter Scale)	.79	.81
Conflict scale, fathers (O'Leary–Porter Scale)	.76	.73
Family cohesion		
Engagement (behavioral observation ratings)	.89	.90
Harmony (behavioral observation ratings)	.86	.85
Youth self-regulation		
Self-control subscale, fathers (SCI)	.53	.53
Self-control subscale, teachers (SCI)	.81	.81
Self-control subscale, mothers (SCI)	.72	.72
Academic competency		
Actual school reading grades	.80	.80
WISC–R vocabulary subscale	.60	.60
Actual school mathematics grades	.76	.76
WISC–R mathematics subscale	.73	.73
Externalizing problems		
Conduct disorder subscale, mothers (CBCL)	.68	.69
Conduct disorder subscale, teachers (CBCL)	.82	.80
Antisocial behavior subscale, mothers (SCI)	.75	.76
Antisocial behavior subscale, teachers (SCI)	.83	.82
Socialized aggression subscale, teachers (CBCL)	.62	.60
Misconduct grade expectation ratings, teachers	.70	.71
Internalizing problems		
CDI ratings, fathers	.56	.57
CDI ratings, mothers	.80	.79
CDI ratings, teachers	.62	.63

Note. SCI = Self-Control Inventory; WISC-R = Wechsler Intelligence Scale for Children—Revised; CBCL = Child Behavior Checklist; CDI = Child Depression Inventory.

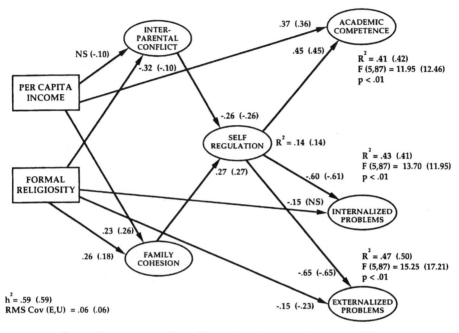

Figure 2. The structural model. Path coefficients for the mother model are in parentheses. RMS Cov = root-mean-square covariance.

To preclude the possibility that the family financial resources variable was confounded with mothers' and fathers' formal religiosity, we included per capita income in the model along with formal religiosity. All of the paths from formal religiosity to family processes and youth outcomes remained robust. In addition, direct effects from financial resources to family cohesion and academic competence emerged. An indirect effect also emerged between family resources and youth self-regulation, through family cohesion.

Discussion

Several questions were posed concerning the associations among religiosity, family processes, and youth outcomes in rural, two-parent African American families. First, what are the observed relations of religiosity with family processes and youth outcomes? Second, what are the direct or indirect paths through which religiosity plays a role in young adolescents' academic and socioemotional outcomes? Third, do the links among parental religiosity, family processes, and youth outcomes remain robust when family financial resources are taken into consideration?

We hypothesized both direct and indirect relations between parental religiosity and youth outcomes, and the data are consistent with these hypotheses. Greater formal religiosity is related directly to more cohesive family relationships, lower levels of interparental conflict, and fewer externalizing and internalizing problems among young adolescents. Formal religiosity also indirectly influenced youth self-regulation through its positive relationship with family cohesion and negative relationship with interparental conflict. These results are consistent with the hypothesis that formal religiosity enhances norms that govern close interpersonal relationships. These observed effects reinforce the prevailing notion that African Americans' religious involvement promotes supportive and responsive family relationships, which in turn help the family cope with the economic and social stressors that accompany life in the rural South.

These results suggest further questions about the ways in which religiosity affects family processes. One of the most plausible hypotheses we can advance at this point is that religiosity affects family processes at both intraindividual and interpersonal levels. At the intraindividual level, religious beliefs could affect family members' attentional processes. The Judeo-Christian religious tradition, to which the families in our study belong, promotes prosocial attitudes such as love, forgiveness, concern for the needs of others, and avoidance of judging others. Accordingly, it is possible that religious family members may selectively attend to positive or neutral cues coming from other members and choose to filter out negative ones. Religiosity may also influence judgmental processes through attributional means. Religious adults and children may be more inclined to attribute family members' conflictual behavior to situational rather than personal characteristics. The literature suggests that situational attributions are less likely than personal ones to provoke negative emotionality during family disputes (Fincham & Bradbury, 1987). It is also plausible that family cohesion is enhanced because family members are less likely to render negative judgments during disagreements; in turn, the withholding of judgments may facilitate the negotiation of family problems. At the interpersonal level, religiosity may promote the open discussion of disagreements without the reciprocation of negative and hostile behaviors, thus avoiding the coercive exchanges that can undermine family relationships (cf. Patterson, 1976).

An alternative explanation for the effects observed in this study centers around social support processes. The results could be attributed to feelings of connection and social support experienced by those who attend church regularly. According to this view, the value of church attendance in promoting positive family relationships comes from its provision of a place for families to gather and socialize. One might argue that those families who do not attend church regularly have greater difficulties because they lack this social support. Future studies should include measures of social support to determine how much of the effects attributed to religiosity can be accounted for by the social support that church participation provides, apart from religious beliefs.

In this study, parental formal religiosity had no direct effect on youth self-regulation. We hypothesized that the norms promoted by formal religiosity would be linked directly with youth self-regulation, internalizing problems, and externalizing problems. The pattern of results that we obtained suggests that parental formal religiosity in and of itself is not associated with youth self-regulation; simply knowing the levels of parents' formal religiosity will not predict youths' ability to regulate their own behavior. Parental formal religiosity is associated, however, with the quality of those family relationships that are associated with youth self-regulation. Note that the relations that emerged between formal religiosity and the youth adjustment problems measures were negative. Again, the data are consistent with the hypothesis that parental formal religiosity is linked with norms and family relationship qualities that decrease the likelihood that youths will experience internalizing and externalizing problems. It is beyond the scope of this study to identify the processes that are associated with the norms that covary with formal religiosity. Future research should consider constructs such as conventionality, prosocial motivations, the interests and norms of peer groups, and parental monitoring processes.

The links between formal religiosity and interparental conflict were stronger for fathers than for mothers. That fathers report lower levels of interparental conflict when they report higher levels of formal religiosity is particularly interesting when considered within the context of the participants' lives. Many fathers worked several jobs to earn enough money to support their families. The norms for interpersonal behavior that accompany formal religiosity may have enabled the fathers to interact with their spouses without succumbing to the effects of fatigue. Another plausible explanation for this finding is that involvement in organized religion enhances self-perceptions, which in turn enhance the spousal relationship. Krause and Tran (1989) reported that involvement in organized religion mitigates assaults on self-esteem and enhances feelings of personal efficacy among African Americans.

A final issue concerned the extent to which the links among formal religiosity, family processes, and youth outcomes were confounded with the availability of family financial resources. All of the paths described earlier were computed with the contribution of family financial resources taken into account, indicating that differences in family financial resources did not account for the obtained results involving parental formal religiosity. As predicted, family financial resources were directly linked to family cohesion and youth academic competence. In addition, parental formal religiosity was directly linked to family cohesion and to youth internalizing and externalizing problems and indirectly linked to youth academic competence. One noteworthy difference concerned the links to interparental conflict from family financial resources and formal religiosity for the fathers' model. No link emerged involving family financial resources, whereas the link involving formal religiosity was quite robust. The literature suggests that the effect of family financial resources on interparental conflict may be mediated by higher levels of depressive symptoms (cf. Brody et al., 1994; Conger et al., 1992; Conger et al., 1990), whereas the path involving formal religiosity may be governed by interpersonal relationship norms. At the very least, the differences in paths involving family financial resources and parental formal religiosity suggest that they contribute to variation in the outcomes of rural African American youths in different ways.

Limitations of this study and some caveats must be noted. First, it is not known whether the model of religiosity, family processes, and youth competence would generalize to urban families or to White families living in the same rural communities. The model examined in this study was developed with particular sensitivity to the demands of rearing African American children in rural areas. We do believe that the processes examined in this study may be important for families from other groups. It is clear that religiosity, family cohesion, and interparental conflict can affect youths from diverse ecological niches. It is possible that the weight of the influence of the processes may vary from sample to sample; this has yet to be examined empirically. Second, the proposed model is not intended to be exhaustive. Models that include different parameters than those included in the present model could also account for variation in the outcome assessments. Third, although the paths between variables in the model may imply causality, at this point we can only test the extent to which the observed variables can be predicted from the hypothesized model without respect to direction of effects. Finally, most of the families in this study were Southern Baptists; therefore, the results cannot be generalized to other religious groups whose beliefs may create different patterns of associations among formal religiosity, family processes, and youth outcomes.

References

Bahr, H. M., & Chadwick, B. A. (1985). Religion and family in Middletown, USA. *Journal of Marriage and the Family, 47,* 407–414.

Balk, D. (1983). How teenagers cope with sibling death: Some implications for school counselors. *School Counselor, 31.* 150–158.

Block, J. H. (1971). *Lives through time.* Berkeley, CA: Bancroft.

Brody, G. H., & Stoneman, Z. (1992). Child competence and developmental goals among rural Black families: Investigating the links. In I. E. Sigel, A. V. McGillicuddy-DeLisi, & J. J. Goodnow (Eds.), *Parental belief systems: The psychological consequences for children* (2nd ed., pp. 415–431). Hillsdale, NJ: Erlbaum.

Brody, G. H., Stoneman, Z., Flor, D., McCrary, C., Hastings, L., & Conyers, O. (1994). Financial resources, parent psychological functioning, parent co-caregiving, and early adolescent competence in rural two-parent African-American families. *Child Development, 65,* 590–605.

Brown, D. R., & Gary, L. E. (1988). Unemployment and psychological distress among Black American women. *Sociological Focus, 21,* 209–221.

Bruce, M. L., Takeuchi, D. T., & Leaf, P. (1991). Poverty and psychiatric status: Longitudinal evidence from the New Haven Epidemiological Catchment Area Study. *Archives of General Psychiatry, 48,* 470–474.

Conger, R. D., Conger, K. J., Elder, G. H., Lorenz, F. O., Simons, R. L., & Whitbeck, L. B. (1992). A family process model of economic hardship and adjustment of early adolescent boys. *Child Development, 63,* 526–541.

Conger, R. D., Elder, G. H., Lorenz, F. O., Conger, K. J., Simons, R. L., Whitbeck, L. B., Huck, S., & Melby, J. N. (1990). Linking economic hardship to marital quality and instability. *Journal of Marriage and the Family, 52,* 643–656.

Coward, R. T., & Smith, W. M. (1983). *Family services: Issues and opportunities in contemporary rural America.* Lincoln: University of Nebraska Press.

Durkheim, E. (1951). *Suicide.* New York: Free Press.

Epstein, S. (1979). The stability of behavior: I. On predicting most of the people much of the time. *Journal of Personality and Social Psychology, 37,* 1097–1126.

Falk, F., & Miller, N. (1991). A soft models approach to family transitions. In P. A. Cowan & E. M. Hetherington (Eds.), *Family transitions* (pp. 273–301). Hillsdale, NJ: Erlbaum.

Filsinger, E., & Wilson, M. (1984). Religiosity, socioeconomic rewards, and family development: Predictors of marital adjustment. *Journal of Marriage and the Family, 46,* 663–670.

Fincham, F. D., & Bradbury, T. N. (1987). The impact of attributions in marriage: A longitudinal analysis. *Journal of Personality and Social Psychology, 53,* 487–489.

Garmezy, N., Masten, A. S., & Tellegen, A. (1984). The study of stress and competence in children: A building block for developmental psychopathology. *Child Development, 55,* 97–111.

Goldman, A. L. (1991, April 10). Portrait of religion in U.S. holds dozens of surprises. *New York Times,* pp. A1, A11.

Greenberger, E. (1982). Education and the acquisition of psychosocial maturity. In D. McClelland (Ed.), *The development of social maturity* (pp. 155–189). New York: Irvington.

Hirschi, T. (1969). *Causes of delinquency.* Berkeley: University of California Press.

Humphrey, L. L. (1982). Children's and teachers' perspectives on children's self-control: The development of two rating scales. *Journal of Consulting and Clinical Psychology, 50,* 624–633.

Jacob, T. (1987). Family interaction and psychopathology: Historical overview. In T. Jacob (Ed.), *Family interaction and psychopathology* (pp. 3–22). New York: Plenum.

Kessler, R. (1982). A disaggregation of the relationship between socio-economic status and psychological distress. *American Sociological Review, 47,* 752–764.

Kovacs, M. (1981). Rating scales to assess depression in school-aged children. *Acta Paedopsychiatry, 46,* 305–315.

Krause, N., & Tran, T. V. (1989). Stress and religious involvement among older Blacks. *Journals of Gerontology: Social Science, 44,* 4–13.

Lewis, E. (1989). Role strain in African-American women: The efficacy of social support networks. *Journal of Black Studies, 20,* 155–167.

Lewis, R. J., Dlugokinski, E. L., Caputo, L. M., & Griffin, R. B. (1988). Children at risk for emotional disorders: Risk and resource dimensions. *Clinical Psychology Review, 8,* 417–420.

Lick, D. (1986, April). *Children and families in the South: Trends in health care, family services, and the rural economy.* [Prepared statement for a hearing before the U.S. House of Representatives Select Committee on Children, Youth, and Families, Macon, GA]. Washington, DC: U.S. Government Printing Office.

Lohmoeller, J. B. (1989). *Latent variable path modeling with partial least squares.* New York: Springer-Verlag.

McIntosh, D., & Spilka, B. (1990). Religion and physical health: The role of personal faith and control beliefs. In M. L. Lynn & D. O. Moberg (Eds.), *Research in the social scientific study of religion* (Vol. 2, pp. 167–194). Greenwich, CT: JAI Press.

McIntosh, W. A., Fitch, S. D., Wilson, J. B., & Nyburg, K. L. (1981). The effect of mainstream religious social controls on adolescent drug use in rural areas. *Review of Religious Research, 23,* 54–75.

McLoyd, V. C. (1989). Socialization and development in a changing economy. *American Psychologist, 44,* 293–302.

McLoyd, V. C. (1990). The impact of economic hardship on Black families and children: Psychological distress, parenting, and socioemotional development. *Child Development, 61,* 311–346.

Palmer, C. E., & Noble, D. N. (1986). Premature death: Dilemmas of infant mortality. *Social Casework, 67,* 332–339.

Pargament, K. I. (1990). God help me: Towards a theoretical framework for the psychology of religion. In M. L. Lynn & D. O. Moberg (Eds.), *Research in the social scientific study of religion* (Vol. 2, pp. 195–224). Greenwich, CT: JAI Press.

Patterson, G. R. (1976). The aggressive child: Victim and architect of a coercive system. In E. J. Mash, L. A. Hammerlynch, & L. C. Hardy (Eds.), *Behavior modification and families* (pp. 35–62). New York: Brunner/Mazel.

Patterson, G. R., Reid, J. B., & Dishion, T. J. (1992). *Antisocial boys.* Eugene, OR: Castalia.

Porter, B., & O'Leary, K. D. (1980). Marital discord and childhood behavior problems. *Journal of Abnormal Child Psychology, 8,* 287–295.

Princeton Religion Research Center. (1980). *Religions in America, 1979–1980.* Princeton, NJ: Princeton University Press.

Quay, H. B., & Peterson, D. R. (1987). *Manual for the Revised Behavior Problem Checklist.* Unpublished manuscript, University of Miami, Coral Gables, FL.

Rutter, M. (1990). Commentary: Some focus and process considerations regarding effects of depression on children. *Developmental Psychology, 26,* 60–67.

Seligman, M. E. P. (1991). *Learned optimism.* New York: Simon & Schuster.

Shrum, W. (1980). Religious and marital stability: Change in the 1970s? *Review of Religious Research, 21,* 135–147.

Steinberg, L., Elmen, J. D., & Mounts, N. S. (1989). Authoritative parenting, psychosocial maturity, and academic success among adolescents. *Child Development, 60,* 1424–1436.

Steinberg, L., Lamborn, S. D., Darling, N., Mounts, N., & Dornbusch, S. N. (1994). Over-time changes in adjustment and competence among adolescents from authoritative, authoritarian, indulgent, and neglectful families. *Child Development, 65,* 754–770.

Stevens, J. H., & Duffield, B. N. (1986). Age and parenting skill among Black women in poverty. *Early Childhood Research Quarterly, 1,* 221–235.

Taylor, R. J. (1988). Structural determinants of religious participation among Black Americans. *Review of Religious Research, 30,* 114–125.

Taylor, R. J., & Chatters, L. M. (1991). Non-organizational religious participation among elderly Blacks. *Journals of Gerontology: Social Science, 46,* 103–111.

Thomas, D. L., & Henry, G. C. (1988). The religion and family connection: Increasing dialogue in the social sciences. In D. L. Thomas (Ed.), *The religion and family connection: Social service perspectives* (pp. 3–23). Provo, UT: Brigham Young University, Religious Studies Center.

Udry, J. R. (1988). Biological predispositions and social control in adolescent sexual behavior. *American Sociological Review, 53,* 709–722.

U.S. Bureau of the Census. (1992, September). *Poverty in the U.S., 1991.* Washington, DC: U.S. Department of Commerce.

Wachs, T. D. (1992). *The nature of nurture.* Beverly Hills, CA: Sage.

Wilson, M. N. (1984). Mothers' and grandmothers' perspectives of parental behavior in three-generational Black families. *Child Development, 55,* 1333–1339.

Wilson, M. R., & Filsinger, E. E. (1986). Religiosity and marital adjustment: Multidimensional interrelationships. *Journal of Marriage and the Family, 48,* 147–151.

Wold, H. (1975). Path models with latent variables: The NIPALS approach. In H. Blalock (Ed.), *Quantitative sociology: International perspectives on mathematic and statistical model building* (pp. 307–357). New York: Academic Press.

Wuthnow, R. (1991). *Acts of compassion: Caring for others and helping ourselves.* Princeton, NJ: Princeton University Press.

Received February 16, 1995
Revision received May 26, 1995
Accepted May 26, 1995 ■

Development During Adolescence

The Impact of Stage–Environment Fit on Young Adolescents' Experiences in Schools and in Families

Jacquelynne S. Eccles, Carol Midgley, Allan Wigfield, Christy Miller Buchanan, David Reuman, Constance Flanagan, and Douglas Mac Iver

Although most individuals pass through adolescence without excessively high levels of "storm and stress," many do experience difficulty. Why? Is there something unique about this developmental period that puts adolescents at risk for difficulty? This article focuses on this question and advances the hypothesis that some of the negative psychological changes associated with adolescent development result from a mismatch between the needs of developing adolescents and the opportunities afforded them by their social environments. It provides examples of how this mismatch develops in the school and in the home and how it is linked to negative age-related changes in early adolescents' motivation and self-perceptions. Ways in which more developmentally appropriate social environments can be created are discussed.

Over the past 10 to 15 years there has been a dramatic increase in the attention paid to adolescence. Few developmental periods are characterized by so many changes at so many different levels—changes due to pubertal development, social role redefinitions, cognitive development, school transitions, and the emergence of sexuality. The nature and pace of these changes make adolescence an ideal focus for the study of human development. This has become increasingly evident to many developmental scientists.

For a variety of historical and policy-related reasons, much of the work in developmental science has focused on adolescence as a time of risk. With rapid change comes a heightened potential for both positive and negative outcomes. Although most individuals pass through this developmental period without excessively high levels of storm and stress, many individuals do experience difficulty during this period. Between 15% and 30% of adolescents in the United States, depending on the ethnic group, drop out of school before completing high school; adolescents have the highest arrest rate of any age group; and an increasing number of adolescents consume alcohol and other drugs on a regular basis (Office of Educational Research and Improvement, 1988).

Many of these problems appear to begin during the early adolescent years (Carnegie Council on Adolescent Development, 1989). Is there something unique about this developmental period that puts individuals at greater risk for difficulty as they pass through it? This article focuses on this question. Consistent with the view elaborated by Higgins and Parsons (1983), we suggest that the unique transitional nature of early adolescence results, at least in part, from an interaction between developmental changes in both the individual and social environmental levels. In particular, we advance the hypothesis that some of the negative psychological changes associated with adolescent development result from a mismatch between the needs of developing adolescents and the opportunities afforded them by their social environments. We provide examples of how this mismatch develops and operates in two specific social environments, the school and the home. We begin by reviewing the evidence of "problematic" change at the individual level.

"Problematic" Changes Associated With Early Adolescent Development

Research suggests that the early adolescent years mark the beginning of a downward spiral for some individuals, a spiral that leads some adolescents to academic failure and school dropout. For example, Simmons and Blyth (1987) found a marked decline in some early adolescents' school grades as they move into junior high school. Furthermore, the magnitude of this decline was predictive of subsequent school failure and dropout. Similarly timed developmental declines have been documented for such

Jacquelynne S. Eccles, Universities of Colorado and Michigan; Carol Midgley and Constance Flanagan, University of Michigan; Allan Wigfield, University of Maryland; Christy Miller Buchanan, Wake Forest University; David Reuman, Trinity College; and Douglas Mac Iver, Johns Hopkins University.

This research was made possible by grants from the National Institute of Child Health and Human Development (HD31724) and the Spencer Foundation to Jacquelynne S. Eccles and from the National Science Foundation (BNS-8510504) to Jacquelynne S. Eccles and Allan Wigfield.

We wish to thank our colleagues for assistance in designing, running, and analyzing the data from the studies reported herein. Special thanks go to Harriet Feldlaufer, Dave Klingel, and Jan Jacobs as well as to the teachers, school personnel, and students who agreed to participate in these studies.

Correspondence concerning this article should be addressed to Jacquelynne S. Eccles, Institute for Social Research, University of Michigan, Ann Arbor, MI 48106-1248.

motivational constructs as interest in school (Epstein & McPartland, 1976); intrinsic motivation (Harter, 1981); self-concepts and self-perceptions (Eccles, Midgley, & Adler, 1984; Harter, 1982; Simmons, Blyth, Van Cleave, & Bush, 1979); and confidence in one's intellectual abilities, especially following failure (Parsons & Ruble, 1977). There are also reports of age-related increases during early adolescence in such negative motivational and behavioral characteristics as test anxiety (Hill, 1980), learned helplessness responses to failure (Rholes, Blackwell, Jordan, & Walters, 1980), focus on self-evaluation rather than task mastery (Nicholls, 1980), truancy, and school dropout (Rosenbaum, 1976; see Eccles et al., 1984, for full review). Although these changes are not extreme for most adolescents, there is sufficient evidence of a gradual decline in various indicators of academic motivation—such as attention in class, school attendance, and self-perception—over the early adolescent years to make one wonder what is happening (see Eccles & Midgley, 1989, for review).

Similar types of changes have been noted in family interactions. Again, although the findings are neither universal nor indicative of major disruptions for most adolescents and their families, research suggests that there is a temporary increase in family conflict, particularly over issues related to autonomy and control, during the early adolescent years (see Buchanan, Eccles, & Becker, 1992; Collins, 1990; Hauser, Powers, & Noam, 1991; Hill, 1988; Montemayor, 1986; Paikoff & Brooks-Gunn, 1991; Smetana, 1988a, 1988b; Steinberg, 1990, for recent reviews). For example, Hill (1988) and Steinberg (1990), in both their observational and self-report studies, have found increased conflict between mothers and their sons and daughters during the early and middle adolescent years, particularly for early maturing adolescents (e.g., Hill, 1988; Steinberg, 1981, 1987, 1988).

A variety of explanations have been offered to explain these negative changes. Some who have studied child development have suggested that such declines result from the intrapsychic upheaval assumed to be associated with early adolescent development (e.g., Blos, 1965). Others have suggested that it is the coincidence of the timing of multiple life changes. Drawing on cumulative stress theory Simmons and her colleagues (e.g., Blyth, Simmons, & Carlton-Ford, 1983; Simmons & Blyth, 1987) have suggested that the concurrent timing of the junior high school transition and pubertal development accounts for the declines in the school-related measures and self-esteem. To test this hypothesis, Simmons and her colleagues compared the pattern of change on early school-related outcomes for adolescents who moved from sixth to seventh grade in a K–8, 9–12 system with the pattern of change for adolescents who made the same grade transition in a K–6, 7–9, 10–12 school system. This approach unconfounds the conjoint effects of age and school transition operating in most developmental studies of this age period. Simmons and her colleagues found clear evidence of greater negative change among adolescents making the junior high school transition than among adolescents remaining in the same school setting, especially among female adolescents. It is not clear whether these differences are due to the cumulative impact of school transition and pubertal change for young females adolescents who moved to a junior high school at grade seven, to differences in the nature of the school environments in these two educational structures, or to differences in both of these sets of experiences. Simmons and her colleagues (see Simmons & Blyth, 1987) now argue for the latter.

Similarly, Eccles and her colleagues (Eccles & Midgley, 1989; Eccles et al., 1984) have suggested that the change in the nature of the learning environment associated with the junior high school transition is a plausible explanation for the declines in the school-related measures associated with the junior high school transition. Drawing on *person–environment fit* theory (see Hunt, 1975), Eccles and Midgley (1989) proposed that these motivational and behavioral declines could result from inappropriate educational environments for early adolescents in junior high schools. According to person–environment fit theory, behavior, motivation, and mental health are influenced by the fit between the characteristics individuals bring to their social environments and the characteristics of these social environments. Individuals are not likely to do well, or be motivated, if they are in social environments that do not meet their psychological needs. If the social environments in the typical junior high school do not fit with the psychological needs of adolescents, then person–environment fit theory predicts a decline in motivation, interest, performance, and behavior as they move into this environment. We elaborate on this perspective and extend it to the family context, focusing on the possible mismatch between adolescents' need for greater autonomy from parental control and the opportunities for such autonomy provided by the adolescents' parents.

Stage–Environment Fit and School-Related Changes

Various explanations have been offered for the declines in early adolescents' school-related motivational orientations associated with the junior high school transition. In this section, the possible role that the school plays in precipitating these declines is discussed. To understand this role, two types of evidence regarding school effects are presented: evidence drawn from studies that follow the standard environmental influences approach and evidence from studies that adopt a developmental variant on the person–environment fit paradigm, or as Eccles and Midgley (1989) have called it, the *stage–environment fit* approach.

General Environmental Influences

Work in a variety of areas has documented the impact of classroom and school environmental characteristics on motivation. For example, the big school–small school literature has demonstrated the motivational advantages of small schools, especially for marginal students (Barker & Gump, 1964). Similarly, the teacher efficacy and teacher-student relationship literatures document the importance of high teacher efficacy and positive teacher–student relations for positive teacher and student motivation (Brookover, Beady, Flood, Schweitzer, & Wisenbaker, 1979; Fraser & Fisher, 1982; Moos, 1979). Finally, motivational psychology has demonstrated the importance of participation and self-control on motivation (de-Charms, 1980; Deci & Ryan, 1985, 1987). The list of such influences could, of course, go on for several pages. The point is that there may be systematic differences between typical elementary classrooms and schools, and typical junior high classrooms and schools, and that these differences may account for some of the motivational changes seen among early adolescents as they make the transition into middle or junior high school. If so, then some of the motivational problems seen at early adolescence may be a consequence of the negative changes in the school environment rather than characteristics of the developmental period per se (see Higgins & Parsons, 1983, for a full elaboration of this argument).

Stage–Environment Fit

A slightly different analysis of the possible environmental causes of the motivational changes associated with the junior high school transition draws on the idea of person-environment fit. Such a perspective leads one to expect negative motivational consequences for individuals when they are in environments that do not fit well with their needs (Hunt, 1975; Lewin, 1935). At the most basic level, this perspective suggests the importance of looking at the fit between the needs of early adolescents and the opportunities afforded them in the traditional junior high school environment. A poor fit would help explain the declines in motivation associated with the transition to junior high school.

A compelling way to use the person–environment fit perspective is to put it into a developmental framework. Hunt (1975) argued for the importance of adopting a developmental perspective on person–environment fit in the classroom:

Maintaining a developmental perspective becomes very important in implementing person–environment matching because a teacher should not only take account of a student's contemporaneous needs by providing whatever structure he presently requires, but also view his present need for structure on a developmental continuum along which growth toward independence and less need for structure is the long-term objective. (p. 221)

That is, teachers should provide the optimal level of structure for children's current levels of maturity while providing a sufficiently challenging environment to pull the children along a developmental path toward higher levels of cognitive and social maturity.

What we find especially intriguing about Hunt's (1975) argument is its application to an analysis of the motivational declines associated with the junior high school transition. If it is true that different types of educational environments may be needed for different age

groups to meet developmental needs and to foster continued developmental growth, then it is also possible that some types of changes in educational environments may be inappropriate at certain stages of development (e.g., the early adolescent period). In fact, some types of changes in the educational environment may be developmentally regressive. Exposure to such changes is likely to lead to a particularly poor person–environment fit, and this lack of fit could account for some of the declines in motivation seen at this developmental period.

In essence, we are suggesting that it is the fit between the developmental needs of the adolescent and the educational environment that is important. Imagine two trajectories: one a developmental trajectory of early adolescent growth, the other a trajectory of environmental change across the school years. We believe there will be positive motivational consequences when these two trajectories are in synchrony, that is, when the environment is both responsive to the changing needs of the individual and offers the kinds of stimulation that will propel continued positive growth. Transition to a facilitative and developmentally appropriate environment, even at this vulnerable age, should have a positive impact on children's perceptions of themselves and their educational environment. In contrast, negative motivational consequences will result if the two trajectories are not in synchrony. In this case, transition into a developmentally inappropriate educational environment should result in the types of motivational declines that have been associated with the transition into junior high school. This should be particularly true if the environment is developmentally regressive, that is, if it affords the children fewer opportunities for continued growth than previous environments.

This analysis suggests a set of researchable theoretical and descriptive questions: (a) What are the developmental needs of the early adolescent? (b) What kind of educational environment would be developmentally appropriate in terms of both meeting these needs and stimulating further development? (c) What are the most common changes experienced by young adolescents as they move into middle or junior high school? (d) Are these changes compatible with the physiological, cognitive, and psychological changes early adolescents are experiencing? If not, is there a developmental mismatch between maturing early adolescents and the classroom environments they experience before and after the transition to the junior high school—a mismatch that results in a deterioration in academic motivation and performance for some children?

Systematic Changes in School Environments With the Transition into Middle or Junior High School

We believe that there are developmentally inappropriate changes in a cluster of classroom organizational, instructional, and climate variables, including task structure, task complexity, grouping practices, evaluation techniques, motivational strategies, locus of responsibility for learning, and quality of teacher–student and student–student relationships. We suggest that these changes contribute to the negative change in students' motivation and achievement-related beliefs assumed to coincide with the transition into junior high school. Although insufficient research has been done on this subject, the existing research provides support for these suggestions.

Remarkably few empirical studies have focused on differences in the classroom or school environment across grades or school levels. Most descriptions have focused on school-level characteristics, such as school size, degree of departmentalization, and extent of bureaucratization. Although differences in these characteristics can have important effects on teacher beliefs and practices and on student alienation and motivation, until recently these links have rarely been assessed. Most attempts to assess the classroom environment have included only one grade level and have related differences in the environment to student outcomes, particularly scores on achievement tests. Although little research has focused on systematic differences in the classroom environment from elementary to junior high school, six patterns have emerged with a fair degree of consistency.

First, junior high school classrooms, as compared with elementary school classrooms, are characterized by a greater emphasis on teacher control and discipline, and fewer opportunities for student decision making, choice, and self-management (e.g., Brophy & Evertson, 1976; Midgley & Feldlaufer, 1987; Midgley, Feldlaufer, & Eccles, 1988; Moos, 1979). For example, Brophy, Evertson, and their colleagues (e.g., Brophy & Evertson, 1976) have found consistent evidence that junior high school teachers spend more time maintaining order and less time actually teaching than do elementary school teachers. In our own work, sixth-grade elementary school math teachers reported less concern with controlling and disciplining their students than these same students' seventh-grade junior high school math teachers reported one year later (Midgley et al., 1988).

Similar differences emerge on indicators of student opportunity to participate in decision making regarding their own learning. Ward et al. (1982) found that upper elementary school students are given more opportunities to take responsibility for their schoolwork than are seventh-grade students in a traditional junior high school. In our work (Midgley & Feldlaufer, 1987) both seventh graders and their teachers in the first year of junior high school reported less opportunity for students to participate in classroom decision making than did these same students and their sixth grade elementary school teachers one year earlier. In addition, using a measure developed by Lee, Statuto, and Kedar-Voivodas (1983) to assess the congruence between the adolescents' desire for participation in decision making and their perception of the opportunities for such participation, Midgley and Feldlaufer (1987) found a greater discrepancy when the adolescents were in their first year in junior high school than when these same adolescents were in their last year in elementary school. The fit between the adolescents'

desire for autonomy and their perception of the extent to which their classroom afforded them opportunities to engage in autonomous behavior had decreased over the junior high school transition.

Second, junior high school classrooms, as compared with elementary school classrooms, are characterized by less personal and positive teacher–student relationships (see Eccles & Midgley, 1989). For example, in Trebilco, Atkinson, and Atkinson's (1977) study, students reported less favorable interpersonal relations with their teachers after the transition to secondary school than before. Similarly, in our work (Feldlaufer, Midgley, & Eccles, 1988), both students and observers rated junior high school math teachers as less friendly, less supportive, and less caring than the teachers these students had one year earlier in the last year of elementary school. In addition, the seventh-grade teachers in this study reported that they trusted the students less than did these students' sixth-grade teachers.

Third, the shift to junior high school is associated with an increase in practices such as whole-class task organization, between-classroom ability grouping, and public evaluation of the correctness of work (see Eccles & Midgley, 1989). In a study by Ward et al. (1982), whole-group instruction was the norm in the seventh grade, small-group instruction was rare, and individualized instruction was not observed at all. In contrast, the sixth grade teachers mixed whole- and small-group instruction within and across subjects areas (Rounds & Osaki, 1982). Similar shifts toward increased use of whole-class instruction, with most students working on the same assignments at the same time, using the same textbooks, and completing the same homework assignments, were evident in our study of the junior high school transition (Feldlaufer et al., 1988). Several reports have also documented the increased use of between-class ability grouping beginning at junior high school (e.g., Oakes, 1981).

Changes such as these are likely to increase social comparison, concerns about evaluation, and competitiveness (see Eccles et al., 1984; Rosenholtz & Simpson, 1984). They may also increase the likelihood that teachers will use normative grading criteria and more public forms of evaluation, both of which may have a negative impact on many early adolescents' self-perceptions and motivation. These changes may also make aptitude differences more salient to both teachers and students, leading to increased teacher expectancy effects and decreased feelings of efficacy among teachers.

Fourth, junior high school teachers feel less effective as teachers, especially with low-ability students. This difference was one of the largest we found between sixth- and seventh-grade teachers. In mathematics, seventh-grade teachers in traditional junior high schools reported much less confidence in their teaching efficacy than did sixth-grade elementary school teachers in the same school districts (Midgley, Feldlaufer, & Eccles, 1989b). This is true even though the seventh-grade math teachers were more likely to be math specialists than were sixth-grade math teachers.

Fifth, there is evidence that classwork during the first year of junior high school requires lower level cognitive skills than does classwork at the elementary level. One rationale often given for the large, departmentalized junior high school system is its efficiency in providing early adolescents with higher level academic work and more varied academic courses taught by specialists in their fields. It is argued that the early adolescents are ready for more formal instruction in specialized subject areas. Two assumptions are implicit in this argument. First, it is assumed that more formal, departmentalized teaching is conducive to the learning of higher order cognitive processes. Second, it is assumed that children in junior high school are undertaking higher order learning tasks in their departmentalized courses.

Both assumptions are being questioned. In an observational study of 11 junior high school science classes (Mitman, Mergendoller, Packer, & Marchman, 1984), only a small proportion of tasks required higher level creative or expressive skills. The most frequent activity involved copying answers from the board or textbook onto worksheets. Similarly, Walberg, House, and Steele (1973) rated the level of complexity of student assignments across Grades 6 through 12. The proportion of low-level activities peaked at Grade 9, the first year after the students in this district made the transition into secondary school. Both of these studies, as well as other studies, suggest that the actual cognitive demands made on adolescents may decrease rather than increase as they make the transition from primary school into secondary school.

Finally, junior high school teachers appear to use a higher standard in judging students' competence and in grading their performance than do elementary school teachers (see Eccles & Midgley, 1989). There is no stronger predictor of students' self-confidence and sense of efficacy than the grades they receive. If grades change, then we would expect to see a concomitant shift in adolescents' self-perceptions and academic motivation. There is evidence that junior high school teachers use stricter and more social comparison-based standards than do elementary school teachers to assess student competency and to evaluate student performance, leading to a drop in grades for many early adolescents as they make the junior high school transition. For example, Finger and Silverman (1966) found that 54% of the students in New York State schools experienced a decline in their grades when they moved into junior high school. Similarly, Simmons and Blyth (1987) found a greater drop in grades between sixth and seventh grades for adolescents making the junior high school transition than for adolescents who remained in K–8 schools. The decline in grades is not, however, accompanied by a similar decline in the adolescents' scores on standardized achievement tests, which suggests that the decline reflects a change in grading practices rather than a change in the rate of the students' learning (Kavrell & Petersen, 1984). Imagine what this decline in grades might do to young adolescents' self-confidence, especially if the material is less intellectually challenging.

Such changes are likely to have a negative effect on children's motivational orientation toward school at any grade level. However, we believe these types of school environment changes are particularly harmful at early adolescence, given what is known about psychological development during this stage of life. Past research suggests that early adolescent development is characterized by increases in desire for autonomy and self-determination, peer orientation, self-focus and self-consciousness, salience of identity issues, concern over heterosexual relationships, and capacity for abstract cognitive activity (see Simmons & Blyth, 1987).

Simmons and Blyth (1987) have argued that adolescents need a reasonably safe, as well as an intellectually challenging, environment to adapt to these shifts—an environment that provides a zone of comfort as well as challenging new opportunities for growth. In light of these needs, the environmental changes often associated with transition to junior high school seem especially harmful in that they emphasize competition, social comparison, and ability self-assessment at a time of heightened self-focus; they decrease decision making and choice at a time when the desire for control is growing; they emphasize lower level cognitive strategies at a time when the ability to use higher level strategies is increasing; and they disrupt social networks at a time when adolescents are especially concerned with peer relationships and may be in special need of close adult relationships outside of the home. We believe the nature of these environmental changes, coupled with the normal course of individual development, results in a developmental mismatch so that the fit between the early adolescent and the classroom environment is particularly poor, increasing the risk of negative motivational outcomes, especially for adolescents who are having difficulty succeeding in school academically. In the next section we review research findings relevant to these predictions.

It is important, however, to step back and briefly consider why junior high school classrooms might have these characteristics. Several sources have suggested that these characteristics result, in part, from the size and bureaucratic nature of the junior high school as an institution (e.g., Barker & Gump, 1964; Bryk, Lee, & Smith, 1990; Carnegie Council on Adolescent Development, 1989; Simmons & Blyth, 1987). These sources argue that such school characteristics as size, connection to the community, and system of governance, as well as such instructional organization characteristics as departmentalized teaching, ability grouping, normative grading, and large student load, undermine the motivation of both teachers and students. It is difficult for teachers to maintain warm, positive relationships with students if they have to teach 25–30 different students each hour of the day. For the same reason, it is difficult for teachers to feel efficacious about their ability to monitor and help all of these students. Consequently, teachers often resort to more controlling strategies when supervising such a large number of students. These problems are likely to be exacerbated by the negative stereotypes about adolescents propagated in this culture by presumed experts and by the mass media (see Miller et al., 1990).

Turning Points: Preparing American Youth for the 21st Century (Carnegie Council on Adolescent Development, 1989) outlines a variety of changes in the structure of middle-grades educational institutions (e.g., junior highs, middle schools, and intermediate schools) that would make it easier for teachers to maintain a high sense of self-efficacy, and for both students and teachers alike to have a strong sense of a shared community. In turn, these changes could make it easier for teachers to provide a more positive learning environment for early adolescents.

Impact of Classroom Environmental Changes on Early Adolescents' Motivation: The Michigan Study of Adolescent Life Transitions

To test the predictions outlined above, we conducted a large-scale, two-year, four-wave longitudinal study of the impact of changes in the school and classroom environments on early adolescents' achievement-related beliefs, motives, values, and behaviors (The Michigan Study of Adolescent Life Transitions [MSALT]). The sample was drawn from 12 school districts located in middle-income communities in southeastern Michigan. Approximately 1,500 early adolescents participated at all four waves of the study, moving from the sixth grade in an elementary school into the seventh grade in a junior high school. As is typically the case, the students did not move as a group into the junior high school; they were assigned to various different classes when they arrived at the junior high school. Questionnaires were administered at school during the fall and spring terms of the two consecutive school years.

Teacher Efficacy

One of the largest differences we found between the sixth- and seventh-grade teachers was in their confidence in their teaching efficacy: The seventh-grade teachers reported less confidence than did the sixth-grade teachers. Although the relation between teacher efficacy and student beliefs and attitudes is yet to be firmly established, Brookover et al. (1979), using schools as the unit of analysis, found negative correlations between teachers' sense of efficacy and students' self-concept of ability and self-reliance. Given these associations, differences in teachers' sense of efficacy before and after the transition to junior high school could contribute to the decline in early adolescents' beliefs about their academic competency and potential.

To test this hypothesis, we divided our adolescent sample into four groups based on median splits of their math teachers' ratings of their personal teaching efficacy (see Midgley et al., 1989b, for a full description of this study). The largest group, 559 of the 1,329 included in these analyses, moved from a high-efficacy sixth-grade math teacher to a low-efficacy seventh-grade math teacher. Another 474 adolescents had low-efficacy teachers both

years, 117 moved from low- to high-efficacy teachers, and 179 had high-efficacy teachers both years. Thus, 78% of the early adolescents in our sample moved to classrooms with low-efficacy teachers in the seventh grade. The potential impact of such a shift on the motivation and self-perceptions of early adolescents, especially those having difficulty mastering the academic material, is frightening. We know, in particular, that teachers' low expectations for their students undermine the motivation and performance of low-achieving students (Eccles & Wigfield, 1985). Moving from a high- to a low-efficacy teacher may produce a similar effect.

As predicted, the adolescents who moved from high-efficacy to low-efficacy math teachers during the transition (the most common pattern) ended their first year in junior high school with lower expectations for themselves in math, lower perceptions of their performance in math, and higher perceptions of the difficulty of math than did the adolescents who experienced no change in teacher efficacy or who moved from low- to high-efficacy teachers. Also as predicted, teacher efficacy beliefs had a stronger impact on the low-achieving adolescents' beliefs than on the high-achieving adolescents' beliefs. By the end of the junior high school year, low-achieving adolescents who had moved from high- to low-efficacy math teachers suffered a dramatic decline in confidence in their ability to master mathematics. This drop may signal the beginning of the downward spiral in school motivation that eventually leads to school dropout among so many low-achieving adolescents. It is important to note, however, that this same decline was not characteristic of the low-achieving adolescents who moved to high-efficacy seventh-grade math teachers, suggesting that the decline is not a general feature of early adolescent development but rather a consequence of the learning environment experienced by many early adolescents as they make the junior high school transition. Whether a similar pattern characterizes other subject areas remains to be demonstrated.

Teacher–Student Relationships

As noted earlier, we also found that student–teacher relationships deteriorate after the transition to junior high school. Research on the effects of classroom climate indicates that the quality of student–teacher relationships is associated with students' academic motivation and attitudes toward school (e.g., Fraser & Fisher, 1982; Moos, 1979; Trickett & Moos, 1974). Consequently, there is reason to believe that transition into a less supportive classroom will have a negative impact on early adolescents' interest in the subject matter being taught in that classroom. In a sample of 1,300 students, we looked at the effect of differences in perceived teacher support before and after the transition to junior high school on the value early adolescents attach to mathematics (see Midgley, Feldlaufer, & Eccles, 1989a, for a full description of this study). As predicted, the early adolescents who moved from elementary teachers they perceived to· be low in support to junior high school math teachers they perceived to be high in support showed an increase in the value they attached to math. In contrast, the early adolescents who moved from teachers they perceived to be high in support to teachers they perceived to be low in support showed a decline in the value they attached to mathematics. Again we found evidence that low-achieving students are particularly at risk when they move to less facilitative classroom environments after the transition.

Both of these studies show that the declines often reported in studies of early adolescents' motivational orientation are not inevitable. Instead, these declines are associated with specific types of changes in the nature of the classroom environment experienced by many early adolescents as they make the junior high school transition. The studies also show that a transition into more facilitative classrooms can induce positive changes in early adolescents' motivation and self-perceptions. Unfortunately, our findings also indicate that most adolescents experience a negative change in their classroom experiences as they make the junior high school transition.

Person–Environment Fit in Classroom Decision Making

Neither of these studies, however, directly tests our stage–environment hypothesis. To do so, one must directly assess person–environment fit and relate this fit to changes in adolescents' self-perceptions and motivation. Data from MSALT provide an opportunity to do this analysis. Both the adolescents and the teachers in this study were asked to rate whether students were allowed to have input into classroom decisions regarding seating arrangements, classwork, homework, class rules, and what to do next and whether students ought to have input into each of these decisions (as developed by Lee et al., 1983). These questions can be used in the following ways: (a) to plot the developmental changes in adolescents' preferences for decision-making opportunities in the classroom, (b) to determine changes in the opportunity for them to participate in decision making, and (c) to determine the extent of match or mismatch between their preferences and the opportunities actually afforded them in the school environment. Grade-related changes in this match can then be related to developmental changes in the adolescents' self-perceptions and school-related motivation.

Developmental Changes in Fit

Grade-related changes. As noted earlier, both the early adolescents and their teachers reported that there was less opportunity for participation in classroom decision making at the seventh grade than at the sixth grade level. In contrast, there was an increase over time and over the school transition in the early adolescents' desires for participation in classroom decision making. As a consequence of these two divergent patterns, the congruence between early adolescents' desires for participation in classroom decision making and their perceptions of the opportunities available to them was lower in the seventh grade than in the sixth grade (Midgley & Feldlaufer, 1987).

Maturational differences in the desire for autonomy. Another way to look at developmental

change is to look for interindividual differences at the same time point between same-aged children of different maturational levels. At this age, the extent of pubertal development provides a good indicator of individual differences in physical maturation for female adolescents. We related an indicator of physical maturation to the female adolescents' desire for input into classroom decisions using the Lee et al. (1983) items. Consistent with the intraindividual longitudinal pattern of age-related change reported above, the more physically mature female adolescents expressed a greater desire for input into classroom decision making than did their less physically mature female peers (Miller, 1986). Unfortunately, as was true for the longitudinal results, the more physically mature female adolescents did not perceive greater opportunities for participation in classroom decision making. Although the female adolescents with varying degrees of pubertal development were in the same classrooms, the more physically mature female adolescents (i.e., the early developers) reported fewer opportunities for participation in classroom decision making than did their less mature peers (i.e., the on-time and late developers).

These maturational differences were even more striking when we looked at the within-year changes in these female adolescents' perceptions of the opportunities they had to participate in classroom decision making. We calculated the mean change in their perceptions of opportunities from the fall to the spring testing waves. We then looked at this change as a function of their pubertal status. The early-maturing female adolescents reported less opportunity to participate in classroom decision making in the spring term than they had reported in the previous fall term. In contrast, the late-maturing female adolescents in these same classrooms showed an increase over the course of the school year in these opportunities (Miller, 1986). How can this be, given that these adolescents were in the same classrooms? Did the teachers actually treat these female adolescents differently (i.e., did the teachers respond to earlier physical maturity with more controlling behavior)? Or did the female adolescents perceive a similar environment differently (i.e., did the early-maturing female adolescents perceive the same level of adult control as providing less opportunity for self-determination than did the late-maturing female adolescents)?

Research in educational psychology, developmental psychology, and general psychology suggests that either or both of these explanations could be accurate: Teachers do respond differently to various children in the same classroom depending on a variety of characteristics (Brophy & Evertson, 1976), and people do perceive similar environments differently depending on their cognitive or motivational orientation (see Baron & Graziano, 1991). More detailed classroom observations are needed to determine the exact nature of the relation between teachers' behavior and adolescents' perceptions.

More important for the issues central to this article, the degree of mismatch between these female adolescents' desires for input and their perceptions of these opportunities in their classroom environment was related to their pubertal status: There was a greater degree of mismatch among the more physically mature female adolescents than among the less mature female adolescents. In fact, by the end of the school year, almost twice as many early-maturing female adolescents reported experiencing the "can't but should" type of mismatch (e.g., answering no to the question "Do you get to help decide what math you work on during math class?" but yes to the question "Should you have a say about this?") as did their less physically mature classmates.

This last set of results is especially interesting in light of the findings of Simmons and her colleagues (e.g., Simmons & Blyth, 1987; Simmons et al., 1979), who found that the pubertal status of female adolescents at the time of the junior high school transition is related to changes in their self-esteem and their self-reports of truancy and school misconduct. The more physically mature female adolescents reported the highest amount of truancy and school misconduct after they made the junior high school transition. Simmons and her colleagues suggested that experiencing both school and pubertal transitions simultaneously puts these female adolescents at particular risk for negative outcomes. Alternatively, it is possible that it is the size of the mismatch between their desire for a less controlling adult environment and their perceptions of the actual opportunities for participation that puts them at risk for the most negative motivational outcomes.

Motivational Consequences of a Poor Developmental-Stage-Environment Fit

As previously discussed, person–environment fit theory suggests that the mismatch between young adolescents' desires for autonomy and control and their perceptions of the opportunities in their environments should result in a decline in the adolescents' intrinsic motivation and interest in school. From a developmental perspective, the exact nature of the mismatch should also be important. Given the appropriate developmental progression toward increased desire for independence and autonomy during the early adolescent period, adolescents who experience decreased opportunities for participation in classroom decision making along with an increased desire for participation in such decisions (i.e., a "can't but should be able to" mismatch) should be more at risk for negative motivational outcomes than adolescents experiencing other forms of mismatch (such as the "can but shouldn't be able to" mismatch).

In a longitudinal analysis of the Lee et al. (1983) items, Mac Iver and Reuman (1988) provided some support for this prediction. Mac Iver and Reuman compared the changes in intrinsic interest in mathematics for adolescents reporting different longitudinal patterns in their responses to the actual and preferred decision-making items across the four waves of data. Consistent with the prediction, some adolescents perceived their seventh-grade math classrooms as putting greater constraints on their preferred level of participation in classroom decision making than their sixth-grade math classrooms. These

adolescents evidenced the largest and most consistent declines in their intrinsic interest in math as they moved from the sixth grade into the seventh grade. They are the students who are experiencing the type of developmental mismatch we outlined in our discussion of the stage–environment fit paradigm.

Stage–Environment Fit in Perceived Control in the Family

Research from several investigators (e.g., Buchanan et al., 1992; Palkoff & Brooks-Gunn, 1991; Steinberg, 1990) suggests that adolescents' relationships with their parents also undergo a stressful period during early and middle adolescence. This stress is often focused on issues of control and autonomy within the family, which are renegotiated during this developmental period. By necessity, children's relationships with their parents are asymmetrical in terms of power and authority; but as children mature, they need to take more and more responsibility for themselves until they eventually leave their natal home and take full responsibility for their own lives. In the optimal situation, parents will reinforce and stimulate this process of growing autonomy, self-determination, and independence. However, it is likely that the renegotiation processes associated with these developmental trajectories will not be smooth. It is not easy for parents to determine the optimal level of autonomy versus control for their children at all ages. According to a stage–environment fit perspective, one would predict strained relationships wherever there is a poor fit between the child's desire for increasing autonomy and the opportunities for independence and autonomy provided by the child's parents.

Early adolescence seems a likely developmental period for asynchrony to emerge within the family context. Social changes in the world of adolescents substantially increase the opportunity for them to experience independence outside the home. The transition to junior high school, and cultural beliefs regarding appropriate amounts of adult supervision for children of different ages, lead to a dramatic increase in the amount of unsupervised age-mate contact during this developmental period (Higgins & Parsons, 1983). This increase creates the opportunity for adolescents to spend a lot of time in relationships that are likely to be more symmetrical in terms of interpersonal power and authority. Such experiences may lead early adolescents to expect greater power symmetry in their relationships at home. The opportunity to be exposed to a broader range of families is also likely to increase with the junior high school transition, because these schools are typically larger and draw their attendance from a more diverse range of neighborhoods and communities. This broadened exposure may lead early adolescents to question the legitimacy of their parents' rules (Higgins & Parsons, 1983; Laupa & Turiel, 1986; Smetana, 1988a, 1988b; Tisak, 1986). Exposure to a broader range of belief systems, along with increasing cognitive maturity, may, in turn, lead adolescents to try to integrate and coordinate diverse social perspectives and to evaluate interpersonal relationships (Damon & Hart, 1982; Selman, 1980).

81

These changes, in turn, may lead early adolescents to question their parents' authority and to push for a more symmetrical relationship with their parents. Finally, parents, in response to their child's emerging sexuality, may become more concerned about his or her safety and may actually become more restrictive than they were during the period of middle childhood, further exacerbating the perceived asynchrony in the adolescent's mind. However, as the family adjusts to these changes, one would expect new authority relationships to emerge and the strain to decrease over the adolescent years (see Montemayor, 1983).

Perhaps the best support for this analysis comes from the work of Smetana (1988a, 1988b, 1989). Drawing on evidence regarding age changes in children's understanding of both moral versus social conventional reasoning and the legitimacy of adult authority, Smetana has conducted in-depth interviews with adolescents and their parents about authority relationships within the family and about the nature and origin of conflicts in the family. Like others, Smetana found that most parent–adolescent conflicts focused on mundane issues, such as cleaning one's room and curfew. The conflicts often resulted because adolescents now defined these issues as personal issues, issues that the individual should decide, whereas the parents still defined these issues as conventional issues, issues for which parents have some right to establish rules. In cross-sectional comparisons, Smetana found a linear age-related increase in the adolescents' view that most of these issues are personal rather than conventional. Shifts in the parents' views were less systematic. Of particular importance for the stage–environment fit hypothesis, the greatest increase in mismatch between the adolescents' and their parents' views occurred during the early adolescent period (Grades 5–8) and mirrored increases in reported conflict (Smetana, 1989).

We are in the process of examining similar issues in our study of adolescent development (the MSALT study described earlier). We assessed family decision making in two ways. Both the adolescents and their parents responded to two items derived from the Epstein and McPartland (1977) scale of family decision making: "In general, how do you and your child arrive at decisions?" *I tell my child just what to do* (1), *We discuss it and then we decide* (3), *I usually let my child decide* (5); and "How often does your child take part in family decisions that concern her/himself? *never* (1); *always* (4). The adolescents were also asked to rate how they thought decisions ought to be made in their family, and the extent to which they think "their parents treated them more like a kid than like an adult."

Consistent with the analyses reported earlier, we found both an increase over time in adolescents' desire for greater participation in family decision making, and positive associations between the extent of the adolescents' participation in family decision making and indicators of both intrinsic school motivation and positive self-esteem (Flanagan, 1985, 1986, 1989; Miller & Taylor, 1986; Yee, 1986, 1987; Yee & Flanagan, 1985). Even more inter-

estingly from the stage–environment fit perspective, the parents reported that they included their children more in family decision making than the adolescents perceived to be true (Flanagan, 1986; Yee, 1987). For girls in particular, the discrepancy between the adolescents' and the parents' perception of the opportunities for the adolescents to participate in family decision making increased over the four waves in our study (Yee, 1987). Most important, the pattern of changes in early adolescents' self-esteem and intrinsic versus extrinsic motivation for school work were systematically, and predictably, related to changes in their perceptions of the opportunity to participate in family decision making at home. As our developmental stage–environment fit perspective on adult control implies, the adolescents who reported decreasing opportunities to participate in family decision making showed a decrease in their self-esteem and intrinsic motivation over the period of this study; the opposite pattern of change occurred for the adolescents who reported increasing opportunities to participate in the decision-making process (Flanagan, 1985, 1989; Yee, 1987). The opportunity to participate in family decision making also predicted better adjustment to the junior high school transition (Eccles et al., 1990). Thus, not only may a mismatch between authority relationships in the home precipitate increased conflict, it may also be detrimental to the adolescents' self-esteem and school-related motivation.

Similar results characterize our data on interindividual pubertal status effects. Miller and Taylor (1986) tested the relationship between female pubertal status and self-esteem. Consistent with other studies (e.g., Simmons & Blyth, 1987), the early-maturing sixth-grade girls reported lower self-esteem than did their less physically mature classmates. However, consistent with the person-environment fit perspective, only early-maturing girls who felt they had relatively little opportunity to participate in family decision making reported lower self-esteem. There was no effect of pubertal status on self-esteem among those sixth-grade female adolescents who reported relatively high opportunity to participate in their family's decision making.

Conclusion

We have argued that optimal development takes place when there is good stage–environment fit between the needs of developing individuals and the opportunities afforded them by their social environments. We have provided evidence of the negative effects of the decrease in personal and positive relationships with teachers after the transition to junior high school and have argued that this decline is especially problematic during early adolescence when children are in special need of close relationships with adults outside of their homes. We have also noted the increase in ability grouping, comparative and public evaluation, and whole-class task organization at a time when young adolescents have a heightened concern about their status in relation to their peers. We have described studies that suggest that the first year of junior high school

82

is characterized by a decrease in the emphasis on higher level thinking skills at a time when cognitive development would suggest the need for more complex academic tasks. Finally, we discussed, and provided evidence where available, the negative consequences of these kinds of developmentally inappropriate environmental changes on early adolescents' school motivation and academic self-concepts.

The role of opportunity for self-determination and participation in rule making was also discussed, and the importance of the need for a match between the individual's increasing desires for autonomy and self-determination and the opportunities for such autonomy provided in the home and at school was emphasized. Although adolescents desire more freedom from adult control than children do, they do not want total freedom and they do not want to be emotionally detached from their parents. Instead, they desire a gradual increase in the opportunity for self-determination and participation in decision making and rule making. Furthermore, research suggests that adolescents develop best when these increasing opportunities occur in environments that are emotionally supportive (Baumrind, 1971; Ryan & Lynch, 1989).

Unfortunately, our research suggests that many early adolescents do not have these experiences in either the school or family setting. After the transition to junior high school, early adolescents are often confronted with a regressive environmental change: They experience a decrease in the opportunity to participate in classroom decision making when they move into junior high school. Not surprisingly, there is also a decrease in intrinsic motivation and an increase in school misconduct associated with this transition, and these changes are most apparent among the adolescents who report experiencing the greatest mismatch between their needs and their opportunities to participate in classroom decision making. Such motivational changes are not apparent in adolescents who report the more developmentally appropriate increase in opportunity for participation in classroom decision making.

Although our analysis of the family data is not as complete as our analysis of the classroom data, we have found evidence suggesting that a similar process is occurring in the family. Excessive parental control is linked to lower intrinsic school motivation, to more negative changes in self-esteem following the junior high school transition, to more school misconduct, and to relatively greater investment in peer social attachments. However, because this study is correlational, it is possible that excessive parental control is the consequence rather than the cause of these negative adolescent outcomes. Nevertheless, the preliminary longitudinal analyses suggest that the causal links are at least bidirectional. Although we have focused on excessive parental control, other studies have documented the negative consequences of too little parental control at this age (see Dornbusch et al., 1985; Fuligni & Eccles, 1990; Steinberg, 1990).

Clearly, these results point to the importance of designing educational and family environments for early adolescents that provide a better match to their developing needs and desires. The existing structure of many junior high schools appears to create a climate that undermines both teacher and student motivation. The large size of the schools, coupled with departmentalized teaching and large student loads, makes it difficult for teachers and students to form close relationships. In turn, a lack of close student–teacher relationships and a generally negative stereotyping of adolescents could be responsible for the prevalence of low teacher efficacy and high use of controlling motivational strategies in junior high school classrooms. Field studies of the more successful middle and junior high schools provide numerous examples of classrooms and schools that have more positive and developmentally appropriate learning environments—classrooms and schools with higher teacher efficacy, greater opportunity for meaningful student participation in both school and classroom decision making, and more positive student–teacher relationships (see Bryk et al., 1990; Carnegie Council on Adolescent Development, 1989; Dryfoos, 1990; Eccles & Midgley, 1989; Lipsitz, 1981). Early adolescents in these schools do not demonstrate the same declines in intrinsic motivation and school attachment stereotypically associated with students in junior high schools; they also do not engage in the same amount of school misconduct as students in more traditional junior high schools. However, many junior high schools do not provide such a developmentally appropriate environment (see Eccles & Midgley, 1989).

There is a similar need for developmentally responsive family environments. Existing research suggests that there is variability in how families adapt to their children's movement into adolescence and that adolescents fare best in family environments that provide a good fit to their increasing need for autonomy. Adolescents fare more poorly in families that respond to their development either by throwing up their hands and relinquishing control or by cracking down too much. Families, like schools, are confronted with a difficult problem: providing an environment that changes in the right way and at the right pace. Unfortunately, we know less about how to help families achieve this balance than we know about how to design schools that help teachers achieve the right balance. There is a great need for programs that will help parents with this difficult task.

REFERENCES

Barker, R., & Gump, P. (1964). *Big school, small school: High school size and student behavior.* Stanford, CA: Stanford University Press.
Baron, R. M., & Graziano, W. G. (1991). *Social psychology.* Chicago: Holt, Rinehart & Winston.
Baumrind, D. (1971). Current patterns of parental authority. *Developmental Psychology Monograph, 4* (1, Pt. 2).
Blos, P. (1965). The initial stage of male adolescence. *The Psychoanalytic Study of the Child, 20,* 145–164.
Blyth, D. A., Simmons, R. G., & Carlton-Ford, S. (1983). The adjustment of early adolescents to school transitions. *Journal of Early Adolescence, 3,* 105–120.
Brookover, W., Beady, C., Flood, P., Schweitzer, J., & Wisenbaker, J. (1979). *School social systems and student achievement: Schools can make a difference.* New York: Praeger.

83

Brophy, J. E., & Evertson, C. M. (1976). *Learning from teaching: A developmental perspective*. Boston: Allyn & Bacon.

Bryk, A. S., Lee, V. E., & Smith, J. B. (1990). High school organization and its effects on teachers and students: An interpretative summary of the research. In W. H. Clune & J. F. Witte (Eds.), *Choice and control in American education* (Vol. 1, pp. 135–226). Philadelphia: Falmer Press.

Buchanan, C. M., Eccles, J. S., & Becker, J. B. (1992). Are adolescents the victims of raging hormones? Evidence for the activational effects of hormones on moods and behavior at adolescence. *Psychological Bulletin, 111,* 62–107.

Carnegie Council on Adolescent Development. (1989). *Turning points: Preparing American youth for the 21st century.* New York: Carnegie Corporation.

Collins, W. A. (1990). Parent–child relationships in the transition to adolescence: Continuity and change in interaction, affect, and cognition. In R. Montemayor, G. Adams, & T. Gullotta (Eds.), *Advances in adolescent development: Vol. 2. From childhood to adolescence: A transitional period?* (pp. 85–106). Newbury Park, CA: Sage.

Damon, W., & Hart, D. (1982). The development of self-understanding from infancy through adolescence. *Child Development, 53,* 841–864.

deCharms, R. (1980). The origins of competence and achievement motivation in personal causation. In L. J. Fyans, Jr. (Ed.), *Achievement motivation: Recent trends in theory and research* (pp. 22–23). New York: Plenum Press.

Deci, E. L., & Ryan, R. M. (1985). *Intrinsic motivation and self determination in human behavior.* New York: Plenum Press.

Deci, E. L., & Ryan, R. M. (1987). The support of autonomy and the control of behavior. *Journal of Personality and Social Psychology, 53,* 1024–1037.

Dornbusch, S. M., Carlsmith, J. M., Bushwall, S. J., Ritter, P. L., Leiderman, H., Hastorf, A. H., & Gross, R. T. (1985). Single parents, extended households, and the control of adolescents. *Child Development, 56,* 326–241.

Dryfoos, J. G. (1990). *Adolescents at risk: Prevalence and prevention.* London: Oxford University Press.

Eccles, J. S., McCarthy, K. A., Lord, S. E., Harold, R., Wigfield, A., & Aberbach, A. (1990, April). *The relationship of family factors to self-esteem and teacher-rated adjustment following the transition to junior high school environment.* Paper presented at the meeting of the Society for Research on Adolescence, Atlanta, GA.

Eccles, J. S., & Midgley, C. (1989). Stage/environment fit: Developmentally appropriate classrooms for early adolescents. In R. E. Ames & C. Ames (Eds.), *Research on motivation in education* (Vol. 3, pp. 139–186). San Diego, CA: Academic Press.

Eccles, J., Midgley, C., & Adler, T. (1984). Grade-related changes in the school environment: Effects on achievement motivation. In J. G. Nicholls (Ed.), *The development of achievement motivation* (pp. 283–331). Greenwich, CT: JAI Press.

Eccles, J., & Wigfield, A. (1985). Teacher expectations and student motivation. In J. Dusek (Ed.), *Teacher expectancies* (pp. 185–217). Hillsdale, NJ: Erlbaum.

Epstein, J. L., & McPartland, J. M. (1976). The concept and measurement of the quality of school life. *American Educational Research Journal, 13,* 15–30.

Epstein, J. L., & McPartland, J. M. (1977). *The Quality of School Life Scale and administrative and technical manual.* Boston: Houghton Mifflin.

Feldlaufer, H., Midgley, C., & Eccles, J. S. (1988). Student, teacher, and observer perceptions of the classroom environment before and after the transition to junior high school. *Journal of Early Adolescence, 8,* 133–156.

Finger, J. A., & Silverman, M. (1966). Changes in academic performance in the junior high school. *Personnel and Guidance Journal, 45,* 157–164.

Flanagan, C. (1985, April). *The relationship of family environments in early adolescence and intrinsic motivation in the classroom.* Paper presented at the meeting of the American Educational Research Association, Chicago.

Flanagan, C. (1986, April). *Early adolescent needs and family decision-making environments: A study of person–environment fit.* Paper pre-

sented at the meeting of the American Educational Research Association, San Francisco.

Flanagan, C. (1989, April). *Adolescents' autonomy at home: Effects on self-consciousness and intrinsic motivation at school.* Paper presented at the meeting of the American Educational Research Association, Montreal, Quebec, Canada.

Fraser, B. J., & Fisher, D. L. (1982). Predicting students' outcomes from their perceptions of classroom psychosocial environment. *American Educational Research Journal, 19,* 498–518.

Fuligni, A. J., & Eccles, J. S. (1990). *Early adolescent peer orientation and parent–child relationships.* Unpublished manuscript, Institute for Social Research, University of Michigan, Ann Arbor.

Harter, S. (1981). A new self-report scale of intrinsic versus extrinsic orientation in the classroom: Motivational and informational components. *Developmental Psychology, 17,* 300–312.

Harter, S. (1982). The Perceived Competence Scale for Children. *Child Development, 53,* 87–97.

Hauser, S., Powers, S. I., & Noam, G. G. (1991). *Adolescents and their families.* New York: Free Press.

Higgins, E. T., & Parsons, J. E. (1983). Social cognition and the social life of the child: Stages as subcultures. In E. T. Higgins, D. W. Ruble, & W. W. Hartup (Eds.), *Social cognition and social behavior: Developmental issues* (pp. 15–62). Cambridge, England: Cambridge University Press.

Hill, K. T. (1980). Motivation, evaluation, and educational test policy. In L. J. Fyans (Ed.), *Achievement motivation: Recent trends in theory and research* (pp. 34–95). New York: Plenum Press.

Hill, K. T. (1988). Adapting to menarche: Familial control and conflict. In M. Gunnar & W. A. Collins (Eds.), *Minnesota symposia on child development* (Vol. 21, pp. 43–77). Hillsdale, NJ: Erlbaum.

Hunt, D. E. (1975). Person–environment interaction: A challenge found wanting before it was tried. *Review of Educational Research, 45,* 209–230.

Kavrell, S. M., & Petersen, A. C. (1984). Patterns of achievement in early adolescence. In M. L. Maehr (Ed.), *Advances in motivation and achievement* (pp. 1–35). Greenwich, CT: JAI Press.

Laupa, M., & Turiel, E. (1986). Children's conceptions of adult and peer authority. *Child Development, 57,* 405–412.

Lee, P., Statuto, C., & Kedar-Voivodas, G. (1983). Elementary school children's perceptions of their actual and ideal school experience: A developmental study. *Journal of Educational Psychology, 75,* 838–847.

Lewin, K. (1935). *A dynamic theory of personality.* New York: McGraw-Hill.

Lipsitz, J. (1981). Educating the early adolescent: Why four model schools are effective in reaching a difficult age group. *American Education, 17,* 13–17.

Mac Iver, D., & Reuman, D. A. (1988, April). *Decision-making in the classroom and early adolescents' valuing of mathematics.* Paper presented at the annual meeting of the American Educational Research Association, New Orleans, LA.

Midgley, C., & Feldlaufer, H. (1987). Students' and teachers' decision-making before and after the transition to junior high school. *Journal of Early Adolescence, 7,* 225–241.

Midgley, C., Feldlaufer, H., & Eccles, J. S. (1988). The transition to junior high school: Beliefs of pre- and post-transition teachers. *Journal of Youth and Adolescence, 17,* 543–562.

Midgley, C., Feldlaufer, H., & Eccles, J. S. (1989a). Student/teacher relations and attitudes toward mathematics before and after the transition to junior high school. *Child Development, 60,* 375–395.

Midgley, C., Feldlaufer, H., & Eccles, J. S. (1989b). Change in teacher efficacy and student self- and task-related beliefs during the transition to junior high school. *Journal of Educational Psychology, 81,* 247–258.

Miller, C. L. (1986, April). *Puberty and person–environment fit in the classroom.* Paper presented at the meeting of the American Educational Research Association, San Francisco.

Miller, C. L., Eccles, J. S., Flanagan, C., Midgley, C., Feldlaufer, H., & Harold, R. D. (1990). Parents' and teachers' beliefs about adolescents: Effects of sex and experience. *Journal of Youth and Adolescence, 19,* 363–394.

Miller, C. L., & Taylor, R. (1986, March). *Pubertal development, self-concept, and behavior: The role of family decision-making practices.* Paper presented at meeting of the Society for Research on Adolescence, Madison, WI.

Mitman, A. L., Mergendoller, J. R., Packer, M. J., & Marchman, V. A. (1984). *Scientific literacy in seventh-grade life science: A study of instructional process, task completion, student perceptions and learning outcomes: Final report.* San Francisco: Far West Laboratory.

Montemayor, R. (1983). Parents and adolescents in conflict: All families some of the time and some families most of the time. *Journal of Early Adolescence, 3,* 83–103.

Montemayor, R. (1986). Family variation in parent–adolescent storm and stress. *Journal of Adolescent Research, 1,* 15–31.

Moos, R. H. (1979). *Evaluating educational environments.* San Francisco: Jossey-Bass.

Nicholls, J. G. (1980, June). *Striving to develop and demonstrate ability: An intentional theory of achievement motivation.* Paper presented at Conference on Attributional Approaches to Human Motivation, Center for Interdisciplinary Studies, University of Bielefeld, Bielefeld, Germany.

Oakes, J. (1981). *Tracking policies and practices: School by school summaries. A study of schooling* (Tech. Rep. No. 25), Los Angeles: University of California Graduate School of Education.

Office of Educational Research and Improvement. (1988). *Youth indicators 1988.* Washington, DC: U.S. Government Printing Office.

Paikoff, R. L., & Brooks-Gunn, J. (1991). Do parent–child relationships change during puberty? *Psychological Bulletin, 110,* 47–66.

Parsons, J. E., & Ruble, D. N. (1977). The development of achievement-related expectancies. *Child Development, 48,* 1975–1979.

Rholes, W. S., Blackwell, J., Jordan, C., & Walters, C. (1980). A developmental study of learned helplessness. *Developmental Psychology, 16,* 616–624.

Rosenbaum, J. E. (1976). *Making inequality: The hidden curriculum of high school tracking.* New York: Wiley.

Rosenholtz, S. J., & Simpson, C. (1984). The formation of ability conceptions: Developmental trend or social construction? *Review of Educational Research, 54,* 301–325.

Rounds, T. S., & Osaki, S. Y. (1982). *The social organization of classrooms: An analysis of sixth- and seventh-grade activity structures* (Report No. EPSSP-82-5). San Francisco: Far West Laboratory.

Ryan, R. M., & Lynch, J. H. (1989). Emotional autonomy versus detachment: Revisiting the vicissitudes of adolescence and young adulthood. *Child Development, 60,* 340–356.

Selman, R. L. (1980). *The growth of interpersonal understanding: Developmental and clinical analyses.* San Diego, CA: Academic Press.

Simmons, R. G., & Blyth, D. A. (1987). *Moving into adolescence: The impact of pubertal change and school context.* Hawthorne, NY: Aldine de Gruyter.

Simmons, R. G., Blyth, D. A., Van Cleave, E. F., & Bush, D. (1979). Entry into early adolescence: The impact of school structure, puberty, and early dating on self-esteem. *American Sociological Review, 44,* 948–967.

Smetana, J. G. (1988a). Adolescents' and parents' conceptions of parental authority. *Child Development, 59,* 321–335.

Smetana, J. G. (1988b). Concepts of self and social convention: Adolescents' and parents' reasoning about hypothetical and actual family conflicts. In M. Gunnar & W. A. Collins (Eds.), *Development during the transition to adolescence: Minnesota symposia on child development* (Vol. 21, pp. 79–122). Hillsdale, NJ: Erlbaum.

Smetana, J. G. (1989). Adolescents' and parents' reasoning about actual family conflict. *Child Development, 60,* 1052–1067.

Steinberg, L. (1981). Transformation in family relations at puberty. *Developmental Psychology, 17,* 833–840.

Steinberg, L. (1987). The impact of puberty on family relations: Effects of pubertal status and pubertal timing. *Developmental Psychology, 23,* 451–460.

Steinberg, L. (1988). Reciprocal relations between parent–child distance and pubertal maturation. *Developmental Psychology, 24,* 122–128.

Steinberg, L. (1990). Interdependence in the family: Autonomy, conflict, and harmony in the parent–adolescent relationship. In S. S. Feldman & G. R. Elliott (Eds.), *At the threshold: The developing adolescent* (pp. 255–276). Cambridge, MA: Harvard University Press.

Tisak, M. S. (1986). Children's conception of parental authority. *Child Development, 57,* 166–176.

Trebilco, G. R., Atkinson, E. P., & Atkinson, J. M. (1977, November). *The transition of students from primary to secondary school.* Paper presented at the annual conference of the Australian Association for Research in Education, Canberra, Australia.

Trickett, E. J., & Moos, R. H. (1974). Personal correlates of contrasting environments: Student satisfactions in high school classrooms. *American Journal of Community Psychology, 2,* 1–12.

Walberg, H. J., House, E. R., & Steele, J. M. (1973). Grade level, cognition, and affect: A cross-section of classroom perceptions. *Journal of Educational Psychology, 64,* 142–146.

Ward, B. A., Mergendoller, J. R., Tikunoff, W. J., Rounds, T. S., Dadey, G. J., & Mitman, A. L. (1982). *Junior high school transition study: Executive summary.* San Francisco: Far West Laboratory.

Yee, D. K. (1986, April). *Family decision-making, classroom decision-making, and student self- and achievement-related attitudes.* Paper presented at the meeting of the American Educational Research Association, San Francisco.

Yee, D. K. (1987, April). *Participation in family decision-making: Parent and child perspectives.* Paper presented at the meeting of the Society for Research in Child Development, Baltimore, MD.

Yee, D. K., & Flanagan, C. (1985). Family environments and self-consciousness in early adolescence. *Journal of Early Adolescence, 5,* 59–68.

85

Family Ecologies of Ethnic Minority Children

Algea O. Harrison
Oakland University

Melvin N. Wilson
University of Virginia

Charles J. Pine
Sepulveda VA Medical Center and UCLA School of Medicine

Samuel Q. Chan
University Affiliated Program, Children's Hospital of Los Angeles

Raymond Buriel
Pomona College

HARRISON, ALGEA O.; WILSON, MELVIN N.; PINE, CHARLES J.; CHAN, SAMUEL Q.; and BURIEL, RAYMOND. *Family Ecologies of Ethnic Minority Children.* CHILD DEVELOPMENT, 1990, **61**, 347–362. This article discusses a proposed interconnectedness between the ecologies of ethnic minority families, adaptive strategies, socialization goals, and child behavioral outcomes. The ethnic minority groups included are African American, American Indian/Alaskan Native, Asian Pacific Americans, and Hispanics. Demographic information on population size, geographic area of concentration, and preferred identity terms is provided. It is argued that adaptive strategies, including extendedness of families and role flexibility, biculturalism, and ancestral worldview, emerge from the ecological challenges of ethnic stratification status. These adaptive strategies foster the child-rearing goals of positive orientation to the ethnic group and socialization for interdependence, which in turn enhance the developmental outcomes of cognitive flexibility and sensitivity to discontinuities among ethnic minority children.

Using an ecological framework, this article explores the relation between ecologies of ethnic minority families, adaptive strategies, socialization goals, and developmental outcomes for ethnic minority children. The article is divided into four sections: (*a*) demographic information on ethnic minority families, (*b*) a discussion of the strategies groups have used to adapt to their social status, (*c*) a presentation of socialization goals that have emerged from the adaptive strategies, and (*d*) a discussion of child outcomes. The theoretical conceptions of the ecological orientation extend beyond the behavior of individuals to encompass functional systems both within and between settings, nested structures, and a complex interaction between the developing person and the environment

(Bronfenbrenner, 1979). In short, an ecological perspective considers how the individual develops in interaction with the immediate social environment and how aspects of the larger social context affect what goes on in the individuals' immediate settings (Garbarino, 1982). Ethnic minority families in America have faced similar ecological challenges from larger social systems and have developed similar adaptive strategies.

Adaptive strategies refer to observable social behavioral cultural patterns that are interpreted as socially adaptive or maladaptive within the social nexus (DeVos, 1982). Importantly, when a strategy is effective in facilitating adaptation for a minority group, it involves some aspect of the dominant culture's

Except for the first two, authors are listed in the order of joining the project. Special thanks to Charles Nakamura, Hector Myers, Barbara Rogoff, Teresa LaFromboise, Kenyon Chan, Sue Gottschalk, and unknown reviewers for their helpful comments in the preparation of this manuscript. Requests for reprints should be sent to Algea O. Harrison, Department of Psychology, Oakland University, Rochester, MI 48309-4401.

mores and the knowledge that one is a minority at some specified level in a social hierarchy (DeVos, 1982). As members of groups learn which strategies are effective and appropriate, they also learn how best to inculcate these competencies in their children (Ogbu, 1981). The socialization goals of a people are partially derived from their cultural knowledge of their adult tasks, of essential competencies for adequate functioning, and of the methods of transmitting these competencies to succeeding generations (Ogbu, 1981). These cultural patterns are a part of the family ecologies of ethnic minority groups. Family ecology refers to important family functionings that are a reflection of the interactions between the family as a social' system and other societal institutions and systems. The family ecologies of ethnic minority children will differ somewhat from those of majority children, where compromising with minority group status is not needed. Consequently, the family ecologies of ethnic minority, when compared to majority, families have the potential of differential outcomes in the development of children. This is especially true if development is viewed as a person's evolving conception of the ecological environment, one's relation to it, as well as one's growing capacity to discover, sustain, or alter its properties (Bronfenbrenner, 1979).

The aim of this article is to explore the interconnectedness between the status of ethnic minority families, adaptive strategies, socialization goals, and child outcomes. Historically, ethnic minority children were not included in samples of subjects studied for establishing normative trends or investigating theoretical questions. Most often data on ethnic minority children came from comparative studies with a controversial deficit explanation (Harrison, Serafica, & McAdoo, 1984; McLoyd & Randolph, 1985). Currently, social scientists are aware of the methodological and conceptual shortcomings of those studies. This article offers a different conceptual perspective for considering ethnic minority families and their children.

Issues in the Study of Family Ecologies of Ethnic Minority Children

The discussion is organized around four general questions, the first of which addresses which groups of people we refer to as ethnic minorities. Minority groups are subordinate segments of their respective societies. However, "Once people perceive ethnic differences and ethnic groups compete against each other, the crucial variables in majority-minority relations is the differential power of one group relative to another" (Yetman, 1985, p. 2). Ethnocentrism, competition, and differential power are the salient ingredients for the emergence and initial stabilization of ethnic stratification. Ethnic stratification refers to a system of arrangements where some relatively fixed group membership (e.g., race, religion, or nationality) is used as one of the standards of judgment for assigning social position with its attendant differential rewards (Noel, 1985). This article focuses on groups of people in the position of minorities in America's ethnic stratification: African Americans, American Indians/Alaskan Natives, Asian Pacific Americans, and Hispanic Americans. Some of these groups are referred to as castelike minorities by Ogbu (1987, p. 258); "minorities incorporated into a society more or less involuntarily and permanently through slavery, conquest, and colonization." Each group's story is different but includes a common element of exploitable resources: (a) the enslavement of Africans and, after emancipation, their segregation and perceived inferior status based on race; (b) military conflicts over land and territory between American Indians and European Americans, and the forced removal and transfer of Indians to reservations; and (c) Asian Americans whose recent immigrants from Indochina sometimes suffer from the same subordination and exploitation endured by earlier immigrants from China, Philippines, and Japan (the latter were incarcerated during World War II); (d) Hispanics who were incorporated through conquest and displacement. In this article, we present a brief demographic summary of the current status of each of these groups.

The second question concerns the strategies these minority families use to adapt to their social environments. Historically, the selected ethnic minority groups have suffered from discrimination and racism. Yet they have formed communities, social institutions, and other organizations for adapting and adjusting to these ecological challenges. What are some of the adaptive strategies of these ethnic minority families? These adaptive strategies form the basis of the family ecologies of ethnic minorities.

The third question concerns the relation between families' adaptive strategies and socialization goals. Adults in families have formed beliefs about what it means to be a member of that ethnic group and what behaviors and attitudes are reflective of adaptations to that status (DeVos, 1982; Ogbu, 1981). These beliefs shape the socialization goals and techniques of ethnic minority families. What socialization goals of ethnic minority families derive from their adaptive strategies?

The final question concerns whether there are developmental patterns among ethnic minority children as a function of their family ecologies. In other words, are there any empirically based trends or patterns among ethnic minority children that can be attributed directly or indirectly to distinct cultural behavioral patterns found among their families? The review will be limited to literature in the cognitive area, where research on ethnic minority children is concentrated. However, there are other developmental domains where empirical studies have been completed but are not as expansive or focused on the relation between family ecologies and child outcomes (e.g., Gibbs, Huang, & Associates, 1989; Irvine & Berry, 1986; McShane, 1988; Powell, Morales, Romero, & Yamamoto, 1983; Rogoff, Gauvain, & Ellis, 1984; Spindler & Spindler, 1987). Shortcomings and the lack of relevant information are highlighted and directions for future research are discussed.

Ethnic Minorities

The ecological challenges facing ethnic minorities are not sudden temporary economic calamities, but derive from a long history of oppression and discrimination. Currently it is reported that one-third of the nation, constituting mainly ethnic minorities, are afflicted by the ills of poverty and discrimination (Report on Minorities in Higher Education, 1988). On all of the major social indicators (e.g., employment, housing, health, etc.) of individual and social well-being, gaps persist—and in some instances are widening—between members of minority groups and the majority population (U.S. Department of Commerce Series, 1988). Nevertheless, when confronted with these challenges, ethnic minority families and communities still strive toward goals and accomplishments as they have done historically. Educational achievement, economic development in the community, political power, affordable housing, and maintaining cultural and religious traditions are some of the goals of these groups (U.S. Department of Commerce Series, 1988).

Demographic Status

African Americans, 96% of whom are descendants of slaves, are currently the largest ethnic minority group in the United States (Reed, 1982). Only recently has the term

"African American" been preferred by some persons in the group rather than the term "black." American Indians are the smallest ethnic minority group, although there are more than 500 tribes or nations in the United States (LaFromboise, 1988). Typically, American Indians prefer their tribal designation to the term American Indian (Burgess, 1980). Asian Pacific Americans comprise the fastest-growing population group in the United States (Gardner, Robey, & Smith, 1985). This dramatically accelerated growth is attributable to the continuing influx of immigrants and refugees (for a more detailed discussion of Asian American demographics, see Bouvier & Agresta, in press; Gardner et al., 1985; National Indochinese Clearinghouse, 1980; Pan Asian Parent Education Project, 1982; Peterson & Yamamoto, 1980; Powell et al., 1983). Persons in this group prefer ethnic terms that identify their country of origin. Hispanics are projected to become the largest minority group by the turn of the century. The Hispanic population consists primarily of *mestizo* peoples born of the Spanish conquest of the Americas who intermixed with populations indigenous to the geographic areas. Persons in this group also prefer ethnic terms that identify their country of origin, and when it is necessary to refer to themselves collectively, they prefer the terms Latino or *la Raza* (Buriel, 1987). More detailed demographics of the groups are presented in Table 1.

Currently, a majority of ethnic minority families live in urban areas. American Indians were the exception for urban residence patterns, residing mainly in rural areas and on reservations. Demographic trends, however, suggest an increase in the number of American Indians migrating to large metropolitan areas (Snipp & Sandefur, 1988). In 1980, 55% of American Indians resided in urban locations. Also, these ethnic minority families are younger and have higher birthrates in comparison to majority families.

Adaptive Strategies

Ethnic minority status has potent meaning for persons in the group because of the difficulties these groups have experienced in attempting to coexist with the European American culture. Examples are prevalent in history, literature, and psychology of persons with political and social power and members of the intelligentsia creating negative stereotypes for members of other groups (Padilla & O'Grady, 1987). The groups usually targeted for negative attributions and stereotypes are those in economically subservient positions

TABLE 1

TOTAL NUMBER, COMPOSITION OF SUBGROUPS, AND GEOGRAPHIC LOCATION OF
ETHNIC MINORITY GROUPS

Ethnic Group	Total Number	Composition of Subgroups	Geographic Concentration
African-American	28.2 million	African-Caribbean, recent immigrants from Africa	South, Northeast
American Indian/ Alaskan Native	1.5 million/ 64,103	Largest tribes: Cherokee, Navajo, Sioux, Chippewa/ Aleuts, Eskimos	Northwest, West
Asian Pacific Americans	10.0 million	Chinese, Japanese, Korean, Vietnamese, Cambodian, Thai, Filipino, Laotian, Lao-Hmong, Burmese, Samoan, Guamanian	West, Northeast
Hispanic	18.8 million	Mexican, Puerto Rican, Cuban, Central and South Americans	Southwest, Midwest, Northeast, Florida, and California

within the society, as well as groups outside the society that are perceived as political, military, and economic threats. These experiences have influenced the individual and group beliefs about what it means to be a member of an ethnic minority group. There is agreement among psychologists that beliefs form an important psychological guide to action (Sigel, 1985); therefore, it is assumed that these beliefs have been a factor in shaping the strategies that members of low-status groups develop.

Adaptive strategies are proposed cultural patterns that promote the survival and well-being of the community, families, and individual members of the group. The term "adaptive strategies" as used refers to observable social behavior, not to personality dynamics (DeVos, 1982). A review of the literature describing the values, attitudes, and behaviors of ethnic minority families highlights the adaptive strategies these groups have in common. Although there are differences in the salience of a strategy, the similarities across family ecologies are striking. Family extendedness and role flexibility, biculturalism, and ancestral worldviews are all part of the life-styles of these groups. Al-

though ethnic minority groups share a commonality in minority status and ethnic stratification, there have been differences in the impact of ecological challenges from the majority population on these groups. Some of the factors that have mediated the experiences of these different groups are motives for coming to America (Suzuki, 1980), time of immigration (Serafica, in press), educational opportunities (Olmedo, 1981), attitude toward educational establishment (Ogbu, 1981), voluntarily or involuntarily coming to America (Harding, 1980), and the American caste system (Ogbu, 1985). Nevertheless, limited access to societal resources has forged a similarity among ethnic minority families. All have had to develop ways of gaining access to European American cultural and social institutions (e.g., educational, medical, political, legal) for services, employment, power, etc.

Family Extendedness and Role Flexibility
The pattern of establishing extended families is an adaptive strategy common to ethnic minority peoples. Although there are traditional and nontraditional types of families in ethnic minority communities, the extended family form is frequently mentioned by social scientists as a typical family struc-

ture in ethnic minority communities (Mindel & Habenstein, 1981). For example, Langston (1980) reported that 85% of her African American elderly sample shared their residence with someone who was either a spouse, an adult child, or a grandchild. Nationally, panel and census data analyses (Beck & Beck, 1989; Sweet, 1977) have indicated that 53% of the African American elderly population shared a residence with a relative, as compared to 40% of the white elderly population. In fact, about 10 percent of African American children below the age of 18 lived with their grandparents and 25 percent of young African American adults between the ages of 18–26 lived with their parents (Beck & Beck, 1984, 1989; Sweet, 1977). Three times as many African American children under age 18 lived with their grandparents than white children, whereas the proportion of African American and white young adults living with parents was about equal (Soldo & Lauriat, 1976; U.S. Bureau of the Census, 1989).

The extended family is a problem-solving and stress-coping system that addresses, adapts, and commits available family resources to normal and nonnormal transitional and crisis situations (Wilson, 1989). Family resources involve family members' ability to contribute tangible help, such as material support, income, childcare, and household maintenance assistance, and nontangible help, such as expressive interaction, emotional support, counseling, instruction, and social regulation (Wilson, 1986, 1989). Through patterns of kin contact and interactions that are proximal, available, frequent, and functional (Gibson, 1972), a family provides its members with a sense of group and personal identities, behavioral rules, roles and responsibilities, and emotional affiliations and attachments (Goode, 1964; Schneider, 1968, 1980). Indeed, extended family refers to family composition, structure, and interaction that go beyond the nuclear family unit to include consanguine, affinal, and fictive relationships (Foster, 1984; Wilson, 1986). Wilson (1986, 1989) asserts that in the African American family, experiencing nonnormal changes and events is a primary reason for the formation of extended family support networks. A common stressful situation in the African American community is the lack of adequate adult resources in single-parent family units. The formation occurs when one family unit absorbs another one. Once formed, the extended family occupies most of the family life span. Martin and Martin (1978) describe the characteristics of

extended families as found among African Americans as interdependent, bilateral, and multigenerational; headed by a dominant family figure; having a family-based household; reaching across geographical boundaries; and processing a built-in mutual aid system providing material aid and moral support. Historically, the African American extended family system supports a familial tradition that existed throughout the periods of slavery, emancipation, and mass rural southern exodus (Agesti, 1978; Aoyagi, 1978; Flanagan, 1978; Fogel & Engelman, 1974; Genovese, 1976; Gutman, 1976; Martin & Martin, 1978; Meachan, 1983; Nobles, 1978).

Similarly, American Indian families may be characterized as a collective, cooperative social network that extends from the mother and father union to the extended family and ultimately to the community and tribe (Burgess, 1980). Although such a family structure is not as prevalent as it once was (Ryan, 1981), it has not disappeared (Burgess, 1980; LaFromboise, 1988; Medicine, 1981), and it has endured many changes brought about by influences of the European-American culture. The typical family has several forms, but the basic social unit consisted of the man, woman, and their children and is embedded in the community, multigenerational, collateral, and comprised sibling groupings of different types. Generally, a strong extended family system characterizes many urban and rural contemporary American Indian families (Goodluck & Eckstein, 1978; Medicine, 1981; Red Horse, 1983). American Indian patterns of extended family include several households representing significant relatives along both vertical and horizontal lines, therefore assuming village-type characteristics (Light & Martin, 1986; Red Horse, 1983).

In the same manner, among Asian Pacific American families, selected practices have persisted throughout the process of increasing acculturation in successive generations and are further maintained by recent immigrants (Chan, 1986). The traditional Asian Pacific family is characterized by well-defined, unilaterally organized, and highly interdependent roles within a cohesive patriarchal vertical structure (Serafica, in press). Prescribed roles and relationships emphasize subordination and interdependence. Familial and social behaviors are thus governed by esteem for hierarchical roles and relationships and the virtue of filial piety (Tseng, 1973).

Likewise, familism among Hispanics involves strong feelings of identification, loyalty, and solidarity with the parents and the extended family, and behaviors associated with these feelings, such as frequent contact and reciprocity among members of the same family (Marin, 1986; Ramirez & Castaneda, 1974; Sabogal, Marin, Otero-Sabogal, Marin, & Perez-Stable, 1987). Much like the Asian Pacific family, the Hispanic family is characterized by strong familism. In addition, the Hispanic extended family is similar to the African American family in that it is bilaterally organized and includes nonrelative members (e.g., compadres).

It is clear from empirical writings and discussions that the extended family system is a value and ideal among ethnic minorities. Do demographic changes within ethnic minority groups alter the structure and importance of family extendedness to family members? McAdoo's (1978) investigations found that the extended family structure was still prevalent among upwardly mobile African American families, while community activists from the same community noted that its effectiveness was declining among low socioeconomic status families because of the tremendous burdens of contemporary social problems (Height, 1985). Further empirical studies are needed to delineate when, how, and under what conditions extended families are adaptive or serve as a source of conflict. For example, involvement in extended families increases economic resources among low-income families but reduces consumable income among middle- and working-class families. Stack (1981) found that extended family relationships often produced conflictual feelings among young African American females. Young African American females were often torn between their commitment and loyalties to the extended family and their feelings and commitments to their boyfriends. Similar findings were noted by Dressler (1985) in his study of families in a southern community. Extended kin support appeared to be less effective in reducing the risk of depression among young women compared to young men. Opposite-sex differences were found by Brown and Gary (1987) in their sample of urban northern African American families. Young females were provided more benefits from the extended family in comparison to young males. Clearly more systematic studies are needed on how this adaptive strategy functions in modern life for all ethnic minority groups.

In addition, ethnic minority families have used social role flexibility as a coping mechanism out of historic necessity (Munoz &

Endo, 1982). Familial social roles can be regarded as flexible in definition, responsibility, and performance. Parenting of younger siblings by older siblings, sharing of the breadwinner role among adults, and alternative family arrangements have been found to be more prevalent in ethnic minority communities than in majority communities (Allen, 1978; Allen & Stukes, 1982).

Biculturalism

A bicultural orientation is not new or unique to ethnic minority groups. Historically, America's formal and informal policies toward non-English-speaking immigrants were to Americanize people as fast as possible (Wagner, 1981). Most immigrant groups go through the process of acculturation, a cultural change that is initiated by the conjunction of two or more autonomous cultural systems (Bing, 1980). For ethnic minorities in America this has presented a problem because of the devaluing of their ethnic culture by the majority culture. Further, the cultures of African Americans and American Indians have been presented frequently from the European perspective rather than from the writings of persons from the respective ethnic group dominating the prevailing perspectives. One of the ways some ethnic minorities have adapted to the conflictual situation is a bicultural orientation to the acculturation process. (See McShane [1983] or McShane & Berry [1986] for an expanded discussion of alternative pathways [e.g., integration, assimilation, rejection, or marginality].)

Szopocznik and Kurtines (1980) proposed that if the cultural context within which acculturation takes place is bicultural, then acculturation will tend to take place along two dimensions. A linear process of accommodating to the host culture is the first dimension, and the second dimension is a complex process of relinquishing or retaining characteristics of the culture of origin. The person learns to function optimally in more than one cultural context and to switch repertoires of behavior appropriately and adaptively as called for by the situation (Laosa, 1977). Although all ethnic groups have expressed biculturalism as an important adaptive strategy (Harrison et al., 1984), a majority of the empirical investigations of the process have studied Hispanic Americans.

Nonetheless, African Americans and American Indians have a set of beliefs and behaviors that have their origins in their ancestral cultures (Nobles, 1978, 1988; Red Horse, 1983). These cultures are distinct from

European American culture (Myers, 1982) as a result of the desire to continue the values and traditions of previous generations, and the limited access to the larger society and its social institutions. Yet there are no extensive systematic investigations of biculturalism among these two groups.

Shon and Ja (1983) describe two interrelated levels of adaptive cultural transaction as part of Asian Pacific immigrants' experiences. At the first level of physical or material transition, immigrants must consistently struggle to overcome language barriers and to achieve economic security and educational and occupational success. The second level of cultural transition involves cognitive and affective changes in which the family attempts psychologically to incorporate various features of their new environment. One of several empirical questions from this process is whether these families continue to maintain a bicultural orientation or select other pathways of adaptation.

Sabogal et al. (1987) examined the effects of acculturation on three attitudinal components of Hispanic familism: (1) familiar obligations, (2) perceived support from family, and (3) family as referents. They found that attitudes concerning familial obligations and family as referents diminished with increasing levels of acculturation (as measured by language preference and usage), but that perception of family support remained constant. The selective effect of acculturation on familism is further supported by the research of Reuschenberg and Buriel (1988), who used the Family Environment Scale (FES) (Moos, Insel, & Humphrey, 1974) to study Mexican American families who were either short- or long-term arrivals from Mexico or U.S. born. The FES is primarily a behavioral rather than attitudinal scale and can be scored to distinguish between interactions involving only family members and those involving family members and outside social systems. Reuschenberg and Buriel (1988) found that acculturation was related to differences in families' interaction patterns with outside social agencies, but not to internal family system variables. In other words, acculturation may change the way individual family members interact and present themselves to outside agents, but internal family dynamics remain mostly intact. This finding suggests the dual existence of public and private domains of family life among Hispanic Americans. Hispanics often achieve a bicultural adaptation that uniquely combines aspects of European American and Hispanic cultures, leading to

behaviors that are not entirely characteristic of either culture (Buriel, 1987). According to Ramirez (1983), the diversity inherent in Hispanics' heritage has provided this group with a worldview that values integration and synthesis of new cultural experiences rather than complete assimilation.

Biculturalism has been the topic of edited books and reviews of empirical studies. The effects of biculturalism have been investigated from the conceptual frameworks of bilingualism and the need for changes in the delivery of mental health services to ethnic minority groups (e.g., Hakuta & Garcia, 1989; Penalosa, 1980; Powell et al., 1983; Ramirez, 1986; Spindler & Spindler, 1987; Serafica et al., in press; Willig, 1985; Wolfson & Manes, 1985). What is needed for more in-depth understanding of biculturalism is more information on the psychological mechanisms involved and the resulting positive or negative effects for individuals as well as the group.

Ancestral Worldviews

American culture is dominated by the belief in individualism, that is, the notion that "each of us is an entity separate from every other and from the group and as such is endowed with natural rights" (Spence, 1985, p. 1288). One of the ways the concept of individualism is incorporated into American cultural heritage is through the lauding of the protestant work ethic as the pathway to success for individuals (Sampson, 1985). The social order of the majority culture is guided by an acceptance of individualism, which is reflected in encouragement and recognition of individual achievements and accomplishments, especially the attainment of material property (Spence, 1985). Given the status of ethnic minorities, generally individualism has not been their pathway to the American Dream. Further, individualism is incompatible with the ancestral worldviews of ethnic minorities.

The indigenous psychology of ethnic minority cultures differs from the majority culture in how interwoven the interest and well-being of the self is with the ethnic group to which one belongs. Self-contained individualism is an indigenous psychology of the majority culture (Heela & Lock, 1981; Nobles, 1978; Ramirez, 1983; Sampson, 1988). In contrast, the degree of fluidity of boundaries between self- and non-self-interests among ethnic minorities is based on a more inclusive conception of the person or self, that is, persons are attached to families, households, communities, and the group (Heela & Lock, 1981; Sampson, 1988). Thus, when confronted in American society with racism, discrimination, occupational barriers, and negative portrayals of the ethnic group, ethnic minorities have used their ancestral worldviews as an adaptive strategy for pathways to achievement and sense of personal worth.

The salience of ancestral worldviews as reflected in spirituality/religiosity and philosophical orientations in contemporary ethnic minority communities is well documented (Garbarino, 1976; Gill, 1982a; Medicine, 1980; Ramirez & Castaneda, 1974; Shon & Ja, 1983; Taylor, 1988; Taylor, Thornton, & Chatters, 1988; Thornton & Taylor, 1988). The term "religiosity" is used in the scholarly orientation to refer to images, actions, and symbols that define the extent and character of the world for the people and provide the cosmic framework for which their lives find meaning, purpose, and fulfillment (Gill, 1982b).

Sudarkasa (1988) and Nobles (1988) have noted that African Americans possess a worldview that is akin to an African belief in collectivism rather than a European belief in individualism. However, research has not been conducted on these concepts among African Americans, and it is not known whether such orientations affect family functioning. On the other hand, research has documented the persistence of some African cultural patterns among contemporary African American families for both rural and urban areas (Sudarkasa, 1988). For example, emphasis on consanguinity, kinship that is biologically based, is a salient feature of African and African American family organization. Researchers have noted the role of religion in enhancing life satisfaction among a national sample of African Americans (e.g., Taylor, 1988).

In American Indian traditions, all aspects of life take on religious significance, and religion and culture are intimately connected (Medicine, 1981; Michaelsen, 1983). American Indians do not share a single dominant religion (Gill, 1982b; Hultkrantz, 1981; Hurdy, 1970), yet a common practice across a variety of American Indian tribal cultures is the quest for a guardian spirit (Garbarino, 1976; Hamer, 1980; Lewis, 1981). The attaining of a guardian spirit is seen as a confidence builder, which at the very least would result in the capability to manage most of life's stresses and demands.

Traditional cultural orientations and values among many Asian Pacific American subgroups are deeply rooted in the doctrines and philosophies of Buddhism, Confucianism,

and Taoism; each offers a worldview and prescription for living that emphasizes selected virtues and adherence to codes of behavior. Confucian thought, important to Asian/Pacific families, is guided by a philosophical orientation wherein *harmony* is the core of existence, and persons' obligation is to sustain harmony within the social order (Chan, 1986; Sampson, 1988; Sue & Sue, 1987). The Hispanic value system of familism is supported and reinforced by the pervasive religious practices in the community. For example, the image of the Virge de Guadalupe (the *Mestizo* equivalent of the Virgin Mary) is both a religious and an unofficial national symbol of *la Raza* (Ramirez & Castaneda, 1974).

In short, the worldviews of ethnic minorities have emphasized collectivism or loyalty to the group in some form. One of the interesting empirical questions needing investigation is how prevalent is the regard for collectivism as compared to individualism among ethnic minorities groups. Do attitudes about collectivism predict behavior? What are the contributing factors to intra- and intergroup differences on these dimensions?

Socialization Goals

Adaptive responses to ecological challenges have shaped the family ecologies of ethnic minorities and affected the socialization of children. Socialization refers to the processes by which individuals become distinctive and actively functioning members of the society in which they live (Elkin & Handel, 1984; Zigler, Lamb, & Child, 1982). The family ecologies of ethnic minority children differ from majority children's and partially provide the basis for variations in the context of socialization. The mechanisms of transmittal of the culture are the same for both ethnic minority and majority children (e.g., reinforcement, modeling, identification, etc.). Yet ethnicity is potent in the socialization process of families since it includes group patterns of values, social customs, perceptions, behavioral roles, language usage, and rules of social interactions that group members share in both obvious and subtle ways (Phinney & Rotheram, 1987).

Attribution theory (Dix & Grusec, 1985), distancing theory (which reflects the theories of Piaget, Kelley, & Weiner [Johnson & Martin, 1985; McGillicuddy-DeLisi, 1985]), and social learning theories have provided the conceptual underpinning for the assumption that parental beliefs are important determinants in the socialization process. In addition, other theoretical orientations have expanded beyond the consideration of parental beliefs and behaviors to include the cultural context in which those processes occur (Bronfenbrenner, 1979; Rogoff, 1982). Ogbu's cultural-ecological model of child rearing is a part of this trend and offers a viable conceptual framework for understanding the relation between the strategies ethnic minorities have adopted to meet the group's ecological challenges and the selection of certain socialization goals.

Ogbu (1981) proposes that child rearing in the family and similar micro settings during the periods of infancy, childhood, and adolescence is geared toward the development of instrumental competence. Instrumental competence refers to the ability to perform culturally specific tasks that are required for adult economic, political, and social roles. Indeed, Ogbu (1981, p. 417) notes, "child categories and instrumental competencies resulting from child-rearing techniques eventually develop into adaptive adult categories and instrumental competencies in the population." In the sections that follow, we identify some of the socialization goals espoused by ethnic minority families. We argue that these goals emerge from the adaptive strategies of ethnic minority families identified earlier. The child-rearing goals so identified and described are positive orientation toward ethnic group and socialization for interdependence.

Positive Orientation toward Ethnic Groups
One goal of the socialization practices among ethnic minority families is to foster a positive orientation among children toward their ethnic group as a means of promoting biculturalism and acceptance of the orientations of the ancestral worldview. Children are taught to view their role within the family and society in terms of relationships and obligations to the family (Chan, 1986; Tseng, 1973). In one of the few empirical studies investigating family socialization of ethnic attitudes, Bowman and Howard (1985) offer insightful information regarding the effect on children of parents actively socializing them regarding the consequences of their ethnicity in the larger society. This study of a national sample of African American three-generational families indicated that the manner in which parents oriented their children toward racial barriers was a significant element in children's motivation, achievement, and prospects for upward mobility. Parents of successful children emphasized ethnic pride, self-development, awareness of racial barriers, and egalitarianism in their socialization practices.

A large percentage of ethnic minority children are growing up in homes where English is not the dominant language and where American culture does not govern most aspects of family life, especially child rearing (Gutierrez, Sameroff, & Karrer, 1988). These children are oriented toward the family group as a source of information regarding their ethnic identity and culture. There is a body of literature on socialization of ethnic identification and the social-behavioral correlates of ethnic identity (e.g., Phinney & Rotheram, 1987).

Socialization for Interdependence
Ethnic minority families typically stress interdependence as a socialization goal for children as a logical accompaniment to emphasis on extended families and the ancestral worldview of collectivism. Parents tend to reinforce personality traits that are consistent with this goal. Given ecological challenges for achievement and accomplishment in American society, the pathway for individual and group members of ethnic minorities has been generally through collective actions that open opportunities for individual achievement. Thus socializing children toward interdependence with the group fosters the continuation of that pathway.

Generally, ethnic minority children are taught to think, feel, and act in ways that involve the development of a cooperative view of life, rather than one of a singularly competitive nature (Chan, 1986; Green, Sack, & Pambrum, 1981). Individuals are instructed to view themselves as an integral part of the totality of their family and the larger social structure and experience a social/psychological dependence on others. Cooperation, obligation, sharing, and reciprocity are essential elements of social interaction (Delgado-Gaitan, 1987; Serafica, in press). These values sharply contrast with Western ideals of competition, autonomy, and self-reliance (Sampson, 1988).

Sims (1978, 1979), in an empirical study concerned with sharing among African American children, found that children were more willing to share their toys and possessions when the request was made in the context of group reference. Establishing an ethnic minority reference facilitated more personal concern on the part of children and thus heightened children's motivation to share. Also, sharing was identified as an appropriate behavior of an ethnic group member. Children were probably affected by the expected group norm that sharing and cooperation were to be done with other group members. Although the number of studies on the topic is limited, there is evidence that American Indian and Hispanic American children are more cooperative and conciliatory in resolving potential interpersonal conflicts than are majority children (Delgado-Gaitan, 1987; Kagan & Madsen, 1971; Knight & Kagan, 1977; Osborne, 1985). There are no comparable studies for Asian American children.

Cognitive Developmental Outcomes

How do socialization goals stemming from adaptive strategies of ethnic minority families influence children's cognitive development? The socialization process is complex, and it is difficult to ascribe developmental outcomes to specific factors. The research evidence for these and similar questions is diffuse, sparse, uneven across ethnic minority groups, and lacking for some (McShane, 1988), yet some insights can be obtained from the general literature on ethnic minority children and families. Caution should be exercised in generalizing from group data to individuals within any single ethnic minority group (Laosa, 1977). Further, within-group differences are an important source of variance when studying developmental outcomes on child behavioral measures. Investigators have examined the variables of social class (Carter, 1983; DeVos, 1973; Hakuta, 1987; Shon & Ja, 1983), identification with ethnic culture (Buriel, 1984; McShane, 1983), generation status (Buriel, Calzada, & Vasques, 1982), geographic origin (Shon & Ja, 1983), father absence (Powell et al., 1983; Scott-Jones, 1987), gender (Hare & Castenell, 1985), home environment (Slaughter & Epps, 1987), and geographical habitats (McShane & Berry, 1986) as examples of important determinants of intragroup heterogeneity.

Theories abound explaining the determinants, course, and trends of cognitive development. Currently, the concepts of Vygotsky (1978) are receiving increased attention as a framework for investigating the importance of culture to cognitive development. Vygotsky viewed children as active participants who attempted to master and competently function in the world around them. One of the ways they mastered their world was through the use of auxiliary stimuli. Auxiliary stimuli are introduced as a means of active adaptation and include the tools of the culture into which the child is born, the language of those who relate to the child, and other means produced by the child himself. Thus, Vygotsky con-

cluded that in order to study development in children one must begin with an understanding of two principally different entities, the biological and the cultural.

The ideas of Vygotsky (1978) have been expanded and serve as a source of fresh insights in the area of developmental psychology (e.g., Irvine & Berry, 1986). Bronfenbrenner (1989) summarized the essence of this trend as proposing that the attributes of the person most likely to shape the beginning of the course of one's cognitive development are those that induce or inhibit dynamic dispositions toward the immediate environment, referred to as developmentally instigative characteristics. For an elaborate discussion of these complex ideas, see Bronfenbrenner (1989). In the section that follows, we examine cognitive flexibility and sensitivity to discontinuity as aspects of cognitive development shaped by the socialization goals of ethnic minority families.

Cognitive Flexibility

Researchers have consistently found that ethnic minority families are concerned with biculturalism—or preparing children to function in both the ethnic and nonethnic communities (Harrison et al., 1984; Peters, 1988). Theoretical and empirical evidence (Ramirez, 1983) indicates that biculturalism often involves more than using two cultural modalities in a simple additive manner (Gutierrez et al., 1988). The process of integrating two cultural systems involves greater cognitive and social flexibility that eventuates in a unique synthesis of both ethnic and nonethnic cultures as well as separateness of both cultures. Achieving the new synthesis is a complex process fraught with many obstacles and conflicts.

Biculturalism can be expressed in values, identity, and customs. Nonetheless, bilingualism is perhaps the most investigated indicator (Hakuta & Garcia, 1989). Balanced bilingual children show more cognitive flexibility than monolingual children (McShane & Berry, 1986; McShane & Cook, 1985; Osborne, 1985; Ramirez & Castaneda, 1974; Seifert & Hoffnung, 1985), that is, the ability to detect multiple meanings of words and alternative orientations of objects. Studies also indicate that bilingualism fosters metalinguistic awareness, the cognitive ability to attend to language as an object of thought rather than just for the content or idea (Diaz, 1983). In the same manner, Boykin (1979) investigated cognitive flexibility by exploring whether differences in the format variability of a set of problem-solving tasks affected the problem-solving performance of ethnic and majority school children. He found that African American children as compared to majority children performed better on tasks that were presented in a varied, as opposed to an unvaried, format. The majority children performed equally well with both formats. The differences between the performance of African American and majority children are explained by Boykin with the concept of psychological/behavioral verve. Psychological/behavioral verve is a unique adaptation to the high-energy pace of home experiences that is manifested in one's attitude, orientation, and responsiveness to varied, constantly changing stimulation.

Sensitivity to Discontinuity

Discontinuity has been defined as an abrupt transition from one mode of being and behaving to another accompanied by noticeable differences in social role assignments and expectations (Marcias, 1987). The problems generated by discontinuity between the home environments of ethnic minority children and the school environment are of concern. Discontinuity has the possibility of negative consequences on cognitive functioning because it affects academic achievement and social adjustment (Osborne, 1985; Spindler & Spindler, 1987). Ethnic minority children are more likely to be exposed to discontinuities between their family ecologies and school environment than majority children, whose family ecologies are more likely to be similar to the academic setting. In her studies of the social ecologies of African American children, Holliday (1985) observed that the discontinuity between home, neighborhood, and school facilitated the development of situational problem solving among young persons. In the home and neighborhood, children's roles most frequently demanded problem-solving skills, that is, the ability to recognize, adapt to, circumvent, or change an encountered predicament. In the school environment, however, children's interpersonal skills—the ability to become a participant, to gain leadership, and to cooperate and collaborate—as well as academic excellence were in greatest demand. Continuity between learning environments of home and school is an important element in the performance of children on problem-solving tasks (Delgado-Gaitan, 1987; Laosa & Sigel, 1982; Marcias, 1987). Research studies have found that ethnic minority children show improvements in their achievement levels, memory, and problem-solving abilities when the context of

the learning environment is consistent with their background (Boykin, 1979; Hare, 1985; Holliday, 1985; Spindler & Spindler, 1987). This phenomenon is highlighted in the teaching strategies parents use in interactions with children. The teaching/learning strategies used in the home influences how children perform on problem-solving situations in school (Laosa, 1980; Laosa & DeAvila, 1979; Steward & Steward, 1973).

Summary and Discussion

Recent population projections of the increase in the proportion of Americans who are members of an ethnic minority group have heightened the need for social scientists to understand these populations. The purpose of this article was to consider the interconnectedness of ecologies of ethnic minority families, adaptive strategies, socialization goals, and child behavioral outcomes. Ethnic minority groups have adaptive strategies that developed as responses to ecological challenges. The adaptive strategies discussed were family extendedness and role flexibility, biculturalism, and ancestral worldview. Adult members of the group have as their socialization goals fostering a positive orientation to the ethnic group and interdependence for children. Cognitive flexibility and sensitivity to discontinuities in children were viewed as developmental outcomes. We hope that this article will stimulate research that can be utilized by those who educate, parent, socialize, and support ethnic minority children.

Although progress has been made in initiating writings and empirical investigations of ethnic minority families and children, a majority of the publications focus on mental health rather than on developmental issues. There is also unevenness in the quality of the research efforts on ethnic minorities, and the social sciences have serious shortcomings in this area.

In the future, researchers need to attend to the extreme heterogeneity among various ethnic groups. It is important to identify the specific ethnic/demographic characteristics of the group studied in empirical investigations. It is important to note that although the cognitive domain was selected for review because there were more empirical investigations in that area, other aspects of development should be studied using this conceptual framework. Earlier literature on ethnic minority children concentrated on cognitive issues and subsequently has been criticized for narrowness of focus and shortcomings in methodology.

Researchers need to consider level of acculturation, period of immigration, social class, and appropriateness of comparison group in research designs. Failure to do so are principal pitfalls in the study of development among ethnic minorities. Also, social scientists need to take stock of the ethnocentrism biases in the formulation of research questions and interpretations of data from studies of ethnic minority children. Sampson (1988) and Spence (1985) offer insightful comments on the precursors for this tendency. With increased interest in the cultural context of development, there is hope that more culturally sensitive research will yield more insightful information regarding development among ethnic minority children.

Two examples of research designs that may be fruitful are offered. One is to study the socialization practices of different ethnic minority families that are rearing successful children. What are the similarities and differences in their parenting techniques, and what factors account for them? Second, in every culture there are critical social pathways to success. What were the procedures or pathways taken by adult members of the ethnic groups that led to success? What environmental factors and psychological processes can best explain how ethnic group members have managed to succeed? Finally, more effort needs to be directed to the formulation of conceptual models that can best explain the development of ethnic minority children. The models should not only be explanatory, but also suggestive of empirical investigations. These efforts are worthwhile as we continue our attempts to understand human development in a cultural context.

References

Agesti, B. F. (1978). The first decades of freedom: Black families in a southern county, 1870–1885. *Journal of Marriage and the Family, 46,* 697–706.

Allen, W. R. (1978). Black family research in the United States: A review, assessment, and extension. *Journal of Comparative Family Studies, 2,* 167–189.

Allen, W. R., & Stukes, S. (1982). Black family life-styles and the mental health of black Americans. In F. U. Munoz & R. Endo (Eds.), *Perspectives on minority group mental health* (pp. 43–52). Washington, DC: University Press of America.

Aoyagi, K. (1978). Kinship and friendship in black Los Angeles: A study of migrants from Texas. In D. Shimkin, E. Shimkin, & D. Frate (Eds.), *The extended family in black societies* (pp. 277–355). Chicago: Aldine.

Beck, R. W., & Beck, S. H. (1984). Formation of extended households during middle age. *Journal of Marriage and the Family, 46,* 277–287.

Beck, R. W., & Beck, S. H. (1989). The incidence of extended households among middle-aged black and white women. *Journal of Family Issues, 10,* 147–168.

Bing, J. (1980). Acculturation as varieties of adaptations. In A. M. Padilla (Ed.), *Acculturation: Theory, models and some new findings* (pp. 9–23). Boulder, CO: Westview.

Bouvier, L. F., & Agresta, A. (forthcoming). Projections of the Asian American population. In J. T. Fawcett & B. Carino (Eds.), *Asian and Pacific immigration to the United States.*

Bowman, P. J., & Howard, C. (1985). Race-related socialization, motivation, and academic achievement: A study of black youth in three-generation families. *Journal of the American Academy of Child Psychiatry, 24,* 134–141.

Boykin, A. W. (1979). Psychological behavioral verve: Some theoretical explorations and empirical manifestations. In A. W. Boykin, A. J. Franklin, & J. F. Yates (Eds.), *Research directions of black psychologists* (pp. 351–367). New York: Russell Sage.

Bronfenbrenner, U. (1979). *The ecology of human development.* Cambridge, MA: Harvard University Press.

Bronfenbrenner, U. (1989, June). *The ecology of cognitive development: Research models and fugitive findings.* Paper prepared for presentation as the keynote address for the Nineteenth Annual Symposium of the Jean Piaget Society, Philadelphia.

Brown, D. R., & Gary, L. (1987). Stressful life events, social support networks, and the physical and mental health of urban black adults. *Journal of Human Stress, 13,* 165–174.

Burgess, B. J. (1980). Parenting in the Native American community. In M. D. Fantini & R. Cardenas (Eds.), *Parenting in a multicultural society* (pp. 63–73). New York: Longman.

Buriel, R. (1984). Integration with traditional Mexican-American culture an sociocultural adjustment. In *Chicano psychology* (2d ed, pp. 95–130). New York: Academic Press.

Buriel, R. (1987). Ethnic labeling and identity among Mexican Americans. In J. S. Phinney & M. J. Rotheram (Eds.), *Children's ethnic socialization* (pp. 134–152). Beverly Hills, CA: Sage.

Carter, J. (1983). Vision or sight: Health concerns for Afro-American children. In G. J. Powell (Ed.), *The psychological development of minority children* (pp. 13–25). New York: Brunner/Mazel.

Chan, S. (1986). Parents of exceptional Asian children. In M. K. Kitano & P. C. Chinn (Eds.), *Exceptional Asian children and youth* (pp. 36–53). Reston, VA: Council for Exceptional Children.

Delgado-Gaitan, C. (1987). Tradition and transitions in the learning process of Mexican children: An ethnographic view. In G. Spindler & L. Spindler (Eds.), *Interpretive ethnography of education: At home and abroad* (pp. 333–359). Hillsdale, NJ: Erlbaum.

DeVos, G. A. (Ed.). (1973). *Socialization for achievement*. Berkeley: University of California Press.

DeVos, G. A. (1982). Adaptive strategies in U.S. minorities. In E. E. Jones & S. J. Korchin (Eds.), *Minority mental health* (pp. 74–117). New York: Praeger.

Diaz, R. (1983). Thought and two languages: The impact of bilingualism on cognitive development. In E. Gordon (Ed.), *Review of research in education, Vol. 10*. Washington, DC: American Educational Research Association.

Dix, J. H., & Grusec, J. E. (1985). Parent attribution processes in the socialization of children. In I. E. Sigel (Ed.), *Parental belief systems* (pp. 201–233). Hillsdale, NJ: Erlbaum.

Dressler, W. W. (1985). Extended family relationships, social support, and mental health in a southern black community. *Journal of Health and Social Behavior, 26*, 39–48.

Elkin, F., & Handel, G. (1984). *The child and society: The process of socialization*. New York: Random House.

Flanagan, W. G. (1978, August). *The extended family as an agent of social change*. Paper presented at the Ninth World Congress of the International Sociological Association, Uppsala University, Uppsala, Sweden.

Fogel, R., & Engelman, S. (1974). *Time on the cross* (Vols. 1 and 2). Boston: Little, Brown.

Foster, H. J. (1984). African patterns in Afro-American families. *Journal of Black Studies, 14*, 201–232.

Garbarino, J. (1982). Sociocultural risk: Dangers to competence. In C. B. Kopp & J. B. Krakow (Eds.), *The child: Development in a social context*. Reading, MA: Addison-Wesley.

Garbarino, M. S. (1976). *Native heritage*. Boston: Little, Brown.

Gardner, R. W., Robey, B., & Smith, P. C. (1985). Asian Americans: Growth, changes and diversity. *Population Bulletin, 40*, 4.

Genovese, E. D. (1976). *Roll, Jordan, roll*. New York: Random House.

Gibbs, J. T., Huang, L. N., & Associates (1989). *Children of color*. San Francisco: Jossey-Bass.

Gibson, G. (1972). Kin family network: Overheralded structure in past conceptualizations of family functioning. *Journal of Marriage and the Family, 34*, 13–23.

Gill, S. D. (1982a). *Beyond "the primitive": The religions of non-literate peoples*. Englewood Cliffs, NJ: Prentice-Hall.

Gill, S. D. (1982b). *Native American religions*. Belmont, CA: Wadsworth.

Goode, W. J. (1964). *The family*. Englewood Cliffs, NJ: Prentice-Hall.

Goodluck, C. T., & Eckstein, F. (1978). American Indian adoption program: An ethnic approach to child welfare. *White Cloud Journal, 1*, 3–7.

Green, B. E., Sack, W. H., & Pambrun, A. (1981). A review of child psychiatric epidemiology with special reference to American Indian and Alaska Native children. *White Cloud Journal, 2*, 22–36.

Gutierrez, J., Sameroff, A. J., & Karrer, B. M. (1988). Acculturation and SES effects on Mexican American parents' concepts of development. *Child Development, 59*, 250–255.

Gutman, H. G. (1976). *The black family in slavery and freedom, 1750–1925*. New York: Vintage.

Hakuta, K. (1987). Degree of bilingualism and cognitive ability in mainland Puerto Rican children. *Child Development, 58*, 1372–1388.

Hakuta, K., & Garcia, E. E. (1989). Bilingualism and education. *American Psychologist, 44*, 374–379.

Hamer, J. H. (1980). Acculturation stress and the functions of alcohol among the forest Potowatomi. In J. Hamer & J. Steinwings (Eds.), *Alcohol and native peoples of the north* (pp. 107–153). Washington, DC: University Press of America.

Harding, V. (1980). *The other American revolution*. Los Angeles: Center for Afro-American Studies, University of California, Los Angeles.

Hare, B. R. (1985). Reexamining the achievement central tendency: Sex differences within race and race differences within sex. In H. P. McAdoo & J. L. McAdoo (Eds.), *Black children* (pp. 139–151). Beverly Hills, CA: Sage.

Hare, B. R., & Castenell, L. A. (1985). No place to run, no place to hide: Comparative status and future prospects of black boys. In M. B. Spencer, G. Brookins, & W. Allen (Eds.), *Beginnings: The social and affective development of black children* (pp. 201–214). Hillsdale, NJ: Erlbaum.

Harrison, A. O., Serafica, F., & McAdoo, H. (1984). Ethnic families of color. In R. D. Parke (Ed.), *The family: Review of child development research* (Vol. 7, pp. 329–371). Chicago: University of Chicago Press.

Heela, P., & Lock, A. C. (Eds.). (1981). *Indigenous psychologies: The anthropology of the self*. London: Academic Press.

Height, D. (1985, March). What must be done about children having children. *Ebony*, p. 76.

Holliday, B. G. (1985). Developmental imperative of social ecologies: Lessons learned from black children. In H. P. McAdoo & J. L. McAdoo (Eds.), *Black children* (pp. 53–71). Beverly Hills, CA: Sage.

Hultkrantz, A. (1981). *Belief and worship in Native North America*. Syracuse, NY: Syracuse University Press.

Hurdy, J. M. (1970). *American Indian religions*. Los Angeles: Sherbourne.

Irvine, S. H., & Berry, J. W. (Eds.). (1986). *Human abilities in cultural context*. Cambridge: Cambridge University Press.

Johnson, J. E., & Martin, C. (1985). Parents' beliefs and home learning environments: Effects on cognitive development. In I. E. Sigel (Ed.), *Parental belief systems* (pp. 25–50). Hillsdale, NJ: Erlbaum.

Kagan, S., & Madsen, M. C. (1971). Cooperation and competition of Mexican, Mexican-American, and Anglo-American children of two ages under four instructional sets. *Developmental Psychology, 5*, 32–39.

Knight, G. P., & Kagan, S. (1977). Development of prosocial and competitive behaviors in Anglo-American and Mexican-American children. *Child Development, 48*, 1385–1394.

LaFromboise, T. D. (1988). American Indian mental health policy. *American Psychologist, 43*, 388–397.

Langston, E. J. (1980). Kith and kin; natural support systems: Their implications for policies and programs for the black aged. In E. P. Stanford (Ed.), *Minority aging policy issues for the '80s* (pp. 125–145). San Diego: University Center on Aging, College of Human Services, San Diego State University.

Laosa, L. M. (1977). Cognitive styles and learning strategies research. *Journal of Teacher Education, 28*, 26–30.

Laosa, L. M. (1980). Maternal teaching strategies in Chicano and Anglo American families: The influence of culture and education on maternal behavior. *Child Development, 51*, 759–765.

Laosa, L. M., & DeAvila, E. A. (1979). Development of cognitive styles among Chicanos in traditional and dualistic communities. *International Journal of Psychology, 14*, 91–98.

Laosa, L. M., & Sigel, I. E. (1982). *Families as learning environments for children*. New York: Plenum.

Lewis, R. (1981). Patterns of strengths of American Indian families. In F. Hoffman (Ed.), *The American Indian family strengths and stresses* (pp. 101–107). American Indian Social Research and Development Associates, Inc., P.O. Box 381, Iskta, NM 87022.

Light, H. K., & Martin, R. E. (1986). American Indian families. *Journal of American Indian Education, 26*, 1–5.

Marcias, J. (1987). The hidden curriculum of Papago teachers: American Indian strategies for mitigating cultural discontinuity in early schooling. In G. Spindler & L. Spindler (Eds.), *Interpretive ethnography of education: At home and abroad* (pp. 363–380). Hillsdale, NJ: Erlbaum.

Marin, G. (1986, October). *The process of acculturation of Latinos in the U.S.* Paper presented at the Second Puerto Rican Convention of Psychology and Mental Health, Rio Piedras, Puerto Rico.

Martin, E., & Martin, J. (1978). *The black extended family*. Chicago: University of Chicago Press.

McAdoo, H. (1978). Factors related to stability in upwardly mobile black families. *Journal of Marriage and the Family, 40*, 761–776.

McGillicuddy-DeLisi, A. V. (1985). The relationship between parental beliefs and children's cognitive level. In I. E. Sigel (Ed.), *Parental belief systems* (pp. 7–24). Hillsdale, NJ: Erlbaum.

McLoyd, V., & Randolph, S. (1985). Secular trends in the study of Afro-American children: A review of child development, 1936–1980. *Monographs of the Society for Research in Child Development, 50*(4–5, Serial No. 211).

McShane, D. (1983). Explaining achievement patterns of American Indian children: A transcultural and developmental model. *Peabody Journal of Education, 61*, 34–48.

McShane, D. (1988). An analysis of mental health research with American Indian youth. *Journal of Adolescence, 11*, 87–116.

McShane, D., & Berry, J. W. (1986). Native North Americans: Indian and Inuit abilities. In J. H. Irvine & J. W. Berry (Eds.), *Human abilities in cultural context* (pp. 385–426). Cambridge: Cambridge University Press.

McShane, D., & Cook, V. (1985). Transcultural intellectual assessment: Hispanic performance on the Wechslers. In B. Wolman (Ed.), *Handbook of intelligence: Theories, measurements, and applications*. New York: Wiley.

Meacham, M. (1983). The myth of the black matriarchy under slavery. *Mid-American Review of Sociology, 8*, 23–41.

Medicine, B. (1980). American Indian women: Spirituality and status. *Bread and Roses, 2*, 14–18.

Medicine, B. (1981). American Indian family: Cultural change and adaptive strategies. *Journal of Ethnic Studies, 8*, 13–23.

Michaelsen, R. S. (1983). "We also have a religion": The free exercise of religion among Native Americans. *American Indian Quarterly, 7*, 111–142.

Mindel, C. H., & Habenstein, R. W. (Eds.). (1984). *Ethnic families in America: Patterns and variations*. New York: Elsevier.

Moos, R. H., Insel, P. M., & Humphrey, B. (1974). *Manual for the Family Environment Scale*. Palo Alto, CA: Consulting Psychologists Press.

Munoz, F. U., & Endo, R. (Eds.). (1982). *Perspectives on minority group mental health*. Washington, DC: University Press of America.

Myers, H. F. (1982). Research on the Afro-American family: A critical review. In B. Bass, G. Wyatt, & G. Powell (Eds.), *The Afro-American family: Assessment treatment and research issues* (pp. 35–69). New York: Grune & Stratton.

National Indochinese Clearinghouse (1980). *Indochinese refugee education guides, general information series.* Washington, DC: National Indochinese Clearinghouse.

Nobles, W. W. (1978). African root and American fruit: The black family. *Journal of Social and Behavioral Sciences,* 20, 1–18.

Nobles, W. W. (1988). African-American family life: An instrument of culture. In H. P. McAdoo (Ed.), *Black families* (2d ed., pp. 44–53). Beverly Hills, CA: Sage.

Noel, D. L. (1985). A theory of the origin of ethnic stratification. In N. R. Yetman (Ed.), *Majority and minority* (pp. 109–120). Boston: Allyn & Bacon.

Ogbu, J. V. (1981). Origins of human competence: A cultural-ecological perspective. *Child Development,* 52, 413–429.

Ogbu, J. V. (1985). The consequences of the American caste system. In V. Neisser (Ed.), *The school achievement of minority children: New perspectives* (pp. 19–56). Hillsdale, NJ: Erlbaum.

Ogbu, J. V. (1987). Variability in minority responses to schooling: Nonimmigrants vs. immigrants. In G. Spindler & L. Spindler (Eds.), *Interpretive ethnography of education: At home and abroad* (pp. 255–280). Hillsdale, NJ: Erlbaum.

Olmedo, E. L. (1981). Testing linguistic minorities. *American Psychologist,* 36, 1018–1085.

Osborne, B. (1985). Research into Native North Americans' cognition: 1973–1982. *Journal of American Indian Education,* 24, 9–25.

Padilla, E. R., & O'Grady, K. E. (1987). Sexuality among Mexican-Americans: A case of sexual stereotyping. *Journal of Personality and Social Psychology,* 52, 5–10.

Pan Asian Parent Education Project (1982). *Pan Asian child-rearing practices: Philipino, Japanese, Korean, Samoan, Vietnamese.* San Diego: Union of Pan Asian Communities.

Penalosa, F. (1980). *Chicano sociolinguistics.* Rowley, MA: Newbury House.

Peters, M. F. (1988). Parenting in black families with young children: A historical perspective. In H. P. McAdoo (Ed.), *Black families* (2d ed., pp. 228–241). Beverly Hills, CA: Sage.

Peterson, R. O., & Yamamoto, B. Y. (Eds.). (1980). *Understanding the Pan Asian client: Book II.* San Diego: Union of Pan Asian Communities.

Phinney, J. S., & Rotheram, M. J. (Eds.). (1987). *Children's ethnic socialization: Pluralism and development.* Beverly Hills, CA: Sage.

Powell, G. J., Morales, A., Romero, A., & Yamamoto, J. (Eds.). (1983). *The psychosocial development of minority group children.* New York: Brunner/Mazel.

Ramirez, J. D. (1986). Comparing structural English immersion and bilingual education: First year

results of a national study. *American Journal of Education,* 95, 122–148.

Ramirez, M. (1983). *Psychology of the Americas.* Elmsford, NY: Pergamon.

Ramirez, M., & Castaneda, A. (1974). *Cultural democracy, bicognitive development, and education.* New York: Academic Press.

Red Horse, J. (1983). Indian family values and experiences. In G. J. Powell, A. Morales, A. Romero, & J. Yamamoto (Eds.), *The psychosocial development of minority group children* (pp. 258–272). New York: Brunner/Mazel.

Reed, J. (1982). Black Americans in the 1980s. *Population Bulletin,* 37, 1–37.

Report on minorities in higher education (1988). Hearing before the Committee on Education and Labor, House of Representatives, One-Hundredth Congress, Serial No. 100-192. Washington, DC: Government Printing Office.

Reuschenberg, E. J., & Buriel, R. (1988). *The effects of acculturation on relationship patterns and system variables within families of Mexican descent.* Unpublished manuscript, the Claremont Graduate School, Claremont, CA.

Rogoff, B. (1982). Integrating context and cognitive development. In M. E. Lamb & A. L. Brown (Eds.), *Advances in developmental psychology* (Vol. 2, pp. 125–170). Hillsdale, NJ: Erlbaum.

Rogoff, B., Gauvain, M., & Ellis, S. (1984). Development viewed in its context. In M. H. Bornstein & M. E. Lamb (Eds.), *Developmental psychology: An advanced textbook.* Hillsdale, NJ: Erlbaum.

Ryan, R. A. (1981). Strengths of the American Indian family: State of the art. In F. Hoffman (Ed.), *The American Indian family: Strengths and stresses.* American Indian Social Research and Development Associates, Inc., P.O. Box 381, Isleta, NM 87022.

Sabogal, F., Marin, G., Otero-Sabogal, R., Marin, B., & Perez-Stable, E. J. (1987). Hispanic familism and acculturation: What changes and what doesn't? *Hispanic Journal of Behavioral Sciences,* 9, 397–412.

Sampson, E. E. (1985). The decentralization of identity. *American Psychologist,* 40, 1203–1211.

Sampson, E. E. (1988). The debate on individualism. *American Psychologists,* 43, 15–22.

Schneider, D. M. (1968). *American kinship: A cultural account.* Englewood Cliffs, NJ: Prentice-Hall.

Schneider, D. M. (1980). *American kinship: A cultural account* (2d ed.). Englewood Cliffs, NJ: Prentice-Hall.

Scott-Jones, D. (1987). Mother-as-teacher in the families of high- and low-achieving, low-income black first graders. *Journal of Negro Education,* 56, 21–34.

Seifert, K. L., & Hoffnung, R. J. (1987). *Child and*

362 Child Development

adolescent development. Boston: Houghton Mifflin.

Serafica, F. C. (in press). Counseling Asian-American parents: A cultural-developmental framework. In F. C. Serafica et al. (Eds.), *Mental health of ethnic minorities*. New York: Praeger.

Shon, S. P., & Ja, D. Y. (1983). Asian families. In M. McGoldrick, J. K. Pearce, & J. Giordano (Eds.), *Ethnicity and family therapy*. New York: Guilford.

Sigel, M. (1985). A study of maternal beliefs and values within the context of an intervention program. In I. E. Sigel (Ed.), *Parental belief systems* (pp. 271–286). Hillsdale, NJ: Erlbaum.

Sims, S. A. (1978). Effects of modeling processes and resources on sharing among black children. *Psychological Reports, 43*, 463–473.

Sims, S. A. (1979). Sharing in black children: The impact of reference group appeals and other environmental factors. In A. W. Boykin, A. J. Franklin, & J. F. Yates (Eds.), *Research direction of black psychologists* (pp. 146–162). New York: Russell Sage.

Slaughter, D. T., & Epps, E. G. (1987). Home environment and academic achievement of black American children and youth: An overview. *Journal of Negro Education, 56*, 3–20.

Snipp, C. M., & Sandefur, G. O. (1988). Earnings of American Indians and Alaskan Natives: The effects of residence and migration. *Social Forces, 66*, 994–1008.

Soldo, B., & Lauriat, P. (1976). Living arrangements among the elderly in the United States: A loglinear approach. *Journal of Comparative Family Studies, 7*, 351–366.

Spence, J. T. (1985). Achievement American style: The rewards and costs of individualism. *American Psychologist, 40*, 1285–1295.

Spindler, G., & Spindler, L. (1987). *Interpretive ethnography of education*. Hillsdale, NJ: Erlbaum.

Stack, C. (1981). Sex roles and survival strategies in an urban black community. In F. C. Steady (Ed.), *The black woman cross-culturally* (pp. 349–367). Cambridge, MA: Schinkman.

Steward, M., & Steward, D. (1973). The observation of Anglo-Mexican and Chinese-American mothers teaching their young sons. *Child Development, 44*, 329–337.

Sudarkasa, N. (1988). Interpreting the African heritage in Afro-American family organization. In H. P. McAdoo (Ed.), *Black families* (2d ed., pp. 27–43). Beverly Hills, CA: Sage.

Sue, D., & Sue, S. (1987). Cultural factors in the clinical assessment of Asian Americans. *Journal of Consulting and Clinical Psychology, 55*, 479–487.

Suzuki, B. H. (1980). The Asian American family.

In M. D. Fanti & R. Cardenas (Eds.), *Parenting in a multicultural society* (pp. 76–101). New York: Longman.

Sweet, J. A. (1977, October). *Further indicators of family structure and process for racial and ethnic minorities*. Paper presented at the Conference on the Demography of Racial and Ethnic Groups, Austin, TX.

Szopocznik, J., & Kurtines, W. (1980). Acculturation, biculturalism, and adjustment among Cuban Americans. In A. M. Padilla (Ed.), *Acculturation: Theory, models and some new findings* (pp. 139–161). Boulder, CO: Westview.

Taylor, R. J. (1988). Structural determinants of religious participation among black Americans. *Review of Religious Research, 2*, 114–125.

Taylor, R. J., Thornton, M. C., & Chatters, L. M. (1988). Black Americans' perceptions of the sociohistorical role of the church. *Journal of Black Studies, 18*, 123–138.

Thornton, M. C., & Taylor, R. J. (1988). Black Americans' perceptions of black Africans. *Ethnic and Racial Studies, 11*, 140–150.

Tseng, W. (1973). The concept of personality in Confucian thought. *Psychiatry, 50*, 76–86.

U.S. Bureau of the Census (1989). *Household and family characteristics: March, 1988* (Current Population Report, Series P-20, No. 437). Washington, DC: Government Printing Office.

U.S. Department of Commerce Series, Bureau of the Census (1988). *We, the Asian and Pacific Islander: We, the Black Americans; We, the first American; and We, Nosotros*. Washington, DC: Government Printing Office.

Vygotsky, L. S. (1978). *Mind in society*. Cambridge, MA: Harvard University Press.

Wagner, S. T. (1981). The historical background of bilingualism and biculturalism in the United States. In M. Ridge (Ed.), *The new bilingualism* (pp. 29–52). New Brunswick, NJ: Transaction Books.

Willig, A. (1985). A meta-analysis of selected studies on the effectiveness of bilingual education. *Review of Educational Research, 55*, 269–317.

Wilson, M. N. (1986). The black extended family: An analytical review. *Developmental Psychology, 22*, 246–258.

Wilson, M. N. (1989). Child development in the context of the black extended family. *American Psychologist, 44*, 380–385.

Wolfson, N., & Manes, J. (Eds.). (1985). *Language of inequality*. New York: Mouton.

Yetman, N. R. (Ed.). (1985). *Majority and minority*. Boston: Allyn & Bacon.

Zigler, E. F., Lamb, M. E., & Child, I. L. (1982). *Socialization and personality development*. New York: Oxford University Press.

Patterns of Interaction in Family Relationships and the Development of Identity Exploration in Adolescence

Harold D. Grotevant and Catherine R. Cooper

University of Texas at Austin

GROTEVANT, HAROLD D., and COOPER, CATHERINE R. *Patterns of Interaction in Family Relationships and the Development of Identity Exploration in Adolescence.* Child Development, 1985, 56, 415–428. The purpose of this research was to develop a model of individuation in family relationships that focuses on communication processes, and to assess the links between them and adolescent identity exploration. Expressions of the 4 dimensions of the model—self-assertion, separateness, permeability, and mutuality—were predicted to be positively associated with identity exploration in adolescents. A sample of 84 Caucasian, middle-class, 2-parent families, each including an adolescent and 1 or 2 siblings, was observed in a Family Interaction Task designed to elicit the expression and coordination of a variety of points of view. Multiple regression analyses revealed differentiated results concerning father-son, father-daughter, mother-son, mother-daughter, and marital relationships as well as positive and negative contributions of communication variables to identity exploration when verbal ability and sociability were controlled. Results are discussed in terms of recent formulations of the progressive redefinition of the parent-child relationship during adolescence.

An important developmental task of adolescence, in societies offering choices in these areas, is the formulation of a sense of identity, a cohesive set of personal values regarding career goals, relationships, and political and religious beliefs (Erikson, 1950, 1968). Surprisingly, few studies have addressed issues concerning the development of individual differences in this accomplishment. Although a number of researchers have proposed a link between patterns of family functioning and adolescent identity formation (e.g., Adams & Jones, 1983; Cushing, 1971; LaVoie, 1976), these investigations have assessed perceptions of past or present child-rearing styles rather than actual family interaction. In addition, in these studies, identity formation has been assessed in terms of identity *status* (Marcia, 1966, 1980), a construct for which no one developmental sequence has been established (Waterman, 1982). However, identity *exploration*, the process of considering alternatives in the various domains of personal values (Jordaan, 1963; Matteson, 1977), plays a central role in identity formation during the late high school years. In recent work, identity exploration is increasingly viewed as a process that can be facilitated within the context of relationships (Grotevant, Thorbecke, & Meyer, 1982; Thorbecke & Grotevant, 1982).

The present study examines the relations between individual differences among adolescents in their identity exploration and the interaction patterns of their families. In contrast to traditional conceptualizations of adolescence as a time of breaking the parent-child bond, recent evidence supports a view of this period as one of gradual renegotiation between parents and children from the asymmetrical authority of early and middle childhood toward, potentially, a peerlike mutuality in adulthood (White, Speisman, & Costos, 1983). Just how these transactions occur is not well understood, but accounts of the maturing parent-adolescent relationship require going beyond unilateral concepts such as parental warmth or restrictiveness to more reciprocal relational constructs (Maccoby & Martin, 1983).

This work was supported by grants from the National Institute of Child Health and Human Development (HD-92819 and HD-17983) and the Hogg Foundation for Mental Health and from the University Research Institute and the Institute of Human Development and Family Studies of the University of Texas at Austin. We express our appreciation to the families who generously shared their time by participating in the Family Process Project. We especially acknowledge the contributions of Susan Ayers-Lopez and Kathryn Kramer to the completion of this report. In addition, we thank three anonymous reviewers for their constructive suggestions. Reprint requests may be sent to either author at: Department of Home Economics, Division of Child Development and Family Relationships, University of Texas at Austin, Austin, TX 78712.

The present investigation is based on developmental and clinical conceptualizations of the family that emphasize the importance of both *individuality* and *connectedness* within family relationships for the well-being of its members (Grotevant & Cooper, in press; Karpel, 1976; Lewis, Beavers, Gossett, & Phillips, 1976; Minuchin, 1974; Olson, Sprenkle, & Russell, 1979; Riskin & Faunce, 1970; Sroufe, 1983). The goal of this program of research has been to develop a testable model of parent-adolescent relationships and to explore the links between these family constructs and measures of psychosocial competence in normal adolescents.

Specifically, this investigation is based on a model of *individuation* in relationships (Cooper, Grotevant, & Condon, 1983; Grotevant & Cooper, in press). Historically, the construct of individuation has been used to characterize relational as well as interpersonal levels of analysis (Grotevant & Cooper, in press). For example, Blos (1979) described adolescence as a second period of individuation similar to toddlerhood (Mahler, 1979), in which autonomy is attained by disengaging from infantile object relations with parents. Other scholars (e.g., Beavers, 1976; Bell & Bell, 1983) consider individuation as a quality of family relationships.

In the program of work of which the present investigation is a part, individuation is comprised of the two components of individuality and connectedness. In this model, individuality is reflected by separateness (seen in expressions of the distinctiveness of self from others) and self-assertion (seen, e.g., in the expression of one's own point of view and in taking responsibility for communicating it clearly). For the adolescent, separateness and self-assertion in family interaction have been regarded as key qualities of healthy family relationships because they concern the ability of family members to have opinions that may differ from those of others (Beavers, 1976; L'Abate, 1976; Minuchin, 1974). Connectedness is reflected by mutuality (seen in an individual's sensitivity to and respect for the views of others) and permeability (openness and responsiveness to the views of others). Mutuality can provide adolescents with support, acknowledgment, and respect for developing their own beliefs, whereas permeability involves the management of the boundaries between self and others, and may be of special significance during the process of identity formation (Carter & McGoldrick, 1980; Fischer, 1978). According to this conception of relationships, evidence of both individuality and connectedness (i.e., an individuated relationship) would be predicted as providing for its members the context for exploring and clarifying individual points of view.

In earlier work on the Family Process Project (described in more detail later in the paper), empirical evidence for the validity of this conceptual model of family interaction was obtained. A sample of 121 families with adolescent children (total $N = 444$) was observed in a situation designed to elicit the expression and coordination of a variety of points of view (Cooper et al., 1983). Each family's interaction was coded according to 14 communication categories hypothesized to reflect the four constructs of self-assertion, separateness, mutuality, and permeability, and factor analysis was performed on the intercorrelation matrix of these behaviors. Principal factors analysis followed by varimax (orthogonal) rotation yielded four factors with eigenvalues greater than 1.0; together they accounted for 51.3% of the variance. The communication behaviors loading on each of the four factors are outlined in the Appendix.

Whereas our earlier work from this project has been concerned with individual family communication behaviors, the present paper reports an investigation of the link between patterns of interaction in relationships within the family and adolescent identity exploration. First, correlational analyses are used to examine the dimensions of self-assertion, separateness, permeability, and mutuality separately for each relationship (adolescent-father, adolescent-mother, adolescent-sibling, and marital). Based on the conceptual model of individuation and the evidence of the independence of its four factors, the exploratory prediction was made that adolescents' identity exploration would be positively related to the frequency of each dimension observed in the Family Interaction Task. It was anticipated that within each relationship in which the adolescent participated, as well as in the marital relationship, variables representing each dimension of individuation would be associated with identity exploration. No causal direction of effects was posited. In the case of separateness, for example, freedom to disagree in family interaction may facilitate the adolescent's ability to explore outside the family, or adolescents who have explored more outside the family may feel more confident or competent to display that sense of self within the family. Second, a multiple regression approach is used to compare the relative contributions of communication behaviors within each relationship while controlling for the possible confounding effects of verbal ability and sociability.

Method

Subjects

The subjects in this study were members of 84 Caucasian, middle-class, two-parent families, each including an adolescent who was a high school senior and either one or two siblings. Subjects were volunteers who responded to letters sent to families of seniors in local public high schools (87% of sample), letters to families with a high school senior in local churches (2% of sample), or referrals from other sources, including participating families (11% of sample). Those families were included who had up to three children and who were either biologically intact or had been together for at least the past 5 years. Socioeconomic status of the families was assessed by Hodge-Siegel occupational prestige ratings of fathers' occupations (Mueller & Parcel, 1981). The mean rating for the sample was 57.4 (range = 35.4–81.2), with most of the fathers being employed in professional work. The target adolescents (mean age = 17.6 years) included 46 females, 34 of whom were firstborns, and 38 males, 30 of whom were firstborns; the siblings (mean age = 15.2 years) included 47 females and 37 males. The families were drawn from a larger sample of 121 families who participated in the Family Process Project, a study directed by the coauthors. The subsample of 84 families was chosen for this report because in each of these families four members (both parents, the target adolescent, and a sibling) participated in the Family Interaction Task.

Procedures

Data collection for the measures reported in this study involved both parents, the target adolescent, and one sibling, and took place in the family's home. Among the measures administered were the Family Interaction Task (to the whole family), the Ego Identity Interview (to the target adolescent), the Extended Range Vocabulary Test (to each family member), and the Strong-Campbell Interest Inventory (to each family member). In addition to the measures discussed in this report, the study also included several questionnaires measuring perceptions of self and family, several social-cognitive tasks, an activity checklist kept by each family member for 4 days, an audiotaped role-taking measure, and an audiotaped interaction task between the target adolescent and an unacquainted peer.

Measures

Family Interaction Task.—The Family Interaction Task involved the family in making plans together for a fictional 2-week vacation for which they had unlimited funds. Their task was to plan the day-by-day itinerary, listing both the location and the activity planned for each day. The research assistant gave the family 20 min to reach their decisions, turned on an audiotape recorder, and left the room.

The task, designed in terms of key methodological considerations current in family problem-solving research (Klein & Hill, 1979), was an adaptation of the Plan Something Together Task first introduced by Watzlawick (1966). It was designed to elicit the expression and coordination of the viewpoints of all family members on a topic on which the adolescent's interests and expertise could legitimately contribute to the family's decisions. Thus, it was anticipated that such a task would enhance the families' potential for exhibiting both individuality (as seen in suggestions for activities or disagreements) and connectedness (as seen in agreements, questions, or initiating compromises).

Concern for optimizing the adolescent's participation guided several decisions concerning the structure of the task. A Plan Something Together Task, which allows multiple ideas to be incorporated into a final plan, was chosen rather than a Revealed or Unrevealed Differences Task, which typically allows only one viewpoint to prevail; the Plan Something Together Task facilitates "power sharing" rather than "power wielding" interactions that often result from tasks that intentionally stimulate conflict (Cromwell & Olson, 1975). In addition, unlimited funds were permitted for the hypothetical vacation so as not to activate pre-established family roles concerning the allocation of money, such as might occur when the purchase of a car was considered. Finally, in order to stimulate participation of all family members, the task required multiple decisions rather than a single decision. The task appeared to be ecologically valid for these families, as most became highly engaged in the task, and many mentioned trips to places they had visited or discussed previously. Still, generalization of the findings should be made with caution since family communication was observed in only one context, and since the task was designed to elicit optimal patterns of power sharing.

As described earlier, the coding of family interaction variables was guided by developmental and clinical research, as well as by

418   Child Development

principles of speech and conversational analysis (Coulthard, 1977; Dore, 1979). Details of the principles governing the preparation of transcripts, unitizing of discourse, definitions of communication behaviors, and conduct of the coding itself are given in Condon, Cooper, and Grotevant (1984). Using transcripts and tapes, coders assigned each of the first 300 utterances of the family interaction to one of 14 categories operationalizing the dimensions of individuation. A previous study indicated that the first 300 utterances were sufficiently representative of the whole session to serve as the basis for data analysis (Cooper, Grotevant, & Condon, 1982). Interjudge reliabilities (percent agreement in coding specific utterances) exceeded .75 for all but three utterance types (initiates compromise, acknowledgment, and agreement). Reliability of coding for each transcript was reviewed by a single trainer (a linguist working on the project), and all coding discrepancies were resolved by consultation with the coding manual (Condon et al., 1984); these procedures were recommended by Gottman (1979). Coders were blind with respect to the adolescents' performance on the Ego Identity Interview and all other measures.

Ego Identity Interview.—The Ego Identity Interview, developed by Marcia (1966) and revised and extended by Grotevant and Cooper (1981), operationalizes Erikson's (1950, 1968) construct of identity in six domains that are pertinent developmentally for both male and female high school students in the United States (Grotevant et al., 1982): occupational choice, religion, politics, friendship, dating, and sex roles. The interview was administered by an interviewer of the same sex as the subject and was audiotaped. Each tape was rated independently by two coders who were blind to the hypotheses of the study and to the performance of the subjects they rated on any other task. Disagreements were resolved by a third rater. Percent exact agreement between two raters averaged 80.7% for interviews of females and 79.6% for interviews of males. Percent agreement for two out of three raters averaged 97.3% for female subjects and 96.6% for male subjects. The identity exploration score used as a key measure in this study was the sum of the exploration ratings across these six domains. Adolescents receiving the highest scores had actively considered a variety of options for themselves (reflecting breadth) by exploring each option in a variety of ways (reflecting depth).

Vocabulary.—The Extended Range Vocabulary Test (Ekstrom, French, Harman, & Derman, 1976) was administered to each family member to determine the association of individual differences in performance on other measures with verbal ability. In another study, this measure was shown to correlate .78 with the verbal section of the Scholastic Aptitude Test (Grotevant & Adams, in press).

Strong-Campbell Interest Inventory.—The Strong-Campbell Interest Inventory (Campbell, 1974) is the 1974 revision of the Strong Vocational Interest Blank, which has been used since 1927 to assess vocational interests. Besides the occupational scales, the Strong also includes an Introversion-Extraversion scale, which assesses the degree to which the subject expresses a preference for occupations and social environments that emphasize interpersonal interaction. Low scores on this scale indicate a preference for activities and situations involving interpersonal contact; thus it is used as an indicator of sociability.

Results

The findings provide evidence of the link between relational properties of family interaction and adolescent identity exploration, with some unexpectedly differentiated results concerning family subsystems. The results are presented in three major sections. In the first two sections, descriptive statistics concerning adolescent identity exploration and family communication behaviors are given. In the third section, results examining the hypothesized relations between dimensions of family communication and identity exploration are presented.

Adolescent Identity Exploration

The identity exploration rating was the sum of individual ratings of identity exploration across six domains: occupational choice, religion, politics, friendship, dating, and sex roles. The theoretical range of scores for each subject was 6–24 points. Actual scores in this sample ranged from 9 to 19 for males and from 10 to 19 for females; the mean difference between males and females was not significant, $t(81) = 1.02$, N.S. Ratings of exploration were also examined for a possible relation with verbal ability. The correlation between identity exploration and adolescents' vocabulary scores was .04 (N.S.). In addition, identity exploration was examined with respect to subjects' birth order. When ratings of only children, firstborns, and second-borns

106

were compared, no significant difference emerged, $F(2,87) = 1.90$, N.S.

Family Interaction Task

Means and ranges of the 14 communication behaviors coded from the Family Interaction Task are contained in Table 1. *T* tests were performed to assess sex differences between target adolescent males and females and between fathers and mothers. Only two significant differences emerged between adolescent males and females: males made more requests for information, $t(82) = 2.60$, $p < .05$, whereas females gave more answers to requests for information, $t(82) = -2.48$, $p < .05$. Five significant mean differences emerged for parents: fathers expressed more relevant comments, $t(83) = 3.15$, $p = .002$; indirect suggestions, $t(83) = 3.61$, $p = .001$; answers to request for information, $t(83) = 3.04$, $p = .003$; and requests for action, $t(83) = 2.36$, $p = .021$; whereas mothers more frequently showed compliance with requests for action, $t(83) = -2.08$, $p = .041$.

Family Communication and Identity Exploration

In this section, analyses linking qualities of family communication and adolescent identity exploration will be presented.[1] In the first set of analyses, correlations were computed between identity exploration ratings of the adolescents and the frequencies of communication behaviors directed from one person to another family member for each possible dyad in the family. Separateness scores included the sum of direct disagreements, indirect disagreements, and requests for action. Permeability scores included the sum of agreements, acknowledgments, and requests for action. Mutuality scores included the sum of initiations of compromise, statements of other's feelings, and answers to requests for information. Means and ranges for these scores in each dyad are presented in Table 2 for all adolescents, as well as for males and females separately; correlations between these scores and identity exploration are presented in Table 3.

For separateness, modest positive correlations with identity exploration were found for most dyads. When correlations for males and females were examined separately, only those for females were significant. Separateness expressed by each parent to the female adolescent and separateness expressed by the adolescent to her sibling were significantly related to identity exploration.

The patterns of correlations relating identity exploration to permeability and mutuality were more differentiated by dyad. In the mother-adolescent dyad, exploration was negatively related to permeability from the mother to the adolescent and negatively related to mutuality from the adolescent to the mother. This pattern suggests that the communication between adolescents higher in identity exploration and their mothers involved higher frequencies of reciprocated separateness (i.e., both from the mother to adolescent and the adolescent to mother) and lower degrees of reciprocated connectedness. For adolescent boys and their fathers, significant correlations suggested the potential role of reciprocated connectedness in identity exploration (permeability from adolescent to father and mutuality from father to adolescent). Correlations relating exploration to permeability and mutuality in the adolescent-sibling dyad were not significant.

The communication in the marital relationship observed by the adolescents was also modestly correlated with their identity exploration. The trend observed in the correlations suggested that adolescent males rated higher in exploration observed reciprocated separateness between their parents. For females, identity exploration was negatively related to reciprocated connectedness (permeability from each parent to the other and mutuality from father to mother).

---

[1] Two alternate approaches to the use of actual frequencies of communication variables were examined. First, to consider the possible attenuation of correlations between communication behaviors and identity exploration (because of skewedness of the communication behaviors), the square root transformation was applied to the communication variables. Correlations were then computed between the transformed and untransformed variables; all exceeded .90. Correlations of transformed and untransformed variables with identity exploration were then compared. These correlations were virtually identical, differing on the average by <.02. Second, because different family members contributed different proportions of total utterances to the interaction, frequencies of each person's 14 communication behaviors were divided by the number of total utterances for each person. These proportional scores were then correlated with the raw frequencies of each communication behavior. Median correlations were .89 for adolescents, .86 for mothers, .84 for fathers, and .83 for siblings. Thus, on the basis of these analyses, actual frequencies of communication behaviors were judged as appropriate for the basis of the subsequent analyses.

TABLE 1

MEANS AND RANGES FOR COMMUNICATION BEHAVIORS IN FAMILY INTERACTION TASK

	Father	Mother	Male Adolescent	Female Adolescent	Male Sibling	Female Sibling
Self-assertion:						
Direct suggestion:						
Mean........	3.5	3.5	5.2	4.9	4.1	4.6
Range	0–15	0–17	0–21	0–15	0–12	0–17
Permeability:						
Acknowledgment:						
Mean........	12.6	13.2	8.5	8.3	5.4	5.7
Range	0–43	1–36	0–24	2–22	0–16	0–18
Request for infor-						
mation:						
Mean........	10.7	11.0	8.8	5.8	4.7	5.9
Range	0–39	1–34	1–24	0–30	0–16	0–18
Agreement:						
Mean........	11.9	12.6	13.1	10.9	9.4	10.8
Range	1–32	2–29	2–26	2–24	0–29	0–27
Relevant comment:						
Mean........	14.1	11.0	9.5	10.0	6.3	5.9
Range	2–48	1–25	1–29	2–21	0–16	0–19
Compliance with						
request for action:						
Mean........	.7	1.0	.8	.7	.6	.5
Range	0–5	0–4	0–3	0–3	0–3	0–3
Mutuality:						
Indirect suggestion:						
Mean........	20.4	15.4	15.4	14.8	11.3	11.6
Range	2–60	3–33	3–37	2–31	2–28	1–35
Initiation of com-						
promise:						
Mean........	1.0	.9	1.0	.6	.4	.7
Range	0–5	0–5	0–4	0–3	0–2	0–4
Statement of others'						
feelings:						
Mean........	.7	.7	.5	.6	.1	.5
Range	0–8	0–5	0–4	0–4	0–1	0–6
Answer to request						
for information:						
Mean........	6.6	4.8	5.7	7.7	5.8	4.5
Range	0–20	0–18	1–12	1–19	2–15	0–11
Separateness:						
Request for action:						
Mean........	3.5	2.7	2.9	2.1	2.0	1.8
Range	0–17	0–10	0–12	0–10	0–9	0–7
Direct disagreement:						
Mean........	2.2	2.4	3.0	2.7	2.3	3.9
Range	0–9	0–9	0–9	0–12	0–8	0–18
Indirect disagreement:						
Mean........	3.8	3.8	4.3	4.9	3.9	3.5
Range	0–15	0–11	0–15	0–22	0–16	0–11
Irrelevant comment:						
Mean........	.2	.4	.5	.2	.2	.4
Range	0–7	0–13	0–6	0–6	0–2	0–3

The second set of analyses was designed to examine sex differences, relational differences (e.g., between mother-son and mother-daughter dyads), and the possible role of the adolescent's verbal ability and sociability in explaining the association between communi- cation variables and identity exploration. A series of hierarchical stepwise multiple regressions was performed, with identity exploration as the dependent variable. For each regression analysis, sociability and verbal ability scores were entered in the first step.

TABLE 2

MEANS AND RANGES FOR SEPARATENESS, PERMEABILITY, AND MUTUALITY IN DYADS

	SEPARATENESS			PERMEABILITY			MUTUALITY		
DYAD	All[a]	M[a]	F[a]	All	M	F	All	M	F
Adolescent to mother:									
Mean	3.4	4.2	2.7	8.7	7.6	9.6	3.1	3.4	2.9
Range.......	0–20	0–20	0–8	0–31	0–31	1–25	0–11	0–11	0–10
Mother to adolescent:									
Mean	3.0	3.2	2.8	9.9	10.1	9.7	2.1	1.5	2.6
Range.......	0–14	0–14	0–11	0–40	0–40	0–26	0–12	0–7	0–12
Adolescent to father:									
Mean	3.2	2.9	3.5	11.8	10.6	12.8	3.1	3.9	2.5
Range.......	0–21	0–21	0–15	1–40	2–26	1–40	0–13	0–13	0–10
Father to adolescent:									
Mean	3.2	3.5	2.9	10.9	11.7	10.2	2.6	2.2	3.0
Range.......	0–21	0–17	0–21	1–41	1–36	1–41	0–11	0–11	0–10
Adolescent to sibling:									
Mean	2.6	2.3	2.8	4.8	4.7	4.9	1.7	1.6	1.7
Range.......	0–10	0–6	0–10	0–18	0–18	0–15	0–10	0–9	0–10
Sibling to adolescent:									
Mean	2.8	2.3	3.3	6.0	6.7	5.5	1.2	1.1	1.4
Range.......	0–18	0–13	0–18	0–19	0–19	0–18	0–5	0–5	0–5
Mother to father:									
Mean	2.7	2.7	2.8	13.8	12.7	14.6	2.6	2.7	2.6
Range.......	0–10	0–8	0–10	2–39	3–22	2–39	0–17	0–17	0–7
Father to mother:									
Mean	2.2	2.1	2.3	11.0	11.9	10.2	3.3	3.4	3.2
Range.......	0–11	0–9	0–11	0–30	1–27	0–30	0–14	0–11	0–14

NOTE.—Separateness = direct disagreements + indirect disagreements + requests for action; Permeability = requests for information + agreements + acknowledgments; Mutuality = initiations of compromise + statements of others' feelings + answers to requests for information.
[a] Sex of adolescent.

The second step included all directional communication composite scores (separateness, permeability, and mutuality) for that particular dyad as well as the following nondirectional communication behaviors for both members of the dyad: direct suggestions, indirect suggestions, relevant comments, and irrelevant comments. The results of the five regression analyses that accounted for significant proportions of variance in identity exploration are presented in Tables 4 and 5 for males and females, respectively.

For males, communication variables in the father-son dyad accounted for 58.4% of the variance in identity exploration after variance accounted for by sociability and verbal ability was subtracted. (The adjusted R^2 for the full equation was .376.) In no other relationship were the communication variables predictive of identity exploration for males. The predictors in the final significant equation, $F(12,18) = 2.51$, $p = .038$, with significant beta weights included mutuality from father to adolescent (beta = .75), separateness from father to adolescent ($-.99$), and separateness from adolescent to father (.97). In addition, adolescent's direct suggestions (.39) and father's indirect suggestions ($-.42$) had moderately high beta weights that approached statistical significance.

For females, communication variables in all four relationships accounted for significant proportions of variance in identity exploration after controlling for sociability and verbal ability: adolescent-father = 22.7%; adolescent-mother = 22.5%; adolescent-sibling = 5.4%; and mother-father = 39.2%.

In the father-daughter relationship, the final significant equation, $F(8,33) = 2.34$, $p = .041$, included one predictor with a significant beta: father's indirect suggestions (beta =

TABLE 3

CORRELATIONS BETWEEN IDENTITY EXPLORATION RATINGS AND FREQUENCIES OF SEPARATENESS, PERMEABILITY, AND MUTUALITY FOR EACH DYAD

DIRECTION OF COMMUNICATION	SEPARATENESS			PERMEABILITY			MUTUALITY		
	All[a]	M[a]	F[a]	All	M	F	All	M	F
Mother to adolescent......	.12	-.03	.26*	-.19*	-.24	-.16	.11	.21	.10
Adolescent to mother......	.20*	.22	.14	.09	.05	.17	-.23*	-.14	-.35**
Father to adolescent.......	.19*	.02	.32*	.05	-.03	.11	.14	.41**	-.08
Adolescent to father.......	.13	.21	.07	.15	.39**	.03	-.00	-.16	.11
Sibling to adolescent	.19*	.21	.22	-.07	-.26	.10	.06	.15	.02
Adolescent to sibling......	.26**	.22	.30*	.05	-.06	.16	.08	.06	.10
Mother to father...........	.08	.20	.01	-.15	.10	-.26*	.09	.03	.18
Father to mother..........	.13	.22	.08	-.15	-.11	-.21	-.17	.17	-.43**

NOTE.—Separateness = direct disagreements + indirect disagreements + requests for action; Permeability = requests for information + agreements + acknowledgments; Mutuality = initiations of compromise + statements of others' feelings + answers to requests for information.

[a] Sex of adolescent.

* $p < .05$.

** $p < .01$.

TABLE 4

STEPWISE MULTIPLE REGRESSION OF IDENTITY EXPLORATION ON COMMUNICATION BEHAVIORS,
CONTROLLING FOR SOCIABILITY AND VERBAL ABILITY: MALES $(N = 31)$

| PREDICTOR | FATHER-SON RELATIONSHIP | | | |
	Cumulative R^2	B	Beta	OVERALL F
Control variables:				
Sociability	.037	.004	(.028)	.02	1.10
Verbal ability	.042	−.029	(.045)	−.10	.61
Communication variables:				
Mutuality F to A	.195	.583	(.175)	.75**	2.19
Separateness F to A	.256	−.597	(.190)	−.99**	2.23
Separateness A to F	.319	.577	(.207)	.97*	2.34
F irrelevant comment.....	.412	.430	(.512)	.23	2.80*
A direct suggestion ......⌐	.515	.243	(.118)	.39	3.49*
F indirect suggestion	.573	−.098	(.066)	−.42	3.69**
A relevant comment	.604	.075	(.079)	.16	3.56**
A indirect suggestion	.613	−.082	(.083)	−.26	3.17*
F direct suggestion	.620	−.093	(.159)	−.13	2.82*
Mutuality A to F	.626	.109	(.204)	.13	2.51*

NOTE.—Numbers in parentheses are standard errors.
F = father; A = adolescent. Variance accounted for by communication variables = .626 − .042 = 58.4%.
Adjusted R^2 for full equation = .376.
* $p < .05$.
** $p < .01$.

−.43). Father's relevant comments (.31) and adolescent's indirect suggestions (.29) also approached significance.

In the mother-daughter relationship, the final significant equation, $F(8,33) = 2.31$, $p = .044$, included the following significant predictor: mutuality from adolescent to mother (beta = −.36). Adolescent's direct suggestions (−.28) and indirect suggestions (.28) and mother's direct suggestions (.26) approached significance.

In the adolescent-sibling relationship, the final significant equation, $F(3,38) = 2.93$, $p = .046$, included the adolescent's sociability score (beta = −.34). In addition, separateness expressed from the adolescent to her sibling (beta = .23) approached significance.

Finally, for the marital relationship, the final significant equation, $F(14,27) = 2.14$, $p = .044$, included the following predictors with significant betas: mutuality from father to mother (beta = −.42) and separateness from father to mother (.40). In addition, father's direct suggestions (−.33), mutuality from mother to father (.32), and father's relevant comments (.30) approached significance.

In sum, adolescents' interactions with their fathers were associated with identity exploration, but in different ways for sons and daughters. Sons scoring higher in identity exploration were more likely to be expressing direct suggestions and separateness with their

fathers, and their fathers reciprocated with more expressions of mutuality and less frequent expressions of separateness. In contrast, daughters rated higher in identity exploration were more likely to be expressing suggestions indirectly. Their fathers showed higher frequencies of relevant comments and lower frequencies of indirect suggestions.

In the mother-daughter relationship, identity exploration was negatively associated with expressions of mutuality from the adolescent to her mother. Higher-scoring daughters were expressing higher frequencies of indirect and lower frequencies of direct suggestions, whereas their mothers were more likely to express their suggestions directly than indirectly. Finally, higher-scoring daughters were more likely to express separateness toward their siblings.

In the marital relationship of the parents of higher-scoring daughters, fathers expressed higher separateness and lower mutuality to their wives as well as higher frequencies of relevant comments and lower frequencies of direct suggestions. Perhaps in a complementary pattern, mothers of the higher-scoring daughters more frequently expressed mutuality to their husbands.

Discussion

On the Family Interaction Task, measures of all four dimensions of the individua-

TABLE 5

STEPWISE MULTIPLE REGRESSION OF IDENTITY EXPLORATION ON COMMUNICATION BEHAVIORS, CONTROLLING FOR SOCIABILITY AND VERBAL ABILITY: FEMALES ($N = 42$)

Predictor	Cumulative R^2	B		Beta	Overall F
Father-daughter relationship:					
Control variables:					
Sociability	.131	−.065	(.038)	−.25	6.02*
Verbal ability	.134	.029	(.038)	.11	3.01
Communication variables:					
F indirect suggestion	.174	−.100	(.039)	−.43*	2.67
Separateness F to A	.239	.199	(.162)	.21	2.91*
A indirect suggestion	.277	.093	(.051)	.29	2.75*
F relevant comment	.342	.125	(.066)	.31	3.03*
A irrelevant comment.......	.352	−.236	(.324)	−.11	2.64*
Permeability F to A	.361	.040	(.058)	.12	2.34*
Mother-daughter relationship:					
Control variables:					
Sociability	.131	−.046	(.040)	−.18	6.02*
Verbal ability	.134	.004	(.037)	.01	3.01
Communication variables:					
Mutuality A to M...........	.204	−.368	(.160)	−.36*	3.24*
A indirect suggestion	.266	.090	(.052)	.28	3.35*
M direct suggestion	.288	.175	(.110)	.26	2.91*
A direct suggestion	.320	−.171	(.107)	−.28	2.75*
M indirect suggestion.......	.338	−.066	(.051)	−.21	2.48*
Permeability A to M........	.359	.065	(.063)	.17	2.31*
Adolescent-sibling relationship:					
Control variables:					
Sociability	.131	−.087	(.038)	−.34*	6.02*
Verbal ability	.134	−.021	(.038)	.08	3.01
Communication variable:					
Separateness A to sib	.188	.210	(.132)	.23	2.93*
Marital relationship:					
Control variables:					
Sociability	.131	−.008	(.042)	−.03	6.02*
Verbal ability	.134	.010	(.043)	.04	3.01
Communication variables:					
Mutuality F to M...........	.233	−.414	(.163)	−.42*	3.84*
Mutuality M to F...........	.277	.397	(.203)	.32	3.55*
Permeability F to M........	.339	−.088	(.060)	−.24	3.69**
F direct suggestion	.364	−.235	(.117)	−.33	3.34**
Separateness F to M........	.409	.423	(.187)	.40*	3.36**
M indirect suggestion.......	.448	−.057	(.048)	−.18	3.35**
M direct suggestion	.467	.134	(.101)	.20	3.12**
F relevant comment	.492	.120	(.073)	.30	3.00**
Separateness M to F........	.503	−.086	(.155)	−.09	2.76*
M relevant comment........	.510	−.065	(.069)	−.17	2.51*
F irrelevant comment.......	.519	−.846	(1.105)	−.12	2.33*
F indirect suggestion	.526	−.025	(.040)	−.11	2.14*

NOTE.—F = father; M = mother; A = adolescent. Variance accounted for by communication variables: father-daughter: .361 − .134 = 22.7%, adjusted R^2 for equation = .207; mother-daughter: .359 − .134 = 22.5%, adjusted R^2 for equation = .203; adolescent-sibling: .188 − .134 = 5.4%, adjusted R^2 for equation = .124; marital: .526 − .134 = 39.2%, adjusted R^2 for equation = .280.

* $p < .05$.
** $p < .01$.

tion model of family interaction were found to be associated with ratings of the breadth and depth of adolescent identity exploration, with the effects of verbal ability and sociability controlled. Although positive associations between all communication variables and identity exploration were initially predicted, the results have provided a more differentiated view of these dimensions, in that some associations were positive and others negative. Communication variables related to identity exploration not only differed for males and females, but also were significant for them in different family relationships. For girls, communication patterns in all four relationships were associated with identity exploration, whereas for boys, only father-son interaction patterns were related to exploration ratings. These differences suggest that sources of family influence on identity exploration may be more diverse for female adolescents than for males.

Our data suggest that somewhat different family interaction styles are associated with identity exploration for male and female adolescents. With their fathers, higher-scoring males expressed their disagreements as well as their suggestions directly. Fathers' communication patterns complemented those of their sons by contributing mutuality, which can be seen as serving a coordinating function in interaction, and by disagreeing infrequently. These fathers were also less likely than those of lower-scoring males to express their own ideas, either directly or indirectly, perhaps in order to allow their sons the opportunity to contribute to the family's vacation plans. Thus, fathers seem to be encouraging or at least tolerating their sons' assertiveness and directness in the task.

In contrast, fathers of higher-scoring daughters expressed higher frequencies of separateness and relevant comments, and lower frequencies of indirect suggestions. With their wives, these men expressed higher separateness, lower mutuality, and lower permeability. Their wives, in a potentially mediating pattern, expressed higher mutuality to their husbands. The picture in these families is of fathers who appear to comment on others' suggestions rather than express their own, and who disagree with both their wives and daughters. That mothers in these families were not simply mollifying the family conflict is indicated by their greater likelihood of expressing their own ideas directly as well as coordinating the family discussion. Thus, sons' relationships with their fathers and daughters' relationships with each parent

appear to provide the context for experiencing both individuality and connectedness, although in different forms.

As a whole, these findings are consistent with Erikson's (1968) view that identity formation involves the definition of a sense of self as distinctive from others. Our results suggest that in late adolescence, acknowledgment and coordination of such differences in family interactions, as seen in permeability and mutuality, offer a context in which adolescents may consider and refine options for their identity. In families whose adolescents engage in more exploration, these supportive qualities seem to be expressed primarily from the parents to their adolescents rather than vice versa. However, current studies of young adults and their parents have documented a developmental trend toward increasing mutuality in their relationships (White et al., 1983).

Because this is a correlational study, it is impossible to make claims about the direction of effects in adolescent identity formation. One plausible interpretation is that observing and participating in family relationships foster clarity in the adolescent's developing sense of self. It may be that experience in family relationships does indeed give adolescents the confidence and skills necessary to explore away from the family. At the same time, adolescents who have had such opportunities for exploration are likely to gain experience and expectations which may in turn affect their communication with family members.

The arguments of the present study regarding the significance of both individuality and connectedness are supported by evidence from a number of recent investigations that adolescent maturity is gained in the context of progressive and mutual redefinition of the parent-child relationship rather than by the adolescent simply leaving the relationship (Hill & Steinberg, 1976) or else redefining it by the solitary use of formal operational reasoning (Youniss, 1983). Hauser, Powers, and their colleagues (e.g., Hauser, Powers, Noam, Jacobson, Weiss, & Follansbee, 1984; Powers, Hauser, Schwartz, Noam, & Jacobson, 1983) have used both psychoanalytic and cognitive approaches to the study of these issues. They have found that adolescents' level of ego development was associated with patterns of family interaction involving high amounts of sharing of perspectives, and challenges in the context of support. Likewise, White et al. (1983) reported evidence of the continuing significance of individuality and connectedness in parent-child relationships into young adulthood. Although each of these studies is limited in terms of its sample and the number of contexts in which family interaction is observed, the convergence of conclusions from these studies is most striking.

In addition, the present findings of family interaction patterns differentiated by gender are consistent with other recent reports. Steinberg (1981) observed greater conflict between young adolescent males and their mothers than with their fathers. In addition, Youniss (in press) found that older adolescents reported differentiated patterns of relating to each parent in everyday social interaction. In the present investigation, it should be noted that few sex differences in mean frequencies of utterance types were observed for adolescents. However, the patterns of association between communication variables and identity exploration were very different for males and females.

In conclusion, the findings of this study support the usefulness of monitoring both individuality and connectedness in family relationships as predictors of individual competence. Important progress in theoretical and empirical work on family relationships will involve further analyses of individual relationships within the family, developmental changes in these relationships, and the contribution of development in family members to their relationships. Although the present study has established a link between individuation in relationships and identity exploration in late adolescence, it is likely that the balance between individuality and connectedness will vary over the course of the parent-child relationship.

Because the present sample was relatively small and included only Caucasian, middle-class, two-parent families, and because family interaction was observed in only one context, generalization should be made with caution, especially to cultural groups in which power sharing and identity exploration are not valued as highly as they likely were in this middle-class sample. In addition, since the characterizations of relationships in these families have been based on whole-family interaction, it will be important to understand how these dyads function independently as well as when the whole family is together. This exploratory study has provided an important starting point for differentiating our view of family process as a relational context for adolescent development.

Appendix

Conceptual Dimensions and Behavioral Indices of Individuation

Self-assertion: Displays awareness of own point of view and responsibility for communicating it clearly
1. Direct suggestion (.63)[2]
    a. Something I've always wanted to do, to go up to the northwest part of the country.
    b. I'd like to go to Italy.

Permeability: Expresses responsiveness to the views of others
1. Acknowledgment (.78).
    a. You said go to Canada.
    b. Oh.
    c. Uh-huh.
    d. OK.
2. Request for information (.72)
    a. In what perspective?
    b. What is a rail?
    c. How far is it from Rome to Athens?
3. Agreement (.46)
    a. I'd like to go there, too.
    b. Yeah, Yellowstone.
    c. Let's use Kim's idea of Spain and go to Madrid.
4. Relevant comment (.39)
    a. So we have two weeks and unlimited funds.
    b. Spain is next to France.
    c. Rail express (elaborates response)
5. Compliance with request for action (.28)
    a. I'll write that down right now.
    b. OK.

Mutuality: Shows sensitivity and respect for others' views
1. Indirect suggestion (.92)
    a. Let's go to Canada.
    b. Would either of you like to go back to Italy?
2. Initiation of compromise (.41)
    a. While Mom's in the antique shop, we can hike for a while.
    b. We can take Cindy to the Bahamas and then we can go wherever you want to go.
3. Statement of others' feelings (.32)
    a. The kids will love to see Disneyworld.
    b. Your mother has always wanted to go to England.
4. Answer to request for information (.30)
    a. A rail you go by train.
    b. It's about 400 miles.

Separateness: Expresses distinctiveness of self from others
1. Request for action (.51)
    a. Write that down there.
    b. Wait a minute.
    c. Let's vote on it.
2. Direct disagreement (.46)
    a. I don't want to go on a train.
    b. No.

[2] Factor loading of communication behavior on its primary factor.

3. Indirect disagreement (.29)
   a. But two or three months?
   b. We don't have time to do all that.
   c. Why would you want to go to that kind of place?
4. Irrelevant comment (.33)
   a. I'd like some more tea.
   b. You know, we're missing my favorite TV show.

References

Adams, G. R., & Jones, R. M. (1983). Female adolescents' identity development: Age comparisons and perceived child-rearing experience. *Developmental Psychology, 19,* 249–256.

Beavers, W. R. (1976). A theoretical basis for family evaluation. In J. M. Lewis, W. R. Beavers, J. T. Gossett, & V. A. Phillips, *No single thread: Psychological health in family systems* (pp. 46–82). New York: Brunner/Mazel.

Bell, D. C., & Bell, L. G. (1983). Parental validation and support in the development of adolescent daughters. In H. D. Grotevant & C. R. Cooper (Eds.), *Adolescent development in the family: New directions for child development* (pp. 27–42). San Francisco: Jossey-Bass.

Blos, P. (1979). The second individuation process of adolescence. In P. Blos, *The adolescent passage: Developmental issues* (pp. 141–170). New York: International University Press.

Campbell, D. P. (1974). *Manual for the Strong-Campbell Interest Inventory T325 (merged form).* Stanford, CA: Stanford University Press.

Carter, E. A., & McGoldrick, M. (1980). *The family life cycle: A framework for family therapy.* New York: Gardner.

Condon, S. M., Cooper, C. R., & Grotevant, H. D. (1984). Manual for the analysis of family discourse, *Psychological Documents, 14,* 8. (Ms. No. 2616.)

Cooper, C. R., Grotevant, H. D., & Condon, S. M. (1982). Methodological challenges of selectivity in family interaction: Assessing temporal patterns of individuation. *Journal of Marriage and the Family, 44,* 749–754.

Cooper, C. R., Grotevant, H. D., & Condon, S. M. (1983). Individuality and connectedness in the family as a context for adolescent identity formation and role taking skill. In H. D. Grotevant & C. R. Cooper (Eds.), *Adolescent development in the family: New directions for child development* (pp. 43–59). San Francisco: Jossey-Bass.

Coulthard, M. (1977). *An introduction to discourse analysis.* Essex: Longman.

Cromwell, R. E., & Olson, D. H. (1975). *Power in families.* New York: Halsted.

Cushing, D. C. (1971). *Identity status: A developmental model as related to parental behaviors.* Unpublished doctoral dissertation, State University of New York at Buffalo.

Dore, J. (1979). Conversational acts and the acquisition of language. In E. Ochs & B. B. Schieffelin (Eds.), *Developmental pragmatics* (pp. 339–361). New York: Academic Press.

Ekstrom, R. B., French, J. W., Harman, H. H., & Derman, D. (1976). *Manual for kit of factor-referenced cognitive tests.* Princeton, NJ: Educational Testing Service.

Erikson, E. H. (1950). *Childhood and society.* New York: Norton.

Erikson, E. H. (1968). *Identity: Youth and crisis.* New York: Norton.

Fischer, J. L. (1978). *A systems theory of dyadic relationships: The case of adolescent friendships.* Paper presented at the Theory Development and Methodology Workshop, National Council of Family Relations Annual Meeting, Philadelphia.

Gottman, J. M. (1979). *Marital interaction: Experimental investigations.* New York: Academic Press.

Grotevant, H. D., & Adams, G. R. (in press). Development of an objective measure to assess ego identity in adolescence: Validation and replication. *Journal of Youth and Adolescence.*

Grotevant, H. D., & Cooper, C. R. (1981). Assessing adolescent identity in the areas of occupation, religion, politics, friendship, dating, and sex roles: Manual for administration and coding of the interview. *JSAS Catalog of Selected Documents in Psychology, 11,* 52. (Ms. No. 2295.)

Grotevant, H. D., & Cooper, C. R. (in press). Individuation in family relationships: A perspective on individual differences in the development of identity and role taking skill in adolescence. *Human Development.*

Grotevant, H. D., Thorbecke, W. L., & Meyer, M. L. (1982). An extension of Marcia's identity status interview into the interpersonal domain. *Journal of Youth and Adolescence, 11,* 33–47.

Hauser, S. T., Powers, S. I., Noam, G., Jacobson, A. M., Weiss, B., & Follansbee, D. J. (1984). Familial contexts of adolescent ego development. *Child Development, 55,* 195–213.

Hill, J. P., & Steinberg, L. D. (1976). The development of autonomy during adolescence. In *Jornadas sobre problematica juvenil.* Madrid: Foundacion Faustino Orbegoza Eizaguerre.

Jordaan, J. P. (1963). Exploratory behavior: The formation of self and occupational concepts. In D. E. Super, R. Starishevsky, N. Matlin, & J. P. Jordaan (Eds.), *Career development: Self-concept theory* (pp. 42–78). Princeton, NJ: College Entrance Examination Board.

Karpel, M. (1976). Individuation: From fusion to dialogue. *Family Process, 15,* 65–82.

Klein, D. M., & Hill, R. (1979). Determinants of family problem-solving effectiveness. In W. R. Burr, R. Hill, F. I. Nye, & I. L. Reiss (Eds.), *Contemporary theories about the family* (Vol. 1, pp. 493–548). New York: Free Press.

L'Abate, L. (1976). *Understanding and helping the individual in the family.* New York: Grune & Stratton.

LaVoie, J. C. (1976). Ego identity formation in middle adolescence. *Journal of Youth and Adolescence,* 5, 145–160.

Lewis, J. M., Beavers, W. R., Gossett, J. T., & Phillips, V. A. (1976). *No single thread: Psychological health in family systems.* New York: Brunner/Mazel.

Maccoby, E. E., & Martin, J. A. (1983). Socialization in the context of the family: Parent-child interaction. In E. M. Hetherington (Ed.), P. H. Mussen (Series Ed.), *Handbook of child psychology: Vol. 4. Socialization, personality, and social development* (pp. 1–101). New York: Wiley.

Mahler, M. S. (1979). Thoughts about development and individuation. In M. S. Mahler, *The selected papers of Margaret S. Mahler, M.D.: Vol. 2. Separation and individuation.* New York: Jason Aronson.

Marcia, J. E. (1966). Development and validation of ego identity status. *Journal of Personality and Social Psychology,* 3, 551–558.

Marcia, J. E. (1980). Identity in adolescence. In J. Adelson (Ed.), *Handbook of adolescent psychology* (pp. 159–187). New York: Wiley.

Matteson, D. R. (1977). Exploration and commitment: Sex differences and methodological problems in the use of identity status categories. *Journal of Youth and Adolescence,* 6, 349–370.

Minuchin, S. (1974). *Families and family therapy.* Cambridge, MA: Harvard University Press.

Mueller, C. W., & Parcel, T. L. (1981). Measures of socioeconomic status: Alternatives and recommendations. *Child Development,* 52, 13–30.

Olson, D. H., Sprenkle, D. H., & Russell, C. S. (1979). Circumplex model of marital and family systems: I. Cohesion and adaptability dimensions, family types, and clinical applications. *Family Process,* 18, 3–28.

Powers, S. I., Hauser, S. T., Schwartz, J. M., Noam,

G. G., & Jacobson, A. M. (1983). Adolescent ego development and family interaction: A structural-developmental perspective. In H. D. Grotevant & C. R. Cooper (Eds.), *Adolescent development in the family: New directions for child development* (pp. 5–25). San Francisco: Jossey-Bass.

Riskin, J., & Faunce, E. E. (1970). Family interaction scales: I. Theoretical framework and method. *Archives of General Psychiatry,* 22, 504–512.

Sroufe, L. A. (1983). Infant-caregiver attachment and patterns of adaptation in preschool: The roots of maladaptation and competence. In M. Perlmutter (Ed.), *Minnesota symposia on child psychology* (Vol. 16). Hillsdale, NJ: Erlbaum.

Steinberg, L. D. (1981). Transformation in family relations at puberty. *Developmental Psychology,* 17, 833–840.

Thorbecke, W., & Grotevant, H. D. (1982). Gender differences in adolescent interpersonal identity formation. *Journal of Youth and Adolescence,* 11, 479–492.

Waterman, A. S. (1982). Identity development from adolescence to adulthood: An extension of theory and a review of research. *Developmental Psychology,* 18, 341–358.

Watzlawick, P. (1966). A structured family interview. *Family Process,* 5, 256–271.

White, K. M., Speisman, J. C., & Costos, D. (1983). Young adults and their parents: Individuation to mutuality. In H. D. Grotevant & C. R. Cooper (Eds.), *Adolescent development in the family: New directions for child development* (pp. 61–76). San Francisco: Jossey-Bass.

Youniss, J. (1983). Social construction of adolescence by adolescents and parents. In H. D. Grotevant & C. R. Cooper (Eds.), *Adolescent development in the family: New directions for child development* (pp. 93–109). San Francisco: Jossey-Bass.

Youniss, J. (in press). *Adolescents: Their parents and friends.* Chicago: University of Chicago Press.

Developmental Psychology
1996, Vol. 32, No. 4, 744-754

Changes in Adolescents' Daily Interactions With Their Families From Ages 10 to 18: Disengagement and Transformation

Reed W. Larson
University of Illinois at Urbana-Champaign

Maryse H. Richards
Loyola University of Chicago

Giovanni Moneta
Institute of Occupational Health

Grayson Holmbeck and Elena Duckett
Loyola University of Chicago

In a cross-sequential study spanning 5th-12th grade, 220 White working-and middle-class youth provided reports on their experience at 16,477 random moments in their lives. Amount of time spent with family was found to decrease from 35% to 14% of waking hours across this age period, indicating disengagement. However, transformation and continued connection were evident in stability across age in time talking and alone with parents; an age increase in family conversation about interpersonal issues, particularly for girls; and with age, adolescents' more frequent perception of themselves as leading interactions. After a decrease in early adolescence, older teens reported more favorable affect in themselves and others during family interactions. Last, the age decline in family time was found to be mediated not by internal family conflict but by opportunities and pulls an adolescent experiences from outside the family.

Two prominent theses have been advanced about developmental changes in adolescents' family relationships. The traditional view was that adolescence is a time of growing disengagement from family, associated with the process of becoming an independent adult. Havighurst (1953) identified emotional autonomy from parents as a developmental task of Western adolescence, and psychoanalytic writers portray adolescents as driven to individuate from their parents (Blos, 1967; Freud, 1946; Lidz, 1969). Steinberg and Silverberg (1986) obtained evidence that, with age, a sample of U.S. adolescents perceived themselves to be more emotionally and behaviorally independent of their parents.

A more recent thesis asserts that even as disengagement occurs, there is a transformation in adolescents' relationships with their parents that maintains continued closeness and warmth. Offer and Offer (1975) found continuity in most adolescent–parent relationships through the teenage years. Youniss (1980) found evidence that adolescent–parent relationships improve in later adolescence and hypothesized that a process of renegotiation takes place, leading to a more symmetric and mutual rela-

Reed W. Larson, Department of Human and Community Development, University of Illinois at Urbana-Champaign; Maryse H. Richards, Department of Psychology, Loyola University of Chicago; Giovanni Moneta, Institute of Occupational Health, Helsinki, Finland; Grayson Holmbeck and Elena Duckett, Department of Psychology, Loyola University of Chicago.

This research was partially supported by National Institute of Mental Health Grant 1 R01 MH38324. We are grateful to Marcelo Diversi for assistance on the manuscript.

Correspondence concerning this article should be addressed to Reed W. Larson, Department of Human and Community Development, University of Illinois, 1105 West Nevada Street, Urbana, Illinois 61801. Electronic mail may be sent via Internet to larsonr@uiuc.edu.

tionship, at least with mothers (Youniss & Smollar, 1985). Numerous authors have contended that the developmental task of adolescents is achievement of psychological independence from parents but with continued connectedness (Grotevant & Cooper, 1986; Hauser, 1991; Hill & Holmbeck, 1987; Youniss & Smollar, 1985).

An important yet neglected level at which these two developmental theses must be evaluated is that of daily interactions. Interactions are the forum in which relationships are enacted: It is through interactions that relationships are maintained, improve, or go sour (Kelley et al., 1983). Although it is useful to know that older adolescents continue to feel warm toward their families, it may be more valuable to know how often they actually see or talk with them. Whereas it is helpful to know that adolescents come to view their relationship with their parents as more mutual, it may be more important to know whether they experience themselves to be on an equal footing during actual interactions. To evaluate disengagement and transformation, we need information on how often and in what circumstances teenagers engage with their families: Is there disengagement and transformation within their daily interactions?

This article examines how basic parameters of adolescents' daily family interactions change across the 5th to 12th grade period. We used time-sampling data, obtained from a longitudinal sample of European American middle and working class youth, first, to examine developmental changes in the quantity of time and contexts of adolescents' family interactions, and second, to examine age changes in adolescents' subjective experience of these interactions: what they feel and how they perceive family members. Third, we evaluate the role of variables such as puberty, family conflict, and adolescents' opportunities outside the family in driving these changes.

This article is a follow-up to a prior article that examined age changes in social interactions across early adolescence (Larson

& Richards, 1991). The earlier article used Time 1 data from the current study to map age differences in the full range of social (and asocial) experience—including time with friends, with family, and alone—across the span from the fall of 5th grade to the winter of 9th grade. Several findings from that article are pertinent to the issues of this article: (a) Across this age span, amount of time spent with family declined by 40%; (b) this decline was largely due to less time in group interactions with family and was attributable to more time spent alone rather than more time away from home; and (c) the emotional states adolescents reported during family interactions became less positive across this age period, although for boys these states were more positive again in the ninth grade. The large decline in time and the less favorable affect suggest disengagement; however, continued engagement was suggested by the findings that amount of one-on-one time with parents did not decrease with age and that boys' emotional states with their families appeared to improve in middle adolescence.

The current article covers the 8-year period from 5th through 12th grade and focuses solely on family interactions, going into more depth. By extending the analysis to comprise the high school years, we include an important period when access to cars and the granting of new freedoms by parents (Feldman & Quatman, 1988) may further diminish family interaction; yet it is also a period when, according to prior research, renegotiation of family relationships is likely to occur. To detect changes in adolescents' level of engagement in family interactions, we evaluate age differences in the activities teens share with their families. In particular, we are interested in whether the amount of time spent communicating with family members decreases along with time in less interactive activities. To examine renegotiation, we examine age differences in how friendly adolescents perceive other family members to be and whom they perceive to be the leader during family interactions.

In addition to describing processes of disengagement and renegotiation within daily interactions, we evaluate variables that might drive these changes. The process of disengagement is often attributed to factors that are internal to adolescents' family relationships, factors that repel teens out of the family sphere. Psychoanalysts have sometimes put this in extreme terms, arguing that a felt need to individuate drives adolescents to partly or wholly repudiate their families (Freud, 1946; Lidz, 1969). Steinberg (1989, 1990) took a more moderate view, arguing that bickering and conflict increase at the age of puberty and lead to somewhat greater psychological distance between parents and adolescents. In one article, he suggested that there may be a built-in biological mechanism, across primate species, that stimulates distancing between offspring and parents at puberty in order to discourage endogenous mating (Steinberg, 1989). To evaluate this line of reasoning, we test whether puberty, family conflict, and other qualities of family relationships might be mediators of age differences in adolescents' family interactions.

Factors external to the family, however, may also play a role in changing adolescents' family interactions: Disengagement might result from as much pull as push. Older adolescents may spend less time with their families simply because they have more competing opportunities apart from the family sphere, either at home or away from home. If this is the case, diminished family time might be linked to life-situational factors that make it more attractive or easier for older adolescents to spend time apart from the family, such as having a private bedroom and a phone or TV in one's room, a later curfew, a job, or a driver's license and a car. In this study, therefore, we evaluate whether these kinds of life-situational factors are mediators of age differences in family interactions. Given the limits of our data set, these analyses of mediators should not be seen as conclusively testing a causal model but only as providing preliminary evidence.

In sum, the objective of this article is to examine processes of disengagement and transformation at the level of adolescents' everyday family interactions. We look at three sets of questions: (a) Does the amount of time and context of family interactions change across this age period? (b) Does adolescents' subjective experience of these interactions change? (c) Are these age changes related to factors internal to the adolescent and family relationships, or are they related to external factors that may pull the adolescent away from the family? Past research leads us to expect that boys' and girls' interactions with their families may differ (Collins & Russell, 1991; Youniss & Smollar, 1985), hence we consider gender as a moderating variable throughout the analyses.

Method

Sample

Participants were 220 middle- and working-class youth from a cross-sequential longitudinal study of adolescent development. At Time 1 of the study, these youth were in the 5th to 8th grades (ages 10–14). At Time 2, 4 years later, they were in the 9th to 12th grades (ages 13–18).

The initial sample was randomly selected from four elementary or junior high schools in the Chicago suburbs. Two schools were in a working-class, blue-collar community on the edge of the city, and two were in an outlying, middle-class bedroom community. The population of both communities was European American. A stratification procedure was used to obtain equal numbers of students by grade, gender, and community. The students in the longitudinal sample, analyzed here, were a subset from those in a larger cross-sectional Time 1 sample (see Larson, 1989a; Larson & Richards, 1989). Students from this larger sample who were ninth graders at Time 1 or who participated during the summer at Time 1 were not studied at Time 2.

Attrition reduced the number of students in the final longitudinal sample. From an initial pool of 438 randomly drawn students, 328 (75%) participated at Time 1, and 220 (67%) of these participated at Time 2. Reasons for nonparticipation included refusal or failure to obtain parental permission ($n = 110$), family moved and was unreachable at Time 2 ($n = 67$), death between Time 1 and 2 ($n = 3$), and providing data at Time 1 or Time 2 that was judged to be of poor quality ($n = 38$). Population data at Time 1 indicated that attrition was not related to community, parents' socioeconomic status (SES), or sociometric ratings of the youth made by other students; however, attrition was somewhat higher among youth with lower self-esteem and those in remarried families (Larson, 1989a). Nonparticipation at Time 2 was somewhat higher among boys (the final sample consists of 97 boys and 123 girls) and among youth with scores at 13 or above on Kovacs's (1985) Children's Depression Inventory (attrition between Time 1 and 2 was 39% for these depressed youth, as compared with 33% for nondepressed).

Census data showed the divorce rates in these two communities to be considerably below the national average. At Time 1, 179 of the youth lived with both of their original parents, 15 lived in remarried families, and 26 lived in one-parent families. At Time 2, 173 lived with both parents, 13 lived in remarried families, and 34 lived in one-parent families.

Procedure

At both Times 1 and 2, participants carried pagers for 1 week and provided reports on their situation and experience at random times when signaled, following the procedures of the experience sampling method (ESM; Csikszentmihalyi & Larson, 1987). One signal was sent at a random time within each 2-hr block of time, with 7 to 8 signals per day. At Time 1, signals were sent between 7:30 a.m. and 9:30 p.m. for all days of the week. This closely approximated their waking hours (Larson, 1989a). At Time 2, signals were sent between 7:30 a.m. and 10:30 p.m. on weekdays and between 8:00 a.m. and 12:00 a.m. on weekends. Although this approximated their waking hours, small amounts of waking time before and after these hours were missed by this schedule for some youth.[1]

Reports were provided for the great majority of the ESM time samples. Participants responded to an average of 85% of the signals at Time 1 and 76% of the signals at Time 2 by completing a report. About 6% of these missed signals were attributable to mechanical failure of the pager, with the remaining attributable to a wide range of reasons from forgetting the pager at home or in one's room to the signal occurring during an activity that could not be interrupted, such as a test or participation in a sporting event (Larson, 1989a). In total, the students provided an average of 40.2 reports per person at Time 1 and 34.7 reports per person at Time 2, resulting in a grand total of 16,477 reports across the two data collections.

After completing the ESM procedure at each time, participants filled out a packet of questionnaires. Data were also obtained from one parent, typically the mother, and from the schools. To randomize time-of-year effects, some students participated in the fall, some in the winter, and some in the spring.

ESM Measures

Being with family. At the time of each ESM signal, participants checked off whom they were with from a list of possible companions. For the purposes of these analyses, we divided their reports into times they indicated being with and not with family members. In addition, we divided occasions with family into seven mutually exclusive categories: (a) being with a parent group (this includes any combination of family members that includes both mother and father); (b) being alone with mother only; (c) being alone with father only; (d) being with one or more siblings; (e) being with mother and one or more siblings; (f) being with father and one or more siblings; and (g) being with extended family (includes any extended family member, and nuclear family members may or may not be present).

Activity, topic of conversation, location. On the ESM questionnaire, participants also responded to open-ended questions asking their activity, topic of conversation, and location each time they were signaled. Their activities were coded into 127 categories (interrater agreement was maintained at 94%). We have collapsed these into nine categories representing major groupings of family activities: homework, chores, eating, transportation, personal maintenance, watching TV, active leisure, talking, and idling. On occasions when students were talking, they were asked to report their topic of conversation. Responses to this item have been divided into two categories: times they were and times they were not talking about an interpersonal topic. Interrater agreement for this coding was 97%. Locations were initially coded into 68 categories (interrater agreement = 99%). For this variable, we were solely concerned about whether they were at home or away from home.

Subjective experience. Students rated their emotional state at each ESM signal on a scale of Affect, computed from three 7-point semantic

differential items (happy–unhappy, cheerful–irritable, friendly–angry). This scale has strong internal reliability (α = .75 at the level of the self-report) and construct validity (Larson, 1989b). Values for this scale were z scored within person separately for Time 1 and Time 2 such that a value of 0.0 corresponds to each person's mean for that time and an increment of 1.0 corresponds to that person's standard deviation. With this transformation, values for affect represent a person's feeling relative to his or her overall distribution of affect scores.

Students also rated their perception of the people they were with at the time of each signal. They were given a 7-point semantic differential scale to rate people from *very unfriendly* (1) to *very friendly* (7). These values were also converted to z scores. In addition, participants were asked on the ESM form who was "the leader" at the moment of the signal. The fixed response choices were "nobody," "yourself," and "someone else."

Questionnaire Measures

Pubertal status. Data on each participant's pubertal status were collected at Time 1 only. Students rated their level of physical development by comparing themselves with drawings created by Morris and Udry (1980) that represent five stages of development articulated by Tanner (1975). Boys rated themselves on two sequences of drawings depicting stages of pubic hair and genitalia development. We created a single puberty scale for boys by summing these two highly correlated (.85) ratings. Girls rated themselves on two sequences of drawings depicting pubic hair and breast development. We summed these two highly correlated (.71) ratings to create a single puberty scale for girls. Boys' and girls' ratings on these drawings have shown correlations with physicians' ratings ranging from .57 to .81 (Morris & Udry, 1980).

Family relationships. Information on family conflict and family relationships was obtained from the adolescent and parent questionnaires. Both adolescents and parents responded to the Conflict and Cohesion scales of the Family Environment Scale (Moos & Moos, 1986). In addition, adolescents responded to a scale assessing how close they felt to their mother (α = .89) and father (α = .91; Blyth, 1982).

Life-situation variables. At Time 2 students completed a questionnaire asking about situational factors in their lives that might be related to the amount of time they spent with their families. We have grouped these to create two scales. The first includes factors related to being apart from the family at home. It includes items asking whether they had their own bedroom and whether they had their own TV, VCR, CD player or stereo, phone, and phone number. The scale assessing factors related to being away from home includes whether they had a driver's license, whether they owned or had access to a motorcycle or car, whether they had a job and how many hours they worked per week, and the hour at which their parents expected them to be home on weekdays and weekends. Responses were adjusted according to the standard deviations for each item and summed to create the two scales.

School grade (versus chronological age). Because grade in school was part of the sampling design, we used it as our index of age. Our prior analyses suggested that this measure of social age is often a better index of developmental status than is chronological age.

Analyses

Analytic techniques were chosen to accommodate the nested or multilevel structure of the ESM data. Our data set included reports on

---

[1] On a questionnaire administered at Time 2, students were asked when they usually got up and went to bed. For weekdays, the average wake-up time was 6:26 a.m. and bedtime was 10:45 p.m. For weekends, the average wake-up time was 9:31 a.m. and bedtime was 12:46 p.m. There were significant grade trends, with 12th graders reporting bedtimes of 38 min later than 9th graders on weekdays and 80 min later on weekends.

16,477 moments in time, but these reports were not statistically independent; they were provided by 220 adolescents, each of whom may have shown distinct patterns. Thus the structure of the data involves two levels: Level 1, constituted by the 16,477 ESM reports, and Level 2, constituted by the 220 adolescents.

When possible we have used multilevel modeling, a regression procedure for modeling data with this hierarchical structure (Goldstein, 1987; Prosser, Rabash, & Goldstein, 1991; see also hierarchical linear modeling, developed by Bryk & Raudenbush, 1992). Through an iterative process, multilevel modeling fits separate regressions for each higher level grouping (in our case, each person) as a step toward arriving at a regression solution for the entire sample. The advantage of this procedure is that it makes full use of the degrees of freedom provided by the 16,477 time samples while taking into account the variation in patterns among the 220 persons. More extensive discussion of the use of multilevel modeling with ESM data is provided by Moneta and Csikszentmihalyi (in press).

Our hypotheses concern the relationship between day-to-day experience and developmental level as indexed by school grade. We were also interested in how these relationships might vary by gender. Thus for our central analyses, we tested multilevel models with the following form:

$$Y = \beta 1 + \beta 2 * \text{Grade} + \beta 3 * \text{Sex} + \beta 4 * (\text{Grade} * \text{Sex}),$$

in which Y was some aspect of family experience. The dependent variable, Y, was based on ESM reports, thus it was a Level 1 variable; sex was a Level 2 variable; and because participants took part in the study at two periods, 4 years apart, their grade in school varied both within a participant's reports and across participants, making it both a Level 1 and a Level 2 variable. Grade and the intercept were defined as random effects for Level 2.

Our strategy with each dependent variable was to first test this fundamental model, then to evaluate whether addition of other independent variables contributed significantly. In addition to this basic set of predictor variables, we evaluated a quadratic variable for school grade and the interaction of this quadratic variable with sex. Before computing these quadratic terms, we subtracted the mean for grade (8.5), so that these variables were orthogonal to the linear variable for grade (Draper & Smith, 1981). In preliminary analyses, we also evaluated a variable, time, that indicated whether a data point came from Time 1 or Time 2. This variable was not significant when grade was also included, thus we concluded that there was at most a minimal test–retest effect from participating in the ESM twice.

To make our findings most useful, we report the raw values for betas (except where otherwise indicated), and we report them using the same units we use to discuss Y. Thus in the example in which Y is the likelihood of being with one's family at each ESM signal—a variable we report as a percentage—values for beta are reported as the percentage change in the likelihood of being with one's family for each grade increment. In other words, a raw beta value of -2.00 indicates that time with family drops by two percentage points per year. To obtain beta values comparable to percentages, we used dichotomous dependent variables that were coded 0 and 100 rather than the typical 0 and 1.

In several instances multilevel modeling could not be used, so we used more conventional analyses, following guidelines described by Larson and Delespaul (1992) for analyzing ESM data. In some analyses that used only a subset of the ESM data points, the multilevel program, ML3 (Prosser et al., 1991), could not converge on a solution because there were insufficient data points per person. In these instances we used standard regression, disregarding the hierarchical structure of the data but using a more stringent alpha of $p < .01$ to compensate for the inflated N. In other instances in which our questions dealt primarily with the person as the unit of analysis, we created person-level variables from the ESM data (e.g., amount of time spent with family) and performed analyses at that level.

Results

Age Changes in the Amount of Time, Context, and Content of Family Interactions

Total time. Our first question was whether the amount of time adolescents spent with their families decreased across the adolescent years. To evaluate this prediction, we performed a multilevel regression equation in which being with family was the dependent variable, and grade, sex, and the interaction of grade and sex were the independent variables.

This analysis showed a large linear decline in time spent with family that continued from early through late adolescence. In the regression, grade was found to be a significant predictor of spending time with family. The value of beta for grade was -2.74 ($SE = .40, p < .001$), indicating that the amount of time spent with family decreased by an estimate of 2.74% per year across the 5th to 12th grade period. Twelfth graders spent approximately two fifths as much of their waking hours with their families as did 5th graders. The addition of a quadratic term for grade did not add significantly to the equation, and the interaction between grade and sex was not significant.

This large drop in family time was evident across all times of the week. The largest decline in family time was on Friday and Saturday nights, with large declines also evident for weekday afternoons and evenings and during daytime hours on weekends. The most frequent time for family interaction for both age groups was Sunday evening after 6:00 p.m.

Time in family subsystems. The next question was whether this decline in family time occurred across all groupings of family members. To test this, a dichotomous dependent variable was created for each of the seven categories of family members, and separate multilevel regressions were run for each.

We found that time spent alone with mother and alone with father did not decline significantly across this 8-year age period. Time spent with mother only remained stable across grade at approximately 3.0% of waking time; time spent with father only remained stable at approximately 1.6% of waking time. Time spent in all other family groupings showed linear declines with age. Grade was a significant predictor for time with parent group ($\beta = -.79, SE = .14, p < .001$); mother and one or more siblings ($\beta = -.44 \, SE = .10, p < .001$); father and one or more siblings ($\beta = -.08, SE = .03, p < .05$); one or more siblings only ($\beta = -.60, SE = .15, p < .01$); and extended family ($\beta = -.41, SE = .16, p < .01$). For the regression predicting time with father and one or more siblings, there was also a significant sex effect ($\beta = -.58, SE = .23, p < .05$) attributable to boys spending more time in this family subsystem. For all of these equations, the addition of a quadratic term for grade was not significant.

The full set of age changes in adolescents' time with each family subsystem is summarized in Figure 1. The graph as a whole shows the substantial cumulative decrease in the total volume of time spent with family.

Activities and topic of conversation with family. Our next question was whether the decline in family time would be uniform across all activities or whether there might be less decline in activities that involve communication. To evaluate this we created dichotomous dependent variables to represent each of the nine categories of activities and included these as dependent

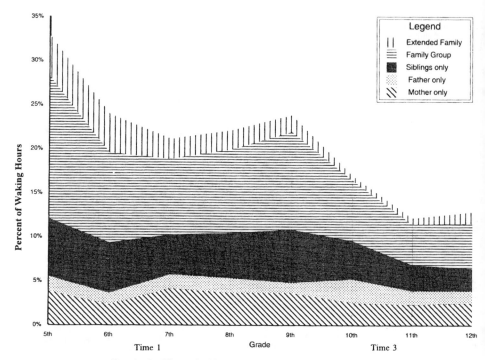

Figure 1. Age differences in adolescents' amount of time spent with family members.

variables in separate multilevel regression analyses in which grade, sex, and their interaction were predictors.

These analyses revealed significant linear declines with grade for all activities with family, except talking and transportation (Table 1). The most substantial decline appeared in leisure activities with family, including TV viewing and active leisure. These analyses also revealed a significant sex effect for frequency of talking ($\beta = 1.35$, $SE = .36$, $p < .001$), with girls reporting more frequent talking. None of the sex by grade interactions and none of the quadratic trends for grade were significant.

We next evaluated whether the rate of talking was stable across all family subsystems. For this analysis, only ESM self-reports when the students were in each subsystem were included, thus the findings address the rate of talking within that subsystem (not as a proportion of all time). Talking versus not talking was the dichotomous dependent variable; because of the reduced sample sizes for these analyses, multilevel regressions did not converge, so we used standard regressions, with an alpha level of .01.

These analyses suggested that talking increased within family subsystems that included mother (Table 2). Rate of talking rose at a significant rate when the adolescent was with mother and one or more siblings. It increased at a close-to-significant rate when the adolescent was with a parent group or with mother only. These analyses also suggested that girls reported talking more frequently than did boys when with mother only and when with one or more siblings only. A close-to-significant interaction between grade and sex for parent groups was attributable to an increased rate of talking for girls (from 10% in the 5th–6th grades to 21% in the 11th–12th grades) with little change for boys (8% and 11%, respectively).

Further analysis showed that the topics of this talk became more interpersonal with age, particularly for girls. The pool of self-reports for this analysis included all occasions with family in which a topic of conversation was reported. The dichotomous dependent variable represented whether the topic was interpersonal or not. Again, the limited number of cases prevented us from testing this trend with multilevel regressions, so we used standard regression with the more stringent alpha of .01. This analysis found that grade was a significant predictor of interpersonal conversation, $\beta = 1.04$, $SE = .25$, $p < .001$. This regression also yielded a significant main effect for sex, $\beta = 7.05$, $SE = 1.20$, $p < .001$, attributable to girls talking more about inter-

Table 1
Percentage of ESM Reports in Different Activities With Family, by Grade

Activity	% of ESM reports by grade level								β for grade trend
	5	6	7	8	9	10	11	12	
Homework	3.1	1.4	1.5	2.2	1.7	0.9	0.3	0.4	−.31***
Chores	1.5	1.8	1.7	1.4	2.0	1.2	0.9	1.1	−.11*
Eating	3.9	2.6	1.8	2.6	2.2	1.6	1.4	1.8	−.22***
Transportation	1.5	1.5	0.9	1.1	1.6	1.4	0.9	0.8	−.06
Personal maintenance	3.5	2.1	1.7	2.0	2.1	1.6	1.1	1.7	−.18**
Watching TV	9.9	7.6	6.0	6.7	6.9	4.5	2.9	3.4	−.87***
Active leisure	5.4	3.4	3.5	2.0	2.4	1.2	0.5	1.2	−.56***
Talking	2.3	3.1	2.8	2.7	3.0	2.2	2.1	2.3	−.11
Idling	2.1	1.3	1.3	0.8	1.6	1.1	0.5	0.4	−.18***

Note. ESM = experience sampling method.
* $p < .05$. ** $p < .01$. *** $p < .001$.

personal topics. It also yielded a significant grade by sex interaction, $\beta = 1.86$, $SE = .95$, $p < .05$; separate regressions for girls and boys found that the grade increase was significant for girls, $\beta = 2.90$, $SE = .75$, $p < .001$, but not for boys, $\beta = −.23$, $SE = 1.04$, *ns.*

In sum, although total time with family declined substantially across adolescence, the amount of time spent in communication with family, especially with mothers, did not drop, and for girls, the proportion of this communication addressed to interpersonal issues increased.

Age Changes in Adolescents' Experience of Family Interactions

Our next question was whether adolescents' subjective experience of their interactions with family changed with age. Did their emotional state become less positive, did they perceive family members to be more friendly, and did they experience greater equality in who was leading the interactions? It should be noted that individuals' aggregated scores for these experience variables were found to be unrelated to the amount of time each spent with his or her family, thus age changes in the quality of family experience appear to be independent of age changes in quantity of time.

Affect. To evaluate whether adolescents' emotional states with family changed as a function of age, we tested a series of multilevel regressions in which ESM reports of affect constituted the dependent variable. Age changes in adolescents' overall emotional states were controlled by using z scored values for affect, as described in the *Analyses* section earlier. Only self-reports during family interactions were included.

These analyses indicated that adolescents' affect with family decreased in early adolescence and then increased in late adolescence. We first tested a simple model with linear terms for grade, sex, and their interaction as the independent variables. This multilevel regression yielded no significant findings. We then added a quadratic term for grade, which was strongly significant ($\beta = 1.24$, $SE = .37$, $p < .01$). Affect with family decreased in the early adolescent years. When we added a cubic term to the equation, we found a significant interaction between this cubic term and gender ($\beta = .89$, $SE = .41$, $p < .05$). A graph of the age by sex interaction indicates that boys and girls both showed a drop in affect with their families between the 5th–6th and 7th–8th grades; however, in the 9th–10th grade period girls' affect remained low, whereas boys' affect improved (Figure 2). The decrease in affect appeared to last longer for girls.

Further analyses suggested that this early adolescent decrease in affect was more evident in some family activities than others.

Table 2
Grade and Sex Differences in Rates of Talk Within Family Subsystems

Family subsystem	Number of reports	Rate of talk (%)	Regression predicting rate of talk (unstandardized β)		
			Grade	Sex of child	Sex by grade
Parent groups	877	10.9	.96*	5.61*	1.86*
Mother only	502	16.3	1.49*	9.88**	−.07
Mother and sibling(s)	538	11.2	2.45***	.13	1.37
Father only	257	12.5	−.33	9.13*	1.57
Father and sibling(s)	123	8.9	.74	6.27	1.37
Sibling(s) only	783	9.8	.47	8.76***	1.86
Extended family	375	15.2	1.45	8.01	1.27

* $p < .05$. ** $p < .01$. *** $p < .001$.

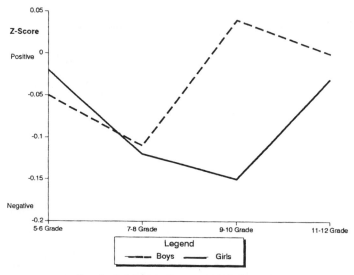

Figure 2. Grade trends in affect reported with family members.

We examined the relationship of grade and sex to affect within each of the nine categories of family activities. In a standard regression, we found that affect during family talk was significantly related to a quadratic term for grade (β = 3.16, SE = 1.17, $p < .01$). This quadratic effect did not approach significance for any of the other activities, including activities with ns that were similar to or larger than for talking (i.e., eating, personal maintenance, media, active leisure). Thus this early-adolescent decrease in affect appeared to be most apparent during talk, an activity in which interaction with family is probably most direct. Similar analyses failed to differentiate trends by family subsystem.

Friendliness of others. Age change in the perceived friendliness of family members was evaluated in multilevel regressions identical to those used to evaluate affect and showed a similar decrease in early adolescence. The regression yielded a significant quadratic effect for grade (β = 1.28, SE = .43, $p < .01$) that was due to a drop in the perceived friendliness of family members in early adolescence. It also yielded a significant main effect for sex (β = −.117, SE = .048, $p < .01$) attributable to girls' perceiving family members to be less friendly than boys. Other terms, including the cubic term for grade and interactions between sex and grade, were not significant.

Perceived leader. Consistent with the hypothesis of renegotiation, we found an age trend, with older adolescents perceiving themselves to be the leader more often during family interactions. We first tested whether there were age changes in adolescents' reporting that there was a leader. The grade term for this multilevel regression was not significant: No leader was reported for approximately 66% of reports across all grades. We

then evaluated a similar multilevel regression with a dependent variable of self versus other as leader. In this analysis there was a significant linear effect for grade (β = 1.50, SE = .72, $p < .05$), with all other effects nonsignificant. In 5th-6th grade, the students reported themselves to be leader in 6.1% of their family reports; in 11th-12th grade this number was 12.8%.

This age trend in adolescents' perception of themselves as the leader was most evident in interactions with siblings. Standard regressions, conducted for the reports within each subsystem, revealed significant trends for time with mother and one or more siblings (β = 2.20, SE = .46, $p < .001$) and time with one or more siblings only (β = 2.50, SE = .73, $p < .001$). The regressions for other family subsystems yielded betas for grade that were smaller and did not approach significance.

Factors Mediating Grade Changes in Family Interaction

The most prominent grade changes we found earlier are a dramatic decline in the amount of time adolescents spent with their families and a curvilinear pattern in the affect they reported during this time. Grade per se, however, is probably not the cause of these changes, but rather variables that are related to grade. Our final question is whether these grade trends are attributable to variables that are internal or external to adolescents' family relationships; that is, are they related to factors that affect family relationships from within, such as puberty and family conflict, or are they related to factors that pull adolescents out of the family, such as opportunities in one's bedroom or away from home?

In essence we wanted to know whether these internal and ex-

Table 3
Regressions Evaluating Possible Mediators of the Relationship
Between Grade and Family Time

	Regression prediction (standardized β)				
		Family time		Family time from	
Mediator	Mediator from grade	from mediator	Family time from grade	Grade	Mediator
Pubertal status[a]					
Boys	.63***	−.41***	−.39***	−.18	−.32**
Girls	.62***	−.23*	−.22*	−.12	−.16
Family conflict					
Reported by adolescent	.19***	−.06	−.45***	−.45***	.03
Reported by parent	−.05	−.03	−.45***	−.45***	−.06
Life-situation factors[b]					
For separation at home	.12	−.16*	−.29***	−.28***	−.14*
To be away from home	.56***	−.32***	−.26***	−.12	−.26**

[a] 5th–8th grade only. [b] 9th–12th grade only.
* p < .05. ** p < .01. *** p < .001.

ternal variables mediated the relationship we have found between grade and family experience. Baron and Kenny (1986) defined a mediator as "a third variable, which represents the generative mechanism through which the focal independent variable [grade, in this case] is able to influence the dependent variable of interest [family experience]" (p. 1173). We used Baron and Kenny's criteria to evaluate mediation (Table 3). For each possible mediating variable we asked the following questions: Is it associated with the independent variable, grade (Column 1)? Is it related to the dependent variable, amount of family time or average experience with family (Column 2)? Is the beta for the independent variable, grade, reduced or eliminated in a regression that includes the mediator (is the beta in Column 4 smaller than the beta in Column 3)? And does the mediator significantly predict family time or experience in a regression that includes grade (Column 5)? Given the limits of our data, these tests cannot prove that a mediator is the "generative mechanism," but failure to meet all four tests is evidence that it is not the mechanism, or that it is, at best, a weak contributor.

Mediators of changes in family time. We first evaluated whether the internal factors met criteria as mediators of the grade changes in family time. These analyses suggested that in early adolescence pubertal status was a mediator of the decline in family time for boys but not girls. For boys, pubertal status met all four criteria (Table 3): It was strongly related to grade; negatively related to amount of time spent with family; and in a regression including grade as a predictor, the contribution of grade became nonsignificant and pubertal status was a strong independent predictor of family time. These findings are consistent with the hypothesis that puberty rather than grade drives boys' decline in family time during early adolescence. For girls, the fourth criteria was not met: With grade included in the equation, pubertal status was not an independent predictor of family time. However, grade was also not a significant predictor in this equation, leaving it ambiguous whether grade or pubertal status might drive the age decline in family time for girls. Separate analyses with our larger sample of fifth to ninth graders

indicated that grade but not pubertal status was an independent predictor of family time for girls during this age period.[2] Thus puberty may make little contribution to girls' diminished time with family.

Next we found that family conflict was not related to the age changes in family time, nor did any of the other family relationship variables meet criteria as mediators of this change. Our analyses of these relationship variables included the entire 5th to 12th grade period and used data for each person at each time period as the unit of analysis (n = 440). Surprisingly, family conflict (as reported by the adolescent and by the parent) was not related to amount of family time—youth with more conflict did not spend less time with their families (Table 3)—thus, it could not be a mediator. Similar analyses with the other relationship variables also failed to meet the criteria as mediators (not shown). Tests of quadratic trends for grade also failed to show mediation. Because the literature has sometimes found different patterns for girls and boys, we also tested these relationships separately for each gender and found that the patterns differed little for boys and girls.

Factors that are "external" to family relationships fared better as mediators of the age changes in adolescents' family time. For the 9th to 12th grade period, the score representing life situation opportunities for separation at home did not meet all the criteria. However, the score representing opportunities to be away from home did (Table 3). This later score included whether the student had a driver's license, a job, and other factors that might make him or her more likely to be away from home. Consistent with mediation, this score was related positively to grade and negatively to family time. In a regression

---

[2] We repeated the final step of these pubertal analyses with the larger Time 1 sample of 483 young adolescents that we have used in other publications (cf. Larson & Richards, 1989). For girls, grade was found to be a significant independent predictor of family time, with a standardized $\beta = -.38$, $p < .001$, but not pubertal status, $\beta = -.03$, ns. For boys, pubertal status was found to be a significant predictor of family time, $\beta = -.31$, $p < .001$, but not grade, $\beta = -.14$, $p < .10$.

including both this score and grade as independent variables, only this score was a significant predictor of family time. Thus, for the senior high school period, this score—which represents opportunities and pulls to be away from home—meets criteria as a mediator of the decline in family time.

An additional set of analyses helped illuminate this last finding. We found that amount of time spent away from home did not change during the 5th to 9th grade period, remaining stable at about 55% of waking hours. During this early adolescent period, declining family time was replaced primarily by time spent alone at home. It was only in the high school years that time apart from home showed an increase, rising to 63% in the 10th grade and to 66% in the 11th and 12th grades. This suggests that pulls away from home mediate the age decline in family time only for the older age period; during early adolescence, factors that draw an adolescent to be alone may be more important.

Mediators of changes in family experience. None of the internal and external factors met the criteria as mediators of the early adolescent decrease in affect and perceived friendliness with family nor the age changes in perceived leader.

Discussion

The focus of this research was on age changes in the mundane, daily interactions between adolescents and their families for this sample of European American youth. We were interested in the quality and quantity of contact that take place after school, at the supper table, or when family members do chores on the weekend. The findings showed that, with age, there is both disengagement and transformation in these kinds of daily interactions.

Disengagement

Disengagement was evident in the total quantity of time teens spent with their families. These working- and middle-class youth exhibited a steady and dramatic drop in their family time: from 35% of waking hours in 5th grade to 14% in 12th grade. By the end of senior high school, these teenagers were spending much less time in leisure and daily maintenance activities with their families. The decline was greatest for time with groups of family members and time with siblings. Evidence from other studies cautions that we should not generalize this pattern to adolescents from non-European backgrounds, for whom centripetal forces to the family may be stronger (Cooper & Baker, 1991; Feldman & Quatman, 1988). Nonetheless, for these European American adolescents, the progressive withdrawal from daily family life is striking.

Contrary to some theories, this disengagement did not appear to be driven by factors internal to family relationships that repel adolescents outward. We failed to find that measures of family relationships met criteria as mediators of this age decline in family time. Our questionnaire measures of family conflict were unrelated to the age differences in amount of family time (see also Montemayor, 1982), as were our measures of family cohesion and adolescents' closeness to mother and father. The immediate affect that adolescents reported with their families was also not correlated with their amount of family time. Such

findings suggest that negative experience with family is as likely to be a stimulus for continued interaction—like one might see in an embattled, enmeshed family—as it is to be a stimulus for physical withdrawal.

The findings did indicate that in early adolescence this disengagement was related to puberty for boys. This relationship resembles, in less extreme form, the pattern for many other primates, among whom there is a dramatic drop for male individuals in time spent with family members at puberty (Caine, 1986; Pusey, 1983). In other primates, however, this disengagement is related to bickering and conflict, which appear to drive pubertal males from the natal group (Caine, 1986; Steinberg, 1989). But for the male human adolescents in this study, family conflict appeared not to be related to the reduction in family time.

Instead, the decline in adolescents' family time was related to pulls from outside the family. In early adolescence, diminishing family time was replaced by time spent alone at home. At this age, teens begin spending more time alone in their bedrooms, and although this time typically brings less favorable affective states, they appear to be drawn to it (Larson, 1990; Larson & Richards, 1991). During the high school years, the continuing decline in family time within our sample was related to increasing pulls from outside the home. After the ninth grade, these adolescents begin spending more time away from home: They stay late at school or go out with friends and thus are with their families less often. Our findings showed that life-situation factors that required or made it easier to be away from home were related to the decline in family time for this older age period. A composite of variables, including having a car, having a job, and having permission from parents to stay out later, met the criteria to be considered a mediator of the age reduction in family time, indeed it eliminated the contribution of grade to predicting family time.

We are thus led to the conclusion that most adolescents do not feel driven out of their families, rather their increasing involvement in outside activities may crowd out or displace family time. In short, the decline with age in family interactions appears to have little to do with the family. In fact, our findings suggest various ways in which teens and their families may try to compensate for loss of shared time.

Continuity and Transformation

Concurrent with this disengagement from daily interactions, we see elements of continued engagement and transformation in the time these adolescents did spend with their families. Although overall family time declined, certain categories of family time did not, suggesting that withdrawal from family was discriminate. The quantity of time these adolescents spent alone with their mothers and the smaller quantity of time they spent alone with their fathers both remained stable across this age period. The stability of this one-on-one time with parents suggests that adolescents, or their parents, may be deliberately selecting their shared time in order to maintain more intimate interaction.

This priority of maintaining direct interaction was further suggested by shifts in the activities that older adolescents reported with their families. With age, adolescents showed the largest declines in family activities involving less communication, such as TV watching, whereas time spent talking did not decline. In fact, for girls, amount of time spent in conversations about interpersonal issues increased significantly. This shift for girls is parallel to shifts in their interactions with peers (Raffaelli & Duckett, 1989), suggesting that it reflects a general growth in girls' capacity for and interest in interactions around interpersonal issues.

Transformation was also indicated by age shifts in adolescents' perceptions of who was leading family interactions. Across ages, these youth reported that no one was leading for about two thirds of the time. However, at older ages they saw themselves as the leader more often during the remaining one third of the time, and by age 18 they saw themselves as the leader nearly as often as they saw other family members to be the leader, especially when they were with siblings or with mother and siblings. This finding provides support, at the level of daily interactions, for Youniss's (1980) thesis that adolescents' relationships with their parents, at least with their mothers, change in the direction of becoming less unilateral and more symmetric in late adolescence.

Finally, we saw signs of transformation in these adolescents' changing emotional experience with their families. The emotional states they reported became less positive in early adolescence, especially during talk, and they experienced family members as less friendly. But these states and perceptions of others became more favorable in the early high school years for boys and in the late high school years for girls. These curved trends—based on adolescents' in vivo experiences—reinforce findings from interview, questionnaire, and observational studies suggesting that early adolescence is often the most strained period in adolescent–parent relationships (Holmbeck & Hill, 1991; Offer & Offer, 1975; Steinberg, 1981). The more positive affect we found in late adolescence is a sign that the renegotiation described by other scholars has led to improved relationships at this age period. Older adolescents report becoming better able to tolerate or even enjoy their parents' company as a result of better communication and greater mutual understanding and respect (Freeman, Csikszentmihalyi, & Larson, 1986).

Therefore, even as these adolescents' family time is diminishing, it is being transformed. The shrinking portion of time that adolescents spend with their families involves more dyadic and direct interaction with parents; it is perceived as less unilateral; and after an early adolescent period of less favorable affect, it is experienced more favorably in late adolescence. Of course, these findings reflect only group trends: Some individuals did not demonstrate transformation; for some, irritability and conflict continues into late adolescence and beyond (cf. Hauser, 1991). We also cannot be certain whether these trends would have been evident for the substantial group of students from the original random sample who declined to take part or for adolescents other than the working- and middle-class European Americans whom we studied. Nonetheless, within the confines of our sample, the findings clearly support the thesis that adolescents are not just disengaging from daily family interaction, but rather these interactions are being altered to maintain family connectedness.

References

Baron, R. M., & Kenny, D. A. (1986). The moderator–mediator variable distinction in social psychological research: Conceptual, strategic, and statistical considerations. *Journal of Personality and Social Psychology, 51,* 1173–1182.

Blos, P. (1967). The second individuation process of adolescence. *The Psychoanalytic Study of the Child, 22,* 162–186.

Blyth, D. A. (1982). Mapping the social world of adolescents: Issues, techniques, and problems. In F. Serafica (Ed.), *Social cognition, context, and social behavior: A developmental perspective* (pp. 240–272). New York: Guilford Press.

Bryk, A., & Raudenbush, S. W. (1992). *Hierarchical linear models: Applications and data analysis methods.* Newbury Park, CA: Sage.

Caine, N. G. (1986). Behavior during puberty and adolescence. In J. Erwin (Series & Vol. Ed.) & G. Mitchel (Vol. Ed.), *Comparative primate biology: Vol. 2, Part A. Behavior, conservation, and ecology* (pp. 327–361). New York: Liss.

Collins, W. A., & Russell, G. (1991). Mother–child and father–child relationships in middle childhood and adolescence: A developmental analysis. *Developmental Psychology, 25,* 550–559.

Cooper, C. R., & Baker, H. (1991, July). *Ethnic perspectives on individuality and connectedness in adolescents' relationships with family and peers.* Paper presented at the meetings of the International Society for the Study of Behavioral Development, Minneapolis.

Csikszentmihalyi, M., & Larson, R. (1987). The experience sampling method. *Journal of Nervous and Mental Disease, 175,* 526–536.

Draper, N. R., & Smith, H. (1981). *Applied regression analyses.* (2nd ed.). New York: Wiley.

Feldman, S. S., & Quatman, T. (1988). Factors influencing age expectations for adolescent autonomy: A study of early adolescents and parents. *Journal of Early Adolescence, 8,* 325–343.

Freeman, M., Czikszentmihalyi, M., & Larson, R. (1986). Adolescence and its recollection: Toward an interpretive model of development. *Merrill-Palmer Quarterly, 32,* 167–185.

Freud, A. (1946). *The ego and the mechanisms of defence.* New York: International Universities Press.

Goldstein, H. (1987). *Multilevel models in educational and social research.* New York: Oxford University Press.

Grotevant, H. D., & Cooper, C. R. (1986). Individuation in family relationships: A perspective on individual differences in the development of identity and role-taking skill in adolescence. *Human Development, 29,* 82–100.

Hauser, S. T. (with Powers, S. I., & Noam, G. G.). (1991). *Adolescents and their families: Paths of ego development* (pp. 231–243). New York: Free Press.

Havighurst, R. J. (1953). *Human development and education.* New York: McKay.

Hill, J. P., & Holmbeck, G. N. (1987). Familial adaptation to biological change during adolescence. In R. M. Lerner & T. T. Foch (Eds.), *Biological-psychosocial interactions in early adolescence* (pp. 207–223). Hillsdale, NJ: Erlbaum.

Holmbeck, G. N., & Hill, J. P. (1991). Conflictive engagement, positive affect, and menarche in families with seventh-grade girls. *Child Development, 62,* 1030–1048.

Kelley, H. H., Berscheid, E., Christensen, A., Harvey, J. H., Huston, T. L., Levinger, G., McClintock, E., Peplau, L. A., & Peterson, D. R. (Eds.). (1983). *Close relationships.* New York: Freeman.

Kovacs, M. (1985). The Children's Depression Inventory. *Psychopharmacology Bulletin, 21,* 995–998.

Larson, R. W. (1989a). Beeping children and adolescents: A method for studying time use and daily experience. *Journal of Youth and Adolescence, 18,* 511–530.

Larson, R. W. (1989b). *The factor structure of moods and emotions in a sample of young adolescents.* Unpublished manuscript, University of Illinois, Urbana–Champaign.

Larson, R. W. (1990). The solitary side of life: An examination of the time people spend alone from childhood to old age. *Developmental Review, 10,* 155-183.

Larson, R. W., & Delespaul, P. (1992). Analyzing experience sampling data: A guidebook for the perplexed. In M. deVries (Ed.), *The experience of psychopathology: Investigating mental disorders in their natural setting* (pp. 58-78). Cambridge, England: Cambridge University Press.

Larson, R. W., & Richards, M. H. (Eds.). (1989). The changing life space of early adolescence (Special issue). *Journal of Youth and Adolescence, 18,* 501-626.

Larson, R. W., & Richards, M. H. (1991). Daily companionship in late childhood and early adolescence: Changing developmental contexts. *Child Development, 62,* 284-300.

Lidz, T. (1969). The adolescent and his family. In G. Caplan & S. Lebovici (Eds.), *Adolescence: Psychosocial perspectives* (pp. 105-112). New York: Basic Books.

Moneta, G. B., & Csikszentmihalyi, M. (in press). The effect of perceived challenges and skills on the quality of subjective experience. *Journal of Personality, 64.*

Montemayor, R. (1982). The relationship between parent–adolescent conflict and the amount of time adolescents spend alone and with parents and peers. *Child Development, 53,* 1512-1519.

Moos, R. H., & Moos, B. S. (1986). *Family environment scales manual* (2nd ed.). Palo Alto, CA: Consulting Psychologists Press.

Morris, N. M., & Udry, J. R. (1980). Validation of a self-administered instrument to assess stage of adolescent development. *Journal of Youth and Adolescence, 9,* 271-280.

Offer, D., & Offer, J. B. (1975). *Teenage to young manhood: A psychological study.* New York: Basic Books.

Prosser, R., Rasbash, J., & Goldstein, H. (1991). *Software for three-level analysis.* London: University of London, Institute of Education.

Pusey, A. E. (1983). Mother–offspring relationships in chimpanzees after weaning. *Animal Behavior, 31,* 363-377.

Raffaelli, M., & Duckett, E. (1989). "We were just talking . . .": Conversations in early adolescence. *Journal of Youth and Adolescence, 18,* 567-582.

Steinberg, L. (1981). Transformations in family relations at puberty. *Developmental Psychology, 17,* 833-840.

Steinberg, L. (1989). Pubertal maturation and parent–adolescent distance: An evolutionary perspective. In G. R. Adams, R. Montemayor, & T. P. Gullotta (Eds.), *Biology of adolescent behavior and development* (pp. 71-97). Newbury Park, CA: Sage.

Steinberg, L. (1990). Autonomy, conflict, and harmony in the family relationship. In S. S. Feldman & G. R. Elliot (Eds.), *At the threshold: The developing adolescent* (pp. 255-276). Cambridge, MA: Harvard University Press.

Steinberg, L., & Silverberg, S. B. (1986). The vicissitudes of autonomy in early adolescence. *Child Development, 57,* 841-851.

Tanner, J. M. (1975). Growth and endocrinology of the adolescent. In L. J. Gardner (Ed.), *Endocrine and diseases of childhood* (2nd ed., pp. 14-64). Philadelphia: Saunders.

Youniss, J. (1980). *Parents and peers in social development.* Chicago: University of Chicago Press.

Youniss, J., & Smollar, J. (1985). *Adolescent relations with mothers, fathers, and friends.* Chicago: University of Chicago Press.

Received March 3, 1995
Revision received July 24, 1995
Accepted November 3, 1995 ■

JOURNAL OF RESEARCH ON ADOLESCENCE, 1(1), 19-36
Copyright © 1991, Lawrence Erlbaum Associates, Inc.

Authoritative Parenting and Adolescent Adjustment Across Varied Ecological Niches

Laurence Steinberg
Temple University

Nina S. Mounts and Susie D. Lamborn
University of Wisconsin–Madison

Sanford M. Dornbusch
Stanford University

This study examines whether the widely reported positive relation between "authoritative" parenting and adolescent adjustment is moderated by the ecological context in which adolescents live. A socioeconomically and ethnically diverse sample of approximately 10,000 high school students completed measures concerning their family background; their parents' behavior; and four indicators of adjustment: school performance, self-reliance, psychological distress, and delinquency. The students were grouped into 16 ecological niches defined by ethnicity, socioeconomic status, and family structure, and analyses were conducted within each niche to contrast the adjustment scores of adolescents from authoritative versus nonauthoritative homes. Analyses indicate that the positive correlates of authoritative parenting transcend ethnicity, socioeconomic status, and family structure. Virtually regardless of their ethnicity, class, or parents' marital status, adolescents whose parents are accepting, firm, and democratic earn higher grades in school, are more self-reliant, report less anxiety and depression, and are less likely to engage in delinquent behavior.

This study extends previous work on the relation between authoritative parenting and adolescent development and behavior (Dornbusch,

---

Requests for reprints should be sent to Laurence Steinberg, Department of Psychology, Temple University, Philadelphia, PA 19122.

129

Ritter, Liederman, Roberts, & Fraleigh, 1987; Steinberg, Elmen, & Mounts, 1989). Authoritative parenting, initially described by Baumrind (1967, 1971, 1973, 1978), is characterized by high levels of responsiveness and high levels of demandingness. According to several comprehensive reviews, authoritative parenting, as opposed to permissive (high in responsiveness, but low in demandingness) or authoritarian (high in demandingness, but low in responsiveness) parenting, is associated with the development of competence in children and adolescents, virtually however indexed (Maccoby & Martin, 1983; Steinberg, 1990). As these reviews have pointed out, however, nearly all research on authoritative parenting and its benefits has focused on White, middle-class families, and it is not known whether these same parenting practices are equally advantageous among other groups of youngsters. In this study we examine whether the ecological context in which adolescents live—defined by their ethnicity, socioeconomic status, and family structure—moderates the relation between parental authoritativeness and adolescent behavior and adjustment.

The theoretical impetus for this study comes mainly from the work of Bronfenbrenner (1979, 1986, 1989; Bronfenbrenber & Crouter, 1983), who suggested that researchers pay more attention to "process-by-context interactions"—the ways in which developmental processes vary as a function of the broader context in which they occur. Although psychologists interested in socialization have paid a good deal of attention to intrafamilial processes and their effects on children's development, and although sociologists interested in families have studied contextual differences in children's development and well-being, studies that look simultaneously at process and context are quite rare. Indeed, in most studies of socialization processes, contextual factors, such as socioeconomic status or ethnicity, are treated as "nuisance" variables: sources of error which are held constant through selective sampling (typically, the selected group is White and middle class) or statistical control. These studies may tell us how various socialization techniques contribute to the child's development above and beyond the contribution of demographic factors, but they do not reveal whether the processes that are important in one context are equally so in others.

There is good reason to believe that the effects of specific parenting practices on children's development may in fact be moderated by the larger context in which a child lives. In particular, one would hypothesize that the specific socialization techniques associated with healthy child development are those that are most consistent with the values and demands of the broader environment in which the family lives. From this perspective, authoritative parenting, with its decidedly middle-class emphasis on democratic parent–child communication and the encouragement of autonomy (see Kohn, 1977) should most benefit children from mainstream, middle-class homes, whereas its positive effects may be less obvious for children from other demographic groups. Conversely, although it is widely held that authoritarian parenting, with its emphasis on obedience to authority, has deleterious consequences for the child (Maccoby & Martin, 1983), one might hypothesize that this style of parenting may have fewer costs, and perhaps some benefits, among minority and poor children (see Baldwin & Baldwin, 1989; Baumrind, 1972). Poor and minority youngsters are more likely to live in relatively more dangerous environments than their White, middle-class peers, and they may benefit from levels of parental control that would appear excessively strict in other environments.

The Dornbusch et al. (1987) study provides some support for the contention that authoritative parenting may be more effective in White households than in others, at least in the prediction of adolescents' school performance. The research examined adolescent school achievement and three indices of parenting practices—authoritative parenting, authoritarian parenting, and permissive parenting—in a sample of 8,000 students separated into four major ethnic groups: African-American, Asian-American, Hispanic-American, and non-Hispanic White. Across the sample as a whole, as hypothesized, parental authoritativeness was associated with higher grades, and parental authoritarianism and permissiveness were associated with lower grades. When the sample was disaggregated into ethnic groups, however, the index of authoritativeness was significantly predictive of achievement only among White adolescents; the index was marginally predictive among Hispanic-American adolescents and not at all predictive in the Asian-American or African-American subsamples. The index of permissiveness was inversely related to grades among White students, but unrelated to grades in the other groups. And the index of authoritarianism was negatively predictive of grades among White and Asian-American students and Hispanic-American girls, but not among African-American youngsters or Hispanic-American boys. The analyses controlled for the effects of socioeconomic status (indexed via parental education levels) and family structure.

By the end of this decade, nearly one-third of all adolescents in the U.S. will be from African-American, Asian-American, or Hispanic-American families (Wetzel, 1987). In light of the changed and changing demography of youth, researchers can no longer afford to study socialization processes and outcomes solely within White samples. Yet, despite an extensive literature documenting variations in parenting behaviors across cultural groups (Whiting & Whiting, 1975), the Dornbusch et al. (1987) study is, as far as we can determine, the only attempt to date to look systematically at the way in which ethnicity moderates the effects of specific parenting practices on adolescent development (see Spencer & Dornbusch, 1990).

131

The broader context in which a youngster lives is defined only in part by his or her ethnicity, of course. Within ethnic groups there are substantial variations in both family structure and socioeconomic status, each of which has been shown to affect parenting practices (e.g., Bronfenbrenner, 1958; Dornbusch et al., 1985; Hess & Shipman, 1967; Hetherington, 1979; Kohn, 1977). Because the Dornbusch et al. (1987) study used parental education and family structure as covariates, it did not permit an analysis of the moderating effects of these variables, either separately or in conjunction with ethnicity. In addition to our interest in further examining the moderating impact of ethnicity on socialization outcomes, we sought in this study to look at the parallel effects of socioeconomic status and family structure.

Our operationalization of authoritativeness is based on three dimensions of parenting initially identified by Schaefer (1965): acceptance/ involvement, firm control, and psychological autonomy. In a previous study of a sample of White, middle- and working-class adolescents, Steinberg et al. (1989) demonstrated that scores on each of these three dimensions were significantly predictive of adolescent school performance. Given the apparent utility of this model in predicting academic achievement among "mainstream" adolescents, these dimensions seemed to be an appropriate place to begin the more ecologically sensitive analyses of this study.

In this investigation, three demographic characteristics—ethnicity, socioeconomic status, and family structure—were used to define a series of 16 ecological niches. Rather than control for these demographic variables, we conducted separate analyses within each ecological niche in order to examine whether the relation between authoritative parenting and adolescent development is comparable across groups. In order to extend this inquiry beyond the prediction of school performance, we examine the relation between parental authoritativeness and adolescent adjustment within four conceptually distinct domains of adolescent functioning: school performance, psychosocial maturity, psychological distress, and behavior problems (see Lamborn, Mounts, Steinberg, & Dornbusch, in press). We predicted that the relation between authoritative parenting and these indices of adjustment would be strongest for adolescents from White, middle-class, intact families and weaker for adolescents growing up in different social ecologies.

METHOD

Sample

The data for this report come from two self-report questionnaires administered to approximately 10,000 9th- through 12th-grade students attending one of nine high schools in Wisconsin and California. The schools were selected to produce a diverse sample in terms of ethnicity, family structure, socioeconomic status, and type of community (rural, suburban, and urban). In the sample, 9% of the students were Black, 14% were Asian, 12% were Hispanic, and 60% were White (the remainder belong to other ethnic groups). All of the students in attendance on the day of testing were asked to complete the questionnaires, and completed questionnaires were obtained each time from approximately 80% of the sample.

Measures

Of interest in these analyses are the demographic variables used to assign youngsters to the various ecological niches, the three parenting dimensions used to operationalize authoritative parenting, and our indices of adolescent adjustment.

Demographic variables. Students provided information on their parents' educational attainment, on their current family structures, and on their ethnic background. Socioeconomic status was operationalized in terms of the mean education level of the adults with whom the adolescent resided, and coded into two categories: working class (less than college completion) and middle class (college completion or higher). We chose parental education as an index of social class for several reasons. First, recent data suggest that indices of class based on composite measures of occupation, income, and education fluctuate frequently over the course of an individual child's lifetime because of parental job changes and fluctuations in family finances; indeed, one analysis indicates that more than half of U.S. children experience between two and five different class environments before age 6 (Featherman, Spenner, & Tsunematsu, 1988). Parental education is probably the most stable component of the family's social class. In addition, since 1950 there has been a decline in the significance of parental occupation, and an increase in the significance of parental education, in explaining beliefs and values about childrearing (Alwin, cited in Featherman et al., 1988). Similarly, most of the relation between parental income and children's achievement is accounted for by parent's education (Dornbusch, cited in Weston & Weston, 1987).

Students provided information on their current family structure, which was used to group individuals into two categories: two-parent biologically intact, and nonintact (primarily, adolescents living with a single mother or in a stepfamily). Unfortunately, it was not possible to look at single-parent homes and stepfamilies separately, because of small cell sizes within certain ethnic/socioeconomic groups. Given previous findings suggesting that the psychological functioning of adolescents from single-parent homes is similar to that of adolescents from stepfamilies, with both groups differing from adolescents from two-parent, intact households (Furstenberg, 1990), we grouped all adolescents from nonintact homes together for purposes of this article.

Students also provided information on their ethnicity, which was used to categorize individuals into one of four major ethnic groups (African-American, White, Asian-American, and Hispanic-American).[1] Ecological niches were formed by creating a 2 (Socioeconomic Status) × 2 (Family Structure) × 4 (Ethnicity) matrix and assigning students to one of the resulting 16 cells.

Authoritative parenting. The questionnaires contained many items on parenting practices that were taken or adapted from existing measures (e.g., Dornbusch et al., 1985; Patterson & Stouthamer-Loeber, 1984; Rodgers, 1966) or developed for this program of work. Based on the previous work of Steinberg et al. (1989), a number of items were selected to correspond with the three dimensions of authoritative parenting identified earlier, and these were subjected to exploratory factor analyses using an oblique rotation. Three factors emerged, corresponding to the dimensions of acceptance/involvement, firm control, and psychological autonomy. These factors are identical to those suggested in the earlier work of Schaefer (1965) and parallel, respectively, the Supportive Control, Assertive Control, and Directive/Conventional Control scales employed by Baumrind (in press) in her ongoing study of socialization and adolescent competence. Factor analyses were repeated separately for the four ethnic groups, and the basic structure was identical. We have labeled these scales in ways that both capture the item content of each and that emphasize parallels between our measures and those used by other researchers (e.g., Schaefer, 1965).

The acceptance/involvement scale measures the extent to which the adolescent perceives his or her parents as loving, responsive, and involved (sample items: "I can count on her to help me out if I have some kind of problem"; "She helps me with my school work if there is something I don't understand"; and "How often does your family do something fun together?"; 15 items, $\alpha = .72$). The firm control scale assesses parental monitoring and limit setting (sample items: "How much do your parents try to know where you go at night?"; "In a typical week, what is the latest you can stay out on school nights (Monday to

---

[1]There were insufficient numbers of students in the American Indian, Middle Eastern, and Pacific Islander groups to conduct analyses; these students were dropped from the sample in this investigation.

Thursday)?"; and "How much do your parents really know what you do with your free time?"; 9 items, $\alpha = .76$). The psychological autonomy scale assesses the extent to which parents employ noncoercive, democratic discipline and encourage the adolescent to express individuality within the family (sample items, reversed scored: "How often do your parents tell you that their ideas are correct and that you should not question them?"; "How often do your parents answer your arguments by saying something like 'You'll know better when you grow up'?"; and "When you get a poor grade in school, do your parents try to make your life miserable?"; 12 items, $\alpha = .72$). Composite scores were calculated on each of these dimensions. For most of the items, students were asked to describe the parent(s) with whom they lived. On those items for which students in two-parent homes answered separately for their mother and their father, scores were averaged before forming composites.

Correlations among the dimensions suggest that they are related but conceptually distinct aspects of parenting: (acceptance with firm control, $r = .34$; acceptance with psychological autonomy, $r = .25$; firm control with psychological autonomy, $r = -.07$). Reliability coefficients for the three dimensions were also calculated within each ecological group; the alpha coefficients are satisfactory across the 16 groups (see Table 1).

Based on previous work and the theoretical model of authoritative

TABLE 1

Sample Sizes, Percent Authoritative Families, and Internal Consistency of Parenting Dimensions Within Ecological Niches

Ecological Niche	N	Percentage Authoritative	Internal Consistency of Dimension		
			Acceptance	Control	Autonomy
White, Working-class, Intact	559	17.2	.69	.76	.71
White, Working-class, Nonintact	436	11.5	.68	.78	.69
White, Middle-class, Intact	2609	25.0	.71	.74	.74
White, Middle-class, Nonintact	1267	17.6	.72	.78	.73
Black, Working-class, Intact	82	13.4	.75	.61	.65
Black, Working-class, Nonintact	205	12.2	.71	.77	.60
Black, Middle-class, Intact	178	14.1	.74	.75	.62
Black, Middle-class, Nonintact	313	16.0	.71	.78	.62
Hispanic, Working-class, Intact	336	10.7	.67	.76	.72
Hispanic, Working-class, Nonintact	254	9.8	.68	.82	.71
Hispanic, Middle-class, Intact	202	15.8	.64	.74	.64
Hispanic, Middle-class, Nonintact	171	12.9	.63	.73	.62
Asian, Working-class, Intact	159	7.5	.78	.70	.66
Asian, Working-class, Nonintact	66	6.1	.55	.67	.66
Asian, Middle-class, Intact	597	15.6	.73	.77	.71
Asian, Middle-class, Nonintact	166	10.8	.70	.75	.73

parenting tested in this study, authoritative families were defined as those scoring above the sample median on acceptance/involvement, firm control, and psychological autonomy scales. Any family scoring below the sample median on any of the three dimensions were classified as "nonauthoritative."[2] The percentages of authoritative families, so defined, across the 16 ecological groups, is presented in Table 1. In general (and consistent with previous research), authoritativeness is more common among middle-class than among working-class families, more common among White than among minority families, and more common among intact than among nonintact families. The highest proportion of authoritative families (25%) is found in the White, intact, middle-class group, whereas the lowest (6%) is found in the Asian-American, nonintact, working-class group.

Adolescent adjustment. The questionnaire battery contained four sets of outcome variables chosen to index four domains of adolescent adjustment: school performance, psychosocial maturity, internalized distress, and behavior problems. Preliminary analyses indicated that these represented conceptually and empirically distinct aspects of adolescent functioning, and that within each outcome set, specific measures were significantly intercorrelated. Because of the large number of planned comparisons in the analysis (see next), we selected one illustrative outcome from each domain, based on previous work linking these aspects of adolescent adjustment to authoritative parenting in White, middle-class, intact, two-parent households (see Maccoby & Martin, 1983; Steinberg, 1990).

Our index of school performance was students' self-reported grade point average (GPA), scored on a 4-point scale. Dornbusch et al. (1987) reported a correlation of .75 between self-reported grades and actual grades taken from official school records. We indexed psychosocial maturity via the self-reliance subscale of the Psychosocial Maturity Inventory (Form D; Greenberger & Bond, 1976; Greenberger, Josselson, Knerr, & Knerr, 1974; α = .81). Our index of psychological distress comes from a series of items from the Center for Epidemiologic Studies Depression Scale (CES-D; Radloff, 1977), which were used to form an index of psychological distress (anxiety, depression, tension, fatigue, insomnia, etc.; α = .88). To examine behavior problems, adolescents' reports on their frequency of involvement in such delinquent activities as theft, carrying a weapon, vandalism, and using a phony ID were used to form an index of delinquency (α = .82; Gold, 1970).

---

[2]This article specifically examines differences between authoritative and nonauthoritative homes. We recognize that the nonauthoritative group includes a variety of family types, including authoritarian, indulgent, and neglectful families.

Means and standard deviations for four outcome variables are presented separately for each of the 16 ecological niches in Table 2.

Plan of Analysis

In order to examine the relation between authoritative parenting and the outcome measures of interest, a series of planned t tests were conducted within each ecological niche. According to Rosnow and Rosenthal (1989), when specific two-group contrasts are of interest, this strategy is preferred over one in which an omnibus analysis of variance (ANOVA) is used to examine interaction terms (e.g., between parenting style and ethnicity), because such tests of interactions are excessively conservative and vulnerable to Type II error. In each contrast, the scores of adolescents from authoritative households were compared with the scores of adolescents from nonauthoritative households. In addition, an estimation of the effect size (r) for each contrast was computed, following Rosenthal and Rubin (1982). Because the sample size varies considerably across ecological groups (and, consequently, the power to discern differences between adolescents from authoritative and nonauthoritative families varies as well), examining effect sizes in addition to the significance levels of the various contrasts provides a more complete picture of the extent to which authoritative parenting is advantageous in different family ecologies.

TABLE 2
Mean Scores (and Standard Deviations) of Dependent Measures Within Each
Ecological Niche

Ecological Niche	GPA	Self-Reliance	Psychological Distress	Delinquency
White, Working-class, Intact	2.61 (.79)	3.01 (.51)	2.61 (.83)	1.22 (.40)
White, Working-class, Nonintact	2.51 (.83)	3.03 (.52)	2.67 (.84)	1.24 (.38)
White, Middle-class, Intact	3.07 (.71)	3.15 (.48)	2.57 (.77)	1.16 (.34)
White, Middle-class, Nonintact	2.80 (.80)	3.16 (.50)	2.68 (.75)	1.18 (.33)
Black, Working-class, Intact	2.59 (.77)	3.18 (.61)	2.13 (.86)	1.12 (.28)
Black, Working-class, Nonintact	2.47 (.78)	3.15 (.60)	2.41 (.82)	1.16 (.32)
Black, Middle-class, Intact	2.57 (.72)	3.10 (.56)	2.38 (.82)	1.19 (.46)
Black, Middle-class, Nonintact	2.48 (.72)	3.12 (.61)	2.44 (.83)	1.19 (.33)
Hispanic, Working-class, Intact	2.47 (.80)	2.95 (.55)	2.42 (.83)	1.25 (.45)
Hispanic, Working-class, Nonintact	2.28 (.84)	2.96 (.59)	2.44 (.86)	1.20 (.40)
Hispanic, Middle-class, Intact	2.62 (.83)	3.00 (.53)	2.32 (.80)	1.20 (.43)
Hispanic, Middle-class, Nonintact	2.50 (.77)	3.00 (.55)	2.57 (.85)	1.26 (.44)
Asian, Working-class, Intact	3.06 (.78)	2.82 (.50)	2.49 (.83)	1.10 (.19)
Asian, Working-class, Nonintact	3.02 (.69)	2.81 (.51)	2.39 (.88)	1.10 (.24)
Asian, Middle-class, Intact	3.35 (.68)	3.02 (.48)	2.54 (.76)	1.10 (.27)
Asian, Middle-class, Nonintact	3.12 (.72)	3.00 (.48)	2.51 (.79)	1.12 (.25)

RESULTS

The results of the 64 contrasts (four outcome variables across 16 ecological groups) are presented in Table 3. Forty of the 64 contrasts are statistically significant, each favoring adolescents from authoritative homes. Compared with their counterparts from nonauthoritative homes, authoritatively reared adolescents earn higher grades in school, are more self-reliant, report less psychological distress, and are less involved in delinquent activity. Of the 24 contrasts not reaching significance, all but three are in the expected direction. Most of the effects in Table 3 are between $r = .1$ and $r = .2$ —what most experts would consider to be "small" effects (Rosenthal & Rosnow, 1984).

Are the benefits of authoritative parenting greater in White, middle-class, intact households? Table 3 suggests that this question is difficult to answer. Significant differences between youngsters from authoritative and nonauthoritative homes are most consistently observed among White youngsters, middle-class youngsters, and youngsters from intact households, as hypothesized. An inspection of magnitude of the effect sizes, however, indicates that this pattern of differential significance may be due mainly to differences in our ability to detect comparable effects in subsamples of different sizes (e.g., we have three times the power to detect an effect of .20 in the subsample of White, middle-class youngsters from intact homes, with an approximate $N = 2,600$, than we do to detect an effect of the same size within the subsample of African-American, working-class youngsters from nonintact homes, with an approximate N of 200; see Cohen, 1977, pp. 92–93). We are especially hampered by the fact that in this case the effect we are trying to detect is quite small, because the detection of small effects requires relatively more statistical power. Indeed, three of the groups in which it appears at first glance that authoritativeness is not especially advantageous (African-American, working class, intact; Asian-American, working class, nonintact; and Asian-American, middle class, nonintact) have subsamples in this study whose size may preclude the detection of the effect we are attempting to find.

In order to examine this issue further, we carried out post-hoc analyses of the heterogeneity of effect sizes across the ecological niches (Rosenthal & Rosnow, 1984). These analyses indicate that the effect sizes are homogeneous for self-reliance, psychological distress, and delinquency, for all three χ^2s, $p > .10$, but not for GPA, $\chi^2(15) = 28.76$, $p < .01$. Further post-hoc contrasts indicate that this heterogeneity in the case of grade-point-average is due to the moderating effect of ethnicity: The effect of parental authoritativeness on GPA is greater among White adolescents than among African-American or Asian-American adolescents ($z = 1.88$, $p < .05$ and $z = 2.59$, $p < .005$, respectively).

138

TABLE 3
Mean Differences on Four Indicators of Adjustment Among Adolescents From
Authoritative Versus Nonauthoritative Homes Across Sixteen Ecological Niches Defined
by Ethnicity, Socioeconomic Status, and Family Structure

Ecological Niche	GPA	Self-Reliance	Psychological Distress	Delinquency	N
White					
Working Class					
Intact					
Authoritative	2.79**	3.14**	2.43**	1.11***	96
Nonauthoritative	2.57	2.97	2.65	1.24	463
r	.11	.13	.10	.12	
Nonintact					
Authoritative	2.82**	3.12	2.55	1.14*	50
Nonauthoritative	2.47	3.02	2.68	1.25	386
r	.14	.12	.05	.09	
Middle Class					
Intact					
Authoritative	3.34***	3.27***	2.37***	1.07***	652
Nonauthoritative	2.98	3.10	2.64	1.18	1957
r	.22	.15	.15	.15	
Nonintact					
Authoritative	3.14***	3.34***	2.50***	1.08***	224
Nonauthoritative	2.73	3.11	2.72	1.20	1045
r	.20	.18	.11	.15	
Black					
Working Class					
Intact					
Authoritative	2.50	3.36	1.80	1.07	11
Nonauthoritative	2.60	3.15	2.18	1.13	71
r	−.04	.12	.14	.07	
Nonintact					
Authoritative	2.78*	3.58***	2.26	1.05*	25
Nonauthoritative	2.42	3.07	2.43	1.79	180
r	.15	.32	.07	.15	
Middle Class					
Intact					
Authoritative	2.84*	3.35*	2.23	1.07**	25
Nonauthoritative	2.52	3.06	2.40	1.21	153
r	.15	.19	.07	.11	
Nonintact					
Authoritative	2.61	3.35*	2.26*	1.17	50
Nonauthoritative	2.45	3.08	2.48	1.97	263
r	.08	.16	.10	.03	
Hispanic					
Working Class					
Intact					
Authoritative	2.83**	3.26**	2.41	1.15*	36
Nonauthoritative	2.43	2.91	2.42	1.26	306
r	.16	.20	.00	.06	

(Continued)

TABLE 3 (continued)

Ecological Niche	GPA	Self-Reliance	Psychological Distress	Delinquency	N
Nonintact					
Authoritative	2.50	3.19*	1.95**	1.13	25
Nonauthoritative	2.25	2.93	2.50	1.21	229
r	.09	.15	.20	.06	
Middle Class					
Intact					
Authoritative	2.88*	3.03	2.01*	1.17	32
Nonauthoritative	2.57	2.98	2.39	1.21	170
r	.13	.04	.18	.03	
Nonintact					
Authoritative	2.75*	3.20*	2.34	1.14*	22
Nonauthoritative	2.46	2.95	2.60	1.28	149
r	.13	.17	.10	.12	
Asian					
Working Class					
Intact					
Authoritative	3.21	3.02	2.09*	1.00***	12
Nonauthoritative	3.05	2.80	2.52	1.10	147
r	.05	.12	.14	.13	
Nonintact					
Authoritative	3.00	3.13	2.28	1.00***	4
Nonauthoritative	3.02	2.79	2.39	1.11	62
r	−.01	.16	.03	.11	
Middle Class					
Intact					
Authoritative	3.51**	3.23***	2.35**	1.04***	93
Nonauthoritative	3.33	2.98	2.57	1.11	504
r	.10	.20	.10	.09	
Nonintact					
Authoritative	3.22	2.92	2.30	1.01***	18
Nonauthoritative	3.10	2.97	2.53	1.13	148
r	.05	−.03	.09	.16	

*$p < .05$. **$p < .01$. ***$p < .001$.

DISCUSSION

The results of this study provide evidence that the widely reported positive correlation between parental authoritativeness and adolescent adjustment appears to transcend ethnicity, socioeconomic status, and family structure. Virtually regardless of their family background, adolescents whose parents are warm, firm, and democratic enjoy psychological and behavioral advantages over their peers. Compared to their nonauthoritatively reared counterparts, adolescents from authoritative

140

homes generally do better in school, are more self-reliance, report less psychological distress, and engage in less delinquent activity. Although further research is obviously needed, the notion that parental authoritativeness is linked with healthy adolescent development may have what Weisz (1978) called "transcontextual validity"—at least within the contemporary U.S.

Although one of the strengths of this study is its large and heterogeneous sample, the conclusions one can draw from the research are limited by its cross-sectional design and reliance on self-report data. Because the data are cross-sectional, it is impossible to say with any certainty that the parenting practices examined have in fact caused or even preceded the outcomes assessed. It could well be the case, for example, that well-adjusted adolescents elicit authoritativeness from their parents, or that less well-adjusted youth provoke parental neglect or hostility (see Lewis, 1981). Although reverse causality can not be ruled out, other research employing similar measures has indicated that parental authorativeness actually promotes competence among White, middle- and working-class young people (Steinberg et al., 1989). The correlational findings reported in this study indicate that longitudinal work on other populations is indeed warranted.

Our reliance on self-report data is also a limiting factor. Because the data all derive from youngsters' reports, we can only say that youngsters who characterize their parents in certain ways show particular patterns of behavior and psychological functioning. What this may indicate is that youngsters' subjective experience of parental behavior is an important influence on their own development and well-being. It is important to know, for methodological as well as theoretical reasons, whether parents' actual behavior toward their children is associated in similar ways with the outcomes assessed, and whether the association between parents' behavior and children's reports of parents' behavior varies as a function of ethnicity, class, or family structure.

Although we acknowledge the important contribution that observational work on families has made to the study of adolescent development, we do not subscribe to the view that objective (i.e., independent) assessments of parenting behavior are the only valid indicators of what takes place in the family (see also Jessor & Jessor, 1977, for a similar argument). Indeed, one might very reasonably argue that if a child experiences his or her parents as authoritative (regardless of how parents may characterize themselves, or how they may appear to outside observers), then this is what they in fact are, at least as far as the child's psychological development is concerned. Ultimately, one can only say that subjective and objective assessments of parental behavior each provide an important window on the child's experience in the family, and that no one approach to the study of socialization is inherently superior to the other.

The comparability of our results to findings reported by investigators using observational measures of parenting (e.g., Baumrind, in press) lends additional support to the contention that the self-report data used in this study have not resulted in unusual biases in the findings. Among other advantages, self-report measures enable investigators to include substantially larger samples in their research than is typically the case in observational studies, and, as we discuss next, larger samples permit the detection of theoretically important findings that may go unnoticed in smaller scale research.

Our findings indicate that the effects of authoritativeness, while statistically significant, are small in magnitude—at least according to statistical convention. Before dismissing these effects as too small to be of practical significance, however, a number of considerations must be raised. First, the actual magnitude of the effect sizes is likely to be diminished by unreliability in the measures. Although the reliability coefficients of the measures employed all exceeded conventional cutoffs, the reader should keep in mind that any unreliability in measurement will attenuate effect sizes.

Second, the hypothesis that adolescents raised in authoritative homes would score higher than their peers on the measures of adjustment was tested in an exceedingly conservative manner, because all families who did not meet the criteria for the authoritative classification were grouped together in the nonauthoritative group. This heterogeneous group contained families who scored above the sample median on two of the three parenting dimensions, for example, and who therefore may be considered relatively well functioning. When we contrast adolescents raised in authoritative homes with their counterparts from families scoring below the median on all three dimensions, the observed effect sizes are substantially larger. For example, within the White, middle-class, intact subsample, the contrast between the mean GPA in families scoring above the median on all three dimensions and their counterparts scoring below the median on all three dimensions yields an effect size of $r = .39$ (as compared with .22 when the nonauthoritative contrast group is more heterogeneous). Similarly, restricting the contrast group within the African-American, working-class, nonintact subsample to the least authoritative families yields an effect size of $r = .28$ (as opposed to .15).

Third, it is important to note that our measure of authoritative parenting taps only certain elements of the parent–child relationship. Other important factors, such as the consistency of parents' behavior over time, the nature and quality of parent–child communication, and the ways in which child-rearing tasks are apportioned between mothers

142

and fathers, all contribute to the adolescent's development. Our estimate of the "effect" of authoritative parenting should be viewed as an estimate of the effect of authoritativeness as operationalized in this study, and not an indicator of the degree to which variations in the parent–adolescent relationship matter.

Finally, whether we consider the observed effects – however modest – to be of practical significance is, after all, a subjective matter. One way to gauge their real-world significance is to generate a Binomial Effect Size Display (BESD; Rosenthal & Rubin, 1982). This procedure allows one to better estimate whether an observed difference between two groups is likely to have real-world significance.

In the case of GPA, for example, suppose we assume that a cutoff is used by educational practitioners to distinguish between students whose grades are "adequate" versus "inadequate." (In practice, such a threshold might be used to make decisions about a student's track placement, or about whether a given student is admissable to a given university.) Knowing the effect size permits us to estimate the percentage of students in each of the groups we are interested in (e.g., those from authoritative homes versus those from nonauthoritative homes) falling above or below an established threshold.[3] In the case of White, middle-class youngsters from intact homes, the BESD indicates that 61% of youngsters from authoritative homes, but only 39% of youngsters from nonauthoritative homes, would be expected to exceed an established cutoff. In contrast, in the case of Asian-American middle-class youngsters from nonintact homes, the percentages of adolescents above the cutoff from authoritative versus nonauthoritative homes are virtually identical (52% vs. 48%). Parallel computations can be made in order to estimate the practical significance of the effect sizes observed in the analyses of self-reliance (where a cutoff might determine which youngsters were selected for a job opportunity), psychological distress (where a cutoff might be used to determine which adolescents were referred for treatment), and delinquency (where a cutoff might determine how an adolescent was treated within the juvenile justice system).

Beyond these practical considerations, however, the consistently small effect sizes reported here suggest important methodological implications. Unfortunately, the news is not good for researchers interested in contrasting socialization consequences across demographic

---

[3]Adding one-half of the effect size coefficient to .50 gives us the percentage of the higher scoring group who would be expected to exceed the threshold; subtracting one-half of the coefficient from .50 estimates the percentage of the lower scoring group who would be expected to exceed the threshold.

groups, because the analyses indicate that relatively large samples may be needed to uncover what appear to be fairly modest, albeit consistent, effects. Future research on parenting practices and adolescent outcomes should anticipate this problem and select sample sizes accordingly.

Thus far, our discussion has focused on the transcontextual validity of authoritative parenting as a predictor of adolescent adjustment. We must note, however, that the relation between authoritativeness and school performance is greater among White and Hispanic-American adolescents than among their African-American or Asian-American peers. This finding replicates the Dornbusch et al. (1987) study, in which the relation between authoritative parenting and students' grades was less consistent among African-American and Asian-American adolescents than among others. We do not know whether other models of parenting would be more predictive of school performance in these samples than was the model tested here. In this study, however, this differential pattern did not emerge in the prediction of the other outcome variables (i.e., authoritatively related African-American and Asian-American adolescents appear to enjoy advantages in the domains of psychosocial maturity, psychological distress, and behavior problems), which suggests that the diminished predictive significance of parental authoritativeness among African-American and Asian-American youngsters may be limited to the domain of school performance.

ACKNOWLEDGMENTS

The research was supported by a grant to Laurence Steinberg and B. Bradford Brown from the U.S. Department of Education, through the National Center on Effective Secondary Schools at the University of Wisconsin–Madison; from the Spencer Foundation to Sanford Dornbusch and P. Herbert Leiderman of the Stanford University Center for Families, Children, and Youth; and from the Lilly Endowment to Laurence Steinberg.

This article was based in part on papers presented at the biennial meeting of the Society for Research in Child Development, Kansas City, MO, April 1989, and the annual meeting of the American Psychological Association, Boston, August 1990.

We are exceedingly grateful to Diana Baumrind and Urie Bronfenbrenner for their comments on an earlier draft of this article and to Ralph Rosnow for his suggestions concerning the plan of analysis.

REFERENCES

Baldwin, C., & Baldwin, A. (1989, April). *The role of family interaction in the prediction of adolescent competence.* Symposium presented at the meeting of the Society for Research in Child Development, Kansas City, MO.

Baumrind, D. (1967). Child care practices anteceding three patterns of preschool behavior. *Genetic Psychology Monographs, 75,* 43–88.

Baumrind, D. (1971). Current patterns of parental authority. *Developmental Psychology Monographs, 4*(1, Pt. 2).

Baumrind, D. (1972). An exploratory study of socialization effects on black children: Some black-white comparisons. *Child Development, 43,* 261–267.

Baumrind, D. (1973). The development of instrumental competence through socialization. In A. Pick (Ed.), *Minnesota symposium on child psychology* (Vol. 7, pp. 3–46). Minneapolis: University of Minnesota Press.

Baumrind, D. (1978). Parental disciplinary patterns and social competence in children. *Youth and Society, 9,* 239–276.

Baumrind, D. (in press). Parenting styles and adolescent development. In J. Brooks-Gunn, R. Lerner, & A. C. Petersen (Eds.), *The encyclopedia of adolescence.* New York: Garland.

Bronfenbrenner, U. (1958). Socialization and social class through time and space. In E. Maccoby, T. Newcomb, & E. Hartley (Eds.), *Readings in social psychology* (pp. 400–425). New York: Holt.

Bronfenbrenner, U. (1979). *The ecology of human development: Experiments by nature and design.* Cambridge, MA: Harvard University Press.

Bronfenbrenner, U. (1986). Ecology of the family as a context for human development. *Developmental Psychology, 22,* 723–742.

Bronfenbrenner, U. (1989). Ecological systems theory. *Annals of Child Development, 6,* 187–249.

Bronfenbrenner, U., & Crouter, A. C. (1983). The evolution of environmental models in developmental research. In W. Kessen & P. H. Mussen (Eds.), *History, theory, and methods: Handbook of child psychology* (Vol. 1, pp. 357–414). New York: Wiley.

Cohen, J. (1977). *Statistical power analysis for the behavioral sciences.* New York: Academic.

Dornbusch, S., Carlsmith, J., Bushwall, S., Ritter, P., Leiderman, H., Hastorf, A., & Gross, R. (1985). Single parents, extended households and the control of adolescents. *Child Development, 56,* 326–341.

Dornbusch, S., Ritter, P., Liederman, P., Roberts, D., & Fraleigh, M. (1987). The relation of parenting style to adolescent school performance. *Child Development, 58,* 1244–1257.

Featherman, D., Spenner, K., & Tsunematsu, N. (1988). Class and the socialization of children: Constancy, change, or irrelevance. In E. M. Hetherington, R. Lerner, & M. Perlmutter (Eds.), *Child development in life-span perspective* (pp. 67–90). Hillsdale, NJ: Lawrence Erlbaum Associates, Inc.

Furstenberg, F., Jr. (1990). Coming of age in a changing family system. In S. Feldman & G. Elliot (Eds.), *At the threshold: The developing adolescent.* Cambridge, MA: Harvard University Press.

Gold, M. (1970). *Delinquent behavior in an American city.* Belmont, CA: Brooks/Cole.

Greenberger, E., & Bond, L. (1976). *Technical manual for the Psychosocial Maturity Inventory.* Unpublished manuscript, University of California, Irvine, Program in Social Ecology.

Greenberger, E., Josselson, R., Knerr, C., & Knerr, B. (1974). The measurement and structure of psychosocial maturity. *Journal of Youth and Adolescence, 4,* 127–143.

Hess, R., & Shipman, V. (1967). Cognitive elements in maternal behavior. *Minnesota Symposium on Child Psychology, 1,* 57–81.

Hetherington, E. M. (1979). Divorce: A child's perspective. *American Psychologist, 34,* 851-858.

Jessor, R., & Jessor, S. (1977). *Problem behavior and psychosocial development: A longitudinal study of youth.* New York: Academic.

Kohn, M. (1977). *Class and conformity* (2nd ed.). Chicago: University of Chicago Press.

Lamborn, S., Mounts, N., Steinberg, L., & Dornbusch, S. (in press). Patterns of competence and adjustment among adolescents from authoritative, authoritarian, indulgent, and neglectful homes. *Child Development.*

Lewis, C. (1981). The effects of parental firm control. *Psychological Bulletin, 90,* 547-563.

Maccoby, E., & Martin, J. (1983). Socialization in the context of the family: Parent-child interaction. In E. M. Hetherington (Ed.) & P. H. Mussen (Series Ed.), *Handbook of child psychology: Socialization, personality, and social development* (Vol. 4, pp. 1-101). New York: Wiley.

Patterson, G., & Stouthamer-Loeber, M. (1984). The correlation of family management practices and delinquency. *Child Development, 55,* 1299-1307.

Radloff, L. S. (1977). The CES-D scale: A self-report depression scale for research in the general population. *Applied Psychological Measurement, 1,* 385-401.

Rodgers, R. R. (1966). *Cornell Parent Behavior Description—An interim report.* Unpublished manuscript, Cornell University, Ithaca, NY, Department of Human Development and Family Studies.

Rosenthal, R., & Rosnow, R. (1984). *Essentials of behavioral research: Methods and data analysis.* New York: McGraw-Hill.

Rosenthal, R., & Rubin, D. (1982). A simple general purpose display of magnitude of experimental effect. *Journal of Educational Psychology, 74,* 166-169.

Rosnow, R., & Rosenthal, R. (1989). Statistical procedures and the justification of knowledge in psychological science. *American Psychologist, 44,* 1276-1284.

Schaefer, E. (1965). Children's reports of parental behavior: An inventory. *Child Development, 36,* 413-424.

Spencer, M., & Dornbusch, S. (1990). Ethnicity and adolescence. In S. Feldman & G. Elliot (Eds.), *At the threshold: The developing adolescent.* Cambridge, MA: Harvard University Press.

Steinberg, L. (1990). Interdependency in the family: Autonomy, conflict, and harmony. In S. Feldman & G. Elliot (Eds.), *At the threshold: The developing adolescent.* Cambridge, MA: Harvard University Press.

Steinberg, L., Elmen, J. D., & Mounts, N. S. (1989). Authoritative parenting, psychosocial maturity, and academic success among adolescents. *Child Development, 60,* 1424-1436.

Weisz, J. (1978). Transcontextual validity in developmental research. *Child Development, 49,* 1-12.

Weston, S., & Weston, W. (1987, October). *Education and the family.* Mimeo available from the Office of Educational Research and Improvement, U.S. Department of Education, Washington, DC.

Wetzel, J. (1987). *American youth: A statistical snapshot.* New York: William T. Grant Foundation Commission on Work, Family and Citizenship.

Whiting, B., & Whiting, J. (1975). *Children of six cultures: A psycho-cultural analysis.* Cambridge, MA: Harvard University Press.

Received May 18, 1990
Revision received September 18, 1990
Accepted September 24, 1990

Stress Levels, Family Help Patterns, and Religiosity in Middle- and Working-Class African American Single Mothers

Harriette Pipes McAdoo
Michigan State University

In this survey of 318 middle- and working-class African American mothers, stress and female-related stress were found to be intense and frequent. Women experienced serious life changes. Younger mothers, with younger children, had more stress than older mothers, and college-educated women had more stress than those without a college education. Religion was important; women prayed frequently but tended not to attend church services. Faith provided strong emotional support, especially for the working class and those in stress, but women who were not religious had the lowest stress.

Unmarried mothers are a growing phenomenon in the United States as divorce and pregnancy without marriage increase in all segments of our society. Now that single parenting has been recognized as a problem that faces all U.S. women, including Black and White alike, empirical studies are needed to address the issues of an increasingly typical family type: a mother alone with her children. Poverty, and its attending stresses, is a major consequence of single parenting (D'Ercole, 1988; Edelman, 1991; Farley & Allen, 1987; Kamerman & Kahn, 1988). Poverty causes many of the strains of single parenting, not just the fact of rearing children alone without a husband. Black children in single-parent households are among the poorest in the nation (Edelman, 1987). This article examines how women of different

AUTHOR'S NOTE: *Funds for this research were provided by the National Institutes of Mental Health, Department of Health and Human Services, Grant 5 R10 MN32159. Appreciation is given to John McAdoo, Erlsie Zdanis, Gayle Weaver, Willette Ewing, Judi Yahkavi, Beulah Newby, and Young-Shi Ou for their assistance in completing this project.*

JOURNAL OF BLACK PSYCHOLOGY, Vol. 21 No. 4, November 1995 424-449
© 1995 The Association of Black Psychologists

economic and marital status cope with the acute stresses they face as household head. It is proposed that the support of extended family and friends and religiosity are important factors for single mothers.

National attention has been focused on the problems of Black single mothers, and various myths have been mixed with reality (such as matriarchy, the welfare mother) to explain the demographic changes that have occurred in the past 20 years (Kaplan, 1988). These stereotypes often became "truth" in policy discussions, and the result is curtailed federal assistance funds.

Family trends for all groups are similar, but for African Americans it appears that patterns emerge a generation earlier than for Whites (Farley & Allen, 1987; McAdoo, 1988). Whereas the unmarried adolescent pregnancy rate for Blacks is higher than for Whites, the rate dropped for several years and then rose for Black girls in comparison to White girls (Alan Guttmacher Institute, 1981; Edelman, 1987; Hayes, 1987; Kaplan, 1988). Other family patterns that have converged are childbearing expectations and childlessness rates (Glick, 1988). There are indications that late first marriages and the long period between divorce and remarriage are the result of young men having difficulty gaining permanent employment (Edelman, 1987; Farley & Allen, 1987; Wilson & Neckerman, 1986).

More than half of all African American children under age 18 live with their mother alone (Danziger & Danziger, 1993). Divorce is the greatest contributor to Black mothers being single (Kamerman & Kahn, 1988; McAdoo, 1988). The second source is birth of a child to young unmarried women, and a small but growing source is birth by choice to stable, older unmarried women (Mechaneck, 1987). As the number of single mothers of all races has increased, the literature has moved from condemnation to the realization that single parenting is here to stay, that one can socialize and rear children effectively without being married (D'Ercole, 1988; Yankelovich, 1981).

Mothers who parent alone are confronted with multiple role demands, financial issues, and child-rearing concerns that require social support and resources. An inadequate standard of living and role overload have been found to be significant predictors of stress in single mothers (D'Ercole, 1988). McLanahan and Booth (1989) offer a comprehensive explanation of the issues and stressors that single mothers face. They point out that stress in a single-parent home is greater than in other forms of family structure. The major stressor is financial, particularly when the father of the child does not provide sufficient support.

An extensive support network among family members and fictive kin, who become as family, is true for people of all socioeconomic statuses (Farley & Allen, 1987; McAdoo, 1988) and different family structures (Taylor,

Chatters, Tucker, & Lewis, 1990). The extended family network can be especially helpful to single mothers, as it can mean options in schooling or career (Martin & Martin, 1978).

Social support apparently buffers stress, and friendships or secondary relationships with other women, family members, and coworkers have been found to be helpful to single mothers (Garfinkel & McLanahan, 1986; Brown & Gary, 1985). If stress becomes too great upon mothers, either mental or physical illness soon follows (Holmes & Masuda, 1974). Women survive by adopting certain patterns of support from the family situations in which they find themselves. Women receive help more frequently from female relatives. When family is available and the relationship with kin is harmonious, the family can be the source of support. Single mothers tend to be more involved with their parents, and this pattern is extended to increased interaction with kin (Marks & McLanahan, 1993).

Although not present in all families, kin help absorb the life stresses of family members and provide emotional support for kin and fictive kin (Aschenbrenner, 1973; McAdoo, 1991a, 1991b; Stack, 1974). The cohesion of families often has a direct linear relationship with positive outcomes. Because the needs of single mothers may exceed the resources of kin, nonrelatives often become closely aligned to the family and also provide support. These fictive kin (McAdoo, 1988; Stack, 1974) become as close to the mother as her own kin and in some cases closer. Because the helping arrangements are similar for kin and fictive kin, both relatives and friends must be examined in looking at the help given to single mothers. There is no agreement on the support patterns that are present in single-mother families, although the work of Horowitz (1992) indicates that a hierarchy of obligations determines which kin provide care to family members. To look only at actual kin ignores an important source of support, however, and female fictive kin should not be overlooked.

Social support from extended family and fictive kin is associated with the involvement of fathers in child rearing. The more support the father gives and the more invested he becomes, the more involved he becomes with the child. The support system among family and fictive kin has been titled *generalized mutual obligations* (Scanzoni & Marsiglio, 1993). If a mother requests assistance from one person in her network and that person is unable to help, then she can turn to another individual. But there are reciprocal obligations (McAdoo, 1988). Mothers who receive help find that their resources must be kept available for others in the network. Family support systems are sometimes overextended and overwhelmed with increasing economic and social pressures and chronic illness (McAdoo, 1993; Reiss,

1989). Interactions with relatives may be problematic for single mothers (Belle, 1982).

Grandparents play an important role in many African American families. They are a source of support and also an important link in the intergenerational history and knowledge within the family (Cherlin & Fustenberg, 1986; Kivett, 1993). Yet many grandmothers are themselves trapped in low-paying jobs with no hope of upward mobility. They may not be able to provide financial aid, but there are many ways that help can be exchanged; sometimes it is important to have a shoulder to cry on.

In a study of very poor urban families, Burton (1992) found that if a parent was addicted to drugs and the grandmother had to step in and rear the children, other kin did not provide the necessary help. These families are extremely stressed and overwhelmed by the grandmother's assumption of the main parenting role. The situation is not typical of African American families, and it also is not typical that the grandmother not receive the help she needs. Indeed, her assumption of the parenting role illustrates the concept of extended kin help common in African American families.

STRESSORS OF SINGLE PARENTING

The stressors related to being African American and to being female have been well noted. The stress faced by single mothers, whether divorced or never married, has become more evident as more women move into this status. The severity of that stress is affected by the economic and emotional resources available. Poor mothers must deal with poverty, high-crime areas, and poor educational facilities, whereas mothers who do not have the same basic economic needs may be more concerned with child care and household tasks. Quinn (1989) found that single mothers were concerned about lack of time and child care. Their sample represented all three socioeconomic groups, similar to the study sample here. The chronic shortage of time was experienced by employed single mothers.

There is an emotional adjustment to single mothering and bearing the sole responsibility for children. Women with young children and women who are no longer married have more stress than other women (McAdoo, 1991b; McLanahan & Booth, 1989). Blacks have a high divorce rate, and divorced women undergo many changes in roles and social position that cause stress to them and their children (Garfinkel & McLanahan, 1986; Hannam & Eggebeen, 1993; McAdoo, 1991a). Future marriage or remarriage often is unlikely for single mothers because of the imbalance in the sex ratios (Darity & Myers, 1991; Tucker & Mitchell-Kernan, 1992). The patterns and interactions of the extended family often work against the entry of another spouse into very poor families (Stack, 1974). The family needs the younger member's help, which would be lost if a marriage were to occur. And some families may interfere with the mother's child-rearing style (Fine, McKinry, Donnelly, & Voydanoff, 1992).

The stressors are affected by any change or significant life event. The lifestyle changes that are found when women move in and out of marriage or go in or out of poverty are significant and cause changes in both women and their children. These changes have been found to be disruptive to women and their children (McAdoo, 1991b).

Taylor, Henderson, and Jackson (1991) found that the stressors leading to depression and poor health emanated from the many life changes that the women in their sample faced. Any change in the environment may cause depressive symptoms and stress. When these changes occur, the perceived availability and involvement of friends are very important. Females in general are more vulnerable than men, and African American women are more vulnerable to depression than are Caucasian females. Single mothers have fewer psychological problems than those who are married (Taylor et al., 1991).

RELIGIOSITY

A religious orientation is a belief in a supreme being, and religiosity may not mean church attendance or membership. As used in this study, religiosity refers to the importance of religion in the woman's life. The traditional Black churches offer solace, warmth, and nurturance, and the "church family" may assume many functions of a kinship network: informal adoptions, job referrals, emotional support, and social contacts. This assistance is in addition to the religious function.

The importance of religion and the church in coping in the lives of African Americans has been well documented (Billingsley, 1968, 1992; Frazier, 1963; Hill, 1971; Pipes, 1992). Brown and Gary (1985) found that religious participation is a source of support with anxiety-related problems. Other studies have shown that the church provides emotional well-being (Neighbors & Jackson, 1984) and that women are more religiously involved than men (Taylor, Thornton, & Chatters, 1987). Therefore, it is important to understand religion as one of the coping strategies available to single mothers.

Although one would expect religiosity to have a direct and positive effect on stress and coping, the women who are very stressed have the greatest religiosity (McAdoo, 1988). A high religious orientation has a direct relationship with depressive symptoms in mothers; that is, the more religious a mother is, the greater is her depression. Women high in religiosity tend to be less involved in their social support network (Taylor, 1991), and a religious orientation seems to have a culturally oppressive rather than liberating effect on women. This finding was corroborated in two other large-scale studies (Jackson, 1991; Taylor & Jackson, 1990).

In summary, as noted in McAdoo (1994), extended family support is available in many families, but help from kin becomes more activated when the mothers are single, when families are facing greater stress, or when economic resources are more limited. Socioeconomic status (SES) and family structure are directly related because the resources that are available to parents as they rear their children are diminished when mothers are parenting alone.

THE HYPOTHESES

This study examines how women of different status cope with the acute stresses they face as household head. What are their sources of support and how do these sources differ for women of different social class and marital status? Four issues were addressed: (a) the factors in personal and family backgrounds that contribute to the ability to face stress; (b) the levels of stress; (c) whether female-related stressors are an addition to regular stress; and (d) the roles of religion.

> *Hypotheses 1:* Stress levels will be similar for both the previously married and never-married women.
> *Hypotheses 2:* Working-class mothers will have significantly higher stress levels than will middle-class mothers.
> *Hypotheses 3:* The roles of religion will be similar for women in both marital status and SES groups.

METHODOLOGY

PROCEDURES

National probability studies with large samples (Jackson, 1991) can provide representative samples, but this research involved a regional sample. Interviewers were able to take time to develop a relationship with the mothers, to follow up on the answers, and to probe in detail for more information. All the interviewers were African American, and half were single mothers. The interviews ranged from 2.5 to 3 hours.

A systematic sampling procedure could not be used because residences of single Black mothers were not randomly distributed across the city. Three methods were used to obtain subjects. First, a sample was drawn from an income-stratified list of all the day care centers approved by the Baltimore Department of Social Service that had an approximate Black enrollment of at least 25. That procedure resulted in a predominance of mothers with younger children. Second, to obtain the names of mothers with older children, ads asking for participants were placed in the local White and Black newspapers. Third, volunteers were obtained from the Women's Center, an employment service center.

Telephone contact was made to explain the project and establish eligibility criteria. Subjects were interviewed at home, but in a few instances, because of privacy, mothers preferred to be interviewed on their job or in our Baltimore office. Each mother was given $20 as a small gift of appreciation for her time and effort. The interviewers were trained, and most had previous interview experience.

INSTRUMENTS

Stress intensity. The Significant Life Events (SLE) scale was used to obtain an intensity score. The Holmes and Rahe (1967; Holmes & Masuda, 1974) Scale of Recent Events was used to secure universal events, that is, 49 events weighted on actual populations across the country. This scale gives a higher score for major changes (divorce, 73; death of a child, 63) and a lower score for less traumatic events (vacation, 13). Based on clinical follow-ups, Holmes grouped the scores into three stress categories: mild (150-199), moderate (200-299), and major (300+). Those in the higher stress groups had a greater probability of becoming physically or mentally ill within a shorter period.

Stress frequency. Frequency was a simple count of whether a stressful event had occurred in a specified period. The Holmes and Rahe SLE scale used 2 years as the time during which change is measured. For this study, that period was used, and an additional two-step temporal scale was developed. Mothers were asked to indicate whether the event had occurred within the past 6 months or the past 7 to 24 months. For example, a family may be subjected to one major event (such as personal injury, 53 points) in 2 years or may have five smaller events (with lower stress scores each) within 6 months. The latter may yield a lower Holmes and Rahe score but may be equally or more traumatic for the family because they all occur within a shorter period.

Female stress. Because many of the stress events on the SLE were oriented toward men and families but not women, 16 events from Belle's (1980) study were added. These items were going on or off welfare; starting an intimate relationship; having an unfaithful lover; widowhood; marriage of a former husband or lover; undesired miscarriage or abortion; unwanted pregnancy and birth; adoption or taking in of a child; changed child care arrangements; giving up custody of a child; death of a child; menopause; rape or molestation; becoming a crime victim; nervous breakdown; and joining a self-help group. These items could not be weighed as were the others on the SLE, but the frequency of occurrences was noted, as in the stress frequency scoring.

Religion. Five areas were examined: religious denomination membership; religiosity; church attendance; frequency of prayer; and what religion does for one. Religiosity was a subjective assessment of how religious the women felt they were and the importance of spirituality in their lives.

SAMPLE CHARACTERISTICS

The sample of 318 single Black women lived in the Baltimore area, where they maintained independent households. All were employed and had full custody of their children, all of whom were under age 19. The women had an average of 1.53 children (.89 boys and 1.02 girls); the younger the mother at her first pregnancy, the more children she tended to have. The average age in the sample was 30.24 years, ranging from 20 to 50 years. More than half (54%) had been age 19 or older when their first child was born.

Forty-four percent had never been married, and 56% had been married at one time; of these latter, 29% were divorced, 26% were separated and considered their marriage to be over, and 2% were widowed (see Table 1). Most of the women (70%) had grown up in two-parent homes, and their present single-parent status was not due to direct modeling of their families of procreation. Their parents had been in their mid-20s (mothers) or late 20s (fathers) when these women were born. They tended to be either the first and only or the second child born to their parents.

Two thirds of the subjects (73%) were not married at the birth of their first child. Half of that group later married, not always to the father of their first child. Very few of the women (5%) had men living within the home. Their

TABLE 1
Demographic Characteristics of
African American Mothers in Sample (*N* = 318)

| | Marital Status | | Socioeconomic Status | | |
	Ever (%)	Never (%)	Middle Class (%)	Working Class (%)	Total (%)
Variable					
Total	56	44	31	69	100
Marital status					
Separated	26	46	0	24	27
Divorced	29	51	0	40	24
Widowed	2	3	0	3	1
Never married	44	0	100	34	48
Total	101	100	100	101	100
Education					
Junior high	3	4	2	3	3
High/trade school	37	31	44	0	53
1-2 years college	29	26	32	5	39
3-4 years college	19	21	17	53	4
Graduate/professional	12	17	6	39	0
Total	100	99	101	100	99
Occupation					
Executive/major professional	25	29	19	77	1
Administrative personnel	12	10	14	10	12
Clerical/business owner	47	47	48	13	63
Skilled/semiskilled	14	12	16	0	20
Unskilled	3	2	4	0	4
Total	101	100	101	100	100
Income ($)					
3,000-8,999	17	17	36	4	35
9,000-11,999	12	22	27	18	27
12,000-14,999	18	18	20	20	19
15,000-23,999	33	33	15	47	16
24,000-40,000	7	10	3	13	4
Total	100	100	100	101	101
Religion					
Baptist	45	49	53	41	52
Methodist	18	20	15	29	13
Catholic	14	13	16	15	14
Other Protestant (combined)	11	13	9	4	14
Fundamentalist	4	6	2	8	2
No religion	4	3	5	2	5
Total	100	100	100	99	100

NOTE: Rounding errors resulted in subtotals of 99 and 101.

present family structures were diverse. The forms were as follow: attenuated nuclear (mother and children, 66%), attenuated extended (mother, children, and relatives, 25%), augmented attenuated nuclear (mother, children, and nonrelative, 7%), and augmented extended (mother, children, relative, and nonrelative, 2%) (see Table 2).

Socioeconomic status (SES). SES was assessed in two different ways. All subjects were coded using the Hollingshead-Redlick Social Position Scale (1958), which places greater emphasis on the occupation than on the education of an individual. This method allowed comparisons with other data sets. The approach does not seem satisfactory, however, for those who face gender and racial discrimination in the occupational market (McAdoo, 1988; Scanzoni, 1977). Therefore, a method suggested by Baldwin (1973) was used, which gives more weight to education than to occupation.

With the modified scoring, the distribution of the sample by SES status was as follows: 11% Class I; 20% Class II; 53% Class III; 15% Class IV; and 1% Class V. For this study, the classes were combined into two groups: middle-class mothers, Classes I and II (31%), and working-class mothers, Classes III, IV, and V (69%).

The education levels were high school (37%), 1 or 2 years of college (29%), 3 or 4 years of college (19%), and graduate or professional degree (12%). Eighty-nine percent worked full time, 11% part time. Most of the women were clerical workers (47%), followed by executives or professionals (25%) and administrative/personnel (12%). Many had been unemployed at some time in their life; being in college (32%) and pregnancy and child rearing (22%) were the most frequent reasons for unemployment.

Those who had never married tended to be working class, $\chi^2 = 5.69$, $p < .02$, had fewer children, $\chi^2(1) = 68.27$, $p < .000$, and lived within a three-generation family. Middle-class women who had never married had more people in the home, $F(3, 314) = 4.58$, $p < .03$. This large household size was due to the fact that these women had taken in more elderly persons, $F(3, 310) = 7.15$, $p < .008$, than had those who were working class. They were in a better financial position to do so and were older than the working-class women. These elderly adults were often the persons who had helped the middle-class women when they were young single mothers.

Income. The median income was $12,000; the range was from $3,000 to more than $40,000. The net income for previously married mothers was higher than for those never married, $\chi^2(7) = 20.64$, $p < .004$. As expected, the middle-class mothers had higher net incomes, $\chi^2(7) = 67.44$, $p < .000$; the working-class mean was $9,500, and the middle-class mean was $16,500. The mother's income was the major source of support (94% of the sample)

TABLE 2
Frequency Distribution of Structure of Family of Orientation and Family of Procreation by Socioeconomic Status and Marital Status

Family Structure	Total f	Total %	Socioeconomic Status Middle %	Socioeconomic Status Working %	χ^2	df	p	Marital Status Ever %	Marital Status Never %	χ^2	df	p
Family of origin					2.71	2	ns			5.54	2	ns
Nuclear	169	53	51	55				48	60			
Extended	130	41	47	39				47	34			
Augmented	17	5	3	7				5	6			
Total	316	99	101	101				100	100			
N			99	217				177	139			
Simple nuclear	126	40	43	38	20.55	7	.005	38	42	11.46	7	ns
Attenuated nuclear	41	13	6	16				9	19			
Simple extended	83	26	37	21				32	19			
Attenuated extended	46	15	8	18				15	14			
Augmented nuclear	6	2	3	1				2	1			
Augmented extended	6	2	1	2				2	2			
Augmented attenuated nuclear	5	2		1				1	1			
Augmented attenuated extended	3	1	1	1				1	1			
Total	316	101	100	99				100	99			
N			99	217				177	139			

158

Present family of procreation

Present family of procreation	N	%	%	%	χ²	df	p	%	%	χ²	df	p
Attenuated nuclear	211	66	64	68	2.65	4	ns	72	59	14.54	5	.01
Simple extended	23	7	10	6				5	11			
Attenuated nuclear	55	17	16	18				15	21			
Augmented attenuated nuclear	23	7	8	6				8	5			
Augmented attenuated extended	6	2	2	2				1	4			
Total	318	99	100	100				101	100			
N			98	216				179	139			

NOTE: Structural definitions: augmented = parents, child, nonrelative; augmented attenuated extended = 1 parent, child, relative, nonrelative; nuclear = parents, child; attenuated nuclear = 1 parent, child; augmented attenuated nuclear = 1 parent, child, nonrelative; extended = parents, child, relative; attenuated extended = 1 parent, child, relative.

for her family. Child support was received by half the mothers, but it was more irregular (51%) than regular (49%).

Because of the low wages they were paid, 84 (26%) of the women received welfare despite their working. Of those receiving welfare, 57% received it regularly, 43% irregularly.

Religion. The largest group was Baptist (59%), followed by Methodist (18%), Catholic (14%), and all other Protestants combined (15%). The change in denomination over three generations on both the paternal and maternal side was examined. The pattern of distribution among denominations had remained constant, but membership had steadily decreased. For example, among Baptists, 70% of grandparents, 62% of parents, and 49% of the present generation were members of this denomination (see Table 1).

Regular church attendance, weekly or at least three times a month, was reported by 25% of the sample; 12% attended once a month. The largest number of women (35%) went only a few times a year, and 15% reported that they never attended church; 52% reported little contact with an organized denomination. Yet frequent prayers were reported by 72% of the women, 25% prayed sometimes, and only 3% said they never prayed.

Social class was associated with different religious memberships, $\chi^2(5) = 25.50, p.0001$. Most of the Baptists (74%) and Catholics (67%) were working class. Methodists (51%) and other Protestants (Episcopalian, Presbyterian, Lutheran, 62%) tended to be middle class. Chi-square analyses were used to compare occupations. The majority were clerical for all religious groups except other Protestants, who were predominately middle class (62%). Methodists were evenly divided between middle class (51%) and working class (49%) (see Table 3).

Marital status at the first pregnancy was associated with religious denomination, $\chi^2(5) = 13.93, p < .02$. The majority of mothers in each religious group were not married, except for the combined Protestants group (other than Baptist), Methodists, and Catholics.

RESULTS

STRESS

Hypothesis 1 was not supported, for even though all of the women had very high stress intensity scores, stress levels did differ based on marital status.

TABLE 3
Cross-Tabulations of Type of Religion and Occupation, Socioeconomic Status, and Marital Status at 1st Pregnancy

	Total	Baptist	Methodist	Fundamentalist Catholic	Other Protestant[a]	No Protestant[b]	Religion	χ^2	df	p
Occupation								45.39	10	.000
Executive	25	19	46	24	11	54	8			
Clerical	60	63	49	67	51	39	92			
Unskilled	15	18	5	9	37	8	0			
Total	100	100	100	100	100	100	100			
N	318	155	57	45	35	13	13			
Socioeconomic status								25.50	5	.0001
Middle class	31	27	51	33	11	62	15			
Working class	69	74	49	67	89	39	85			
Total	100	101	100	100	100	101	100			
N	318	155	57	45	35	13	13			
Marital status at 1st pregnancy								13.93	5	.02
Married	27	22	35	20	23	62	39			
Not married	73	78	65	80	77	39	62			
Total	100	100	100	100	100	101	101			
N	316	153	57	45	35	13	13			

NOTE: Rounding errors resulted in subtotals of 99 and 101.
a. Fundamental Protestants = Pentecostal, Jehovah's Witness, Moorish, Seventh-Day Adventist
b. Other Protestants = Episcopal, Presbyterian, Lutheran.

The mothers had a mean stress score of 367.33, considered to be a very high level (see Table 4). Holmes would consider this entire group to be under major stress (300+) and vulnerable to physical or mental illness, which have been found significantly related to the level of stressful changes in life. Stress intensity levels were high for all subgroups and were not related to age, SES, or age and marital status at first pregnancy. For the 2-year period, previously married mothers ($M = 186.27$) had higher stress intensity scores than those never married ($M = 154.00$), $F(313) = 3.88$, $p < .05$. The stress score that was assigned to divorce (73) is a factor. Those who did not experience a marriage that had gone bad and a subsequent divorce would, indeed, have lower stress.

The second measure of stress was the frequency of stressful life events that had occurred, regardless of intensity. The average was 16.31 events over 2 years, 9.13 within the 6 months prior to the interview. The mothers had, in addition, experienced an average of 2.05 female stress events during the 2-year period. The average for the combined measures over the 2 years was 18.26 events (see Table 4).

All the stress measures for the three periods intercorrelated significantly ($p < .001$) with all the other stress scores. Mothers who experienced stress in one area were high in all other stress.

The demographic variables were regressed against stress intensity, and all were significant. Mothers who were under less stress had residential stability, sufficient income and occupation, were never married, were older, had few people and children in the home, and were moderately educated (see Table 5). A positive direct relationship was found for the number of years the mother had lived in the same house, $r(308) = .174$, $p = < .01$, and for sufficient income, $r(308) = .144$, $p < .01$.

Women who were older and more experienced with the demands of their lives, who had time to work out their living arrangements, who had children who were older and less physically demanding, who were educated enough to have stable jobs, and who were responsible for fewer people in their homes perceived their lives as less stressful.

Mothers who had been married and given birth during their teen years had experienced more female stress life events, $F(3, 294) = 3.74$, $p < .05$, than those who had never married or who were older than 19 years when first giving birth. College-educated women had experienced more stress intensity, $F(1, 311) = 5.52$, $p < .004$, than those with less education.

When incomes were considered, those who made less were under greater strain. Women who earned less than $9,000, $F(1, 310) = 5.47$, $p < .02$, and those who earned less than $12,000 were higher in all three stress scores. Women who needed income from a number of sources were higher in stress intensity, frequency, and female stress over each of the three periods (signifi-

TABLE 4
Means and Standard Deviations of Stressful Life Events (SLE):
Intensity and Frequencies of Experiences (N = 317)

Stress Variables	M	SD
Stress intensity		
Past 6 months	194.81	125.73
Past 6 months-2 years	172.22	149.63[1]
Entire 2 years (original SLE scoring)	367.33	205.92
Stress frequency		
Past 6 months	9.31	5.39
Past 6 months-2 years	7.03	5.88
Entire 2 years	16.31	8.54
Female-related stress frequency		
Past 6 months	1.01	1.14
Past 6 months-2 years	1.05	1.18
Entire 2 years	2.05	1.77
Total stress frequency		
Past 6 months	10.32	6.03
Past 6 months-2 years	8.08	6.48
Entire 2 years	18.26	9.61

NOTE: SLE was score of stress intensity over the entire three year period. A temporal dimension was added: stress over the past six months; stress experienced between 7 months and 2 years.

cant at the .01 level or higher). Mothers who were highly stressed had fewer people contributing to the family income and living in the house with them. Mothers experienced fewer stress events in either the 6-month or 2-year period when more people lived in and helped out financially ($r = -.094, p < .05$).

Younger mothers were higher on the stress intensity scores; age was negatively correlated with stress in the past 6 months ($r = -.127, p < .01$) and over the 2-year period ($r = -.150, p < .03$). Younger mothers had experienced more frequent stress events in the past 6 months ($r = -.174, p < .001$) and over the whole 2 years ($r = -.132, p < .000$). The younger mothers had even more female stress ($r = -.235, p < .000$). Older mothers experienced less stress in all areas.

In addition to the regression, analyses of variance were used to determine the relation between age at first pregnancy and stress. Age at first pregnancy (below or above 19 years) did not relate to stress levels. As noted earlier, however, mothers who had been married and had given birth during their teens had experienced more female stress life events, $F(3, 294) = 3.74, p < .05$, than those who had married but gave birth later, those who never married but gave birth as teens, or those who never married but gave birth later.

TABLE 5
Regression Analyses of Stress Intensity

	Cumulative			
	r	R^2	β	F
Number of years in same house	.174*	.03	−.11	8.80*
Family income	.144*	.05	−.16	6.87*
Marital status	.109	.06	.22	6.40**
Age	−.079	.07	−.13	5.78**
Number of people in house	−.125	.09	−.11	5.59**
Education	.086	.09	.08	5.05**
Number of children	−.039	.09	−.04	4.36**
Occupation	−.035	.10	−.01	3.81**

NOTE: df = 8,274.
*$p < .01$. **$p < .09$.

The age of the woman's parents at her birth was related to female stress. Women had higher female stress scale scores when their own fathers (r = .158) and mothers (r = .136) were younger. Women who reported more frequent female stress also had young mothers (r = −.146, $p < .007$). The younger the mother at her first pregnancy, the more children she tended to have. These women had more girls than boys. The ages of the children appeared to make a difference in female-related stress but not in stress intensity in general. Mothers with higher scores on the female stress events scale, in the past six months (r = .101, $p < .04$) and in the entire two years, had more young children between the ages of 2-5 years old. The older the children, the lower the stress, which was borne out by the fact that mothers with older children had less stress of all kinds. Mothers of older children, 15- to 18 years old, tended to have lower frequency scores in the 6-month period (r = −.132, $p < .009$) and in the 2-year period (r = −.113, $p < .02$). Mothers had experienced fewer female-related stress events in the period of 6 months to 2 years when their children tended to be 10-14 years old.

The more children living at home the less stress intensity was reported in the past 6 months to 2 years (r = −.112, $p < .02$). Women with more children living at home had also experienced fewer female-related stress events in the immediate previous 6 months (r = −.122, $p < .02$); 6 months to 2 years (r = −.105, $p < .04$); and over the whole period (r = −.107, $p < .03$). Mothers with more children in the 15-to-18 age group had lower stress intensity scores for the previous 6 months (r = −.121, $p < .03$) and over the 2-year period (r = −.105, $p < .03$). These same mothers had lower female stress scores for the 6-month (r = −.143, $p < .007$) and 2-year (r = −.130, $p < .01$) periods as well as fewer female stress occurrences in the 6-month to 2-year period ($r = -.102$, $p < .04$) and for the whole 2 years ($r = -.121, p < .02$).

THE ROLE OF RELIGION

Most of the women reported that they were fairly religious (75%), some said very religious (19%), and some not religious at all (6%). The importance of religion was shown in that it provided emotional support for 86% of the women. Moral support was mentioned by 11%. Two percent said that religion answered prayers, and the same percentage said that it did nothing. When the women were asked what religion did for their family, the most frequent responses were that it provides emotional support (39%) and moral support (36%). Religion was considered to help by fostering family unity (6%), by just being there (5%), and by answering prayers (3%). Eleven percent of the sample felt that religion did nothing for their family.

Most of the mothers felt that the church had helped Blacks function in this society (76%). The positive comments were that churches gave strong support to families (42%) and provided a system of beliefs (21%). Mention was also made of persons who had stopped drugs and alcohol, and emphasis was placed on the churches' role in fostering civil rights. The negative comments referred to hypocritical practices, insensitivity, and the promotion of beliefs that cloud reality and pacify Blacks into accepting less (see Table 6).

Stress intensity differed significantly by the three major denominations that represented 83% of the sample, $F(2, 253) = 3.61, p < .03$. Baptists, the largest group, had the highest stress scores ($M = 390.29$), much higher than the overall mean for the sample ($M = 367.33$). Catholics ($M = 338.96$) and Methodists ($M = 310.22$) had much lower scores. The working-class predominance among the Baptists and the middle-class status of many of the Methodists could account for the difference.

Religiosity was also related to stress intensity, $F(2, 312) = 3.10, p < .05$. Those who were fairly religious had higher stress scores ($M = 18.71$) than those who were very religious ($M = 18.14$). The lowest stress was found among women who were not at all religious ($M = 12.87$).

DISCUSSION

This sample of middle-class and working-class Black single mothers was highly stressed. Within the past 6 months they had experienced enough stressful events ($M = 194.81$) to be considered under moderate stress on the

TABLE 6
Description of the Role of Religion

Variable	%
How religious	
Very	19
Fairly	75
Not at all	6
Total	100
N	316
How often pray	
Often	72
Sometimes	25
Never	3
Total	100
N	315
Attends services	
Once a week	18
3 times a month	17
Once a month	12
Few times a year	37
Never	15
Total	99
N	314
What religion does for subject	
Emotional support	86
Moral support	11
Answers prayers	2
Nothing	2
Total	101
N	303
What religion does for subject's family	
Emotional support	39
Moral support	36
Nothing	11
Helps family unity	6
Just helps	5
Answers prayers	3
Total	100
N	305
How church affects Blacks	
Positive	
Strong support	42
Something to believe in	21
Only alternative	6
People stopped using drugs/alcohol	4
Supported civil rights	4

continued

166

TABLE 6 continued

Variable	%
Negative	
Hypocritical practices	7
Insensitive to needs of people	4
Pacifies, clouds reality	4
No difference	8
Total	100
N	275

Holmes and Rahe (1967) scale, even if it was spread over 2 years. They were experiencing stress that can be considered destructive. It was so intense and occurring so frequently that one wonders how they managed to function from day to day.

Intensity scores were higher for more recent (last 6 months) than more distant (7 months to 2 years) stress. This would indicate that their stress was accelerating or that they had forgotten more distant stress after a certain amount of time. Regardless of the measurement issues, this sample had experienced life changes sufficiently serious to become debilitating without intervention or some form of external support (Holmes & Masuda, 1974).

Stress intensity and frequency were important measures of changes within their lives that required adjustment. Only 2.05 of the 16 female stress items had occurred, on the average, but female stress appeared to be an important issue, as it differentiated the women in many respects.

One interesting pattern was that a woman with younger parents, regardless of her present age or her age when she became pregnant, experienced more female stress but not stress intensity. These women born to young parents were experiencing the most difficulty with their own stress related to child-bearing, their lovers, and other female stress. They may not have had the benefit of parents who had learned a few of life's lessons before they had children, and therefore these women were relatively unprepared. This could be related to our finding that previously married women who had given birth in their teen years had higher female stress. Young marriage, especially when hastened by an impending pregnancy, may not be wise. The young girl may lose some family support and the wisdom that comes from having parents around a little longer.

Younger mothers had more stress than older women. Women who had younger children (aged 2 to 5 years) at home had more female stress but not more stress intensity. Younger women may still be finding themselves while facing the multiple pressures of parenting alone. They may be experiencing the changes that come with their age, they may face exploitation in the work place, and they may be more dependent. Older women with older children may have learned how to fend for themselves, may not be as attractive, and may be more experienced at not putting themselves in situations where they can be exploited. They have learned their lessons and may be retreating to their family and children. Children make fewer demands on a mother when they become older; the demands may be emotionally taxing, but at least the physical care is easier.

College-educated women experienced more stress. Although this appears contrary to the data on income, one must also look at the household arrangements under which they lived. There are fewer marriage partners with comparable education available to them (McAdoo, 1988), a situation complicated by the presence of children. In comparison to the older women, more of them had taken elderly people into their homes. Those middle-class women who had never married had a home significantly longer, allowing them to amass the resources that enabled them to be more supportive of more relatives. These women, who had been pregnant and not married, had earlier been dependent on their family members and now were obligated to assist them in their old age, a reversal of roles.

Never-married women tended to be working class, have fewer children, and live in three-generational families. Low income did contribute to higher stress, as was found by Edelman (1987). But stress was lower when the mother could depend on many people for support.

Women who were Baptist or Catholic were working class; Methodists and other Protestants tended to be middle class. Baptists had the highest stress intensity levels, much higher than the overall average score of the women. Whereas most women were single at the birth of their first child, those in the combined Protestants group tended to be married, probably because of the higher social class of the participants in those denominations.

Our subjects were basically unchurched, as attested by their lack of attendance regardless of denomination. This indicates a need that the churches, especially in the Black community, should address. More attention needs to be paid to this population because of the high levels of single parenting within these communities. The women reported praying frequently, so religion still plays an important role in their life (Frazier, 1963). They may be overwhelmed by responsibilities and unable to attend church.

These single mothers, of both middle and working class, felt that they were fairly religious and that their religion provided emotional support. Yet, the fairly religious women had higher stress scores. In fact, the lowest mean score belonged to the women who were not religious at all. But for those with stress, though they may not go to a church service, praying and having faith appears to be a readily available coping strategy.

This is consistent with the role that religion has played through the years (Pipes, 1992). Women under great stress have used religion as a resource, not unlike the way they have used the other members of their family. Consistent with the findings of Brown and Gary (1985), religion appears to be a recourse for the women studied here. They pray often to release anxiety. They may not be able to solve their problems, but they have the strength to go on and face up to their life.

IMPLICATIONS

The overall impression is that these women are facing tremendous stress. Its alleviation should be a priority, for more families in all communities are adopting the family structure of single mothers. The financial stress could be lessened by court-ordered and -enforced child support payments. Only half of African American women are granted such an order, and only half of those ever receive any money (Pearce & McAdoo, 1981). More recent data are similar, and this situation accounts for the increased poverty of million of women and children.

There are implications from these findings for counselors and therapists, the churches, social service deliverers, and family life educators. For these who provide counseling and advisory services, it is important to be aware of the family support and helping systems. Providers should attempt to become familiar with the literature about these families (Boyd-Franklin, 1989). Services should not try to replace but should augment the existing cultural patterns. Reciprocal help is a tradition in many African American families, and the *familism* among Hispanics is very similar. One cannot generalize, however, for there are real differences in the overall patterns. Whereas most families are available to help, not all African Americans are involved in their family network, not all live in close proximity, and not all have lifestyles consistent with their other relatives.

Services should meet the diversity of family support patterns. One cannot make assumptions about a woman's social network. Women differ in their approaches to receiving help; some are in intensive family help patterns, some are in cooperative arrangements with women in similar situations, and a few women are going it all alone. It will be necessary to gather background data, more than is needed for most service providers.

One cannot make assumptions about why a single mother is in her situation. Myths should not cloud our thinking. It is often difficult for service providers to remain free of the stereotypes that prevail about Black women, welfare, and teen pregnancy. Most Black mothers were formerly married, and only 30% were mothers while unmarried in their teens (Edelman, 1991). The rate of divorce is twice that of Whites and has risen to an alarming extent. The important point is that Black single mothers are not a monolithic group (Campbell & Moen, 1993; McAdoo, 1991b).

Counselors should look at the importance of female stress, for this is more problematic than the type measured by the typical male-oriented scales. The female component should always be used when assessing stressful significant life changes. Support groups could be started to address relevant concerns. Effective use of time is an important topic, for time is what the mothers do not have. Indeed, support groups must be made highly relevant, or the women will not make time for them. Groups should meet in the neighborhoods or the homes of the women. Those running the programs should provide child care and perhaps transportation. I found in an intervention project for single mothers that once these women are interested in what is going on in a support group, they will not let anything stop them from getting there.

The religious institutions, whether Protestant, Catholic, or Muslim, need to work more with single mothers through targeted programs and outreach in which other women, preferably single mothers, visit the homes to disseminate pertinent information and supportive services. Churches should look at the attendance of single mothers, for they are religious but do not go to services. Religious groups sometimes are reluctant to work with a divorced woman or a young girl who becomes pregnant when unmarried, but there is work to be done in the churches, for the level of single mothers is increasing. Churches can be sources of support beyond the religious aspect, such as augmenting existing family patterns or forming supportive networks where none exist.

As mothers are provided help, there must be emphasis on related policy issues: child support enforcement; adequate quality child care available 24 hours; housing discrimination that prevents women with children and African Americans from moving to convenient locations with good schools; and the maintenance of income above the poverty level. There will be more single African American mothers in the future, and it is imperative that efforts are made to help them be self-sufficient and able to cope with their many roles.

REFERENCES

Alan Guttmacher Institute. (1981). *Fact book on teenage pregnancy*. New York: Author.

Anne E. Casey Foundation. (1992). *Kids count data book*. Washington, DC: Center for the Study of Social Policy.

Aschenbrenner, J. (1973). Extended families among Black Americans. *Journal of Comparative Families Studies, 4*, 257-268.

Baldwin, C. (1973, March). "Comparison of mother-child interaction at different ages and in families of different education levels and ethnic backgrounds." Paper presented at the annual meeting of the Society for Research in Child Development, Philadelphia.

Belle, D. (1982). Social ties and social support. In D. Belle (Ed.), *Lives in stress: Women and depression* (pp. 133-144). Newbury Park, CA: Sage.

Billingsley, A. (1968). *Black families in White America*. Englewood Cliffs, NJ: Prentice-Hall.

Billingsley, A. (1992). Climbing Jacob's ladder: The enduring legacy of African-American families. New York: Simon & Schuster.

Boyd-Franklin, N. (1989). *Black families in therapy: A multisystems approach*. New York: Guilford.

Brown, D., & Gary, L. (1985). Social support network differentials among married and nonmarried Black females. *Psychology of Women Quarterly, 9*, 229-241.

Burton, L. (1992). Black grandparents rearing children of drug-addicted parents: Stressors, outcomes, and social service needs. *The Gerontologist, 32*, 744-751.

Campbell, M., & Moen, P. (1993). Job-family role strain among employed mothers of pre-schoolers. *Family Relations, 41*, 205-211.

Cherlin, A., & Fustenberg, F. (1986). *The new American grandparents*. New York: Basic Books.

Danziger, S. & Danziger, S. (1993). Child poverty and public policy: Toward a comprehensive antipoverty agenda. America's childhood. *Daedalus: Journal of the American Academy of Arts and Sciences. 122*(1), 57-84.

Darity, W., & Myers, S. (1991, March). Sex ratios, marriageability, and the marginalization of Black males. Paper presented at the biennial meeting of the Society for Research in Child Development, Seattle, WA.

D'Ercole, A. (1988). Single mothers: Stress, coping, and social support. *Journal of Community Psychology, 16*, 41-54.

Edelman, M. (1987). *Families in peril: An agenda for social change*. Cambridge, MA: Harvard University Press.

Edelman, M. (1991). *The measure of our success: Letter to my children and yours*. Boston: Beacon Hill.

Farley, R., & Allen, W. (1987). *The color line and the quality of life in America*. New York: Russell Sage.

Fine, M., McKinry, P., Donnelly, B., & Voydanoff, P. (1992). Perceived adjustment of parents and children: Variations by family structure, race, and gender. *Journal of Marriage and the Family, 54*, 118-127.

Frazier, F. (1963). *The Negro church in America*. New York: Schocken.

Garfinkel, I., & McLanahan, S. (1986). *Single mothers and their children*. Washington, DC: Urban Institute.

Glick, P. (1988). A demographic picture of Black families. In H. McAdoo (Ed.), *Black families* (2nd ed., pp. 116-137). Newbury Park, CA: Sage.

Hayes, C. (Ed.). (1987). *Risking the future: Adolescent sexuality, pregnancy, and childbearing*. Washington, DC: National Academy Press.

Hill, R. (1971). *The strengths of Black families*. New York: Prentice Hall.

Hollingshead, A. & Redlich, F. (1958). *Social class and mental illness: A community study. The index of social position*. New York: Wiley.

Holmes, T., & Masuda, M. (1974). Life changes and illness susceptibility. In B. Dohrenwend & B. Dohrenwend (Eds.), *Stress life events, their nature and effects* (pp. 45-72). New York: John Wiley.

Holmes, T., & Rahe, R. (1967). The social readjustment rating scale. *Journal of Psychosomatic Research, 11*, 213-218.

Horowitz, F. D. (1992). John B. Watson's legacy: Learning and environment. *Developmental Psychology, 28*, 360-367.

Jackson, J. (1991). *Life in Black America*. Newbury Park, CA: Sage.

Kamerman, S., & Kahn, A. (1988). *Mothers alone, strategies for a time of change*. Dover, MA: Auburn House.

Kaplan, E. (1988). Where does the Black teenage mother turn? *Feminist Issues, 8*(1), 51-83.

Kivett, V. (1993). Racial comparisons of the grandmother role: Implications for strengthening the family support system of older Black women. *Family Relations, 42*, 165-172.

Marks, N., & McLanahan, S. (1993). Gender, family structure, and social support among parents. *Journal of Marriage and the Family, 55*, 481-493.

Martin, E., & Martin, J. (1978). *The Black extended family*. Chicago: University of Chicago Press.

McAdoo, H. (1988). *Changes in the formation and structure of Black families: The impact of Black women* (Working Paper No. 182). Wellesley, MA: Wellesley College Center for Research on Women.

McAdoo, H. (1991a). The ethics of research and intervention with ethnic minority parents and their children. 1990. In Fisher & Tryon (Eds.), *Ethics in applied developmental psychology* (pp. 273-283). Norwood, NJ: Ablex.

McAdoo, H. (1991b). Portrait of African American families in the United States. In S. Rix (Ed.), *The American women: A status report* (pp. 71-93). New York: Norton.

McAdoo, H. (1993). The social cultural contexts of ecological developmental family models. In P. Boss, W. Doherty, R. LaRossa, W. Schumm, & S. Steinmetz (Eds.), *Sourcebook of family theories and methods: A contextual approach* (pp. 298-301). New York: Plenum.

McAdoo, H. (1994). Family equality and ethnic diversity. In K. Altergott (Ed.), *One world, many families* (pp. 52-55). Minneapolis, MN: National Council on Family Relations.

McLanahan, S., & Booth, K. (1989). Mother-only families: Problems, prospects, and politics. *Journal of Marriage and the Family, 55*, 557-580.

Mechaneck, R. (1987). Single mothers by choice: A family alternative. *Women and Therapy, 6*(1/2), 263-281.

Neighbors, H., & Jackson, J. (1984). The use of informal and formal help: Four patterns of illness behavior in the Black community. *American Journal of Community Psychology, 12*, 629-644.

Pearce, D., & McAdoo, H. (1981, September). Women and children: Alone and in poverty. Washington, DC: National Advisory Council on Economic Opportunity, September.

Pipes, W. (1992). *Say amen, brother!* Detroit: Wayne State University Press.

Quinn, W., & Allen. (1989). Family treatment of adolescent drug abuse: Transitions and maintenance of drug-free behavior. *American Journal of Family Therapy, 17*(3), 229-243.

Reiss, D. (1989). Families and their paradigms: An ecological approach to understanding the family in its social world. In C. Ramsey (Ed.), *Family systems in medicine* (pp. 298-301). New York: Guilford.

Scanzoni, J. (1977). *The Black family in modern society: Patterns of stability and security*. Chicago: University of Chicago Press.

Scanzoni, J., & Marsiglio, W. (1993). New action theory and contemporary families. *Journal of Family Issues, 14,* 1005-1032.

Stack, C. (1974). *All my kin: Strategies for survival in a Black community.* New York: Harper & Row.

Taylor, J. (1991). Extended family networks of older Black adults. *Journal of Gerontology, 46,* S210-S217.

Taylor, R., Chatters, L., Tucker, B., Lewis, E. (1990). Developments in research on Black families: A decade review. *Journal of Marriage and the Family, 52,* 993-1014.

Taylor, J., Henderson, D., & Jackson, B. (1991). A holistic model for understanding and predicting depressive symptoms in African American women. *Journal of Community Psychology, 19,* 306-320.

Taylor, J., & Jackson, B. (1990). Factors affecting alcohol consumption in Black women. *International Journal of Addictions, 25,* 1407-1419.

Taylor, R., Thornton, M., & Chatters, L. (1987). Black Americans' perceptions of the sociohistorical role of the church. *Journal of Black Studies, 18,* 123-138.

Tucker, B., & Mitchell-Kernan, C. (1992). Sex ratio imbalance among Afro-Americans: Conceptual and methodological issues. In R. Jones (Ed.), *Advances in Black Psychology, 1.* Berkeley, CA: Cobb & Henry.

Wilson, W., & Neckerman, K. (1986). Poverty and family structure: The widening gap between evidence and public policy issues. In S. Danziger & D. Weinburg (Eds.), *Fighting poverty: What works and what doesn't* (pp. 237-262). Cambridge, MA: Harvard University Press.

Yankelovich, D. (1981). A world turned upside down. *Psychology Today, 15*(4), 35-91.

notes for practice

Strengths of Black Families: A Black Community's Perspective

DAVID D. ROYSE AND GLADYS T. TURNER

Since the publication of Frazier's classic studies of black family life, investigators have often maintained there is more pathology in black families than in white families.[1] The pathology focus is more recently characterized in the controversial Moynihan report. Moynihan cited as evidence of greater dysfunctioning in black families the high incidence of illegitimate births, households headed by females, welfare enrollment, and broken marriages.[2] While some blacks have fiercely responded to Moynihan's charge that the black family was deteriorating, little literature is available on black families which is not presented from the pathology perspective. Too rarely have researchers attempted to identify the virtues or strengths of black family life. This study attempts to do that by identifying family strengths as perceived by blacks.

The majority of blacks are self-supporting, have stable marriages, and "manage to keep out of trouble, often despite the grossest kinds of discrimination and provocation," yet there has been a scarcity of research on them, as Billingsley was among the first to note.[3] Ladner has also called for researchers to examine black families from a nondeviant perspective and to consider the strengths that have enabled blacks to adapt to poverty and racism.[4] Hill responded to this call by analyzing and interpreting census data and other types of information and identifying five strengths found in black families:

David D. Royse, MSW, is Director of Research and Evaluation, Greene-Clinton Mental Health and Retardation Board, Xenia, Ohio. Gladys T. Turner, MSW, is Coordinator of Quality Assurance, Daymont West Community Mental Health Center, Dayton, Ohio.

strong kinship bonds, work orientation, adaptability of family roles, achievement, and religious orientation.[5]

A review of the literature suggests that the characteristics identified by Hill are not widely recognized and that there is a dearth of scholarly research on the specific topic of the strengths of black families. The study described here appears to be the first one that empirically examines blacks' perceptions of those family traits identified by Hill.

It is important that the strengths found in black families be revealed so that social workers and other professionals will be able to utilize those traits in the helping process. The documentation of such strengths assists the white social worker in coming closer to understanding blacks and to bridging the racial barrier. Also, it is essential for blacks—in terms of their self-identity—to discover evidence of strengths in their culture and not just signs of social pathology.

RESEARCH DESIGN

In the study reported here, the researchers developed a questionnaire based on the list of strengths identified by Hill and on a review of the literature on black families. The questionnaire required interviewees to respond to statements in a Likert-type format with one of the following responses: "strongly agree," "agree," "undecided," "disagree," or "strongly disagree." Three black women and one black man conducted all of the interviews during the winter of 1977.

The researchers identified the twelve census tracts in Dayton, Ohio, containing the highest concentration of blacks. They then made a random selection of four of these tracts and of

fifty blocks within the four tracts. Black households were randomly selected within these blocks, and one adult resident from each household was interviewed.

Of the 128 respondents, 22 percent reported incomes of less than $5,000, 47 percent had incomes between $5,050 and $10,000, 13 percent had incomes between $10,050 and $15,000, and 18 percent had incomes of more than $15,050. Respondents' educational levels ranged from no formal education to graduate work. Only 24 percent had not received a high school diploma, and 43 percent had attended or finished college. Approximately one-third of the respondents were between the ages of 26 and 45, and one-third were between 46 and 64. Fourteen percent were 65 or older, and 18 percent were between 18 and 25.

Slightly more than half of the interviewees were married, and almost a fifth were single. The balance of the respondents were divorced, separated, or widowed. Twenty-four percent of the respondents had no children, 56 percent had one, two, or three children, and 20 percent had four or more children. Fifteen percent of the sample reported their chief occupation as "housewife." Twenty percent of the sample were retired, and 14 percent of the respondents reported being unemployed. Those employed in professional and technical occupations made up 11 percent of the sample. Thirty-one percent of the respondents were male.

The research team produced cross-tabulations of all variables by selected variables in preparation for analysis of these data. Examination revealed no essential differences in modal response categories by marital status, sex, or

[1] See, for example, E. Franklin Frazier, The Negro Family in the United States (Chicago: University of Chicago Press, 1966); and Frazier, The Black Bourgeoisie (New York: Free Press, 1965).

[2] Daniel Moynihan, The Negro Family: The Call for National Action (Washington, D.C.: U.S. Department of Labor, 1965).

[3] Andrew Billingsley, Black Families in White America (Englewood Cliffs, N.J.: Prentice-Hall, 1968), p. 206.

[4] Joyce Ladner, Tomorrow's Tomorrow: The Black Woman (New York: Doubleday & Co., 1971).

[5] Robert Hill, The Strengths of Black Families (New York: Emerson Hall Publishers, 1971).

0037-8046/80/2505-0407 $0.50 © 1980, National Association of Social Workers, Inc. **407**

number of children. Consequently, this report specifies only the percentage of responses per category.

FINDINGS

Hill defines kinship bonds in terms of the "adopting" of the elderly and of children born out of wedlock. He documents this strength with data demonstrating the higher frequency with which black families take relatives into their homes. Twenty-five percent of the respondents in the present study strongly agreed and 60 percent agreed with the statement, "Black families are more likely than white families to take in their children born out of wedlock." Less than 6 percent of the respondents disagreed or strongly disagreed. Ten percent were undecided. (Because of rounding, the percentages cited in some groups do not total 100 percent.) Nineteen percent of the respondents strongly agreed and 67 percent agreed with the other part of Hill's operational definition of strong kinship bonds as reflected in the statement, "Black

families, more than white families, are likely to take in their elderly black family members." Eight percent disagreed and 6 percent were undecided.

Hill maintains that a strong work orientation exists among blacks and that self-help is a characteristic pattern of most black families. He supports this with statistics demonstrating that more of the black poor work than do the white poor. When blacks in the study reported here were asked to respond to the statement, "Most black families encourage their children to become industrious workers," 7 percent strongly agreed and 65 percent agreed. Seven percent were undecided, 18 percent disagreed, and 3 percent strongly disagreed with the statement. When this statement was rephrased and expressed in the negative, about the same percentage of respondents disagreed as had previously agreed. The rephrased statement was, "Black families do not teach their children that success comes from hard work." Sixty-five percent disagreed and 8 percent strongly disagreed. Six percent were undecided, 19

percent agreed, and 2 percent strongly agreed. A related finding was that 15 percent strongly agreed and 73 percent agreed with the statement, "Blacks have had to exert extraordinary efforts, such as the joint employment of both husband and wife, to achieve economic stability and financial success as a family." Approximately 6 percent were undecided and 6 percent disagreed.

The data that Hill examined suggested to him that the typical pattern of decisions among black families was not "matriarchal" but egalitarian. Black husbands were seen as being actively involved in both decision-making and the performance of household tasks. In the present study, however, only a slight majority of the respondents (52 percent) agreed or strongly agreed with the statement, "Black husbands often help their wives with household tasks." Nine percent strongly agreed, 43 percent agreed, 18 percent were undecided, 24 percent disagreed, and 6 percent strongly disagreed. Approximately the same percentage (55 percent) disagreed or strongly disagreed with the following statement phrased in the negative: "One strength missing in black families is that both husband and wife seldom share equally in making important family decisions." Five percent strongly disagreed, 50 percent disagreed, 12 percent were undecided, 27 percent agreed, and 6 percent strongly agreed.

Hill believed that a tendency to seek achievement was demonstrated by his finding that higher proportions of black students than white students cited parental pressure to finish college, and that higher occupational aspirations existed among blacks from lower-status broken homes than among whites from lower-status intact homes. In the current study, almost three-fourths of the respondents either agreed or strongly agreed with the statement, "A higher percentage of black families than white families want their children to attend college." Ten percent strongly agreed, 63 percent agreed, 14 percent were undecided, 11 percent disagreed, and 2 percent strongly disagreed. About the same proportion (78 percent) disagreed with the statement, "Black families do not stress the importance of education" as agreed with the previous statement. Two percent strongly agreed, 13 percent agreed, 7 percent were undecided, 57 percent disagreed, and 21 percent strongly disagreed.

The fifth and final family strength identified by Hill was that of religious orientation. Hill did not use empirical evidence to support his argument for the presence of this characteristic but cited the historical role of the black church. A religious orientation can be inferred from the results of this study, as 21 percent of the respondents strongly disagreed and 58 percent disagreed with the statement, "Most black families do not teach their children that religion is important." Six percent were undecided, 13 percent agreed, and 2 percent strongly agreed.

Responses to the following statements suggested that black families have strengths beyond those described by Hill.

■ Seventy-five percent of respondents agreed and 18 percent strongly agreed with the statement, "Black families teach their children to respect themselves." Two percent were undecided and 6 percent disagreed.

■ Ten percent of the subjects strongly agreed and 80 percent agreed that "black families teach their children how to be happy, even when times are hard." Two percent were undecided, 7 percent disagreed, and 1 percent strongly disagreed.

■ Three percent strongly agreed and 84 percent agreed that "black families stress cooperation within the family." Eight percent were undecided and 5 percent disagreed.

■ Twenty-eight percent of the respondents strongly disagreed and 50 percent disagreed with the statement, "Black parents do not strictly discipline their children." Three percent were undecided, 17 percent agreed, and only 2 percent strongly agreed with this statement.

■ Two-thirds of the respondents were optimistic about the future for black youths. This optimism was shown in the finding that 9 percent of subjects strongly disagreed and 55 percent disagreed with the statement, "In the next twenty years it does not look like many black children will be able to reach middle-class status. Six percent of the respondents were undecided, 29 percent agreed with the statement, and 1 percent strongly agreed.

DISCUSSION

Much more work remains to be done in the documentation of the strengths that exist in black families. This initial study suggests that blacks perceive themselves as having the same family strengths as those identified by Hill. There does not appear, however, to be any reason to suspect that the publication of Hill's studies has in any way influenced the responses of those people interviewed in this study. Also, there would not seem to be any basis for believing that family strengths are limited to those listed by Hill or those added to the list in the course of this study. The authors hope that more researchers will begin to study black family life from a nondeviant perspective. As this occurs, numerous other strengths will doubtlessly be found.

It is necessary to note that some of the characteristics outlined here as family strengths can also act as detriments. For example, a family's financial resources can suffer when too many children or elderly persons are taken in. Nevertheless, the identified traits are *perceived* as strengths by a majority of blacks in this study. It remains the social worker's responsibility to make an individual assessment based on the particular client's strengths and weaknesses. The strengths reported here may provide a starting place for all social workers who need to identify the strengths of black families and to understand how those strengths influence social and environmental aspects of behavior. ◀

0037-8046/80/2505-0409 $0.50 © 1980, National Association of Social Workers, Inc.   **409**

JOURNAL OF RESEARCH ON ADOLESCENCE, 5(1), 31–53
Copyright © 1995, Lawrence Erlbaum Associates, Inc.

Parental Ethnic Socialization and Adolescent Coping With Problems Related to Ethnicity

Jean S. Phinney and Victor Chavira

California State University, Los Angeles

This study investigated ethnic socialization by parents of minority group adolescents, the adolescents' ethnic identity and strategies for coping with stereotypes and discrimination, and the interrelationships among these and demographic variables. In-depth interviews were carried out with 60 American-born Japanese-American, African-American, and Mexican-American high-school students, aged 16 to 18 years, and one parent of each adolescent. There were significant ethnic group differences in parental ethnic socialization, with African-American parents more frequently reporting discussing prejudice with their child and Japanese-American and African-American parents emphasizing adaptation to society more than Mexican-American parents. Adolescent use of a proactive style of coping with stereotypes and discrimination was associated with higher self-esteem, and use of verbal retorts was related to lower self-esteem. Parental socialization did not have a strong relationship to adolescent outcomes.

As the numbers of ethnic minority children continue to increase, the socialization of ethnic minority children and adolescents has become a topic of growing interest and concern (e.g., Boykin & Toms, 1985; Harrison, Wilson, Pine, Chan, & Buriel, 1990; Knight, Bernal, Garza, Cota, & Ocampo, 1993; Phinney & Rotheram, 1987; Thornton, Chatters, Taylor, & Allen, 1990). Interest in the development of minority children was indicated by a recent issue of *Child Development* (1990) that focused

---

Requests for reprints should be sent to Jean S. Phinney, Department of Psychology, California State University, Los Angeles, CA 90032.

on this topic. However, many of the articles in that issue stressed the dearth of information and the need for additional research.

This need for research on the role of ethnicity and minority status in socialization stems from two concerns. First, there is widespread recognition that much of the literature on socialization has been based on White, middle-class samples (Graham, 1992; Harrison et al., 1990). Because adolescents from other cultural and ethnic backgrounds face different developmental issues, conclusions from research that does not include ethnic minorities cannot be generalized to include them. Indeed, there is evidence that socialization patterns differ among ethnic groups with regard to issues such as child rearing (Ellis & Petersen, 1992; Lin & Fu, 1990), gender roles (Davenport & Yurich, 1991), and school performance (Dornbusch, Ritter, & Steinberg, 1991; Steinberg, Dornbusch, & Brown, 1992).

These differences could be explained by the concept of the developmental niche (Super & Harkness, 1986), which stresses the role of the cultural context in which the socialization of the child takes place. Developmental outcomes are a result of complex interactions between the developing individual and his or her environment (Bronfenbrenner, 1979, 1986). In the United States, a key component of this interactive process is the ethnicity of the individual. Each ethnic group has a different history, cultural heritage, and status within contemporary society; and these differences are likely to influence a range of developmental processes and outcomes (e.g., Gibbs & Huang, 1989; Spencer & Dornbusch, 1990).

Although research has begun to examine the role of ethnicity in socialization regarding general developmental issues such as gender roles and school performance, there has been little attention to a second concern: the unique socialization issues faced by minority parents. Because members of ethnic minorities experience lower power and status in society and face stereotyping and discrimination (Harrison et al., 1990), preparing children to understand and deal with these issues is an important component of the parenting process. Very little is known about parental socialization regarding ethnicity and minority status.

These issues are likely to become particularly salient during adolescence. Developmentally, minority adolescents are beginning to explore identity issues generally (Marcia, 1980) and ethnic identity in particular (Phinney, 1989). Although children acquire an ethnic label and knowledge about their ethnic group at a younger age (Aboud, 1987; Bernal, Knight, Ocampo, Garza, & Cota, 1993), during adolescence, minority youths begin to examine the meaning of their ethnicity and of minority status. During the high-school years, they may be exposed to racism and prejudice as they move into a wider world through jobs, sports, and other activities. Parents are likely to be aware of this process and to initiate discussions; they may also respond to questions raised by their son or daughter. In any case, many adolescents report discussing these issues with their parents (Phinney, 1989). Thus, the primary purpose of the present study was to identify the ethnic socialization issues that minority parents emphasize with their children and the impact of these parental messages on adolescent outcomes.

On the basis of research primarily with African-American families, it appears that minority parents are faced with three distinct challenges. Their children need to be socialized both to their own culture and the mainstream culture, and they need to understand prejudice and discrimination. In a widely cited conceptual framework, Boykin & Toms (1985) identified three themes that form the basis for the socialization of African-American children: understanding African-American culture, getting along in mainstream society, and dealing with racism. These three themes recur in various forms throughout the literature on African-American socialization.

The first theme, the learning of one's own culture, would seem to be the least problematic, in that it is presumably learned naturally in the home. However, it is not clear to what extent culture is deliberately taught to children as opposed to simply being learned through practice and observation. Boykin and Toms (1985) suggested that much of African-American culture is transmitted to children through tacit socialization. Yet we know from several studies of African-American families that there is also explicit cultural teaching. According to Bowman and Howard (1985), 6% of their sample of African-American youths (ages 14 to 24 years) stated that they had been explicitly taught about Black history and culture and an additional 17% had been socialized regarding racial pride and African-American unity and commitment. Thornton et al. (1990) reported similar percentages among parents who were asked about their socialization messages to their children: African-American heritage and the historical tradition of African Americans were emphasized by 8.6% of the parents, and racial pride was stressed by 17.2%. These results suggest that about one quarter of African-American parents teach their children about their cultural heritage and/or racial pride. There is little empirical evidence regarding cultural teaching in other ethnic groups.

A second socialization theme involves teaching children to get along in the mainstream culture or helping them to succeed in society at large. For example, Demo and Hughes (1990) identified among African-American parents a socialization theme termed *integrative/assertive*, which involved both African-American pride and getting along with Whites. Other African-American writers have pointed out that African-American parents generally teach their children to be bicultural (e.g., Cross, 1987). Part of getting along in society involves developing the skills necessary to be successful; to accomplish this, children are encouraged to work hard and do well in general. Thornton et al. (1990) found that 22.2% of African-American parents stressed the importance of achieving and working hard. Bowman and Howard (1985) reported that 14% of African-American youths received messages focusing on self-development and individual achievement. Again, little is known about groups other than African Americans.

A final theme common to all the research on African-American socialization is explicit teaching or preparation of children to be aware of prejudice and discrimination. Racial barriers and blocked opportunity were emphasized by 13% of the youths studied by Bowman and Howard (1985) and by 8.2% of parents in the study by Thornton et al. (1990). Demo and Hughes (1990) used the category *cautious/defensive* to describe a style of African-American socialization that stressed deference, social distance, and recognition of White prejudice. Socialization on this issue appears to have a strong impact. Bowman and Howard (1985) found that youths socialized to be aware of racial barriers and cautioned about appropriate interracial behavior attained higher grades and had a greater sense of personal efficacy.

While ethnic minority groups in the United States share some similarities, they differ in important ways, including history, religion, and cultural values and traditions. The very limited existing research on socialization in groups other than African Americans has focused on these cultural factors (e.g., Mindel, Habenstein, & Wright, 1988) and has paid little attention to socialization related to minority status. Thus, it is unclear to what extent the socialization themes outlined above apply across ethnic groups. The first goal of the present study was to examine socialization related to ethnicity among African-American, Japanese-American, and Mexican-American parents.

In addition to the need for a better understanding of the ways minority parents prepare their children for understanding their ethnicity, it is important to study the impact of such preparation. Although ethnic or racial socialization has received relatively little research attention, the outcomes in terms of adolescent behaviors and attitudes have received even less. Given the fact that ethnic minority youths are likely to experience negative stereotypes and discrimination (Mont-Reynaud, Ritter, & Chen, 1990), the way these adolescents cope with negative discriminatory experiences and the way they think about their ethnicity (i.e., their ethnic identity) are two important socialization outcomes.

Minority group reactions to prejudice and discrimination have been studied primarily at a sociological level (e.g., Ogbu, 1985). There is little evidence in the psychological literature regarding the way minority youths cope with negative experiences related to their ethnicity and minority status. In his sociological framework, Parrillo (1985) proposed several strategies that characterize the way ethnic minorities, as groups, respond to discrimination. Some of these strategies can be used to discuss personal coping behaviors.

According to Parrillo (1985), ethnic group members may respond to discrimination with *defiance*, that is, by actively challenging the discriminatory practice. A second strategy is *deviance*, engaging in behaviors that the minority group considers reasonable but that violate the norms or laws of the dominant society. Another way of coping with discrimination is through *avoidance*, or refusing to deal with the discriminatory act or with the perpetrator of the act. Finally, groups may rely on *acceptance*, a process whereby minority group members accept and conform to the discriminatory norms of the dominant society. These strategies are conceptually meaningful, especially for studying the relationship between race-related experiences and mental health among minority group members. However, because of the paucity of empirical data, it is not certain whether these strategies accurately describe minority individuals' responses. Thus, the second and third goals of this study were to describe the strategies used by minority adolescents in responding to prejudice and discrimination and to examine the relationship between these strategies and both self-esteem (a common indicator of psychological adjustment) and ethnic identity (a key component of self-concept for minority group members; Phinney, 1990).

A final question of this study was how parental socialization may influence adolescent outcomes, including coping strategies and ethnic identity. Research on outcomes of socialization has focused on school achievement. For example, Bowman and Howard (1985) found that racial socialization contributed to the maintenance of higher school grades and a sense of personal efficacy. The family is also likely to be an important influence on adolescent coping strategies, even though such strategies are the results of many influences (Bronfenbrenner, 1986; Ogbu, 1985; Seiffge-Krenke & Shulman, 1990). Studies have shown that ethnic minority parents talk to their children about how to cope with prejudice and racism (e.g., Bowman & Howard, 1985; Thornton et al., 1990), but it is not known whether this socialization influences the kind of coping strategies minority children actually use.

In addition to specific strategies vis-à-vis their ethnicity, minority youths develop a sense of themselves as ethnic group members. Although parents may convey to children a positive sense of their culture, children are increasingly exposed to the dominant culture by the media, school, and their peers. They inevitably become aware that their own group is often viewed less favorably than the dominant group; and they may, therefore, develop negative feelings about their group (Aboud, 1987). However, through a developmental process of questioning, learning about, and coming to appreciate their own ethnicity and culture, most minority youths achieve a secure and confident ethnic identity (Cross, 1991; Phinney, 1989, 1990; Phinney & Rosenthal, 1992).

The role of parental socialization in this process is unclear, because only a few studies—mainly with African-American samples—have addressed the topic. Spencer (1983) reported that among young African-American children, Eurocentric racial attitudes (i.e., attitudes less favorable toward African-American culture) were associated with the lack of parental discussion of racial discrimination and teaching about civil rights. Similarly, Branch & Newcomb (1986), in interviews with young African-American children and their parents, found that children with high racial awareness, knowledge, and preference had parents who taught them positive aspects of their race. In a study of African-American adults, Demo and Hughes (1990) found a low but significant correlation between a feeling of closeness to other African-Americans and earlier socialization from parents involving racial pride, the importance of African-American heritage, and getting along with Whites.

Only a few studies have looked at other ethnic groups. Knight et al. (1993) examined the relationship of teaching about Mexican culture, ethnic pride, and discrimination to ethnic knowledge, behavior, and preference among 6- to 10-year-old Mexican-American children. Few significant relationships were found, although several trends suggested that mothers who are more comfortable with Mexican culture may have children who are more ethnically identified. In a study with Chinese-American and Chinese-Australian adolescents, Rosenthal and Feldman (1992) found that ethnic pride was fostered by parental environments characterized as warm, controlling, and autonomy-promoting. They did not, however, assess socialization specifically related to ethnicity.

In summary, it is clear that minority parents face a complex task in socializing their children. However, there has been only limited research on this process. The majority of existing data concerns African Americans, and little is known about ethnic socialization in other minority groups. Few studies have looked at adolescent outcomes of ethnic socialization, particularly outcomes related to ethnicity, such as ethnic identity and ways of coping with discrimination. In order to provide data on such socialization and its impact, this study investigated parental ethnic socialization and adolescent outcomes in Japanese-American, African-American, and Mexican-American families and examined the relationships among parental socialization and adolescent coping and ethnic identity.

METHOD

Participants

There were 120 participants: 60 American-born adolescents, aged 16 to 18 years, and either the mother or father of each adolescent. The families were from one of three ethnic groups: African American, Japanese American, or Mexican American. The sample was drawn from a predominantly minority high school in a stable middle- and working-class community that is ethnically diverse. Located in the suburban Los Angeles area, the community was formerly largely Japanese American but has been changing with the influx of middle- and working-class African-American and Mexican-American families. The community closely resembles Los Angeles County in per capita income, education level, and unemployment rate and is in sharp contrast to inner-city minority communities on these indicators. For example, compared to a specific (typical) inner-city community in Los Angles, the per capita income of the community is twice as high and its unemployment rate is nearly one third (Bureau of the Census; 1992; Slater & Hall, 1992). The socioeconomic status (SES) of the participating families reflects this middle class status. SES was determined on the basis of parental report of occupation and education. Families were assigned to either middle-class (professional or white collar, some college education) or working-class (unskilled or semiskilled work, no college education). The demographic characteristics of the sample are shown in Table 1.

Questionnaire Measure and Procedures

The questionnaire was administered to a sample of 417 high-school students who were participants in another study (Phinney, 1992). It included the following measures:

Ethnic identity.   Ethnic identity was assessed by the 14-item Multigroup Ethnic Identity Measure (Phinney, 1992). The measure has a reported reliability of .81 with high-school students and assesses

185

TABLE 1
Demographic Description of the Sample

Description	Japanese American	African American	Mexican American
Adolescent's Gender			
Male	9	7	10
Female	9	9	16
Mean age in years	16.7	16.3	16.5
Parent interviewed			
Mother	14	13	24
Father	4	3	2
Parental birthplace			
Both U.S.	7	16	1
1 U.S., 1 foreign	8	0	4
Both foreign	3	0	21
Parental marital status			
Married	17	7	20
Single	1	9	6
Social class			
Middle	94.4%	93.8%	53.9%
Working	5.6%	6.2%	46.1%

three aspects of ethnic identity: a sense of belonging to and attitudes toward one's ethnic group (5 items; e.g., "I have a strong sense of pride in my ethnic group and its accomplishments"); ethnic behaviors and customs (2 items; e.g., "I participate in the cultural practices of my own group, such as special food, music or customs"); and ethnic identity achievement, based on exploration and commitment (7 items; e.g., "I have spent time trying to find out more about my own ethnic group, such as its history, traditions and customs" and "I have a clear sense of my own ethnic group and what it means to me"). Items are rated on a four-point scale, ranging from *strongly disagree* (1) to *strongly agree* (4). An ethnic identity score is derived by reversing negative items, summing across the 14 items, and obtaining a mean. Scores can range from 1 to 4, indicating very low to very high ethnic identity, respectively.

Self-esteem. This variable was measured by Rosenberg's (1986) 10-item self-esteem inventory. Participants respond on a 4-point scale ranging from *strongly disagree* (1) to *strongly agree* (4). The score is obtained by reversing negative items and obtaining the mean.

Demographic variables. The questionnaire asked participants to indicate their ethnicity and that of their parents, as well as their gender, age, and birthplace (whether American- or foreign-born).

Interview Procedures

Students who completed the questionnaire as part of a larger study (Phinney, 1992), who were American-born, and who were from one of the three targeted ethnic groups were invited to participate in the interview study and were requested to provide a telephone number if interested. Three months after collecting the questionnaires, an attempt was made by a research assistant from the same ethnic background to contact the families of all students who had expressed interest. Among those who could be reached by phone, about one half of each ethnic group agreed to participate. However, subsequent problems in scheduling interviews at times convenient to both the adolescent and parent resulted in lower actual participation rates, especially for the Japanese Americans and African Americans (50% and 36%, respectively, of those who agreed to participate). Participation rates were highest among the Mexican Americans (69%).

Each adolescent and one of his or her parents were individually interviewed by an interviewer of the same ethnic background as the family. Generally, the mother was interviewed; but in cases where she was not available, the father was interviewed. Interviews were carried out in the adolescent's home, at a time convenient to the adolescent and the parent. The interviews were carried out separately, with neither parent nor adolescent hearing the responses of the other. Adolescents were paid five dollars each for their participation. The interviews were tape recorded, transcribed, and coded. Codes were developed by a team of research assistants also representing the ethnic groups of the participants.

Parent interviews and coding.   An in-depth interview consisting of both open-ended and closed questions was used with the parents. Four specific questions concerned ethnic socialization:

1. Do you try to teach your son or daughter about the cultural practices of your ethnic group?
2. Have you tried to teach you son or daughter how to get along in mainstream American culture?
3. Have you talked to him or her about how to deal with experiences like name calling or discrimination?
4. Have you personally tried to prepare your son or daughter for living in a culturally diverse society?

Affirmative responses were followed up with probes concerning the specific things that the parents said to the adolescent and activities carried out with him or her related to the topic. In addition, open-

TABLE 2
Parental Socialization Themes and Examples

Theme	Examples
Achievement	"You have to work a lot harder to get ahead." "If you have the education and the skills, you can do just about anything you want." "You have to struggle to better yourself and not fall behind."
Culture	"It is important (for Blacks) to say, we have roots and they start here." "I talk to them about traditions, customs and celebrations."
Adaptation	"To get where you want to, you have to mingle with all races." "I tell them to get involved with all different groups of people." "I've told my child to learn to live side by side with other people, of our race and of other races."
Pride	"Once you are proud of who you are, you want to proclaim it." "It all has to do with pride." "We need to perceive ourselves in a positive role."
Prejudice as a problem	"My son tells me there is still—and will always be—discrimination; I see that it hurts him." "As long as there is prejudice there are going to be problems. We must deal with rejection every day."
Coping with prejudice	"I have always told my daughter she is going to have to learn how to cope." "I have told him to face the issues." "It is important to teach kids how to deal with it, how to cope."

ended questions assessed the parents' views on a range of topics related to ethnicity, such as issues faced by minority youths, the qualities needed for minority adolescents to get along in society, and the ways the parents sought to maintain their ethnic heritage. Each parent also was asked demographic questions concerning occupation, education, marital status, and place of birth (of both parents).

Data from the parent interviews consisted of yes/no responses to the four socialization questions, which were scored dichotomously, and responses to the open-ended questions. For the latter, initial codes were developed covering all the types of responses obtained to each question. Transcripts were coded independently by two research assistants, and disagreements were resolved by discussion with a third coder. This initial coding yielded a very large and frequently overlapping list of the types of messages parents conveyed to their children in various contexts. An examination of the responses revealed six socialization themes that covered virtually all the socialization messages of parents. Therefore, in the final coding process, each transcript was coded for the presence or absence of each theme. Each interview was coded by two coders; agreement between coders was above 83%. The themes, with illustrative examples, are shown in Table 2.

Adolescent interviews and coding.   The adolescent interview was similar in form to the parent interview and explored the following issues: (a) what the participants saw as the characteristics of their own ethnic group, (b) whether they experienced a conflict between ethnic and mainstream culture, (c) how they dealt with living in two cultures, (d) what images (stereotypes) they believed most people had of their group and how the participants reacted to these images, (e) whether and the extent to which the participants had experienced discrimination, and (f) what they believed to be the best way of dealing with discrimination.

As with the parent interviews, initial coding involved developing categories of responses to each of the issues discussed in the interview. Although several of the issues are conceptually distinct, the adolescents' responses generally fell into one of five categories, or strategies, used to deal with issues raised by their ethnicity. The strategies are shown in Table 3. In the final coding, each interview was coded for the presence or absence of each strategy; thus, more than one strategy could be coded per interview. All interviews were coded by two independent raters; agreement was above 82%.

RESULTS

Our results are presented in three sections. First, we present the parental socialization practices and examine them in relation to demographic variables. Next, we describe the adolescents' strategies in relation to demographic variables and to their ethnic identity and self-esteem. Finally, we explore the relation of parental practices to adolescent strategies.

Because the sample sizes were small, cross-tabular analyses tended to generate too many cells with small expected frequencies. Because this makes the results of the usual chi-square test somewhat questionable, we have used an exact probability test, similar to Fisher's Exact Test, available from SAS. For the most part, the *p* values from these tests were similar to those from chi-square tests.

Parental Socialization Practices

Data regarding parental socialization were of three types: (a) yes/no responses to four socialization questions, (b) socialization themes derived from the coding of open-ended responses to general questions about ethnic socialization, and (c) four mutually exclusive socialization styles derived from examining patterns within the socialization

TABLE 3
Adolescent Strategies for Dealing With Discrimination or Stereotypes

Strategy	Examples
Discussion	"[I] try to talk to the person, to clarify things with them about the common misconceptions about ethnic backgrounds." "I try to talk to them . . . to tell them that we are not like that." "I would express and share my view with them. We kind of shared each other's views . . . then it works out O.K."
Self-affirmation	"I know that I am good, and I don't care what people think." "I love being Hispanic; to me it seems like a privilege, because I know how to speak Spanish."
Disprove	"It makes me angry, and it just makes me want to work harder to prove them wrong." "I feel like I have something to prove if I do good in class."
Verbal retort	"They'll start saying stuff . . . most of the time I just say something back." "I would just leave and maybe say something that they deserve to hear." "If they talk to you rudely . . . I'd probably answer back with the same rudeness."
Ignore	"I think you should forget about it and go on with your life." "It makes you mad, but you really can't do anything. I wouldn't want to do anything." " I do not like being teased for being Japanese, but I usually do not do anything. It is very mean, but it happens."

themes. In each case, because of the demographic differences among the three ethnic groups, preliminary analyses were carried out to explore the impact of the main demographic variables.

Parental responses to the socialization questions are shown by ethnic group at the top of Table 4. Analyses of each socialization question revealed no statistically significant differences in terms of gender of adolescent, gender of parent interviewed, SES or marital status of the parents, or parents' birthplace (i.e., United States or foreign country). There were significant ethnic group differences in three of the four questions, with African-American and Mexican-American parents indicating more teaching for getting along in mainstream society compared to Japanese-American parents, $p < .01$; more preparation for living in a diverse society, $p < .001$; and more discussion of dealing with prejudice, $p < .01$.

The percentage of parents reporting each socialization theme, by ethnic group, is shown at the bottom of Table 4. It should be noted that the themes are not mutually exclusive. Parents could express any number of themes, so that the percentages total more than 100. Themes are listed in order of frequency of occurrence. A large majority of parents mentioned culture, and over half stressed achievement and discussed prejudice.

There were no differences in themes related to the gender of the adolescent or the parent. With ethnicity controlled, there were no differences in themes related to SES, marital status, or parental birthplace. Statistical analyses revealed significant ethnic group differences in three of the themes, with many more African-American parents mentioning prejudice as a problem, $p < .001$, and talking to their teen about handling it, $p < .02$. African-American and Japanese-American parents emphasized adaptation to society more than Mexican-American parents, $p < .05$.

In order to create a single socialization variable to be used in further analyses, four mutually exclusive socialization styles were developed from the themes. *Achievement* style was based on parental report of the achievement theme, without mention of prejudice. In *Social Problems* style, parents reported either one or both of the themes dealing with prejudice and discrimination, but did not mention personal achievement. *Combined* style involved discussing both achievement and social problems. *Neither* applied to parents who did not discuss either achievement or prejudice. (Because a very large proportion of parents from all groups discussed culture, this was not included in the styles.)

The percentages of parents from each group who used each style are shown in Table 5. The socialization styles differed significantly among the three groups, $p < .05$. Compared to the other groups, African-American parents were most likely to use the Combined style, whereas Japanese-American parents were most likely to use the Achievement

TABLE 4
Percentage by Ethnic Group of Parents Responding Positively to Socialization Questions and Reporting Socialization Themes

Questions/Themes	Japanese American[a]	African American[b]	Mexican American[c]
Socialization questions			
Q1: Teach cultural practices	66.7	81.3	88.0
Q2: Teach how to get along***	22.2	75.0	69.2
Q3: Talk about discrimination***	22.2	75.0	58.3
Q4: Prepare for diversity****	16.7	68.7	68.2
Socialization themes			
Culture	94.4	81.3	92.3
Achievement	55.6	75.0	50.0
Prejudice: coping**	27.8	75.0	57.7
Prejudice as problem****	16.7	81.3	46.2
Adaptation**	38.9	56.3	19.2
Pride*	5.6	25.0	34.6

[a]$n = 18$. [b]$n = 16$. [c]$n = 26$.
*$p = .08$. **$p < .05$. ***$p < .01$. ****$p < .001$.

TABLE 5
Percentage of Parents Using Each Socialization Style

Socialization Style	Japanese American[a]	African American[b]	Mexican American[c]
Achievement	27.8	0	11.5
Social problems	16.7	18.8	34.6
Both	27.8	75.0	38.5
Neither	27.8	6.3	15.4

Note. Exact test, $p < .05$.
[a]$n = 18$. [b]$n = 16$. [c]$n = 26$.

style or Neither. Mexican Americans were intermediate. Logistic regression analyses carried out for each of the styles individually did not reveal any additional demographic factors related to parental socialization.

Adolescent Strategies, Ethnic Identity, and Self-Esteem

Preliminary analyses revealed no ethnic group differences in the percentage of adolescents reporting each strategy in response to stereotypes and discrimination. A majority of adolescents stated that at times they would *Ignore* the issue (65.0%). *Discuss* was mentioned as the most frequent proactive response (53.3%), followed by *Disprove* (33.3%), *Self-Affirmation* (15.0%), and *Verbal Retort* (13.3%). (Because individuals could mention more than one strategy, the percentages totaled more than 100.)

The strategies were further coded into a single variable consisting of three mutually exclusive styles for coping with prejudice and discrimination. The coping styles and the number of adolescents using each style were as follows: *Proactive* coping style ($n = 44$) included adolescents who reported Discuss, Self-Affirmation, and Disprove as ways of dealing with these issues; over half of these respondents also mentioned Ignore as a possible strategy. *Passive* coping style ($n = 11$) included all adolescents who mentioned only Ignore as a way of dealing with prejudice and discrimination. *Aggressive* coping style ($n = 5$) involved the use of Verbal Retort, together with the absence of any of the proactive strategies. An exact probability table revealed no significant ethnic group differences in these coping styles.

Although they did not differ on strategies or coping styles, adolescents from the three ethnic groups reported different experiences with prejudice and discrimination. A majority of each group reported personal experience with prejudice. However, discriminatory treatment was reported by 81.3% of the African Americans, in contrast to 45.9.%

of the Mexican Americans and 27.8% of the Japanese Americans. In contrast, verbal slurs were reported much more frequently by the Japanese Americans (38.9%) than by Mexican Americans (29.2%) or by African Americans (6.3%).

In order to examine the relationships among the adolescent variables, exploratory analyses were carried out for each of the strategies and the coping styles, using a pool of adolescent variables (gender, SES, self-esteem, and ethnic identity) in a logistic regression. (Parental variables were also entered in the analysis; these results are discussed later.) On the basis of preliminary results, significant variables were examined in further logistic regression analyses. Statistically significant effects are shown in Table 6. With increasing self-esteem, adolescents were less likely to use Verbal Retort and more likely to use the Proactive coping style. There were nonsignificant trends for those with higher self-esteem to use Discuss, $p = .082$, and Self-Affirmation, $p = .094$. The logistic regression results for Ignore as a strategy show that, as ethnic identity increased, adolescents were less likely to use Ignore. Strategies and coping styles did not differ significantly by SES or gender.

Analyses of variance, with Tukey paired comparisons, were carried out to explore further the differences in ethnic identity and self-esteem based on coping styles (see Table 7). The adolescents using the Aggressive coping style were significantly lower in ethnic identity than those using either the Passive coping style or the Proactive coping style, $F(2, 57) = 3.50$, $p < .05$. Similarly, those using the Aggressive coping style were lower in self-esteem than the other two groups, $F(2, 56) = 8.17$, $p < .001$).

TABLE 6
Significant Effects From Logistic Regression of Adolescent Strategies and Coping Styles

Variables	Parameter Estimate	p
Strategy		
Verbal retort		
Intercept	1.82	.264
Self-esteem	−1.24	.028
Ignore		
Intercept	6.62	.008
Ethnic identity	−1.19	.036
Q3: Discuss discrimination	1.65	.014
Marital status	−1.70	.054
Strategic approaches		
Proactive		
Intercept	−2.04	.167
Self-esteem	0.99	.040

46   PHINNEY AND CHAVIRA

TABLE 7
Ethnic Identity and Self-Esteem Scores by Strategic Approach

Variable	Passive[a]	Proactive[b]	Aggressive[c]	F
Ethnic identity	3.05	3.07	2.33	3.50*
Self-esteem	3.13	3.22	2.16	8.17**

$^a n = 11.$ $^b n = 44.$ $^c n = 5.$
*$p < .05.$ **$p < .001.$

Parental Socialization and Adolescent Outcomes

An exact probability table of parental socialization styles by adolescent coping styles revealed no statistically significant relationship between parental socialization and adolescent strategic approaches for the sample as a whole or for the Japanese-American or Mexican-American families. For the African-American families, there was a trend for the parents who used the Combined style to have adolescents who used the Proactive coping style, $p = .099$.

The logistic regression analysis shown in Table 6 included the parental variables of socialization questions, socialization themes, marital status, and gender of parent. Results indicated that parents who talked about discrimination had children who were more likely to use Ignore as a strategy. There was also a trend for children of married (as compared to single) parents to be less likely to use Ignore. Other relationships were suggested by descriptive statistics but did not attain statistical significance in the small sample. The percentage of adolescents who would try to prove that stereotypes and discrimination are wrong (Disprove) was higher among those whose parents perceived prejudice as a problem (46.4%) than among those whose parents did not (21.9%). Verbal Retort was reported to be used less by adolescents whose parents reported talking about prejudice (3.1%) than by those whose parents did not discuss the subject (25%).

Ethnic identity scores of adolescents whose parents reported each socialization theme were compared to scores of adolescents whose parents did not report each theme, and ethnic identity scores were compared between those whose parents responded positively and those whose parents responded negatively to each socialization question. Results revealed a trend toward higher ethnic identity among adolescents whose parents prepared them for diversity, $t = 1.85$, $p = .07$. A step-wise linear regression of ethnic identity carried out using a pool of parental predictors (socialization questions and themes, marital status, SES, and gender of parent) showed a trend for higher SES and positive parental response to question 4 to be related to higher adolescent ethnic identity. A model including these variables is shown in Table 8.

TABLE 8
Results of Stepwise Linear Regression of Parental Variables on Adolescent Ethnic Identity

Predictor	Regression coefficient	Standard error
Intercept**	.95	.12
Q4: Prepare for diversity*	.28	.16
Low socioeconomic status*	−.32	.18

Note. Overall R^2 = .109. N = 60.
*p < .08. **p < .001.

DISCUSSION

The socialization themes that have been identified in other research were apparent among the Japanese-American, African-American, and Mexican-American parents in the present study. Most of the parents taught their adolescents about their culture, over half emphasized achievement, and substantial numbers expressed concern about the problems of prejudice and discrimination that their children would face.

While there were virtually no differences in parental socialization related to social class, marital status, or place of birth, there were significant differences based on ethnicity. Across virtually all indices, the African-American parents reported providing the most extensive ethnic socialization, the Japanese-American parents generally provided the least, and the Mexican-American parents were intermediate. The African-American parents, far more than the others, emphasized the positive goals of personal achievement and fitting into mainstream society, but were also keenly aware of the social problems their child would face and discussed with them ways of dealing with prejudice and discrimination. The Mexican-American parents paid relatively less, but still considerable, attention to social problems and to achievement; in addition, they emphasized cultural pride more than the other groups. The Japanese-American parents stressed achievement alone more than the other two groups and exceeded the Mexican Americans in their emphasis on adaptation to society.

Although the three ethnic groups differed in socioeconomic status, SES was unrelated to parental socialization when ethnicity was controlled. In fact, the African-American and Japanese-American parents, although most similar in SES, were most divergent in socialization. These results are congruent with those of Thornton et al. (1990) who, using data from a large survey of African-American adults, found no effects of education or income on racial socialization.

No other demographic variables, including gender of parent or adolescent and parental marital status and place of birth, were significantly related to socialization, when ethnicity was controlled. As in the present study, Thornton et al. (1990) found that marital status was not a strong predictor of ethnic socialization. In general, ethnic group membership appears to be a factor of far greater importance than other demographic variables in determining the types of socialization parents report.

The reasons for differences among parental socialization practices can be understood in terms of the ecological influences on each ethnic group. Even though significant progress has been made in eliminating discrimination in legal terms, African-American Americans in particular continue to be subject to discrimination (Hacker, 1992; Sigelman & Welch, 1991). African-American parents respond to the reality of the kinds of experiences their children will face and attempt to prepare them to deal with that reality. In addition to discussing prejudice and discrimination, African-American parents in this study stressed achievement more than the other parents; many African-American parents reported telling their child that he or she would need to work harder and do better than other adolescents in order to be successful.

This reality is supported by the comments of the African-American adolescents, four fifths of whom reported personal experiences of being treated in a discriminatory fashion. This result is similar to other evidence that African-American youths experience the most discrimination among ethnic minorities (Mont-Reynaud et al., 1990). Interestingly, the African-American youths reported fewer verbal racial slurs than the Japanese Americans or Mexican Americans. This finding may reflect modern racism, as described by Dovidio and Gaertner (1986). These authors suggested that people have become increasingly aware that overt racism against African Americans is unacceptable; therefore, they avoid overt remarks that might seem racist, although more subtle forms of discrimination toward African Americans persist. In contrast, there may be less general awareness of and sensitivity about racist remarks toward other minority groups.

A majority of the adolescents interviewed had experienced some form of prejudice. The results of this study provide important insights into the ways they cope with these experiences, a topic about which there has been little prior information. Unlike the parental socialization variables, which showed clear ethnic differences, there were no significant differences among the three ethnic groups in adolescent strategies or coping styles. Almost three quarters of the students took a basically active stance toward prejudice and discrimination by discussing it with the perpetrator, disproving stereotypes, and using self-affirmation. Mena, Padilla, and Maldonado (1987), similarly, found an active coping style to be the most frequent response to stereotypes and discrimination among college students. In the present study, less than one fifth used an exclusively passive style, and only 8% responded aggressively. However, the fact that ignoring the issue was mentioned by two thirds of the students indicates that, even among the proactive respondents, negative incidents were ignored when that was deemed the most appropriate response.

An important question is whether these strategies provide minority youths with adaptive means of coping. The Proactive, Passive and Aggressive coping styles that we identified closely parallel the strategies introduced in Parrillo's (1985) sociological framework discussed earlier. Responding to incidents of discrimination and prejudice with a proactive approach (such as discussion, disproving, or self-affirmation) appears to be the most psychologically adaptive way of coping, as evidenced by the higher self-esteem among adolescents who used this approach. Responding with an aggressive approach, on the other hand, is clearly the least adaptive. Interestingly, however, we found that self-esteem among adolescents who responded with a passive approach was nearly as high as that of adolescents who responded with a proactive coping style. It should be noted, as well, that over half of the adolescents classified as proactive reported the use of Ignore under some circumstances.

These results are consistent with a growing body of research that suggests that the effectiveness of a given coping strategy, whether active or passive, is not simply a function of the strategy itself; rather, it is mediated by complex personal and situational factors (Roth & Cohen, 1986; see also Folkman, 1984, for a theoretical analysis). Further, because the data reported here are correlational, it is not clear whether self-esteem is an outcome of coping strategies or a factor that contributes to the use of these strategies.

The impact of parental socialization on adolescents did not show up strongly in this study. For example, parental discussion or teaching about culture was unrelated to ethnic identity. This lack of effect may be due in part to the small sample. In addition, the family is only one of many factors affecting children, and its influence declines in adolescence. For minority youths in particular, peers appear to play a particularly important role and one that may, to some extent, counteract parental influence (Steinberg et al., 1992).

Nevertheless, several relationships between parental and adolescent factors are of interest. Compared to parents who did not report discussing discrimination, those who did discuss the topic had adolescents who were more likely to ignore incidents of prejudice and somewhat less likely to use verbal retort. A nonsignificant trend also suggested that parents who perceived prejudice as a problem had children who were more likely to try to disprove the negative attitudes they encountered. Frankness by parents in recognizing and discussing discrimination may help adolescents to be more aware of various possible ways of dealing with the experience, such as proving it wrong or, where appropriate, ignoring it. As suggested above, these may be better choices than an aggressive verbal response.

In addition, parents who said they prepare their child for living in a diverse society tended to have adolescents with higher ethnic identity. Presumably these parents are themselves aware of issues related to ethnicity, and they provide a context in which the adolescent can develop an understanding of his or her own ethnicity. Of course, direction of effect cannot be determined from these data; it is possible that adolescents who are actively exploring their ethnicity raise questions to which their parents respond. Longitudinal studies are needed to clarify this relationship.

In the present study, we investigated socialization in families from three specific minority groups that have an American-born adolescent and live in a stable, middle- and working-class, minority community in an ethnically diverse region of the country. Obviously, the results cannot be generalized to other ethnic groups, to other regions of the country, to immigrant youths, or to inner-city families. However, given the absence of differences related to demographic variables other than ethnicity, the results strongly suggest that ethnicity is a crucial factor in parental socialization. The findings provide a good starting point for future research on ethnic and racial socialization within and across ethnic groups. As suggested by the idea of the developmental niche (Super & Harkness, 1986), parental ethnic socialization responds to the realities that adolescents face. Furthermore, there is suggestive evidence that parents can be most helpful to their adolescents by being open in discussing potential problems. There is clearly need for further research to examine these relationships in greater detail and with other populations. If we wish to promote the successful transition of minority youths to adulthood, we need to understand the socialization experiences that they encounter and the effects these experiences have on their lives.

ACKNOWLEDGMENTS

Portions of this research were presented at the meeting of the Society for Research in Child Development, Seattle, WA, April, 1991.

This research was supported in part by Public Health Service Grant RR–08101 from the Minority Biomedical Research Support Program Division of the National Institutes of Health.

We thank Sterling Alexander and Stephanie Nakayama for their contribution to this study and Rita Englehart for her assistance with the data analyses.

REFERENCES

Aboud, F. (1987). The development of ethnic self-identification and attitudes. In J. Phinney and M. Rotheram (Eds.), *Children's ethnic socialization: Pluralism and development* (pp. 32–55). Newbury Park, CA: Sage.

Bernal, M., Knight, G., Ocampo, K., Garza, C., & Cota, M. (1993). Development of Mexican American identity. In M. Bernal & G. Knight, (Eds.), *Ethnic identity: Formation and transmission among Hispanics and other minorities* (pp. 31–46). Albany: State University of New York Press.

Bowman, P., & Howard, C. (1985). Race-related socialization, motivation, and academic achievement: A study of Black youth in three-generation families. *Journal of the American Academy of Child Psychiatry, 24,* 134–141.

Boykin, A. W., & Toms, F. (1985). Black child socialization: A conceptual framework. In H. McAdoo & J. McAdoo (Eds.), *Black children: Social, educational, and parental environments* (pp. 33–51). Newbury Park, CA: Sage.

Branch, C., & Newcomb, N. (1986). Racial attitude development among young Black children as a function of parental attitudes: A longitudinal and cross-sectional study. *Child Development, 57,* 712–721.

Bronfenbrenner, U. (1979). *The ecology of human development.* Cambridge, MA: Harvard University Press.

Bronfenbrenner, U. (1986). Ecology of the family as a context for human development: Research perspectives. *Developmental Psychology, 22,* 723–742.

Bureau of the Census. (1992). *1990 census of population and housing: Summary social economic, and housing characteristics for California.* Washington, DC: U.S. Department of Commerce.

Cross, W. (1987). A two-factor theory of Black identity: Implications for the study of identity development in minority children. In J. Phinney and M. Rotheram (Eds.), *Children's ethnic socialization: Pluralism and development* (pp. 117–133). Newbury Park, CA: Sage.

Cross, W. (1991). *Shades of Black: Diversity in African-American identity.* Philadelphia: Temple University Press.

Davenport, D., & Yurich, J. (1991). Multicultural gender issues. *Journal of Counseling and Development, 70,* 64–71.

Demo, D., & Hughes, M. (1990). Socialization and racial identity among Black Americans. *Social Psychology Quarterly, 53,* 364–374.

Dornbusch, S., Ritter, P., & Steinberg, L. (1991). Community influences on the relation of family statuses to adolescent school performance: Differences between African Americans and non-Hispanic Whites. *American Journal of Education, 99,* 543–567.

Dovidio, J, & Gaertner, S. (1986). *Prejudice, discrimination, and racism.* Orlando, FL: Academic.

Ellis, G., & Petersen, L. (1992). Socialization values and parental control techniques: A cross-cultural analysis of child rearing. *Journal of Comparative Family Studies, 23,* 39–54.

Folkman, S. (1984). Personal control and stress and coping processes: A theoretical analysis. *Journal of Personality and Social Psychology, 46,* 839–952.

Gibbs, J., & Huang, L. (1989). *Children of color: Psychological interventions with minority youth.* San Francisco, CA: Jossey-Bass.

Graham, S. (1992). "Most of the subjects were White and middle class...": Trends in published research on African Americans in selected APA journals, 1970–1989. *American Psychologist, 47,* 629–639.

Hacker, A. (1992). *Two nations: Black and White, separate, hostile, unequal.* New York: Scribner's.

Harrison, A., Wilson, M., Pine, C., Chan, S., & Buriel, R. (1990). Family ecologies of ethnic minority children. *Child Development, 61,* 347–362.

Knight, G., Bernal, M., Garza, C., Cota, M., & Ocampo, K. (1993). Family socialization and the ethnic identity of Mexican-American children. *Journal of Cross-Cultural Psychology, 24,* 99–114.

Lin, C.-Y., & Fu, V. (1990). A comparison of child–rearing practices among Chinese, immigrant Chinese, and Caucasian-American parents. *Child Development, 61,* 429–433.

Marcia, J. (1980). Identity in adolescence. In J. Adelson (Ed.), *Handbook of adolescent psychology* (pp. 159–187). New York: Wiley.

Mena, F., Padilla, A., & Maldonado, M. (1987). Acculturative stress and specific coping strategies among immigrant and later generation college students. *Hispanic Journal of Behavioral Sciences, 9,* 207–225.

Mindel, C., Habenstein, P., & Wright, R., Jr. (1988). *Ethnic families in America: Patterns and variations.* New York: Elsevier.

Mont-Reynaud, R., Ritter, P., & Chen, Z. (1990, April). *Correlates of perceived discrimination among minority and majority youth in the Dornbusch-Steinberg data set.* Paper presented at the meeting of the Society for Research on Adolescence, Atlanta, GA.

Ogbu, J. (1985). A cultural ecology of competence among inner-city Blacks. In M. Spencer, G. Brookins, & W. Allen (Eds.), *Beginnings: The social and affective development of Black children* (pp. 45–66). Hillsdale, NJ: Lawrence Erlbaum Associates, Inc.

Parrillo, V. (1985). *Strangers to these shores.* New York: Wiley.

Phinney, J. (1989). Stages of ethnic identity development in minority group adolescents. *Journal of Early Adolescence, 9,* 34–49.

Phinney, J. (1990). Ethnic identity in adolescents and adults: Review of research. *Psychological Bulletin, 108,* 499–514.

Phinney, J. (1992). The Multigroup Ethnic Identity Measure: A new scale for use with diverse groups. *Journal of Adolescent Research, 7,* 156–176.

Phinney, J., & Rosenthal, D. (1992). Ethnic identity formation in adolescence: Process, context, and outcome. In G. Adams, T. Gulotta, & R. Montemayor (Eds.), *Adolescent identity formation* (pp.145–172). Newbury Park, CA: Sage.

Phinney, J., & Rotheram, M. (Eds.) (1987). *Children's ethnic socialization: Pluralism and development.* Newbury Park, CA: Sage.

Rosenberg, M. (1986). *Conceiving the self.* Melbourne, FL: Krieger.

Rosenthal, D., & Feldman, S. (1992). The relationship between parenting behavior and ethnic identity in Chinese-American and Chinese-Australian adolescents. *International Journal of Psychology, 27,* 19–31.

Roth, S., & Cohen L. (1986). Approach, avoidance and coping with stress. *American Psychologist, 41,* 813–819.

Seiffge-Krenke, I., & Shulman, S. (1990). Coping style in adolescence: A cross-cultural study. *Journal of Cross-Cultural Psychology, 21,* 351–377.

Sigelman, L., & Welch, S. (1991). *Black Americans' views of racial inequality: The dream deferred.* New York: Cambridge University Press.

Slater, C., & Hall, G. (1992). *1992 county and city extra: Annual metro, city and county data book.* Lanham, MD: Bernan.

Spencer, M. (1983). Children's cultural values and parental child rearing strategies. *Developmental Review, 3,* 351–370.

Spencer, M., & Dornbusch, S. (1990). Challenges in studying minority youth. In S. Feldman & G. Elliott (Eds.), *At the threshold: The developing adolescent* (pp. 123–146). Cambridge, MA: Harvard University Press.

Steinberg, L., Dornbusch, S., & Brown, B. (1992). Ethnic differences in adolescent achievement. *American Psychologist, 47,* 723–72.

Super, C., & Harkness, S. (1986). The developmental niche: A conceptualization at the interface of child and culture. *International Journal of Behavioral Development, 9,* 545–569.

Thornton, M., Chatters, L., Taylor, R., & Allen, W. (1990). Sociodemographic and environmental correlates of racial socialization by Black parents. *Child Development, 61,* 401–409.

Received December 2, 1992
Revision received May 10, 1993
Accepted October 13, 1993

JOURNAL OF RESEARCH ON ADOLESCENCE, 1(4), 323-348

Presidential Address:
Families, Lies, and Videotapes

E. Mavis Hetherington
University of Virginia

This article compares the results of two longitudinal studies on the effects of divorce and remarriage on children's adjustment, one involving preadolescent children and one involving early adolescent children. With younger children the adverse effects of divorce and life in a single parent household headed by a divorced custodial mother are more marked and enduring for sons than for daughters. In contrast, although both male and female preadolescent children initially are disrupted by and resistant to the entry of a stepfather, boys may eventually adapt to and benefit from a close relationship with the stepfather. Few gender differences are found in adolescents' responses to their parents divorce or remarriage. Early adolescence is an especially difficult time in which to have a remarriage occur. No improvement in stepfather–adolescent relationships or in adolescents' behavior problems occurs in stepfamilies over the first 26 months of remarriage.

Some of you who heard me give my presidential address for the Society for Research in Child Development (SRCD) in Baltimore 3 years ago may think that I am repeating the same talk (Hetherington, 1989). Both talks report the results of longitudinal studies of the effects of divorce and remarriage on family functioning and on children's adjustment. Both take a family systems perspective where it is assumed that reorganizations in the family resulting from divorce and remarriage are associated with alterations in the functioning of and relationships among all family subsystems. Both assume that the quality of family relationships will be one of the main contributors to children's adjustment. In addition, both talks consider that adaptation to family transitions depends on the

---

Requests for reprints should be sent to E. Mavis Hetherington, Department of Psychology, Gilmer Hall, University of Virginia, Charlottesville, VA 22903.

experiences that have preceded these changes. The response to divorce will be influenced by pre-divorce family relationships, and roles and relationships in the one-parent household will shape family members' subsequent responses to the addition of a stepparent. Finally, both talks address issues relating to gender differences in adjustment and changes in adjustment over time.

So why give this talk? The two talks describe two different longitudinal studies involving children in different age groups. The SRCD talk reported the results of a study that I began in collaboration with Martha and Roger Cox (Hetherington, Cox, & Cox, 1982). The children in that study which I will call Study I were an average of 4 years of age at the beginning of the study and 10 at the time of the last wave of data collection to be reported in this article. A subsequent wave of data collection when the children were 15 has been completed but not yet analyzed. The study I am going to describe, which I will call Study II involved early adolescents and was done in collaboration with Glenn Clingempeel and a team of wonderful undergraduate, graduate, and post-doctoral students. I draw freely on the results of these young collaborators' work in this article.

In this article I compare and contrast the findings in the two studies in order to illuminate some of the unique responses of early adolescents to their parents' marital transitions and the challenges family members confront in trying to establish a harmonious and fulfilling life in a remarried family. This article addresses four main questions. First, how does divorce and living in a one parent household headed by a divorced non-remarried custodial mother or living in a remarried family with a stepfather affect children's adjustment? Second, are there gender differences in children's responses to their parents' marital transitions? Third, what family factors influence the development and adjustment of children following divorce or remarriage? Fourth, how do children's adjustment and family relations change over time following parents' divorce or remarriage?

STUDY I

Let me briefly describe the two studies that involved very similar methods and similar subjects. Both studies involved White middle class families. Study I, included 144 families, half were divorced mother custody families and half non-divorced families who were seen four times in the 6-year course of the study at 2 months, 1 year, 2 years, and 6 six years after divorce. As might be expected, there were many shifts in marital status that occurred over the 6-year period with some of our original parents from intact families divorcing and over half of our custodial mothers remarrying. It was apparent that their parents' remarriage and the addition of a stepfather to the family had a profound effect on the adjustment of children in the divorced families. However, because we had no control over the timing of the remarriage, our analysis of the course of remarriage was less refined than we desired and most of our analyses involved a breakdown of children whose parents had been remarried more or less than 2 years at the final assessment 6 years beyond the time of their parents' initial divorce when the children were 10 years old. Although 122 of the original 144 families were available for the final wave, in order to facilitate cross sectional analyses at age 10, the sample at age 10 was expanded to 180 children equally divided among non-divorced, divorced mother custody, and remarried stepfather families.

STUDY II

Study II was designed to answer issues raised in the early study and to see whether the findings with younger children would be replicated on a sample of early adolescents and their families. Early adolescent children were selected for this study, because it has been found that early adolescence girls in mother custody one parent households who previously appeared well adjusted, may begin to show increasing non-compliant acting out behavior, precocious sexuality, and conflict with their mothers at this time (Hetherington, 1972, 1989; Newcomer & Udry, 1987; Rogers, 1983; Udry, Talbert, & Morris, 1986). Furthermore, it has been suggested that this may be a time when children have the most difficulty in adjusting to their parents' remarriage and benefit least from the entry of a stepparent (Brand, Clingempeel, & Bowen-Woodward, 1988; Hetherington & Anderson, 1987).

Study II examined the family relationships and adjustment of family members in stepfather families, non-divorced families, and in families with a divorced non-remarried custodial mother. There were 202 families at the beginning of the study and 164 at the end. Stepfamilies were assessed at 4 months, 17 months, and 26 months following remarriage. Families in the other two groups were assessed at equivalent times. The target child in this study was an average of 11.5 years old at the beginning of the study, and an average of 13.5 years old at the conclusion of the study. Divorced non-remarried mothers and remarried mothers in the stepfather families had been separated and divorced for approximately equivalent periods of time; they were approximately 5.5 years post separation and 3.5 years post divorce. It should be noted then

205

that these divorced mothers in the one parent households were well past the initial 2-year crisis transitional period of divorce and were in restabilized single parent households. Furthermore, in comparison to Study I, this study involved older parents and older children who were entering adolescence, and permitted a more controlled examination of adjustment to remarriage over the course of the first 26 months of remarriage.

METHODS

In both Study I and Study II each assessment wave involved a large set of interview, observational, and standardized test measures. Measures were selected and constructed so that similar information was assessed with different methods and by multiple respondents usually by mother, father, and child, and additionally by teachers when assessing the child's competence and behavior problems. Younger children in Study I were observed in structured tasks and in free play with parents as well as in unstructured interactions extending from predinner to bedtime. In Study II families were videotaped at dinner and during family problem-solving sessions in dyadic and triadic combinations of family members. These interactions were coded on twenty 5-point rating scales describing the quality of the husband and wife relationship, the behavior of each parent to the target child and of the target child to each parent and the behavior of the target child interacting with the sibling who was closest in age. In addition, in Study I sequential coding of all family interactions were done and in Study II sequential coding of conflict was done on a subset of interactions. Although analyses on separate measures were performed and we were interested in different family member's perceptions of family relations and the children's adjustment, we also composited across tests and reports and observational measures of the marital, parent/child, and sibling relationships and of the child's adjustment. Composite scores were calculated by converting all scales to z–scores, summing across scales and dividing by the number of available scales for that dimension. Scores were averaged rather than summed since no residential spouse reports were available for single mother households. Composite measures were derived of parental warmth/involvement, conflict/coercion, control and monitoring, children's positivity or negativity with parents and siblings and spouses' positivity and negativity in the marital relationship. The molar measures of child adjustment of interest were externalizing, internalizing and social and cognitive competence. Composite measures of children's externalizing and competence were derived, however we could not obtain a composite internalizing measure with a satisfactory Cronbach alpha. Evidently, anxious, depressed, withdrawn behaviors are perceived differently by parents, teachers, children, and observational coders. In addition to these measures when possible, information was gathered from the non-residential fathers, grandparents, and step grandparents to assess frequency and quality of contact between the child and relations outside of the home. Finally, measures of stresses and supports available to parents and children were assessed.

Cautionary Comments

Because of time constraints, this presentation focuses mainly on family relations within the home and on children's adjustment. Let me underscore a few points to keep in mind when considering the results of these studies. First, these studies involved White middle class families. The single parent households had a divorced custodial mother, and the stepfamilies had a divorced custodial mother and a stepfather. The results may not be generalizable to other ethnic or socioeconomic groups or to families having other custodial arrangements or differing stepfamily structures. Second, although both studies involved a group of stepfather families and a group of families with divorced custodial mothers, Study I involved younger children who were preschoolers at the start of the study and who were aged 10 at the time the data to be reported in this article were collected. Thus children were 1.5 years younger at wave four in Study I than the average age of children in the first wave of Study II. The children in all family groups in Study II were going through the transition to early adolescence and its concomitant social, emotional and cognitive changes. However, in addition, children in the stepfamilies were coping with alterations in family roles and relationships associated with the entry of a stepfather and adaptation in the early years of remarriage. In those remarried families the normative developmental changes associated with the transition to early adolescence are compounded by disruptions associated with the non-normative transition of remarriage.

In this article I describe the results found in Study I with younger children and compare them with the results found in Study II with early adolescent children.

I am first going to discuss the adjustment of children in non-divorced families, in one parent households with a divorced custodial mother, and in families with a divorced remarried custodial mother and stepfather. Then I turn to an examination of differences in family functioning and relationships that may contribute to the adjustment of children in our different family groups.

207

The Adjustment of Children

On the basis of past research, it was expected that children would show an increase in behavior problems associated with their parents' marital transitions and that these problems would decline overtime as the reorganized families stabilized and new roles and relationships were established. Furthermore, it was predicted that boys in one parent mother custody households would show more intense and enduring problems than would girls, but that as girls in divorced families moved further into adolescence disruptions in mother child relations and increases in behavior problems, especially in antisocial behavior and in precocious sexual activity would occur. It also was anticipated that if a stepfather was reasonably competent and involved, both the mother and children but especially stepsons, would benefit from his support. Although an increase in children's problems might occur in the early stages of remarriage, these were expected to decrease over the course of the first few years of the remarriage as the remarriage attained a new equilibrium.

Because there is little available research on patterns of gender differences in adolescents responses to their parents remarriage we had less well-defined expectations about the gender differences that would be found.

Werner (1987) proposed that the first 10 years of life may be the most stressful for boys and the second for girls. She suggests that the normative challenges in the first 10 years of life such as those associated with self control, restrained activity, and focused and sustained attention in the academic situation are more difficult for boys whereas those in the second decade associated with sexuality and the balancing of achievement, career, and family aspirations and feminine social role demands are more difficult for girls. If so girls might be especially distressed by a remarriage occurring in early adolescence when they are facing a broad array of other normative life stresses.

A second way in which gender differences may be manifested is in boys' and girls' dominant coping styles. It has been suggested that boys are more likely to respond to stress with externalizing behavior and girls with internalizing behavior and that these gender differences in the style of responding to stress are more likely to emerge as children grow older (Emery, 1982). Thus higher rates of internalizing in the response of girls to their parents remarriage in adolescence may occur.

The adjustment of younger children in Study I. With the younger children in Study I our hypotheses were generally confirmed. In the first year following divorce, children from divorced families showed increases in externalizing in the form of aggressive, impulsive, destructive, non-compliant behaviors; in internalizing in the form of anxious, whining, dependent, withdrawn behaviors; and declining social competence in the home and in the school. These effects were most marked for externalizing in both boys and girls. Both boys and girls adjustment markedly improved after the first year following divorce and remarriage. By 2 years after divorce, girls with divorced non-remarried custodial mothers were showing no more problems than girls in non-divorced families. Boys' behavior after the first year also improved, however, even 6 years after divorce when the boys were 10, they were still showing more externalizing and internalizing behavior problems than boys in non-divorced families. Furthermore, problems in academic achievement were beginning to emerge in these boys in divorced families. The girls continued to function well at age 10 except for a subset of very early maturing girls who were associating with older peers. These girls were exhibiting more antisocial non-compliant behavior problems and conflict with their mothers than were either the later maturing girls in one parent households or the girls in the non-divorced families. Teachers, peers, and the girls themselves reported these girls as being involved in more anti-social activities. Divorced mothers, however, did not seem to know what was going on.

Following remarriage, boys and girls were initially resistant to their mother and stepfather and showed disrupted behavior, especially in externalizing, but both adapted over time to their new life in a stepfamily. However, in contrast to divorce, the adverse effects of remarriage were more marked and sustained for girls than for boys. Two years after the remarriage boys in stepfamilies were showing no more problems than boys in non-divorced families and many fewer problems, especially in externalizing than boys whose divorced mothers had not remarried. Although girls also were adapting to the remarriage, even 2 years after it they were showing more externalizing than were girls either with non-divorced parents or with a divorced non-remarried mother.

Some support was found for Werner's (1987) proposition that boys experience more stress than do girls in the first 10 years of life. We found that boys were more likely to be exposed to and involved in family conflicts, less likely to be protected from adversity or provided with support during times of duress, and less likely to seek or utilize available support. Furthermore, the noxious behavior of tempermentally difficult boys under stress was especially likely to elicit aversive behavior from parents. Mothers, especially divorced and remarried mothers, reported more parenting stress with sons than with daughters. Thus, boys appeared to be not only the most stressed but also the most stressful to

209

those around them in the first 10 years of life. There was no support for Emery's (1982) suggestion that if adverse responses to parents' marital transitions occurred they were most likely to be found for boys in externalizing and girls in internalizing. In this study when problems occurred in response to divorce and remarriage they were most likely to be manifested in externalizing and boys rather than girls were more likely to show higher internalizing than their counterparts in non-divorced families.

The adjustment of early adolescent children in Study II. There were two striking differences between the findings related to the adjustment of children in Study I with younger children and those in Study II with early adolescents. First, and perhaps most surprisingly, in contrast to the findings in the early study where boys were especially likely to eventually benefit from the presence of a stepfather, the anticipated improvement over time in the adjustment of early adolescent children in stepfamilies, even in boys, as they tried to cope with their new family situation did not occur. Sometimes there was an increase in behavior problems at time two and some recovery from time two to three, however there were no significant improvements in our stepchildren's adjustment from Wave 1 to Wave 3. It may be that early adolescents take longer to adjust than do younger children, and that 26 months following remarriage is not a sufficient time for adaptation to occur. Or it may be, as proposed, that early adolescence is an especially inauspicious time to have a remarriage occur and that these adolescents may never accept or benefit from their new family situation and a relationship with a stepfather.

The second difference between the results of the two studies was that in Study II with young adolescents we obtained many significant main effects for families and many for gender but many fewer family type by gender interactions than we had with younger children. In general girls were seen as more competent and as having fewer behavior problems than boys. When significant family differences in adjustment among these early adolescents were obtained they were almost invariably in the direction of children in the non-divorced group being perceived as more competent and showing fewer problems in adjustment than those in either the remarried or divorced mother headed household. More frequent differences were found between children in step families and non-divorced families, than divorced and non-divorced families. These differences were found in measures of social competence, externalizing and internalizing. The ordering of means was usually with non-divorced and remarried at the two extremes and divorced single parent families in the middle.

Indices constructed by compositing across methods and informants indicated that not only were children in divorced and remarried families less socially competent than those in non-divorced families they also are exhibiting more non-compliant disruptive, aggressive acting out behavior. Girls and boys with divorced non-remarried mothers look increasingly similar as they move into adolescence with the exception that these boys have more academic problems.

We were unable to construct a composite with adequate internal consistency for internalizing, however mothers and fathers reports on the Child Behavior Checklist (Achenbach & Edelbrock, 1983), that is the most frequently used measure of childhood psychopathology, yielded main effects for family type and for gender with boys showing more internalizing than girls and with children in remarried families and divorced families exhibiting more internalizing than children in non-divorced families. There were high and sustained levels of internalizing for boys in remarried families. Again there was no support for the proposal that girls are more likely than boys to respond to their parents marital transitions with internalizing.

Another way to examine the apparently high incidence of deviant behavior in children whose parents have gone through marital transitions is to look at the percent of children in the different family groups who score in extreme groups above the clinical cut off's on standardized tests. On total behavior problems on the Child Behavior Checklist (Achenbach & Edelbrock, 1983) mothers in remarried families reported almost one third of their children and stepfathers reported over 40% of their stepchildren to be exhibiting serious levels of psychopathology in contrast to 10% of children in our non-divorced group. Ten percent is in accord with normative data on the percent of children expected to score above the clinical cutoff. According to maternal reports the percent of children with divorced non-remarried mothers fell between the two with about 25% above the clinical cutoff. Furthermore as was predicted differences between girls in divorced and non-divorced families increased as they moved further into adolescence.

An interesting example of the increase in behavior problems in the girls in the families with non-remarried custodial mothers is found in the self reports of children on a predelinquent subscale scale of the 24-hr behavior checklist where parents and children were asked to report which behavior on a list had occurred in the past 24 hr. The predelinquent subscale involves such things as sexual activities, drinking, drug use, and so on. Girls in the one parent households reported that they were involved in more of these activities than did girls in the non-divorced families. Furthermore, their mother did not know about it, a reflection either of deception on the part of the adolescent daughter or of the less effective monitoring of their children's activities by divorced mothers which are discussed later.

There were some discrepancies among reports of children's behavior problems. Girls tended to report themselves as being involved in more antisocial behavior than other informers saw them being involved in. Mothers and stepfathers reported children in remarried families as showing the most problem behaviors, whereas teachers reported the children with divorced, non-remarried mothers as the most problematic. The aversive antisocial behavior of children in the first 2 years of remarriage may be more intense but confined to disruption in family relationships, whereas the antisocial behavior in the families with a divorced non-remarried mother may be generalized across situations and found in family, school, and peer relations.

Let me briefly summarize the findings on the adjustment of children. First, children in divorced and remarried families were likely to show multiple behavior problems and have fewer psychological resources or competencies on which to draw in times of stress than did children in non-divorced families. Second, there was no indication that internalizing was more likely to occur in girls than in boys in response to their parents' marital transitions. Third, although younger children gradually adjusted to their parents remarriage early adolescents in newly remarried families did not show fewer problems over the course of the first 26 months of remarriage, and there was some indication that girls in one parent households were developing more problems and becoming more similar to boys in these families as they advanced further into adolescence. Finally gender differences in response to divorce and remarriage were more often found in preadolescent than in early adolescent children.

Parent–Child Relations

Perhaps some understanding of the high rates of problem behaviors in children in divorced, mother headed families, and remarried families can be gleaned by examining their family relationships. The results of Study I are presented and the experiences of the younger children and their relationships in the single parent household are used to clarify why the later transition of parental remarriage in early adolescence may be an especially difficult one. In part, this is related to the shifts in roles and relationships from a one parent mother headed household to a remarried family with a stepfather. In part, it is related to the conjunction of these shifts and the normative challenges of early adolescence.

Divorced mothers and children Study I.   In Study I where we had been able to carefully explore short- and long-term effects of divorce, it was apparent that in the immediate aftermath of divorce an anxious, stressed, preoccupied custodial mother and a confused, demanding, angry, apprehensive child were often unable to offer each other mutual solace and frequently exacerbated each others problems. In Study I, in the first year following divorce, mothers made fewer maturity demands of their children, communicated less well, were less affectionate and more punitive with children, and showed marked inconsistency in discipline and lack of control with their children in comparison to mothers in non-divorced families. These effects were most marked when divorced mothers were interacting with sons. Divorced mothers and sons frequently became involved in escalating, angry, coercive exchanges. Divorced mothers became increasingly competent in their parenting in the second year following divorce. However, even 6 years after divorce, the relationship between divorced mothers and sons continued to be ambivalent and conflicted. Divorced mothers continued to nag, natter, and complain to their 10-year-old sons with little follow through and enforcement of their demands.

Although divorced mothers thought they were controlling and monitoring their 10-year-old children's behavior well, neither children nor observers concurred with this view. Divorced mothers knew less about where their children were, who they were with, and what they were doing than did mothers in two parent households. On their 24 hr behavior checklists, 10-year-old boys in divorced families reported being involved in more antisocial behavior that the mother did not know about than did children in any other group, although this discrepancy was also high in the mother daughter reports in the stepfamily groups. In addition, 10-year-old children in the one parent households were less likely than those in the two parent households to have adult supervision in their parent's absence. Both Weiss (1979) and Wallerstein and Kelly (1980) reported that one way that children may cope with their parents' divorce is by becoming disengaged from the family. In Study I, by age 10, 6 years after the divorce, boys from divorced families were spending significantly less time in the home with their parents or other adults and more time alone or with peers than were any of the other groups of children. In contrast to divorced mothers and sons, even by 2 years following divorce, there were few differences in the relationship between divorced mothers and preadolescent daughters and that of mothers and daughters in non-divorced families.

In Study I, by the time the children were 10, both sons and daughters in divorced families were allowed more responsibility, independence, and power in decision making than were children in non-divorced families. Sequence analysis of videotaped family interactions showed they successfully interrupted their divorced mother and their mother yielded to their demands more often than in the other family types. In some cases, this greater power and independence resulted in an egalitarian mutually supportive relationship. In other cases, where the emotional demands or responsibilities required by the mother were age inappropriate, were beyond the capabilities of the child, or interfered with normal activities of the child (e.g., in peer relations or school activities), resentment, rebellion, or behavior problems followed. Thus, children in divorced mother custody households had more power and were assigned more responsibilities. They did, in the words of Weiss (1979) "grow up faster" (p. 107).

In Study I, divorced mothers and 10-year-old daughters in stabilized mother-headed households expressed considerable satisfaction with their congenial relationship. However, there was an exception to this happy picture. Measures of pubescent status had been obtained from the parents, interviewer, and children at age 10. As might be expected, few children had entered puberty by this time since they were only 10 years old, however, 26 of our 90 girls were early maturers and were beginning to show some signs of puberty. Family conflict was higher in all three family types for these early-maturing girls versus late-maturing girls, however, it was most marked between mothers and daughters in the single parent households. Early maturity in girls was associated with a premature weakening of the mother–child bonds. These early maturing girls, especially in the mother-headed families, were alienated and disengaged from their families, talked less to their mothers but interrupted them more and became involved in activities with older peers. Past research suggests that divorced mothers and daughters may experience problems as daughters become pubescent and that these girls become sexually active earlier than girls in non-divorced families (Hetherington, 1972; Newcomer & Udry, 1987). The pattern of interaction between early maturing girls at age 10 and their divorced mothers was an indication of what occurred in Study II when older girls from divorced families moved further into adolescence.

Divorced mothers and children Study II. Relationships between divorced mothers and early adolescent sons in Study II were remarkably similar to those found in Study I. Relationships between divorced mothers and daughters however were reminiscent of those found with the early maturing girls in Study I. Furthermore, the levels of conflict and punitive discipline by divorced mothers have become increasingly similar toward adolescent sons and to daughters. The relationship between divorced mothers and their adolescent children is an intensely emotional and ambivalent one. Both mothers and adolescents reported that the divorced mothers were more involved and spent more time doing things with them than was reported for mothers and children in either non-divorced or remarried families. However we now also found high levels of punitive discipline by the divorced mothers and of increasingly coercive, acrimonious, conflictual exchanges between both boys and girls and their divorced non-remarried mothers. This conflict increased over time and became much higher than that found in either non-divorced or remarried families. Remarried mothers' conflict with daughters decreased over the 26 months of the study. Since I began working on divorce and one parent families 30 years ago, I have consistently been impressed by the highly charged affective quality in parent child relations in families with an unremarried, divorced custodial mother. The sense of intimacy, affection, camaraderie, concern, involvement even enmeshment accompanied by anger and conflict was notable in these families with adolescent children.

Over the course of these early adolescent years, divorced mothers were becoming more active in attempting to control and monitor their children's behavior, especially their daughter's behavior. However, the attempt seemed to be initiated too late and seemed to have been initiated in response to the daughters anti-social behavior that was already on going. It is reactive rather than proactive and preventive. Children and observers now saw divorced mothers as involved but as ineffectual in monitoring and control.

Parent–child relations in remarried families.   It is against the background of the divorced mother's relationship with her preadolescent children in the single parent household that the transition to remarriage and the addition of a stepfather must be considered, the background of the closeness of divorced mothers and daughters, conflict and coercion between divorced mothers and sons, and independence and power for both boys and girls. Preadolescent sons who are involved in coercive cycles with their divorced mothers in the long run may have little to lose and something to gain from the addition of a warm involved adult male. The stepfather may serve as an emotional support, companion and male role model as well as a means of deflecting the negativity of divorced mothers that seems focused on preadolescent sons. Preadolescent girls on the other hand have an unusually close relationship with their mothers and may experience the stepfather as an intruder or competitor for their mother's affection. In addition, with these precociously autonomous children, efforts at control by the stepfather may be problematic especially in adolescence.

Two of the major tasks confronting early adolescents that may make remarriage at this time especially difficult, are the development of independence while maintaining appropriate levels of attachment to family members and coping with sexual changes, feelings, and fantasies. Children who have attained early independence in single parent households may be particularly sensitive to infringements on their autonomy by step parents at this time. Furthermore, early adolescents who are increasingly preoccupied with sexuality may find the presence of an adult to whom they are not biologically related distressing. Even with biologically related parents and children, there is an alteration or decrease in intimacy and physical affection as children move into the pubertal apex. Fathers with pubescent girls reflect this in less touching, kissing, direct gaze, and more averted body orientation. Hill (1988) reported that sometimes with fathers and daughters it also may be reflected in a teasing flirtatiousness. Steinberg (1990) and Hill (1988) also suggested that with boys and mothers it is more likely to be found in conflict as boys move into the pubertal apex. Both the teasing, flirtatiousness, and the conflict may be distancing mechanisms that avoid direct or threatening expressions of affection. Children, especially early adolescents, do not like to think of their parents as being sexually active and the recognition of this may be difficult to avoid when confronting their mothers' new remarriage. In the areas of intimacy, sexuality, and appropriateness of displays of affection between family members, the early adolescent may be troubled by the introduction of a stepfather and disruptions in family relations may be more marked and sustained at this time than they are with younger children.

Remarried mothers and children. In both Study I and Study II remarried mothers were as warm to their children as were mothers in other types of families. In both studies it was in low maternal control and monitoring that differences were found from mothers in non-divorced families. With the younger children maternal control and monitoring increased and conflict decreased over time as the family adjusted to the remarriage. In contrast, with the early adolescent children, maternal monitoring and control by remarried mothers in Waves 2 and 3 stabilized at levels significantly lower than that found in either divorced, non-remarried or non-divorced mothers. With the early adolescent children, no improvement in maternal parenting over time occurred with the exception of a decrease in conflict over time from an initially very high level of conflict between daughters and their remarried mothers. Although active altercations between remarried mothers and daughters decreased observers rated both sons and daughters as communicating less, being less warm and more coercive in interactions with their remarried mothers than were children in non-divorced families. This suggests that the intimacy in the one parent household that preceded remarriage has been replaced with detachment by early adolescents. In general younger girls dealt with their parents remarriage with more directly antagonistic, disruptive behavior whereas the adolescent girls were increasingly non-communicative, sullen, and avoidant.

Stepfathers and stepchildren. Differences between biological fathers' and stepfathers' relations with children were even more marked than for mothers in non-divorced and remarried families. Furthermore, the pattern of differences were similar in the two studies with the younger and older children.

In both studies, stepfathers in contrast to biological fathers were more likely to be emotionally disengaged and less likely to have an authoritative parenting style involving warm, responsive but firm discipline, and high control and monitoring.

In the first 2 years following remarriage, in both studies stepfathers reported themselves to be low on felt or expressed affection for their stepchildren although they spent time with them attempting to establish a relationship. They both expressed less strong positive affect and in Study I showed fewer negative, critical responses than did the non-divorced fathers. In the early stage of remarriage they were like polite strangers, self-disclosing, asking questions, sometimes trying to relate the child's experience to their own, often valiantly attempting to establish a relationship or at least a truce in the face of aversive behavior by their stepchildren. Biological fathers were freer both in expressing affection and in criticizing their children for poor personal grooming, for not doing their homework, not cleaning up their rooms or for fighting with their siblings. However, they also reported more rapport and closeness to their children. Initially, stepfathers were far less supportive to stepsons than to stepdaughters, however, with the younger but not the early adolescent children this reversed in longer established remarriages. In the early stage of the remarriage stepfathers remained relatively pleasant in spite of the aversive behavior they encountered from their stepdaughters. However with adolescent children this honeymoon period rapidly passes and by 2 years after remarriage they were more impatient. Although they tried to remain disengaged they got into extremely angry and prolonged interchanges with their stepdaughters. This contrasted markedly with the harmonious and warm relationship found between non-divorced fathers and their daughters. These conflicts tended to focus on issues of parental authority and respect for the mother. Stepdaughters viewed their stepfathers as hostile, punitive and unreasonable on matters of discipline. Stepfathers made significantly fewer monitoring or control attempts and were less successful in gaining control with both sons and daughters than were non-divorced fathers.

With younger but not older children, stepfathers' control of stepsons but not stepdaughters was better in longer remarriages. With the younger children in Study I although authoritative parenting by stepfathers increased over time with boys, authoritative behavior by stepfathers with daughters decreased and disengagement doubled as the remarriage went on. In addition, even with the younger boys in Study I after 2 years of remarriage, disengagement remained the predominant parenting style of stepfathers. In Study II, stepfathers with adolescent stepchildren remained disengaged over the 26 months after remarriage, their participation across multiple dimensions of parenting stabilized at levels far below that of either their wives or non-divorced fathers on rapport, warmth, control, and monitoring. In contrast to the findings in Study I, stepfathers did not grow increasingly more disengaged with girls than boys.

Effects of Parent–Child Relationship on Children's Adjustment

Steinberg et al. (1991) recently completed a meta analysis of the effects on children's adjustment of authoritative parenting. They concluded that across social class, race, and family structure, authoritative parenting consistently leads to more salutary outcomes for children. Does this hold true in our families with stepfathers? In contrast to the effects of parenting styles on children's behavior in non-divorced families, where authoritative parenting by both mothers and fathers is associated with positive child outcome, with the younger children in Study I, both authoritative parenting involving warm, responsive control, and authoritarian parenting involving hostile, rigid control in stepfathers were related to high rates of behavior problems and to hostile, angry, resistant behavior in both stepdaughters and in stepsons in the initial stage of remarriage. After 2 years, authoritative parenting by stepfathers was related to fewer behavior problems and greater acceptance of the stepfather by stepsons but was not at this time significantly related to stepdaughters' behavior. In Study I, the best long-term strategy for the stepfather in gaining acceptance by the younger stepchildren seemed to be one where there was no initial attempt to take over and try to actively control the child's behavior through either authoritarian or authoritative techniques. Instead, the stepfather who was ultimately successful first worked at establishing a relationship with the child and supported the mother in her parenting and only later became a more active authoritative parent. This pattern was associated both with acceptance of the stepfather by stepchildren and with positive adjustment in boys.

This contrasts with the findings in Study II that suggest that with early adolescents immediate authoritativeness in parenting by stepfathers is desirable. Children entering adolescence eventually showed increased competence and lower levels of behavior problems when there was early awareness, warmth, involvement, concern, and monitoring of their activities and low negativity in stepfathers. The results of both studies found that it was those stepfathers who were very disengaged and remained so who were associated with the poorest outcomes for children. Surprisingly, direct attempts to control adolescents' behavior were not associated with adolescent adjustment although they had been with the adjustment of younger children. Adolscent adjustment was more closely associated with the affective quality of the parent–child relationship and to monitoring than with rules, regulations, and discipline attempts. If a close relationship between parent and child and internalized norms of behavior and self control have not been established in the child by adolescence, it is difficult for a parent to shape the child's behavior by initiating control attempts in adolescence.

Furthermore, both cross-lagged panel analyses and a structural equation modeling analysis based on the Social Relations Model of Kenny and LaVoie (1984) indicated that in younger children and in non-divorced families, although there was reciprocity in negative exchanges between parents and children, rejection, punitiveness, and negativity in parents was more powerful in shaping children's negative behaviors than the reverse. The effects of aversive behavior in children in eliciting anger and coercion from parents was more powerful in older children and in stepfamilies especially with the stepfather. In Study II negative behavior in mothers and especially in stepfathers in remarried families appeared to result largely from adolescents provoking the conflicted, coercive hostile behavior in parents.

In the face of their stepchildren's aversive behavior many well intended stepfathers were unable to initiate or sustain authoritative parenting or even to establish a close relationship with their stepchildren. The establishing of a close mutually valued relationship between the stepfather and stepchildren was especially difficult and often unsuccessful with adolescents. Not only was the stepfather's rapport and closeness to stepchildren significantly lower than that of non-divorced fathers and children, but also stepchildren's closeness to stepfathers was lower than that of children with non-divorced biological fathers, and the closeness between stepfathers and adolescent stepchildren did not increase over time as they became better acquainted. Even after 26 months many stepfathers and stepchildren did not mention each other when asked to identify members of their family. This is unfortunate because, even with adolescents, closeness to fathers in non-divorced families and in stepfamilies in Wave 3 after children have had an opportunity to establish a relationship with the stepfather was associated with greater social and scholastic competence in boys. Boys who enjoyed being with their stepfathers or fathers, who wanted to be similar to them, and valued their opinions and advice, benefitted from the relationship.

Let me summarize the findings on parent–child relations thus far. With the younger children following an initial period of disrupted parenting in the first year following divorce, divorced mothers became less inept in dealing with their children although they were ineffective in monitoring and controlling their children's behavior. Divorced mothers and daughters formed close harmonious relationships whereas boys and their mothers were involved in escalating coercive interchanges. As daughters moved into adolescence divorced mother daughter–relations became more similar to those with sons with an increase in conflict. Divorced mothers also were making frantic but ineffectual attempts to monitor and control their early adolescent daughters deviant behavior.

In remarried families, monitoring and control by both mothers and stepfathers was low. With younger children after an initial period of low maternal warmth and mother–child conflict parent–child relations improved. There was no improvement in the relations of remarried mothers and early adolescent children over the 26-month period following remarriage with the exception of a decline in mother–daughter conflict and this seemed to be associated with disengagement on the part of daughters. In both studies, disengagement was the predominant parenting style of stepfathers and stepfathers stabilized at much lower levels of warmth, control, and monitoring, and higher levels of conflict than did fathers in non-divorced families. With stepfathers of younger sons, there was an increase in authoritative parenting over time and sons eventually were able to benefit from a close relationship with the stepfathers. Stepfathers and stepdaughters became increasingly acrimonious over time. There was no improvement in stepfathers' relations with their adolescent stepchildren over time. In remarried families the acrimony between parents especially stepfathers and adolescent children was largely provoked by hostility, resistance, and coerciveness in children. This negativity in children interfered both with the development of authoritative parenting by stepfathers and with the formation of a close stepfather–stepchild relationship.

Closeness to the Stepfather

We are going to turn now to a discussion of two factors that may influence the child's ability to get close to the stepfather and to benefit from the remarriage, the first is the attributes of the child, the second the quality of the marital relationship.

Characteristics of the child and acceptance of the stepfather. Scholars such as Rutter (Rutter, 1987) and Block and his colleagues (Block, Block, & Gerde, 1986) suggested that children who have difficult temperaments or who have behavior problems may be most vulnerable to the effects of stressful life events and have the most difficulty in adjusting to new experiences. In part, this is because difficult children are more likely to be the elicitors and targets of their parents negativity under stress and are less able to cope with stressful or aversive behavior when it hits. In contrast, there may be an enhancement or steeling effect where easy or well adjusted children may actually increase their coping skills and benefit from encountering moderate levels of stress under supportive conditions. Thus under stress, the psychologically poor get poorer, and the psychologically rich may get richer.

We were interested in how the characteristics of the child might influence his or her acceptance of the stepfather and the child's subsequent adjustment. In Study I we had assessments both of infant and current temperament which we did not have in Study II. Sons who had easy temperaments, who were high in self-esteem, assertiveness, and social competence before the remarriage, that is the well-adjusted feisty boys were more likely to initially resist the remarriage. At first these boys were more acrimonious and negative toward stepfathers but as the remarriage progressed, this relationship reversed itself so that the competent well-adjusted boys were more likely in the long run to accept and benefit from the presence of a stepfather. The temperamentally easy, well-adjusted boy may be less fearful and more capable than the temperamentally difficult boy in his initial interactional assaults on the stepfather, but eventually is more adaptive and able to accept and benefit from a new relationship with an adult male. In contrast there was no effect for temperament and competence in the response of stepdaughters to stepfathers either initially or even after the marriage had lasted for 2 years. When the stepfather first entered the family both easy and difficult girls behaved in an agonistic, resistant fashion. Younger girls may perceive the father as a greater threat to their close relationship with their mothers and the trauma of their mothers remarriage may be greater for preadolescent girls than for boys and may suppress any possible effects of temperament and personality.

We did not have measures of the children's adjustment prior to the remarriage available in Study II, however we did do an analysis of how externalizing and competence of the child at Wave 1 related to initial negativity and positivity toward the stepfather and acceptance of the stepfather at Wave 1 and to long-term acceptance at Wave 3. For both adolescent boys and girls, externalizing and competence at Wave 1 were associated with both the concurrent and the future relationships with the stepfather at Wave 3. Acting out, socially incompetent adolescents were initially most resistant and less warm to the stepfather and in the long run continued to be unable to establish or benefit from a close congenial relationship with the stepfather.

The marital relationship and parent–child relations.   I now turn to an examination of the second factor that may affect children's responses to their mothers remarriage. Papernow (1984) commented that the typical starting point for the remarried couple would be considered pathological in a first marriage "a weak couple subsystem, a tightly bonded parent–child alliance and potential interference in family functioning from an outsider" (p. 360). In spite of the challenges confronting remarried couples in both studies we found that the marital relation in first marriages and remarriages had more similarities than differences. In the early honeymoon stages of remarriage the remarried couple reported more marital satisfaction than did the longer married couples in first marriages and over time the marital satisfaction in the two types of marriages began to converge. Although satisfaction in the two types of marriages were increasingly similar, there were some differences in the association between the marital relationship and parent–child relationship and these differed for the younger children and adolescents.

It has been suggested that a close marital relationship is a strong cornerstone for the family, that it serves to facilitate more positive parenting behavior and promotes the psychological well being of parents and children. In the first study of young children different correlations between closeness and satisfaction in marital relations and children's responses were found in non-divorced and remarried families. As has been found in many other studies in non-divorced families a close marital relationship, was related to parental warmth and involvement and low parent–child conflict with both boys and girls, but the relations were larger and more consistent for boys. However, in the stepfamilies there occurred what might appear to be an anomalous finding. In remarried families in contrast to non-divorced families a close marital relationship was associated with high levels of parent–child conflict with both mother and stepfathers, and lack of acceptance of the stepfather especially when the stepchild was a girl. For sons, this relationship was significant in the early but not later stages of remarriage. The closer and more satisfying was the marital relationship the greater the children initially perceived the threat of the remarriage to be. Again, we find that young boys but not girls seem to be more able to adapt to the remarriage over time. In Study I evidence for the greater threat to the close mother–daughter relationship and resentment of the remarriage by daughters is found in the very high correlation between closeness to the mother before the remarriage and subsequent conflict of daughters with the mother ($r = .65$, $p < .001$) and with the stepdaughter's negative sulky, hostile behavior and lack of acceptance of the stepfather ($r = .71$, $p < .001$). The closer the pre-divorce mother–daughter relationship was the greater the perceived threat and resistance by daughters to a close marital relationship. It is notable that the positive behavior of the stepfather toward younger stepdaughters did not correlate with her acceptance of the stepfather in the early stages of remarriage. No matter how hard the stepfather tried the stepdaughter rejected him.

In Study I, in the longer remarried families a close marital relationship was associated with acceptance of the stepfather and with lower externalizing for boys but an increase in acting out behavior and in depression in stepdaughters.

In Study II with adolescents, a different pattern of associations between the marital relationship and parent–child relationship emerged. In non-divorced families again, the quality of the marital relationship played a central role in family relations and the adjustment of boys. A marital relationship characterized by mutual warmth and support and low negativity was consistently associated with less conflictual relations between both mothers and fathers and their adolescent sons and with fewer behavior problems and greater competence in boys. This strong pattern however, was not obtained for girls with non-divorced parents. The parents' behavior toward daughters was not influenced by the quality of the marital relationship and only scattered associations between the marital relation and daughters behavior toward parents or the daughters adjustment were found for girls.

A reverse pattern was found in the remarried families in that the quality of the marital relationship played a more central role in family relations with stepdaughters than stepsons. Low conflict and high positivity in the marital relationship were related to the quality of parenting of daughters by both mothers and fathers, to the daughters' response to the parents and to the daughters' adjustment. Furthermore, this relation was the reverse of that found with the younger stepdaughters in Study I. A close marital relationship was associated with less negativity in parent child relations and with positive adjustment in adolescent daughters.

In these remarried families in Study II the marital relationship showed no consistent association with parent child relations or the adjustment of adolescent stepsons. However, in Wave 2 when boys were beginning to move into puberty a close marital relationship was associated with more aversive and less positive behavior toward mothers and stepfathers by sons. This negative relationship was not found in Wave 1 or Wave 3.

Let me attempt to summarize these findings. In non-divorced families, the quality of the marital relationship was more closely related to the parent–child relationship and children's adjustment in boys than girls and this pattern of gender differences was more marked with adolescent than younger children. In non-divorced families with boys, the marital relationship did indeed serve as the cornerstone for positive parent–child relations and child adjustment. In remarried families, however, the role of the marital relationship was more pervasive in parent child relations and children's adjustment for girls than for boys. In young girls, a close marital relationship appeared to disrupt parent–child relationships and to be associated with poor adjustment in girls. In adolescent girls however a reverse pattern was obtained where a close marital relationship was associated with more positive, less conflictual parent–child relationships and better adjustment in girls. It may be that in adolescence a close marital relationship in stepfamilies is seen as a buffer or protection against the threat of inappropriate intimacy between stepfathers and stepdaughters.

Sibling Relationships

I now examine a final and very salient relationship within the family, the sibling relationship. Although considerable research has been done on parent–child relationships in divorced and remarried families, there is little work on the role siblings may play in exacerbating or buffering the effects of marital transitions. Two alternative hypotheses might be offered about siblings and the marital transitions of their parents. One would be that siblings become increasingly rivalrous and hostile as they compete for scarce resources of parental love and attention following their parents' divorce or remarriage. Alternatively, siblings in families that have gone through marital transitions may view relationships with adults as unstable, untrustworthy, and painful and turn to each other for solace, support, and alliance.

On the whole, the findings on sibling relationships were similar in Study I and Study II, however, there were a few differences that should be noted. First, in both studies, siblings in stepfamilies and boys in divorced families had more problematic relationships than siblings in non-divorced families or girls in divorced families. Boys in divorced and remarried families and girls in the early stage of remarriage were not only less warm and involved than other siblings, they also were more aggressive, avoidant, and rivalrous. Negative start-ups, reciprocated aggression, and long chains of aggressive, coercive behaviors with siblings were more common among stepchildren and among sons in divorced families than among children in non-divorced families. Second, with the younger siblings in Study I, relationships in stepfamilies improved over time but remained more disturbed than those in non-divorced or divorced families. Disengagement and avoidance of younger female children toward their siblings remained more common in stepfamilies than other families, even 2 years after remarriage. In contrast, with adolescents, sibling relations of stepsons deteriorated over time with decreasing warmth and increased conflict and distance whereas siblings relations for girls in both divorced and remarried families improved over time. It seems that over time adolescent girls in divorced and eventually in remarried families were able to serve as confidants and supports for their siblings whereas boys in these families had increasingly conflictual distant relationships. Third, any sibling dyad involving a boy was more troubled than those involving only girls. Not only were boys seen as exhibiting more aversive behaviors than girls, but girls behaved in a less congenial fashion when interacting with brothers than sisters. Both sons and daughters in stepfamilies and daughters in divorced families were less likely to initiate conversations or activities and more likely to refuse or ignore overtures on the part of a male than a female sibling. Brothers were not getting much support from their female siblings in these families.

If we reevaluate the alternative proposals on what may happen to sibling relations in response to stress and marital transitions, the most prevalent response of boys during the adjustment to divorce or remarriage is likely to be competition for scarce resources, in the form of diminished support, involvement, and guidance, and increased aggression, rivalry, and avoidance. As has been found in previous studies (Dunn, 1988), family transitions were most strongly associated with disrupted, negative, and aggressive sibling relationships rather than enhanced, positive, supportive sibling relationships. There is little evidence in this study to indicate enhanced support among most siblings during times of family transition. Although adolescent girls in remarried families demonstrated increased support toward their siblings over time, this was a recovery from an initial period of disruption rather than enhanced support from the outset. Even in adolescence, the girls in divorced and remarried families did not show closer or more positive relations than those found in non-divorced families with their siblings. Moreover for boys, the disruption seen in the sibling relationship appears to worsen over time with the advance into adolescence. Perhaps the concurrent family reorganization for remarried families serves to exacerbate a normative process of disengagement during early adoles-

225

cence, and the combination of these two transitions brings a more negative quality to the sibling relationship.

Furthermore, sibling relationships tend to play a relatively independent and unique role in the family. For boys, conflict in the sibling relationship is independent of conflict in the parent child dyad or the marital dyad. For girls, the quality of the sibling relationship is related to the quality of parent–child relationships but not to the marital relationship.

Some of our structural models looking at the associations among family relationships and children's adjustment suggested that sibling relations played an especially important role in the development of externalizing. We wondered what the differences in levels of externalizing might be if no siblings were present in the home. When the means for externalizing for only children were compared to those of children who had at least one sibling, there were no effects of family type but the presence of a sibling was associated with higher externalizing for girls but not for boys. Perhaps boys have more opportunities to hone their antisocial coercive skills in situations and groups outside of the family such as the peer group. The uniquely intense, vulnerable, inescapable, persistent, and often ambivalent relations found between siblings may play a more critical role in the development of aggressive, coercive behavior in girls than in boys.

CONCLUSION AND SUMMARY

After this laborious review of two longitudinal studies what can we conclude about the effects of divorce and remarriage? First children who undergo their parents marital transitions are at greater risk for developing behavior problems than are children who remain in non-divorced families. Second, adolescence is a time when children are least adaptable and are most vulnerable to the adverse effects of their parents' remarriage. It is also a time when problems increase in daughters and are sustained in sons with divorced, custodial, non-remarried mothers. Third, younger sons are more likely than younger daughters or adolescent children to accept or benefit from the presence of a stepfather. Fourth, a disengaged parenting style is the one most frequently found in stepfathers and this disengagement may increase over time especially with adolescent children. Finally, the effects of marital transitions and the consequent restructuring of the family affect the entire family system and the relationships among subsystems. These effects on family relations and their interrelationships vary with the age and gender of the child.

I conclude with a theme I am frequently reiterating. Divorce and remarriage are often associated with experiences that place children at increased risk for developing social, psychological, behavioral, and academic problems. Yet divorce and remarriage also can remove children from stressful or acrimonious family relationships and provide additional resources for children. There is great diversity in children's responses to their parents marital transitions. Many children eventually emerge from their parents divorce or remarriage as competent or even enhanced individuals. It is only by focussing on this diversity in response to marital transitions that we are going to be able to identify factors that facilitate or disrupt the functioning of these families. This information is essential in planning policies and intervention strategies to make these transitions less stressful and to promote the psychological well being of family members in divorced or remarried families.

ACKNOWLEDGMENTS

This article was presented at the Presidential Address at the Meeting of the Society for Research in Adolescence, March 1990, in Atlanta, GA.

Among the young scholars who made major contributions to this study, I especially wish to acknowledge Ed Anderson, Layne Bennion, James Deal, Peggy Hagan, Ann Hollier, Marjorie Lindner, and Sam Vuchinich.

REFERENCES

Achenbach, T., & Edelbrock, C. S. (1983). *Manual for the Child Behavior Checklist and revised Child Behavior Profile.* New York: Queen City Printers.
Block, J. H., Block, J., & Gerde, P. F. (1986). The personality of children prior to divorce: A prospective study. *Child Development, 57,* 827–840.
Brand, E., Clingempeel, W. E., & Bowen-Woodward, K. (1988). Family relationships and children's psychological adjustment. In E. M. Hetherington & J. D. Arasteh (Eds.), *Impact of divorce, single-parenting and step-parenting on children* (pp. 299–324). Hillsdale, NJ: Lawrence Erlbaum Associates, Inc.
Dunn, J. (1988). Connections between relationships: Implications of research on mothers and siblings. In R. A. Hinde & J. Stevenson-Hinde (Eds.), *Relationships within families: Mutual influences* (pp. 168–180). Oxford, England: Oxford University Press.
Emery, R. E. (1982). Interparental conflict and the children of discord and divorce. *Psychological Bulletin, 92,* 310–330.
Hetherington, E. M. (1972). Effects of fathers' absence on personality development in adolescent daughters. *Developmental Psychology, 7*(3), 313–326.
Hetherington, E. M. (1989). Coping with family transitions: Winners, losers and survivors. *Child Development, 60,* 1–14.

Hetherington, E. M., & Anderson, E. R. (1987). The effects of divorce and remarriage on early adolescents and their families. In M. D. Levine & E. R. McAnarney (Eds.), *Early adolescent transitions* (pp. 49–67). Lexington, MA: Heath.

Hetherington, E. M., Cox, M. J., & Cox, R. (1982). Effects of divorce on parents and children. In M. E. Lamb (Ed.), *Nontraditional families* (pp. 233–288). Hillsdale, NJ: Lawrence Erlbaum Associates, Inc.

Hill, J. P. (1988). Adapting to menarche: Familial control and conflict. In M. Gunnar (Ed.), *21st Minnesota symposium on child psychology* (pp. 43–77). Hillsdale, NJ: Lawrence Erlbaum Associates, Inc.

Kenny, D. A., & LaVoie, L. (1984). The social relations model. In L. Berkowitz (Ed.), *Advances in experimental social psychology* (Vol. 18, pp. 141–182). New York: Academic.

Newcomer, S. F., & Udry, J. R. (1987). Parental marital status effects on adolescent sexual behavior. *Journal of Marriage and the Family, 49*, 235–240.

Papernow, P. L. (1984). The step-family cycle: An experiential model of stepfamily development. *Family Relations, 33*, 355–363.

Rogers, J. L. (1983). Family configuration and adolescent sexual behavior. *Population and Environment, 6*, 73–83.

Rutter, M. (1987). Psychosocial resilience and protective mechanisms. *American Journal of Orthopsychiatry, 57*, 316–331.

Steinberg, L. (1990). Autonomy, conflict, and harmony in the family relationship. In S. Feldman & G. Elliott (Eds.), *At the threshold: The developing adolescent* (pp. 255–276). Cambridge, MA: Harvard University Press.

Steinberg, L., Mounts, N., Lamborn, S., & Dornbusch, S. (1991). Authoritative parenting and adolescent adjustment across varied ecological niches. *Journal of Research on Adolescence, 1*, 19–36.

Udry, J. R., Talbert, L. M., & Morris, N. M. (1986). Biosocial foundations for female adolescent sexuality. *Demography, 23*, 217–230.

Wallerstein, J. S., & Kelly, J. B. (1980). *Surviving the breakup*. New York: Basic Books.

Weiss, R. S. (1979). Growing up a little faster: The experience of growing up in a single-parent household. *Journal of Social Issues, 35*, 97–111.

Werner, E. E. (1987). Vulnerability and resiliency in children at risk for delinquency: A longitudinal study from birth to young adulthood. In J. D. Burchard & S. M. Burchard (Eds.), *Prevention of delinquent behavior* (pp. 68–84). Beverly Hills, CA: Sage.

Received March 25, 1991
Accepted March 25, 1991

JOURNAL OF RESEARCH ON ADOLESCENCE, 3(1), 19-39
Copyright © 1993, Lawrence Erlbaum Associates, Inc.

Conceptions of Parental Authority in Divorced and Married Mothers and Their Adolescents

Judith G. Smetana
University of Rochester

Conceptions of parental authority were assessed in 28 divorced, unremarried mothers and 66 married mothers and their 6th–11th graders. Participants were presented with 15 items pertaining to family transgressions, 4 moral, 4 conventional, 3 personal, and 4 multifaceted (containing conventional and personal components). For each act, participants judged the legitimacy of parental jurisdiction, justified its wrongness or permissibility, and assessed its contingency on parental authority. As expected, regardless of family structure, mothers and adolescents treated both moral and conventional issues as being more legitimately subject to parental jurisdiction than multifaceted and personal issues. However, married mothers of boys and divorced mothers of girls treated all rules as being more legitimately subject to parental jurisdiction than did divorced mothers of boys. Correspondingly, married families of mid-adolescent girls and divorced families of mid-adolescent boys treated personal and multifaceted items as under personal jurisdiction more than did married families with younger girls and divorced families with mid-adolescent girls, respectively. Adolescents' personal reasoning and sorting of items as issues of personal jurisdiction increased with age and conventional reasoning about the multifaceted items decreased with age in married families but not in divorced families. Findings are discussed in terms of the effects of divorce on adolescent–parent relationships and the development of autonomy in adolescence.

Research on the effects of parental divorce on adolescents has consistently shown that family functioning in divorced, unremarried families

---

Requests for reprints should be sent to Judith G. Smetana, Graduate School of Education and Human Development, Lattimore Hall, University of Rochester, Rochester, NY 14627.

and two-parent families differs. Single-parent families have been found to be less hierarchical than married families (Hetherington, 1989; Hetherington, Stanley-Hagan, & Anderson, 1989; Weiss, 1979). Furthermore, unremarried mothers are more permissive, less controlling, and provide less chaperonage than mothers in intact families (Anderson, Hetherington, & Clingempeel, 1989; Baumrind, 1989; Flanagan, 1987; Hetherington, 1989; Santrock, Warshak, Lindbergh, & Meadows, 1982). Correspondingly, adolescents in divorced families have been found to have more independence, power, and responsibility than do adolescents in married families (Baumrind, 1989; Dornbusch et al., 1985; Hetherington, 1989).

It is unclear whether these functional differences are associated with differences in the way that parents and children conceptualize their roles and, in particular, their conceptions of parental authority. Divorced and married mothers' conceptions of parental authority may not differ, but divorced mothers simply may become less attentive to the needs of their children as they handle the crisis of divorce and the loss of a second parent who reinforces their role. It is also possible that with the reorganization of the family, divorced mothers and their adolescents come to view many childrearing issues as being less legitimately subject to parental jurisdiction than do mothers and children in intact families. Divorced and married families can be seen as providing different social contexts for childrearing, and evaluations of family norms and expectations within those contexts, as well as expectations regarding which issues should be under adolescents' personal jurisdiction, might differ. I examined these questions by comparing conceptions of parental authority in divorced and married mothers and their adolescents.

Previous research on married families indicates that parents' and adolescents' conceptions of parental authority differ according to the type of act under consideration (Smetana, 1988a). Using a domain model of social–cognitive development (Smetana, 1983; Turiel, 1979, 1983; Turiel & Davidson, 1986), distinctions were made between (a) *moral issues* (defined as acts that are prescriptively wrong because they affect the rights and welfare of others); (b) *conventional issues* (defined as the arbitrary and consensually agreed-on behavioral uniformities that structure social interactions within social systems; Turiel, 1979, 1983); and (c) *issues of personal jurisdiction* (defined as actions that have consequences only to the actor and as such are viewed as being beyond societal regulation and moral concern; Nucci, 1981).

This research indicates that across ages, virtually all adolescents and parents judged that parents should retain authority over moral and conventional issues. Adolescents and parents consistently differed, however, in their judgments of personal issues. Previous research has shown that children across a wide age range judge acts that violate a stated rule or norm but that result in consequences primarily affecting the actor to be independent of rules and justified on that basis (Nucci, 1981). The research on parental authority (Smetana, 1988a) indicates, however, that even when the depicted personal acts did not violate parental customs or conventions, and their consequences primarily affected the actor (e.g., an adolescent), parents were less likely than adolescents to evaluate such events as being under the adolescents' personal jurisdiction. Because the inclusion of actions within the personal domain has been hypothesized to represent an important aspect of adolescents' developing autonomy or distinctiveness from others (Nucci, 1981; Smetana, 1988a),[1] the findings suggest that parents and adolescents differ in the extent to which adolescents should be granted autonomy over these issues.[2]

The research also indicates that adolescents and parents differed in their judgments of multifaceted issues that entail both personal and conventional components (Smetana, 1988a). Parents treated personal and multifaceted issues as being more legitimately subject to parental jurisdiction and viewed their wrongness as being more contingent on parental authority than did adolescents, on the basis of concerns with social convention. Adolescents, by contrast, treated these same issues as being more independent of parental authority than did parents, on the basis of concerns with exercising or maintaining personal jurisdiction.

---

[1]Adolescents' claims that they have a right to make autonomous decisions might seem to suggest that claims for autonomy represent moral (rather than personal) judgments. Others (Dworkin, 1978; Gewirth, 1978, 1982; Nucci & Lee, 1990) have argued, however, that the notion of rights is grounded in the establishment and maintenance of personal agency. In this view, personal concepts are those aspects of the psychological domain that identify "freedom" as being necessary for the maintenance of agency and uniqueness. In this view, the content of the personal domain is the content of the individual's identified freedoms. Thus, in this article, appeals to personal jurisdiction can be seen as the source of rights claims.

[2]In previous research examining distinctions in children's social judgments, children have evaluated hypothetical stimuli that were judged by the researchers to be prototypical of the domain. Children's judgments along theoretical criteria hypothesized to distinguish the domains were then examined to determine whether children would make domain distinctions in their social judgments. Thus, the purpose of this research was to determine whether participants would classify events in ways that are consistent with theoretical formulations. Previous research has indicated that from early childhood on, children consistently evaluate a set of issues as being under their personal jurisdiction using the criteria described here (e.g., Nucci, 1981; Nucci et al., 1991; Tisak, in press) and that parents also grant their children personal jurisdiction over some issues (Nucci & Smetana, 1992; Nucci & Weber, 1991). The findings from the previous research on parental authority suggests, however, that adolescents and parents differ in where they draw the boundaries between legitimate parental authority and adolescents' personal jurisdiction.

Adolescents' and parents' reasoning and judgments about moral and conventional issues did not differ significantly across adolescence. However, parental authority regarding multifaceted and personal issues was observed to decline with adolescents' increasing age.

In this study, I assessed divorced mothers' and their adolescents' conceptions of parental authority by using the measures used in the previous research (Smetana, 1988a). I used three tasks assessing different facets of adolescents' and mothers' conceptions of parental authority. Participants assessed the independence or contingency of different hypothetical acts on parental authority and justified the wrongness or permissibility of the acts; these tasks have been used in previous research to distinguish among morality, conventionality, and personal jurisdiction in children's judgments and justifications (Davidson, Turiel, & Black, 1983; Nucci, 1981; Smetana, 1981a, 1981b, 1985; Turiel, 1983). In addition, to determine the boundaries between legitimate parental regulation and adolescents' personal jurisdiction, mothers and adolescents evaluated the legitimacy of parental authority for the different acts.

Divorced mothers' and adolescents' judgments and justifications were compared with a subset of married mothers and adolescents drawn from the original sample of 102 two-parent families with 5th–12th graders interviewed about parental authority. The adolescents were divided into two ages groups: early adolescents (6th–8th graders) and mid-adolescents (9th–11th graders). The divorced sample consisted of "stabilized" divorced families (Hetherington, 1989); divorced mothers typically had been divorced prior to their child's adolescence, had not remarried, and, according to their report, were not currently cohabiting. The two-parent comparison sample consisted of the mothers of and 6th–11th graders who were living with both of their natural parents.

On the basis of previous research (Smetana, 1988a) and because morality is hypothesized to be generalizable across contexts (Smetana, 1983; Turiel, 1983; Turiel & Davidson, 1986; Turiel, Killen, & Helwig, 1987), I hypothesized that married and divorced families would not differ in their reasoning and judgments regarding moral issues. I also hypothesized that married and divorced families' reasoning and judgments about conventional issues would not differ. Regardless of family structure, I expected that adolescents and their mothers would view both moral and conventional issues as being legitimately subject to parental jurisdiction, on the basis of moral or conventional concerns, and that they would evaluate the wrongness of (a) moral acts as being independent of parental authority and (b) conventional acts as being contingent on parental authority.

Prior research has shown that adolescents from divorced families are more independent in their decisions regarding clothing, curfew, choice of friends, and spending money than are adolescents from intact families (Dornbusch et al., 1985). Because these issues can be conceptualized as either personal or multifaceted (in that parents might view them as conventional, whereas adolescents might view them as being outside of the bounds of societal regulation and moral concern and therefore as personal issues), I predicted that divorced mothers and their adolescents would judge multifaceted and personal issues as being less legitimately subject to parental jurisdiction than would married mothers and their adolescents.

Early adolescents from married families have been found to appeal more to exercising or maintaining personal jurisdiction when reasoning about actual family conflicts than do early adolescents from divorced families (Smetana, Yau, Restrepo, & Braeges, 1991). Because early adolescents from divorced families have been granted more independence in decision making than early adolescents from married families (Dornbusch et al., 1985), this finding appears to reflect their greater desire for autonomy. Therefore, I hypothesized that in this study, adolescents from married families would reason more about exercising personal jurisdiction, particularly in early adolescence, when autonomy concerns are especially salient (Steinberg & Silverberg, 1986), than would their counterparts from divorced families.

METHOD

Subjects

The sample consisted of 94 6th–11th graders and their mothers. There were 28 single-parent mother-custodial families, 14 with girls and 14 with boys, and 66 intact, two-parent families, half with boys and half with girls. There were no stepparent families in the sample, and both parents in the two-parent families were the child's natural parents. None of the custodial mothers were currently cohabiting. The families were divided into two groups: those with 6th–8th graders (referred to here as early adolescents) and those with 9th–11th graders (referred to here as mid-adolescents), with equal numbers of divorced families at each age. There were equal numbers of boys and girls from divorced families at each age ($n = 7$); there were 16 male and 17 female early adolescents and 17 male and 16 female mid-adolescents from married families. Early and mid-adolescents were, on average, 12.55 and 15.68 years of age ($SDs = 0.96$ and 0.94, respectively). Divorced mothers typically had been divorced prior to their children's adolescence (see

233

Smetana, Yau, et al., 1991, for more details on the demographic characteristics of the divorced sample). Although children's birth order did not differ significantly by age or family structure, married families (M = 2.46 children) were significantly larger than divorced families (M = 1.93 children), $F(1, 94) = 9.76$, $p < .01$. All families were recruited from a suburban area near a midsized eastern city.[3]

The families were primarily (more than 90%) White, well educated, and middle- to upper-middle class. Divorced and married mothers did not differ significantly in age or educational level, but divorced mothers were significantly lower in socioeconomic status (SES), as measured by the Hollingshead (1977) four-factor index, than married mothers (Ms = 51.50 and 55.97, respectively).

Stimuli

The stimuli for this study were 15 familial transgressions presented on 3-in. × 5-in. cards, 4 moral, 4 conventional, 3 personal, and 4 multifaceted. The definitions of the domains were based on previous research (Nucci, 1981; Smetana, 1981a, 1981b, 1985; Turiel, 1983). The moral items were stealing pocket money from parents, not sharing (communal property) with brothers and sisters, lying to parents, and hitting brothers and sisters. The conventional items were not doing assigned chores, not keeping parents informed of one's activities, calling parents by their first names, and not cleaning up after a party. The personal events were sleeping late on a weekend, talking on the phone (when no one else wants to use it), and watching MTV (Music Video TV). The multifaceted items were dressing in punk clothes, going out with friends instead of going to a family picnic, hanging out with a friend that

---

[3]As described elsewhere (Smetana, 1989; Smetana et al., 1991), I recruited families through the cooperation of a suburban school district. Research assistants first visited classrooms to tell children about the research, and parents were then mailed a letter inviting them to participate. The sample consisted of families who indicated interest by returning a postcard to the research group. The response rate among two-parent and single-parent families was 15% and 40%, respectively. Phone calls to families who declined participation revealed that nonparticipation was caused by a variety of factors, including scheduling difficulties. The lower participation rate of two-parent than single-parent families was primarily due to fathers' general reluctance to participate. The response rate was comparable to other research on adolescent–parent interactions (W. A. Collins, personal communication, 1988; C. Cooper, personal communication, 1988) but was lower than in studies in which adolescents and their parents were interviewed in their homes (L. Steinberg, personal communication, 1988) or schools (S. Hauser, personal communication, 1988). Participants did not differ from the broader school population in socioeconomic status, parental education, or religion, but their academic performance was somewhat better than average.

parents do not approve of, and not cleaning one's room. Each of the multifaceted events could be seen to violate parental conventions (e.g., dressing unconventionally; violating family customs regarding shared activities; violating parental norms regarding acceptable friendships; and, to the extent that the child's room is seen as being part of the house, not contributing to the household or conforming to acceptable maintenance standards). Each of these items also could be seen to entail a personal component (e.g., exercising individuality through dress; maintaining or exercising personal choice over decisions regarding friendships, activities, and, to the extent that the child's room is seen as being his or her own territory, personal space).

Procedure

Families were recruited from two suburban middle schools and high schools located near a northeastern city as part of a larger project on adolescent–parent relationships (see Smetana, 1988a, for details). After obtaining demographic information, family members were each individually interviewed. Participants were presented with a set of cards describing different types of acts. For each act, they first sorted the cards into two categories, "OK (not OK) for parents to make rules," assessing the legitimacy of parental authority. Next, for each act, they were asked, "Why is (the act) wrong (or OK)?", assessing their reasons, or their justifications for the act's wrongness or permissibility. They then sorted the cards into three categories: "Always wrong, whether or not the parent says so," "Wrong only if the parent says so," and "Not an issue of right or wrong—up to the individual," assessing the independence or contingency of the act on parental authority. On the basis of previous research (Nucci, 1981; Smetana, 1981b), these three categories were seen to represent one aspect of distinctions among moral, conventional, and personal issues, respectively. No instructions were given about the basis for their responses.

Scoring

Responses to the legitimacy and contingency of parental authority tasks were recorded on a checklist. Responses indicating that the act was seen as being legitimately under parental jurisdiction were assigned a score of 1, and responses indicating that it was not were assigned a score of 0. Responses pertaining to the contingency of acts on parental authority were scored in one of three categories corresponding to the three response choices noted earlier. Responses were assigned a score of 1 if the category was used and 0 if it was not.

Justifications were audio tape-recorded, transcribed, and coded into 16 standard and reliable categories on the basis of previous research (Davidson et al., 1983; Smetana, 1985, 1988a, 1988b, 1989). More than one justification was permitted per item, with a maximum of two justifications per item scored.[4] Interrater agreement between two coders in coding 20 protocols (332 justifications) was 84%. Justifications were then collapsed into categories for analytic purposes. On the basis of previous research (Davidson et al., 1983; Smetana, 1983, 1988a; Turiel, 1983), justifications pertaining to welfare, obligation, and fairness were combined to form the moral category, and justifications pertaining to appeals to authority, social nonconformity, social coordination, social customs and norms, politeness, responsibility, and punishment avoidance were combined to form the social–conventional category. Appeals to personality characteristics and interpersonal reasons were treated as aspects of the psychological category. On the basis of previous research (Smetana, 1988a, 1988b, 1989) and the focus here on examining judgments regarding personal jurisdiction, personal choice, and autonomy seeking, also aspects of the psychological domain, were treated as a separate personal category. Concerns with prudence (which pertain to nonsocial negative consequences to the child, such as personal comfort and health) and pragmatics (which pertain to practical needs and consequences) have been categorized conceptually as aspects of personal choice in previous research (Nucci, Guerra, & Lee, 1991; Tisak, in press; Tisak & Turiel, 1984), but I combined and examined them separately here because previous research has shown that prudential or pragmatic issues are more likely to be judged as being legitimately regulated by parental or social rules than other personal issues.[5] More detailed definitions of the domains and their relation to the tasks may be found in Table 1.

---

[4]Less than 5% of responses entailed more than two justifications per item. Justifications pertaining to authority or punishment avoidance were not scored when more than two justifications were given, and this accounted for nearly all of these instances. In the remaining cases, only the first two justifications given were scored.

[5]Research indicates that prudential issues, like personal issues, are evaluated as having consequences only for the actor and, consequently, these acts are seen as being under the individual's personal jurisdiction. However, because concerns with prudence may focus on harm to the self (e.g., through carelessness), prudential violations are generally seen as being more serious than personal violations and, in some cases, as serious as moral violations (Tisak, 1991). Thus, external regulation of prudential issues is seen as being justified in some circumstances (e.g., in regulating drug use; Nucci et al., 1991; Tisak & Turiel, 1984). Although psychological reasons, personal choice, and prudence and pragmatics are seen as being conceptually related aspects of psychological knowledge (Turiel & Davidson, 1986), they were separated in this research to provide a clearer understanding of adolescents' and parents' conceptions of parental authority.

TABLE 1
Social Knowledge Domains: Definitions, Criteria, and Study Tasks

Domain Definitions	Criteria	Study Tasks
Moral Acts that are prescriptively wrong because they have intrinsic consequences for others' welfare, rights, trust, or the fair distribution of resources	Rule and authority independence; generalizability; obligatory; unalterable; unchangeable	1. Authority independent (wrong whether or not parents say so)
		2. Justifications: welfare, obligation, fairness
		3. Legitimacy (OK to make rules)
Conventional Arbitrary and agreed-on behavioral uniformities that structure social interactions within different social systems	Rule contingency; subject to authority and rule jurisdiction; alterability; contextual relativity	1. Authority contingent (wrong only because parents say so)
		2. Justifications: authority, punishment, customs, social nonconformity, social coordination, responsibility, politeness
		3. Legitimacy (OK to make rules)
Psychological Understanding of self and others as psychological systems; includes		
Personal: acts that have consequences only for the self and as such, are important for developing self, autonomy, and identity	Act affects only the self; beyond the bounds of social or moral concern	1. Under personal jurisdiction (not an issue of right or wrong; up to the individual)
		2. Justifications: personal choice; autonomy
		3. Legitimacy: not OK to make rules
Prudential: nonsocial negative consequences to the self (e.g., pertaining to health, safety, or personal comfort)	Act affects the self; rule utility, generalizability, rule contingency	2. Justifications: prudential and pragmatic
Psychological: knowledge of self, identity, personality, and attributions for causes of self and others' behavior		2. Justifications: appeals to personality characteristics; interpersonal reasons

Analyses

To ensure the comparability of the parent data from two-parent and single-parent families, I performed all analyses on only mothers' responses; I did not include married fathers' responses in the analyses. Because parent–child and age differences have been reported extensively for the larger two-parent sample, I report only results pertaining to family structure except when hypotheses regarding age, generation (mother vs. adolescent), or domain differences are specified. To control for their effects, I used both SES and family size (number of siblings) as covariates in the analyses. In all analyses conducted on proportions, I performed arcsine transformations because proportions may not be normally distributed (Winer, 1971). When significant findings were obtained, I conducted post hoc comparisons of means using Duncan multiple range tests and Bonferroni t tests for between-subjects and within-subjects effects, respectively.

RESULTS

Legitimacy of Parental Authority

I analyzed responses regarding the legitimacy of parental authority using a 2 (Family Structure) $\times$ 2 (Generation: Mother vs. Adolescent) $\times$ 2 (Age) $\times$ 2 (Child's Sex) $\times$ 4 (Domain) repeated-measures analysis of covariance (ANCOVA) on the mean proportion of responses per domain that affirmed adult authority. Generation and domain were the repeated measures.

As predicted, there was a highly significant main effect for domain, $F(3, 240) = 7.74$, $p < .0001$. Consistent with expectations, mothers and adolescents in both married and divorced families viewed moral and conventional issues as being more legitimately subject to parental jurisdiction than multifaceted or personal issues ($ps < .0001$; see Table 2 for means). Furthermore, multifaceted issues were viewed as being more legitimately subject to parental jurisdiction than were personal issues ($p < .01$).

There were significant Family Structure $\times$ Generation, $F(1, 80) = 4.94$, $p < .05$, and Family Structure $\times$ Sex, $F(2, 80) = 3.34$, $p < .05$, interactions. As can be seen in Table 2, married mothers viewed all rules as being more legitimately subject to parental jurisdiction than did their adolescents, $t = 5.37$, $p < .0001$, but divorced mothers and their adolescents did not differ. Furthermore, married families with boys, $F(1, 42) = 7.84$, $p < .01$, and divorced families with girls, $F(1, 23) = 4.46$, p

TABLE 2
Judgments of the Legitimacy of Parental Authority

	Married Families				Divorced Families				
	Mothers	of	Adolescents		Mothers	of	Adolescents		Total
Items	Boys	Girls	Boys	Girls	Boys	Girls	Boys	Girls	M
Moral	.91	.89	.91	.92	.73	.89	.93	.91	.89
Conventional	.91	.89	.89	.90	.75	.86	.86	.96	.88
Multifaceted	.67	.55	.42	.39	.41	.66	.36	.43	.49
Personal	.61	.57	.21	.29	.45	.60	.27	.29	.41
M	.78	.74	.64	.65	.59	.78	.60	.67	.68

$< .05$, treated all rules as being more legitimately subject to parental jurisdiction than did divorced families with boys. However, these findings were qualified by a significant three-way–Family Structure × Generation × Sex–interaction, $F(2, 80) = 3.24$, $p < .05$. Married mothers of boys, $F(1, 42) = 9.46$, $p < .01$, and divorced mothers of girls, $F(1, 23) = 5.38$, $p < .05$, treated all rules as being more legitimately subject to parental jurisdiction than did divorced mothers of boys, but married mothers of girls did not differ.

Authority Contingency

Table 3 shows the (untransformed) mean proportions of items in each domain sorted as wrong independent of authority, wrong contingent on authority, and under personal jurisdiction. As described later, separate ANCOVAs were performed for each of these three categories on items collapsed within domains.

Items sorted as being independent of authority. As Table 3 indicates, significant frequencies of moral items were sorted as being wrong independent of authority. Overall, 81% of moral items (and 43% of the conventional items) were sorted as being independent of parental authority. Therefore, a 2 (Family Structure) × 2 (Age) × 2 (Sex) × 2 (Generation: Mother vs. Adolescent) mixed ANCOVA with generation as the repeated measure was performed on the arcsine-transformed mean proportion of hypothesized moral items sorted in this category. As expected, mothers' and adolescents' sorting of items as being independent of authority did not vary according to family structure, nor did family structure interact with adolescents' age or sex.

Items sorted as being contingent on authority. As can be seen in Table 3, conventional, multifaceted, and personal items were all sorted

TABLE 3
Proportion of Items (%) Sorted as Being Independent or Contingent on Parental
Authority or Under Personal Jurisdiction

	Wrong Independent of Parental Authority				Wrong Contingent on Parental Authority				Under Personal Jurisdiction			
	Married		Divorced		Married		Divorced		Married		Divorced	
Items	E	M	E	M	E	M	E	M	E	M	E	M
Moral												
Adolescent	86	80	79	83	7	14	17	12	6	6	4	6
Boys	89	90	63	88	5	7	29	4	6	3	5	8
Girls	84	69	88	79	10	22	9	18	6	9	4	4
Mother	79	82	75	81	15	10	20	10	6	8	5	1
Sons	80	82	65	75	14	10	25	8	6	7	6	17
Daughters	78	82	81	86	16	10	16	11	6	8	4	4
Conventional												
Adolescent	53	42	54	48	42	50	42	48	5	8	4	4
Boys	44	46	42	58	48	50	46	42	8	4	10	0
Girls	62	38	56	39	35	50	44	54	3	13	0	7
Mother	35	43	36	35	56	45	48	46	9	12	16	20
Sons	31	47	35	25	63	38	45	46	7	15	19	29
Daughters	38	38	38	43	50	53	50	46	12	8	14	11
Multifaceted												
Adolescent	14	6	15	6	38	32	40	38	48	62	46	56
Boys	13	7	13	8	42	31	42	25	45	62	35	67
Girls	16	4	19	4	34	33	34	50	50	63	54	46
Mother	17	11	16	6	48	38	39	56	36	52	45	38
Sons	17	12	20	0	47	41	40	46	36	47	38	54
Daughters	16	10	19	11	49	33	38	64	35	57	50	25
Personal												
Adolescent	10	2	6	8	25	19	44	21	65	79	50	72
Boys	6	4	11	11	13	24	22	22	81	73	60	67
Girls	14	0	4	5	37	15	54	19	49	85	43	76
Mother	14	11	3	5	36	42	45	51	49	47	52	44
Sons	13	12	0	0	38	47	33	33	50	41	67	67
Daughters	16	11	4	10	35	36	58	67	49	53	43	24

Note. E = early adolescent and M = mid-adolescent.

as being contingent on parental authority in varying frequencies. Therefore, I performed a 2 (Family Structure) × 2 (Adolescent's Age) × 2 (Adolescent's Sex) × 2 (Generation) × 3 (Domain) repeated-measures ANCOVA on the arcsine-transformed proportions of these three types of items sorted as being contingent on authority.

Family structure interacted significantly with domain and sex, $F(2, 162) = 5.63$, $p < .01$. The personal items were treated as being more contingent on parental authority by divorced families with girls ($M =$

.50) than boys (M = .29), $F(1, 25)$ = 5.89, p < .05, but no differences in married families' sorting of personal items were observed. Furthermore, divorced families with girls (M = .50) treated personal items as being more contingent on parental authority than did married families with girls (M = .30), $F(1, 46)$ = 7.80, p < .01, but families with boys did not differ significantly. There was a significant five-way interaction, $F(2, 162)$ = 3.17, p < .05, but I did not examine it further because such higher order interactions are not dependable.[6]

Items sorted as being under personal jurisdiction. As Table 3 indicates, both multifaceted and personal items were sorted as being under personal jurisdiction in significant frequencies by mothers and adolescents. Therefore, I performed a 2 (Family Structure) × 2 (Generation: Mother vs. Adolescent) × 2 (Age) × 2 (Child's Sex) × 2 (Domain) mixed ANCOVA on the arcsine-transformed proportions of multifaceted and personal items sorted in this category.

As might be expected, personal items were sorted as being under personal jurisdiction more than were multifaceted items, as indicated by a significant main effect for domain, $F(1, 81)$ = 4.47, p < .05. Overall, 49% of the multifaceted items and 59% of the personal items were sorted in this category.

A significant Family Structure × Age interaction, $F(1, 81)$ = 9.15, p < .01, revealed that married families' sorting of the personal and multifaceted items as being under personal jurisdiction increased with age, $F(1, 64)$ = 3.15, p < .05 (Ms = .55 and .67, respectively), but comparable age-related increases were not observed in divorced families (Ms = .51 and .57, respectively). These findings were qualified by a Family Structure × Age × Sex interaction, $F(1, 81)$ = 9.79, p < .01, which revealed that age-related changes occurred in married families with girls (M = .50), $F(1, 31)$ = 6.67, p < .05, but not boys (M = .73). In addition, the personal and multifaceted items were sorted as being under personal jurisdiction more by divorced families with mid-adolescent boys (M = .71) than girls (M = .45), $F(1, 12)$ = 4.49, p < .05. Finally, married families with mid-adolescent girls (M = .73) sorted personal and multifaceted items as being under personal jurisdiction more than did divorced families with same-age girls (M = .45), $F(1, 21)$ = 9.94, p < .01. I did not analyze further a significant five-way interaction, $F(1, 81)$ = 4.31, p < .05, because the results are likely to be undependable.

---

[6]Further information on higher order interactions may be obtained by writing to the author.

Justifications

Next, I examined participants' justifications for the wrongness or permissibility of hypothesized moral, conventional, multifaceted, and personal items. The proportions of moral, conventional, and personal justifications given for moral, conventional, multifaceted, and personal items are presented in Table 4.

Moral items. As can be seen in Table 4, moral transgressions were primarily justified using moral justifications. Fifty-six percent of adolescents' responses and 54% of mothers' responses to moral items pertained to moral justifications, with the remaining responses being primarily divided between conventional and psychological justifications. I performed a 2 (Family Structure) × 2 (Age) × 2 (Sex) × 2 (Generation: Mother vs. Adolescent) ANCOVA on the arcsine-transformed proportions of moral justifications for moral items. As hypothesized, there were no significant differences in moral reasoning about the moral items as a function of family structure.

Conventional items. Table 4 indicates that family members primarily offered conventional justifications for the wrongness of the conventional items; 70% of adolescents' responses and 69% of mothers' responses to conventional items pertained to conventional justifications. Therefore, I performed a 2 (Family Structure) × 2 (Age) × 2 (Sex) × 2 (Generation:

TABLE 4
Justifications (in %) for Moral, Conventional, Multifaceted, and Personal Items

Justifications	Moral				Conventional				Multifaceted				Personal			
	Married		Divorced		Married		Divorced		Married		Divorced		Married		Divorced	
	E	M	E	M	E	M	E	M	E	M	E	M	E	M	E	M
Adolescents																
Moral	58	54	56	56	22	20	4	18	4	3	12	0	2	3	3	0
Conventional	27	26	17	24	68	67	77	73	38	21	20	20	5	4	2	3
Psychological	13	15	22	17	5	5	4	0	9	7	15	4	5	3	0	0
Prudential	1	2	2	0	1	2	12	4	6	18	4	12	4	8	8	8
Personal	1	2	2	4	4	6	4	5	43	68	45	73	75	87	87	89
Mothers																
Moral	59	51	57	48	20	12	16	13	8	8	8	6	11	13	5	8
Conventional	19	17	10	12	71	73	56	65	45	35	19	27	10	18	9	8
Psychological	16	25	29	32	1	4	4	2	10	11	2	18	2	4	8	2
Prudential	3	3	2	5	2	1	7	5	3	3	13	6	14	15	8	22
Personal	2	4	2	4	6	10	17	15	34	44	58	43	62	51	71	60

Note. E = early adolescent and M = mid-adolescent.

Mother vs. Adolescent) ANCOVA on the arcsine-transformed proportions of conventional justifications offered for conventional items. Also consistent with hypotheses, there were no significant differences in conventional reasoning as a function of family structure.

Multifaceted items. As expected, participants reasoned about the multifaceted items using both conventional and personal justifications (see Table 4). Therefore, I performed a 2 (Family Structure) × 2 (Age) × 2 (Sex) × 2 (Generation: Mother vs. Adolescent) × 2 (Domain) mixed ANCOVA on the arcsine-transformed proportions of personal choice and conventional justifications given for the multifaceted items. There was a significant Family Structure × Domain × Age interaction, $F(2, 73) = 6.30$, $p < .01$. There was more conventional reasoning about the multifaceted items in married ($M = .47$) than in divorced ($M = .19$) families with early adolescents, $F(1, 42) = 13.50$, $p < .001$. Furthermore, personal reasoning increased with age, and conventional reasoning decreased with age in married ($M = .48$) but not in divorced ($M = .28$) families, $Fs(1, 64) = 10.67$ and 8.41, $ps < .05$, respectively. A significant four-way (Family Structure × Age × Generation × Domain) interaction, $F(2, 73) = 5.34$, $p < .01$, revealed that these effects were due to differences in adolescents' (but not mothers') reasoning.

Personal items. As Table 4 indicates, personal items were justified primarily on the basis of maintaining personal jurisdiction. A 2 (Family Structure) × 2 (Age) × 2 (Sex) × 2 (Generation: Mother vs. Adolescent) mixed ANCOVA performed on the arcsine-transformed proportion of personal choice justifications revealed a three-way–Family Structure × Generation (Adolescent vs. Mother) × Age–interaction, $F(2, 72) = 4.46$, $p < .05$. Mid-adolescents from married families gave more personal-choice justifications than did their mothers ($p < .001$, $Ms = .87$ and $.51$, respectively), but early adolescents and their married mothers and adolescents and divorced mothers did not differ.

DISCUSSION

The results of this study are consistent with a growing body of literature that indicates that children's conceptions of parental authority are differentiated according to the type of act under consideration (Laupa, 1991; Laupa & Turiel, 1986; Smetana, 1988a; Tisak, 1986; Tisak & Tisak, 1990). Regardless of family structure, mothers and adolescents in this study judged moral and conventional issues to be more legitimately subject to parental jurisdiction than multifaceted issues, which were in turn judged to be more legitimately subject to parental jurisdiction than personal issues. Both mothers and adolescents also treated the wrongness of moral issues as being independent of parental authority, on the basis of concerns with justice, welfare, obligations, and rights, whereas they treated the wrongness of conventional issues as being contingent on parental authority, on the basis of conventional concerns with social coordination, social nonconformity, social norms, politeness, and authority. There were no generational differences in these judgments and justifications, nor did they vary according to adolescents' age or sex.

As expected, conceptions of parental authority also differed in married and divorced families with adolescents. The results of the analyses reported here indicate that mother–child differences were more pronounced in married than divorced families. Married mothers treated all rules as being more legitimately subject to parental jurisdiction than did their adolescents, whereas divorced mothers and their adolescents did not differ. Furthermore, married mothers of mid-adolescents gave fewer personal-choice justifications for personal items than their adolescents did, but divorced mothers and their mid-adolescents did not differ. These findings are consistent with the results of previous research, which indicate that parent–child relations are less hierarchical and that children are pushed to grow up faster in divorced than married families (Hetherington et al., 1989; Weiss, 1979). The results of this study suggest that the more permissive and less hierarchical parenting observed in previous research among divorced than married mothers may be related to differences in the way they conceptualize their role and authority in the family (Goodnow, 1988). These conceptions warrant further investigation in future research.

Furthermore, early adolescents from married families reasoned about the conventionality of multifaceted items (which could be conceptualized in either personal or conventional terms) nearly twice as often as did early adolescents from divorced families. These findings are consistent with previous research, which has shown more conventional reasoning about actual family conflicts in married than divorced families (Smetana, Yau, et al., 1991). They suggest that early adolescents in married families place greater emphasis on maintaining conventionality in outward appearance and behavior than do early adolescents from divorced families. Conventional reasoning regarding these items was also found to decline with age among adolescents in married families and, correspondingly, sorting of the personal and multifaceted items as being under personal jurisdiction increased with age among married (but not divorced) families. This decline in conventional reasoning and corresponding increases in appeals to personal jurisdiction may provide one explanation for the greater incidence of adolescent–parent conflict observed among married than divorced families with adolescents (Anderson et al., 1989; Flanagan, 1987; Smetana, Yau, et al., 1991). That is, these qualitative changes in adolescents' reasoning, particularly the decline in conventional reasoning in favor of personal choice, may be interpreted by parents as a sign of rebellion that leads to conflict.

As has been observed consistently in other research on the effects of divorce on children (Zaslow, 1988), interactions between family status and sex were more pervasive in this study than main effects of family status. Divorced mothers of boys were found to treat all rules as being less legitimately subject to parental jurisdiction than did married mothers of boys and divorced mothers of girls. Correspondingly, divorced mothers and their sons treated personal items as being less contingent on parental authority less than did divorced mothers and their daughters, and personal and multifaceted items were treated as being under the adolescent's personal jurisdiction more by divorced families with mid-adolescent boys than girls. These findings may be related to the finding that mothers of sons are ineffectual in their control attempts and do not consistently follow through on their instructions (Hetherington, Cox, & Cox, 1985), but the causal direction of such a relationship is unclear. That is, divorced mothers' more permissive conceptions of parental authority may lead to more ineffectual control or, alternatively, divorced mothers' inability (or unwillingness) to discipline their sons may lead to more permissive conceptions of parental authority. Regardless of the causal direction, it appears that these judgments and behaviors have negative outcomes because other research has demonstrated that boys from divorced families show more externalizing and deviant behavior and less social competence than boys from nondivorced families, even long after divorce (Dornbusch et al., 1985; Hetherington et al., 1985). Thus, the interrelations between judgments and actions bear further examination, preferably in longitudinal research.

Several limitations of this study should be noted. First, the divorced sample was small, especially when considered in terms of adolescents' age and sex. Thus, the interactions between age and sex within the divorced sample need to be interpreted cautiously because these results may not replicate in a larger sample. Furthermore, the response rate was low, particularly among the married families. Although this might have biased the sample toward better functioning families, it is not clear how such sampling biases would affect family members' conceptions of parental authority. Also, the divorced sample included only unremarried, mother-custody families. In future research, conceptions of parental authority should be examined in different family arrangements, including unremarried father-custody families and in stepparent and reconstituted families. In addition, adolescents' and parents' conceptions of parental authority should be examined longitudinally through the process of separation and divorce to determine whether these conceptions are related to parenting behaviors or children's adjustment following divorce and whether they contribute to (or are consequences of) differences in family functioning in divorced as compared with married families. Finally, as others have noted, there is a need for more research on adolescents of varying SESs and ethnicities (Hill, 1987; Steinberg, 1990).

The results of this study also need to be interpreted cautiously because there might have been some overlap in the tasks used here. For instance, judgments of the legitimacy and contingency of acts on parental authority may not be completely independent. Thus, further research on adolescents' and parents' conceptions of parental authority should use a broader range of tasks that tap different aspects of subjects' judgments. Nevertheless, the findings of this study are consistent with the view that conceptions of parental authority should be considered according to the domain in which authority is exerted (Smetana, 1988a). Furthermore, they underscore the importance of examining contextual influences on development. Turiel, Smetana, and Killen (1991) have proposed that social contexts can be logically analyzed in the same way as social judgments and that it is necessary to consider their interaction in accounting for development in different "ecological niches" (e.g., Steinberg, Mounts, Lamborn, & Dornbusch, 1991). Such an approach proved fruitful here. As expected, divorced and married families did not differ in their judgments of moral or conventional issues, but family structure differences were found in adolescents' and mothers' evaluations of multifaceted and personal issues, and these differences were consistent with previous research on the effects of divorce on families with adolescents. The results of this study suggest that research examining the boundaries between familial conventions and adolescents' personal jurisdiction, and the behavioral implications for adolescent autonomy, might be a particularly profitable avenue for future research.

ACKNOWLEDGMENTS

This research was supported by National Institute of Mental Health Grant RO1-39142.

I thank the many families who participated in this research and the principals and teachers of the Brighton School District for their assistance in recruiting families. I am also grateful to Roberta Paikoff, Marie Tisak, and Elliot Turiel for their comments on an earlier version of this article.

REFERENCES

Anderson, E. R., Hetherington, E. M., & Clingempeel, W. G. (1989). Transformations in family relations at puberty: Effects of family context. *Journal of Early Adolescence, 9*, 310–334.

Baumrind, D. (1989, May). *Sex-differentiated socialization effects in childhood and adolescence in divorced and intact families.* Paper presented at the biennial meetings of the Society for Research in Child Development, Kansas City, MO.

Davidson, P., Turiel, E., & Black, A. (1983). The effect of stimulus familiarity on the use of criteria and justifications in children's social reasoning. *British Journal of Developmental Psychology, 1*, 49–65.

Dornbusch, S. M., Carlsmith, J. M., Bushwall, S. J., Ritter, P. L., Leiderman, H., Hastorf, A. H., & Gross, R. T. (1985). Single-parents, extended households, and control of adolescents. *Child Development, 56*, 326–341.

Dworkin, R. (1978). *Taking rights seriously.* Cambridge, MA: Harvard University Press.

Flanagan, C. (1987, April). *Parent–child decision making, curfew, and closeness in single-parent, married, and remarried families.* Paper presented at the biennial meetings of the Society for Research on Child Development, Baltimore, MD.

Gewirth, A. (1978). *Reason and morality.* Chicago: University of Chicago Press.

Gewirth, A. (1982). *Human rights: Essays on justification and applications.* Chicago: University of Chicago Press.

Goodnow, J. J. (1988). Parents' ideas, actions, and feelings: Models and methods from developmental and social psychology. *Child Development, 59*, 286–320.

Hetherington, E. M. (1989). Coping with family transition: Winners, losers, and survivors. *Child Development, 60*, 1–14.

Hetherington, E. M., Cox, M., & Cox, R. (1985). Long-term effects of divorce and remarriage on the adjustment of children. *Journal of the American Academy of Child Psychiatry, 24*, 518–530.

Hetherington, E. M., Stanley-Hagan, M., & Anderson, E. R. (1989). Marital transitions: A child's perspective. *American Psychologist, 44*, 303–312.

Hill, J. P. (1987). Research on adolescents and their families: Past and prospect. In C. Irwin (Ed.), *New directions for child development: Adolescent social behavior and health* (pp. 13–32). San Francisco: Jossey-Bass.

Hollingshead, A. B. (1977). *Four factor index of social status.* Unpublished manuscript, Yale University, New Haven, CT.

Laupa, M. (1991). Children's reasoning about three authority attributes: Adult status, knowledge, and social position. *Developmental Psychology, 27*, 321–329.

Laupa, M., & Turiel, E. (1986). Children's conceptions of adult and peer authority. *Child Development, 57*, 405–412.

Nucci, L. (1981). The development of personal concepts: A domain distinct from moral or societal concepts. *Child Development, 52*, 114–121.

Nucci, L., Guerra, N., & Lee, J. (1991). Adolescent judgments of the personal, prudential, and normative aspects of drug usage. *Developmental Psychology, 27*, 841–848.

Nucci, L., & Lee, J. (1990, July). *Morality and personal autonomy.* Paper presented at the Third International Ringberg Conference on morality and the self, Ringberg, Bavaria, Federal Republic of Germany.

Nucci, L., & Smetana, J. G. (1992). *Mothers' reasoning about children's personal issues.* Manuscript in preparation.

Nucci, L., & Weber, E. (1991). *Mothers' conceptions of personal issues.* Paper presented at the biennial meetings of the Society for Research in Child Development, Seattle, WA.

Santrock, J. W., Warshak, R., Lindbergh, C., & Meadows, L. (1982). Children's and parents' observed social behavior in stepfather families. *Child Development, 53,* 472–480.

Smetana, J. G. (1981a). Preschool children's conceptions of moral and social rules. *Child Development, 52,* 1333–1336.

Smetana, J. G. (1981b). Reasoning in the personal and moral domains: Adolescent and young adult women's decision making regarding abortion. *Journal of Applied Developmental Psychology, 2,* 211–226.

Smetana, J. G. (1983). Social-cognitive development: Domain distinctions and coordinations. *Developmental Review, 3,* 131–147.

Smetana, J. G. (1985). Preschool children's conceptions of transgressions: The effects of varying moral and conventional domain-related attributes. *Developmental Psychology, 21,* 18–29.

Smetana, J. G. (1988a). Adolescents' and parents' conceptions of parental authority. *Child Development, 59,* 321–335.

Smetana, J. G. (1988b). Concepts of self and social convention: Adolescents' and parents' reasoning about hypothetical and actual family conflicts. In M. R. Gunnar & W. A. Collins (Eds.), *21st Minnesota Symposium on Child Psychology: Development during the transition to adolescence* (pp. 79–122). Hillsdale, NJ: Lawrence Erlbaum Associates, Inc.

Smetana, J. G. (1989). Adolescents' and parents' reasoning about actual family conflict. *Child Development, 60,* 1052–1067.

Smetana, J. G., Yau, J., Restrepo, A., & Braeges, J. (1991). Adolescent–parent conflict in married and divorced families. *Developmental Psychology, 27,* 1000–1010.

Steinberg, L. (1990). Interdependency in the family: Autonomy, conflict, and harmony in the parent–adolescent relationship. In S. S. Feldman & G. R. Elliot (Eds.), *At the threshold: The developing adolescent* (pp. 255–276). Cambridge, MA: Harvard University Press.

Steinberg, L., Mounts, N. S., Lamborn, S. D., & Dornbusch, S. M. (1991). Authoritative parenting and adolescent adjustment across varied ecological niches. *Journal of Research on Adolescence, 1,* 19–36.

Steinberg, L., & Silverberg, S. B. (1986). The vicissitudes of autonomy in early adolescence. *Child Development, 57,* 841–851.

Tisak, M. (1986). Children's conceptions of parental authority. *Child Development, 57,* 166–176.

Tisak, M. (in press). Preschool children's judgments of moral and personal events involving physical harm and property damage. *Merrill-Palmer Quarterly.*

Tisak, M., & Tisak, J. (1990). Children's conceptions of parental authority, friendship, and sibling relations. *Merrill-Palmer Quarterly, 36,* 347–367.

Tisak, M., & Turiel, E. (1984). Children's reasoning about moral and prudential events. *Child Development, 55,* 1030–1039.

Turiel, E. (1979). Distinct conceptual and developmental domains: Social convention and morality. In C. B. Keasey (Ed.), *1978 Nebraska Symposium on Motivation* (pp. 77–116). Lincoln: University of Nebraska Press.

Turiel, E. (1983). *The development of social knowledge: Morality and convention.* Cambridge, England: Cambridge University Press.

Turiel, E., & Davidson, P. (1986). Heterogeneity, inconsistency, and asynchrony in the development of cognitive structures. In I. Levin (Ed.), *Stage and structure: Reopening the debate* (pp. 106–143). Norwood, NJ: Ablex.

Turiel, E., Killen, M., & Helwig, C. C. (1987). Morality: Its structure, function, and vagaries. In J. Kagan & S. Lamb (Eds)., *The emergence of morality in young children* (pp. 155-243). Chicago: University of Chicago Press.

Turiel, E., Smetana, J. G., & Killen, M. (1991). Social contexts in social cognitive development. In J. L. Gewirtz & W. M. Kurtines (Eds.), *Moral behavior and development: Advances in theory, research, and applications* (pp. 307-332). Hillsdale, NJ: Lawrence Erlbaum Associates, Inc.

Weiss, R. S. (1979). Growing up a little faster: The experience of growing up in a single-parent household. *Journal of Social Issues, 35,* 97-111.

Winer, B. T. (1971). *Statistical principles in experimental design.* New York: McGraw-Hill.

Zaslow, M. J. (1988). Sex differences in children's response to parental divorce: 1. Research methodology and postdivorce family forms. *American Journal of Orthopsychiatry, 58,* 355-378.

Received September 25, 1991
Revision received March 18, 1992
Accepted October 21, 1992

Developmental Psychology
1985. Vol. 21, No. 6, 1157–1164

Maternal Role Satisfaction, Mother–Child Interaction, and Child Temperament: A Process Model

Jacqueline V. Lerner
The Pennsylvania State University

Nancy L. Galambos
The Pennsylvania State University and Technical
University of Berlin

Using data from the New York Longitudinal Study, this study tested the hypothesis that the relation between maternal role satisfaction and child adjustment is mediated by the quality of the mother–child relationship. Using the child's temperamental difficulty as an index of adjustment, results of several path analyses indicated that mothers who were dissatisfied with their roles showed more rejection of the child, and in turn, had more difficult children. These results illustrate the use of a process model in the explanation of the relation between maternal role satisfaction and child development.

Among the most dramatic demographic changes that have taken place in the United States over the past quarter century, and especially during the past 10 years, is the increase in maternal employment. Paralleling this increase has been scientific interest in how this phenomenon influences the development of children. Recent reviews indicate that maternal employment has few consistent effects on child development (Bronfenbrenner & Crouter, 1982; Lamb, 1982), and both scientists and policymakers conclude that the experience of maternal employment is not the same for everyone (Crouter, Belsky, & Spanier, 1984). As such, a differentiated analysis of maternal employment influences, one that considers mediating processes, is required.

In this study we focus on one construct that has been emphasized most as mediating between maternal employment and child development: maternal role satisfaction. Findings from the early studies of Yarrow, Scott, de Leeuw, and Heinig (1962) and Hoffman (1963) converge with more recent studies in suggesting that a mother's satisfaction with her role, whether she is employed or not, has positive

effects on her children. In contrast, dissatisfaction is associated with negative effects on children. For example, in elementary school children and adolescents, research findings show that congruence between the mother's attitude and her employment status is associated with such positive child outcomes as better personality adjustment and more egalitarian sex role concepts (Baruch, 1972; Gold & Andres, 1978; Pearlman, 1981; Williamson, 1970; Woods, 1972).

Research with infants and preschoolers also points to maternal role satisfaction as a critical variable in predicting aspects of the child's behavior. Hock (1980), for example, observed 12-month-old infants after brief separations from their mother and encounters with a stranger in a laboratory. She found that infants with mothers whose beliefs about the infant's need for exclusive maternal care were incongruent with the mother's work status were less likely to maintain proximity with the mother during the stressful laboratory situation and showed signs of conflict on reunion with the mother. In addition, Farel (1980) reported that the most poorly adjusted children were those who had mothers who did not work but wanted to. Specifically, there was no relation between the mother's work status and school adjustment and competence; however, incongruence between mother's attitude and her work status was related to lower competence in the child.

Because the above findings converge in suggesting that maternal role satisfaction is linked more directly to child outcomes than is moth-

Jacqueline V. Lerner's work on this article was supported in part by grants from the John D. and Catherine T. MacArthur Foundation and the W. T. Grant Foundation.
The authors thank Richard M. Lerner for his critical reading of an earlier version of this article.
Reprint requests should be sent to Jacqueline V. Lerner at the College of Human Development, The Pennsylvania State University, University Park, Pennsylvania 16802.

251

er's work status per se, many researchers have begun to speculate about what underlying process may account for the positive child outcomes associated with mother's role satisfaction. Many writers suggest that the process of influence is one in which role satisfaction leads to positive parenting, which in turn, enhances child development. For example, Stuckey, McGhee, and Bell (1982), found that incongruence between attitudes and maternal employment status is related to *parent* behaviors. Specifically, they report that for a sample of preschoolers, both mothers and fathers were more likely to exhibit negative behaviors toward their children when the parents' attitudes were not congruent with the mother's work status. Thus, some studies have linked role satisfaction directly to child development outcomes (Farel, 1980; Gold & Andres, 1978; Hock, 1978, 1980; Hoffman, 1963; Williamson, 1970; Woods, 1972), whereas others link role satisfaction to parental functioning (Stuckey et al., 1982; Yarrow et al., 1962). Thus, given these findings, it is plausible to posit the existence of a process of influence model, one which has two components: (a) The quality of the mother–child relationship is influenced by maternal role satisfaction; (b) The quality of the mother–child relationship has an impact on the child's development.

Why does role satisfaction affect the mother–child relationship? Lamb, Chase-Lansdale, and Owen (1979) propose that role satisfaction leads to self-fulfillment and to the enhancement of self-esteem in the mother, qualities that lead her to be a more sensitive mother. Maternal sensitivity and responsiveness to an infant's cues are important dimensions of a high-quality mother–child relationship. Differences in aspects of the mother–child relationship other than maternal responsiveness have also been linked to role satisfaction. For example, Warr and Parry (1982) find a general mood difference in employed mothers who are happy or unhappy·with their job situations. They have found strong relations among working class women of the United Kingdom between employed mothers' overall attitudes to their job and measures of positive and negative affect and life satisfaction. Mood differences may indeed become evident in parent–child interactions, as Stuckey et al. (1982) found differences in parental affect expression

according to attitude–employment congruence. Thus, there is evidence that maternal role satisfaction is exhibited in the kinds of interactions between mothers and their children. This is the first part of a "process of influence" model.

Evidence for the remaining part of this process of influence model stems from research that links positive parenting to child outcomes. The area of literature that lends the most support to the notion that positive mother–child relationships lead to enhanced child development is research on attachment. Although most work on attachment has not specifically addressed what the developmental antecedents of various forms of attachment may be (Lamb, Thompson, Gardner, Charnov, & Estes, 1984), statements have emerged that link secure infant–mother attachment with the mother's sensitive responsiveness to the infant's signals and communications (Ainsworth, Blehar, Waters, & Wall, 1978). Secure attachment is viewed as an indication of positive child functioning, therefore, and is thought to be mediated by the mother's sensitivity to the infant, a positive aspect of parenting.

Although the above findings show evidence for the pieces of this model, they fail to specify and document a process of influence linking maternal role satisfaction, mother–child interaction, and child outcomes. We attempt such an integration in this study and, as such, test through path analytic procedures the hypothesis that role satisfaction is related to mother–child interaction and, in turn, to child development.

The feature of child development focused on in the present study is the Thomas and Chess (1977) notion of temperamental difficulty. Temperament is defined by Thomas and Chess as the "style of behavior," not *what* a child does, but *how* he or she goes about doing it. For example, all children eat, sleep, and play; however, some do these things regularly, with a lot of activity, and with a negative mood; other children may be irregular, have low activity, and positive moods. The focus on temperament is taken because Thomas and Chess (1977) found that the particular characteristics defining a "difficult temperament" (negative mood, frequent withdrawal, low rhythmicity, low adaptability, and high intensity responses) were emblematic of child adjustment difficulties in the sample of children who participated in their New York Longitudinal Study (NYLS). It was this sample that was used in the present research.

Thomas and Chess (1977) have maintained that when the child's temperamental characteristics do not "fit" parental demands for temperament, adjustment problems are likely to result. They propose that a given set of temperamental characteristics should not be predictive of adjustment problems when these characteristics provide a "goodness of fit" with environmental demands. Indeed, Korn (1978) has demonstrated that in an independent lower class Puerto Rican sample, some of the attributes of the "difficult" child "fit" parental demands and these "fit" children showed no evidence of adjustment difficulties. However, in the white upper middle-class sample of the NYLS, parental demands were quite different. Although Thomas and Chess did not measure demands directly, the interview data they collected revealed that parents of the NYLS children demanded temperamental styles that were "easy"—showing high rhythmicity of biological functions, positive mood, low to moderate intensity of reactions, positive approach behaviors in new situations, and rapid adaptability. Indeed, most of the "easy" children of the NYLS sample did not develop behavior problems, whereas most of the "difficult" children did (Thomas, Chess, & Birch, 1968). It is for this reason that we used "difficult" temperament as an index of poor adjustment.

Method

Sample

The subjects for this study were part of a sample of those parents and children who have participated in the NYLS from the child's early infancy. The NYLS was initiated in 1956 by Thomas and Chess, and is continuing at this time. The major sample is composed of 133 children (66 males, 67 females). For the present study, complete data existed for 89 subjects (48 males, 41 females). Fifty-one of the subjects were from nonemployed mother families, and 38 subjects were from employed mother families. The families of this sample are of middle- to upper middle-class backgrounds and are 78% Jewish, 7% Catholic, and 15% Protestant, with 40% of the mothers and 60% of the fathers having both college educations and postgraduate degrees. Ninety-eight percent of the nonworking mothers and 84% of the working mothers were from intact families. Although twice as many employed mothers held postgraduate degrees, another recent study with this sample, by

Galambos and Lerner (1985), revealed that mother's educational level was not predictive of the likelihood of her being employed.

The prestige of the father's occupations was similar for both samples, with most fathers holding highly prestigious jobs (e.g., medical doctors, university professors). In turn, there was considerable homogeneity in the socioeconomic status of the total sample (middle to upper middle class). It is likely, therefore, that the employed mothers were employed for reasons of personal fulfillment. We are aware of the fact that the homogeneity of our sample limits the generalizability of the results to other groups of lower SES, where many mothers may be employed for reasons of economic need. However, all major, long-term longitudinal studies in the United States have nonrepresentative samples (e.g., the Berkeley/Oakland data sets, the Fels data set), and although sampling bias may impose limitations in making generalizations about mean levels or possibly, variability, it does not necessarily constrain generalizations about structural patterns within or across time (Jessor, 1982). In this regard, Eichorn (1984) indicated that no finding derived from a major longitudinal study has been concluded to be incorrect on the basis of subsequent cross-sectional research with more representative samples. Thus, we believe that the homogeneity of our sample should not preclude our ability to discern the processes by which mothers' role satisfaction influences child development.

Procedure

The characteristics of this sample and the methods used throughout the study are detailed in several previous publications (e.g., Chess & Thomas, 1984; Thomas, Chess, Birch, Hertzig, & Korn, 1963; Thomas et al., 1968; Thomas & Chess, 1977, 1980). We present here an overview of those features of the NYLS methods that are relevant to the present study.

Beginning in the first month of the child's life, the parents were interviewed periodically (about every 3 months) for the first 2 years, and every 6 months until age 5, after which they were interviewed in adolescence and young adulthood. The interviews concerned the child's behaviors and functioning in several content areas (e.g., sleeping, eating, social behaviors, school behaviors). In the early months, interviews were approximately 1 hr in length and increased as the child got older and entered new domains of functioning. An emphasis on obtaining descriptions of actual behaviors rather than subjective parental ratings of the child was maintained throughout the interviews. Parents were also asked about any problems that the child displayed in the following areas: eating, fears, relationships with parents and siblings, school difficulties, motor problems, discipline, and school and social functioning. These regular interviews were the source for the temperament ratings. The techniques used to derive the temperament scores are described below.

Here, however, it is important to note that when the child was approximately 3 years of age the mothers and fathers in the sample were interviewed for approximately 3 hr about their child care practices, parental and spousal roles, and the effects of the child on them and the family. Each parent was interviewed and audiotaped independently by two interviewers who had no exposure to data already gathered. The semi-structured interview sought to obtain information pertinent to parental permissiveness, consistency of rules, and discipline strategies. In addition, a portion of the interview was devoted to discussing the mother's employment situation, feelings about working, father's support of the mother working, and other supports in the home that help the mother to fulfill her role obligations (e.g., availability of child care or household help). It is primarily from this interview that the maternal and mother–child interaction variables used in this study were obtained. However, in the few cases where detailed interviews were not conducted and variables could not be obtained directly, data from other maternal interviews (e.g., the interviews conducted by Thomas and Chess at regular intervals) were used.

We realize that the issue of common method variance may be raised because all of the variables we use are taken from maternal interviews. Direct observations of mother–child interaction would have provided us with a relatively unbiased measure of this interaction. Our use of data collected 25 years ago precluded the possibility of obtaining direct observational measures. However, we should note that throughout the NYLS, Thomas and Chess have put a strong emphasis on obtaining descriptions of behaviors rather than subjective opinions by parents. It is these descriptions that are then used by objective raters to code variables of interest. In addition, we believe that there are several advantages to using parental interviews. As Maccoby and Martin (1983) have noted, a child's behavior varies widely across situations, and some behaviors are not publicly displayed. The parent, therefore, becomes the source for this kind of information. Moreover, although Maccoby and Martin (1983) caution us about the unreliability of parental reports of retrospective information, we should note that in this study we have used the maternal interviews to obtain only concurrent information about the mother and about mother–child interaction.

Development of the Coding Protocol

In order to obtain data regarding maternal role satisfaction and the mother's employment situation from the 3-year-interviews, a coding protocol was developed by the authors. Based on recent reviews of the literature (e.g., Zaslow, Rabinovich, & Suwalsky, 1983), we outlined first what are regarded as important domains of the mother's employment and family situation. Thus, we included items to measure aspects of the mother's work situation, for example, the type of job held and the flexibility of work hours. We obtained information regarding the mother's employment status during each of the child's first five years (not employed, employed part-time, employed full-time). Additional items included information about child care and household help, father's participation in child care and housework, and mother's satisfaction with child care and household help. Last, we rated the mother's perceived role strain and role satisfaction.

The protocol was given to five researchers and graduate students in human development and was discussed with them regarding face validity. Changes were made based on their suggestions. The next step in the process was a training session with four raters (the authors and two students) in which the protocols were discussed and completed for two of the actual mother interviews. Individual raters proceeded to listen to the remaining audiotaped interviews and rated them.

After the tapes were rated, 20% were chosen in order to determine interrater reliabilities. Reliabilities for the items ranged from .88 to .98. Following are more detailed descriptions of the items used in the present study.

Maternal role satisfaction. One item of the coding protocol asked raters to assess the mothers "feelings about being an employed mother or not." The possible responses ranged on a 5-point-scale from *strongly negative* (1) to *ambivalent* (3) to *strongly positive* (5). The interrater reliability for this item was .89.

Mother–child interaction. The scores relevant to mother–child interaction that were used in the present study were obtained from the above-described 3-year maternal interviews and were established in previous research with the NYLS data set. That is, Cameron (1977) selected 70 items pertaining to parenting practices and entered them into a cluster analysis using the Tryon and Baily (1966) system. Eight oblique parental clusters resulted from the 70-item matrix; three of these are used here because they most clearly resemble constructs used in other studies of role satisfaction. These three are as follows: (a) Rejection—the mother's tolerance for and disapproval of the child; (b) Limit setting—the degree of restrictiveness and strictness of discipline when dealing with the child; and (c) Inconsistency—the consistency with which the child is disciplined. Scores were standardized with a mean of 50 and a standard deviation of 10. Factor scores were computed by the "simple sum" method: the standardization of the sums of the defining items were divided by the number of items with nonmissing data.

The rejection cluster was made up of six items pertaining to the mother's tolerance and feelings for the child, her approval of the child, and the quality of the mother–child relationship. A high score on this factor indicates high bias and intolerance toward the child and a high amount of rejection. These scores ranged from 38 to 83 with a M of 48.83 and a SD of 9.33.

The limit-setting cluster was made up of three items pertaining to parental permissiveness and discipline. A high score on this factor indicates strict discipline on the part of the mother. Scores for this factor ranged from 30 to 77, with a M of 50.03 and a SD of 10.08.

The inconsistency cluster was made up of two items that pertained to the consistency/inconsistency in disciplining the child. Scores on this factor ranged from 40 to 92, with a M of 49.7 and a SD of 7.9.

As is true for all eight clusters from the Cameron (1977) ratings, the three we used had quite low interscale correlations. For example, rejection had a $-.08$ correlation with limit-setting and a .34 correlation with inconsistency, and limit-setting had a $-.16$ correlation with inconsistency. Such low intercorrelations indicate the absence of any general response bias or halo effect operating in the ratings used. The validity of these ratings are supported by data reported by Cameron (1977), which indicate that rejecting mothers tended to have daughters who were significantly ($p < .05$) less persistent and active in their reactions and had higher thresholds for responsiveness. In addition there was a significant ($p < .05$) relationship between sons' adaptability and maternal rejection, indicating that the more rejecting mothers had sons who were slow at adapting. Cameron (1977) also reported that characteristics of negative mood and high intensity of reactions were present in the daughters of inconsistent mothers. Low rhythmicity was also associated with inconsistency in both sons and daughters in the first 2 years of life. In terms of the limit-setting dimension, sons of highly strict parents were more adaptable at age 2, but at age 5 the opposite relation emerges. Among daughters, low persistence was related to high parental strictness.

Temperament. Each subject's temperament or behavioral style was measured at ages 2 and 4 for each of the following dimensions: activity level (the amount of motor activity present in a child's functioning); rhythmicity (the regularity of a child's functions such as sleep–wake cycles, hunger, feeding patterns or elimination); approach/withdrawal (the nature of the initial response to a new stimulus); adaptability (the ease with which the child adjusts to new or altered situations); threshold of responsiveness (the intensity level of stimulation needed to evoke a response); intensity of reaction (the energy level of a response, irrespective of its quality or direction); quality of mood (the amount of pleasant or unpleasant behavior); distractibility (the effectiveness of extraneous stimuli in interfering with or altering the direction of the ongoing behavior); and attention span/persistence (attention span refers to the length of time a child pursues a particular activity; persistence refers to the continuance of an activity in the face of obstacles).

Temperament scores were obtained for each subject by rating the descriptions of behavior contained in the parental interviews for Years 2 and 4. Multiple interviews were used at each age, and scores were generated by Thomas and Chess (1977). The usefulness of these ratings has been documented in previous research using the NYLS data set (e.g., Chess & Thomas, 1984; Thomas et al., 1963, 1968). In addition to receiving a score on each of the nine characteristics of temperament listed above, each subject received a "difficulty" score. The signs of the Difficult Child (Thomas & Chess, 1977) are low rhythmicity, low adaptability, withdrawal responses, negative mood, and high intensity of reactions. Each subject's scores on these five attributes made up a "difficulty" score (a low score was indicative of an "easy" temperament, and a high score was indicative of a "difficult" temperament); it was this score that was used in the present analyses. Information pertinent to the reliability and validity of the temperament ratings have been reported by Thomas et al. (1963) and Thomas and Chess (1977). For example, interrater agreements for the temperament categories from birth to age two were 90%. In addition, temperament ratings during the same age span were related to direct observational data ($p < .01$). Because of our interest in the antecedent–consequent relation between role satisfaction and child difficulty, we made use of the longitudinal nature of the data set and chose to use child difficulty at Age 4 as our outcome measure.

Analyses

Figure 1 details our "process" model of the relation between maternal role satisfaction and a child temperament. To test our proposed "process of influence" model we investigated, through the use of path analytic models, the relation among early child difficulty (Age 2), maternal role satisfaction, mother–child in-

teraction (rejection, limit-setting, and inconsistency), and later child difficulty (Age 4). Path analysis appeared to be well-suited to the problem under investigation and the nature of the data. That is, previous research indicated a plausible causal ordering of variables that could be specified a priori and tested using the NYLS data. The model in Figure 1 is a just-identified recursive model. Specifically, the number of correlations between the observed variables is equal to the number of paths in the model. Moreover, the number of subjects per variable is over 10 for the total and nonemployed samples and just under 10 for the employed sample; these ratios correspond to the one frequently recommended in the literature. In addition, the reliability of the measures was acceptable, and the variables exhibited no multicollinearity, thus meeting several other assumptions of path analysis (Kenny, 1979; Schumm, Southerby, & Figley, 1980).

Because of the longitudinal nature of the data set, we were able to include an early measure of child difficulty (Age 2) in order to investigate the effect that the child's early temperament may have on the mother's role satisfaction and on later child difficulty (Age 4). Furthermore, the inclusion of this "difficulty" measure at Age 2 enabled us to investigate possible bidirectional effects of the child on the mother and the mother on the child. That is, we wanted to explore the notion that the mother's satisfaction influences her interactions with her child and her child's subsequent adjustment and that the child (in this case, his or her "difficulty") can exert an equally strong influence on the mother's satisfaction. Maternal role satisfaction was only measured at Age 3, because it was derived from the detailed 3-year parental interviews.

It was hypothesized that a stronger relation would exist for the indirect path—from role satisfaction → mother–child interaction → child difficulty (Age 4)—than for the direct paths—of child difficulty (Age 2) → child difficulty (Age 4); role satisfaction → child difficulty; early child difficulty → role satisfaction; or early child difficulty → mother–child interaction. Preliminary analyses revealed that two of the mother–child interaction measures, limit-setting and inconsistency, did not bear any relation to the outcome measure of child difficulty. Maternal rejection, however, was re-

1162   JACQUELINE V. LERNER AND NANCY L. GALAMBOS

lated to the outcome, and, therefore, it was retained for use in the final analysis.

A path analytic model was tested that included the direct paths from child difficulty (Age 2) → role satisfaction; child difficulty (Age 2) → child difficulty (Age 4); role satisfaction (Age 3) → child difficulty (Age 4); and child difficulty (Age 2) → maternal rejection (Age 3); the tested model included, too, the indirect path of role satisfaction (Age 3) → maternal rejection (Age 3) → child difficulty (Age 4). This model was tested using the total sample ($N = 89$), the nonemployed mother sample ($N = 51$), and the employed mother sample ($N = 38$) separately.

Results

Consistent with the hypothesis, for the total sample the direct paths were insignificant, but the indirect path of role satisfaction → maternal rejection → child difficulty was significant. Figure 1 presents the models for the total sample, for the nonemployed mother sample, and for the employed mother sample, with their respective path coefficients and significance levels. As seen in the figure, neither early child difficulty nor mother's role satisfaction was significantly related to later child difficulty; nor was early child difficulty related to role satisfaction or maternal rejection. However, role

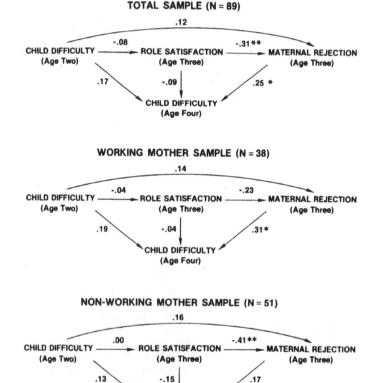

Figure 1. Path models and coefficients for the direct and mediated relationships between maternal role satisfaction and child temperament.

256

satisfaction was significantly related to maternal rejection, and maternal rejection was significantly related to later child difficulty. When the nonemployed mother group and the employed mother groups were tested separately, the same trends emerged; however, in the nonemployed sample only the path coefficient from role satisfaction to maternal rejection reached significance, and in the employed sample only the path coefficient from maternal rejection to child difficulty (Age 4) reached significance. In each case, however, the coefficients for the indirect path were greater than any of the coefficients for the direct paths, indicating that the smaller sample sizes may be responsible for the insignificant coefficients.[1]

Discussion

In this article we presented a "process" model of maternal employment influences, using longitudinal data from the NYLS. Our results lend support to the notion that the relation between maternal role satisfaction and child outcomes may be mediated by a third factor—that of mother–child interaction. Researchers (Hock, 1980; Hoffman, 1963; Zaslow et al., 1983) have speculated that maternal role satisfaction leads to more positive mother–child interactions that, in turn, enhance child development. Our analyses of the NYLS data demonstrate that neither early child difficulty nor role satisfaction significantly relates to later difficulty; however, highly dissatisifed mothers have high levels of rejection and, in turn, more difficult children. At least for the present sample then, a process-of-influence model that links maternal role satisfaction → parent–child interaction → child development finds some support. In addition, mothers who were highly satisfied with their roles, whether they were working or not, displayed higher levels of warmth and acceptance than did dissatisfied mothers. Our results suggest that the mother's satisfaction with her role, employed or not, influences her relationship with her child. This relationship, in turn, may influence her child's subsequent development.

We should point out here that the NYLS is a very homogeneous sample; therefore our results may not be generalizable across race and socioeconomic class. In addition, the data were collected in an era when social attitudes toward employed women were generally quite different than they are today. We recognize that these attitudes could have influenced these mothers' feelings and their interactions with their children. Unfortunately, these influences were not directly measured, and we have no way of assessing their impact. In addition, the relations found in the present study could have been the result of other, unmeasured factors. However, we should emphasize that the opportunity to examine maternal employment influences in *any* longitudinal data set is rare. Thus, if the process model that we are forwarding can be supported in more current data sets—if it can be demonstrated that this model depicts the way in which maternal role satisfaction functions to influence child development—support will thereby be provided for the existence of the idea that a historically *general* process of human development describes the relation between maternal role satisfaction and child development in the early childhood years. In sum, our results suggest that research aimed at determining what factors influence child development, be it maternal employment research or otherwise, need to focus on the parent–child relationships and what variables affect that relationship.

---

[1] It should be noted that these analyses involve separately comparing whether each of three potential paths differ significantly from the null hypothesis. Although this test of competing paths is representative of procedures conventionally employed in the literature, other types of statistical tests are possible. For instance, one can test whether one path significantly differs from another (in this case, whether the indirect paths significantly differ from the direct path), as opposed to whether each separately differs from zero. However, such tests are not ordinarily feasible in *extant* major longitudinal research, given that exceedingly more power is needed to discriminate a significant difference between two correlations than to test whether a single correlation is significantly different from zero (e.g., Cohen, 1977). For example, given an expected effect size of .30, the N required to ascertain if a single correlation is significantly different from zero is approximately 90. However, an N of approximately 400 would have to exist to test for the significance of the difference between two correlations given an expected difference size of .20 (a difference that we would expect to be present in our data). The latter N is not one found in the major extant American long-term longitudinal studies (Kagan, 1964).

References

Ainsworth, M. D. S., Blehar, M. C., Waters, E., & Wall, S. (1978). *Patterns of attachment.* Hillsdale, NJ: Erlbaum.

Baruch, G. K. (1972). Maternal influences upon college women's attitudes toward women and work. *Developmental Psychology, 6,* 32–37.

Bronfenbrenner, U., & Crouter, A. C. (1982). Work and family through time and space. In S. B. Kamerman & C. D. Hayes (Eds.), *Families that work: Children in a changing world* (pp. 39–83). Washington, DC: National Academy of Sciences.

Cameron, J. R. (1977). Parental treatment, children's temperament, and the risk of childhood behavioral problems: 1. Relationships between parental characteristics and changes in children's temperament over time. *American Journal of Orthopsychiatry, 47,* 568–576.

Chess, S., & Thomas, A. (1984). *Origins and evolution of behavior disorders.* New York: Brunner/Mazel.

Cohen, J. (1977). *Statistical power analysis for the behavioral sciences.* New York: Academic Press.

Crouter, A. C., Belsky, J., & Spanier, G. B. (1984). The family context of child development: Divorce and maternal employment. In G. Whitehurst (Ed.), *The annals of child development.* Greenwich, CT: JAI Press.

Eichorn, D. (1984, October). Comments made at the Radcliffe Conference on "The use of archival data to study women's lives." Cambridge, MA.

Farel, A. N. (1980). Effects of preferred maternal roles, maternal employment, and sociographic status on school adjustment and competence. *Child Development, 50,* 1179–1186.

Galambos, N. L., & Lerner, J. V. (1985). *Child characteristics and the employment of mothers with young children: A longitudinal study.* Unpublished manuscript, The Pennsylvania State University.

Gold, D., & Andres, D. (1978). Developmental comparisons between ten year old children with employed and nonemployed mothers. *Child Development, 49,* 75–84.

Hock, E. (1978). Working and nonworking mothers with infants: Perceptions of their careers, their infants' needs, and satisfaction with mothering. *Developmental Psychology, 14,* 37–43.

Hock, E. (1980). Working and nonworking mothers and their infants: A comparative study of maternal caregiving characteristics and infant social behavior. *Merrill-Palmer Quarterly, 26,* 79–101.

Hoffman, L. W. (1963). Mother's enjoyment of work and effects on the child. In F. I. Nye & L. W. Hoffman (Eds.), *The employed mother in America* (pp. 95–105). Chicago: Rand McNally.

Jessor, R. (1982, December). *Psychosocial development in adolescence: Continuities with young adulthood.* Paper presented at Social Science Research Council Subcommittee on "Child Development in Life-Span Perspective" Conference on "Pubertal and Psychosocial Change." Tucson, AZ.

Kagan, J. (1964). American longitudinal research on psychological development. *Child Development, 35,* 1–32.

Kenny, D. A. (1979). *Correlation and causality.* New York: Wiley.

Korn, S. J. (1978). *Temperament, vulnerability, and behavior.* Paper presented at the Louisville Temperament Conference, Louisville, Kentucky, September.

Lamb, M. E. (1982). Maternal employment and child development: A review. In M. E. Lamb (Ed.), *Nontraditional families: Parenting and child development* (pp. 45–69). Hillsdale, NJ: Erlbaum.

Lamb, M. E., Chase-Lansdale, L., & Owen, M. T. (1979). The changing American family and its implications for infant social development: The sample case of maternal employment. In M. Lewis & L. A. Rosenblum (Eds.), *The child and its family* (pp. 267–291). New York: Plenum Press.

Lamb, M. E., Thompson, R. A., Gardner, W. P., Charnov, E. L., & Estes, D. (1984). Security on infantile attachment as assessed in the "strange situation": Its study and biological interpretation. *The Behavioral and Brain Sciences, 7,* 127–171.

Maccoby, E. E., & Martin, J. A. (1983). Socialization in the context of the family: Parent-child interaction. In E. M. Hetherington (Ed.), *Handbook of child psychology: Vol. 4. Socialization, personality, and social development* (pp. 1–101). New York: Wiley.

Pearlman, V. A. (1981). Influences of mothers' employment on career orientation and career choice of adolescent daughters. *Dissertation Abstracts International, 41* (11-A), 4657–4658.

Schumm, W. R., Southerby, W. T., & Figley, C. F. (1980). Stumbling block or stepping stone: Path analysis in family studies. *Journal of Marriage and the Family, 42,* 251–262.

Stuckey, M. F., McGhee, P. E., & Bell, N. J. (1982). Parent-child interaction: The influence of maternal employment. *Developmental Psychology, 18,* 635–644.

Thomas, A., & Chess, S. (1977). *Temperament and development.* New York: Brunner/Mazel.

Thomas, A., & Chess, S. (1980). *The dynamics of psychological development.* New York: Brunner/Mazel.

Thomas, A., Chess, S., & Birch, H. G. (1968). *Temperament and behavior disorders in children.* New York: New York University Press.

Thomas, A., Chess, S., Birch, H. G., Hertzig, M., & Korn, S. (1963). *Behavioral individuality in early childhood.* New York: New York University Press.

Tryon, R., & Baily, D. (1966). The BC TRY computer system of cluster and factor analysis. *Multivariate Behavioral Research, 1,* 95–111.

Waters, E., Wippman, J., & Sroufe, L. (1979). Attachment, positive affect, and competence in the peer group: Two studies in construct validation. *Child Development, 50,* 821–829.

Warr, P., & Parry, G. (1982). Paid employment and women's psychological well-being. *Psychological Bulletin, 91,* 498–516.

Williamson, S. Z. (1970). The effects of maternal employment on the scholastic performance of children. *Journal of Home Economics, 62,* 609–613.

Woods, M. B. (1972). The unsupervised child of the working mother. *Developmental Psychology, 6,* 14–25.

Yarrow, M. R., Scott, P., DeLeeuw, L., & Heinig, C. (1962). Child-rearing in families of working and nonworking mothers. *Sociometry, 25,* 122–140.

Zaslow, M., Rabinovich, B., & Suwalsky, J. (1983). *The impact on the child of maternal employment: An examination of mediating variables.* Paper presented at the Lecture series on Developmental Plasticity "Social Context and Human Development," Boulder, Colorado.

Received October 8, 1984
Revision received February 12, 1985 ∎

Caught Between Parents: Adolescents' Experience in Divorced Homes

Christy M. Buchanan, Eleanor E. Maccoby, and Sanford M. Dornbusch

Stanford University

BUCHANAN, CHRISTY M., MACCOBY, ELEANOR E., and DORNBUSCH, SANFORD M. *Caught Between Parents: Adolescents' Experience in Divorced Homes.* CHILD DEVELOPMENT, 1991, 62, 1008–1029. This study examined adolescents' feelings of being caught between parents to see whether this construct helps to explain (1) variability in their postdivorce adjustment and (2) associations between family/child characteristics and adolescent adjustment. Adolescents 10 to 18 years old ($N = 522$) were interviewed by telephone 4½ years after their parents' separation. Feeling caught between parents was related to high parental conflict and hostility and low parental cooperation. Being close to both parents was associated with low feelings of being caught. The relation between time spent with each parent and feeling caught depended on the coparenting relationship. Adolescents in dual residence were especially likely to feel caught when parents were in high conflict, and especially unlikely to feel caught when parents cooperated. Feeling caught was related to poor adjustment outcomes. Parental conflict was only related to adjustment outcomes indirectly, through adolescents' feelings of being caught.

In recent years there has been much interest in discovering characteristics of families and children that aid or inhibit the adjustment of children to divorce. In the current study we explore adolescents' feelings of being caught between parents in an effort to shed light on their adaptation to parental divorce. Two different literatures suggest the potential importance of this concept. First, the family systems literature—specifically, that on triangulation and boundary diffusion—suggests that when parents try to form alliances with a child against the other parent, or when the boundaries between the parent-parent and parent-child subsystems become unclear, children are likely to be drawn into parental negotiations, tensions, or active conflicts. For example, the child might become a confidant to one or both parents, or carry messages between parents. Stress and confusion are the expected consequences for the child (Aponte & Van Deusen, 1981; S. Minuchin, 1974).

Second, some of the divorce literature points to loyalty conflicts as a source of distress and difficulty for children after divorce (e.g., Clingempeel & Segal, 1986; Goldstein, Freud, & Solnit, 1979; Johnston & Campbell, 1987; Levy & Chambers, 1981; Wallerstein & Blakeslee, 1989; Wallerstein & Kelly, 1980), although the concept of loyalty conflicts has seldom been explored empirically. The most detailed discussions of loyalty conflicts following divorce are clinical in nature (e.g., Johnston & Campbell, 1987; Wallerstein & Kelly, 1980). These authors discuss the difficulties they observe for children who feel love for and allegiance to both parents, and yet fear the consequences of loyalty to both. These children try to maintain fair, equitable relationships with both parents, but—given the nature of the interparental relationship—experience guilt and anxiety as a result.

Both the family systems and the divorce literatures suggest that the extent to which a child feels caught between parents—practically and/or emotionally—may impede difficulty in adjusting to the divorce. Understanding when and why children feel caught between parents may thus help us to under-

This research was supported by the W. T. Grant Foundation, Grant no. 88119688 to Eleanor E. Maccoby and Sanford M. Dornbusch. We would like to thank the interviewers and the adolescents who made the Stanford Adolescent Custody Study possible. We are grateful for the statistical advice of Lee Cronbach and for the comments of Kate Funder and three anonymous reviewers on this manuscript. Special thanks also go to Sue Dimicelli, Pat Weaver, and Sue Monahan for their help at various phases of the project. Requests for reprints should be sent to Christy M. Buchanan, Center for the Study of Families, Children and Youth, Building 460, Stanford University, Stanford, CA 94305-2135.

stand the variability in their adjustment to divorce. In addition, exploring this concept may shed light on previously documented relations between family or child characteristics (e.g., child sex, level of parental conflict) and adjustment outcomes.

In the present study, then, we investigated the following questions: (1) What postdivorce circumstances predict adolescents' feelings of being caught between parents? (2) Are feelings of being caught between parents predictive of adjustment outcomes? and (3) Does an understanding of adolescents' feelings of being caught between parents help us to understand relations between other postdivorce circumstances and adolescent adjustment? As suggested above, our measure of adolescents' being caught between parents (described in more detail in the Method section) was based both on adolescents' *feelings* of being caught in the middle and on their perceptions of *parental behaviors or attitudes* related to those feelings.

Similarly, our choice of predictors to explore was based on factors suggested in theoretical and policy discussions as being related to children's loyalty conflicts and to the family systems concepts of "triangulation" and "boundary diffusion." Thus, we examined: age and sex of the child, positive and negative aspects of coparenting, the amount of time children spent with each parent, and parent-child closeness. Time since parental separation, although potentially interesting, was not examined because families in our sample did not differ on this dimension.

Age of Child
Based on balance theory and stages of social-cognitive development, Johnston and Campbell (1987) argued that loyalty conflicts will be most common in the middle childhood years (approximately ages 6 to 8) and drop off in the 9–11-year age period as children become more likely to form alliances with one parent or the other. Their data on children 2 to 14 years old—all from families in relatively high conflict over issues of custody—lend support to these expectations (Johnston, Campbell, & Mayes, 1985; Johnston, Kline, & Tschann, 1989). It is less clear from their predictions or their data what one might expect as children proceed through adolescence. They argued that adolescents become increasingly able to distance themselves from parental disputes, implying that loyalty conflicts should either level off or continue to decrease after early adolescence.

On the other hand, it may be that increases in the ability to see multiple points of view heighten the likelihood of feeling caught between parents over the adolescent years. In addition, as children get older, parents may become more willing to act in ways that may make them feel caught in the middle, for example, asking them to convey messages, or confiding in them regarding the other parent's alleged faults.

Sex of Child
Boys were more likely to be caught in parents' conflict in the Johnston et al. (1989) study, perhaps because parents expose boys to more conflict than girls (Hetherington, Cox, & Cox, 1982). If girls, however, are more often concerned with maintaining harmonious interpersonal relationships and with resolving conflict in ways that are mutually satisfying (Gilligan, 1982; Maccoby, 1990; Miller, Danaher, & Forbes, 1986), girls might be more vulnerable to feeling caught between parents than boys.

Loyalty conflicts may also be more acute among children living with their opposite-sex parent. Warshak and Santrock (1983) report that children living with their opposite-sex parent often long to live with their same-sex parent. Children living with their opposite-sex parent might experience more loyalty conflicts than children living with a same-sex parent because the former feel a strong allegiance to their same-sex parent at the same time that they are committed to the caretaking parent.

The Postdivorce Coparenting Relationship
The greater the animosity between parents, the more likely parents will be to triangulate children (i.e., attempt to form an alliance with the child against the other parent) and the greater the likelihood that diffusion of the spousal subsystem boundary will occur, potentially drawing children into what should be parent-parent domains of functioning (Aponte & Van Deusen, 1981). The child's sensitivity to the parental relationship, and fear of negative repercussions of loyalty to one or the other parent, would also be expected to increase with level of parental conflict. In support of these expectations, Johnston et al. (1989), in their study of high-conflict families, found that the higher the conflict between parents, the more children were caught in that conflict. Their measure of being caught, however, assumed the existence of conflict between the parents and measured, quite specifically, the experience of being caught *in that conflict*. In the cur-

rent study, the measure of being caught be-tween parents was not limited to situations of parental conflict. Nonetheless, we ex-pected that more general feelings of being caught would increase with the level of pa-rental conflict.

Conversely, we expected that higher pa-rental cooperation would lessen the likeli-hood of feeling caught in the middle be-tween parents. If parents are actively cooperating with one another, there is less need for parents to use children to achieve objectives of the parent-parent relationship. Within Johnston et al.'s (1989) sample of high-conflict families, however, parental at-tempts to reason together did not lessen the likelihood of children's being caught in par-ents' conflict.

Although the extent to which parents disagree and/or argue after divorce and the extent to which they talk to each other and attempt to work together are surely corre-lated, they can in fact represent two separate dimensions of parenting. The intersection of these two dimensions is likely to be impor-tant when considering effects on children. Maccoby, Depner, and Mnookin (1990) used the term "discord" to indicate how much parents disagreed and tried to undermine one another in parenting and the term "co-operative communication" to indicate how much they tried to communicate and work cooperatively in parenting. These authors identified four coparenting patterns based on a cross-classification of "discord" and "cooperative communication." "Conflicted" parents were those who had high discord and low cooperative communication. "Coop-erative" parents had low discord and high cooperative communication. Parents low on both discord and cooperative communica-tion were called "disengaged." The fourth combination—high on both "discord" and "cooperative communication"—was rela-tively rare.

Based on the literature described ear-lier, we would expect children of conflicted parents to be the most caught between par-ents and children of cooperative parents (in this case defined not just by attempts to co-operate but also by low discord) to be the least caught. It is less clear what one would expect for children of "disengaged" par-ents—a relatively large group. Children of disengaged parents may feel caught if the disengagement is related to diffuse parental subsystem boundaries. For example, the lack of communication and cooperation be-

tween parents might put children in the role of carrying out whatever negotiations are re-quired between parents or between house-holds. Alternatively, if conflict is the overrid-ing factor, children from disengaged families would not be expected to feel caught be-tween parents.

Amount of Contact with Each Parent

Conflicting arguments have been made regarding the potential impact on loyalty conflicts of allowing a child to spend consid-erable amounts of time with *both* parents— as distinct from living mainly with one par-ent and only occasionally visiting the other. For instance, Levy and Chambers (1981) ar-gue that high levels of contact between chil-dren and both parents exacerbate parental conflict and increase opportunities for par-ents to use children in attempts to under-mine one another. On the other hand, Fol-berg (1979) recounts arguments that the legal and/or de facto recognition that both parents can remain involved with their chil-dren reduces the need for parents to use children to gain power. Others argue that joint custody arrangements in fact promote cooperation between parents (Roman & Haddad, 1978); as suggested earlier, when parents cooperate, loyalty dilemmas may be less likely to occur.

More frequent access to both parents was related to a higher likelihood of being caught in parents' conflict in the Johnston et al. (1989) study. Because these data were collected only from individuals in high con-flict, however, they may reflect one side of an interaction whereby amount of contact with a nonresidential parent (or, in other words, considerable contact with each par-ent) is associated with negative outcomes when parents are in conflict but with posi-tive outcomes if parents are not in conflict (Hetherington, Cox, & Cox, 1978, 1982). Al-though Steinman (1981) describes the expe-rience of torn loyalties for children in joint custody among well-functioning and cooper-ative families, her data do not address whether those torn loyalties are higher among joint-custody children than among sole-custody children. In another study (Shiller, 1986), although parents reported more loyalty conflicts for boys in joint cus-tody than boys in mother custody, assess-ments of loyalty conflicts from the boys themselves did not differ by residence. Thus, we cannot conclude from the existing research how (or whether) feelings of being caught are related to the way the child's time is divided between the two parents. The effect of the division of time may depend on the coparenting relationship, with increased feelings of being caught for adolescents in high contact with both parents mainly or only when those parents are in high conflict.

The Parent-Child Relationship
The clinical literature (Johnston & Campbell, 1987; Wallerstein & Kelly, 1980) suggests that creating an alliance with one or the other parent relieves the stress of loyalty conflicts for children, implying that children who have a close relationship with only one parent will be less torn between parents. A close relationship with *both* parents seems to be at the heart of the experience of loyalty conflicts. Closeness to only the nonresidential parent, however, may lead to more feelings of being caught than closeness to only the residential parent.

These, then, are some of the potential predictors of being caught between parents among children of divorce. Presumably, the consequences of being caught between parents are negative: anxiety, guilt, and confusion. If loyalty conflicts are, in fact, predictors of negative adjustment outcomes, do they help explain associations between various postdivorce circumstances and adjustment outcomes? For example, can the negative relation between parental conflict and children's adjustment after divorce be, in part, explained by children's experience of loyalty conflicts? Literature examining how parental conflict translates into negative outcomes for children repeatedly suggests that parental conflict alters some facet of parent-child interaction (Fauber, Forehand, Thomas, & Wierson, 1990; S. Minuchin, 1974; Patterson, 1982). Perhaps parental conflict alters parent-child relationships so that the child is more likely to be caught between parents, which in turn predicts other negative outcomes. Emery (1988), pointing to the great variability in children's reactions to parental conflict, has also suggested that individual differences in adjustment to parents' conflict may in part be explained by how children respond to that conflict (e.g., their tendency to form alliances, to try to mediate the conflict, or to withdraw).

Evidence from Johnston et al. (1989) lends support to the hypothesis that being caught between parents mediates between parental conflict and outcomes. The authors found that when parental aggression and the child's experience of being caught in parents' conflict were examined separately,

both were related to higher levels of behavior problems in children. In multivariate analyses, however, levels of interparental aggression were only indirectly related to certain outcomes (total behavior problems, withdrawn behavior, and somatic complaints) through their association with children's experience of being caught. These results imply that the extent to which children become caught in parents' conflict may mediate the effects of that conflict on some child outcomes, but the findings are limited to families where parents are experiencing substantial conflict. As noted previously, the Johnston measure of being caught itself assumes conflict between parents. No previous study has examined whether feelings of being caught, conceptualized more broadly, also mediate associations between parental conflict and outcomes, or whether such relations would emerge in a more representative (i.e., less conflictual) sample.

In sum, we did not have specific predictions about the relations between age or sex and feeling caught in our adolescent sample, although we did anticipate that adolescents living with their opposite-sex parent might feel more "caught" than adolescents living with their same-sex parent. We also hypothesized that feelings of being caught between parents would be associated with high parental discord, lack of parental communication and cooperation, and high levels of closeness to both parents or to only the nonresidential parent. It was not clear to us how the amount of time spent with each parent would influence feelings of being caught, although we did expect that a fairly equal division of time (i.e., dual residence or high visitation) would be associated with a higher likelihood of feeling caught when parents were in high conflict.

In addition, we predicted that feelings of being caught between parents would be associated with adolescent maladjustment and would, at least in part, mediate the effects of age, sex, coparenting, time spent with each parent, and parent-child relationships on outcomes. The adjustment outcomes examined were depression/anxiety and deviant behavior.

Method

SAMPLE

Participants in the Stanford Adolescent Custody Study were recruited from families that had taken part in an earlier study of parents' custody decisions and postdivorce functioning (the Stanford Child Custody Study), in which only parents were interviewed. These parents were recruited from the population of parents who filed for divorce in two northern California counties between September 1984 and March 1985. At the time of filing, parents had been separated for about 3 months in the usual case, and not more than 13 months (see Maccoby et al., 1990, for a more thorough description of that sample). Parents who agreed to participate were interviewed up to three times, at approximately 6 months (Time 1), 1½ years (Time 2), and 3½ years (Time 3) after separation. Adolescents from these families were interviewed between November 1988 and June 1989, approximately 4½ years after their parents' separation.

The target sample for the adolescent study consisted of children between the ages of 10½ and 18 years, inclusive. Ten-year-olds were interviewed if they were in fifth grade and would be 11 by June 1, 1989. A recruitment packet was mailed to one parent in each family with eligible adolescents. The parent chosen to receive the initial mailing was the parent who had participated in the Stanford Child Custody Study. When both parents had participated in the earlier study, the mailing, with rare exceptions, was sent to the parent with whom the child was living.

Interviews were conducted by telephone. In research on adults, few problems have been encountered concerning amount and type of information disclosed over the telephone when good interviewing techniques are employed (Groves & Kahn, 1979). Investigators who have used this method with adolescent populations find that adolescents are familiar and comfortable with the telephone as a mode of communication, and that information obtained in this manner is reliable and valid (e.g., Furstenberg, Nord, Peterson, & Zill, 1983; Montemayor & Brownlee, 1987). Although it may be more difficult to establish rapport in telephone interviews as opposed to face-to-face interviews, there are also potential advantages of a telephone interview with teenagers. Adolescents may feel less inhibited in talking about sensitive issues over the phone; in addition, the telephone makes it possible to reduce the salience of talking with an older person. In order to maximize reliability and

validity of the information we collected, interviewers went through a minimum of 35 hours of training, much of which focused on developing and maintaining rapport with adolescents.[1] Interviews averaged 1 hour in length. At the conclusion of the interview, each adolescent was sent a check for 10 dollars and a letter thanking him or her for participating.

Of 647 potential adolescent respondents, 522 (81%) individuals from 365 families agreed to be interviewed. In 12% of the target cases, a parent or child refused participation. Five percent of the cases were not locatable, and 2% were not eligible for the study due to parents' reconciliation, a death of a parent or child, or the existence of a mental handicap that precluded participation. Analyses were conducted comparing the interviewed and not interviewed (those who refused or could not be located) groups on parent-reported variables from the earlier interviews. There were no differences between these groups on most of the parent and child characteristics examined. We were, however, somewhat more successful in recruiting families in which parents had more education. And we were slightly less successful in recruiting adolescents who had been living primarily with their fathers at the time of the last parent interview than adolescents who had been living primarily with their mothers or splitting time living with both parents. Further descriptive information about the sample can be found in Table 1.

MEASURES

Adolescent Report

Caught between parents.—See Table 2 for descriptive data on each item and correlations among items used in the "caught" composite. All adolescents answered the question "How often do you feel caught in the middle between your mother and your father"? (1 = never, 2 = once in a while, 3 = fairly often, 4 = very often). This item, which represented adolescents' subjective feelings of being caught, was moderately but significantly associated with other items intended to capture dimensions of parental behavior indicating potential triangulation or boundary diffusion (i.e., parents' attempts to use the adolescent as either a message carrier or an informer), and adolescents' feel-

---

[1] Detailed information about the training and interviewing procedures can be obtained from the authors.

TABLE 1

TABLE 1

DESCRIPTIVE SAMPLE INFORMATION

	% of Families (N = 365)		% of Adolescents (N = 522)
Number of adolescents interviewed from the same family:		Male	51
		≥ 14 years old	55
One	63	High school dropout	2
Two	32	High school graduate	9
Three or four	5		
Parental ethnicity:		Residential Arrangement:[a]	
Both parents non-Hispanic white	73	Mother residence	70
Both parents Hispanic	7	Father residence	19
Both parents Asian	4	Dual residence	10
Both parents black	2	Other residence	1
Parents of different ethnicities	14		
Parental education:			
Mother a college graduate	27		
Father a college graduate	42		
Mother's earnings:			
<$20,000	56		
$20,000–$39,999	38		
≥$40,000	6		
Father's earnings:			
<$20,000	15		
$20,000–$39,999	37		
≥$40,000	48		

[a] Mother-resident adolescents were defined as those who spent 11 or more overnights in a typical 2-week period with mother; father-resident adolescents spent 11 or more overnights in a 2-week period with father. Dual-resident adolescents spent at least four overnights in a 2-week period, at least 1 week out of each month, or at least 3 months (not all vacation) each year, with each parent. Other-resident adolescents were living primarily with someone other than their mother or father during the year prior to the interview. Although 23 respondents—mostly high school graduates—had moved out of the home prior to being interviewed, the move had taken place recently enough that we were able to obtain information about their recent past and to classify them according to their previous residential arrangement.

TABLE 2

DESCRIPTIVE DATA FOR ITEMS USED IN "CAUGHT" COMPOSITE

	DESCRIPTIVE DATA					CORRELATIONS AMONG ITEMS					
ITEMS	N	M	SD	Min	Max	2	3	4	5	6	7
1. How often do you feel caught?	522	2.0	1.0	1	4	.31	.26	.27	.22	.27	.20
2. How often does mother ask you to carry messages?	494	2.0	.9	1	4		.56	.15	.22	.26	.21
3. How often does father ask you to carry messages?	494	2.0	.8	1	4			.13	.35	.23	.28
4. Does mother ask questions you wish she wouldn't ask?	495	.4	.5	0	1				.22	.32	.08
5. Does father ask questions you wish he wouldn't ask?	495	.3	.5	0	1					.19	.30
6. How often do you hesitate to talk about father in front of mother?	518	2.1	.9	1	4						.46
7. How often do you hesitate to talk about mother in front of father?	494	2.2	1.0	1	4						...

ings of needing to hide emotions or information regarding one parent from the other. Such hesitancy suggests fears that expressions of loyalty for one parent in front of the other, or merely providing information (e.g., "Dad has a new car"; "there's a lady living at dad's house") about the other parent, will have negative repercussions. To measure specific parental behaviors, the following questions were asked about each parent if the adolescent had seen or spoken to both parents within the last year: "How often does your mother [father] ask you to carry messages to your father [mother]?" (1 = never, 4 = very often), and "Does your mother [father] ever ask questions about your father's [mother's] home that you wish she [he] wouldn't ask?" (1 = yes, 0 = no). Adolescents' feelings of needing to hide information or emotions regarding father from mother were assessed if the adolescent had seen his or her mother in the last year: "When your mother is around, how often do you hesitate to talk about things concerning your father?" (1 = never, 4 = very often). Similarly, hesitation to talk about mother in front of father was assessed for adolescents who had seen their father in the last year.

For purposes of reducing data into one "caught" composite, we first considered how to combine information from the pairs of items about interactions with each of the two parents (e.g., being asked to carry messages by mother and by father). We thought that frequent problems wih one parent might be of greater subjective significance to a child in terms of feeling caught in the middle than less frequent problems with two parents. To check this assumption, we correlated the item "How often do you feel caught in the middle?" first with a composite of the paired items using scores summed across parents and second with a composite using only the score for whichever parent had the higher score (maximum score). The composite using maximum scores correlated slightly higher with feeling caught in the middle than the summed composite; thus, we took that approach.

To create the final "caught" composite, then, the maximum scores for being asked to carry messages, being asked questions by one parent about the other, and hesitating to talk about one parent in front of the other and the single item about feeling caught in the middle were standardized and summed together. For easier readability, a constant (five) was added to the total score to bring all scores above zero. The final composite

ranged from 0 to 12, with a mean of 4.8 and a standard deviation of 2.9. Cronbach's alpha for this composite was .64.

Visitation with the outside parent.—A measure of visitation with the nonresidential parent was constructed for adolescents in mother or father residence. This measure ranged from 1 to 4, where 1 = contact rare or absent; 2 = 2 weeks or more of vacation time but low contact during the school year, 3 = at least 8 hours of daytime contact or one overnight—but less than two overnights—every 2 weeks during the school year, and 4 = two or three overnights every 2 weeks during the school year. This measure was available only for adolescents who were living with one or both parents at the time of the interview and not for adolescents who had moved out of the home within the past year. Thus, analyses incorporating time spent with the nonresidential parent were based on a slightly reduced sample (347 mother-resident cases and 98 father-resident cases).

Closeness to parents.—The following questions were asked about each parent using a scale from 1 (not at all) to 5 (very):

How openly do you talk with your [mother/father]? How careful do you feel you have to be about what you say to your [mother/father]? How comfortable do you feel admitting doubts and fears to your [mother/father]? How interested is your [mother/father] in talking to you when you want to talk? How often does your [mother/father] express affection or liking for you? How well does your [mother/father] know what you are really like? How close do you feel to your [mother/father]? How confident are you that your [mother/father] would help you if you had a problem? If you needed money, how comfortable would you be asking your [mother/father] for it? How interested is your [mother/father] in the things you do?

Some of these items were drawn from previously reported scales of parent-adolescent relationships (Amato, 1987; Fine, Worley, & Schwebel, 1985; Smollar & Youniss, 1985), while others were newly created for this study. In a principal component analysis, all items except "How careful do you have to be about what you say" loaded above .40 on one factor; thus, the nine remaining items were summed to form a "closeness to parent" composite for each parent. For mothers, the scale mean was 36.1 and the standard deviation was 7.5. For fathers, the mean was 33.0 and the standard deviation was 8.1. Cronbach's alpha was .89 for mothers and .90 for fathers.

In addition, a median split was performed on the closeness to mother and closeness to father composites to create "High" and "Low" closeness categories. Adolescents at the median were included in the "Low" closeness group. These categorical "closeness to mother" and "closeness to father" variables were then combined into a "closeness to both parents" composite with three categories: close to two parents, close to only one parent, and close to neither parent.

Depression/anxiety.—Adolescents were asked how often in the past month they had experienced 15 mental (e.g., felt lonely) and physical (e.g., had a headache) symptoms typically used to measure depression and anxiety (Dornbusch, Mont-Reynaud, Ritter, Chen, & Steinberg, 1991). The scale for each item ranged from 0 (never) to 3 (three or more times). Initial exploration of the data suggested that two of the items—"lost your appetite" and "felt as if you were eating too much"—could be combined to create a measure of "eating problems." Because we were not interested in predicting specific types of symptoms (somatic vs. psychological), we used principal components analysis to assess the feasibility of creating one scale indicating general psychosomatic adjustment. This analysis indicated that 10 of the items loaded above .50 on one factor (with the rest loading below .40). These items were: eating problems, felt overtired, had a headache, had a stomach ache, felt nervous, felt depressed, felt tense or irritable, had trouble sleeping, felt lonely, and felt like running away.

The reliability (Cronbach's alpha = .83) for these 10 items was higher than for any potential subscales. Given the high reliability, together with our interest in having one general adjustment scale, scores on these items were summed to form one depression/anxiety composite, with a mean of 15.2 and a standard deviation of 7.0.

Deviance.—Using a scale from 1 (never) to 4 (often), adolescents told us about their involvement in a variety of deviant acts over the past 12 months (Dornbusch et al., 1991). An overall deviance scale ($M = 21.8$, $SD = 5.7$) was created by summing responses to the following items (Cronbach's alpha = .83): smoked cigarettes, or used marijuana, or used chewing tobacco; bought beer or asked someone to buy it for you; used a phony ID; been drunk; smoked marijuana; used a drug other than marijuana, for example, "uppers" or cocaine; copied homework

or an assignment from somebody else; cheated on a class test; came to class late; cut a class; took something of value from somebody else; got in trouble with the police; carried a weapon to school; got into a physical fight at school; purposely damaged school property.

Parent Report: Coparenting

In the Time 3 parent interview (approximately 1 year prior to the adolescent interviews), parents whose children had at least 4 hours of face-to-face contact per week with the nonresidential parent answered questions about their coparenting efforts. Two composites were created based on factor analyses (see Maccoby et al., 1990, for a more detailed description of items as well as composites). "Discord" consisted of items asked separately of each parent about: frequency of arguments, logistical problems in managing visitation and alternation, undermining of one another's parenting, refusals to allow visitation (or threats to do so), and attempts by ex-spouses to upset one another when they disagreed. For the first three of these items, if both parents were interviewed and they differed in their response, the more discordant score was used because of the expectation that if one of the two parents saw these things as a problem, they were in fact a problem for the relationship. The remaining items were averaged across parents, and then all combined items were averaged into a total discord score ($M = 4.1$, $SD = 1.5$). Cronbach's alpha for this scale was .69.

"Cooperative communication" (Cronbach's alpha = .56) consisted of the mean of three items that were averaged across parents: how often parents talked about children, attempts to coordinate rules between homes, and the degree to which parents did not try to avoid contact with each other. The scale mean was 4.5 and the standard deviation was 1.9.

"Discord" and "cooperative communication" were cross-classified (by dividing each at the median) to create the major *coparenting patterns* used by Maccoby et al. (1990) and described earlier. Parents who were high on both discord and cooperative communication were excluded from analyses given their small number ($N = 18$).

In addition to these parent-reported measures of coparenting, interviewers at Time 3 rated the general hostility of each parent toward the ex-spouse, using a scale where 1 = someone who speaks quite favorably about the ex-spouse, and 10 = someone who is extremely bitter, hostile, and critical. For the purposes of this article, if both parents were interviewed and they differed in their response, the higher score was used as the measure of hostility. This maximum hostility scale had a mean of 5.6 and a standard deviation of 2.2. An assessment of interrater reliability was not available for this measure. Despite this drawback, the measure of hostility was included as an alternative to the parent-reported measure of conflict.

ANALYSES

First we examined the associations between age (using correlation) and sex (using *t* test) and feelings of being caught between parents. For the remaining analyses relating predictor variables (e.g., coparenting, contact, parent-child closeness) to "caught," we used analysis of variance (for categorical predictors) and regression (for continuous predictors) models. Age and sex were controlled in the ANOVA models by entering them as covariates (ANCOVA). In regression models, age and sex were entered as part of the full model predicting "caught" in order to control for their effects. Regression was also used to examine the associations between feeling caught and adjustment outcomes. Finally, we used path analysis to examine the role of being caught between parents as a mediator of family or adolescent characteristics and adolescent adjustment. We discuss further details of particular analyses in the Results section.

In our analyses, we faced the problem of having interviewed more than one sibling in some families. Siblings almost always lived in the same residence and usually had the same schedule of visits to the nonresidential parent. They shared the same divorce history, as reflected in the data obtained from parental interviews during the first 3½ postdivorce years. With respect to these measures, then, siblings cannot be considered as independent cases. Yet sibling correlations on most of our outcome variables were low. Thus, it was clear to us that siblings often responded quite differently to the antecedent conditions we wanted to use as predictors. They differed in a number of ways that were pertinent to our model: on sex and age, and on the nature of the relationship with each parent (e.g., closeness to parents or feelings of being caught between parents). In these respects, then, they *were* independent cases. Because of this, we were reluctant to select only one adolescent per family for analysis.

An additional problem with selecting one adolescent per family involved choosing the adolescent to be included. To follow the strategy of taking only the oldest child would overrepresent older children and restrict the age range. Even a random choice—a popular solution—raises the question of *which* random choice (since different random samples will, by chance, sometimes produce different results).

We considered two additional solutions that would allow us to use all cases: (1) doing analyses with data from all children but using the number of families as our degrees of freedom, and (2) weighting each individual's scores by the inverse of the number of siblings represented in the analysis. Both of these solutions could become unwieldy in carrying out the complex analytic tasks planned for the study. Furthermore, we were not convinced that either of them actually solved the problem of correlated error among our cases.

The primary focus of our research is on individual adolescents and their adaptations; family variables are of interest in terms of their impact on individual adolescents, filtered through those adolescents' experiences and characteristics. Furthermore, we have something approaching a representative sample of the preadolescent and adolescent children in our catchment area whose parents were divorced. Because the number of adolescents interviewed in a given family was highly correlated with the number of children of the marriage, to select one adolescent per family, or to weight inversely by number of adolescents, would be to bias the distribution with regard to family size. By excluding more than half of the children in larger families, we would seriously underrepresent adolescents growing up in families with more than one child—something we did not want to do. Yet it is not legitimate to ignore sibling ties altogether in establishing our criteria for accepting a finding as statistically significant.

In the end, we have taken the following approach: to analyze all cases and then to analyze a subsample, using all adolescents in families where only one was interviewed, and taking only one adolescent per family, chosen on a random basis, where more than one was interviewed. When results from both samples are significant at $p \leq .05$, we interpret this as a significant finding and report the statistics from the full sample. When results for the two analyses differ, we repeat the analyses on at least one and sometimes two additional random samples. If results using all cases and at least one of the additional random samples are significant at $p < .05$, we also report this as a significant finding; in such cases, the results from any "nonsignificant" random samples are typically close to being significant at $p \leq .05$. If a result using all cases is significant, but statistical significance is weakened slightly when using subsamples (i.e., $.05 \leq p \leq .10$ for results that were significant at $p \leq .05$ with all cases, or $.10 \leq p \leq .15$ for results that were significant at $p \leq .10$ with all cases), we examine the magnitude of effect. If the magnitude of effect remains approximately the same in subsamples as with all cases, we report this as a borderline result. If statistical significance weakens as much or more than that described above, and/or the magnitude of effect changes substantially, we consider the original result an artifact of our nonindependent cases (e.g., correlated error, family size).

In a similar manner, we explore results that are not significant in the full sample but are significant using a random sample. In general, we look for consistency across all cases and random subsamples in statistical significance and in the magnitude of effect. Where there is either marginal or substantial disagreement between analyses using all cases and analyses using random subsamples, we report this to the reader along with our interpretation of the strength of the result. Where there is no discussion of results using random subsamples, the reader may assume that results using at least one subsample did not differ from the result using all cases, as discussed earlier.

In addition to these series of analyses, we have also repeated major analyses controlling for the number of adolescents interviewed in the family and for the number of children of the marriage. Controlling for these variables changed none of the results we report.

Results

Age and Sex of Adolescent

Older adolescents were somewhat more likely to report feelings of being caught between parents than younger adolescents ($r = .12$, $p = .005$). Girls ($M = 5.1$, SD $= 3.0$) reported more feelings of being caught than boys ($M = 4.4$, SD $= 2.7$), $t(520) = -2.69$, $p = .007$. Because age and sex were significantly related to feeling caught, these variables were controlled in subsequent analyses. For relations between age and

sex and the other variables examined, see Table 3.

To test whether feelings of being caught were more acute among adolescents living with their opposite-sex parent, we excluded dual-resident adolescents and used ANCOVA to predict "caught" with child's sex, residence (mother vs. father), and the interaction of sex and residence, controlling for age. The means indicated that while girls in father residence ($M = 6.2$, SD $= 3.3$, $N = 38$) had somewhat higher means on feeling caught than girls in mother residence ($M = 4.9$, SD $= 2.8$, $N = 198$), there was no evidence that boys in mother residence ($M = 4.4$, SD $= 2.8$, $N = 168$) felt more caught than boys in father residence ($M = 4.6$, SD $= 2.6$, $N = 62$). Further, the interaction effect was just barely significant at a trend level using all cases, $F(1,461) = 2.73$, $p = .10$, and did not hold up at $p < .10$ using random samples. Thus, we do not find that feelings of being caught are significantly worse for adolescents living with their opposite-sex parent.

Coparenting

Results of analyses using the different coparenting measures were similar to one another. Thus, for brevity's sake when reporting analyses that involve coparenting measures, we describe only details of analyses using the "discord" and "cooperative communication" measures, except in cases where the results using hostility best demonstrate an effect. In such cases, we report details for all three measures.

Separate regressions were used to predict "caught" with each coparenting measure, age, and sex. Controlling for age and sex, higher discord, $t(335) = 5.14$, $p = .0001$ ($\beta = .27$), and lower cooperative communication, $t(334) = -3.56$, $p = .0004$ ($\beta = -.19$), were related to more feelings of being caught between parents. ANCOVA and follow-up t tests using the cross-classification of these two scales (i.e., the coparenting pattern) showed that adolescents from conflicted families were more likely to feel caught ($M = 6.1$, SD $= 2.9$, $N = 76$) than adolescents from disengaged families ($M = 4.6$, SD $= 2.6$, $N = 166$), who were in turn more likely to feel caught than adolescents from cooperative families ($M = 3.7$, SD $= 2.3$, $N = 78$), $F(2,315) = 16.22$, $p = .0001$.

Amount of Contact with Each Parent

ANCOVA, with age and sex as covariates, was used to examine the relations between residence (mother, father, or dual)

TABLE 3

RELATIONS BETWEEN AGE AND SEX AND OTHER VARIABLES USED IN ANALYSES

CONSTRUCT	N	AGE	SEX Males	SEX Females	STATISTICAL SIGNIFICANCE
		CONTINUOUS VARIABLES			
		(r)	(Mean)	(Mean)	
Discord	339	$-.12$*	4.1	4.1	sex: $t(337) = -.30$
Cooperative communication	338	$-.02$	4.7	4.3	sex: $t(336) = 1.65$†
Hostility	513	$-.04$	5.5	5.6	sex: $t(511) = -.73$
Closeness to mother	521	$-.12$**	36.9	35.4	sex: $t(519) = 2.31$*
Closeness to father	494	$-.17$****	34.3	31.8	sex: $t(492) = 3.49$***
Depression/anxiety	522	$.25$****	13.7	16.8	sex: $t(520) = -5.12$****
Deviance	522	$.51$****	22.4	21.2	sex: $t(520) = 2.37$*
		CATEGORICAL VARIABLES			
		(Mean in Years)	(%)	(%)	
Sex:					
Males	265	14.1	...	...	age: $t(520) = -.26$
Females	257	14.2	...	...	
Coparenting pattern:					
Conflicted	76	13.8	48	53	sex: $\chi^2(2, N = 320) = 1.02$
Cooperative	78	14.2	55	45	age: $F(2,317) = .76$
Disengaged	166	14.2	53	47	
Residence:					
Mother	366	14.2	46	54	sex: $\chi^2(2, N = 522) = 11.44$**
Dual	51	13.2	63	37	age: $F(2,514) = 3.99$*
Father	100	14.3	62	38	
Closeness to both parents:					
Close to both	149	13.6	53	47	sex: $\chi^2(2, N = 491) = 2.75$
Close to one	179	14.0	53	47	age: $F(2,490) = 7.66$***
Close to neither	165	14.7	45	55	

† $p \leq .10$.
* $p \leq .05$.
** $p \leq .01$.
*** $p \leq .001$.
**** $p \leq .0001$.

and feeling caught. When using all cases, residence was marginally related to being caught between parents, $F(2,512) = 2.52$, $p = .08$, with dual-resident adolescents feeling least caught and father-resident adolescents feeling most caught. The means for mother residence, father residence, and dual residence were 4.7, 5.3, and 4.3, respectively. In three random samples taking only one case per family, however, residence was never significantly related to being caught at $p \leq .10$. Because our hypothesis was that adolescents who had high contact with both parents would look different from adolescents who lived primarily with one parent or the other, we also did analyses combining mother- and father-resident adolescents into a "sole residence" group and comparing them to dual-resident adolescents. Residence defined in this way was still not significantly related to feeling caught.

We also examined the association between amount of visitation with the nonresidential parent (for sole-resident adolescents) and feelings of being caught. The relation between this measure of contact and "caught" was also not significant.

To look at whether effects of contact on feeling caught between parents were dependent on the coparenting relationship, we conducted three separate regressions. In each, we predicted "caught" with age, sex, one of the three coparenting measures, a dummy variable indicating whether or not the adolescent was in dual residence, and the interaction of being in dual residence with the coparenting measure. We used stepwise regression in order to assess the change in variance explained when the interaction term was added to the predictive equation. See Table 4 for a summary of the final regression equations. The interaction of dual residence and coparenting was significant for each coparenting measure. The slopes of the interaction terms indicate that negative coparenting (discord and hostility) is more strongly related to being caught between parents for adolescents in dual residence than adolescents in sole residence, and that cooperative communication is especially beneficial for dual-resident adolescents.

Although significance levels are presented for all predictors in each equation, one must be cautious in interpreting the main effects of the coparenting variables and the dummy variable for dual residence, given their correlation with the interaction

term and the significance of the interaction term. In the case of the coparenting scores, this does not seem problematic, since the results are consistent with those we reported earlier. However, the effects of being in dual residence need to be interpreted in the context of the entire equation. For instance, in the equation with cooperative communication, dual residence appears to have a positive (although not significant) relation to being caught between parents, whereas its effect is negative in all other equations. And, in fact, its effect in the cooperative communication analysis was negative until the interaction term was entered. By estimating the equation at different values of cooperative communication (with age and sex held constant), it becomes evident that at low levels of cooperative communication, dual-resident adolescents are more likely to be caught between parents than sole-resident adolescents, and that at high levels dual-resident children are less likely to be caught.

Closeness to Parents

Separate regressions were used to predict "caught" with closeness to mother or closeness to father (and sex and age). The results for closeness to mother were highly significant: adolescents who were closer to their mothers were also less likely to feel caught between parents, $t(517) = -5.26$, $p = .0001$ ($\beta = -.23$). Feeling closer to father was also associated with fewer feelings of being caught between parents, although the relation was of borderline significance using all cases, $t(490) = -1.82, p = .07$ ($\beta = -.08$). Closeness to father had a somewhat stronger association with feeling caught in two of three random subsamples, but even in these, the beta weight for closeness did not exceed $-.12$, much smaller than that for closeness to mother.

Because we were interested in whether closeness to the residential parent was more strongly associated with feeling caught between parents than closeness to mother or father per se, we repeated the regressions separately for mother-resident, dual-resident, and father-resident adolescents. Interestingly, closeness to mother was strongly related to feeling caught in all three residential groups (although the effect is not significant for the dual-residence group, the magnitude of effect is as high or higher than in the sole-residence groups), while closeness to father was not significantly related to feeling caught in any residential group (see Table 5). Only for dual-resident adolescents did the relation between closeness to father

TABLE 4

RESULTS OF REGRESSION ANALYSES PREDICTING FEELINGS OF BEING CAUGHT BETWEEN PARENTS WITH AGE, SEX, COPARENTING, RESIDENTIAL ARRANGEMENT, AND THE INTERACTION OF RESIDENTIAL ARRANGEMENT WITH COPARENTING

Variables Entered	b	t	β	F	R^2	ΔR^{2a}	N
				7.95****	.11	.01	336
Intercept	.99	. . .					
Sex	.67	2.33*	.12				
Age	.13	2.22*	.12				
Discord	.41	4.08****	.23				
Dual residence	−2.82	−2.27*	−.36				
Dual residence × discord	.56	1.91$^+$	.30				
				5.97****	.08	.02	335
Intercept	4.20	. . .					
Sex	.53	1.80$^+$	.10				
Age	.09	1.51	.08				
Cooperative communication	−.19	−2.31*	−.13				
Dual residence	1.65	1.60	.21				
Dual residence × cooperative communication	−.51	−2.45*	−.32				
				8.70****	.08	.02	509
Intercept	.73						
Sex	.65	2.67**	.11				
Age	.14	2.91**	.13				
Hostility	.19	3.18**	.15				
Dual residence	−2.81	−2.86**	−.29				
Dual residence × hostility	.56	2.97**	.30				

^{a} This is the difference between R^2 with and without the interaction term in the model.
$^+$ $p \leq .10$.
* $p \leq .05$.
** $p \leq .01$.
**** $p \leq .0001$.

and feeling caught approach the same magnitude as that between "caught" and closeness to mother.

Next we examined the association between feeling caught and the three-level variable of closeness to both parents (e.g., close to two parents, close to one parent only, close to neither parent) using ANCOVA. Controlling for sex and age, adolescents who were close to both parents reported fewer feelings of being caught between parents than adolescents who were close to only one parent or who were not close to either parent, $F(2,488) = 7.72$, $p = .0005$ (see Table 6).

The earlier analyses of closeness to mother and father by residence group did not indicate that a closer relationship with the nonresidential parent was related to increased feelings of being caught; however, we conducted a further analysis to see whether adolescents who were close to only the nonresidential parent felt more caught between parents than adolescents who were close to only the residential parent. Using the mother- and father-resident adolescents who felt close to only one parent, subjects were classified according to whether they felt close to their residential or nonresidential parent. Controlled for age and sex, difference in feelings of being caught between parents between these two groups of adolescents, $F(1,155) = .42$, $p > .10$, was not significant. In fact, the means did not even go in the direction predicted. Adolescents who were only close to the residential parent had somewhat higher "caught" scores ($M = 5.3$, $SD = 2.7$, $N = 95$) than those who were only close to the nonresidential parent ($M = 5.0$, $SD = 2.8$, $N = 64$).

Adjustment Outcomes

Regression was used to examine relations between feeling caught and the two adjustment outcome measures, controlling for age and sex. The more "caught" adolescents felt, the more depressed and anxious they were, $t(518) = 9.18$, $p = .0001$ ($\beta = .36$) and the more they engaged in deviant behavior, $t(518) = 4.86$, $p = .0001$ ($\beta = .18$).

Path Analyses

Two sets of multivariate analyses were used to examine the question of whether

TABLE 5

RESULTS OF REGRESSION ANALYSES PREDICTING FEELINGS OF BEING CAUGHT BETWEEN PARENTS WITH AGE, SEX, AND CLOSENESS OF RELATIONSHIP TO MOTHER OR FATHER BY RESIDENTIAL GROUPING

Variables Entered	b	t	β	F	R^2	N
Mother residence:						
				6.02***	.05	366
Intercept	5.35					
Age	.08	1.38	.07			
Sex	.45	1.56	.08			
Closeness to mother	−.07	−3.31***	−.17			
				2.67*	.02	337
Intercept	3.71					
Age	.08	1.40	.08			
Sex	.47	1.55	.08			
Closeness to father	−.03	−1.46	−.08			
Father residence:						
				8.65****	.21	99
Intercept	3.29					
Age	.29	2.64**	.24			
Sex	1.06	1.85⁺	.18			
Closeness to mother	−.11	−3.33**	−.32			
				4.66**	.13	100
Intercept	−.40					
Age	.28	2.37*	.23			
Sex	1.59	2.69**	.26			
Closeness to father	−.02	−.38	−.04			
Dual residence:						
				1.29	.08	51
Intercept	11.74					
Age	−.20	−1.05	−.15			
Sex	.28	.32	.05			
Closeness to mother	−.14	−1.83	−.27			
				.59	.04	51
Intercept	9.81					
Age	−.19	−.97	−.14			
Sex	.17	.20	.03			
Closeness to father	−.09	−1.13	−.17			

⁺ $p \le .10$.
* $p \le .05$.
** $p \le .01$.
*** $p \le .001$.
**** $p \le .0001$.

TABLE 6

POST HOC t TESTS FROM ANALYSES PREDICTING FEELINGS OF BEING CAUGHT BETWEEN PARENTS WITH CLOSENESS TO PARENTS (Close to Two vs. Close to One vs. Close to Neither)

				CAUGHT BETWEEN PARENTS		
				t for Difference in Means		
CLOSENESS TO PARENTS	N	M	SD	1	2	3
1. Close to neither parent	165	5.1	2.8	. . .	−.12	3.32***
2. Close to one parent	179	5.2	2.8			3.55***
3. Close to both parents	149	4.1	2.8			. . .

NOTE.—Means and standard deviations are adjusted for sex and age.
*** $p \le .001$.

273

feeling caught between parents mediated effects of family and adolescent characteristics on adjustment outcomes. The first set focused on "caught" as a mediator of coparenting, age, sex, and outcomes. The second focused on "caught" as a mediator of closeness to parents and outcomes. Zero-order correlations among the various predictor and outcome variables are presented in Table 7.

Coparenting.—In path analysis, causal relations between variables are posited and tested using a series of multiple regressions. Each dependent variable in the model is predicted, simultaneously, with all independent variables preceding it (see Johnson & Wichern, 1988). In our analyses, we first predicted either depression or deviance with: "caught," two dummy variables representing whether an adolescent was in dual residence (vs. all others) or whether he or she was in father residence (vs. all others), one of the coparenting measures (discord, cooperative communication, or hostility), age, and sex (female = 1, male = 0). Next, we predicted "caught" with the residence dummy variables, the coparenting measure, age, and sex. Third, we predicted the residence dummy variables with coparenting, age, and sex. Last, we correlated coparenting, age, and sex.

We included the measures of residence in this model—even though there had not been effects of residential arrangement on feeling caught between parents in our earlier analyses—in order to see whether any effects would emerge once coparenting was controlled. We entered the three coparenting measures in separate models because, although the correlations among coparenting measures were theoretically not large enough to produce multicollinearity problems, they were high enough to produce possible misleading results about their relative effects.

The results we report are those using "discord" as the measure of coparenting. Results using "cooperative communication" and "hostility" are similar. Standardized regression coefficients from these analyses are presented as path coefficients; coefficients are presented for the full sample and for one random sample of sibling cases, in order to show which effects are tenuous.

Results of these path analyses support the hypothesis that coparenting is related to outcomes via adolescents' feelings of being caught between parents. As indicated in the zero-order correlations (Table 7) and as shown in Figures 1 and 2, there was no direct association between interparental discord and depression or deviance. Discord was, however, related to feeling caught, which was, in turn, related to the outcomes. Thus, parental discord did not appear to augment either depression or deviance among adolescents in this sample unless the adolescent felt caught between parents as a result of the conflict.

Age and sex also had indirect effects on adjustment through their relations with feeling caught, although the associations between these variables and "caught" appeared to be of borderline significance when other variables in the model were controlled. The direct paths between age and sex and the outcomes were much stronger and more stable than the indirect paths.

Adolescents' closeness to parents.—Analyses examining whether feeling caught between parents mediates between closeness to parents and outcomes were not as clear as the analyses described above, primarily because the direction of effect with regard to "closeness" and "caught" could not easily be resolved. In the path analyses for coparenting, measures of coparenting were reported at an earlier point in time and by different reporters than the measure of feeling caught. It was logical to hypothesize that parents' coparenting influenced adolescents' feelings of being caught. In the case of closeness to parents, however, "closeness" and "caught" were reported by adolescents at the same point in time; it is plausible that feelings of being caught could influence feelings of closeness to parents as well as the reverse.

Furthermore, the correlations between closeness to parents and outcomes were of the same magnitude as those between closeness to parents and "caught" (see Table 7), and both closeness and caught continued to predict outcomes when entered into a regression equation where the effects of one were controlled for the other. Thus, unlike with coparenting, we did not have a strong argument for presenting a model in which "closeness" predicted "caught," which in turn predicted outcomes, as opposed to a variety of alternative models (e.g., "caught" predicts "closeness," which predicts outcomes; "closeness" predicts both "caught" and "outcomes," etc.). We believe there are some intriguing relations here that need to be tested using longitudinal data.

TABLE 7
ZERO-ORDER CORRELATIONS AMONG COMPOSITES USED IN PATH ANALYSES

Composites	Deviance	Caught	Dual Residence	Father Residence	Discord	Cooperative Communication	Hostility	Closeness to Mother	Closeness to Father
Depression..................	.38	.41	-.12	.02	.08	-.04	.03	-.28	-.22
Deviance....................		.23	-.06	.13	.01	.00	.06	-.22	-.09
Caught.......................			-.08	.08	.26	-.20	.19	-.25	-.12
Dual residence				-.16	-.02	.01	-.14	.10	.17
Father residence					-.00	-.00	.11	-.16	.08
Discord......................						-.39	.57	-.07	-.16
Cooperative communication ...							-.46	.05	.14
Hostility								-.07	-.09
Closeness to mother....									.26

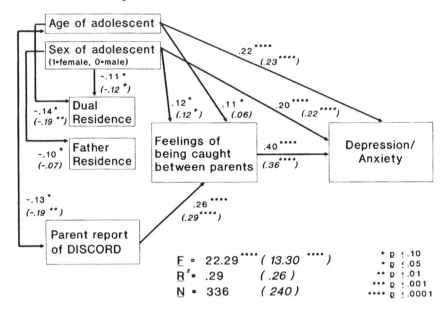

Note: Numbers in parenthesis are from analyses using all adolescents in families where only one adolescent was interviewed and one randomly chosen adolescent from families where more than one adolescent was interviewed.

FIG. 1.—Predicting depression with feelings of being caught between parents, residential arrangement, parental discord, sex of adolescent, and age of adolescent.

Discussion

Previous research has found that adjustment outcomes vary among children in seemingly similar postdivorce circumstances (Clingempeel & Repucci, 1984; Emery, 1988; O'Leary, 1984). Both the divorce and family systems literatures suggest that a possible reason for diverse outcomes is the extent to which a child becomes caught between parents. This article provides evidence that feeling caught is related to postdivorce variability in adjustment, and that, in addition, it may help to explain and refine previously documented relations between family or child characteristics and adjustment outcomes.

What factors increase the likelihood that adolescents will feel caught between parents? The most powerful predictor of feeling caught in this sample was the coparenting relationship. High discord and hostility and low cooperative communication between parents predicted more feelings of being caught between parents. Adolescents of parents who had disengaged from one another were less likely to feel caught than adolescents whose parents were still fighting, but

more likely to feel caught than adolescents whose parents were actively cooperating.

Despite the strong relation between feeling caught and the quality of the interparental relationship, not all adolescents whose parents had poor relationships felt caught between their parents, and some adolescents felt caught even though their parents scored on the positive end of our coparenting measures. For example, two-fifths of the adolescents whose parents had high discord scores were nevertheless below the median on feeling caught. A similar percentage of adolescents whose parents were in low conflict had "caught" scores equal to or above the median. Further, even though siblings always experienced the same amount of parent-described conflict, the correlation between siblings on feeling caught was .31—a moderately high correlation, but lower than one might expect if parental conflict were the main determining factor in such feelings. The implications of this are twofold: (1) some parents in high conflict refrain from the types of behaviors indicated in our composite as important in determining how "caught" a child feels (e.g., interro-

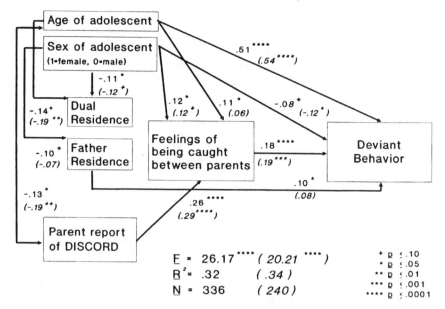

FIG. 2.—Predicting deviance with feelings of being caught between parents, residential arrangement, parental discord, sex of adolescent, and age of adolescent.

gating the child about the other home or asking the child to relay messages) while others in low conflict do not; and (2) characteristics of individual adolescents or their families—other than the coparenting relationship—affect the likelihood of feeling caught between parents. Our data indicate that other potential predictors of feeling caught include the amount of time spent with each parent (in interaction with the coparenting relationship), closeness of the parent-adolescent relationship, and age and sex of the adolescent.

Although there were no main effects of the amount of time spent with each parent on feeling caught, the effects of the coparenting relationship were particularly strong for adolescents in dual residence. Thus, spending considerable time with both parents after divorce does not seem to be especially beneficial or harmful in itself (see Folberg, 1979; Levy & Chambers, 1981). Dual residence arrangements, however, do appear harmful when parents remain in high conflict. Conversely, adolescents in dual residence seem to benefit from interparental cooperation more than do adolescents in

sole residence arrangements. Our results suggest that the direct relation between frequent contact and being caught in parents' conflict found by Johnston et al. (1989) is a finding limited to high-conflict families.

Adolescents who had close relationships with their parents were less likely to feel caught between their parents. When parents have close relationships with their children they may be more sensitive to their children's feelings and be, therefore, less likely to behave in ways that put their children in the middle. With our data, however, we cannot rule out the alternative hypothesis that children who feel caught between their parents are more likely to develop and maintain close relationships with them after divorce. Why was the association especially strong for closeness to mothers? Hetherington (1979) reported that a child's relationship with mother was more important in predicting outcomes after divorce than his or her relationship with father, but in her study all children were in mother's physical custody. Our study points to the important place of the mother-child relationship 4½ years after divorce, even in cases where mother-child contact is limited. Perhaps the tendency for children to have more intimate relationships with their mothers than their fathers means that mothers' behaviors have a stronger influence on children's feelings of being caught, or, alternatively, that mothers are more likely to bear the brunt of negative feelings of children who feel caught.

We had anticipated that being close to *both* parents would increase loyalty conflicts and, hence, feelings of being caught between parents. This was not the case. Adolescents who were close to both parents were the least likely to feel caught between parents, even in comparison to adolescents who were close to only one parent. Further research is needed to clarify the direction of this effect.

Age and sex of adolescent were also related to feeling caught between parents. Older adolescents in our sample were slightly more likely to feel caught, suggesting that increases in social and cognitive maturity across the adolescent years may increase one's opportunities or tendencies to become caught between parents. Our age effect was small, however, and other circumstances (e.g., the coparenting relationship) appear to be more important predictors of feeling caught between parents than age.

Girls were more likely to feel caught between parents than boys. We had anticipated that this might be the case, for girls show greater concern with maintaining interpersonal relationships and with developing mutually satisfying resolutions to conflict (e.g., Maccoby, 1990; Miller et al., 1986). Additionally, although findings on sex differences among adolescents of divorce are inconsistent (Zaslow, 1988, 1989), there is some evidence that girls have more negative reactions to life stress during adolescence than do boys (Compas, 1987; Petersen, Sarigiani, & Kennedy, in press).

We did not find, however, that living with one's opposite-sex parent predicted more feelings of being caught in the middle. Although girls living with fathers had somewhat higher means of feeling caught than girls living with mothers, boys living with mothers felt no more caught than boys living with fathers, and the sex of child–sex of parent interaction was not statistically significant.

Having identified some postdivorce factors that predicted feelings of being caught

between parents, the remaining aims of this study were to see whether feeling caught in the middle was related to poor adjustment and whether it mediated relations between other characteristics of the postdivorce family (e.g., parental conflict) or child (e.g., age, sex) and adolescent outcomes. Feelings of being caught were related to higher levels of depression/anxiety and more deviant behavior. Furthermore, for the adolescents in our sample, the effects of the coparenting relationship on adolescent adjustment were completely accounted for by its relation to feeling caught between parents. In this sense, feelings of being caught mediated between the interparental relationship and adolescent outcomes. To our surprise, however, there were no direct associations between coparenting and outcomes in our sample, even when feeling caught was not controlled. This inconsistency with previous literature on the effects of parental conflict may be due to the somewhat different measures used in our study, the low reliability of our coparenting measures, or perhaps to the fact that our coparenting measures do not distinguish between conflicts to which adolescents are exposed and are not exposed. For instance, correlations between adolescent-reported coparenting and outcomes were larger than between parent-reported coparenting and outcomes (although substituting adolescent-reported conflict or cooperation in the path analyses does not change the results of those analyses).

Thus, although adolescents of parents in high conflict do not always end up feeling caught between parents, the fact that many of them do may help to explain why adjustment problems are often found among such adolescents. Our results suggest that parental conflict has negative effects by altering family interaction in such a way that either the child is explicitly drawn into the conflict and/or becomes fearful of what effect a positive relationship with one parent will have on the other parent. Stress from the parent-parent relationship is, in this sense, shared with or diverted to the parent-child relationships, and this stress appears to have negative consequences in terms of adjustment. These results also indicate, however, that parental conflict need not affect children negatively. If children do not feel caught between battling parents, they are less likely to manifest negative adjustment outcomes. Thus, children's experience of feeling caught helps to explain both the average relation between parental conflict and child outcomes and the variability in adjustment to parental conflict.

Evidence that feelings of being caught between parents mediate other facets of family or individual characteristics was not as strong. Direct effects of age and sex on outcomes were stronger than their indirect effects through feeling caught. Methodologically, we could not distinguish between the possibilities of "caught" mediating the effect of closeness to parents on outcomes versus closeness mediating the effect of "caught." Both constructs were clearly related to each other and to adjustment outcomes.

Several caveats need to be considered when interpreting these results. For instance, the fact that we did not have measures of the same constructs by different reporters at the same point in time raises questions about bias in reporting. The little information we do have, however, suggests that our constructs are reasonably valid. For instance, the correlations between parent-reported measures of coparenting and interviewer-reported hostility were fairly large and in the direction expected. In addition, correlations between parent (Time 3) and adolescent (Time 4) reports of similar—though not identical—constructs are also in the expected direction. We asked adolescents about how often their parents argued and how often their parents told them to do different things. A composite of these items correlated .34 with the parent-reported discord measure. Similarly, an adolescent-reported measure of cooperation (how often do your parents talk, how often do they try to cooperate in decisions, and how often do they try to have the same rules) correlated .41 with the "cooperative communication" composite.

What about the fact that we have no convergent validation for our core construct—feeling caught between parents? Although we do not know how the adolescents' reports would agree with others' (i.e., parents') reports on this measure, we were specifically interested in the adolescents' perspective. We would argue that the adolescents' own feelings of being caught—regardless of whether others would notice these feelings and would report them similarly—are most likely to influence their adjustment. It will be important, however, to see how adolescents' reports of the types of parental behavior measured here relate to parents' or others' reports of the same behaviors.

With regard to depression and deviance, we are also clearly relying on adolescents' own perceptions. Although we cannot rule out the possibility that reports of "caught," depression, and deviance simply represent a negative response set, if this were so, we would have expected associations between predictors and outcomes similar to those between predictors and "caught." In particular, the much stronger association of coparenting variables with "caught" than with outcomes suggests that "caught" measures something beyond poor adjustment. A logical next step, however, would be to test these hypotheses using longitudinal data and data from multiple respondents. The measure of "caught" should also be validated by comparison with other measures of loyalty conflicts, parental triangulation, and/or boundary diffusion. When more indices of each are available, it would be fruitful to separate the behavioral and emotional aspects that we incorporated into one measure and to study more explicitly which parental behaviors are related to the emotional experience of loyalty conflicts.

The low reliabilities of the scales measuring discord, cooperative communication, and caught indicate that there is measurement error in these assessments; such error, however, means that the results we have reported are probably conservative. Given the seeming importance of feeling caught in the middle between parents, attention should be given to better delineating the dimensions of this construct and how best to measure those dimensions. Replicating the path analyses with a more reliable measure of parental conflict—which might show stronger relations with outcomes—should also be a priority. Finally, an attempt to replicate these results using methods of interviewing other than telephone interviewing would also be informative.

We have already indicated that an intriguing task for future research is to disentangle the relations among closeness to parents, feelings of being caught, and adjustment outcomes. Determining other predictors of feeling caught would also be fruitful. For instance, temperamental characteristics of the child may affect his or her willingness to be a go-between. In addition, developmental changes in the predictors of feeling caught and in the strength of the connection between feeling caught and adjustment should be explored. For instance, among younger children (preschool through early adolescence), boys were more likely to be caught in parents' conflict than were girls (Johnston et al., 1989), while in our adolescent sample boys were less likely to feel caught between parents. Is this because of the different methods used in the two studies, or is there a developmental change in the likelihood that boys versus girls feel caught between parents?

Taken together, the findings reported in this study add to our knowledge about when and why children adjust poorly to parental divorce and conflict. Factors identified in previous studies as buffering children from the effects of divorce (e.g., low interparental conflict and possibly positive parent-child relationships) may have their beneficial effects at least in part through reducing the extent to which children feel caught between parents. Our results also suggest, however, that even when parents are in high conflict, if children can escape feeling caught between parents they are to some extent buffered from the impact of that conflict.

Our findings also point to the importance of considering the family as a system (P. Minuchin, 1985; Vuchinich, Emery, & Cassidy, 1988). Examining triadic interactions and relationships (i.e., among mother, father, and child) may be necessary not only for understanding child adjustment but for understanding the course of interparental relationships after divorce.

References

Amato, P. R. (1987). Family processes in one-parent, stepparent, and intact families: The child's point of view. *Journal of Marriage and the Family, 49,* 327–337.

Aponte, H. J., & Van Deusen, J. M. (1981). Structural family therapy. In A. S. Gurman & D. P. Kniskern (Eds.), *Handbook of family therapy* (pp. 310–360). New York: Brunner/Mazel.

Clingempeel, W. G., & Reppucci, N. D. (1984). Joint custody after divorce: Major issues and goals for research. *Psychological Bulletin, 91,* 102–107.

Clingempeel, W. G., & Segal, S. (1986). Stepparent-stepchild relationships and the psychological adjustment of children in stepmother and stepfather families. *Child Development, 57,* 474–484.

Compas, B. E. (1987). Stress and life events during childhood and adolescence. *Clinical Psychology Review, 7,* 275–302.

Dornbusch, S. M., Mont-Reynaud, R., Ritter, P. L., Chen, Z., & Steinberg, L. (1991). Stressful events and their correlates among adolescents of diverse backgrounds. In M. E. Colten & S. Gore (Eds.), *Adolescent stress: Causes*

and consequences (pp. 111–130). Hawthorne, NY: Aldine de Gruyter.

Emery, R. E. (1988). *Marriage, divorce, and children's adjustment* (Developmental Clinical Psychology and Psychiatry, Vol. 14). Newbury Park, CA: Sage.

Fauber, R., Forehand, R., Thomas, A. M., & Wierson, M. (1990). A mediational model of the impact of marital conflict on adolescent adjustment in intact and divorced families: The role of disrupted parenting. *Child Development, 61,* 1112–1123.

Fine, M. A., Worley, S. M., & Schwebel, A. I. (1985). The parent-child relationship survey: An examination of its psychometric properties. *Psychological Reports, 57,* 155–161.

Folberg, H. J. (1979). Joint custody of children following divorce. *University of California, Davis, Law Review, 12,* 523–581.

Furstenberg, F. F., Nord, S. W., Peterson, J. L., & Zill, N. (1983). The life course of children of divorce: Marital disruption and parental contact. *American Sociological Review, 48,* 656–668.

Gilligan, C. (1982). *In a different voice: Psychological theory and women's development.* Cambridge, MA: Harvard University Press.

Goldstein, J., Freud, A., & Solnit, A. J. (1979). *Beyond the best interests of the child.* New York: Free Press.

Groves, R. M., & Kahn, R. L. (1979). *Surveys by telephone: A natural comparison with personal interviews.* New York: Academic Press.

Hetherington, E. M. (1979). Family interaction and the social, emotional, and cognitive development of children following divorce. In V. Vaughn & T. Brazelton (Eds.), *The family: Setting priorities* (pp. 71–87). New York: Science and Medicine.

Hetherington, E. M., Cox, M., & Cox, R. (1978). The aftermath of divorce. In J. H. Stevens, Jr., & M. Matthews (Eds.), *Mother-child, father-child relations* (pp. 149–176). Washington, DC: NAEYC.

Hetherington, E. M., Cox, M., & Cox, R. (1982). Effects of divorce on parents and children. In M. Lamb (Ed.), *Nontraditional families* (pp. 233–288). Hillsdale, NJ: Erlbaum.

Johnson, R. A., & Wichern, D. W. (1988). *Applied multivariate statistical analysis* (2d ed.). Englewood Cliffs, NJ: Prentice-Hall.

Johnston, J. R., & Campbell, L. E. G. (1987). Instability in family networks of divorced and disputing parents. In E. J. Lawler & B. Markovsky (Eds.), *Advances in group processes* (Vol. 4, pp. 243–269). Greenwich, CT: JAI.

Johnston, J. R., Campbell, L. E. G., & Mayes, S. S. (1985). Latency children in post-separation and divorce disputes. *Journal of the American Academy of Child Psychiatry, 24,* 563–574.

Johnston, J. R., Kline, M., & Tschann, J. M. (1989). Ongoing post-divorce conflict in families contesting custody: Effects on children of joint custody and frequent access. *American Journal of Orthopsychiatry*, 59, 576–592.

Levy, B., & Chambers, C. (1981). The folly of joint custody. *Family Advocate*, 3, 6–10.

Maccoby, E. E. (1990). Gender and relationships. *American Psychologist*, 45, 513–520.

Maccoby, E. E., Depner, C. E., & Mnookin, R. H. (1990). Coparenting in the second year after divorce. *Journal of Marriage and the Family*, 52, 141–155.

Miller, P. M., Danaher, D. L., & Forbes, D. (1986). Sex-related strategies for coping with interpersonal conflict in children aged five and seven. *Developmental Psychology*, 22, 543–548.

Minuchin, P. (1985). Families and individual development: Provocations from the field of family therapy. *Child Development*, 56, 289–302.

Minuchin, S. (1974). *Families and family therapy.* Cambridge, MA: Harvard University Press.

Montemayor, R., & Brownlee, J. R. (1987). Fathers, mothers, and adolescents: Gender-based differences in parental roles during adolescence. *Journal of Youth and Adolescence*, 16, 281–291.

O'Leary, K. D. (1984). Marital discord and children: Problems, strategies, methodologies, and results. In A. B. Doyle, D. Gold, & D. S. Moskowitz (Eds.), *New directions for child development: No. 24. Children in families under stress* (pp. 35–46). San Francisco: Jossey-Bass.

Patterson, G. R. (1982). *Coercive family process.* Eugene, OR: Castalia.

Petersen, A. C., Sarigiani, P. A., & Kennedy, R. E. (in press). Adolescent depression: Why more girls? *Journal of Youth and Adolescence.*

Roman, M., & Haddad, W. (1978). *The disposable parent: The case for joint custody.* New York: Holt, Rinehart & Winston.

Shiller, V. M. (1986). Loyalty conflicts and family relationships in latency age boys: A comparison of joint and maternal custody. *Journal of Divorce*, 9, 17–38.

Smollar, J., & Youniss, J. (1985). Parent-adolescent relations in adolescents whose parents are divorced. *Journal of Early Adolescence*, 5, 129–144.

Steinman, S. (1981). The experience of children in a joint custody arrangement: A report of a study. *American Journal of Orthopsychiatry*, 51, 403–414.

Vuchinich, S., Emery, R., & Cassidy, J. (1988). Family members as third parties in dyadic family conflict: Strategies, alliances and outcomes. *Child Development*, 59, 1293–1302.

Wallerstein, J. S., & Blakeslee, S. (1989). *Second chances: Men, women and children a decade after divorce.* New York: Ticknor & Fields.

Wallerstein, J. S., & Kelly, J. B. (1980). *Surviving the breakup: How children and parents cope with divorce.* New York: Basic.

Warshak, R. A., & Santrock, J. W. (1983). The impact of divorce in father-custody and mother-custody homes: The child's perspective. In L. A. Kurdek (Ed.), *New directions for child development: No. 19. Children and divorce* (pp. 29–46). San Francisco: Jossey-Bass.

Zaslow, M. J. (1988). Sex differences in children's response to parental divorce: 1. Research methodology and postdivorce family forms. *American Journal of Orthopsychiatry*, 58, 355–378.

Zaslow, M. J. (1989). Sex differences in children's response to parental divorce: 2. Samples, variables, ages, and sources. *American Journal of Orthopsychiatry*, 59, 118–141.

Socialization and Development in a Changing Economy

The Effects of Paternal Job and Income Loss on Children

Vonnie C. McLoyd   *University of Michigan*

ABSTRACT: Research on the impact of paternal job and income loss on the child is reviewed. Although some direct effects have been found, most effects are indirect and mediated through the changes that economic loss produces in the father's behavior and disposition. Fathers who respond to economic loss with increased irritability and pessimism are less nurturant and more punitive and arbitrary in their interactions with the child. These fathering behaviors increase the child's risk of socioemotional problems, deviant behavior, and reduced aspirations and expectations. The child also may model the somatic complaints of the father. The child's temperament, physical attractiveness, relationship with the mother, and degree of contact with the father are discussed as factors that condition the father's treatment of the child following economic loss. Economic hardship also may influence the child's development indirectly through the events that it potentiates (e.g., divorce) and discourages (e.g., marriage). High maternal support and experiences that encourage maturity and autonomy appear to be critical sources of psychological resilience in children who have experienced economic hardship.

This review focuses on the effects on socialization and child development of economic decline that stems from paternal job and income loss. Declines in the relative income status and economic well-being of individuals in the United States are not uncommon. In the Panel Study of Income Dynamics, 31% of individuals lived in families whose relative income position moved down at least one quintile between 1971 and 1978, and 11% moved down at least two quintiles. During the same period, about one fifth of individuals lived in families whose income relative to need declined dramatically. These fluctuations are primarily due to changes in family composition, movement into and out of the labor force, and changes in employment status, although changes in work hours and hourly wages among the continuously employed also are contributing factors (Duncan, 1984).

High rates of unemployment and job loss for fathers are a social change that characterizes the 1980s and distinguishes the decade from the previous 40 years. Back-to-back recessions in 1980 and 1981–1982, combined with management decisions to retrench and alter production methods in major manufacturing industries in

response to foreign competition, resulted in an unemployment rate of 10.6% in late 1982, the highest since the Depression of the 1930s (Flaim & Sehgal, 1985). Between 1981 and 1986, 10.8 million American workers 20 years of age and over lost jobs because of plant closings, business failures, and layoffs. Those with 3 or more years of tenure on the jobs they lost (displaced workers) were without work for a median period of 18 weeks. In many cases, because wages were not restored to their previous level, reemployment only lessened rather than reversed economic decline. Of the displaced workers who found employment after losing jobs between 1981 and 1986, 30% had earnings that were 20% or more below their predisplacement earnings (Horvath, 1987).

Because most recent retrenchments have been in the manufacturing sector, where male workers predominate, rather than in the service sector, where women are more likely to be employed, most of the job loss in recent years has been among men. Afro-American men and their families experience a vastly disproportionate share of job and income loss, though we know least about how they cope with these events. This increased vulnerability to economic decline is the result of several factors including less education, less skill training, less job seniority, fewer transportable job skills, and institutional barriers deriving directly from past or present discrimination (e.g., housing patterns and information about job opportunities) (Buss & Redburn, 1983). Moreover, recent structural changes in the economy have hit Afro-American men especially hard: (a) Rates of displacement are higher and reemployment rates are lower in precisely those blue-collar occupations in which Afro-Americans are overrepresented (Simms, 1987); (b) the shift of manufacturing employment from central cities to outlying areas has been more injurious to Afro-Americans because they reside in central cities in disproportionate numbers (in 1980, 58% compared with 25% for the rest of the population); and (c) the transformation of central cities from centers of production to centers of administration has generated rapid increases in white-collar employment, but Afro-Americans rely disproportionately on blue-collar employment (Fusfeld & Bates, 1984).

Manufacturing employment is projected to decline by more than 800,000 jobs during the 1986–2000 period. As the shift from a goods-producing economy to a service economy continues, a substantial number of fathers are

Copyright 1989 by the American Psychological Association, Inc. 0003-066X/89/$00.75
Vol. 44, No. 2, 293–302

Figure 1
Conceptual Model of How Paternal Economic Loss Affects the Child

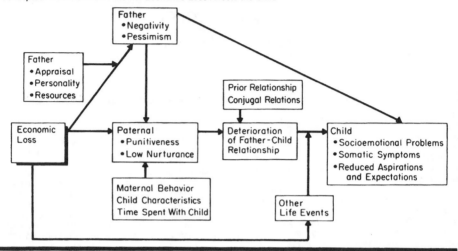

Preparation of this article was supported in part by a Faculty Scholar Award in Child Mental Health from the William T. Grant Foundation.

The author is grateful to Lois Wladis Hoffman and anonymous reviewers for valuable comments on the original version of this article.

Correspondence concerning this article should be addressed to Vonnie C. McLoyd, Department of Psychology, 3433 Mason Hall, University of Michigan, Ann Arbor, MI 48109.

expected to be displaced, and the geographic concentration of many of the declining industries portends mass unemployment and economic decline in some localities (Kutscher, 1987). Research on the impact of paternal job and income loss on children is limited but growing, and it is largely from two periods—the 1930s and the 1980s.

Conceptual Model

The organization of this review is guided by a conceptual model, shown in Figure 1, that assumes that economic loss is a stressor, or crisis-provoking event, if it poses a situation for which the family has had little or no prior preparation. Whether job or income loss is transformed from a stressor event into a crisis that seriously undermines the functioning of the father and his family is assumed to depend on his appraisal of the event and his crisis-meeting resources (Hill, 1958; Voydanoff, 1983).

Although the workplace where job and income loss occur typically is external to the child's environment, economic loss can influence the child's development primarily through the changes it produces in the father's behavior and disposition (father mediation). This conclusion is drawn from the pioneering studies conducted

by Elder and his colleagues of families that experienced economic decline during the Depression. These studies indicated that fathers who sustained heavy financial loss became more irritable, tense, and explosive, which in turn increased their tendency to be punitive and arbitrary in the discipline of their children. These fathering behaviors were predictive of temper tantrums, irritability, and negativism in young children, especially boys, and of moodiness and hypersensitivity, feelings of inadequacy, and lowered aspirations in adolescent girls (Elder, 1979; Elder, Liker, & Cross, 1984; Elder, Nguyen, & Caspi, 1985). The parenting behavior of mothers generally was not influenced by economic hardship.

Several economic and social changes since the Depression (e.g., unemployment compensation, severance pay, and employment of spouse) are thought to mitigate the negative impact of job and income loss in today's context (Jahoda, 1979; LeGrande, 1983). Nonetheless, Elder et al.'s causal pathway linking economic loss to the child through the father's behavior has been replicated in recent studies of contemporary children (Galambos & Silbereisen, 1987a; Kelly, Sheldon, & Fox, 1985; Lempers, Clark-Lempers, & Simon, in press). Wives of unemployed men appear to be affected through a similar mediational process (Dew, Bromet, & Schulberg, 1987). The robustness of this causal pathway suggests the importance of understanding those factors that buffer psychological impairment in economically deprived fathers and contravene harsh discipline. The impact of economic loss on father–child interaction and relations is seen as variable rather than constant and is assumed to be influenced by child characteristics and the nature of the family system. The model also assumes that economic decline may influence the child's development as a result of the kinds of events it potentiates (e.g., divorce) and discourages (e.g., marriage).

In keeping with the model, the first section of this review considers the impact of job and income loss on fathers. In the second section, father–child interaction and relations in economically strapped families as well as moderating factors are discussed. The third section briefly examines selected life events potentiated by economic decline that increase children's psychological risk. Finally, the effects of economic setbacks on children's socioemotional functioning, aspirations and expectations, and physical health are reviewed.

Effects on the Father

Although most studies of psychological effects of unemployment disregard parental status, their findings concur with effects reported specifically for unemployed fathers. Besides providing material support, work structures time and provides social contacts, a sense of identity and purpose, and evidence that one is needed by others (Jahoda, 1982). It is not surprising, then, that unemployed men are more depressed, anxious, and hostile and have elevated feelings of victimization and dissatisfaction with themselves and their lives, compared with employed men. They consume more alcohol, have more somatic complaints and eating and sleeping problems, and are at higher risk of neurosis, psychoticism, and suicide (Buss & Redburn, 1983; Gary, 1985; Kasl & Cobb, 1979; Liem, 1981; Theorell, Lind, & Floderus, 1975). Decreased psychosocial adjustment is evident among Afro-American men who expect to fail in the role of primary breadwinner, father, or husband (Bowman, in press). There also is evidence that fathers are more pessimistic about life as income loss increases (Galambos & Silbereisen, 1987a). Some negative effects of unemployment are more pronounced in heads of households with dependent children, compared with those without dependents (Schlozman & Verba, 1978), probably because financial strain and feelings of failure are more acute. The findings of studies of individuals are consistent with those of aggregate studies. For example, fluctuations in unemployment rates have been linked to aggregate indices of psychological distress (e.g., admissions to psychiatric hospitals, Dooley & Catalano, 1980; Horwitz, 1984).

Recent research has demonstrated cogently that these are true effects and not simply selective factors that lead to job loss (Dew et al., 1987; Kessler, House, & Turner, 1987). Not only has unemployment been shown to be directly responsible for increasing stress symptoms, but reemployment has been demonstrated to have health-promoting, restorative effects on fathers (Liem, 1983). Collectively, these studies present strong evidence that economic decline can adversely affect mental and physical well-being. Effects appear to occur through two mechanisms. First, unemployment results in increased financial strain, which in turn undermines physical and mental

health. Second, it leaves the individual more vulnerable to the impact of unrelated life events. When financial strain is controlled, unemployed workers who have not experienced some other stressful event in the previous year have been reported to be in no worse health than the stably employed (Kessler, Turner, & House, in press-a).

Appraisal and Personality Factors

The psychological and physical health outcomes of job and income loss are not uniform, but vary depending on several cognitive, personality, and social factors. Economic loss poses a greater risk to the mental and physical health of the father and consequently the child, if the father defines job or income loss as a negative, crisis-producing event (Horwitz, 1984; Perrucci & Targ, in press), blames himself for these events (Buss & Redburn, 1983; Cohn, 1978; Ginsburg, 1942; Kasl & Cobb, 1979; Komarovsky, 1940), is prone to self-denigration (Kessler, Turner, & House, in press-b), and has rigid, traditional conjugal and family role ideologies that make role changes difficult to implement and accept (Komarovsky, 1940; Powell & Driscoll, 1973; Voydanoff, 1983). If loss of employment or income is seen as a positive event or as an event caused by external forces, it may actually strengthen family ties and boost the father's morale (Caplovitz, 1979; Little, 1976; Moen, Kain, & Elder, 1983).

Social and Financial Support

Social support has been found to insulate fathers against the negative psychological impact of unemployment (Gore, 1978; Kasl & Cobb, 1979; Kessler et al., in press-b). Because they lessen the economic hardship caused by unemployment, greater financial assets and shorter periods of unemployment also ameliorate stress symptoms (Bakke, 1940; Gore, 1978; Kasl & Cobb, 1979; Kessler et al., in press-a, in press-b; Little, 1976). The latter two factors, combined with a reduced tendency to define job loss as a crisis of either identity or economic survival (Cohn, 1978), probably account for reduced levels of symptomatology among middle-class men (compared with working-class men) and nonminority men (compared with Afro-American men) (Buss & Redburn, 1983) who have lost jobs. As married women have entered the labor force, the proportion of unemployed husbands with a working wife (55% in 1981) has increased significantly (Klein, 1983). The wife's employment mitigates economic hardship following paternal job and income loss (Moen, 1983), though there is some tentative evidence that employment of the wife that is instigated by the husband's job loss can intensify the husband's feelings of failure (Tauss, 1976). Furthermore, if the ratio of wife's to husband's labor income increases, the restorative effects of the husband's reemployment may be attenuated (Cohn, 1978).

During the Depression, the employment of the adolescent son often eased the economic crisis for the family and appeared to facilitate the adolescent's long-term ego development (Elder, 1974). However, because children

285

tended to give their wages to the mother rather than the father, further eroding the father's status, the child's employment often increased family tension (Cavan, 1959). Today, children's employment is less likely to reduce the family's financial strain because of a major change in the meaning of children's work. The acquisition of discretionary items for themselves, not necessities or the family's subsistence needs, is the primary reason that today's adolescent works (Greenberger, 1987). Conflict is likely to erupt if parents attempt to alter the allocation of the child's wages in favor of the family's subsistence needs.

Effects on Father–Child Interaction

Because their disposition is more likely to be gloomy and hostile, parents who have experienced job or income loss have a tendency to be less nurturant and more punitive and arbitrary in their interactions with their children (Elder et al., 1984, 1985; Goldsmith & Radin, 1987; Lempers et al., in press). However, economic setbacks do not uniformly result in this kind of paternal treatment of the child. Several factors have been found to influence the quality of father–child interaction following job and income loss.

Temperament of the Child

Elder et al. (1985, 1986) found that father mediation of economic hardship through harsh discipline was conditioned by the child's temperament. Children who were temperamentally difficult (irritable, negative, and inclined toward tantrums) at 18 months were more likely to be disciplined in an extreme (severe punishment or indifference) and arbitrary manner by financially pressed fathers 3 years later. This was true even when the father's initial level of irritability (i.e., when the child was 18 months old) was controlled, a finding that is in accord with Rutter's (1979) research with multiproblem families. It is also interesting to note that fathers who were hostile toward the child before the economy crashed were arbitrary and punitive irrespective of how the child behaved, but initially affectionate fathers behaved arbitrarily and harshly primarily in response to problematic child behavior.

Physical Attractiveness of the Child

Elder et al.'s research also showed that economically deprived fathers became more punitive and less supportive of the daughter only if she was physically unattractive. If the daughter was attractive, in some cases economic hardship actually increased supportiveness and lessened paternal harshness. It has been suggested that perhaps physical unattractiveness is a risk factor because adults assign more blame to physically unattractive children and because unattractive girls are less self-confident and assertive because they think less highly of themselves (Elder et al., 1985, 1986). In Elder et al.'s work, boys' attractiveness made no difference in the parenting outcomes of economic hardship, perhaps because physical attractiveness is less critical to boys' sense of self and less salient in others' evaluations of them.

Increase in Father–Child Contact

Unemployed fathers often cite the opportunity for increased contact with their children as a positive aspect of an otherwise negative experience. They report significant increases in the amount of time devoted to child care when asked about changes in their behavior following job loss (Warr & Payne, 1983). Jobless fathers of preschoolers report spending more time as primary caregiver and greater involvement in child rearing overall than employed fathers, and data from their wives corroborate these reports (Radin & Goldsmith, in press). However, fathers differ in the amount of time they spend with their children, and this factor may influence the impact of economic setbacks on father–child interaction and consequently the child. Because it increases the opportunity for conflict and harsh treatment of the child, greater father–child contact makes it more likely that the child will be affected by economic hardship through the changes it produces in the father.

During the Depression, adolescent girls in economically deprived families suffered considerable socioemotional distress in response to the father's harshness. In contrast, adolescent boys' functioning, which reflected greater resiliency and ego strength, was not influenced by the behavior of the father. Elder and his colleagues posit two plausible explanations for this sex difference in father mediation. First, economically strapped fathers may have directed more punitive behavior toward daughters than sons, perhaps because of the daughter's lesser size and strength and/or a greater acceptance of such abusive behavior compared with adolescent sons. Second, and more germane to this discussion, adolescent girls may have spent more time with the father and, thus, may have been exposed to more abusive parenting and family discord than adolescent boys. Adolescent girls spent substantially more time in the home doing chores to compensate for the absence of mothers who took jobs to supplement family income, whereas adolescent boys often found employment outside the home (Elder, 1974; Elder et al., 1985, 1986).

Increased father–child contact following job loss may give rise to a heightened awareness of the child's negative attributes and a less favorable perception of the child. This may contribute to withdrawal of nurturance and an increase in punitiveness by the father. In a study of involuntarily unemployed fathers previously employed in predominantly blue-collar and lower level professional occupations, Johnson and Abramovitch (1985) found that those who were primary caretakers of their children were less positive in the description of their children, attached less importance to parenting skills, and saw their unemployment as less beneficial to the child, the longer they had been unemployed. The corresponding correlations were not significant for unemployed fathers whose children were cared for primarily by someone other than the father. Because selective factors were not ruled out and the sample was small ($n = 30$), these provocative findings must be interpreted cautiously. In a follow-up study of

296

286

these men six months later, Johnson and Abramovitch (1986) found a nonsignificant tendency for still-unemployed fathers to be more negative than reemployed men in the descriptions of their children, but they did not report differences between fathers who were primary caregivers and those who were nonprimary caregivers.

Unemployed fathers who assume the role of primary caregiver of preschoolers may feel behaviorally incompetent or psychologically unfit for the role (e.g., insufficient patience) or resentful about being forced into it. Even if the role of primary caregiver is viewed more positively at the outset, the new role may wear thin. As the demands of child care become more apparent and if child care responsibilities interfere with job search activities, what was initially an opportunity for greater involvement with the child may come to be seen as a burden. In addition, as the duration of unemployment increases, the father's negative feelings about his joblessness may spill over into his parenting role and rob him of the ability to enjoy the time with his child (Johnson & Abramovitch, 1985; Kanter, 1977). Increased participation in child care has been found to be associated with more positive mental health in highly educated unemployed fathers in dual-wage families—a finding that may reflect a waning of the tendency to regard caring for children as a sign of demasculinization (Shamir, 1986). However, the causal direction of this relationship is unclear, and the finding is probably not generalizable to working-class men such as those in Johnson and Abramovitch's (1985) study, who tend to have more traditional sex-role ideologies.

Extrapolating from Johnson and Abramovitch's (1985) findings, increased negative affect toward the child stemming from increased contact may be one of the mechanisms that mediate the well-documented link between unemployment and child abuse (Parke & Collmer, 1975). There are several other pathways by which the father's unemployment can lead to child abuse: (a) an increase in the father's role as disciplinarian, (b) a heightened need in fathers to exercise power because of a real or perceived status loss, (c) increased frustration brought on by financial strain, and (d) an increase in marital disputes and displacement of anger onto the child, especially if the child forms a coalition with the mother (Herrenkohl, Herrenkohl, & Egolf, 1983; Parke & Collmer, 1975). During the Depression, children whose fathers lost the greatest amount of income were most likely to perceive the mother as someone to rely on and most likely to align themselves with the mother when the parents quarreled (Elder, 1974). Taken together, this work and evidence that unemployed heads of household feel less positively about their children (Sheldon & Fox, 1983) appear to suggest that under certain conditions paternal unemployment lowers the worth of children to fathers (Siegal, 1984).

Role of the Mother

During the Depression, mothers played a pivotal role in determining how economically deprived fathers treated their children. If the mother's relationship with the child prior to the Depression was warm and affectionate, harsh treatment of the child by the father was reduced. In the face of economic loss, a family system distinguished by an aloof mother was most likely to lead to the father's maltreatment of the child. The quality of the mother-child relationship also made a difference in how income loss affected the child's behavior. Severe temper tantrums occurred only if the young child lacked a warm affective bond with the mother (Elder et al., 1986). Mothers were less supportive and protective of their young sons than their daughters, and this difference seems to explain why economic hardship during early childhood markedly increased the risk of psychological impairment in boys but was linked to personal strength and resourcefulness in girls (Elder, 1979).

Effects on the Father–Child Relationship

Given the increased tendency of unemployed fathers to behave toward their children in a rejecting, arbitrary manner, it is hardly surprising that economic losses have been found to strain the father's relationship with the child, to reduce his attractiveness to the child as a role model, companion, and confidant, and to increase the tendency of children to affiliate with peers and nonfamilial adults. The father's emotional volatility, combined with role changes and other adaptations to economic hardship, may enhance the affective status of the mother relative to the father (Elder, 1974). However, whether economic setbacks during the Depression threatened the father–child relationship depended on two factors—the quality of the father's relationship with the child before economic setbacks occurred and the affective disposition of the wife toward her husband.

Prior Father–Child Relationship

In Komarovsky's (1940) study, a positive father–child relationship prior to unemployment characterized all cases in which the fathers of young children gained status following job loss and all cases in which the fathers of children 15 years old or older maintained their parental authority (none of the latter fathers gained status). Among those fathers whose authority deteriorated subsequent to job loss, two dominant types of preunemployment father–child relationships were evident: coercive, disinterested fathers who were feared by their children and rigid, interfering fathers who commanded no respect but sought to impose on their children antiquated standards of decorum.

The Wife's Attitude

The attitude of the wife toward her husband exerted a powerful influence on the unemployed father's relationship with his child during the Depression. The mother's prominence in the child's life made it possible for her, first, to shape the child's understanding of the economic crisis and the father's ensuing behavior and, second, to modify the actions of the child toward the father. If she lost respect for her husband and blamed him for the disruption in their lives, she was unlikely either to present a sympathetic interpretation of the father's predicament

287

or to encourage child behaviors that acknowledged the authority of the father. Within this kind of marital context, the child's relationship with the father was likely to suffer (Elder, 1974; Ginsburg, 1942). There is no compelling reason to believe that this conditioner of effects on the father–child relationship would be any less potent in the context of today's economic setbacks (for a discussion of the impact of unemployment on marital relations, see Ray & McLoyd, 1986).

Recent research findings reflect a peculiar inconsistency. Today's middle-class and working-class parents rarely report deterioration of their relationship with the child following job loss when directly asked. In fact, they are as likely or more likely to report improvement in relations with the child following job loss (Perrucci & Targ, in press; Perrucci, Targ, Perrucci, & Targ, 1987; Rayman & Bluestone, cited in Cunningham, 1983; Thomas, McCabe, & Berry, 1980), though this outcome would appear unlikely if relations were markedly distant or contentious prior to job loss (Komarovsky, 1940). In some of these studies, unemployed workers received relatively generous economic assistance following job loss (e.g., severance pay or continuation of health benefits) (Perrucci & Targ, in press), were middle class and had substantial financial assets (Thomas et al., 1980), or typically had spouses who were employed (Little, 1976). All of these factors may have mitigated family tension and discord. Also, it should be pointed out that most of these studies did not have a comparison group of employed workers.

In contrast to these benign reports from unemployed parents, when unemployed and reemployed groups are compared and the estimates of parent–child conflict are based on reports from the child, rather than the parent, differences have been found. In a recent study by Flanagan (1988b), adolescents whose parents were currently unemployed because of job loss reported more conflict with their parents than those whose parents lost jobs and had found new employment. Other researchers have found no relation between the father's employment status and children's reports of family problems (Buss & Redburn, 1983), but these reports may not reflect the quality of parent–child relationships per se. In general, the impact of economic setbacks in recent years on the father–child relationship is poorly understood because few relevant studies have been conducted and because existing studies, with notable exceptions, use severely truncated measures, ignore the child as a potential informant, lack comparison groups of employed families, and ignore conditioning factors.

Life Events Potentiated by Paternal Job and Income Loss

Unemployment may affect the child's development and his or her relationship with the father through its deterrence of marriage and ferment of marital instability. Furstenberg (1981) found that when out-of-wedlock conception occurred, marriage was much more likely to occur during the prenatal period if the father had a full-time job than if he was unemployed. Compared with those who deferred marriage, women who married prior to delivery were more likely to marry the father of the child. If she married the biological father, rather than another man, the child's cognitive and social skills were more advanced in later years, perhaps because of the continuity of the father–child relationship.

Several studies document the fact that marital dissolution is more likely if the husband is unemployed (Bishop, 1977), though the risk is probably much greater if the marriage was weak before the husband lost employment (Ray & McLoyd, 1986). When marriages end, whether through divorce, separation, or desertion, the child usually spends some time living in a single-parent household, most often (90%) headed by his or her mother (Blechman, 1982). Families headed by previously married mothers typically experience downward economic mobility. These events and circumstances have effects on both the child's development and relationship with the father (Hetherington, 1979; Weiss, 1979).

Effects on the Child

Socioemotional Functioning

Economic setbacks often require denial of money and accoutrements for social activities. These material losses, combined with embarrassment caused by the family's situation, may undermine the child's mental health and lead him or her to withdraw from peers. Children whose families have experienced job or income loss have more mental health problems (Werner & Smith, 1982) and are more depressed, lonely (Lempers et al., in press), and emotionally sensitive (Elder et al., 1985). They are less sociable and more distrustful (Buss & Redburn, 1983) and are more likely (adolescent girls) to feel excluded by peers (Elder, 1974). Parental unemployment also has been linked to low self-esteem in children, especially boys (Coopersmith, 1967; Isralowitz & Singer, 1986) and reduced competence in coping with stress (Flanagan, 1988a). Recent evidence indicates that many of these effects are mediated through the rejection and punitiveness of economically deprived parents (Elder et al., 1985; Lempers et al., in press). High maternal support and experiences that encourage maturity and autonomy appear to be critical sources of psychological resilience in economically deprived children (Elder, 1979).

If economic hardship can decrease peer affiliation, it also can increase it, especially in boys (Elder et al., 1985). The child's dependency on peers may make him or her highly susceptible to negative peer pressure. Children in families experiencing economic loss, compared with children in economically stable families, report performing more socially disapproved acts and violating more school rules (Flanagan, 1988b). Werner and Smith's (1982) longitudinal study of the children of Kauai, Hawaii, indicated that paternal job loss was one of the life events that discriminated between children who developed serious behavior problems (e.g., delinquency) and children who were free of such problems. Lempers et al. (in

298

press) found no direct link between economic hardship and delinquency-drug use. Rather, economic hardship led to more delinquency-drug use by increasing inconsistent and punitive discipline by parents. Research also indicates that problem behavior in children experiencing economic loss is greater if economic strain as perceived by parents is high (Perrucci & Targ, in press), if parental acceptance of the child is low (Galambos & Silbereisen, 1987b), if the family lacks cohesion (Flanagan, 1988b; Walper & Silbereisen, 1987), and if the marriage is weak (Rockwell & Elder, 1982).

Though the paucity of longitudinal data precludes firm conclusions, economic loss during childhood appears to have few long-term psychological effects. Buss and Redburn (1983), who interviewed college-age children of laid-off and employed steelworkers during the four years following the closing of the steel mills, reported no effects. Elder (1979) found few enduring effects of economic hardship on psychological health, though men who were economically deprived as very young children, compared with their nondeprived counterparts, were more worried, emotionally distant, and lethargic at midlife. They also had higher levels of alcohol consumption and were more likely to use professional therapy.

Aspirations and Expectations

Parents experiencing economic hardship are more pessimistic about their lives and the future of their children (Galambos & Silbereisen, 1987a; Ginsburg, 1942), feel less confident about helping their children prepare for future work roles, and are less likely to encourage college matriculation (Flanagan, 1988a). They also report more negative changes in educational plans for their children (Larson, 1984). These parental dispositions and behaviors appear to dampen children's aspirations and expectations. Adolescents in families experiencing economic loss express more financial worries, are less likely to expect to go to a four-year college, and are more likely to expect to go into vocational training after high school (Flanagan, 1988a), though their work values (i.e., ratings of the importance of job prestige and security, monetary rewards, etc.) appear unaffected (Isralowitz & Singer, 1986).

Girls are especially prone to reduce their aspirations and expectations of job success, and this seems to be in response to the father's pessimism and rejection (Elder et al., 1985; Galambos & Silbereisen, 1987a). Furthermore, economic adversity is more likely to lead to a downward shift in parents' educational plans for daughters than for sons (Mott & Haurin, 1982). These factors, combined with parental expectations of lower achievement in daughters than sons even in a favorable economic climate (Parsons, Adler, & Kaczala, 1982) and increased pressure during early adolescence to conform to feminine sex-role stereotypes (Galambos & Silbereisen, 1987a), constrict girls' aspirations and discourage feelings of self-adequacy.

If children's work aspirations diminish, education may come to be seen as irrelevant to the future and the child's academic performance may suffer. As one Detroit student put it after both her mother and father lost jobs:

The future stinks. You're supposed to spend your childhood preparing for the real life of being an adult. But what if that real life is no good? What's the sense? Look at my parents. They always did everything the way you're supposed to. Now look at them—nobody will give them a job. . . . What's the sense of trying in school. There's no jobs for my dad or my mom. Why should I believe there will be jobs for me when I get out [of school]? ("Children of the Unemployed," 1983, p. 3)

Research from the 1930s and the 1980s reports declines in the academic performance of children in families experiencing economic hardship. This may be the result of reduced educational and occupational expectations, emotional problems that reduce attention span, poor physical health, lack of parental assistance with homework, or a combination of these factors (Eisenberg & Lazarsfeld, 1938; Elder, 1979). Teachers perceive children from families experiencing economic loss to be less well adjusted to school than children from economically stable families (Flanagan, 1988a).

However, economic hardship may not be a strong predictor of occupational success. Elder (1979) found that though men from economically deprived families were less likely to complete college, they were more likely than nondeprived men to match or exceed career expectations based on level of education. Factors that appear to have fostered resilience in the deprived men who suffered psychological impairment during adolescence include entry into college, late marriage and child bearing, military service, a rewarding work life, and the emotional support of marriage and family life.

Physical Health

Children of job losers are at increased risk of illness including respiratory infections, gastrointestinal infections, immunological diseases such as asthma and eczema, and trauma (Margolis & Farran, 1981). This may be attributable to a decline in the quality of food, the disruption of social support, and a decrease in the use of medical care because many displaced workers lose employer-financed health insurance along with their jobs (Podgursky & Swaim, 1987). The impact of economic decline on children's physical health also may be mediated through the father's behavior. Children often learn how to behave in different situations and become aware of the consequences of events and behavior by observing the behavior of others (Bandura, 1977). Deterioration in the father's health following job and income loss may become a communicable social phenomenon to the extent that the child models the symptomatic behavior of the father (Kelly et al., 1985). Kelly et al. (1985) found no direct link between parental job loss and the child's physical health status. Rather, job loss adversely affected the child's physical health through its elevation of the parent's health problems. In Buss and Redburn's (1983) study, the somatic complaints of the children of unemployed steelworkers and managers paralleled those of the fathers.

Summary

Studies of contemporary families and families of the 1930s Depression are consistent in demonstrating that paternal job and income loss affect children's development primarily through the changes they produce in the father's behavior and disposition. The amount of psychological distress experienced by unemployed fathers and the extent to which this distress adversely affects the father's treatment of the child depend on several cognitive, personality, and environmental factors. Negative fathering behavior increases the child's risk of socioemotional problems, deviant behavior, and reduced aspirations and expectations.

A great deal more study is needed of those factors that account for variation in the child's response to economic hardship in the contemporary context. Degree of material deprivation, social support, family decision-making style, adolescent employment, developmental status, and the child's causal attributions about the parent's loss of employment or income are obvious factors that need to be considered. The contemporary mother, more so than mothers of the Depression, shares her role as socializer and caregiver with others (e.g., father or day care worker), often because she is employed. Whether she is as potent as mothers of the Depression in insulating the child against the negative impact of economic hardship is not known. Studies are needed to determine long-term effects and how these are related to the child's work values and causal attributions about economic decline. Our knowledge base should be expanded to include Afro-American and Hispanic families because their risk of economic decline is high.

Maternal Job and Income Loss

Research on the impact of economic decline focuses almost exclusively on displaced men and their children, despite significant numbers of married and single mothers who are unemployed and seeking work. Women were less affected than men by the two recent recessions because their employment is concentrated in the steadily growing service-producing sector, but they were not immune. Of those workers displaced between 1981 and 1986 from jobs they had held at least three years, about a third were women (Horvath, 1987). Compared with married men, married women appear to be spared at least some of the psychological costs of unemployment, apparently because the alternative roles of wife and mother provide self-gratification and self-definition that men do not derive from their roles as husbands and fathers (Warr & Parry, 1982). On the assumption that children's responses to job loss are conditioned by parents' responses, one would expect children to be less affected by maternal job loss than paternal job loss if it occurs in the context of marriage. However, more substantial effects may result if work is a major source of a mother's identity, self-esteem, and psychological fulfillment or if her wages are a significant determinant of the family's income and standard of living.

Two factors make it difficult to be sanguine about children living in households headed by single women who have suffered economic losses. First, they have fewer financial resources and face a high risk of falling into poverty (Rosen, 1983). Because there are fewer persons of working age, on average, in female-headed families, these families are less likely to have a second wage earner whose income can cushion the impact of job and income loss. Since 1976, the proportion of unemployed women who head families that include an employed person has never exceeded 22% (Klein, 1983). Second, irrespective of employment status, single mothers generally are at greater risk of anxiety, depression, and health problems than other marital status groups (Guttentag, Salasin, & Belle, 1980; Kelly et al., 1985). Thus, they probably have fewer psychological resources to cope with economic setbacks, and this is likely to increase the risk of punitive and harsh treatment of the child. These considerations justify special concern about the children of single women who experience job and income loss.

REFERENCES

Bakke, E. (1940). *Citizens without work.* New Haven, CT: Yale University.
Bandura, W. (1977). *Social learning theory.* Englewood Cliffs, NJ: Prentice-Hall.
Bishop, J. (1977). *Jobs, cash transfers, and marital instability: A review of the evidence.* Madison: University of Wisconsin Institute for Research on Poverty.
Blechman, E. (1982). Are children with one parent at psychological risk? A methodological review. *Journal of Marriage and the Family, 44,* 179–196.
Bowman, P. (in press). Post-industrial displacement and family role strains: Challenges to the black family. In P. Voydanoff & L. Majka (Eds.), *Families and economic distress.* Beverly Hills, CA: Sage.
Buss, T., & Redburn, F. S. (1983). *Mass unemployment: Plant closings and community mental health.* Beverly Hills, CA: Sage.
Caplovitz, D. (1979). *Making ends meet: How families cope with inflation and recession.* Beverly Hills, CA: Sage.
Cavan, R. S. (1959). Unemployment—crisis of the common man. *Marriage and Family Living, 21,* 139–146.
Cohn, R. (1978). The effect of employment status change on self-attitudes. *Social Psychology, 41,* 81–93.
Coopersmith, S. (1967). *The antecedents of self-esteem.* San Francisco: Freeman.
Cunningham, S. (1983, January). Shock of layoff felt deep inside family circle. *APA Monitor,* p. 14.
Children of the unemployed. (1983, March 8). *Detroit Free Press,* p. 3.
Dew, M., Bromet, E., & Schulberg, H. (1987). A comparative analysis of two community stressors' long-term mental health effects. *American Journal of Community Psychology, 15,* 167–184.
Dooley, D., & Catalano, R. (1980). Economic change as a cause of behavioral disorder. *Psychological Bulletin, 87,* 358–390.
Duncan, G. (1984). *Years of poverty, years of plenty.* Ann Arbor, MI: Institute for Social Research.
Eisenberg, P., & Lazarsfeld, P. E. (1938). The psychological effects of unemployment. *Psychological Bulletin, 35,* 358–390.
Elder, G. (1974). *Children of the Great Depression.* Chicago: University of Chicago Press.
Elder, G. (1979). Historical change in life patterns and personality. In P. Baltes & O. Brim (Eds.), *Life span development and behavior* (Vol. 2, pp. 117–159). New York: Academic Press.
Elder, G., Caspi, A., & Nguyen, T. (1986). Resourceful and vulnerable children: Family influence in hard times. In R. K. Silbereisen, K. Eyferth, & G. Rudinger (Eds.), *Development as action in context* (pp. 167–186). New York: Springer-Verlag.
Elder, G., Liker, J., & Cross, C. (1984). Parent-child behavior in the Great Depression: Life course and intergenerational influences. In P. Baltes & O. Brim (Eds.), *Life span development and behavior* (Vol. 6, pp. 109–158). Orlando, FL: Academic Press.

290

Elder, G., Nguyen, T., & Caspi, A. (1985). Linking family hardship to children's lives. *Child Development, 56,* 361–375.

Flaim, P., & Sehgal, E. (1985). Displaced workers of 1979–83: How well have they fared? *Monthly Labor Review, 108,* 3–16.

Flanagan, C. (1988a, April). *The effects of a changing economy on the socialization of children's academic and vocational aspirations.* Paper presented at the American Educational Research Association, New Orleans.

Flanagan, C. (1988b). *Parents' work security and the young adolescent's development.* Unpublished manuscript, University of Michigan, Dearborn.

Furstenberg, F. (1981). The social consequences of teenage parenthood. In F. Furstenberg, R. Lincoln, & J. Menken (Eds.), *Teenage sexuality, pregnancy, and childbearing* (pp. 184–210). Philadelphia: University of Pennsylvania Press.

Fusfeld, D., & Bates, T. (1984). *The political economy of the urban ghetto.* Carbondale, IL: Southern Illinois University Press.

Galambos, N., & Silbereisen, R. (1987a). Income change, parental life outlook, and adolescent expectations for job success. *Journal of Marriage and the Family, 49,* 141–149.

Galambos, N., & Silbereisen, R. (1987b). Influences of income change and parental acceptance on adolescent transgression proneness and peer relations. *European Journal of Psychology of Education, 1,* 17–28.

Gary, L. (1985). Correlates of depressive symptoms among a select population of black men. *American Journal of Public Health, 75,* 1220–1222.

Ginsburg, S. W. (1942). What unemployment does to people. *American Journal of Psychiatry, 99,* 439–446.

Goldsmith, R., & Radin, N. (1987, April). *Objective versus subjective reality: The effects of job loss and financial stress on fathering behavior.* Paper presented at the biennial meeting of the Society for Research in Child Development, Baltimore, MD.

Gore, S. (1978). The effect of social support in moderating the health consequences of unemployment. *Journal of Health and Social Behavior, 19,* 157–165.

Greenberger, E. (1987). Children's employment and families. In N. Gerstel & H. Gross (Eds.), *Families and work* (pp. 396–406). Philadelphia: Temple University Press.

Guttentag, M., Salasin, S., & Belle, D. (1980). *The mental health of women.* New York: Academic Press.

Herrenkohl, R., Herrenkohl, E., & Egolf, B. (1983). Circumstances surrounding the occurrence of child maltreatment. *Journal of Consulting and Clinical Psychology, 51,* 424–431.

Hetherington, M. (1979). Divorce: A child's perspective. *American Psychologist, 34,* 859–865.

Hill, R. (1958). Generic features of families under stress. *Social Casework, 39,* 139–150.

Horvath, F. (1987). The pulse of economic change: Displaced workers of 1981–85. *Monthly Labor Review, 110,* 3–12.

Horwitz, A. (1984). The economy and social pathology. *Annual Review of Sociology, 10,* 95–119.

Isralowitz, R., & Singer, M. (1986). Unemployment and its impact on adolescent work values. *Adolescence, 21,* 145–158.

Jahoda, M. (1979). The impact of unemployment in the 1930s and the 1970s. *Bulletin of the British Psychological Society, 32,* 309–314.

Jahoda, M. (1982). *Employment and unemployment: A social-psychological analysis.* Cambridge: Cambridge University Press.

Johnson, L., & Abramovitch, R. (1985). *Unemployed fathers: Parenting in a changing labour market* (ISBN 0-919456-30-8). Toronto, Canada: Social Planning Council of Metropolitan Toronto.

Johnson, L., & Abramovitch, R. (1986). *Between jobs: Paternal unemployment and family life* (ISBN 0-919456-29-4). Toronto, Canada: Social Planning Council of Metropolitan Toronto.

Kanter, R. (1977). *Work and family in the United States: A critical review and agenda for research and policy.* New York: Russell Sage.

Kasl, S. V., & Cobb, S. (1979). Some mental health consequences of plant closings and job loss. In L. Ferman & J. Gordus (Eds.), *Mental health and the economy* (pp. 255–300). Kalamazoo, MI: Upjohn Institute for Employment Research.

Kelly, R., Sheldon, A., & Fox, G. (1985). The impact of economic dislocation on the health of children. In J. Boulet, A. M. DeBritto, &

S. A. Ray (Eds.), *The impact of poverty and unemployment on children* (pp. 94–108). Ann Arbor: University of Michigan Bush Program in Child Development and Social Policy.

Kessler, R., House, J., & Turner, J. (1987). Unemployment and health in a community sample. *Journal of Health and Social Behavior, 28,* 51–59.

Kessler, R., Turner, J., & House, J. (in press-a). Intervening processes in the relationship between unemployment and health. *Psychological Medicine.*

Kessler, R., Turner, J., & House, J. (in press-b). The effects of unemployment on health in a community sample: Main, modifying, and mediating effects. *Journal of Social Issues.*

Klein, D. (1983). Trends in employment and unemployment in families. *Monthly Labor Review, 106,* 21–25.

Komarovsky, M. (1940). *The unemployed man and his family.* New York: Dryden Press.

Kutscher, R. (1987). Overview and implications of the projections to 2000. *Monthly Labor Review, 110,* 3–9.

Larson, J. (1984). The effect of husband's unemployment on marital and family relations in blue-collar families. *Family Relations, 33,* 503–511.

LeGrande, L. (1983). *Unemployment during the Great Depression and the current recession* (Report #83-15-E). Washington, DC: Library of Congress Congressional Research Service.

Lempers, J., Clark-Lempers, D., & Simons, R. (in press). Economic hardship, parenting, and distress in adolescence. *Child Development.*

Liem, R. (1981). Unemployment and mental health implications for human service policy. *Policy Study Journal, 10,* 354–364.

Liem, R. (1983). *Unemployment: Personal and family effects.* Unpublished manuscript, Boston College.

Little, C. B. (1976). Technical–professional unemployment: Middle-class adaptability to personal crisis. *Sociological Quarterly, 17,* 262–274.

Margolis, L., & Farran, D. (1981). Unemployment: The health consequences for children. *North Carolina Medical Journal, 42,* 849–850.

Moen, P. (1983). Unemployment, public policy, and families: Forecasts for the 1980s. *Journal of Marriage and the Family, 45,* 751–760.

Moen, P., Kain, E., & Elder, G. (1983). Economic conditions and family life: Contemporary and historical perspectives. In R. R. Nelson & F. Skidmore (Eds.), *American families and the economy: The high costs of living* (pp. 213–259). Washington, DC: National Academy Press.

Mott, F., & Haurin, R. (1982). Variations in the educational progress and career orientations of brothers and sisters. In F. Mott (Ed.), *The employment revolution: Young American women in the 1970's* (pp. 19–44). Cambridge, MA: MIT Press.

Parke, R., & Collmer, C. (1975). Child abuse: An interdisciplinary review. In E. M. Hetherington (Ed.), *Review of child development research* (Vol. 5, pp. 509–590). Chicago: University of Chicago Press.

Parsons, J., Adler, T., & Kaczala, C. (1982). Socialization of achievement attitudes and beliefs: Parental influences. *Child Development, 53,* 310–321.

Perrucci, C., & Targ, D. (in press). Effects of a plant closing on marriage and family life. In P. Voydanoff & L. Majka (Eds.), *Families and economic distress.* Beverly Hills: Sage.

Perrucci, C., Targ, D., Perrucci, R., & Targ, H. (1987). Plant closing: A comparison of effects on women and men workers. In R. Lee (Eds.), *Redundancy, layoffs, and plant closures* (pp. 181–207). Wolfeboro, NH: Croom Helm.

Podgursky, M., & Swaim, P. (1987). Health insurance loss: The case of the displaced worker. *Monthly Labor Review, 110,* 30–33.

Powell, D. H., & Driscoll, P. F. (1973). Middle-class professionals face unemployment. *Society, 10,* 18–26.

Radin, N., & Goldsmith, R. (in press). The involvement of selected unemployed and employed men with their children. *Child Development.*

Ray, S. A., & McLoyd, V. C. (1986). Fathers in hard times: The impact of unemployment and poverty on paternal and marital relations. In M. Lamb (Ed.), *The father's role* (pp. 339–383). New York: Wiley.

Rockwell, R., & Elder, G. (1982). Economic deprivation and problem behavior: Childhood and adolescence in the Great Depression. *Human Development, 25,* 57–64.

Rosen, E. (1983, September). *Laid off: Displaced blue collar women in*

291

New England. Paper presented at annual meeting of the Society for the Study of Social Problems, Detroit, MI.

Rutter, M. (1979). Protective factors in children's responses to stress and disadvantage. In M. Kent & J. Rolf (Ed.), *Primary prevention of psychopathology* (Vol. 3, pp. 49–74). Hanover, NH: University Press of New England.

Schlozman, K. L., & Verba, S. (1978). The new employment: Does it hurt? *Public Policy, 26,* 333–358.

Shamir, B. (1986). Unemployment and household division of labor. *Journal of Marriage and the Family, 48,* 195–206.

Sheldon, A., & Fox, G. (1983, September). *The impact of economic uncertainty on children's roles within the family.* Paper presented at meeting of the Society for the Study of Social Problems, Detroit, MI.

Siegal, M. (1984). Economic deprivation and the quality of parent-child relations: A trickle-down framework. *Journal of Applied Developmental Psychology, 5,* 127–144.

Simms, M. (1987). How loss of manufacturing jobs is affecting blacks. *Focus: The Monthly Newsletter of the Joint Center for Political Studies, 15,* 6–7.

Tauss, V. (1976). Working wife-house husband: Implications for counseling. *Journal of Family Counseling, 4,* 52–55.

Theorell, T., Lind, E., & Floderus, B. (1975). The relationships of disturbing life changes and emotions to the early development of myocardial infarction and other serious illness. *International Journal of Epidemiology, 4,* 281–293.

Thomas, L. E., McCabe, E., & Berry, J. (1980). Unemployment and family stress: A reassessment. *Family Relations, 29,* 517–524.

Voydanoff, P. (1983). Unemployment and family stress. In H. Lopata (Ed.), *Research in the interweave of social roles: Jobs and families* (Vol. 3, pp. 239–250). Greenwich, CT: JAI Press.

Walper, S., & Silbereisen, R. (1987, April). *Economic loss, strained family relationships, and adolescents' contranormative attitudes.* Paper presented at the biennial meeting of the Society for Research in Child Development, Baltimore, MD.

Warr, P., & Parry, G. (1982). Paid employment and women's psychological well-being. *Psychological Bulletin, 91,* 498–516.

Warr, P., & Payne, R. (1983). Social class and reported changes in behavior after job loss. *Journal of Applied Social Psychology, 13,* 206–222.

Weiss, R. (1979). Growing up a little faster: The experience of growing up in a single-parent household. *Journal of Social Issues, 35,* 97–111.

Werner, E., & Smith, R. (1982). *Vulnerable but invincible: A study of resilient children.* New York: McGraw-Hill.

292

Articles

Kinship Support and Maternal and Adolescent Well-Being in Economically Disadvantaged African-American Families

Ronald D. Taylor and Debra Roberts

Temple University

TAYLOR, RONALD D., and ROBERTS, DEBRA. *Kinship Support and Maternal and Adolescent Well-Being in Economically Disadvantaged African-American Families.* CHILD DEVELOPMENT, 1995, 66, 1585–1597. This study tested a conceptual model developed to explain the link between kinship support and the psychological well-being of economically disadvantaged African-American adolescents. The relation of kinship support with maternal and adolescent well-being and mothers' child-rearing practices was assessed in 51 African-American families whose incomes placed them at or below the poverty threshold. Findings revealed that kinship social support to mothers/female guardians was positively associated with adolescent psychological well-being, maternal well-being, and more adequate maternal parenting practices (acceptance, firm control and monitoring of behavior, autonomy granting). Maternal well-being and more adequate maternal parenting practices were positively related to adolescent well-being. Evidence of the mediational role of maternal well-being and parenting practices was revealed. When the effects of maternal well-being and maternal parenting practices were controlled, significant relations between kinship support and adolescent well-being were no longer apparent.

Economic Distress, Psychological Well-Being, and Parenting

Economic disadvantage has been linked to a variety of forms of psychological distress in adults and children (Gibbs, 1986; Lempers, Clark-Lempers, & Simons, 1989; Liem & Liem, 1978; McLoyd, 1990; Neff & Husaini, 1980). Among adults, economic distress is positively related to depression (Dressler, 1985; Pearlin & Johnson, 1977) and other forms of psychiatric impairments (for a review and discussion, see Liem & Liem, 1978). Among children and adolescents economic hardship has been associated with depression (Gibbs, 1986; Lempers et al., 1989), somatic complaints (McLoyd, 1988, cited in McLoyd, 1990), and conduct disorders (Myers & King, 1983).

Poverty and economic distress may impede the completion of important developmental tasks during adolescence. These tasks include the formation of satisfying emotional attachments, the development of autonomy and a clear sense of identity, and the development of skills and values necessary to function adequately as adults (e.g., Steinberg, 1990). As McLoyd (1990) suggests, economically disadvantaged families often live in neighborhoods marked by high crime rates, inadequate housing, and a high proportion of births to teenage mothers. Living in such circumstances may make it difficult for youngsters to accomplish developmental tasks.

Understanding the effects of poverty is especially important when examining the

This research was supported by a postdoctoral fellowship to the first author from the Social Science Research Council. The research was also supported in part by the Office of Educational Research and Improvement (OERI) of the U.S. Department of Education through a grant to the National Center for Education in the Inner City (CEIC) at Temple University. The opinions expressed do not represent the position of the supporting agency, and no official endorsement should be inferred. We are grateful to Lee Jussim, Diane Scott-Jones, and two anonymous reviewers for their helpful comments on an earlier version of the manuscript. Correspondence regarding the report should be addressed to the first author at the Department of Psychology, Temple University, Philadelphia, PA 19122.

development of African-American adolescents, for several reasons. First, African-American adolescents have a higher rate of poverty than adolescents of any other racial or ethnic group in the United States (Sum & Fogg, 1991). Also, because they are more likely to live in single-parent households, African-American adolescents are likely to experience poverty of long duration (Sum & Fogg, 1991).

Taylor (1990) has argued that the conditions engendered by economic disadvantage (disappearing local economy, disintegrating community institutions, social isolation), may lead some segments of poor inner-city adolescents to embrace a "subculture of disengagement from the wider society" (p. 140). The impact of this subculture may be reflected in the levels of youth gang violence, out-of-wedlock births, drug use and abuse, and school-related problems present in many disadvantaged inner-city communities.

In addition to the negative association with the psychological well-being of adults, children, and adolescents, economic hardship has also been linked to less adequate parenting practices. Lempers et al. (1989) found that economic hardship, through its negative impact on parental nurturance and parents' disciplinary practices, was associated with depression/loneliness and delinquency/drug use among adolescents.

As McLoyd (1990) has discussed, poor parents are more likely than more economically advantaged parents to value obedience in children over autonomy and independence, employ power assertive discipline techniques, and display fewer expressions of affection. Given the link between economic disadvantage, psychological distress, and less adequate parenting, it seems reasonable to assume that some of the problems often facing poor children are linked to parenting practices and behaviors compromised by the effects of poverty.

Economic Distress and Kinship Support

In the present study we examined the possibility that kinship social support may enhance the psychological well-being of economically disadvantaged African-American adolescents through its positive effects on mothers' well-being and parenting practices. Anderson (1991) notes that social support to adolescents' families may prevent youngsters' involvement in the "street culture" which can be a source of problematic behaviors in inner-city communities. Research with African-American families has revealed a positive association between economic stress and extended kin support (Dressler, 1985). Dressler (1985) found that in a sample of African-American adults economic strain (e.g., difficulty paying bills, not enough money for health care, etc.) was associated with greater assistance from relatives.

Research has also shown that among black and white families facing economic hardship and other forms of stress, social support may buffer feelings of psychological distress (Colletta & Lee, 1983; McAdoo, 1982; McLoyd, 1990; Zur-Szpiro & Longfellow, 1982), enhance child and adult adjustment (Dressler, 1985; Kellam, Adams, Brown, & Ensminger, 1982), and facilitate parents' child-rearing practices (Colletta, 1981; Furstenberg & Crawford, 1978; Hetherington, Cox, & Cox, 1978; Kellam, Ensminger, & Turner, 1977; Taylor, Casten, & Flickinger, 1993).

Conceptual Model Linking Kinship Support to Adolescent Well-Being

The positive effects of kinship support on adolescent well-being may be mediated by maternal well-being and maternal parenting practices. Specifically, kinship support to mothers may enhance mothers' psychological adjustment and parenting behaviors. When mothers are better adjusted and display more positive parenting behaviors, adolescents may function more adequately. Positive parenting was defined in this study as the extent to which mothers/female guardians displayed attitudes and behaviors associated with authoritative parenting. Authoritative parenting is a parenting style that involves acceptance, demands for mature behavior and autonomy, and firm control and monitoring of behavior. Authoritative parenting has been positively linked to the adjustment of African-American adolescents (e.g., Steinberg, Mounts, Lamborn, & Dornbusch, 1991; Taylor et al., 1993).

In a sample of poor African-American families, we assessed the following hypotheses: (a) kinship support was expected to predict increased psychological well-being among adolescents, increased psychological well-being among mothers/female guardians, and more positive parenting practices by mothers/female guardians; (b) maternal well-being and maternal parenting practices were expected to predict increased adolescent psychological well-being; and (c) the effects of kinship support on adolescent well-being were expected to be mediated by maternal well-being and maternal parenting practices. The conceptual model tested is shown in Figure 1.

Little research exists on the processes linking kinship support to child and adolescent outcomes in poor African-American families. Taylor et al. (1993) showed that, in a mainly working-class, African-American, adolescent sample, kinship support predicted increased authoritative parenting experiences, which, in turn, predicted increased adolescent well-being. The present study extends the work of Taylor et al. (1993) by (a) examining the role of maternal well-being as an additional possible mediator of the association of kinship support and adolescent well-being, (b) gathering information about kinship relations and parenting practices from additional informants (mothers/female guardians), and (c) examining the mediation of kinship support and adolescent adjustment in an economically disadvantaged sample.

Method

SAMPLE

The sample is composed of 51 African-American adolescents and their mothers/female guardians living in a large northeastern city. The term "mothers/female guardians" is used to reflect the fact that six of the adolescents were living with female guardians (e.g., four with grandmothers and two with aunts). Because data from only seven fathers or male guardians were available, information from fathers was not included in the analyses. The adolescents and their mothers/female guardians were part of a group of 100 families whose names and addresses were obtained through the adolescent's school. School officials randomly selected approximately five classes at the school and made the names and addresses of the students available to the research staff. The investigators attempted to contact and recruit each family for participation in the study. The neighborhood in which the school exists and the families reside is economically depressed. According to student data compiled by the school district, 80.3% of the youngsters are from economically disadvantaged homes, based upon census classifications. A comparison of demographic and achievement data from the school district for students living in similar neighborhoods and attending similar types of schools revealed no differences.

We were unable to contact a sizeable number of parents (44) because of frequent changes of residence, lack of a telephone in the home, unreturned phone calls, and unac-

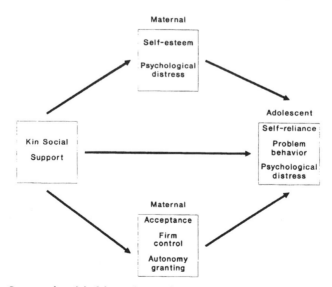

FIG. 1.—Conceptual model of the mediation of the association of kinship support and adolescent well-being.

knowledged mailings. Only five students and their parents refused to participate. The students who did not participate, either because of their refusal or because of their lack of availability, did not differ from the participants in terms of age, sex, or school achievement, based on data obtained from school records. However, according to school officials, the inaccessibility of these families may be a sign of instability and family problems. Thus, it is possible that our sample is overrepresented by more highly functioning economically disadvantaged families.

The adolescents were 31 females and 20 males. Demographic information on the sample is shown in Table 1. The information was examined separately for one-parent and two-parent families. Table 1 reveals that the average and actual income levels of both one- and two-parent families placed them at or below the poverty threshold for families of their size (U.S. Bureau of the Census, 1991). The relation between family structure and the other demographic characteristics was assessed. The difference in the incomes of two-parent and one-parent families approached significance, $F(1, 49) = 3.65$, $p < .06$, with two-parent families having somewhat higher incomes. Also, two-parent families had larger families than one-parent families, $F(1, 49) = 5.77$, $p < .02$.

PROCEDURE

Data on relations with kin, parenting practices, psychological adjustment, and demographic characteristics were collected via interviews administered to the adolescents and the mother/female guardian in a laboratory setting. Five families were unable to travel to the research setting, and interviews were administered at their home. A comparison of the scores for those families administered the measures in the laboratory versus those seen at home revealed no differences. The adolescents and parents at either site were given the interviews in separate rooms. The families were paid for their participation.

MEASURES

Adolescent Variables

a)   *Self-reliance.*—Self-reliance (10 items) was measured using the Psychological Maturity Inventory (Greenberger & Bond, 1986; Greenberger, Josselson, Kneer, & Kneer, 1974). The measure assessed adolescents' lack of dependency, sense of initiative, and control over events. Sample questions reverse coded included; "Luck decides most of the things that happen to me," or "When I do something wrong I depend on my parents to straighten things out

TABLE 1

DEMOGRAPHIC INFORMATION

	FAMILY STRUCTURE	
CHARACTERISTIC	Single-Parent ($n = 24$)	Two-Parent ($n = 27$)[a]
Mean age adolescent (SD)	16.50 (5.07)	17.91 (1.30)
Range	15–19	15–19
Mean age mother/guardian (SD)	42.56 (6.14)	41.54 (5.69)
Range	34–61	31–73
Mean number of household members (SD)	4.01 (1.34)	5.20 (2.25)
Range	1–6	1–9
Mean household income (SD)[b]	1.73 (1.15)	2.59 (1.76)
Range	1–3	1–3
Mean years of schooling (SD)	11.76 (2.05)	11.54 (2.93)
Range	5–12	0–13
Number reporting receiving forms of public assistance (%)[c]	19 (79%)	18 (66%)
Household employment (%)[d]	8 (33%)	11 (40%)

[a] The families in two-parent family structure include six families in which both grandparents were the custodial guardians of the adolescents.

[b] Income level: 1 = less than $5,000/year; 2 = $5,000–$10,000/year; 3 = $10,000–$15,000/year; 4 = $15,000–$20,000/year; 5 = $20,000–$25,000/year; 6 = $25,000–$30,000/year; 7 = $30,000–$35,000/year.

[c] Public assistance included the receipt of welfare, food stamps, or public housing.

[d] Household employment refers to the question of whether there were employed adult(s) within the home.

for me." The adolescents indicated their answers using a Likert-response scale ranging from 4 (strongly agree) to 1 (strongly disagree).

b) Problem behavior.—Problem behavior (15 items) was assessed by obtaining the adolescents' self-report of their frequency of involvement in delinquent activities such as physical assault, drug use, and vandalism (Gold & Reimer, 1975). The response format for the measure is a Likert-scale ranging from 4 (several times) to 1 (never).

c) Psychological distress.—Psychological distress (20 items) was measured with the Center for Epidemiological Studies (CES) Depression Scale (Radloff, 1977). Adolescents reported the frequency of mental or physical states (e.g., feelings of depression, loss of appetite, difficulty sleeping) over the past month. The Likert-response scale ranges from 4 (three or more times) to 1 (never).

Maternal Variables
    a) Kinship relations.—Kinship relations (13 items) was measured with a series of questions taken from Taylor et al. (1993). The measure assesses the mothers'/female guardians' perceptions of the level of social and emotional support they receive from adult kin. The measure examined the areas of socialization and entertainment, advice and counseling, and problem solving. Sample questions in each area included: "We often get together with our relatives for reunions and holidays" (socialization and entertainment); "When I'm worried about something I look to my relatives for advice" (advice and counseling); or "We can count on our relatives to help when we have problems" (problem solving). The participants indicated their answers using a Likert-response scale ranging from 4 (strongly agree) to 1 (strongly disagree).

b) Psychological distress.—Psychological distress for mothers/female guardians, like the adolescents, was assessed with the CES Depression Scale.

c) Self-esteem.—Self-esteem (10 items) was assessed with the Rosenberg Self-Esteem Scale (Rosenberg, 1965). This scale, which has been widely used with adults, assesses the self-acceptance component of self-esteem (sample question: "I feel that I

have a number of good qualities"). The response format for the measure is a Likert-response scale ranging from 4 (strongly agree) to 1 (strongly disagree).[1]

d) Parenting practices.—Parenting practices were examined with the revised short form of the Child's Report of Parental Behavior Inventory (CRPBI, Schludermann & Schludermann, 1977). This measure assesses three aspects of maternal disciplinary practices: Acceptance, Psychological Control (vs. Psychological Autonomy), and Lax Control (vs. Firm Control). The CRPBI is a widely used Likert-scale format, self-report measure of adolescents' assessment of the parents' discipline practices. Both adolescents and the mothers/female guardians completed the measure. The mothers/female guardians completed a version of the measure modified appropriately for administration to parents.

The *Acceptance* subscale (10 items) consists of questions assessing the mother's/female guardian's and adolescent's perceptions of maternal closeness and acceptance of the adolescents. The *Psychological Control* subscale (10 items) consists of questions assessing the mother's/female guardian's and adolescent's ratings of maternal use of anxiety or guilt induction as a method of control of the adolescent. The measure of Psychological Control was coded so that high scores represent the extent to which the adolescents' psychological autonomy was encouraged. The items of the *Lax Control* subscale (10 items) assess mother's/female guardian's and adolescent's ratings of maternal regulation and monitoring of the adolescent's behavior. High scores on the measure of Lax Control represent the perception that adolescent's behavior was under Firm Control. These subscales of the CRPBI have been found to have good discriminant and convergent validity (Schwarz, Barton-Henry, & Pruzinsky, 1985).

A single score for each aspect of parenting assessed was created by averaging the ratings of the mothers/female guardians and adolescents for each of the parenting subscales. Justification for this approach comes from Schwarz et al. (1985), who have shown that the reliability and validity of scores on the subscales of the CRPBI increase as the number of aggregated ratings increases. The

---

[1] Parents were not administered measures of well-being identical to those given to the adolescents because the measures administered to the adolescents were developmentally appropriate for adolescents but not for adults.

subscales of the CRPBI were employed as measures of more positive parenting because they are components of authoritative parenting, which has been linked to adolescent adjustment.

All of the measures included have been utilized in research with African-American parents or adolescents and have had acceptable levels of reliability. The measures appear to operate similarly across ethnic and social class groups in that the correlates of the measures are similar across groups (e.g., Roberts & Taylor, 1994; Steinberg et al., 1991; Taylor et al., 1993). In the present sample the internal reliabilities of all scales were acceptable and highly similar to those reported in previous research using the measures (see Table 2).

ANALYSIS PLAN

Recursive path analysis estimated by ordinary least squares regression was utilized to test the conceptual model shown in Figure 1. This statistical technique allows the assessment of both direct and mediated relations among variables in the model. For each of the three indicators of adolescent psychological functioning, path coefficients were estimated using a series of multiple regression equations.[2] At each step the criterion variables were regressed on all variables with arrows leading directly to the criterion variable. This procedure was followed for each of the separate criterion variables. The demographic factors of age, sex, income, and family structure were included in the analyses to examine and control for their effects.

The data were analyzed in accord with Baron and Kenny's (1986) recommendations for assessing mediator effects. According to Baron and Kenny, mediational effects are apparent when there is evidence that (a) the predictor variable (e.g., kinship support) is significantly associated with the criterion variable (e.g., adolescent self-reliance, problem behavior, psychological distress); (b) the predictor variable and the proposed mediator variable (e.g., maternal acceptance, firm control, autonomy granting, psychological distress, self-esteem) are significantly related; (c) the criterion variables and mediator variables are significantly related; and (d) controlling for the effects of the mediator variable reduces the association of the predictor and criterion variables, while the association of the mediator and criterion variables remains.

Results

The means and standard deviations of the major variables are presented in Table 2. Table 3 shows the correlations among variables. The effects of the demographic factors (age, sex, income, and family structure) were examined and had no significant effect on any of the measures.

Kinship Support and Adolescent Self-Reliance, Problem Behavior, and Psychological Distress

The first step in assessing the mediation of the association between kinship social support and adolescent well-being is to examine the relation of kinship social support and the domains of adolescent psychological well-being assessed. These results are shown in Figure 2. Kinship support is positively associated with self-reliance (beta = .28, $p < .05$), and negatively associated with

---

[2] According to Baron and Kenny (1986) the use of multiple regression to estimate a mediational model requires that the criterion variable not cause the mediator variable. Given the nature of the variables assessed, reciprocal relations between some of the measures are indeed possible (e.g., maternal self-esteem may lead to greater adolescent self-reliance, and increased self-reliance may lead to greater maternal acceptance). Because our data is cross-sectional it is impossible to sort out causal relations among the variables. In addition, our data is not sufficient for the use of other structural modeling techniques that take into consideration the complication of feedback or bidirectional relations in the mediational chains. First, our sample size is too small to utilize procedures such as LISREL-IV (Jöreskog & Sörbom, 1984) or EQS (Bentler, 1982). Bentler and Chou (1987) recommend that the ratio of sample size to number of free parameters be 5:1, though a ratio of 10:1 may be more appropriate. Second, none of our variables meets the recommended criteria for serving as instrumental variables in the estimation of two-stage least squares to examine feedback (James & Singh, 1978). Specifically, the use of two-stage least squares requires the identification of a variable that (a) has a direct or indirect effect on the criterion variable; (b) is not related to the mediator variable; (c) is unrelated to unmeasured causes of the criterion variable, and (d) is not caused by either the criterion or mediator variable. None of the variables measured in the sample unequivocally meet these criteria. Therefore, because the possibility of feedback exists, the mediational relations revealed must be interpreted with caution.

TABLE 2

MEANS, STANDARD DEVIATIONS, AND ALPHAS OF THE MAJOR VARIABLES

Variable	Mean	Standard Deviation	Alpha
Kinship social support	25.49	4.94	.88
Maternal self-esteem	33.08	5.50	.85
Maternal psychological distress	27.78	7.95	.82
Maternal acceptance	38.88	3.71	.72
Psychological autonomy granting	29.71	6.02	.82
Firm behavioral control	27.18	2.50	.77
Adolescent self-reliance	12.01	2.77	.79
Adolescent problem behavior	6.63	2.07	.74
Adolescent psychological distress	12.65	4.63	.82

NOTE.—The alphas reported in the table are from the sample in the present study.

problem behavior (beta = −.28, p < .05). Kinship support and psychological distress are unrelated.

Kinship Support, Maternal Psychological Distress, Self-Esteem, Acceptance, Firm Control, and Psychological Autonomy Granting

The second step in assessing the mediation of the link between kinship support and adolescent well-being is to examine the association among kinship support, maternal well-being, and maternal parenting practices. These findings are shown in Figure 3.

Results indicate that social support by kin is positively associated with maternal self-esteem (beta = .46, p < .01), maternal acceptance (beta = .38, p < .01), and maternal autonomy granting (beta = .38, p < .01).

Maternal Self-Esteem, Psychological Distress, Acceptance, Firm Control, Autonomy Granting and Adolescent Self-Reliance, Problem Behavior, and Psychological Distress

The third step in assessing the mediation of the link between kinship support and adolescent well-being is to assess the associ-

TABLE 3

CORRELATIONS AMONG MAJOR VARIABLES

	1	2	3	4	5	6	7	8	9
1. Kinship social support	...								
2. Maternal self-esteem	.47**	...							
3. Maternal psychological distress	.15	−.23	...						
4. Maternal acceptance	.32*	.28*	−.27*	...					
5. Psychological autonomy granting	.35*	.34*	.09	.21	...				
6. Firm behavioral control	.05	.10	−.30*	.16	−.38**	...			
7. Adolescent self-reliance	.30*	.28*	.02	.28*	.29*	.02	...		
8. Adolescent problem behavior	−.29*	−.34*	−.08	−.34*	.15	.30*	.01	...	
9. Adolescent psychological distress	.16	−.14	.25+	−.03	.08	−.26	−.28*	.05	...

+ p < .10.
* p < .05.
** p < .01.

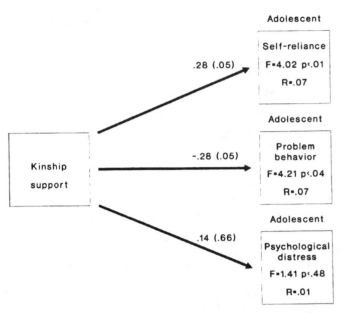

FIG. 2.—Kinship support and adolescent self-reliance, problem behavior, and psychological distress. Standardized regression coefficients are displayed on each path with the corresponding p values in parentheses.

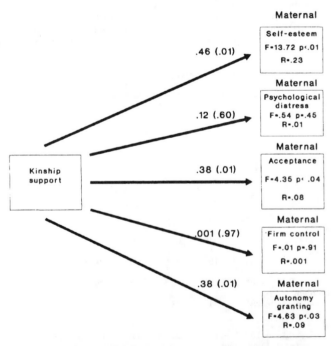

FIG. 3.—Kinship support and maternal self-esteem, psychological distress, acceptance, firm control, and autonomy granting. Standardized regression coefficients are displayed on each path with the corresponding p values in parentheses.

Taylor and Roberts 1593

ation of maternal well-being and maternal parenting practices with adolescent well-being. These results are shown in Figure 4. The findings reveal that maternal self-esteem is positively associated with adolescent self-reliance (beta = .41, $p < .01$) and negatively related to adolescent problem behavior (beta = −.36, $p < .01$). Maternal acceptance is positively associated with adolescent self-reliance (beta = .41, $p < .01$) and negatively related to problem behavior (beta = −.27, $p < .05$). Maternal firm control of behavior is negatively associated with adolescent problem behavior (beta = −28, $p < .05$. Finally, maternal autonomy granting is positively associated with adolescent self-reliance (beta = .44, $p < .01$).

Mediational Effects

The final step in assessing the mediation of the relation between kinship support and adolescent well-being is the evaluation of the link between kinship support and adolescent psychological well-being, when controlling for the effects of maternal well-being and maternal parenting practices. Evidence in support of mediational effects also requires that maternal well-being and parenting practices remain significantly associated

with adolescent well-being when kinship support is controlled. Evidence of mediation emerged for two of the indicators of adolescent psychological functioning. Specifically, for self-reliance the significant standardized regression coefficient linking kinship support and self-reliance (beta = .28) is no longer apparent with the effects of maternal self-esteem, acceptance, and autonomy granting controlled (beta = .05). Furthermore, with the effects of kinship support controlled, maternal self-esteem, acceptance, and autonomy granting remain significantly associated with self-reliance (beta = .35, $p < .01$, beta = .41, $p < .01$, beta = .39, $p < .01$, respectively). Turning to the second indicator, the significant relation between kinship support and adolescent problem behavior (beta = −.28) is no longer apparent when the effects of maternal self-esteem and maternal acceptance are removed (beta = .15). Autonomy granting is not assessed as a mediator here because it was unrelated to problem behavior. With the effects of kinship support controlled, maternal self-esteem and acceptance remain significantly related to problem behavior (beta = −.43, $p < .01$, beta = −.44, $p < .01$, respectively).

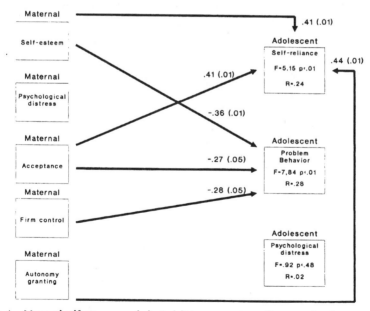

Fig. 4.—Maternal self-esteem, psychological distress, acceptance, firm control and autonomy granting, and adolescent self-reliance, problem behavior, and psychological distress. Standardized regression coefficients are displayed on each path with the corresponding p values in parentheses.

Mediational effects for adolescent psychological distress, and the role of maternal psychological distress and firm control of behavior as mediator variables were not examined because these measures were unrelated to kinship support.

Discussion

The present study adds to the sparse literature on family relations and psychosocial adjustment for economically disadvantaged African-American families. The results obtained generally supported the predictions tested. Specifically, consistent with expectations, the more social support mothers/female guardians report receiving, the greater adolescents' sense of self-reliance and the less they engage in problem behavior. These findings are in accord with previous research linking support from extended family members to individuals' adjustment in poor and nonpoor families (e.g., Dressler, 1985; Kellam et al., 1982; Taylor et al., 1993).

The findings also support the hypothesis of a positive association between kinship support and aspects of mother's/females guardian's well-being and parenting practices. The more support mothers/female guardians reported, the higher their self-esteem, the greater their acceptance of the adolescent, and the more they granted the adolescent autonomy and independence. These findings complement the results of a number of investigations linking kinship social support to maternal adjustment (e.g., Colletta & Lee, 1983; McLoyd, 1990; Zur-Szpiro & Longfellow, 1982) and to better parenting practices (Colletta, 1981; McLoyd, 1990). The results extend previous research by showing that not only are mothers less likely to display aversive behaviors (Colletta, 1981; scolding, nagging, threatening) when they have assistance, but they are also more likely to display supportive behaviors and attitudes.

Evidence supporting the hypothesis that maternal psychological well-being and parenting practices predict adolescent psychological well-being is also present in the findings. Results reveal that to the extent that mothers/female guardians are higher in self-esteem, more accepting of the adolescent, and encouraging of the adolescent's autonomy, the adolescents report greater self-reliance. Higher maternal self-esteem and acceptance are also associated with lower levels of adolescent problem behavior. These findings add to the growing body of research showing that among economically disadvantaged families parents' psychological distress and the adequacy of their parenting practices are linked to children's and adolescents' social and emotional adjustment (McLoyd, 1990).

Finally, evidence supporting the prediction regarding the mediation of the association of kinship social support and adolescent adjustment is apparent in the findings. The results suggest that higher kinship support is associated with higher maternal self-esteem, acceptance of the adolescent, and autonomy granting. Higher acceptance, self-esteem, and autonomy granting, in turn, are associated with higher adolescent self-reliance. Higher acceptance and self-esteem are also associated with lower levels of problem behavior. These findings in particular and the overall pattern of results support portions of McLoyd's (1990) analytic framework linking economic hardship to children's outcomes. McLoyd (1990) suggests that social support may ease parents' emotional distress and may promote more adequate parenting practices, which, in turn, may "foster positive socioemotional development in impoverished children" (p. 315). The results are also in line with Belles's (1984) discussion of the potential benefits of social support as a source of mental health treatment for women "in the midst of oppressive life conditions" (p. 148).

Several limitations in the research should be noted. First, our measures were based on the self-reports of the parent and adolescent. The relations observed would be more firmly established with similar findings using methods that directly assessed the behaviors under study. Having additional informants who might have different perspectives on the functioning of the family would also be beneficial.

Second, the size of the sample included is also an issue that should be considered in interpreting the findings. In particular, in the assessment of mediational effects, the regression coefficients may be less precise than they would be if they were assessed in a larger sample. It is important to note however, that a smaller sample size does not invalidate the regression coefficients but makes the detection of significant effects in fact more difficult.

Third, also regarding the sample, the accessibility of the families in the study and the lack of availability of those not included may be indicative of important distinguishing features of the participants. Care should be taken when applying results across economically disadvantaged African-American families.

Finally, the findings obtained are all correlational, and, therefore, the causal relations of the variables are not known. For instance, it is possible that kinship social support leads to greater parental self-esteem. It is equally plausible, however, that parents who are high in self-esteem or more generally well adjusted may elicit more assistance from kin. Similar arguments can be made for other relations found in this research.

The possibility of bidirectional relations or feedback among the variables is important. In particular, if there is feedback between the mediating variables and the outcome variables, then the relations between the variables may be overestimated. If the relations are overestimated, the mediational findings revealed may not be as strong, and caution must used in interpreting these results.

However, it is important to note that, for several reasons, it is not clear that bidirectional relations exist between the variables in the mediational chains. We know of no research with African-American families showing, for example, that maternal parenting practices and adjustment, and adolescent adjustment are reciprocally related. Also, in a relevant discussion Cairns (1979) notes, "In relationships where there are clear discrepancies between the social roles of the participants, teacher-pupil, therapist-patient, father-son, older-younger—societal biases can support the dominance of one individual's acts relative to another" (p. 313). He suggests, further, that even if a social relationship is bidirectional "its major themes and course can be determined unequally by virtue of societal expectations and institutional constraints that operate on all members of the interchange" (p. 314). Cairns's discussion supports the plausibility of the mediational chains specified in our conceptual model and revealed in our findings. Because parents typically have more power, status, and control in the home than adolescents, bidirectional effects between parent variables (parenting practices and adjustment) and adolescent variables (adjustment) may be either nonexistent or small. Longitudinal data focusing on the issues investigated here are needed to examine the matters of causality and reciprocal relations.

In terms of future research, the ecology associated with poverty and economic disadvantage and its impact on family relations need to examined. Specifically, the manner in which kinship support and family well-being varies as a function of community or neighborhood conditions needs to be evaluated. Also, little is known about the effects on families of extending help to kin. Indeed, Belle (1984) has suggested that for poor women the strain and distress associated with providing support to extended family members may diminish the effectiveness of the help poor women themselves receive.

Finally, more process-oriented work with African-American children and families is needed. We know far too little about the nature of African-American families, their parenting practices, and the outcomes for children. We know less still about the processes underlying relations between important variables. Given the increasing diversity of children and youth in the United States, it is important that greater attention be given to the conditions promoting and inhibiting the competence and well-being of families of color.

References

Anderson, E. (1991). Neighborhood effects on teenage pregnancy. In C. Jencks & P. E. Peterson (Eds.), The urban underclass. Washington, DC: Brookings Institution.

Baron, R. M., & Kenny, D. A. (1986). The moderator-mediator variable distinction in social psychological research: Conceptual, strategic, and statistical considerations. Journal of Personality and Social Psychology, 51, 1173-1182.

Belle, D. (1984). Inequality and mental health: Low income and minority women. In L. Walker (Ed.), Women and mental health policy (pp. 135-150). Beverly Hills, CA: Sage.

Bentler, P. M. (1982). Theory and implementation of EQS: A structural equations program. Unpublished manuscript, University of California, Los Angeles.

Bentler, P. M., & Chou, C. (1987). Practical issues in structural modeling. Sociological Methods and Research, 16, 78-117.

Cairns, R. B. (1979). Social development: The origins and plasticity of interchanges (pp. 297-317). San Francisco, CA: W. H. Freeman.

Colletta, N. (1981). Social support and the risk of maternal rejection by adolescent mothers. Journal of Psychology, 109, 191-197.

Colletta, N., & Lee, D. (1983). The impact of support for black adolescent mothers. Journal of Family Issues, 4, 127-143.

Dressler, W. (1985). Extended family relationships, social support, and mental health in a southern black community. *Journal of Health and Social Behavior*, 26, 39–48.

Furstenberg, F., & Crawford, D. B. (1978). Family support: Helping teenagers to cope. *Family Planning Perspectives*, 11, 322–333.

Gibbs, J. (1986). Assessment of depression in urban adolescent females: Implications for early intervention strategies. *American Journal of Social Psychiatry*, 6, 50–56.

Gold, M., & Reimer, D. (1975). Changing patterns of delinquent behavior among Americans 13 through 16 years old: 1967–1972. *Crime and Delinquency Literature*, 7, 483–517.

Greenberger, E., & Bond, L. (1976). *Technical manual for the Psychosocial Maturity Inventory*. Unpublished manuscript, Program in Social Ecology, University of California, Irvine.

Greenberger, E., Josselson, R., Kneer, C., & Kneer, B. (1974). The measurement and structure of psychosocial maturity. *Journal of Youth and Adolescence*, 4, 127–143.

Hetherington, E. M., Cox, M., & Cox, R. (1978). The aftermath of divorce. In J. Stevens, Jr., & M. Matthew (Eds.), *Mother-child, father-child relations*. Washington, DC: National Association for the Education of Young Children.

James, L. R., & Singh, B. K. (1978). An introduction to logic, assumptions, and basic analytic procedures of two-stage least squares. *Psychological Bulletin*, 85, 1104–1123.

Jöreskog, K. H., & Sörbom, D. (1984). *LISREL-VI-Estimation of linear structural equations by maximum likelihood methods* (3d ed.). Mooresville, IN: Scientific Software.

Kellam, S. G., Adams, R. G., Brown, C. H., & Ensminger, M. A. (1982). The long-term evolution of the family structure of teenage and older mothers. *Journal of Marriage and the Family*, 46, 539–554.

Kellam, S. G., Ensminger, M. A., & Turner, J. T. (1977). Family structure and the mental health of children. *Archives of General Psychiatry*, 34, 1012–1022.

Lempers, J., Clark-Lempers, D., & Simons, R. (1989). Economic hardship, parenting, and distress in adolescence. *Child Development*, 60, 25–49.

Liem, R., & Liem, J. (1978). Social class and mental illness reconsidered: The role of economic stress and social support. *Journal of Health and Social Behavior*, 19, 139–156.

McAdoo, H. P. (1982). Stress absorbing systems in black families. *Family Relations*, 31, 479–488.

McLoyd, V. C. (1988). *Determinants of the mental health of black and white children experienc-*

ing economic deprivation. Paper presented at a study group meeting on poverty and children, University of Kansas, Lawrence.

McLoyd, V. C. (1990). The impact of economic hardship on black families and children: Psychological distress, parenting, and socioemotional development. *Child Development*, 61, 311–346.

Myers, H. F., & King, L. (1983). Mental health issues in the development of the black American child. In G. Powell, J. Yamamoto, A. Romero, & A. Morales (Eds.), *The psychosocial development of minority children* (pp. 275–306). New York: Brunner/Mazel.

Neff, J., & Husaini, B. (1980). Race, socioeconomic status, and psychiatric impairment: A research note. *Journal of Community Psychology*, 8, 16–19.

Pearlin, L., & Johnson, J. (1977). Marital status, life-strains and depression. *American Sociological Review*, 42, 704–715.

Radloff, L. S. (1977). The CES-D Scale: A self-report depression scale for research in the general population. *Applied Psychological Measurement*, 1, 385–401.

Richardson, R. A., Galambos, N. L., Schulenberg, J. E., & Petersen, A. C. (1984). Young adolescents' perceptions of the family environment. *Journal of Early Adolescence*, 4, 131–154.

Roberts, D., & Taylor, R. D. (1994). *Neighborhood characteristics, parenting, psychological well-being and adolescent adjustment among African-American families.* Unpublished manuscript, Temple University, Philadelphia.

Rosenberg, M. (1965). *Society and the adolescent self-image.* Princeton, NJ: Princeton University Press.

Schludermann, E., & Schludermann, S. (1977). Replicability of factors in children's report of parent behavior (CRPBI). *Journal of Psychology*, 96, 15–23.

Schwarz, J. C., Barton-Henry, M. L., & Pruzinsky, T. (1985). Assessing child-rearing behaviors: A comparison of ratings made by mother, father, child, and sibling on the CRPBI. *Child Development*, 56, 462–479.

Steinberg, L. (1990). The logic of adolescence. In P. Edelman & J. Ladner (Eds.), *Adolescence and poverty: Challenge for the 90's* (pp. 19–36). Washington, DC: Center for National Policy Press.

Steinberg, L., Mounts, N. S., Lamborn, S. D., & Dornbusch, S. M. (1991). Authoritative parenting and adolescent adjustment across varied ecological niches. *Journal of Research on Adolescence*, 1, 19–36.

Sum, A. N., & Fogg, W. N. (1991). The adolescent poor and the transition to early adulthood. In P. Edelman & J. Ladner (Eds.), *Adolescence and poverty: Challenge for the 90's* (pp. 37–110). Washington, DC: Center for National Policy Press.

Taylor, R. D., Casten, R., & Flickinger, S. (1993). The influence of kinship social support on the parenting experiences and psychosocial adjustment of African-American adolescents. *Developmental Psychology, 29*, 382–388.

Taylor, R. L. (1990). Poverty and adolescent black males: The subculture of disengagement. In P. Edelman & J. Ladner (Eds.), *Adolescence*

and poverty: Challenge for the 90's (pp. 139–162). Washington, DC: Center for National Policy Press.

U.S. Bureau of the Census. (1991). *Poverty in the United States: 1990 and 1991*. (Current Population Reports, Series A-8). Washington, DC: U.S. Government Printing Office.

Zur-Szpiro, S., & Longfellow, C. (1982). Fathers' support to mothers and children. In D. Belle (Ed.), *Lives in stress: Women and depression*. Beverly Hills, CA: Sage.

JOURNAL OF RESEARCH ON ADOLESCENCE, 2(4), 351-378
Copyright © 1992, Lawrence Erlbaum Associates, Inc.

Linking Family Economic Hardship to Adolescent Distress

Xiaojia Ge, Rand D. Conger, and
Frederick O. Lorenz
Iowa State University

Glen H. Elder, Jr.
University of North Carolina

Ruth B. Montague and Ronald L. Simons
Iowa State University

A study of 451 families living in the rural Midwest examined the negative impact of financial problems on early adolescents' symptoms of psychological distress. The tested model links financial difficulties to adolescent psychological problems through the quality of marital and parent–child relationships. Results show that economic stress has a direct effect on marital quality which, in turn, disrupts or undermines the parent–child relationship. Negative feelings by parents and adolescents about their relationships tend to increase adolescent psychological distress. This general model operates similarly across four family dyads: fathers and sons, fathers and daughters, mothers and sons, and mothers and daughters. Overall, the diminished quality of marital and parent–child relationships represents one pathway by which economic hardship places adolescents at risk for psychological dysfunction.

Children and adolescents in families are often influenced by external events and changes through the personalities of family members and social relationships of affection and control. For example, irritable fathers generally become more explosive under the pressures of economic hardship, and emotionally unstable men become even more

Requests for reprints should be sent to Xiaojia Ge, Center for Family Research in Rural Mental Health, Iowa State University, Research Park, 2625 North Loop Drive, Suite 500, Ames, IA 50010-8296.

erratic in situations of this kind (Elder, Liker, & Cross, 1984). Similar processes have been observed for mothers and their children (Conger, McCarthy, Yang, Lahey, & Kropp, 1984; Patterson, 1988). Among family relationships, marital interaction is especially vulnerable to external pressures and can serve as a link to the quality of parental behavior (Conger et al., 1992; Conger et al., 1991), although little is known about this causal sequence among fathers and mothers in relation to sons and daughters.

This article investigates the importance of family relationship quality for adolescents in families experiencing economic difficulties. Using data from 451 two-parent households in the north central region of Iowa, the analysis traces the effects of economic hardship and pressure on adolescent emotional distress through the varying quality of marital and parent–child relationships. This perspective is consistent to earlier research demonstrating the importance of family mediation in linking economic hardship to children's emotional well-being (Conger et al., 1992; Elder, 1974). Indeed, Coyne and Downey (1991) noted that troubled relationships may, in general, mediate the effect of stressful life experiences on individual distress, as well as operate as stressors in their own right. Moreover, studies on children of divorce and discord (Emery, 1982; Emery, 1988; O'Leary & Emery, 1984) generally have found increased conduct disturbance in children after parental divorce and in response to parental conflict. Other research on the interpersonal context of children's development also demonstrates the importance of the quality of parent–child interactions and feelings for child adjustment (Grotevant & Cooper, 1985, 1986; Hauser et al., 1987; Hinde & Stevenson-Hinde, 1986, 1987). We begin this inquiry with a statement of our theoretical model and a review of relevant literature.

THE THEORETICAL MODEL

Economic Conditions and Family Well-Being

The theoretical model that guides this article is presented in Figure 1. The model begins with several dimensions of family economic circumstance, each evolving from an independent research tradition (Conger et al., 1990; Horwitz, 1984). These traditions view family economic hardship in terms of (a) economic standing as measured by income adjusted for family size (Duncan, 1984); (b) the debt-to-asset ratio reflecting debt load relative to assets and used to measure financial status in rural and farm families (Murdock & Leistritz, 1988); (c) income loss (Elder, 1974; Liker & Elder, 1983), including both losses that result from unstable

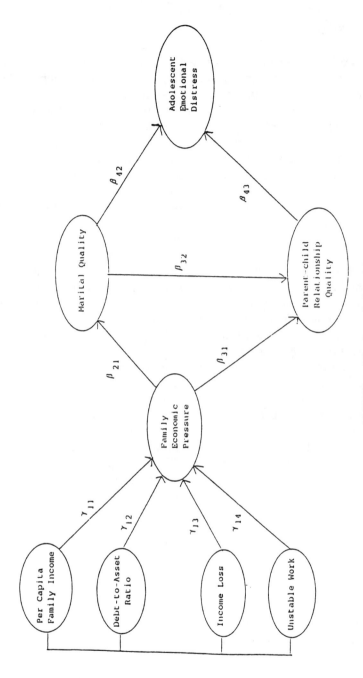

FIGURE 1   The theoretical model.

309

work and other losses of earnings such as reduction in farm sales; and (d) work life status and stability, including both unemployment and job disruptions such as demotion and downward mobility (Shepherd, 1981; Kelvin & Jarrett, 1985). These interrelated dimensions of family finances provide a broad base of exogenous economic variables as the starting point for this article. Although not specifically included in the model, in later empirical analyses we control for the influence of educational attainment in estimating coefficients for the hypothesized processes.

According to our theoretical model (Figure 1), the effects of objective economic conditions on family processes are mediated largely by the family's experience of economic pressure, which includes both the economic constraints felt by family members and their adjustments to financial difficulties. Families suffering from low incomes, high debts, income losses, and unstable work are more likely to feel economically constrained in that resources are inadequate to meet family necessities. They also are more likely to make painful adjustments, such as severe budgetary cutbacks (Conger et al., 1990; Elder, 1974). Thus, we propose that adverse economic conditions affect family well-being through the pressures they create in day-to-day living.

The model in Figure 1 addresses one of several pathways by which financial difficulties could affect family dynamics and thereby child and adolescent outcomes. In a longitudinal study of children growing up during the Great Depression, Elder and his colleagues found that economic stress acts as an amplifier that heightens family conflict and lowers the quality of family interaction, which subsequently leads to child behavior problems (Elder, 1974; Elder, Caspi, & Downey, 1986; Elder, Nguyen, & Caspi, 1985; Liker & Elder, 1983). Patterson (1983) likewise suggested that stressful events such as chronic illness and adverse income change should be viewed as change agents for family process.

We propose that economic pressures and concomitant negative changes in patterns of family interaction violate expectations of family living and create adversities that reduce family relationship quality. Preliminary evidence for this thesis was found in earlier research that demonstrated that economic pressure affects family and marital relationship quality by increasing marital conflict, reducing marital support, and increasing parents' emotional distress (Conger et al., 1992; Conger et al., 1990). This process leads to lower family relationship quality, the focus of this article.

In our theoretical model, we view lowered relationship quality in terms of decreased happiness and satisfaction with family ties that result from the described hardship-related disruptions in behavioral interaction and emotional well-being of parents. As closeness among family members diminishes, adolescents are likely to become emotionally distressed and unhappy with their lives in general. Thus, reduced relationship quality may represent one of several possible family mechanisms that link economic hardship to adolescent well-being.

Quality of Family Relationships and Adolescent Distress

Although some studies (e.g., Niemi, 1988; Wallerstein & Kelly 1980) suggested that the exposure of adolescents to open marital conflict can promote children's psychological health and cognitive development, most studies have shown that marital discord, emotional withdrawal, and open hostility between parents are detrimental to child and adolescent social and psychological functioning (Emery, 1982; Hetherington, Stanley-Hagen, & E. R. Anderson, 1989). From a clinical perspective, one way in which marital discord can impinge on parent–adolescent relationship quality is offered by the *compensatory hypothesis*. Lidz (1969), for example, suggested that in the context of an unsatisfactory marriage, a child can become a substitute source of emotional gratification. Increased parental attention to and physical involvement with the child can, in turn, lead to extreme closeness in parent–child relationships. A similar perspective proposed by Minuchin, Rosman, and Baker, (1978) suggested that parental involvement with children may increase as a result of marital dissatisfaction. Although such processes may be observed in clinical populations, we expect that probably they are not typical of the association between marital dynamics and parent–child relationships in general.

By contrast, most studies have reported a positive association between marital quality and the quality of the parent–child relationship (Belsky, 1981, 1990; Engfer, 1988; Hess & Camara, 1979). These findings support a "spill-over" argument that is reflected in our model. According to this view, parents experiencing marital distress tend to engage in less optimal socialization practices than happily married couples (Belsky, Gilstrap, & Rovine, 1984; Caspi & Elder, 1988; Conger et al., 1992; Easterbrooks & Emde, 1988; Elder et al., 1986; Meyer, 1988). They are more likely to demonstrate increased hostility (Hess & Camara, 1979; S. M. Johnson & Lobitz, 1974) and decreased warmth (Easterbrooks & Emde, 1988) in child-rearing practices. These results have been found to generalize across samples and with time (Belsky, 1990; M. Cox, Owen, Lewis, & Henderson, 1989; Hartup, 1986; Maccoby & Martin, 1983).

Although a variety of studies have demonstrated an association between the quality of marital and parent–adolescent relationships, questions regarding causal direction remain. Previous longitudinal studies support the argument that marital quality acts as an antecedent to parent–child relationship quality (Caspi & Elder, 1988; Meyer, 1988; Olweus, 1980). For example, Caspi and Elder's (1988) study of Berkeley women during the 1930s found that troubled marriages lead to parenting difficulties that are significantly related to children's problem behaviors. Thus, in our model, we propose that increasing economic difficulties first affect the marriage and then generalize to parent–child relationships.

Some theorists have argued that parent–adolescent conflict is necessary and desirable in that it promotes detachment and appropriate independence in adolescent development (e.g., A. Freud, 1958). This position, however, has received little empirical support. The majority of studies suggest that difficulties in the parent–adolescent relationship are associated with a variety of problems some children have, including conduct disorder, substance use, and emotional distress (Conger et al., 1992; Conger et al., 1991; Elder et al., 1985; Lempers, Clark-Lempers, & Simons, 1989; Montemayor, 1983; Robertson & Simons, 1989; Rutter, Graham, Chadwick, & Yule, 1976; Skinner, Elder, & Conger, in press).

Accordingly, our model (Figure 1) proposed that economic pressure resulting from adverse financial circumstances has a negative effect on the quality of both marital and parent–child relationship. Moreover, we expected to find marital quality to be positively related to parent–child relationship quality which, in turn, should have a direct influence on adolescent distress. Finally, we expected to find that marital quality also has a direct impact on adolescent development. The following analyses tested the empirical validity of the proposed theoretical perspective. Because variations in family process often have differential effects dependent on sex, we examined the model separately for fathers, mothers, sons, and daughters. For example, Elder (1974) found that early adolescent girls were more vulnerable to hardship-related adjustment problems than boys of the same age, and that fathers were more distressed by financial difficulties than mothers (Liker & Elder, 1983).

METHOD

Sample and Procedures

The sample included the 451 seventh graders and their biological parents participating in the Iowa Youth and Families Project (IYFP). The IYFP is an epidemiological study of rural two-parent households with a seventh grader (target adolescent) and a near-age sibling, drawn from a contiguous eight-county area in the Midwest (see Kellam, 1990). The participation rate for families meeting these criteria of family structure and geographic location was 78.8%. Data are reported here for three of the four participating family members, the target adolescent, and his or her parents. These families lived in an area of the rural Midwest that had suffered its worst economic decline since the Great Depression of the 1930s. Although the economic situation was improving by the late 1980s, the area still suffered from high rates of business failure, out-migration, and declining wages (Davidson, 1990). When we visited them, these families were faced with very uncertain economic futures.

The seventh graders (215 males, 236 females) were from White, predominantly middle-class families. Family residence was a farm (34%), a non-farm rural area (12%), or a town or a small city with a population under 6,500 (54%). Median family income was $33,700, well below the median of $39,995 for married couples with children in the U.S. in 1988. Moreover, 11% of the families were below the poverty line, twice the national average for two-parent families in 1988 (Bureau of the Census, 1989). Family size ranged from 4 to 13 persons (median = 4.95), exceeding that of the general population due to sampling criteria. The median age of fathers and mothers was 39 and 37 years old, respectively, while median years of schooling was 1 year beyond high school for both parents.

Data collection followed a series of contacts for recruitment, obtaining informed consent, and scheduling. Each family was then visited twice at home by a member of the IYFP field staff trained in interviewing and videotaping. Family visits lasted an average of 2 hr each, and usually occurred within a 2-week period. During the first visit, and between visits, family members completed a set of questionnaires related to economic conditions, family relationships, and individual characteristics. During the second visit, family members were videotaped as they engaged in four structured-interaction tasks, two involving all four family members, one for only the marital dyad, and one for only the two siblings. Each family member's questionnaire responses were kept completely confidential from other family members, and only those participating in a given video task were present during taping. These videotaped recordings were subsequently coded by trained observers and were used to assess several family and individual characteristics employed in subsequent analysis. Because multivariate analyses by structural equations require list-wise deletion, any person with missing values for a variable were deleted from the analyses. Therefore, only 426 cases that had valid values for all variables were included in the subsequent analyses. No significant differences were found between those cases deleted and those in the analyses on major dimensions of sample characteristics.

Measures

A single indicator was used to measure each of the four exogenous economic constructs shown in Figure 1. We calculated *per capita family income* by adjusting total family income from all sources (earnings, interest, dividends, government payments, etc.) for household size. This measure ranged from $ − 10,245 to $51,800, (M = $8,113).[1] *Debt-to-asset ratio* was assessed by dividing all types of debt (home mortgage, auto loans, tuition loans, etc.) by material assets possessed by the family. A natural log was taken to normalize the distribution of this variable. Previous studies of farm families have shown that a debt-asset ratio greater than 40% creates financial difficulties, and a ratio greater than 70% places the farming operation in serious jeopardy (Murdock & Leistritz, 1988).

The measure of *unstable work* focuses on the past year's work experience of parents. Parents were defined as having an unstable work life over the past year if they reported one or more of the following events – *yes* (1) or *no* (0): (a) changed job for a worse one, (b) demoted or had trouble at work, (c) laid off or fired, or (d) involuntarily stopped working for a long period. Because we were interested in assessing family work instability, we combined responses for mothers and fathers. Father's instability alone had a slightly stronger relation to economic pressure than mother's work problems; however, the following analyses would not be substantively altered using separate work measures for spouses. The measure of *family income loss* was an average of independent father and mother estimates of percentage change in income over the past year. It ranged from one (increased more than 30%) to nine (decreased more than 30%), with an average score of 3.52 (i.e., on average families experienced a slight increase in income). Higher scores indicate heavier losses, whereas lower scores indicate increases in income.

According to our theoretical model, the effect of family economic conditions on family well-being occurs through its impact on the daily experiences of family members. That is, adverse financial circumstances produce economic pressure such as having to cutback on spending, and

---

[1]The negative income resulted from the fact that we calculated net farm income by subtracting farm operation expenses from total farm receipts. As a result, there are six farm families with negative income in our sample, that is, families whose farm operating expenses exceeded farm profits resulting in a net loss for 1988.

it is these constraints that should directly affect personal distress and family relationships. We used three measures as indicators of economic pressure: *can't make ends meet* (1), *material needs* (2), and *economic adjustments* (3). The measure of can't make ends meet includes two items: difficulty in paying bills—*a great deal of difficulty* (5)—and a report on whether families had enough money to make ends meet at the end of each month on a 4-point scale ranging from *more than enough* (1) to *not enough* (4). We standardized and combined the answers by fathers and mothers to form a family measure (the correlation between them is 0.65). Thus, this measure ranges from −5.42 to 5.64 with a mean of zero. Material needs consists of seven items that ask whether the family has enough money to meet their needs for a home, clothing, furniture, car, food, medical care, and leisure activities. Fathers and mothers each indicated on a 5-point scale whether they agreed or disagreed that they could meet these needs. A high score indicates they could not. The scale has high-internal consistency (α = 0.89 for fathers and 0.88 for mothers). The scores for parents are highly correlated (r = .54) and, therefore, were combined. The third measure, family economic adjustment, was indexed by summing up either father's or mother's "yes" response on each of 17 items (thus the range of scores is 0 to 17) that indicate economic adjustments made by the family during the past year—*yes* (1) or *no* (0). Adjustments include rather drastic steps (e.g., canceling medical insurance) that were taken to reduce expenditures in response to financial difficulties.

In developing measures of family relationships and adolescent distress, we wanted to avoid the problem of relying on a single source of information. As O'Leary and Emery (1984) pointed out, ratings of marital and parent–child relationships have been largely obtained only from parents. When parent-reported data on relationship quality were correlated with data based on parent ratings of child emotional and behavioral problems, the association between relationship quality and adolescent distress was of greater magnitude than when data on adolescent problems were obtained from independent sources, such as teachers or trained observers (O'Leary & Emery, 1984; Smith & Forehand, 1986). This bias, known as the *method variance problem*, that results from measuring all study variables through reports from a single source, has been discussed elsewhere (Bank, Dishion, Skinner, & Patterson, 1990; Lorenz, Conger, Simons, Whitbeck, & Elder, 1991). Several studies have shown that perceptions of child problems are affected by parents' psychological characteristics (e.g., Brody & Forehand, 1986; Griest, Wells, & Forehand, 1979). Therefore, when all information on family relationships and adolescent problems is obtained from a parent, it is possible that some third variable, such as parent's depression, may

operate to distort the association between family and adolescent constructs (Grych & Fincham, 1990).

To overcome these shortcomings, in this article we use measures of
relationship quality based both on reports by participants in the family
dyads of interest and by trained observers. There are several advantages
to this approach. First, marital and parent–child relationship qualities
represent global measures that capture the subjective essence of the
dyadic relations. Second, unlike the parent–preadolescent relationship,
the relationship between parents and adolescents becomes co-regulated
(Maccoby & Martin, 1983). Like the marital relationship, it involves
highly interdependent and bilateral adjustment sequences by both
parties involved and thus requires ratings by both participants. Third,
husbands and wives, adolescents and their parents can differ in perceptions of their relationships (e.g., Rutter et al., 1976). Employing multiple
sources of information brings in different but overlapping perspectives
that can enhance the understanding of these relationships (Achenbach,
McConaughy, & Howell, 1987). Finally, assessments of relationship
quality by research observers as well as dyadic participants serves as a
cross validation that overcomes, to some degree, the previously discussed problem of method variance.

Each *participant's judgment* of relationship quality was assessed by two
items. Spouses each rated satisfaction with the marital relationship on a
5-point scale ranging from *not at all satisfied* (1) to *completely satisfied* (5),
and happiness with the relationship on a 6-point scale ranging from
extremely unhappy (1) to *extremely happy* (6). These two items were
standardized and summed and used as indicators for marital quality.
Similarly, parents and children were asked to indicate their satisfaction
and happiness with the parent–child relationship on two 4-point scales
ranging from *very unsatisfied* (1) to *very satisfied* (4) and *very unhappy* (1) to
very happy (4). These two questions have been found to be a reliable
measure of relationship quality (Conger et al., 1990). *Observers' ratings* of
relationship quality were defined by subjective judgments of overall
quality on a 5-point scale ranging from *low* (1) to *high* (5). Observations
of the husband–wife interaction task (Task 4) were used by raters to
assess marital quality, and the two interaction tasks involving both
parents and children (Tasks 1 and 2) were used for generating observer
ratings of parent–child relationship quality. Here, we assumed that
feelings of relationship satisfaction and happiness by family members
are, to some extent, public information as indicated through the
gestures and statements they make to each other. Observers are
sensitive to the resulting "emotional tone" in the relationship and are
able to make discriminations about the overall quality of the bond
between participants. For 12% of all tasks, relationship quality was

independently coded by two observers selected at random. Inter-observer reliability for marital quality was 0.77 (Task 4) and for parent–child relationship quality, averaged across Tasks 1 and 2, it was 0.68 (fathers and adolescents) and 0.69 (mothers and adolescents). Although not high, these coefficients for inter-observer reliabilities are acceptable (Suen & Ary, 1989).

Adolescents rated their *emotional distress* on three subscales from the Symptom Checklist-90-revised (*SCL-90-R*; Derogatis, 1983). This instrument has demonstrated reliability and validity (Derogatis & Cleary, 1977) as a measure of psychological distress and has been used in several previous studies of adolescents (e.g., Compas, Slavin, Wagner, & Kathryn, 1985). Two of the subscales include symptoms of internalization (depression and anxiety). One subscale (hostility) assesses symptoms of externalization and is included because previous research suggests that males tend to display more symptoms of externalization whereas females are more likely to display symptoms of internalization (Derogatis, 1983).

The *SCL-90-R* assesses symptoms experienced during the past week on a 5-point scale ranging from *no discomfort* (1) to *extreme discomfort* (5). The depression subscale (12 items) included symptoms such as "feeling blue." Ten items (e.g., feeling fearful) make up the anxiety measure and six items (e.g., having urges to beat, injure, or harm someone) make up the hostility subscale. These subscales were internally consistent (0.87, depression; 0.80, hostility; and 0.83, anxiety). Because no directly comparable items were available from parent or observer reports, the adolescent distress construct was based only on adolescent ratings of self.

RESULTS

Because previous studies have suggested that economic difficulties may have differential effects for men and women (Conger et al., 1990; Liker & Elder, 1983), as well as for boys and girls (Elder et al., 1985; Emery & O'Leary, 1983; Gore & Colten, 1989), we first evaluated the validity of our model by testing it separately for four different dyads (i.e., father–boy, father–girl, mother–boy, and mother–girl). The means, standard deviations, and correlations among all study variables used in model estimation are reported in the Appendix. Table 1 summarizes the results of the latent variable, structural equation analyses using Linear Structural Equation Model, Version 7 (LISREL 7; Joreskog & Sorbom, 1989). To control for response biases across constructs, error terms for

TABLE 1
Completely Standardized Maximum Likelihood Estimates of Model Parameters Controlling for Parents' Education, t tests in Parentheses.

Parameters	Father				Mother			
	Boys		Girls		Boys		Girls	
Measurement coefficients								
Economic pressure								
$\lambda y1,1$; ends meet	0.90	–	0.89	–	0.91	–	0.89	–
$\lambda y2,1$; material needs	0.83	(14.64)	0.80	(13.43)	0.83	(14.65)	0.80	(13.33)
$\lambda y3,1$; adjustment	0.78	(13.47)	0.79	(13.28)	0.78	(13.54)	0.79	(13.27)
Marital quality								
$\lambda y4,2$; father	0.52	–	0.65	–	0.54	–	0.64	–
$\lambda y5,2$; mother	0.72	(4.71)	0.81	(6.07)	0.69	(4.70)	0.82	(5.84)
$\lambda y6,2$; observer	0.54	(4.74)	0.50	(5.87)	0.53	(4.68)	0.50	(5.76)
Parent–child								
$\lambda y7,3$; observer	0.37	–	0.50	–	0.37	–	0.36	–
$\lambda y8,3$; parent	0.35	(2.77)	0.46	(3.76)	0.57	(3.75)	0.46	(3.26)
$\lambda y9,3$; adolescent	0.38	(2.89)	0.58	(3.85)	0.59	(3.84)	0.58	(3.39)
Adolescent distress								
$\lambda y10,4$; anxiety	0.86	–	0.89	–	0.86	–	0.89	–
$\lambda y11,4$; depression	0.88	(14.86)	0.86	(14.08)	0.87	(14.85)	0.87	(14.16)
$\lambda y12,4$; hostility	0.84	(14.24)	0.75	(12.25)	0.84	(14.35)	0.75	(12.17)
Structural coefficients								
$\gamma1,1$; income to pressure	−.46	(−6.90)	−.32	(−5.35)	−.48	(−7.31)	−.35	(−6.04)
$\gamma1,2$; DTA to pressure	0.24	(3.80)	0.40	(6.68)	0.24	(3.80)	0.39	(6.48)
$\gamma1,3$; loss to pressure	0.01	(0.14)	0.28	(4.85)	0.01	(0.02)	0.27	(4.66)
$\gamma1,4$; work to pressure	0.13	(2.13)	0.09	(1.52)	0.13	(2.06)	0.09	(1.45)
$\beta2,1$; pressure to mq	−.28	(−2.76)	−.28	(−3.13)	−.28	(−2.84)	−.28	(−3.10)
$\beta3,1$; pressure to p/c	−.26	(−1.36)	−.14	(−1.36)	−.21	(−2.01)	−.04	(−0.41)
$\beta3,2$; mq to p/c	0.65	(2.85)	0.23	(2.01)	0.46	(2.71)	0.34	(2.29)
$\beta4,2$; mq to distress	−0.20	(−0.72)	0.07	(0.78)	0.05	(0.40)	0.16	(1.50)
$\beta4,3$; p/c to distress	−0.46	(−1.72)	−0.43	(−3.35)	−0.55	(−3.10)	−0.56	(−3.02)
$\chi^2(101)$	118.44		135.90		112.01		133.12	
p	0.113		0.013		0.213		0.058	
GFI[a]	0.941		0.928		0.943		0.932	
N	208		218		208		218	

Note. T tests are in parentheses. Pressure = family economic pressure; DTA = Debt-to-asset ratio; loss = family income loss; work = unstable work; mq = marital quality; p/c = parent–child relationship quality; distress = adolescent emotional distress. T-test values are in parentheses. Dashes identify indicators originally set equal to one. For these indicators, t tests are not provided.
[a]Goodness of fit index.

measures based on the same reporter were allowed to covary (Lavee, McCubbin, & Olson, 1987; Thomson & Williams, 1984).

For the measurement part of the model, loadings for each of the four multiple-indicator constructs (economic pressure, marital quality, parent–child relationship quality, and child emotional distress) are reasonably high across all four models. The three loadings for parent–child relationship quality (λ_{73}, λ_{83}, λ_{93}) are somewhat lower than those for marital quality. This result is consistent with previous research that has shown greater discrepancy among reports by observers, parents, and children than that between parents and observers. For example, the studies by Jossop (1981), Noller and Callan (1988), and Achenbach et al. (1987) found that there were only low to moderate levels of consistency between parents and children in their perceptions about family life. As Achenbach et al. (1987) argued, however, the lower degree of agreement between particular combinations of informants may indicate that one source of information cannot simply be substituted for another because they contribute different information.

Turning to the structural coefficients, each of which was estimated controlling for each parent's level of education. Three of the financial measures (per capita family income, debt-to-asset ratio, and income loss) had significant effects on family economic pressure for the models involving girls.[2] The relationship between parents' unstable work and economic pressure, however, is not significant for families with seventh-grade females. The strongest associations involve debt-to-asset ratio (0.40 for fathers and daughters, 0.39 for mothers and daughters) and income level ($-.32$, fathers and daughters, $-.35$ mothers and daughters).

For the boys' model, family income level, debt-to-asset ratio, and parents' unstable work are significantly related to family economic pressure. For these measures, per capita income produced the highest coefficients ($-.48$ mothers, $-.46$, fathers), unstable work the lowest. Unlike the girls' model, however, the effect of family income loss on family economic pressure is not significant. We examine the possible implications of this sex difference in the discussion.

Taken together, these results are supportive of the first stage of our hypothesis that various dimensions of economic adversity may affect family relationships primarily through parental cognitions and behavioral adjustments that reflect their awareness of and responses to economic difficulties (Conger et al., 1990). More important, the associations among economic circumstances and felt economic pressure are robust, in most instances, even with parents' educational level controlled in the analyses.

Both models for boys and girls show that economic difficulties have an

---

[2]Note that, as shown in the Appendix, parents' levels of education were significantly related to three indicators of economic pressure. This is also true in our structural models that show fathers' and mothers' education levels were significantly related to the latent construct of economic pressure.

adverse impact on marital quality. The results, however, do not lend strong support for the hypothesis that economic pressure directly affects parent–child relationship quality because only relationship quality for mothers and sons is significantly affected by family economic pressure ($-.21$, $t = -2.01$). The path coefficients in the other three models are not statistically significant. The results suggest that the effect of economic pressure on the parent–child relationship may be primarily indirect through lowered marital quality. As expected, the findings also indicate that marital quality is significantly related to parent–child relationship quality for all four models. Marital quality is more strongly related to parents' relationship quality with boys (0.65 for fathers and sons, 0.46 for mothers and sons) than with girls (0.23, fathers and daughters, 0.34 mothers and daughters). These findings suggest that relationship quality for parents and sons is more likely to be disrupted by low-marital quality than parents and daughters relationships. These sex differences, however, should be interpreted with caution because covariance structure comparisons indicated that none of them was statistically significant—X^2 (1) = 0.83 for the difference between father–boy and father–girl models—X^2 (1) = 1.31 for the difference between mother–boy and mother–girl models. Again, we return to the issue of sex differences in the discussion.

In the final stage of the analyses, the results also suggest that the effect of marital quality on children's distress is mainly indirect through parent–child relationship quality. None of the structural coefficients from marital quality to adolescent distress is statistically significant. However, parent–child relationship quality was strongly related to adolescent emotional distress with structural coefficients ranging from $-.43$ ($t = -3.35$) for fathers and daughters to $-.56$ ($t = -3.02$) for mothers and daughters.

The fit indexes reported in Table 1 suggest that our postulated model fits the data reasonably well. However, we wanted to determine whether the model was an equally accurate description of economic influences on both boys and girls. To answer this question, covariance structures were compared using multi-sample analysis procedures outlined by Joreskog and Sorbom (1989). Two models (fathers and boys and fathers and girls) were first stacked and invariant constraints were imposed. The overall chi square for the whole model is 325.78 with 226 df. Next, the invariant constraints were relaxed for the beta matrix in order to test the hypothesis that the structural relations among endogenous constructs were different for boys and girls. The resulting chi square was 320.27 with 221 degrees-of-freedom. Compared to the model of complete invariance, this small decrease in chi square (5.51) with a sacrifice of 5 df indicates that the beta matrices are not significantly different for boys and girls. The same procedure was repeated for models involving mothers. The resulting change in chi square of 6.83 with 5 df again demonstrated no significant sex differences in estimation of the structural equation models.

Having established the model's consistency across four different family dyads, we further tested its accuracy with the overall sample including both parents and boys and girls combined (Figure 2). Three combined measures were formed by adding up mother–child and father–child relationship quality for each of the reporters: observers, parents, and children. Each parent's educational level was controlled in the estimation of all structural coefficients. Figure 2 shows the results of the estimation procedures. In this model, all four economic constructs were significant predictors of parents' economic pressure, with income level ($-.38$) and debt-to-asset ratio (0.31) being the strongest. Family economic pressure was negatively related to both marital ($-.28$) and parent–child relationship quality ($-.11$); the latter coefficient is marginally significant ($t = -1.65$) using the full sample. Consistent with the earlier models, much of the relation between economic pressure and parent–child relationship quality is indirect, mediated by marital quality which is significantly related (0.46) to the quality of parent–child relationships. The coefficient (0.14) for the relationship between marital quality and child emotional distress is also marginally significant ($t = 1.68$) with the full sample. Although parent–child relationship quality is negatively related to adolescent distress when single indicators were used, unexpectedly, marital quality was positively related to adolescent distress when multiple indicators were used. This positive association, controlling for the parent–child relationship, underscores the importance of this family subsystem's total effect on adolescent distress. As earlier, the relationship between marital quality and adolescent distress is largely indirect through parent–child relationship quality, which is the strongest predictor of child emotional distress ($-.55$). The fit indexes for the model using the complete sample, including a critical n of 323.09, suggest a good match between the data and the hypothesized causal processes. Because economic pressure may also differentially influence families at different income levels, we tested for an interaction effect between them by dividing the sample into high income (above \$6,500 for per capita income, $n = 195$) and low income groups (below \$6,500 for per capita income, $n = 231$). No differences were found between the two groups.

Given the fact that only modest levels of consistency were obtained between parent, child, and observer ratings of parent–child relationship quality, a question could be raised as to whether the structural coefficients were sensitive to the specific indicator (or report) being used. To

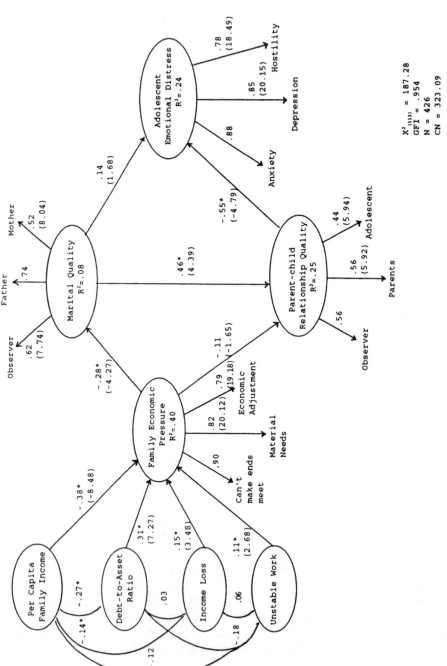

FIGURE 2   The maximum likelihood estimates for the combined model controlling for parents' education. T tests in parentheses. Measurement errors between the same reporting sources across marital quality and parent–child relationship quality were correlated (standardized

answer this question, a sensitivity analysis (Kim, 1984) was conducted to see the extent to which the pattern of coefficients was altered by employing single indicators or pairs of indicators in the analyses. The results of the test show that the pattern of parameter estimates was quite robust no matter which reporter or pair of reporters was used. The effects of marital quality on the parent–child relationship are 0.25 ($t = 3.92$, observer rating), 0.32 ($t = 4.84$, parents rating), and 0.28 ($t = 4.28$, adolescent rating), respectively. The effects of parent–child relationship quality on adolescent emotional distress are $-.12$ ($t = -2.19$, observer rating), $-.19$ ($t = -3.51$, parents rating), and $-.37$ ($t = -7.29$, adolescent rating), respectively. The models with two-indicator constructs of parent–child relationship quality show a similar pattern to the model with three indicators (Figure 2). The results indicate that, although the magnitude of the model parameters may vary by reporter, their statistical significance is quite stable regardless of which combinations of indicators we choose. The model with single indicators is also similar to the three-indicator model except that the magnitude of the coefficients is smaller than for either the two- or three-indicator models. This is due to the nature of single-indicator models that do not correct for attenuation resulting from errors in measurement as do multiple-indicator models.

The adequacy of the overall model was further tested by subjecting it to an incremental fit test (Bentler & Bonett, 1980; Bollen, 1989; Sobel & Bohrnstedt, 1985). In this test, we were interested in answering two questions: First, to what extent is our combined model for both parents and girls and boys consistent with our data in comparison with other alternative models? Second, among the alternative models, is our postulated model the most parsimonious? In order to choose theoretically meaningful models for comparison, six nested models are designated (Table 2). The first is a baseline model with all gammas and beta being fixed to zero. The reason for this designation is that the model represents a hypothetical phenomenon in which all the constructs are unrelated with one another, but in which observed variables were assumed to be determined by their respective constructs. The second, a null beta model, is chosen because this model implies that family economic pressure was affected by objective economic circumstances, but was unrelated to relationship quality as well as to adolescent well-being. The third is a single-pathway model that hypothesizes links from economic pressure to marital quality to parent–child relationship quality to child emotional distress. That is, we asked whether the direct paths from economic pressure to parent–child relationship quality and from marital quality to adolescent distress could be dropped from the originally proposed model to obtain a more parsimonious rendering of the process of interest. The fourth model we tested is the originally hypothesized model that includes paths from economic pressure to parent-child relationship quality and from marital quality to adolescent distress (Figure 1). The fifth, a subdiagonal beta model, was used to test the hypothesis that economic pressure would have a direct effect on adolescent distress in addition to its indirect effects through marital and parent-child relationship quality. And finally, for the sixth model, we tested a fully recursive model that includes all direct and indirect paths between constructs to see whether it would significantly improve the fit of the model.

Table 2 provides the results of these tests. Along with chi-square and degrees of freedom, changes in chi-square and in degrees of freedom are also reported. We included Bentler and Bonett's (1980) normed index and Bollen's (1989) index to show the incremental fits. The results indicate that the null beta model significantly improved the fit over the baseline model $-X^2(5)$ = 190.45 $-$ which lends strong support to the argument that economic adversity leads to heightened family economic pressure. When the single-pathway model was estimated, a further significant improvement over the null beta model $-X^2(3)$ = 104.15 $-$ was obtained, suggesting that it is the route from marital quality to parent-child relationship quality that is largely responsible for mediating the effects of economic pressure on child emotional distress. However, when our originally hypothesized model was tested $-x^2(2)$ = 5.12 $-$ there was little change in the other fit indexes. The insignificant improvement of the hypothesized model over the single-pathway model suggests that, to a large degree, the latter model is adequate to account for the postulated processes from economic pressure to adolescent psychological distress.

The subdiagonal beta model was estimated to see whether there is a significant improvement in the fit of the model when the direct effect of

TABLE 2
Incremental Fit Comparison Across Models

Competing Models	χ^2	df	$\Delta\chi^2$	Δdf	χ^2/df	BBI	BI
Baseline model	487.60	124	–	–	3.93	–	–
Null beta model	297.15	118	190.45*	5	2.52	0.40	0.52
Single pathway model	193.00	115	104.15*	3	1.67	0.62	0.72
Hypothesized model	187.88	113	5.12	2	1.67	0.63	0.80
Subdiagonal beta model	185.92	112	1.36	1	1.66	0.63	0.80
Fully recursive model	159.75	94	26.17	18	1.68	0.68	0.82

Note. BBI = Bentler and Bonett (1980) normed index; BI = Bollen (1989) index; dashes indicate not applicable; starred coefficient: $p < .01$; ΔX^2 = change in X^2; Δdf = change in degrees of freedom.

economic pressure on adolescent distress is also estimated. The results show that the inclusion of this direct path only changes the $X^2(1) = 1.36$, indicating no statistically significant improvement in the model fit and no evidence for a direct effect. The results from estimating the fully recursive model also show that there is no significant improvement in fit using the complete model over the models nested within it.

To complete the analyses, Table 3 presents the total, direct, and indirect effects for the four endogenous constructs in the hypothesized model. The results confirm that economic pressure is significantly and indirectly related to adolescent distress (0.06). Economic pressure also has a detrimental impact on the parent–child relationship both indirectly ($-.12$) and as a total effect ($-.23$). As mentioned earlier, marital quality is positively related to parent–child relationship quality and negatively associated with adolescent distress ($-.25$, indirect effect; $-.11$, total effect).

DISCUSSION

This article examined the effect of family economic circumstances on adolescent psychological distress, particularly the role of family relationship quality in linking these two phenomena. Various dimensions of family finances were found to be associated with the level of economic pressure experienced by husbands and wives. As predicted, economic

TABLE 3
Estimates of Total, Direct, and Indirect Effects in Relations Among the Endogenous Constructs, t Tests in Parentheses

Structural	Type of Effect		
Relationships	Total	Direct	Indirect
Economic pressure to	$-.28$	$-.28$	$-$
marital quality	(4.20)	(4.20)	$-$
Economic pressure to	$-.23$	$-.11$	$-.12$
parent/child quality	(3.33)	(-1.65)	(-3.28)
Economic pressure to	0.06	$-$	0.06
adolescent distress	(2.05)	$-$	(2.50)
Marital quality to parent/child	0.46	0.46	$-$
quality	(4.41)	(4.39)	$-$
Marital quality to	$-.11$	0.14	$-.25$
adolescent distress	(1.79)	(.98)	(-3.79)
Parent/child to adolescent	$-.55$	$-.55$	$-$
distress	(-4.81)	(-4.81)	$-$

Note. Dashes indicate not applicable.

325

pressures have a negative influence on marital quality. Although economic pressures are found to be significantly related to relationship quality for mothers and sons, we did not find strong evidence to support the proposition that family economic pressure would have a direct impact on other parent–child relationships. However, we did find that the detrimental effect of economic pressure on the parent–child relationship was mainly indirect and is largely mediated through marital quality.

The strong effect of marital quality on parent–child relationship quality lends support to the spill-over hypothesis that parents who are unhappy with their marriages tend to have problems with parent–child relationships as well (Belsky, 1981, 1984; Conger et al., 1991; Patterson, 1982). In contrast, no supporting evidence was found for the hypothetical compensatory argument (Minuchin et al., 1978). Marital quality had only a statistically marginal direct effect on adolescent emotional problems in this article. These results are consistent with those of Porter and O'Leary (1980) who found that mother's rating of marital satisfaction was not significantly associated with a range of child problems. This lack of association is also consonant with the work of Hetherington, M. Cox, and R. Cox (1982) and Rutter et al. (1974) who discovered that child psychological problems are more closely related to open marital conflicts than to parents' perceptions of lowered marital quality.

An important finding in this article is that the marital relationship is especially vulnerable to external pressures, and that it is contagious and affects perceptions of satisfaction in parent–child relationships as well. The results of this article suggest that a pathway from marital to parent–child relationship quality represents one of several possible mechanisms through which economic pressures place adolescents at increased risk for problems of psychological distress. In future research, we will be interested in identifying the interactional or perceptual mechanisms that may account for this causal sequence from closeness in the marriage to ties between parents and children.

In this article, the effect of marital quality on adolescent emotional distress was found to be mediated by parent–child relationship quality. This finding is consonant with previous research and recent theoretical emphases on the mediational role of parenting in the stress process (Patterson, DeBaryshe, & Ramsey, 1989). In an early review of studies on children in divorced and discordant families, Emery (1982) suggested that an unhappy marriage might lead to children's maladjustment if it results in a deterioration in parent–child relationships. This position has found support in studies of adolescent males (Conger et al., 1992; Conger et al., 1991; Patterson, 1991), children of divorced families (Tschann, Johnston, Kline, & Wallerstein, 1989), and of early adolescents of both sexes (Fauber, Forehand, Thomas, & Wierson, 1990). This article lends further support to this theoretical argument and expands its applicability to other family dyads (i.e., to fathers as well as mothers, and to relationships between parents and adolescent females as well as boys).

Regarding possible sex differences in the findings, earlier studies on the effects of family relationships on children's adjustment, as reviewed by Emery (1982), suggested that disrupted family relationships have more negative consequences for boys than for females (Hetherington et al., 1982; Porter & O'Leary, 1980). More recent investigations, however, report either that females are equally vulnerable to disrupted family relationships (Elder et al. 1985; Emery & O'Leary, 1984; P. L. Johnson & O'Leary, 1987; Long, Forehand, Fauber, & Brody, 1987) or, that males' greater vulnerability occurs only before early adolescence (Forehand, Neighbor, & Wierson, 1991), an earlier point in development than the children in this study. Indeed, Elder (1974) reported that early adolescent females are more vulnerable to family economic hardship than boys. Recent reviews (Amato & Keith, 1991; Grych & Fincham, 1990) also indicate considerable inconsistency with regard to sex differences in vulnerability. For example, a recent study by Forehand et al. (1991), found that family relationship quality during stressful times has as much influence on females as on boys. Given the variability in previous findings regarding sex differences in vulnerability to family stress, we suspect that our failure to find significant adult or adolescent sex effects may reflect the actual situation for these families rather than some artifact of the sample, measures, or statistical procedures employed.

Although the findings from these analyses are reasonably consistent with the hypothesized model, there are, of course, competing explanations for the results as well as limitations in the research methodology. With cross-sectional data, we cannot be certain that the postulated direction of effects among constructs is appropriate. For example, parent–child relationship quality may affect marital quality or, even more likely, there may be a reciprocal relationship between them (e.g., K. E. Anderson, Lytton, & Romney, 1986; Nihira, Mink, & Myers, 1985). We can say that our model is at least not inconsistent with the observed relationships among constructs and that earlier, longitudinal studies of family economic stress demonstrate similar processes across time (Elder et al., 1986). Future longitudinal studies are needed, though, to increase our confidence in these results. And, even though it might be possible to estimate reciprocal effects with cross-sectional data, instrumental variables are required for such analyses. Such instruments were not available for these analyses.

Other obvious limitations of the study include sample characteristics such as family structure, geographic location, ethnicity, and the absence of urban families. Because these findings parallel in important ways the results of past research with urban samples (Elder, 1974), we are more confident of their generalizability. Nevertheless, replication with more diverse populations is essential. In addition, it will be important to generalize the findings using other approaches to assessment of the constructs of interest. For example, economic hardship might be examined as a dichotomy (above and below the poverty line) as might emotional distress (diagnosis of psychiatric disorder vs. absence of a diagnosis). Because only about 11% of these families were living below the poverty line, and because diagnostic measures were unavailable, we chose to model the hypothesized processes using continuous variables. Future studies will be needed to determine whether the postulated processes hold using dichotomous approaches that identify extreme cases.

Regarding other measurement issues, the sensitivity analyses demonstrated that statistically significant associations between constructs remained whether data from one, two, or three reporters were used as indicators. These findings underscore the robust nature of the results, but lead to confusion regarding which indicators or reporters are to be preferred. Our view is that multiple reporters are to be preferred, unless findings are quite discrepant among them because: (a) They act as a check on the validity as well as reliability of constructs, (b) they provide a correction for attenuation due to measurement error from any single source of information, and (c) they identify a component of variance in the data that is least affected by the unique dispositions of a single reporter.

Finally, worthy of mention is the fact that, for these analyses, there were very few significant zero-order correlations between family economic conditions (income, debts/assets, work instability, income loss) and either family relationship quality or adolescent distress. The results suggest that, unless economic disadvantage actually leads to felt economic pressures in daily living, it will have little influence on either family process or adolescent development. This finding is consistent with a growing body of data suggesting the importance of perceived hardship in economic stress processes (Kessler, Turner, & House, 1989).

ACKNOWLEDGMENTS

This article is based on collaborative research involving the Iowa Youth and Families Project at Iowa State University, Ames, and the Social

Change Project at University of North Carolina, Chapel Hill. The combined research effort is currently supported by National Institute of Mental Health Grant MH43270, National Institute on Drug Abuse Grant DE05347, the John D. and Catherine T. MacArthur Foundation Program for Successful Adolescent Development Among Youth in High-Risk Settings, and Research Scientist Award MH00507. Journal Paper Number 14949 of the Iowa Agriculture and Home Economics Experiment Station, Ames, IA — Project Number 2931.

REFERENCES

Achenbach, T. M., McConaughy, S. H., & Howell, C. T. (1987). Child/adolescent behavioral and emotional problems: Implications of cross-informants correlations for situational specificity. *Psychological Bulletin, 101,* 213–232.

Amato, P. R., & Keith, B. (1991). Parental divorce and the well-being of children: A meta-analysis. *Psychological Bulletin, 110,* 26–46.

Anderson, K. E., Lytton, H., & Romney, D. M. (1986). Mothers' interaction with normal and conduct-disordered boys: Who affects whom? *Developmental Psychology, 22,* 604–609.

Bank, L., Dishion, T., Skinner, M., & Patterson, G. R. (1990). Method variance in structural equation modeling: Living with "GLOP." In G. R. Patterson (Ed.), *Aggression and depression in family interactions* (pp. 247–280). Hillsdale, NJ: Lawrence Erlbaum Associates, Inc.

Belsky, J. (1981). Early human experience: A family perspective. *Developmental Psychology, 17,* 3–23.

Belsky, J. (1984). The determinants of parenting: A process model. *Child Development, 55,* 83–96.

Belsky, J. (1990). Child care and children's socioemotional development. *Journal of Marriage and the Family, 52,* 885–903.

Belsky, J., Gilstrap, B., & Rovine, M. (1984). The Pennsylvania Infant and Family Development Project I: Stability and change in mother–infant and father–infant interaction in a family setting at 1-to-3-to-9 months. *Child Development, 55,* 692–705.

Bentler, P. M., & Bonett, D. B. (1980). Significant tests and goodness of fit in the analysis of covariance structures. *Psychological Bulletin, 88,* 588–606.

Bollen, K. A. (1989). A new incremental fit index for general structural equation models. *Sociological Methods and Research, 17,* 303–316.

Brody, G. H., & Forehand, R. (1986). Maternal perception of child maladjustment as a function of the combined influence of child behavior and maternal depression. *Journal of Consulting and Clinical Psychology, 54,* 237–240.

Bureau of the Census. (1989). *Money income and poverty status in the United States: 1988* (Series P-60 No. 166). Washington, DC: U.S. Department of Commerce.

Caspi, A., & Elder, G. H., Jr. (1988). Emergent family patterns: The intergenerational construction of problem behavior and relationships. In R. A. Hinde & J. Stevenson-Hinde (Eds.), *Relationships within families: Mutual influences* (pp. 218–240). New York: Oxford University Press.

Compas, B. E., Slavin, L. A., Wagner, B. M., & Kathryn, V. (1985). Relationship of life events and social support with psychological dysfunction among adolescents. *Journal of Youth and Adolescence, 15,* 205–221.

Conger, R. D., Conger, K. J., Elder, G. H., Jr., Lorenz, F. O., Simons, R. L., & Whitbeck, L. B. (1992). A family process model of economic hardship and adjustment of early adolescent boys. *Child Development, 63,* 526–541.

Conger, R. D., Elder, G. H., Jr., Lorenz, F. O., Conger, K. J., Simons, R. L., Whitbeck, L. B., Huck, S., & Melby, J. N. (1990). Linking economic hardship to marital quality and instability. *Journal of Marriage and the Family, 52,* 643–656.

Conger, R. D., Lorenz, F. O., Elder, G. H., Jr., Melby, J. N., Simons, R. L., & Conger, K. J. (1991). A process model of family economic pressure and early adolescent alcohol use. *Journal of Early Adolescence, 11,* 430–449.

Conger, R. D., McCarthy, J., Yang, R. K., Lahey, B. B., & Kropp, J. P. (1984). Perception of child, child-rearing values, and emotional distress as mediating links between environmental stressors and observed maternal behavior. *Child Development, 55,* 2234–2247.

Cox, M., Owen, M. R., Lewis, J. M., & Henderson, V. K. (1989). Marriage, adult adjustment, and early parenting. *Child Development, 60,* 1015–1024.

Coyne, J. C., & Downey, G. (1991). Social factors and psychopathology: Stress, social support, and coping processes. In M. R. Rosenzweig & L. W. Porter (Eds.), *Annual review of psychology* (Vol. 42, pp. 401–425). Palo Alto, CA: Annual Review.

Davidson, O. G. (1990). *Broken heartland: The rise of America's rural ghetto.* New York: The Free Press.

Derogatis, L. R. (1983). *SCL-90-R administration, scoring, and procedures manual II.* Townsen, MD: Clinical Psychometric Research.

Derogatis, L. R., & Cleary, P. A. (1977). Confirmation of the dimensional structure of the SCL-90: A study in construct validation. *Journal of Clinical Psychology, 33,* 981–989.

Duncan, G. J. (1984). *Years of poverty, years of plenty.* Ann Arbor, MI: Institute for Social Research.

Easterbrooks, M. A., & Emde, R. N. (1988). Marital and parent–child relationships: The role of affect in the family system. In R. A. Hinde & J. Stevenson-Hinde (Eds.), *Relationships within families: Mutual influences* (pp. 83–103). New York: Oxford University Press.

Elder, G. H., Jr. (1974). *Children of the Great Depression.* Chicago: University of Chicago Press.

Elder, G. H., Jr., Caspi, A., & Downey, G. (1986). Problem behavior and family relationships: Life-course and intergenerational themes. In A. M. Sorensen, F. E. Weinert, & L. R. Sherrod (Eds.), *Human development and life course: Multidisciplinary perspectives* (pp. 293–340). Hillsdale, NJ: Lawrence Erlbaum Associates, Inc.

Elder, G. H., Jr., Liker, J., & Cross, C. (1984). Parent–child behavior in the Great Depression: Life-course and intergenerational influences. In P. B. Baltes & O. G. Brim, Jr. (Eds.), *Life-span development and behavior* (Vol. 6, pp. 109–158). New York: Academic.

Elder, G. H., Jr., Nguyen, T. V., & Caspi, A. (1985). Linking family hardship to children's lives. *Child Development, 56,* 361–375.

Emery, R. E. (1982). Marital turmoil: Interpersonal conflict and the children of discord and divorce. *Psychological Bulletin, 92,* 310–330.

Emery, R. E. (1988). *Marriage, divorce, and children's adjustment.* Beverly Hills, CA: Sage.

Emery, R. E., & O'Leary, K. D. (1983). Children's perception of marital discord and behavior problem of boys and girls. *Journal of Abnormal Child Psychology, 24,* 349–354.

Emery, R. E., & O'Leary, K. D. (1984). Marital discord and child behavior problems in nonclinical sample. *Journal of Abnormal Child Psychology, 12,* 411–420.

Engfer, A. (1988). The interrelatedness of marriage and mother–child relationship. In R. A. Hinde & J. Stevenson-Hinde (Eds.), *Relationships within families: Mutual influences* (pp. 104–118). New York: Oxford University Press.

Fauber, R., Forehand, R., Thomas, A. M., & Wierson, M. (1990). A mediational model of the impact of marital conflict on adolescent adjustment in intact and divorced families: The role of disrupted parenting. *Child Development, 61,* 1112–1123.

Forehand, R., Neighbor, B., & Wierson, M. (1991). The transition to adolescence: The role of gender and stress in problem behavior and competence. *Journal of Child Psychology and Psychiatry, 32,* 929–937.

Freud, A. (1958). Adolescence. *Psychologic Study of the Child, 13,* 255–278.

Gore, S., & Colten, M. E. (1989, August). *Sex differences in symptoms of depression and distress in high school aged youth in three communities.* Paper presented at the annual meeting of the American Sociological Association, San Francisco.

Griest, D. L., Wells, K. C., & Forehand, R. (1979). An examination of predictors of maternal perceptions of maladjustment in clinic-referred children. *Journal of Abnormal Psychology, 88,* 277–281.

Grotevant, H., & Cooper, C. (1985). Patterns of interaction in family relationships and the development of identity exploration in adolescence. *Child Development, 56,* 415–428.

Grotevant, H., & Cooper, C. (1986). Individuation in family relationships. *Human Development, 29,* 82–100.

Grych, J. H., & Fincham, F. D. (1990). Marital conflict and children's adjustment: A cognitive-contextual framework. *Psychological Bulletin, 108,* 267–290.

Hartup, W. W. (1986). On relationships and development. In W. W. Hartup & Z. Rubin (Eds.), *Relationships and development* (pp. 27–50). Hillsdale, NJ: Lawrence Erlbaum Associates, Inc.

Hauser, S., Power, S., Noam, G., Jacobson, A., Weiss, B., & Follansbee, D. (1987). Familial context of adolescent ego development. *Child Development, 55,* 195–213.

Hess, R. D., & Camara, K. A. (1979). Post-divorce family relationships as mediating factor in the consequences of divorce for children. *Journal of Social Issues, 35,* 79–96.

Hetherington, E. M., Cox, M., & Cox, R. (1982). Effects of divorce on parents and children. In M. E. Lamb (Ed.), *Nontraditional families: Parenting and child development* (pp. 233–288). Hillsdale, NJ: Lawrence Erlbaum Associates, Inc.

Hetherington, E. M., Stanley-Hagen, M., & Anderson, E. R. (1989). Marital transitions: A child's perspective. *American Psychologist, 44,* 303–312.

Hinde, R. A., & Stevenson-Hinde, J. (1986). Relating childhood relationships to individual characteristics. In W. W. Hartup & Z. Rubin (Eds.), *Relationships and development* (pp. 27–50). Hillsdale, NJ: Lawrence Erlbaum Associates, Inc.

Hinde, R. A., & Stevenson-Hinde, J. (1987). Interpersonal relationships and child development. *Developmental Review, 7,* 1–21.

Horwitz, A. V. (1984). The economy and social pathology. *Annual Review of Sociology, 10,* 95–119.

Johnson, P. L., & O'Leary, K. D. (1987). Parental behavior patterns and conduct disorder in girls. *Journal of Abnormal Child Psychology, 15,* 573–581.

Johnson, S. M., & Lobitz, G. K. (1974). The personal and marital adjustment of parents as related to observed child deviance and parenting behaviors. *Journal of Abnormal Child Psychology, 2,* 193–207.

Joreskog, K. G., & Sorbom, D. (1989). *LISREL 7: A guide to the program and applications.* Chicago: SPSS Inc.

Jossop, D. J. (1981). Family relationships as viewed by parents and adolescents: A specification. *Journal of Marriage and the Family, 43,* 95–107.

Kellam, S. G. (1990). Developmental epidemiological framework for family research on depression and aggression. In G. R. Patterson (Ed.), *Depression and aggression in family interaction* (pp. 11–48). Hillsdale, NJ: Lawrence Erlbaum Associates, Inc.

Kelvin, P., & Jarrett, J. E. (1985). *Unemployment: Its social psychological effects.* New York: Cambridge University Press.

Kessler, R. C., Turner, J. B., & House, J. S. (1989, August). *Unemployment and mental health in a blue collar community.* Paper presented at the annual meeting of the American Sociological Association, San Francisco.

Kim, J. O. (1984). Sensitivity analysis in sociological research. *American Sociological Review, 49,* 272–282.

Lavee, Y., McCubbin, H. I., & Olson, D. H. (1987). The effect of stressful life events and transitions on family functioning and well-being. *Journal of Marriage and the Family, 49,* 857–873.

Lempers, J. D., Clark-Lempers, D. S., & Simons, R. L. (1989). Economic hardship, parenting, and distress in adolescence. *Child Development, 60,* 25–39.

Lidz, T. (1969). The adolescent and his family. In B. Caplan & S. Lebovich (Eds.), *Adolescence: Psychological perspective* (pp. 67–90). New York: Basic Books.

Liker, J. K., & Elder, G. H. (1983). Economic hardship and marital relations in the 1930s. *American Sociological Review, 48,* 343–359.

Long, N., Forehand, R., Fauber, R., & Brody, G. (1987). Self-perceived and independently observed competence of young adolescents as a function of parental marital conflict and recent divorce. *Journal of Abnormal Child Psychology, 15,* 15–27.

Lorenz, F. O., Conger, R. D., Simons, R. L., Whitbeck, L. B., & Elder, G. H. (1991). Economic pressure and marital quality: An illustration of the method variance problem in the causal modeling of family processes. *Journal of Marriage and the Family, 53,* 375–388.

Maccoby, E. E., & Martin, J. A. (1983). Socialization in the context of the family: Parent–child interaction. In E. M. Hetherington (Ed.), *Handbook of child psychology: Vol 4. Socialization, personality and social development* (pp. 119–141). New York: Oxford University Press.

Meyer, H. J. (1988). Marital and mother–child relationships: Developmental history, parent personality, and child difficultness. In R. A. Hinde & J. Stevenson-Hinde (Eds.), *Relationships within families: Mutual influences* (pp. 119–141). New York: Oxford University Press.

Minuchin, S., Rosman, B. L., & Baker, L. (1978). *Psychosomatic families: Anorexia nervosa in context.* Cambridge, MA: Harvard University Press.

Montemayor, R. (1983). Parents and adolescents in conflict: All families some of the time and some families most of the time. *Journal of Early Adolescence, 3,* 83–103.

Murdock, S. H., & Leistritz, F. L. (Eds.). (1988). *The farm financial crisis: Socioeconomic dimensions and implications for producers and rural areas.* Boulder, CO: Westview.

Noller, P., & Callan, V. J. (1988). Understanding parent–adolescent interactions: Perceptions of family members and outsiders. *Developmental Psychology, 5,* 707–714.

Niemi, P. M. (1988). Family interaction patterns and the development of social conceptions in the adolescence. *Journal of Youth and Adolescence, 17,* 429–444.

Nihira, K., Mink, I. T., & Myers, C. E. (1985). Home environment and development of slow-learning adolescents: Reciprocal relations. *Developmental Psychology, 21,* 784–794.

O'Leary, K. D., & Emery, R. E. (1984). Marital discord and child behavior problems. In M. D. Levine & P. Satz (Eds.), *Middle childhood: Development and dysfunction* (pp. 345–364). Baltimore: University Park Press.

Olweus, D. (1980). Familial and temperamental determinants of aggressive behavior in adolescent boys: A causal analysis. *Developmental Psychology, 16,* 644–660.

Patterson, G. R. (1982). *Coercive family process.* Eugene, OR: Castalia.

Patterson, G. R. (1983). Stress: A change agent for family process. In N. Garmezy & M. Rutter (Eds.), *Stress, coping and development in children* (pp. 235–264). New York: McGraw-Hill.

Patterson, G. R. (1988). Family process: Loops, levels, and linkages. In N. Bolger, A. Caspi, G. Downey, & M. Moorehouse (Eds.), *Persons in context: Developmental processes* (pp. 114–151). New York: Cambridge University Press.

Patterson, G. R. (1991, April). *Interaction of stress and family structure, and their relation to child adjustment: An example of cross-site collaboration.* Paper presented at the meeting of the Society for Research in Child Development, Seattle, WA.

Patterson, G. R., DeBaryshe, B. D., & Ramsey, E. (1989). A developmental perspective on antisocial behavior. *American Psychologist, 44,* 329–335.

Porter, B., & O'Leary, K. D. (1980). Marital discord and childhood behavior problems. *Journal of Abnormal Child Psychology, 8,* 287–295.

Robertson, J. F., & Simons, R. L. (1989). Family factors, self-esteem and adolescent depression. *Journal of Marriage and the Family, 51,* 125–138.

Rutter, M., Graham, P., Chadwick, O., & Yule, W. (1976). Adolescent turmoil: Fact or fiction? *Journal of Child Psychology and Psychiatry, 17,* 35–56.

Rutter, M., Yule, B., Quinton, D., Rowlands, O., Yule, W., & Berger, M. (1974). Attainment and adjustment in two geographical areas: III. Some factors accounting for area differences. *British Journal of Psychiatry, 125,* 520–533.

Shepherd, G. (1981). Psychological disorder and unemployment. *Bulletin of the British Psychological Society, 34,* 345–348.

Skinner, M. L., Elder, G. H., Jr., & Conger, R. D. (in press). Linking economic hardship to adolescent aggression. *Journal of Youth and Adolescence.*

Smith, K. A., & Forehand, R. (1986). Parent-adolescent conflict: Comparison and prediction of perceptions of mothers, fathers, and daughters. *Journal of Adolescence, 6,* 353–367.

Sobel, M. E., & Bohrnstedt, G. W. (1985). Use of null models in evaluating the fit of covariance structure models. In N. B. Tuma (Ed.), *Sociological methodology* (pp. 152–178). San Francisco: Jossey-Bass.

Suen, H. K., & Ary, D. (1989). *Analyzing quantitative behavioral observation data.* Hillsdale, NJ: Lawrence Erlbaum Associates, Inc.

Thomson, E., & Williams, R. (1984). A note on correlated measurement error in wife-husband data. *Journal of Marriage and the Family, 46,* 643–649.

Tschann, J. M., Johnston, J. R., Kline, M., & Wallerstein, J. S. (1989). Family process and children's functioning after divorce. *Journal of Marriage and the Family, 51,* 431–444.

Wallerstein, J. S., & Kelly, J. B. (1980). *Surviving the breakup.* New York: Basic Books.

Received July 29, 1991
Revision received April 13, 1992
Accepted April 20, 1992

Changes in Parents' Work Status and Adolescents' Adjustment at School

Constance A. Flanagan
University of Michigan—Dearborn

Jacquelynne S. Eccles
University of Michigan—Ann Arbor

FLANAGAN, CONSTANCE A., and ECCLES, JACQUELYNNE S. *Changes in Parents' Work Status and Adolescents' Adjustment at School*. CHILD DEVELOPMENT, 1993, **64**, 246–257. The effects of change in parental work status on early adolescents' school adjustment before and after the transition to junior high school were examined in a 2-year longitudinal study. Data were gathered from 883 adolescents, their mothers, and teachers. Based on patterns of change or stability in parental work status during the 2 years of the study, 4 groups were compared: deprived, declining, recovery, and stable families. With parents' education controlled, teachers said that adolescents in deprived and declining families were less competent than their peers in stable or recovery families. In addition, adolescents whose parents experienced a decline in work status were the most disruptive in junior high school. While most students had difficulty adjusting to junior high school, the transition was particularly difficult for those students whose parents were simultaneously dealing with changes in work status.

Economic changes over the past decade have undermined the job security of many American workers and have contributed to a decline in income status among a sizable number of families (Dooley & Catalano, 1988; Harrison & Bluestone, 1988). Such changes in job security or income have disruptive effects on marital and parent-child relationships, increasing parents' depression, arbitrary discipline, and conflict with children and decreasing feelings of nurturance and integration in the family (Conger et al., 1990a; Elder, Van Nguyen, & Caspi, 1985; Flanagan, 1990a, 1990b; Lempers & Clark-Lempers, 1990; Lempers, Clark-Lempers, & Simon, 1989; McLoyd & Wilson, 1990; Radin & Harold-Goldsmith, 1989). The loss of a family's income or a parent's security on the job is also associated with children's adjustment problems. Increases in loneliness, depression, and antisocial tendencies and decreases in academic aspirations and self-esteem have been found (Conger, Elder, Melby, Simons, & Conger, 1990b; Elder et al., 1985; Flanagan, 1990b;

Lempers et al., 1989; Silbereisen, Walper, & Albrecht, 1990).

Most of the research on parental unemployment has centered on the disruptive effects of such changes within families. We know less about how changing conditions at a parent's workplace may affect children's behavior in other settings. In this paper we build on the existing literature by linking patterns of change in parental employment to patterns over time in early adolescents' adjustment to school. By employing a longitudinal design we were able to compare normal developmental patterns of adjustment during the transition to junior high school (from sixth to seventh grade) with the patterns for adolescents whose parents were concurrently dealing with a loss of status on the job.

Family Stressors and Adolescents' Social Adjustment at School

Research on stress and competence has focused on adjustment at school because of its relevance to children's lives (Garmezy,

The assistance of Carol Midgley and our colleagues from the Achievement Research Laboratory in collecting and processing these data is gratefully acknowledged. We thank the editor and several anonymous reviewers for their helpful advice on an earlier draft of this manuscript. The Transitions at Early Adolescence Study was made possible by grants from the National Institute of Mental Health (MH31724) and the National Institute of Child Health and Human Development (HD17296) to Jacquelynne S. Eccles. Please send correspondence and requests for reprints to Connie Flanagan, Behavioral Sciences Department, University of Michigan—Dearborn, Dearborn, MI 48128.

Masten, & Tellegen, 1984; Pellegrini, Masten, Garmezy, & Ferrarese, 1987). Adaptation to junior high school poses special problems for students due to the multiple changes that occur during this developmental period and to the fact that junior high schools are very different settings from elementary schools (Eccles, Midgley, & Adler, 1984; Simmons & Blyth, 1987). Significant declines in students' achievement as well as in students' and teachers' satisfaction, esteem, and sense of efficacy occur during the transition from elementary to junior high school (Eccles et al., 1990; Feldlaufer, Midgley, & Eccles, 1988; Midgley & Feldlaufer, 1987; Midgley, Feldlaufer, & Eccles, 1989). According to students and independent observers, teacher supportiveness is lower in junior high school (seventh grade) compared to elementary school (sixth grade), and relationships between students and teachers deteriorate after the transition to junior high school (Feldlaufer et al., 1988; Hawkins & Berndt, 1985; Hirsch & Rapkin, 1987). If this downward trend in students' achievement and relationships with teachers is characteristic of the junior high transition, a stable home environment might be important in facilitating a smooth adjustment to school. Conversely, adverse changes or uncertainties at home might intensify the normal difficulties that early adolescents experience during this transition.

The question that we were interested in addressing was the following: Since the early adolescent must adapt to a new school environment and new peer networks, do negative changes in the parents' work status compromise this process? Besides its developmental relevance to early adolescents, we concentrated on social adjustment at school for several reasons. First, such a focus enlarges the developmental framework by linking events that have occurred at the parent's workplace (a setting where children are not present) to the adolescent's adjustment in a setting where the parent is not present (Bronfenbrenner, 1986). Second, gathering data about adjustment at school means that the teacher can act as an independent informant, one who is not a member of the family system and whose observations should be unbiased by knowledge of the parents' work situation. The use of teachers' reports alleviates one of the common biases of much of the work on economic change and children's adjustment—that is, that the parents or the adolescent are often the sole reporters of both the independent and the

dependent measures (economic changes, family stress, and adolescent adjustment). To control for respondent bias, we have relied on parents' reports of changes in work status but have used teachers and students to provide independent sources of information about adolescents' social adjustment at school.

Social Adjustment at School

Based on other work which found that a family's economic decline was related to an adolescent's depression but not to his or her grades in school (Clark-Lempers, Lempers, & Netusil, 1990), we chose indicators of social adjustment and not academic achievement. Rather than settling on simple measures of a global construct like adjustment to school, we felt that it was important to use conceptually different measures from different informants. Two outcomes and two independent sources of information (teachers' reports and self-reports) were used to assess adolescents' adjustment in the sixth and then in the seventh grade. Teachers assessed the adolescents' social competence, and adolescents reported on their own disruptive behavior at school. These indicators of adjustment are similar to the constructs of engagement (the quality of a student's involvement with peers and activities) and disruptiveness (the extent to which a student is aggressive and oppositional) used in other work as indicators of adaptation to school (Garmezy et al., 1984).

Social competence as it is used in this study is based on the concept of social tasks —that is, adjustment defined in terms of relevant social tasks in particular developmental settings, in this case, the school. Significant others in those settings, such as teachers, are considered reliable sources for evaluating an individual child's success in negotiating the relevant tasks (Dodge & Murphy, 1984). Items tapping social competence assess the adolescent's ability to get along with peers and to handle stress and frustration at school. In contrast, disruptiveness reflects poor adaptation to the school environment, specifically, the tendency to act out in a noncooperative, aggressive manner in class. Although disruptiveness as we have operationalized it is not as extreme as delinquent behavior, a positive relation between economic stress and adolescents' antisocial behavior, delinquency, and drug use has been found in other work (Conger et al., 1990b; Lempers & Clark-Lempers, 1990; Werner & Smith, 1982). Like other stressors, disruptions in the security of a parent's work or a family's income can compromise parents' capacity to monitor and supervise their children and thus place children and adolescents at risk for delinquency and susceptibility to peer pressure (Loeber & Dishion, 1983; Patterson, DeBaryshe, & Ramsey, 1989; Steinberg, 1987).

The following hypotheses, derived from empirical work on the junior high school transition and on family stress and children's adjustment, were tested in this study. First, consistent with other literature on the junior high transition, we expected a developmental decline in adjustment between the sixth and seventh grades (i.e., a decrease in competence and an increase in disruptiveness). Second, we expected that negative changes in parental work status (e.g., temporary or permanent layoffs, job demotions) would be associated with early adolescents' adjustment problems at school. Our third hypothesis was based on Coleman's (1989) focal theory, which holds that individuals experience stress when they have to negotiate several changes simultaneously. This suggests that if a family was dealing with a decline in parental work status during the same period that the adolescent was making the transition from elementary to junior high school, the normal difficulties associated with the transition would be intensified. Finally, we expected that boys would exhibit more adjustment problems at school than girls, and that negative changes in parental work status would exacerbate this sex difference.

Empirical support for the differential risks of economic changes in the family for sons and daughters has been mixed, possibly due to the different indicators of adjustment used in various studies. Economic declines and parental unemployment have been associated with high levels of conflict between adolescent sons and their parents, with a tendency for sons to reject fathers and turn to peers, and with more delinquency and drug use among adolescent boys versus girls (Elder et al., 1985; Flanagan, 1990a; Lempers & Clark-Lempers, 1990). In contrast, depression, loneliness, pessimism about the future, and a sense of personal inadequacy tend to be reactions of daughters in financially pressed families, but are not found among sons (Elder et al., 1985; Galambos & Silbereisen, 1987; Lempers & Clark-Lempers, 1990). In sum, boys may act out, whereas girls may internalize their reactions to these family stressors. Since adjustment was measured with indicators of overt social

behaviors at school, we expected that girls would have fewer problems than boys, and that this difference would be intensified in families that experienced a negative change in parental work status.

Method

Sample

Data were obtained from a 2-year, four-wave study of early adolescents investigating the effects of normative environmental transitions (e.g., the move to junior high school) on early adolescent adjustment (Eccles, 1988). The study was conducted in 12 working- and middle-class communities where the official unemployment statistics at Wave 1 (1983) ranged between 7.9% and 21%. Cases were selected for inclusion in this study if data from mothers and adolescents obtained in the fall of the child's sixth and in the spring of the child's seventh grade and from the sixth- and seventh-grade teachers were complete. Approximately 96.7% of the sample included in the present study were white, 1.5% African-American, and 1.8% other minorities. According to mothers, 81.7% were married, 8.5% remarried, and 9.8% were divorced, separated, or widowed. Family size ranged from one to nine children; 9.4% of the families had one child, 46.5% two, 27.8% three, and the rest had four or more children. The mean age of students at Time 1 was 11 years, 5 months, and there were 432 girls and 451 boys in the study.

Procedure

Project staff described the study to teachers and sixth graders in their classrooms. A permission letter describing the study was sent home to parents. Participating parents were mailed questionnaires with return postage envelopes. Seventy-one percent of the families and 95% of the teachers completed questionnaires at Time 1. Under the supervision of project staff, questionnaires were group administered to the adolescents in their classrooms while teachers completed individual assessments of each student.

Although the Transitions study was a four-wave design, measures of school adjustment and parental work status were not taken at all waves. For this reason, the present study is confined to Waves 1 (fall of the sixth grade) and 4 (spring of the seventh grade) when these measures were taken. For clarity, these times of measure will be referred to as Time 1 (before the transition to junior high school) and Time 2 (post–junior high school transition) for the remainder of this paper.

Independent Measures

Parents' work status.—Economic recessions have a broad and diverse impact on working adults. The burden of the recession on individuals may take the form of wage and salary cutbacks, deskilling of jobs, or layoffs of a temporary or more permanent nature. Each of these changes, particularly in the context of an uncertain economy, may be stressful for individuals and their families. As others conducting research on economic change and psychological adjustment have done (Kessler, Turner, & House, 1989; Liem & Liem, 1989), we measured work status based on patterns of change in that status (i.e., demotion, layoff, or reemployment) over the 2-year period of the study rather than as a simple status at one point in time. Families were coded into one of four parental work status categories based on the mother's response at Time 1 and Time 2 to the following question: "During the last 2 years, has your family experienced any of the following: a permanent layoff, a temporary layoff, a job demotion, or a rehiring?" Comparing Time 1 with Time 2 reports yielded the following categories: the *deprived* group reported permanent layoffs during the 2 years of the study (N = 95); the *declining* group (N = 104) experienced a layoff or demotion between Times 1 and 2; the *stable* group were families who reported no layoffs or demotions at either time of measure (N = 550); the *recovery* group were families who reported a layoff or demotion at Time 1 and reemployment at comparable jobs at Time 2 (N = 134). We were able to identify which parent experienced the change in work status for 94 of the declining families (among two-parent families there were 50 fathers, 32 mothers, 5 families in which both parents' status declined, and in single-parent families 7 mothers reported a decline); 93 of the deprived families (64 fathers, 10 mothers, and 8 in which both parents in two-parent households experienced a long-term layoff and 11 single-parent mothers); and only 49 of the recovery families. Based on the premise that families ex-

perience stress when they are faced with a disparity between their former assumptions and new realities (Moen, Kain, & Elder, 1983), we coded an involuntary negative change in "parental" work status regardless of which parent experienced the change.[1]

A description of the sample by categories of parental work status is provided in Table 1. As the results show, work status and family income were strongly related at both times. The stable group had significantly higher and the deprived group significantly lower incomes than any other group. While there were no income differences between the declining and recovery groups at Time 1, there was a difference between these groups at Time 2 due to a significant increase for the recovery families. Similar associations were found between parental work status and the adolescent's subjective worries about their family's finances. At Time 1, adolescents in stable families reported significantly less worry than the other three groups. By Time 2, the financial boost for the recovery families was obvious in the adolescents' reports of financial concerns: their concerns had declined to the point where there was no longer a significant difference between the stable and recovery groups. Chi-square tests of independence revealed no relation between parental work status and family structure. However, there was a relation between parental work status and race, $\chi^2(6, N = 883) = 15.81, p < .02$: minorities were overrepresented in the group whose status declined during the study.

In order to test for bias due to attrition between Times 1 and 2, we compared families who met the criteria for inclusion in the study at Time 1 and later dropped out with those that were still present at the end of the study. Within-group comparisons were made based on the reports of stability or loss in status at Time 1. As the comparisons presented in Appendix Table A1 show, there were some consistent patterns that distinguished the attrition group from the families that remained in the study. Regardless of the parents' work status at Time 1, sample attrition was related to race, marital status, and

---

[1] We hypothesized no differential effects of mother's versus father's change in work status. Analyses comparing mothers versus fathers in two-parent families in the declining and deprived groups were done. These showed that, when there were effects for one or the other parent, the negative effects on adjustment were stronger when mothers, not fathers, reported a loss of status. These results are consistent with contemporary literature on unemployed adults that challenges the myth of "benign stress" associated with women's unemployment (Banks & Jackson, 1982; Romero, Castro, & Cervantes, 1988).

TABLE 1

CHARACTERISTICS OF THE FOUR FAMILY WORK STATUS GROUPS

| | PARENTAL WORK STATUS | | | | | | | |
| | Stable (n = 550) | | Declining (n = 104) | | Recovery (n = 134) | | Deprived (n = 95) | |
CHARACTERISTICS	M	SD	M	SD	M	SD	M	SD
Parents' education[a]	4.04_a	1.16	3.75_b	1.37	$3.53_{b,c}$	.97	3.38_c	1.05
Family income time 1[b]	4.09_a	1.08	3.38_b	1.15	3.35_b	1.04	2.71_c	1.17
Family income time 2	4.26_a	1.05	3.43_b	1.28	3.76_c	1.06	3.03_d	1.30
Number of children	2.61	1.15	2.75	1.33	2.63	1.19	2.54	1.07
Adolescent's report of:								
Financial worries Time 1	2.64_a	1.05	2.97_b	1.08	$3.02_{b.}$	1.03	3.29_c	.86
Financial worries Time 2	2.52_a	1.06	$2.86_{b,c}$	1.13	$2.70_{a,b}$	1.02	3.12_c	.97
Race:								
Caucasian (%)	97.6		91.2		96.3		97.9*	
Afro-American (%)	.9		2.9		3.0		1.1	
Other minorities (%)	1.5		5.9		.7		1.1	
Marital status:								
Married (%)	82.9		74.0		83.6		78.9	
Remarried (%)	7.1		10.6		6.0		10.4	
Single parent (%)	10.0		15.4		10.4		13.7	

NOTE.—Means with different subscripts differ significantly at $p < .05$ or stronger.

[a] Response options: 1 = grade school, 2 = some high school, 3 = high school diploma, 4 = some post–high school training, 5 = B.A., 6 = some graduate school, 7 = M.A., 8 = Ph.D./professional.

[b] Scale ($10,000 increments): 1 = under $10,000, to 5 = over $40,000.

* $p < .05$.

mother's employment status. There were more minorities, single-parent and blended families, and working mothers among the group who dropped out of the study. In addition, among families who reported stable work status at Time 1, there were significant differences between those who remained or dropped out of the study. Those who dropped out had lower family incomes and levels of parent education and more financial worries reported by the adolescent.

Parents' education.—An average of the mother's and father's educational level, measured at Time 1, was used as an index of family background. Since individuals with fewer skills and lower levels of education are at greater risk for dislocation during periods of recession, we expected that changes in work status would be related to the mean level of parents' education. An analysis of variance indicated a significant association between parents' average education and the categories of work status, $F(3, 879) = 14.83$, $p < .0001$. On a scale of 1 to 8, the mean levels of parent education were 4.04 (SD = 1.16), 3.75 (SD = 1.17), 3.54 (SD = .97), and 3.38 (SD = 1.05), respectively, for the stable, declining, recovery, and deprived groups. Parents in the stably employed

group had higher levels of education than any other group, and parents in the declining group were better educated than those in deprived families. No other between-group differences were significant. Given the association of parental education with the categories of work status, parents' mean education was used as a covariate to control for family background in later analyses.

Dependent Measures

Adolescent's social competence.—As part of an individual assessment of students, the sixth- and seventh-grade teachers were each asked four items (on a Likert-type scale with 1 = never to 4 = always) about the adolescent's ability to get along with peers and to handle stress and frustration in the classroom. The student's social competence score was the average of these four items. Cronbach's alpha was .76 for the sixth- and .70 for the seventh-grade teachers' assessments. Teachers' assessments of students' social skills as well as their problem behaviors correlate reliably with sociometric measures of children's social competence, as well as with parents', mental health workers', and independent observers' ratings (Achenbach, McConaughy, & Howell, 1987; Hoge & Coladarci, 1989; Hoge & McKay,

1986). The validity of our measure is indicated by its negative correlations with the teacher's report that the student was a discipline problem ($r = -.49$, $p < .0001$) and that emotional problems interfered with his or her academic performance ($r = -.35$, $p < .0001$) and its positive correlation with the seventh-grade teacher's assessment that the student had made a smooth adjustment to junior high school ($r = .60$, $p < .0001$).

Adolescent's reports of disruptiveness at school.—The second measure was based on the adolescent's report of how often (during the past 3 weeks) he or she had engaged in four disruptive behaviors at school: punching another student, writing on school property, disrupting or wising off in class, and refusing to work. An individual's score was based on an average of the four items, with high scores indicating more frequent disruptiveness. These items have been established as valid measures of adolescents' disruptiveness at school in other research (Kulka, Klingel, & Mann, 1980). In this study, the student's self-report of disruptiveness was positively correlated with the teacher's report that the student was a discipline problem ($r = .36$, $p < .0001$) and negatively correlated with the teacher's assessment of the student's social competence ($r = -.25$, $p < .0001$). Cronbach's alpha for this four-item index was .77 in the sixth and .77 in the seventh grade.

Analysis Plan

MANCOVA and ANCOVAs with repeated measures were used to analyze the data. A 4 (parental job status) × 2 (child sex) repeated-measures MANCOVA with time of measurement and source of information as the repeated factors and parents' average education as the covariate was performed. Note that the use of the MANCOVA is a very stringent test in this case. Not only are the dependent measures reported by different informants, but the measures themselves are quite distinct indicators of social adjustment at school.

Results

The MANCOVA revealed significant effects of student's sex, $F(1, 877) = 53.81$, $p < .0001$; time, $F(1, 877) = 3.56$, $p < .05$; and source of information (teacher/student), $F(1, 877) = 10.39$, $p < .01$. There were also significant interactions of the within-subjects factor, source of information, with parental work status, $F(3, 877) = 2.57$, $p < .05$, and sex of student, $F(1, 877) = 75.69$, $p < .0001$.

Teachers' Assessments of Adolescents' Social Competence

The ANCOVA for teachers' assessments of adolescents' social competence revealed significant main effects of student's sex, parental work status, and time of measurement and an interaction of parental work status with time. Simple effects tests indicated that teachers considered girls ($M = 2.59$, $SD = .30$) more competent than boys ($M = 2.46$, $SD = .36$), $F(1, 877) = 33.41$, $p < .0001$. In addition, controlling for the significant effect of parents' education on this outcome, teachers rated the students in stable families more competent, on average ($M = 2.55$, $SD = .33$), than their peers in declining ($M = 2.44$, $SD = .36$) or deprived ($M = 2.47$, $SD = .37$) families, $F(3, 877) = 4.13$, $p < .01$.

As expected, there was an effect of time on teachers' assessments of students' social competence: seventh-grade teachers rated students significantly lower ($M = 2.49$, $SD = .40$) than the sixth-grade teachers had rated these same students ($M = 2.55$, $SD = .42$) in the prior year. Besides the main effect of time, there was a time × parental work status interaction. Repeated-measures ANCOVAs conducted separately for each work status group revealed a decline between the sixth and seventh grades for adolescents in the stable, $F(1, 548) = 15.90$, $p < .001$ and declining, $F(1, 102) = 5.17$, $p < .025$ groups, but no effect of time for adolescents in the recovery or deprived families.

A comparison of the mean social competence scores of the four groups in the sixth and in the seventh grades is presented in Table 2. As the results show, sixth-grade teachers rated the students from stable families as more competent compared to their peers in the other three groups, but seventh-grade teachers did not. Consistent with the negative attitudes toward students found among junior high school teachers in other research (Feldlaufer et al., 1988; Hawkins & Berndt, 1985; Hirsch & Rapkin, 1987), these results show a decline between elementary and junior high school in teachers' assessments for the largest group of students in the study (i.e., those in stably employed families). A comparison between groups in junior high school revealed that seventh-grade teachers assessed students in the declining families as significantly less competent than their peers in stable, $F(1, 871) = 8.91$, $p < .01$ or recovery, $F(1, 871) = 7.20$, $p < .01$ families. The drop between the sixth and seventh grades made this group the least competent of any group in junior high

TABLE 2

RELATION OF PARENTAL WORK STATUS TO STUDENT'S ADJUSTMENT AT SCHOOL
BEFORE AND AFTER THE TRANSITION TO JUNIOR HIGH SCHOOL

ADJUSTMENT MEASURES	PARENTAL WORK STATUS			
	Stable (n = 550)	Declining (n = 104)	Recovery (n = 134)	Deprived (n = 95)
Teacher's assessments of student's social competence:				
Pretransition:				
M	2.59_a	2.49_b	2.50_b	2.48_b
SD	.41	.45	.42	.43
Posttransition:				
M	2.51_a	2.39_b	2.52_a	$2.46_{a,b}$
SD	.38	.41	.40	.45
Adolescents' reports of disruptive behavior:				
Pretransition:				
M	2.45	2.54	2.37	2.72
SD	2.05	2.16	1.88	2.38
Posttransition:				
M	2.65_a	3.33_b	2.69_a	$2.92_{a,b}$
SD	2.19	2.82	1.96	2.60

NOTE.—Adjusted means with different subscripts differ significantly at $p < .05$ or stronger.

school. In contrast, since the students in stable families had the highest scores in the sixth grade, the drop associated with the transition to junior high school meant that they were more similar to their peers after the transition.

There were no effects of time for adolescents in recovery or deprived families, and both of these groups were quite similar to the stable group in the seventh grade. Finally, although there was a main effect of sex, there was no interaction of sex with parental work status on teachers' assessments of adolescents' social competence.

Adolescents' Disruptive Behavior
The repeated-measures ANCOVA revealed main effects of child sex, of time, and an interaction of parental work status with time on disruptiveness. Boys (M = 3.10, SD = 2.12) reported more disruptiveness than girls (M = 2.12, SD = 1.40), $F(1, 877)$ = 65.66, $p < .0001$, and disruptive behaviors increased between the sixth (M = 2.48, SD = 2.08) and seventh grades (M = 2.77, SD = 2.30). An interaction of time with work status was obtained. Repeated-measures ANCOVAs conducted separately for each work status group revealed increases between the sixth and seventh grades for adolescents in the stable, $F(1, 548)$ = 4.12, $p < .05$, declining, $F(1, 102)$ = 8.42, $p < .01$, and

recovery, $F(1, 132)$ = 4.56, $p < .05$ groups. As the results of the simple effects tests in Table 2 show, there were no effects of parental work status on disruptiveness in the sixth grade; however, consistent with the results for social competence, adolescents in declining families reported significantly more disruptiveness in the seventh grade compared to peers in stable, $F(1, 871)$ = 8.09, $p < .01$ or recovery, $F(1, 871)$ = 4.82, $p < .05$ families.

Subsequent to these analyses, additional tests were performed on a subset of the cases in the study (38 cases had missing data on Time 1 income) to assess whether the family's income level accounted for the effects of parental job status on the adolescent outcomes. MANCOVA with repeated measures using family income at Time 1 as a covariate and dummy variable multiple regression procedures to assess the effects of parents' changing job status with or without Time 1 income as a control variable were used.

The MANCOVA revealed significant effects of student's sex, $F(1, 839)$ = 56,32, $p < .0001$; source of information (teacher/student), $F(1, 839)$ = 21.42, $p < .0001$; and time, $F(1, 839)$ = 15.57, $p < .0001$. The test also revealed interactions of the source of information with students' sex, $F(1, 839)$ =

TABLE 3

EFFECTS OF PARENTAL WORK STATUS ON ADOLESCENT ADJUSTMENT WITH AND WITHOUT
TIME 1 INCOME CONTROLLED

DEPENDENT VARIABLES	PREDICTORS OF ADJUSTMENT				
	Decline	Recovery	Deprived	Gender[a]	Time 1 Income
Teachers' assessment of social competence:					
Time 1	$-.08^*$	$-.09^{**}$	$-.10^{**}$	$-.16^{****}$	
	$-.05$	$-.05$	$-.04$	$-.16^{****}$	$.17^{****}$
Time 2	$-.10^{**}$	$-.005$	$-.05$	$-.14^{****}$	
	$-.08^*$	$.02$	$-.02$	$-.14^{****}$	$.10^{**}$
Adolescents' reports of disruptiveness:					
Time 1	$.02$	$-.01$	$.05$	$.25^{****}$	
	$.007$	$-.03$	$.02$	$.25^{****}$	$-.06$
Time 2	$.10^{**}$	$.02$	$.05$	$.22^{****}$	
	$.07^*$	$-.01$	$.005$	$.22^{****}$	$-.14^{***}$

NOTE.—$N = 845$.
[a] Male.
$^* p < .05.$
$^{**} p < .01.$
$^{***} p < .001.$
$^{****} p < .0001.$

76.76, $p < .0001$; with income, $F(1, 839) = 14.92$, $p < .0001$; and with time, $F(1, 839) = 11.60$, $p < .001$; and an interaction of income with time, $F(1, 839) = 6.96$, $p < .01$. With Time 1 income as a covariate, there were no effects of parental work status on the outcomes in this subset of cases.

Table 3 presents the results of the regression of each dependent variable on parental work status and student's sex, with or without controls for income at Time 1. As the results show, family income has a significant effect on teachers' assessments at both times of measure and on students' reports at Time 2. There are negative effects of each work status (relative to the stable group) on teachers' reports at Time 1 when income is not controlled. However, if parents' work status declined during the study, there was a negative effect on teachers' and students' reports at Time 2, even with income controlled. Parents in the declining group were the only ones whose work status worsened between the two times of measurement (and whose Time 2 income did not improve relative to Time 1—see Table 1), and this is the only group of adolescents for whom work status had a negative impact on adjustment at Time 2. In sum, although family income data are not available for the whole sample, we expect that the negative effects of unemployment or job demotion on adolescents' adjustment are, in large part,

due to a decline in the family's standard of living.

Discussion

Theories of stress and coping suggest that children can cope relatively well with single stressors, but the risks to development increase considerably when they face several changes simultaneously (Coleman, 1989; Simmons & Blyth, 1987). Simmons and Blyth (1987) have shown that the early adolescent's adjustment during the transition to junior high school is most problematic for those students who are simultaneously negotiating other physical changes or social demands. For some adolescents in our sample, the transition to junior high school occurred at the same time that their parents were coping with insecurities at their workplace, and the results suggest that developmental difficulties associated with this school transition may be exacerbated under these conditions. According to teachers, adolescents in deprived and especially in declining families exhibited significantly lower social competence than their peers in stable or recovery families. Moreover, a decline in parental work status that occurred during the same period that the adolescent made the transition to junior high school was associated with an increase in school adjustment problems between the sixth and seventh grades. After the transition to junior high school, adolescents in the declining families had the lowest levels of social competence of any group.

Consistent with other work showing increases in teacher-student tension following the transition to junior high school (Feldlaufer et al., 1988; Hawkins & Berndt, 1985; Hirsch & Rapkin, 1987; Miller-Buchanan et al., 1990), seventh-grade teachers considered students less competent than the sixthgrade teachers had rated them in the prior year. The drop was especially marked for the stable group, which may reflect the large size of this group relative to the others. Nonetheless, despite this drop in competence, students in the stable families were judged more competent in junior high school relative to their peers in the declining families.

There was also a developmental decline between elementary and junior high school indicated by students' increased disruptive behavior at school. All students reported more disruptiveness after the transition, although the increase did not reach significance for students in deprived families. While there were no differences between groups in the sixth grade, students in declining families were the most disruptive group in the seventh grade. In sum, based on teachers' assessments and self-reports, students in the declining families had the most difficult time adjusting to junior high school.

These results were obtained with parents' educational level controlled, suggesting that they were not simply artifacts of the adolescent's family background. In fact, parents in the declining families were better educated than those in the deprived and as well educated as those in the recovery group; yet their children had the most adjustment problems of any group in junior high school. Families in the declining category were the only ones whose work status deteriorated and whose income showed no increase between Times 1 and 2. Although the declining group's mean income at Time 1 was significantly higher than that of the deprived group, their drop in status was associated with more problems at school for their junior high school children, even when Time 1 income was controlled.

One interpretation of the stronger effects for the declining compared to the deprived families is that recent or sudden changes in parents' job security may be more disruptive in the short run for families. Although the absolute level of income for this group was not as low as the deprived group's, they were worse off in terms of both income and security relative to their accustomed standards. We do not infer from these results that a drop in income, regardless of the level of family income, is more deleterious than poverty for children. The daily deprivation that poor families face is likely to have more enduring consequences for children, especially if families learn a "resigned adaptation" to their deprived state and lower their goals and aspirations for their children (Warr, Jackson, & Banks, 1988).

Although there was a main effect of sex on adjustment, the hypothesis that family hardship would have more negative implications for boys was not confirmed. Possibly, the very powerful main effect of sex on both measures of adjustment masked any potential interaction effects. This lack of an interaction is consistent with results obtained by Conger et al. (1990b), who found no differential effects of economic constraints on early adolescent boys' or girls' antisocial behavior. Neither the Conger et al. measure of antisocial behavior nor our measure of disruptiveness included extreme acts of aggression. If economic strains in the family have differential effects on girls' and boys' aggressiveness, perhaps more extreme measures might be indicated in future research.

There were certain shortcomings of this study, such as the lack of family process variables that may have accounted for the relations between work status and adjustment. We can only speculate, based on other research, that family stressors such as job demotion or job or income loss undermine parents' effectiveness as agents of socialization, and that the disruption of family processes is the link between economic changes and adolescents' adjustment problems at school (Conger et al., 1990b; Patterson et al., 1989). Attrition was also a problem in this study, as it tends to be in longitudinal research. While the loss of subjects suggests that caution should be exerted in interpreting the results, we expect that if there were demonstrable associations of parental work status with adolescent adjustment for the more "resilient" families who remained during the 2 years of the study, the impact would be at least as strong for those families who dropped out of the study.

Several strengths of the study should be noted as well, especially given the difficulties inherent in research attempts to link macro-level changes in society to micro-level developmental processes. The longitudinal design of this study meant that working could be conceptualized in a more dynamic way than it is usually dealt with as a part of the family's "social address" (Bronfenbrenner, 1986). Furthermore, studying adjustment before and after the junior high transition meant that we could compare normative developmental change during the early adolescent period with developmental patterns for adolescents "at risk" due to a changing economy. By adding indicators of change in parents' lives to a study of adolescent development, we were able to study development within a larger social ecology (Bronfenbrenner, 1979) and to study social change as it was occurring. As the archival analyses of the Oakland Growth and Berkeley Guidance studies from the Great Depression have shown, the impact of labile events in communities on children and families can be uncovered in the course of conducting research on normal development (Elder, 1974).

Given the climate of economic change in the United States and abroad, we can expect increasing numbers of people to face dislocations from their jobs in the future (Dooley & Catalano, 1988). In fact, as this paper was being completed, General Motors announced plans to close several large plants in the communities where these data were collected. While research on the effects of unemployment on adults has grown in the last decade, we know less about how changing economic trends affect the development of children and adolescents (McLoyd, 1989). This study suggests that a changing economy may pose additional risk factors for families and may intensify adjustment problems associated with normal transitions in development.

Appendix

TABLE A1

COMPARISON OF 883 STUDY CASES WITH 896 DROP-OUT CASES BY WAVE 1 FAMILY WORK STATUS

	WAVE 1 FAMILY WORK STATUS						
	Loss of Work Status				Stable Work Status		
	Remain ($n = 225$)		Drop Out ($n = 282$)		Remain ($n = 628$)		Drop Out ($n = 614$)
MEASURES	M	SD	M	SD	M	SD	M	SD
Parents' education[a]	3.47	1.06	3.45	.98	4.02	1.15	3.81	1.14**
Family income[b]	3.09	1.13	2.90	1.24	4.02	1.11	3.81	1.18**
Number of children	2.63	1.14	2.70	1.08	2.61	1.18	2.74	1.25
Adolescent's report of financial worry	3.16	1.03	3.17	.97	2.66	1.06	2.85	1.00**
Race:								
Caucasian (%)	96.5		89.9**		96.8		92.4***	
African-American (%)	2.4		5.8		1.1		4.5	
Other minorities (%)	1.2		4.3		2.1		3.1	
Maritial status:								
Married (%)	82.4		66.7***		81.2		73.2**	
Remarried (%)	5.9		14.0		8.0		10.0	
Single parent (%)	11.8		19.4		10.8		16.8	
Mother's employment status:								
Employed full time (%)	27.0		39.1**		28.2		34.3*	
Employed part time (%)	27.4		22.8		27.8		23.3	
Homemaker full time (%)	45.6		38.0		44.0		42.4	

[a] Response options: 1 = grade school, 2 = some high school, 3 = high school, 4 = some college/technical, 5 = B.A., 6 = some graduate school, 7 = M.A., 8 = Ph.D./professional.
[b] Scale ($10,000 increments): 1 = under $10,000, to 5 = over $40,000.
* $p < .05$.
** $p < .01$.
*** $p < .001$.

References

Achenbach, T. J., McConaughy, S. H., & Howell, C. T. (1987). Child/adolescent behavioral and emotional problems: Implications of cross-informant correlations for situational specificity. *Psychological Bulletin,* 101, 213–232.

Banks, M. H., & Jackson, P. R. (1982). Unemployment and risk of minor psychiatric disorder in young people: Cross-sectional and longitudinal evidence. *Psychological Medicine,* 12, 789–798.

Bronfenbrenner, U. (1979). *The ecology of human development: Experiments by nature and design.* Cambridge, MA: Harvard University Press.

Bronfenbrenner, U. (1986). Ecology of the family as a context for human development: Research perspectives. *Developmental Psychology,* 22, 723–742.

Clark-Lempers, D. S., Lempers, J. D., & Netusil, A. J. (1990). Family financial stress, parental support, and young adolescents' academic achievement and depressive symptoms. *Journal of Early Adolescence,* 9, 21–36.

Coleman, J. C. (1989). The focal theory of adolescence: A psychological perspective. In K. Hurrelmann & U. Engel (Eds.), *The social world of adolescents: International perspectives* (pp. 43–56). New York: Walter de Gruyter.

Conger, R. C., Elder, G. H., Lorenz, F. O., Conger, K. J., Simons, R. L., Whitbeck, L. B., Huck, S., & Melby, J. (1990a). Linking economic hardship to marital quality and instability. *Journal of Marriage and the Family,* 52, 643–656.

Conger, R. C., Elder, G. H., Melby, J. N., Simons, R. L., & Conger, K. J. (1990b, March). *A process model of family economic constraints and early adolescent alcohol use.* Paper presented at the biennial meetings of the Society for Research on Adolescence, Atlanta.

Dodge, K. A., & Murphy, R. R. (1984). The assessment of social competence in adolescents. *Advances in Child Behavioral Analysis and Therapy,* 3, 61–96.

Dooley, D., & Catalano, R. (1988). Recent research on the psychological effects of unemployment. *Journal of Social Issues,* 44, 1–12.

Eccles, J. S. (1988). *Psychological and behavioral underpinnings of performance.* Washington, D.C.: National Institute of Child Health and Human Development Final Report.

Eccles, J. S., Midgley, C., & Adler, T. (1984). Grade-related changes in the school environment: Effects on achievement motivation. In J. G. Nicholls (Ed.), *The development of achievement motivation* (pp. 283–331). Greenwich, CT: JAI.

Eccles, J. S., Wigfield, A., Flanagan, C. A.,

Miller, C., Reuman, D. A., & Yee, D. (1990). Self-concepts, domain values, and self esteem: Relations and changes at early adolescence. *Journal of Personality,* 57, 283–310.

Elder, G. H. (1974). *Children of the Great Depression.* Chicago: University of Chicago Press.

Elder, G. H., Jr., Van Nguyen, T., & Caspi, A. (1985). Linking family hardship to children's lives. *Child Development,* 56, 361–375.

Feldlaufer, H., Midgley, C., & Eccles, J. S. (1988). Student, teacher, and observer perceptions of the classroom environment before and after the transition to junior high school. *Journal of Early Adolescence,* 8, 133–156.

Flanagan, C. A. (1990a). Change in family work status: Effects on parent-adolescent decision making. *Child Development,* 61, 163–177.

Flanagan, C. A. (1990b). Families and schools in hard times. In V. C. McLoyd & C. A. Flanagan (Eds.), *Responses of children and adolescents to economic crisis* (New Directions for Child Development, No. 46). San Francisco: Jossey-Bass.

Galambos, N. L., & Silbereisen, R. K. (1987). Influences of income change and parental acceptance on adolescent transgression proneness and peer relations. *European Journal of Psychology of Education,* 1, 17–28.

Garmezy, N., Masten, A. S., & Tellegen, A. (1984). The study of stress and competence in children: A building block for developmental psychopathology. *Child Development,* 55, 97–111.

Harrison, B., & Bluestone, B. (1988). *The great U-turn: Corporate restructuring and the polarizing of America.* New York: Basic.

Hawkins, J. A., & Berndt, T. J. (1985, April). *Adjustment following the transition to junior high school.* Paper presented at the biennial meeting of the Society for Research on Child Development, Toronto.

Hirsch, B. J., & Rapkin, B. D. (1987). The transition to junior high school: A longitudinal study of self-esteem, psychological symptomatology, school life, and social support. *Child Development,* 58, 1235–1243.

Hoge, R. D., & Coladarci, T. (1989). Teacher-based judgments of academic achievement: A review of literature. *Review of Educational Research,* 59, 297–313.

Hoge, R. D., & McKay, V. (1986). Criterion-related validity data for the Child Behavior Checklist—Teacher's Report Form. *Journal of School Psychology,* 24, 387–393.

Kessler, R. C., Turner, J. B., & House, J. S. (1989). Effects of unemployment on health in a community survey: Main, modifying, and mediating effects. *Journal of Social Issues,* 44, 69–85.

Kulka, R. A., Klingel, D. M., & Mann, D. W.

(1980). School crime and disruption as a function of student-school fit: An empirical assessment. *Journal of Youth and Adolescence, 9,* 353–370.

Lempers, J. D., & Clark-Lempers, D. S. (1990). Family economic stress, maternal and paternal support and adolescent distress. *Journal of Adolescence, 13,* 217–229.

Lempers, J. D., Clark-Lempers, D., & Simons, R. L. (1989). Economic hardship, parenting, and distress in adolescence. *Child Development, 60,* 25–39.

Liem, R., & Liem, J. H. (1989). The psychological effects of unemployment on workers and their families. *Journal of Social Issues, 44,* 87–105.

Loeber, R., & Dishion, T. J. (1983). Early predictors of male delinquency: A review. *Psychological Bulletin, 94,* 68–99.

McLoyd, V. C. (1989). Socialization and development in a changing economy: The effects of paternal job and income loss on children. *American Psychologist, 44,* 293–302.

McLoyd, V. C., & Wilson, L. (1990). Economic stress, coping, and psychological functioning in black adolescents: An ecological perspective. In V. C. McLoyd & C. A. Flanagan (Eds.), *Response of children and adolescents to economic crises and deprivation* (New Directions for Child Development, No. 46). San Francisco: Jossey-Bass.

Midgley, C., & Feldlaufer, H. (1987). Students' and teachers' decision-making fit before and after the transition to junior high school. *Journal of Early Adolescence, 7,* 225–241.

Midgley, C., Feldlaufer, H., & Eccles, J. S. (1989). Change in teacher efficacy and student self- and task-related beliefs in mathematics during the transition to junior high school. *Journal of Educational Psychology, 81,* 247–258.

Miller-Buchanan, C., Eccles, J. S., Flanagan, C., Midgley, C., Feldlaufer, H., & Harold, R. (1990). Parents' and teachers' beliefs about adolescents: Effects of sex and experience. *Journal of Youth and Adolescence, 19,* 363–394.

Moen, P., Kain, E. L., & Elder, G. H. (1983). Economic conditions and family life: Contemporary and historical perspectives. In R. R. Nelson & F. Skidmore (Eds.), *American families and the economy: The high cost of living.* Washington, D.C.: National Academy Press.

Patterson, G. R., DeBaryshe, B. D., & Ramsey, E. (1989). A developmental perspective on antisocial behavior. *American Psychologist, 44,* 329–335.

Pellegrini, D. S., Masten, A. S., Garmezy, N., & Ferrarese, M. J. (1987). Correlates of social and academic competence in middle childhood. *Journal of Child Psychology and Psychiatry and Allied Disciplines, 28,* 699–714.

Radin, N., & Harold-Goldsmith, R. (1989). The involvement of selected unemployed and employed men with their children. *Child Development, 60,* 454–459.

Romero, G. J., Castro, F. G., & Cervantes, R. C. (1988). Latinas without work: Family, occupational, and economic stress following unemployment. *Psychology of Women Quarterly, 12,* 281–297.

Silbereisen, R. K., Walper, S., & Albrecht, H. (1990). Families experiencing income loss and economic hardship: Antecedents of adolescents' problem behavior. In V. C. McLoyd & C. A. Flanagan (Eds.), *Responses of children and adolescents to economic crisis* (New Directions for Child Development, No. 46). San Francisco: Jossey-Bass.

Simmons, R., & Blyth, D. A. (1987). *Moving into adolescence.* New York: Aldine de Gruyter.

Steinberg, L. (1987). Single parents, stepparents, and the susceptibility of adolescents to antisocial peer pressure. *Child Development, 58,* 269–275.

Warr, P., Jackson, P., & Banks, M. (1988). Unemployment and mental health: Some British studies. *Journal of Social Issues, 44,* 47–68.

Werner, E., & Smith, R. (1982). *Vulnerable but invincible: A study of resilient children.* New York: McGraw-Hill.

Characteristics of Married and Unmarried Adolescent Mothers and Their Partners

Michael E. Lamb,[1,2] Arthur B. Elster,[2] Laura J. Peters,[2] James S. Kahn,[2] and Jane Tavare[2]

Received February 27, 1986; accepted September 4, 1986

In a middle-class, urban-clinic sample of 275, mostly Caucasian, adolescent mothers and their partners living in Utah, three groups were identified and their psychosocial characteristics were compared. Couples married at the time of conception (N = 22) enjoyed more positive responses from prospective grandparents and earned more than couples not married at the time of conception. On the other hand, these initially married youths were much more likely to be high-school dropouts, which suggests limits in their lifetime earning capacities, and they were not more likely to identify one another as sources of emotional support. Couples who married between conception and delivery (N = 110) reported that prospective grandparents responded less favorably to news of the pregnancy than did relatives of the initially married couples, but while their current salaries were lower, they were much more likely to be continuing with their education. Those who married after conception also had fewer antisocial and conduct disorders than young men and women who chose to continue in a dating relationship (N = 29). Overall, the couples who married after conception appeared to face less severe problems than either the initially-married couples or the steady daters.

This research was supported by grant number APR 000922-02-0 from the Office of Adolescent Pregnancy Programs to Drs. Elster and Lamb.
[1]To whom correspondence and reprint requests should be addressed at Department of Psychology, University of Utah, Salt Lake City, Utah 84112.
[2]Dr. Lamb (Ph.D., Yale University) is currently Professor of Psychology, Psychiatry and Pediatrics at the University of Utah. Dr. Elster (M.D., University of Texas, Galveston) is Associate Professor of Pediatrics and Director of Adolescent Medicine at the University of Utah, where he and Dr. Lamb conduct research on pregnant teens, teenaged parents, and their children. Ms. Peters and Mr. Kahn are graduate students in School of Education at the University of Utah, while Ms. Tavare is a biostatistician at the University of Utah Medical Center.

487

INTRODUCTION

Despite mounting concern about the "epidemic" of adolescent pregnancies in the United States, little is known about the characteristics of pregnant adolescents and their male partners. Initial research on adolescent mothers emphasized the biological risks associated with premature reproduction (e.g., Battaglia, Frazier, and Hellegers, 1963; Israel and Woutersz, 1963), whereas more recent investigations have emphasized the psychosocial risks associated with premature parenthood (e.g., Elster, McAnarney, and Lamb, 1983). Adolescent mothers are reportedly less sensitive and behave less appropriately than adult mothers (Epstein, 1980; Jones, Green, and Krauss, 1980; Osofsky and Osofsky, 1970; Sandler, Vietze, and O'Connor, 1981), although many of these differences may be attributable to the high degrees of stress and lack of social support that frequently accompany adolescent parenthood (Colletta and Gregg, 1981; Elster *et al.*, 1983; Ragozin, Basham, Crnic, Greenberg, and Robinson, 1982). As pointed out in a recent anthology (Elster and Lamb, 1986), the partners of adolescent mothers are better known by stereotypes than by their actual characteristics; although the evidence shows that a surprising proportion wish to assume some responsibility for their children and partners, and suffer irreversible setbacks in the educational and vocational arenas, popular stereotypes largely portray them as irresponsible and exploitative predators. Researchers have also shown that the differences between the parental behavior of adolescent mothers and fathers are remarkably similar to the differences between adult mothers and fathers (Lamb and Elster, 1985) and that adult and adolescent fathers do not differ on measures of personality and psychopathology (Nakashima and Camp, 1984). Rivara, Sweeney, and Henderson (1985) compared teenage fathers with age-matched peers from comparable black lower-class backgrounds; nonfathers were more likely than fathers to see pregnancy as a disruption of future plans for school, employment, and marriage, and were less likely to have mothers who had themselves been teen parents. With respect to age of first intercourse, frequency of intercourse, knowledge of reproduction, and use of contraception, however, the groups did not differ. In a previous examination of the sample studied here, however, Elster and his colleagues (in press) reported that an unusually high proportion of young fathers and mothers had a history of legal and judicial contact.

In all of these studies the goal has been to compare younger and older parents, or to compare young parents with age-matched peers who are not yet parents. Instead of seeking normative descriptions of adolescent parents, our goal in the present research was to identify and to describe subgroups among the adolescent parents in Utah. In this article we describe the prepregnancy psychosocial characteristics of 275 primiparous adolescent mothers and their male partners. The adolescent women were all enrolled in a comprehensive care program for pregnant adolescents. Like any sample drawn from a single program or source, the subjects cannot be considered typical of adolescent mothers and their partners nationally. At best, they represent a group of largely Caucasian young men and women from lower-middle and middle-class urban backgrounds. Descriptions of "typical" adolescent mothers and their partners may not be especially useful, however, because adolescent parents constitute an extremely heterogeneous group. Consequently, we sought to make three systematic comparisons among groups of adolescent couples: Those who were married at the time of conception compared with those who got married at that time; those who were married at conception compared with those who got married between conception and delivery; and those daters who got married between conception and delivery compared with those who maintained a steady dating relationship but did not get married. Men and women who marry when either or both are adolescents are known to have a greater likelihood of divorce and separation than those who marry in adulthood (Burchinal, 1965; Furstenberg, 1976; Teti, Lamb, and Elster, 1986), and many social scientists have attributed this risk to the fact that these dyads are formed prematurely after precipitation by pregnancy (McCarthy and Menken, 1979). If this is the case, we might expect that those couples who make formal commitments to one another prior to conception would appear psychologically healthier and more stable than those who were unmarried or whose unions were precipitated by pregnancies (Belsky and Miller, 1986). However, the prepregnancy characteristics of young parents-to-be in these different kinds of circumstances have never been explored.

METHOD

Subjects

Records of clinic-intake interviews conducted in a university-based adolescent pregnancy program provided data for the study. Three hundred and five of the pregnant adolescents over a 4½-year period were able to identify the fathers of their offspring; 275 of these women were primiparous, and these women and their partners were included in the study. Data were obtained from interviews with mothers-to-be, fathers-to-be, and/or the couples; t tests and χ^2 tests revealed that the source of information did not affect the quality of the data obtained. The women ranged in age from 12.5 to 19 years (mean = 17 years) at the time of delivery; 85% were Caucasian, and the mean Hollingshead (1976) class status of their families of origin was

3.33 (*SD* = 1.09). The males ranged in age from 14 to 36 years (mean = 21 years) at the time of delivery; 78% were Caucasian, and the mean Hollingshead (1976) class status of their families of origin was 3.22 (*SD* = 1.02). The majority of families of origin were classified in Hollingshead classes 3 and 4, which contain the bulk of middle-class individuals with nonprofessional but skilled white- and blue-collar occupations. There were no group differences with respect to ethnicity, maternal and paternal age, or socioeconomic status (SES) of maternal or paternal families of origin.

Procedures

The information was initially elicited from the subjects using a semistructured interview format. Data for this study were obtained by reviewing the notes made during these interviews and by coding them using a number of predetermined categories. The items coded included the source of information; the fathers' and mothers' reactions, and those of their parents, to the pregnancy (positive/mixed or neutral/negative); change in parents' relationships with their parents (better/no change/worse), father-of-baby's (FOB's) and mother-of-baby's (MOB's) history of drinking, smoking, and substance use; history of physical and sexual maltreatment; educational status (enrolled, graduated, dropped out); grade point average (GPA) in last year; academic and behavioral problems at school; employment status (wage rate, hours worked per week); religion; sources of emotional support; age at which sexual activity (sexarche) began; menarche; history of contraceptive use and judicial involvement; anxieties concerning parenthood; marital status and SES of parents; and history of family involvement in adolescent pregnancies. In the interest of brevity, only variables in which significant differences were found are included in the tables.

RESULTS

For purposes of analysis, *t* tests were used when continuous data were available, and in these cases means are provided in the tables; χ^2 tests were used when the variables were categorical in nature, and in these cases percentages in specified cells are presented in the tables.

The first set of analyses compared those who were married or unmarried at the time of conception; the results of these analyses are displayed in Table I (columns 3, 4, and 5). As might be expected, analyses showed that the couples who were married at the time of conception involved males, and prospective maternal and paternal grandparents, who responded more favorably to the pregnancy than did those who were not married at concep-

Table I. Comparison Between Couples Who Were and Were Not Married at the Time of Conception and/or Delivery

	Married between conception and delivery (N = 110)	Significance of difference	Married at conception (N = 22)	Significance of difference	Not married at conception (N = 253)
FOB's reaction to pregnancy (% positive)	47	d	75	b	38
MOB's reaction to pregnancy (% positive)	30	d	57		27
Reaction of FOB's parents (% positive)	36	b	85	b	34
Reaction of MOB's parents (% positive)	22	a	69	a	20
Change in relationship with FOB's parents (% better)	34		55	d	23
MOB's substance abuse (% never)	76	d	53		71
FOB's educational status (% dropouts)	44	c	73	d	49
FOB's GPA (mean)	3.44	a	1.67	b	3.28
MOB's educational status (% dropout)	45	b	77	b	42
FOB's salary/hour (mean)	4.88	c	7.97	a	4.56
MOB's hours worked/week (workers only) (mean)	19.0	d	26.67		22.67
FOB present as support person during labor (%)	84	c	83	c	55
FOB's sexarche (mean in years)	15.94	c	12.67	c	15.64
MOB's sexarche (mean in years)	16		15.0		15.33
MOB's use of contraceptives at time of conception (% yes)	7	c	19	c	5
History of teen pregnancy in MOB's family (% yes)	31	d	64	d	31

[a] $p < .001$ by t or χ^2 test.
[b] $p < .01$.
[c] $p < .05$.
[d] $p < .10$.

tion. Males and females who were married at conception were more likely to have dropped out before graduation from high school; in the fathers' cases, this may have been because their school performance was poor. However, the groups did not differ with respect to encounters with judicial authorities or identification of one another as sources of emotional support, although initially married fathers were more likely to be present at delivery. Initially married fathers worked more and earned higher wages per hour, and had their first sexual experience significantly earlier than unmarried men. Married women were more likely to have been attempting some form of contraception at the time of conception.

Those couples who married between conception and delivery differed in several respects from those who were married at conception (see Table I, columns 1, 2, and 3), and exactly the same pattern of results was obtained when we considered marriage/living together/engagement as the criterion relationships rather than only formal marriage. Couples who married during pregnancy reported nonsignificantly ($p < .10$) fewer positive responses to the pregnancy on the part of the fathers and mothers, and significantly fewer positive responses on the part of both sets of grandparents. The educational histories of the fathers and mothers who married during pregnancy were significantly better than those of the initially-married couples, but the later-married fathers earned less per hour than the initially-married fathers, and the later-married mothers worked nonsignificantly fewer hours. As a result, the total family income of the couples who married during pregnancy would have been substantially lower than that of the initially-married couples. Initially-married mothers and fathers first experienced sexual intercourse at significantly younger ages than those who married later.

National statistics indicate that a growing percentage of unwed teenage mothers maintain dating relationships with their partners instead of getting married, and we sought to determine whether these couples differed from those daters who chose to get married.

The daters who married during pregnancy differed in a few important respects from those who were dating regularly at the time of conception but chose not to marry before delivery (see Table II).[3] The fathers who married reported fewer behavioral problems in school (truancy, sloughing), were much less likely to have had contact with judicial and legal authorities, and worked more hours per week than the daters. Later marrying mothers (but not fathers) had their first sexual experience later than dating mothers did. Last, later marrying fathers were much more likely to serve as support persons

---

[3]Note that the number of couples who married during pregnancy described in this table is smaller than the number described on Table I. That is because Table II includes only those who described themselves as steady daters at the time of intake; column 1 in Table I also includes those who had more casual relationships at the time of conception, yet chose to get married.

Table II. Comparisons Between Regularly-Dating Couples Who Chose Either to Marry
or Not to Marry by Delivery

	Daters at both points (N = 29)	Significance of difference	Daters who marry (N = 84)
FOB's reaction to pregnancy (% positive)	21	d	45
Change in relationship with FOB's parents (% better)	0	d	37
MOB's history of physical or sexual abuse (% yes)	37	d	16
FOB's behavior problems in school (% yes)	87	b	36
FOB's hours worked/week (whole sample)	11.0	b	26.04
FOB present as support person during labor (%)	45	a	85
MOB identifies FOB as source of emotional support (%)	25	d	51
MOB's sexarche (mean age)	15.4	c	16.25
FOB's arrest history (% yes)	90	a	37
Marital status of MOB's parents (% still married)	41	d	62

$^a p$ < .001 by t test or χ^2 test.
$^b p$ < .01.
$^c p$ < .05.
$^d p$ < .10.

during labor, and then tended (p < .10) to be identified by mothers as sources of emotional support more often than daters were.

DISCUSSION

These results confirm the importance of recognizing the heterogeneity among adolescent mothers and their partners, since different types of young couples appear to face different sorts of problems. It remains necessary, of course, to explore these differences in samples of adolescents and their partners from different socioeconomic, ethnic, and geographic regions, as we must avoid facile assumptions about the similarities among groups of adolescent parents.

In our sample of urban Utahns, those who were already married at conception appeared to enjoy more positive responses from paternal and maternal grandparents than those who were not married. Married fathers-to-be also earned more than nonmarried fathers-to-be. On the other hand, these initially-married young men and their partners were most likely to have terminated their education prematurely, either because they got married (and then needed to support themselves) or because their performance at school was too poor to warrant perseverance. And although the fathers were more likely to be present at delivery when they had been married *ab initio,* initially-married partners were not more likely to identify one another as sources of emotional support than were mothers- and fathers-to-be who were not married at the time of conception. The low rates of identification — overall, 33% of the women and 44% of the men identified their partners as one of two sources of emotional support — suggest that these were not strong marriages to begin with, and that marital distress is likely to occur. In addition, the below-average educational histories of these young parents may presage long-term limitations on the parents' earning power, which may also be a source of stress in the future (Card and Wise, 1978; Teti *et al.,* 1986).

Because of the politically and religiously conservative climate in Utah, a larger proportion of unwed pregnant adolescents choose to marry during pregnancy than is true nationally, and this may affect the generalizability of our findings concerning these adolescents and their partners. Different problems and strengths characterized those in our sample who were married initially and those who chose to marry only when they learned they were to become parents. Both sets of grandparents and both parents ($p < .10$) responded less favorably to news of the pregnancy, although the educational status (and thus future economic and occupational potential) of both parents in couples who married during pregnancy was better than that of those who were initially married. The fathers who married during pregnancy earned less than the initially-married fathers, however, suggesting more intense immediate financial pressures even if their long-range prospects (should they persevere educationally) appeared brighter. Finally, those daters who chose to get married in response to the pregnancy represented a select subgroup when compared with those daters who simply maintained a steady dating relationship: the fathers who married during pregnancy had fewer school-related and legal behavior problems, worked more hours per week, and were much more likely to be present as support persons during labor and delivery than were the dating fathers. These differences suggest that the fathers who married after conception were more responsible and committed young men than were the dating fathers. Indeed, the psychosocial situation of the couples who married during pregnancy appeared substantially better, not only than that of those who were married initially, but also than those who decided to maintain a steady relationship without formal commitment (marriage). Interestingly, differences between mothers in the various groups were much less reliable than differences between the fathers. It is not clear whether this reflects the choice of measures in the present study or the fact that paternal characteristics are more salient than maternal characteristics as discriminators among the groups studied here.

Adolescent marriages are known to face a disproportionate risk of dissolution through divorce (e.g., Burchinal, 1965; Freedman and Thornton, 1979; Furstenberg, 1976; Teti *et al.*, 1986); it remains unclear, however, which of the groups identified in this study is at greatest risk. Viewed prospectively, we would have to predict, somewhat counterintuitively, that the greatest risks attended those who married early even in the absence of a pregnancy: certainly the relationships with their partners appeared deficient in basic respects, and their economic futures appeared bleakest, given the known consequences of premature educational termination (Freedman and Thornton, 1979; Teti *et al.*, 1986). By contrast, the couples who married during pregnancy appeared best qualified to cope with the stresses of parenthood and marriage, provided the immediate financial stresses did not overwhelm them. Prospective and retrospective analyses of the different rates of marital dissolution in families of these two types would be most valuable, as would studies designed to assess these factors and group differences in adolescent parents from different socioeconomic and ethnic backgrounds.

ACKNOWLEDGMENTS

The authors are grateful to Dr. Douglas Teti for his comments on earlier drafts of this paper.

REFERENCES

Battaglia, F. C., Frazier, T. M., and Hellegers, A. E. (1963). Obstetric and pediatric complications of juvenile pregnancy. *Pediatrics* 32: 902-910.

Belsky, J., and Miller, B. C. (1986). Adolescent fatherhood in the context of the transition to parenthood. In Elster, A. B., & Lamb, M. E. (eds.), *Adolescent Fatherhood*. Erlbaum, Hillsdale, NJ.

Burchinal, L. G. (1965). Trends and prospects for young marriages in the United States. *J. Marriage Family* 27: 243-254.

Card, J. J., and Wise, L. L. (1978). Teenage mothers and teenage fathers: The impact of early childbearing on the parents' personal and professional lives. *Family Plan. Perspect.* 10: 199-205.

Colletta, N. D., and Gregg, C. H. (1981). Adolescent mothers' vulnerability to stress. *J. Nerv. Mental Dis.* 169: 50-54.

Elster, A. B., and Lamb, M. E. (eds.). (1986). *Adolescent Fatherhood*. Earlbaum, Hillsdale, NJ.

Elster, A. B., McAnarney, E. R., and Lamb, M. E. (1983). Parental behavior of adolescent mothers. *Pediatrics* 71: 494-503.

Elster, A. B., Lamb, M. E., Peters, K., Kahn, J., and Tavare, J. (in press). Judicial involvement of fathers of infants born to adolescent mothers. *Pediatrics*.

Epstein, A. S. (1980) *Assessing the Child Development Information Needed by Adolescent Parents with Very Young Children*. Final Report, U.S. Department of Health, Education, and Welfare.

Freedman, D. S., and Thornton, A. (1979). The long-term impact of pregnancy at marriage on the family's economic circumstances. *Family Plan. Perspect.* 11: 6-21.

Furstenberg, F. F. (1976). The social consequences of teenage parenthood. *Family Plan. Perspect.* 8: 148-164.

Hollingshead, A. B. (1976). *The Four Factor Index of Social Position.* Unpublished manuscript, Department of Sociology, Yale University.

Israel, S. L., and Woutersz, T. B. (1963). Teenage obstetrics: A comparative study. *Amer. J. Obstetr. Gynecol.* 83: 659-668.

Jones, V. A., Green, V., and Krauss, D. R. (1980). Maternal responsiveness of primiparous mothers during the post partum period: Age differences. *Pediatrics* 65: 579-584.

Lamb, M. E., and Elster, A. B. (1985). Adolescent mother-father-infant interaction. *Develop. Psychol.* 21: 768-773.

McCarthy, J., and Menken, J. (1979). Marriage, remarriage, marital disruption and age at first birth. *Family Plan. Perspect.* 11: 21-30.

Nakashima, I. I., and Camp, B. W. (1984). Fathers of infants born to adolescent mothers: A study of paternal characteristics. *Amer. J. Dis. Children,* 138: 452-454.

Osofsky, H. J., and Osofsky, J. D. (1970). Adolescents as mothers: Results of a program for low-income pregnant teenagers with some emphasis upon infants' development. *Amer. J. Orthopsychiatr.* 40: 825-834.

Ragozin, A. S., Basham, R. B., Crnic, K. A., Greenberg, N. T., and Robinson, N. M. (1982). Effects of maternal age on parenting role. *Develop. Psychol.* 18: 627-634.

Rivara, F. P., Sweeney, P. J., and Henderson, B. F. (1985). A study of low socioeconomic status, black teenage fathers and their nonfather peers. *Pediatrics* 75: 648-656.

Sandler, H. M., Vietze, R. M., and O'Connor, S. (1981). Obstetric and neonatal outcomes following intervention with pregnant teenagers. In Scott, K. G., Field, T., & Robertson, E. (eds.), *Teenage Parents and Their Offspring.* Grune and Stratton, New York.

Teti, D. M., Lamb, M. E., and Elster, A. B. (March, 1986). *Long-Range Educational, Financial, and Marital Consequences of Teen Marriage in Three Cohorts of Adult Males.* Paper presented to the Society for Research in Adolescence, Madison, WI.

JOURNAL OF RESEARCH ON ADOLESCENCE, 1(2), 173–188
Copyright © 1991, Lawrence Erlbaum Associates, Inc.

The Effects of Maternal Age-at-Birth on Children's Cognitive Development

Robert D. Ketterlinus, Sandra Henderson,
and Michael E. Lamb

National Institute of Child Health and Human Development

For nearly 20 years, there has been widespread acceptance of the conclusion that the cognitive development of children born to adolescent parents is deficient relative to that of children born to adult parents. The conclusion may be premature, however, because of sample biases and methodological flaws that characterize much of the research. The purpose of our study was to compare the school achievement scores of elementary-school children born to either adolescent or adult mothers using data obtained from a nationally representative sample of contemporary youth and their children. The effects of maternal age on children's school achievement scores were negligible after controlling for maternal intelligence, sociodemographic status, and the quality of the home environment. Maternal age did have a direct effect on children's math achievement after variations in maternal intelligence were statistically accounted for, but this effect disappeared after entering other variables into the regression equation. Also, after controlling for other variables in the model, maternal age was a significant predictor of Peabody Individual Achievement Tests (PIATs) scores among Blacks but not among Whites and Hispanics. These results, together with new trends in childbearing, suggest that researchers should reexamine conclusions about the effects of adolescent motherhood on children's cognitive development.

For nearly 20 years, researchers, clinicians, and reviewers have concluded that children born to adolescent parents are at greater risk of physical, emotional, and intellectual problems than are other children

Requests for reprints should be sent to Robert D. Ketterlinus, National Institute of Child Health and Human Development, Laboratory of Comparative Ethology, Section on Social and Emotional Development, BSA Building, Room 333, 9190 Rockville Pike, Bethesda, MD 20814.

(Baldwin & Cain, 1980; Furstenberg, Brooks-Gunn, & Chase-Lansdale, 1989; Hofferth & Hayes, 1987; Record, McKeown, & Edwards, 1969). For example, Baldwin and Cain (1980) concluded a review of National Institute of Child Health and Human Development (NICHD) -funded research by noting that:

> All analyses show deficits in the cognitive development of children (especially male children) born to teenagers; much, but not all, of the effect results from the social and economic consequences of early childbearing. Less consistent effects are found for the children's social and emotional development and school adjustment. (p. 34)

Likewise, in a recent review article, Furstenberg et al. (1989) concluded that:

> Generally, children born to teenage mothers are at a developmental disadvantage compared with children born to older mothers. Small but consistent differences in cognitive functioning between offspring of early and later childbearers appear in preschool and continue into elementary school (Broman, 1981; Maracek, 1979, 1985). These decrements are more likely to be observed in the sons than in the daughters of early childbearers. (p. 316)

This conclusion may be premature, however. Most of the research was conducted prior to 1980 on predominantly Black, urban, disadvantaged women who were enrolled in specialized intervention programs. Many studies published after 1981 have similar methodological problems, but sophisticated statistical analyses reveal no effects of young maternal age after the effects of socioeconomic status have been accounted for (Belmont, P. Cohen, Dryfoos, Stein, & Zayac, 1981; Broman, 1981).

The results of two recent studies suggest that maternal age is a less important predictor of children's cognitive development than are factors such as sociodemographic status and maternal intelligence. In a study of the effects of maternal employment on children's cognitive development, for example, Desai, Chase-Lansdale, and Michael (1989) found that maternal age had no significant effect on 4-year-old children's scores on the Peabody Picture Vocabulary Test–R (PPVT–R), after controlling for maternal race/ethnicity, maternal education level, maternal scholastic aptitude, family income level, and child-care arrangements. Maternal verbal aptitude (but not mathematical aptitude) was significantly and positively correlated with PPVT scores. In another study, Dubow and Luster (1990) examined the contribution of risk and protective factors in the academic and behavioral adjustment of 8- to 15-year-old children born to mothers aged 19 years old or younger. The risk factors were primarily sociodemographic indicators (family size, father absence, poverty status, maternal education, urban residency), but also included maternal self-esteem and maternal age (below 17 at the time of the child's birth). Although bivariate results indicated that youthful maternal age was associated with higher scores on a problem behavior index and lower math and reading achievement scores, the effects of maternal age became statistically nonsignificant, except for a weak relationship with reading recognition achievement (standardized regression coefficient = .09, p < .05), in multivariate regression analyses. Although the best predictors of maladjustment were a cluster of sociodemographic variables representing socioeconomic disadvantage, different indicators within the cluster were related to different adjustment problems.

Unfortunately, researchers studying the effects of maternal age have rarely assessed the effects of the quality of the home environment on children's cognitive development. The quality of the home environment is reported to have strong relationships with measures of intellectual performance, language development, and school achievement (Bee et al., 1982; Bradley & Caldwell, 1984; Stevenson & Lamb, 1981). In addition, several investigators have found that children born to adolescent mothers live in less stimulating environments than do children born to adult mothers (Garcia Coll, Hoffman, & Oh, 1987; Luster & Rhoades, 1989; cf. Field, Widmayer, Stringer, & Ignatoff, 1980, who found no differences). It is unclear, however, whether these differences are due to the differing practices and beliefs of adolescent and adult mothers or to the differing sociodemographic conditions (see Lamb & Ketterlinus, 1990). In addition to examining the effects of maternal intelligence, sociodemographic status, and age, we therefore included a standardized measure of the quality of the home environment in our analyses.

The purpose of this study was to provide a comparison of the school achievement scores of elementary-school children born to either adolescent or adult mothers using data obtained from a national sample of contemporary youth and their children. The women in this study were not chosen on the basis of their participation in clinic-based intervention programs, and the database allowed us to isolate the effects of maternal age from environmental and organismic factors among a sociodemographically heterogeneous sample of adolescent and adult mothers and their children. Based on our review of the literature, we predicted that the effects of maternal age on children's school achievement scores would be negligible after controlling for maternal intelligence, sociodemographic status, and the quality of the home environment, and we tested this prediction by means of hierarchical multiple regression analyses.

METHOD

Subjects

Data for this study were obtained from the National Longitudinal Survey of the Work Experience of Youth (NLSY). The NLSY consists of three independent probability samples, two civilian and one military, drawn from a national probability sample of households using standard area probability sampling methods. One sample consisted of the 14- to 21-year-old (as of January 1, 1979) noninstitutionalized youth, the second supplemental sample was designed to oversample Hispanics, Blacks, and poor Whites, and the third military sample, which was oversampled for women, was a clustered probability sample of the 17- to 21-year-old cohort, stratified by branch of service (Frankel, McWilliams, & Spencer, 1983).

In 1986, biological, psychosocial, and behavioral data were collected on 4,971 children (ages 1 through 14) born to the women in the sample. In this study, we examined the 1,880 children (52% males) who were 5 years or older (range = 5 to 12 years; M age = 7.2 years, SD = 2.0); as well as their mothers who were 22 to 30 years old in 1986 (the dates of birth for this sample of women ranged from February 1956 to January 1964).

Note that the restricted age range within the NLSY sample may attenuate the correlation between maternal age and children's cognitive status. The NLSY women and their children are not fully representative of American women and children. Instead, the NLSY children are approximately representative of the first 40% of the children born to a cohort of American women. As a result, children who are born to younger women, and children with less educated and minority mothers, are overrepresented (Baker & Mott, 1989). Any conclusions concerning maternal age effects using this sample, therefore, must be interpreted cautiously and should not be generalized to other samples with age ranges outside those represented by the NLSY sample.

Measures

Maternal age-at-birth-of-child. In this study, 3.2% of the mothers were 13 to 15 years old at the time of delivery, 33.2% were 16 to 18 years old, 44.0% were 19 to 21 years old, and 19.6% were 22 to 25 years old. In the regression models, maternal age-at-birth-of-child (range = 13 to 25; M = 19.4, SD = 2.0) was entered as a continuous variable (i.e., actual years).

Race.   Black (38%), Hispanic (17%), and White (45%) women and their children were included in this study. In the multiple regression analyses that follow, the Whites were chosen as the reference category.

Marital status.   At the time of their children's assessment in 1986, 24% of the mothers had never been married; 23% had been divorced, separated, or widowed; and 53% were married (reference category).

Maternal education.   As of 1986, 49% of the mothers had completed less than 11 years of education, 39% had completed high school, and 12% had completed 13 or more years of education. In the regression models, maternal education in years of schooling was entered as a continuous variable (M = 10.91, SD = 2.06, range = 0 to 18).

Family income.   Mothers were asked to report 1986 income received by all members of the family living in the same household as the mother (M = $17,270.12, SD = $14,239.02, median = $13,180, range = $0.00 to $127,000.00).

Maternal aptitude.   In 1979, all NLSY respondents completed the Armed Services Vocational Aptitude Battery (ASVAB; see Bock & Moore, 1986). This battery includes 10 subtests that measure knowledge and skill in certain areas. Two of the 10 subtests were selected for use in this study—word knowledge (vocabulary), and arithmetic reasoning (word problems requiring the respondent to use mathematical terms to solve questions described in short passages).[1] In this study we used standardized scores which have a range of −3 to +3 with a mean of zero and variance of one. The ASVAB scores predict scores on the

---

[1]The other 8 ASVAB subscales and descriptions of what they were designed to measure: *Paragraph comprehension* measures how well information is acquired from written passages; *general science* measures basic factual knowledge taught in secondary school general science courses; *mathematics knowledge* measures knowledge of subjects taught in secondary school mathematics courses such as geometry, algebra, and trigonometry; *numerial operations* measures speed and accuracy in solving basic arithmetic questions; *coding speed* measures speed and accuracy in completing tasks; *mechanical comprehension* measures the ability to visualize how objects work together; *auto and shop information* tests specific knowledge of the tools and terms used in the repair and maintenance of vehicles; and *electronics information* tests specific knowledge of electrical terms and equipment.

Scholastic Aptitude Test (SAT; Bock & Moore, 1986), and was considered here as a proxy index of maternal intelligence.

Home environment. An abbreviated version of the Home Observation for Measurement of the Environment (HOME) for elementary school children (Caldwell & Bradley, 1984) was used as an index of the quality of the home environment. The HOME yields scores that are stable and reliable over time, and that predict children's subsequent cognitive development (Bradley & Caldwell, 1984; Bradley, Caldwell, & Elardo, 1979). The version of the HOME used in the NLSY, called the HOME-Short Form (HOME-SF), is about half as long as the HOME Inventory and included both interviewer observations and maternal self-reports. Baker and Mott (1989) reported details about the construction, scoring, and psychometric properties of the HOME-SF.

Because the reliability (internal consistency) of the HOME subscales in the NLSY is quite low (α = .65 and .61 for emotional stimulation and cognitive stimulation, respectively, according to Dubow and Luster, 1990), we decided to use only the Total HOME scores (α = .76).

Children's achievement. In 1986, the Peabody Individual Achievement Tests (PIATs; see Dunn & Markwardt, 1970) were administered to children who were 5 years of age or older. Two tests were selected for use in this study, math and reading recognition. The math subscale covers elementary school math training and consists of 84 items of increasing difficulty, from numerical recognition to geometry and trigonometry. The reading recognition subscale also consists of 84 items that measure general reading ability. Subjects are required to name and match letters and read words aloud. In this study, we used the standardized scores which are normed by age and gender. In our sample, the PIAT scores ranged from 65 to 135, with mean scores of 97.43 (*SD* = 12.75) for math, and 103.25 (*SD* = 13.20) for reading recognition.

Statistical Analyses

Because the main purpose of this study was to assess the effect of maternal age on children's school achievement scores after controlling for maternal intelligence, sociodemographic status, and the quality of the home environment, we employed hierarchical multiple regression analysis techniques (J. Cohen & P. Cohen, 1983). In order to assess the extent to which the variance in a dependent variable (e.g., children's cognitive development) is explained by the main independent variable of interest (in this study, maternal age), researchers often enter the main independent variable after all other main effect variables (e.g., maternal intelligence and environmental factors), examining the changes in R^2s at each step, and the significance level of the regression coefficients in the final step. In this dataset, there is a strong relationship between maternal age and maternal cognitive status, however. If maternal age was entered after the mothers' cognitive scores, the effects of all the factors that are jointly correlated with cognitive status and age would be attributed to mothers' cognitive scores rather than to maternal age, and this might lead us to underestimate the effects of maternal age and overestimate the effects of maternal intelligence. In the first step of each analysis (one with PIAT math scores as the dependent variable and one with PIAT reading scores as the dependent variable), therefore, we entered mother's age-at-birth of the target child. In the second step, maternal aptitude as assessed using the ASVAB was entered. If variations in maternal intelligence actually account for previously reported "effects" of young maternal age, as we have predicted, the maternal age effect should become statistically nonsignificant when the maternal aptitude scores are entered into the regression equation.

To control for the effects of children's sex on achievement test performance, we entered the children's gender into the regression equations in the third step. In the fourth step of the regression analyses we entered a block of sociodemographic variables which included race, marital status, maternal education, and family income.[2] The total HOME scores were entered in the fifth step, and in the sixth and final step we added three interaction terms—Race × Maternal Aptitude, Race × Maternal Age, and Maternal Education × Maternal Age.

RESULTS

Bivariate Analyses

Because Blacks, Hispanics, and poor Whites were oversampled in the original study, we were interested in comparing the sociodemographic status of these groups in our sample. The results of these analyses

---

[2]In preliminary analyses, we also included two other indicators of socioeconomic status, *family poverty status*, and the *Duncan Index* of occupational prestige. However, these variables were omitted from the final analyses because their partial regression coefficients were not significant, and because a large number of scores on these variables were missing. Large amounts of data were missing because the codes were computed using a variety of measures; if any of the component scores were missing the variable could not be computed. Young disadvantaged women, especially Blacks, are generally overrepresented among those with missing data on these variables.

suggest that the Blacks in our study were more disadvantaged than were the Hispanics and the Whites. The mean family income of Blacks was lower than those of both Hispanics and Whites (13,792, $16,190, and $20,453, respectively). Although Blacks appeared to be in a lower socioeconomic status group, their educational attainment was, on average, somewhat greater than those of the Whites and Hispanics (*M* number of years of completed education = 11.37, 10.93, and 9.84, respectively), suggesting that factors other than the number of years of completed schooling were responsible for the lower incomes of the Black women. Two possible factors were marital status and age-at-birth-of-child. Blacks were more likely to have never been married than were either Hispanics or Whites (47%, 20%, and 7%, respectively), and were also less likely to be married in 1986 (32%, 61%, and 67%, respectively). Blacks also tended to be younger at-birth-of-child than Hispanics and Whites (18.90, 19.59, and 19.80 years, respectively) and were over-represented in the under-19-years-of-age-at-birth group (62%, 50%, and 46%, respectively). On average, however, Black women were approximately the same age in 1986 as were Hispanic and White women (*M* age in 1986 = 27.04, 27.23, and 27.54 years, respectively). Because there appeared to be important differences among the three racial groups, mean scores for the three groups are provided separately in Table 1 (zero-order correlation matrices are available upon request from Robert D. Ketterlinus).

Multivariate Analyses

The results of both multiple regression analyses for the pooled sample were similar with respect to Rs, R^{2s}, increments in R^2, and significant standardized regression coefficients (betas; see Table 2). The results concerning maternal cognitive status and maternal age, however, differed in the two analyses. In both analyses, maternal age-at-birth accounted for 1% of the variance in children's PIAT test scores (βs = .11). When maternal ASVAB scores were entered into the regression equations (increasing the R^2s by approximately 10 percentage points), however, the coefficient for maternal age dropped below the level of statistical significance for PIAT reading (β = .04), whereas the coefficient for maternal age remained statistically significant for PIAT math scores, although the magnitude dropped from .11 to .06.

Although the addition of child's gender did not significantly increase R^2 for reading or math scores, it should be noted that the coefficient for maternal age became marginally significant in the reading analysis (p = .08) and remained statistically significant in the math analysis (p = .02). The addition of the sociodemographic block of variables increased R^2 for

TABLE 1
Means and Standard Deviations of All Variables by Race

	Total[a]	Hispanics[b]	Blacks[c]	Whites[d]
Gender	1.48	1.45	1.47	1.49
	(.50)	(.50)	(.50)	(.50)
Mom's age-at-birth[e]	19.42	19.59	18.90	19.80
	(2.24)	(2.18)	(2.25)	(2.17)
Marital status[e]	1.99	2.00	1.74	2.18
	(.66)	(.63)	(.78)	(.54)
Mom's education[e]	10.91	9.84	11.37	10.93
	(2.00)	(2.62)	(1.80)	(1.88)
Family income[e]	17272.12	16190.62	13792.38	20453.28
	(14232.09)	(11503.32)	(12717.28)	(15546.97)
HOME[e]	16.42	15.80	15.34	16.56
	(37.92)	(40.15)	(37.47)	(34.05)
ASVAB Math[e]	−0.74	−0.96	−0.10	−0.41
	(.72)	(.70)	(.56)	(.83)
ASVAB Reading[e]	−0.73	−0.11	−0.12	−0.23
	(1.01)	(.98)	(.82)	(.95)
PIAT Math[e]	97.43	95.45	94.28	100.86
	(12.75)	(12.78)	(12.23)	(12.32)
PIAT Reading[e]	103.26	100.33	102.02	105.44
	(13.15)	(13.98)	(12.99)	(12.62)

[a]$N = 1,880$. [b]$N = 323$. [c]$N = 714$. [d]$N = 843$. [e]Groups significantly different by ANOVA, $p < .001$.

both math and reading scores, and at this step in the analyses the coefficient for maternal age dropped well below the level of statistical significance for both reading and math scores. The addition of HOME scores also increased R^2 in both analyses. Finally, the addition of the interaction terms (not shown) to the regression models did not significantly increase R^2 for PIAT reading scores but did increase R^2 slightly (1%) for PIAT math scores. The R^2s for the final model were .18 and .14 for math and reading scores, respectively.

The final models for both math and reading scores were similar. Most importantly, when all of the variables were included, the coefficients for maternal age were negligible in both analyses, whereas the coefficients for maternal cognitive status, some sociodemographic variables, and quality of the home environment were all statistically significant. In addition, the coefficient for gender was statistically significant for reading (higher scores for females) but not for math scores.

Interactions. In both regression analyses, there was a statistically significant coefficient for the Race (Blacks vs. Whites) by Maternal Age-at-Birth interaction term, suggesting that higher maternal age was

TABLE 2
Multiple Regression Results for PIAT Reading and Math Scores for the Pooled Sample

Standardized Regression Coefficients

	Reading					Math				
Mom's age	.11***	.04	.04*	.02	.02	.11***	.06**	.06**	.00	.00
ASVAB		.30***	.31***	.20	.19		.31***	.31***	.16***	.16***
Gender			-.02	-.11***	-.11***			-.02	-.02	-.01
Mom's education				.15***	.13				.17***	.14***
Family income				.03	.02				.07***	.06**
Hispanic				-.05*	-.04				-.09***	-.08***
Black				-.05*	-.03				-.22**	-.19***
Never married				-.02	.00				.02	.05*
Divorced/separated				-.00	.02				.04	.06**
Home					.11***					.13***
R^2	.01	.10	.11	.13	.14	.01	.11	.11	.16	.17

*p < .10. **p < .05. ***p < .01.

related to higher PIAT test scores, but that this association was greater among Blacks than among Whites. The effects for Hispanics fell between those of Whites and Blacks (more similar to those for Blacks), but were not statistically significant. To illustrate the race by maternal age-at-birth interactions we reran the regression analyses separately for the three racial groups (Table 3).[3] Note that for both the PIAT Math and PIAT Reading analyses, the maternal age-at-birth beta is larger for Blacks than for the other racial groups. For both Hispanics and Whites, the maternal age-at-birth betas never reach statistical significance, whereas for Blacks, maternal age-at-birth remains either statistically significant (reading, $p = .04$) or marginally significant (math, $p = .08$) after the addition of the other predictor blocks to the regression equations.

DISCUSSION

Using a nationally representative sample of young women between the ages of 22 and 30 and their children, we found that maternal intelligence and environmental factors may be better predictors of children's cognitive development than is maternal age. In particular, three groups of children appear particularly likely to perform poorly on arithmetic and reading achievement tests: Children of mothers who do not provide a stimulating home environment, children of women who had low math and reading aptitude tests scores, and children with young Black mothers. However, our results also suggest that the children of very young mothers may perform more poorly on tests of quantitative competence than do children of somewhat older mothers, even after controlling for the effects of maternal cognitive status (but the effect of maternal age disappears after accounting for sociodemographic status). Conversely, the effects of maternal cognitive status appears to mitigate any effects of maternal age on children's reading abilities. These findings offer the intriguing possibility that maternal age may have different effects in these two domains of cognitive development.

Our results also suggested that the magnitude of maternal age effects may differ among racial groups. Significant Race × Maternal Age interactions suggested that maternal age is not as important a predictor of children's achievement test scores among Whites as it is among Blacks. Furthermore, regression analyses run separately for the three

---

[3]We removed the Maternal Education × Maternal Age-at-Birth interaction term from the six analyses (Step 6) because the coefficients were not statistically significant (smallest $p = .49$) and the addition of this term to the regression equations did not yield statistically significant increases in R^2s over Step 5.

TABLE 3

Multiple Regression Results for PIAT Reading and Math Scores, for Whites, Blacks, and Hispanics, Separately

	Whites					Blacks					Hispanics				
PIAT Reading Scores: Standardized Regression Coefficients															
Mom's age	.07*	.00	-.04	-.04		.13***	.11***	.11***	.09**	.08**	.04	.05	.00	.02	
ASVAB vocabulary		.27***	.27***	.21***	.20***		.25***	.27***	.19***	.19***		.29***	.29***	.17**	.15**
Gender			-.10***	-.10***	-.10***			-.12**	-.13***	-.13***			-.14**	-.12**	-.11*
Mom's education				.11***	.11**				.18***	.15***				.18**	.12
Family income				.07*	.06				-.01	-.02				-.02	-.01
Never married				.02	.02				.00	.03				-.20***	-.17***
Divorced/separated				.02	.03				-.04	-.02				-.02	-.03
HOME					.07*					.05**					.19***
R^2	.005	.07	.08	.09	.10	.02	.08	.09	.12	.13	.04	.09	.11	.16	.19
PIAT Math Scores: Standardized Regression Coefficients															
Mom's age	.04*	-.02	-.05	-.05		.11***	.11***	.11***	.07*	.07*	.02	.03	.00	.02	
ASVAB arithmetic		.29***	.29***	.23***	.22***		.12***	.13***	.04	.04		.34***	.35***	.20***	.19***
Gender			.00	.00	.00			-.00	-.01	-.02			-.10*	-.07	-.07
Mom's education				.10**	.09**				.20***	.16***				.26***	.21***
Family income				.07*	.06				.06	.05				.09+	.16***
Never married				-.00	.02				.07	.12**				-.00	-.02
Divorced/separated				.02	.04				.05	.08				.06	.11
HOME					.09***					.17***					.14**
R^2	.002	.08	.08	.09	.10	.03	.04	.04	.07	.10	.03	.11	.13	.19	.20

*$p < .10$. **$p < .05$. ***$p < .01$.

368

racial groups suggested that maternal age-at-birth had relatively greater effects on children's cognitive status among Blacks as compared to Whites. At least two other large scale studies have reported Race by Maternal Age interactions (Belmont et al., 1981; Broman, 1981) but the effects are not consistent among those studies and this study, possibly due to cohort effects or differences in sample designs. In any event, the results of all three studies suggest that there are different patterns of correlations between maternal age and children's cognitive development among different racial or ethnic groups. One caution concerning interpretation of this study's results is that the Race by Age interaction may have been attenuated because Black mothers tended to be younger than Whites and Hispanics.

Black, White, and Hispanic children in the U.S. are generally exposed to very different social, economic, cultural, and educational experiences. These differences may explain the differential effects of maternal age on child outcomes among members of these three racial groups. In a similar comparison of the perinatal outcomes of adolescent and adult women, Ketterlinus, Henderson, and Lamb (1990) found that Black children were at greater risk of premature birth and low birthweight than were White children. The children of very young adolescent mothers were also more likely to be born prematurely and to have low birthweights than were children of older adolescent women or adult mothers. Together, the results of these two studies suggest that the effects of maternal age on children's development are most marked when mothers are very young, Black, and are strongly mediated by the socio-demographic or ecological circumstances in which children are reared. In this study, we also found that the quality of the home environment was correlated with indices of the children's school achievement. Mothers who lived in disadvantaged homes (who were disproportionately Black) provided less stimulating home environments (as assessed by the HOME), and their children's PIAT scores were depressed in turn. The fact that 47% of the Black women had never been married and that 32% were not married in 1986 also suggests that father absence may contribute to lower quality home environments, and may in turn help depress children's scores on the PIATs.

Unfortunately, our final models accounted for only for a small amount of the variance in PIAT test scores because we could not adequately assess the contribution of factors which measure paternal influences (e.g., paternal intelligence or involvement), parents' childrearing attitudes, knowledge, and competencies, or the childrens' unique experiences outside of the home (e.g., daycare and early school experiences). Future studies should include these variables in studies designed to assess the relative impact of parental age and other factors on children's physical, social, and cognitive development.

These deficiencies notwithstanding, our results demonstrated the need to re-evaluate the simplistic conclusion that early maternal childbearing has adverse effects on children's cognitive development. The widespread acceptance of this conclusion may reflect ideological disapproval of early childbearing rather than solid empirical support (Melhuish & Phoenix, 1988), or the failure to understand that maternal age probably affects children's cognitive development only indirectly through its influence on more direct determinants of children's intellectual competence. In fact, our analyses suggested that young maternal age, considered in isolation, may play an even smaller role in explaining deficits in children's cognitive development than has been suggested by past reviewers of the literature. Instead, sociodemographic status, maternal intelligence, and the quality of the home environment proved to be most important. These conclusions must be considered tentative, however, until replication studies can be conducted using more representative samples of women and children.

Finally, new sociodemographic trends in adolescent childbearing, such as the increasing numbers of adolescent mothers completing high school (Upchurch & McCarthy, 1989), the smaller completed family size of early childbearers (Balakrishnan, Rao, Krotki, & Lapierre-Adamcyk, 1988), the population-wide reductions in the age at which childbearing is initiated (Eggebeen & Uhlenberg, 1989), and the nationwide increases in rates of marital instability (Martin & Bumpass, 1989) also make evident the wisdom of reexamining conclusions about the consequences of being born to adolescent parents.

ACKNOWLEDGMENT

We are indebted to Doris Entwisle and several anonymous reviewers who provided thoughtful comments and suggestions during the preparation of this article.

REFERENCES

Baker, P. C., & Mott, F. L. (1989). *NLSY Child Handbook 1989.* Columbus: Center for Human Resource Research, Ohio State University.
Balakrishnan, T. R., Rao, K. V., Krotki, K. J., & Lapierre-Adamcyk, E. (1988). Age at first birth and lifetime fertility. *Journal of Biosocial Science, 20,* 167–174.

Baldwin, W. H., & Cain, V. S. (1980). The children of teenage parents. *Family Planning Perspectives, 12,* 34–43.

Bee, H. L., Barnard, K. E., Eyres, S. J., Gray, C. A., Hammond, M. A., Spietz, A. L., Snyder, C., & Clark, B. (1982). Prediction of IQ and language skill from perinatal status, child performance, family characteristics, and mother–infant interaction. *Child Development, 53,* 1134–1156.

Belmont, L., Cohen, P., Dryfoos, J., Stein, Z., & Zayac, S. (1981). Maternal age and children's intelligence. In K. G. Scott, T. Field, & E. G. Robertson (Eds.), *Teenage parents and their offspring* (pp. 177–194). New York: Grune & Stratton.

Bock, R. D., & Moore, E. G. J. (1986). *Advantage and disadvantage: Profile of American youth.* Hillsdale, NJ: Lawrence Erlbaum Associates, Inc.

Bradley, R. H., & Caldwell, B. M. (1984). 174 children: A study of the relationship between home environment and cognitive development during the first five years. In A. W. Gottfried (Ed.), *Home environment and early cognitive development* (pp. 5–56). New York: Academic.

Bradley, R. H., Caldwell, B. M., & Elardo, R. (1979). Home environment and cognitive development in the first two years: A cross-lagged panel analysis. *Developmental Psychology, 15,* 246–250.

Broman, S. H. (1981). Long-term development of children born to teenagers. In K. G. Scott, T. Field, & E. G. Robertson (Eds.), *Teenage parents and their offspring* (pp. 177–194). New York: Grune & Stratton.

Caldwell, B., & Bradley, R. (1984). *Home observation for measurement of the environment.* Little Rock: University of Arkansas at Little Rock.

Cohen, J., & Cohen, P. (1983). *Applied multiple regression/correlation for the behavioral sciences* (2nd ed.). Hillsdale, NJ: Lawrence Erlbaum Associates, Inc.

Desai, S., Chase-Lansdale, L., & Michael, R. T. (1989). Mother or market? Effects of maternal employment on cognitive development of four-year-old children. *Demography, 25,* 545–562.

Dubow, E. F., & Luster, T. (1990). Adjustment of children born to teenage mothers: The contribution of risk and protective factors. *Journal of Marriage and the Family, 52,* 393–404.

Dunn, L. M., & Markwardt, F. C. (1970). *Peabody individual achievement test manual.* Circle Pines, MN: American Guidance Service.

Eggebeen, D. J., & Uhlenberg, P. (1989). Changes in the age distribution of parents, 1940–1980. *Journal of Family Issues, 10,* 169–188.

Field, T. M., Widmayer, S. M., Stringer, S., & Ignatoff, E. (1980). Teenage lower-class black mothers and their preterm infants: An intervention and developmental follow-up. *Child Development, 51,* 426–436.

Frankel, M. R., McWilliams, H. A., & Spencer, B. D. (1983). *National Longitudinal Survey of Labor Force Behavior, Youth Survey (NLS): Technical sampling report.* Chicago: University of Chicago, National Opinion Research Center.

Furstenberg, F. F., Brooks-Gunn, J., & Chase-Lansdale, L. (1989). Teenage pregnancy and childbearing. *American Psychologist, 44,* 313–320.

Garcia Coll, C. T., Hoffman, J., & Oh, W. (1987). The social ecology and early parenting of Caucasian adolescent mothers. *Child Development, 58,* 955–963.

Hofferth, S. L., & Hayes, C. D. (1987). *Risking the future: Adolescent sexuality, pregnancy, and childbearing, Vol. II.* Washington, DC: National Academy Press.

Ketterlinus, R. D., Henderson, S., & Lamb, M. E. (1990). Maternal age, sociodemographics, prenatal health and behavior: Influences on neonatal risk status. *Journal of Adolescent Health Care, 11,* 423–431.

Lamb, M. E., & Ketterlinus, R. D. (1990). Adolescent parental behavior. In R. M. Lerner,

A. C. Petersen, & J. Brooks-Gunn (Eds.), *The encyclopedia of adolescence* (Vol. 2, pp. 735–738). New York: Garland.

Luster, T., & Rhoades, K. (1989). The relation between child-rearing beliefs and the home environment in a sample of adolescent mothers. *Family Relations, 38,* 317–322.

Maracek, J. (1979). *Economic, social, and psychological consequences of adolescent childbearing: An analysis of data from the Philadelphia Collaborative Perinatal Project* (Final report to National Institute for Child Health and Human Development). Washington, DC: U.S. Government Printing Office.

Maracek, J. (1985). *The effects of adolescent childbearing on children's cognitive and psychosocial development.* Unpublished manuscript.

Martin, T. C., & Bumpass, L. L. (1989). Recent trends in marital disruption. *Demography, 26,* 37–51.

Melhuish, E., & Phoenix, A. (1988). Motherhood under twenty: Prevailing ideologies and research. *Children and Society, 1,* 288–298.

Record, R. G., McKeown, T., & Edwards, J. H. (1969). The relations of measured intelligence to birth order and maternal age. *Annals of Human Genetics, 33,* 61–69.

Stevenson, M. B., & Lamb, M. E. (1981). The effects of social experience and social style on cognitive competence and performance. In M. E. Lamb & L. R. Sherrod (Eds.), *Infant social cognition: Theoretical and empirical considerations* (pp. 375–394). Hillsdale, NJ: Lawrence Erlbaum Associates, Inc.

Upchurch, D. M., & McCarthy, J. (1989). Adolescent childbearing and high school completion in the 1980s: Have things changed? *Family Planning Perspectives, 21,* 199–202.

Received June 25, 1990
Revision received October 3, 1990
Accepted February 8, 1991

Acknowledgments

Bronfenbrenner, Urie. "Ecology of the Family as a Context for Human Development: Research Perspectives." *Developmental Psychology* 22 (1986): 723–42. Copyright 1986 by the American Psychological Association. Reprinted by permission.

Baumrind, Diana. "The Influence of Parenting Style on Adolescent Competence and Substance Use." *Journal of Early Adolescence* 11 (1991): 56–95. Reprinted with the permission of Sage Publications, Inc.

Brody, Gene H., Zolinda Stoneman, and Douglas Flor. "Parental Religiosity, Family Processes, and Youth Competence in Rural, Two-Parent African American Families." *Developmental Psychology* 32 (1996): 696–706. Copyright 1996 by the American Psychological Association. Reprinted by permission.

Eccles, Jacquelynne S., Carol Midgley, Allan Wigfield, Christy Miller Buchanan, David Reuman, Constance Flanagan, and Douglas Mac Iver. "Development During Adolescence: The Impact of Stage-Environment Fit on Young Adolescents' Experiences in Schools and in Families." *American Psychologist* 48 (1993): 90–101. Copyright 1993 by the American Psychological Association. Reprinted by permission.

Harrison, Algea O., Melvin N. Wilson, Charles J. Pine, Samuel Q. Chan, and Raymond Buriel. "Family Ecologies of Ethnic Minority Children." *Child Development* 61 (1990): 347–62. Reprinted with the permission of the Society for Research in Child Development.

Grotevant, Harold D., and Catherine R. Cooper. "Patterns of Interaction in Family Relationships and the Development of Identity Exploration in Adolescence." *Child Development* 56 (1985): 415–28. Reprinted with the permission of the Society for Research in Child Development.

Larson, Reed W., Maryse H. Richards, Giovanni Moneta, Grayson Holmbeck, and Elena Duckett. "Changes in Adolescents' Daily Interactions with Their Families from Ages 10 to 18: Disengagement and Transformation." *Developmental Psychology* 32 (1996): 744–54. Copyright 1996 by the American psychological Association. Reprinted by permission.

Steinberg, Laurence, Nina S. Mounts, Susie D. Lamborn, and Sanford M. Dornbusch. "Authoritative Parenting and Adolescent Adjustment Across Varied Ecological Niches." *Journal of Research on Adolescence* 1 (1991): 19–36.

Reprinted with the permission of Lawrence Erlbaum Associates Inc.

McAdoo, Harriette Pipes. "Stress Levels, Family Help Patterns, and Religiosity in Middle- and Working-Class African American Single Mothers." *Journal of Black Psychology* 21 (1995): 424–49. Reprinted with the permission of Sage Publications, Inc.

Royse, David D., and Gladys T. Turner. "Strengths of Black Families: A Black Community's Perspective." *Social Work* 25 (1980): 407–409. Reprinted with the permission of the National Association of Social Workers.

Phinney, Jean S., and Victor Chavira. "Parental Ethnic Socialization and Adolescent Coping With Problems Related to Ethnicity." *Journal of Research on Adolescence* 5 (1995): 31–53. Reprinted with the permission of Lawrence Erlbaum Associates Inc.

Hetherington, E. Mavis. "Presidential Address: Families, Lies, and Videotapes." *Journal of Research on Adolescence* 1 (1991): 323–48. Reprinted with the permission of Lawrence Erlbaum Associates Inc.

Smetana, Judith G. "Conceptions of Parental Authority in Divorced and Married Mothers and Their Adolescents." *Journal of Research on Adolescence* 3 (1993): 19–39. Reprinted with the permission of Lawrence Erlbaum Associates, Inc.

Lerner, Jacqueline V., and Nancy L. Galambos. "Maternal Role Satisfaction, Mother-Child Interaction, and Child Temperament: A Process Model." *Developmental Psychology* 21 (1985): 1157–64. Copyright 1985 by the American Psychological Association. Reprinted by permission.

Buchanan, Christy M., Eleanor E. Maccoby, and Sanford M. Dornbusch. "Caught Between Parents: Adolescents' Experience in Divorced Homes." *Child Development* 62 (1991): 1008–29. Reprinted with the permission of the Society for Research in Child Development.

McLoyd, Vonnie C. "Socialization and Development in a Changing Economy: The Effects of Parental Job and Income Loss on Children." *American Psychologist* 44 (1989): 293–302. Copyright 1989 by the American Psychological Association. Reprinted by permission.

Taylor, Ronald D., and Debra Roberts. "Kinship Support and Maternal and Adolescent Well-Being in Economically Disadvantaged African-American Families." *Child Development* 66 (1995): 1585–97. Reprinted with the permission of the Society for Research in Child Development.

Ge, Xiaojia, Rand D. Conger, Frederick O. Lorenz, Glen H. Elder Jr., Ruth B. Montague, and Ronald L. Simons. "Linking Family Economic Hardship to Adolescent Distress." *Journal of Research on Adolescence* 2 (1992): 351–78. Reprinted with the permission of Lawrence Erlbaum Associates, Inc.

Flanagan, Constance A., and Jacquelynne S. Eccles. "Changes in Parents' Work Status and Adolescents' Adjustment at School." *Child Development* 64 (1993): 246–57. Reprinted with the permission of the Society for Research in Child Development.

Lamb, Michael E., Arthur B. Elster, Laura J. Peters, James S. Kahn, and Jane Tavare. "Characteristics of Married and Unmarried Adolescent Mothers and Their Partners." *Journal of Youth and Adolescence* 15 (1986): 487–96. Reprinted with the permission of Plenum Publishing Corp.

Ketterlinus, Robert D., Sandra Henderson, and Michael E. Lamb. "The Effects of Maternal Age-at-Birth on Children's Cognitive Develoment." *Journal of Research on Adolescence* 1 (1991): 173–88. Reprinted with the permission of Lawrence Erlbaum Associates, Inc.